SIMPSON

IMPRINT IN HUMANITIES

The humanities endowment
by Sharon Hanley Simpson and
Barclay Simpson honors
MURIEL CARTER HANLEY
whose intellect and sensitivity
have enriched the many lives
that she has touched.

The publisher gratefully acknowledges the generous contribution to this book provided by the Art Endowment Fund of the University of California Press Foundation.

ANNA HALPRIN

ANNA HALPRIN EXPERIENCE AS DANCE

Janice Ross

Foreword by Richard Schechner

UNIVERSITY OF CALIFORNIA PRESS
BERKELEY LOS ANGELES LONDON

University of California Press, one of the most
distinguished university presses in the United
States, enriches lives around the world by
advancing scholarship in the humanities, social
sciences, and natural sciences. Its activities are
supported by the UC Press Foundation and by
philanthropic contributions from individuals
and institutions. For more information, visit
www.ucpress.edu.

University of California Press
Berkeley and Los Angeles, California

University of California Press, Ltd.
London, England

Library of Congress Cataloging-in-Publication Data

Ross, Janice.
    Anna Halprin : experience as dance / Janice Ross ;
foreword by Richard Schechner.
        p. cm.
    Includes bibliographical references and index.
    ISBN 978-0-520-26005-4 (pbk. : alk. paper)
    1. Halprin, Anna.   2. Dancers—United States—
Biography.   3. Modern dance.   I. Title.
    GV1785.H255R67   2007
    792.8092—dc22
    [B]   2006034878

Manufactured in the United States

18   17   16   15   14   13   12   11   10   09
10   9   8   7   6   5   4   3   2   1

The paper used in this publication meets the minimum
requirements of ANSI/NISO Z39.48–1992 (R 1997)
(*Permanence of Paper*).

TO SALLY,

who pioneered the 1960s for dance scholarship

CONTENTS

FOREWORD

Richard Schechner

IN THE 2003 FILM *Returning Home,* Anna Halprin, naked, settles into the earth, her whole body drenched in mud. This mud is not filtered or "clean." It is full of clumps of earth and pebbles, dark brown, "primal." As is eighty-year-old-Halprin. She is one with the mud, the landscape . . . and—dare I say it?—with herself. Still vibrantly alive, she enacts her physical return to her—and our—ultimate home in dirt and death. As we see her body immersed, we hear Halprin's voice: "We've been alienated from the natural world. We need to find a way to reenter."

To "reenter" has been Halprin's perduring action through the eight and a half decades of her life. A cancer survivor, dancer, choreographer, performance theorist, community leader, healer, wife, mother—through the stages of life from youth into old age, Halprin has left one stage only to enter another. In the 1960s Halprin pioneered what was to be known as "postmodern dance." Her work was a key that unlocked the door leading to all kinds of experimentation in theater, music, Happenings, and performance art. Over her long and fecund career, Halprin's glory has been to pay scant attention to boundaries. Art, ritual, play, healing, exorcism, personal statement, archetype have all been concatenated in Halprin's participatory work. Nor has she, even as an old woman, sat down satisfied to watch others. Halprin leads by doing. Being one of the pioneers of participation in performance, she passionately follows her own inclination. Where Anna Halprin is, there is movement.

Janice Ross's book treats Halprin as the iconoclast she is: breaking old habits, setting out far from known paths, pioneering, inventing, combining. If Walt Whitman sang the "body electric" (in all its multifarious implications), Halprin moves this vibrant body in very specifically American ways. That is, Halprin—long a California resident—is both stubborn and playful simultaneously, celebrating "the body" as a thing, a temple, an instrument, an erotic force, a part of nature, a construct, a living organism, and a social being. Just as Whitman never tired of listing all that America and Americans might be or become, so Halprin in her concrete physical enactments—her workshops, her dances, her interviews—moves the American body. This body is not always or even primarily a "dancer's body"— slim, young, lithe, athletic. Sometimes it is a diseased body, crippled; or a hurting body, in need of healing; or an old body, with barely breath left, merging into the mud. What Ross shows in her depiction of Halprin's journey is this radical acceptance. But, make no mistake about it, this does not mean that Halprin is softheaded, gentle, or forgiving-for-no-reason. If she embodies Whitmanesque/American idealism, Halprin also lives the life of a hard-nosed pioneer leader, ready to trek into new territory, undertake hard sweaty tasks, make unpleasant decisions, and cut loose when that is called for.

Ross's book is an intellectual biography. Ross traces the outline of Halprin's life. This is especially valuable in relation to Halprin's formative years as a girl and young woman. Ross provides readers with good information concerning Halprin's family, her deeply abiding Jewishness, her turn from reading knowledge to motor knowledge, her resistant and rebellious core (always a plus for an experimental thinker-doer), her nascent feminism ("Ann didn't like taking direction from any men," writes Ross), her exposure to the choreography of Doris Humphrey, and her big awakening at the University of Wisconsin to what dance could be—ordinary and extraordinary at the same time, pedestrian and artful, expressive and healing, aesthetic and ritualized. And her meeting Lawrence Halprin—the start of a lifelong collaboration between two extremely creative people.

Lawrence Halprin, at first a horticulturalist, then an architect profoundly dedicated to organicity, drew Ann (not yet Anna) into the world of the Bauhaus, under the tutelage of Walter Gropius, displaced from Germany by Nazism to Harvard. The 1940s for the Halprins was a period of explosive growth. The Bauhaus perspective opened to the whole world, proposed a reconstruction of human living conditions and consciousness. This was precisely the kind of vision Ann Halprin—at one time a "hick from the mid-West"—thirsted for. Her lifelong task became how to link the ideal universal with the bodily particular of dancing. In Boston, working with schoolchildren, Ann began making dances that were socially aware, even political, even as they were personal and expressive.

In 1943 Lawrence Halprin enlisted in the navy. He was discharged in San Francisco shortly before VJ Day in 1945. Ann joined him there—and the rest, as the saying goes, is history. A carefully told history by Ross. The move to the West Coast—and its bursting sense of new energies, the "new age," the California spirit—suited the Halprins. Ann was to become Anna, relish working outdoors on her famous "dance deck," form the San Francisco Dancers' Workshop, help create postmodern dance, and continue to this day to affect dance, theater, and performance art. Ross's book adds much rich detail to these aspects of Anna Halprin's story. In reflecting on Halprin's life and work, I detect in her a counternarrative to the path taken by members of the Group Theatre. The Group—a half-generation earlier than Halprin—worked through the Great Depression, was to a large degree formed by the Federal Theatre Project, and was then savaged by the anti-Communist red scares of the late 1930s and the 1950s McCarthy period. The Group opened the New York–Hollywood axis, where to this day the Group style dominates American mainstream theater and film. Halprin—and the dancing she embodies—got to California soon enough to participate deeply in counterculture, a connection to the landscape (where Anna and Lawrence converge), and to various alternative religions and ritual practices. These two tendencies—the Group and the Alternative—are the poles of American performance culture. Generally, scholars have paid more attention to the Group story. Ross's book takes a big step in telling the Alternative story in terms of one of its major pioneers and practitioners.

A long journey, that from being Ann Schuman, the granddaughter of an immigrant tailor from Odessa, to becoming Anna Halprin, the iconoclastic icon of the American avant-garde. How much of Ann, the Jewess with Eastern European roots, remains active in Anna, the quintessential Marin County, California, counterculturist? We can change our names, but to what extent can we transform and transcend our personal history? I believe in Buddhistic presence, Heraclitan flux, and American revisionism. And yet . . . we each carry within us our own cultural DNA, a marker. No, not something as sharply defined as a marker. More like a cultural perfume enfragranting our values and behavior. And what might Anna Halprin's scent be? Earthy, from Russia; sweaty from her immigrant hard-working grandparents; expensively perfumed from her father's success as a Chicago businessman; the odor of *talism,* the prayer shawls worn in *shul,* where Ann admired the men swaying back-and-forth in their ritual prayer dance. But for all this, Ann Schuman was a child of privilege. A girl among more than a dozen boys; the daughter of a well-to-do clothing manufacturer who had risen far above his own father's immigrant status. An American success story. This success story is the core narrative of Ross's book.

PREFACE

ONE SUMMER EVENING in June 1961 Anna Halprin (or Ann, as she was then called)[1] related the following story during a lecture-demonstration at Stanford University:

> There was a little boy whose teacher had a precious teacup, a rare antique. The boy happened to break this cup and was greatly perplexed and agitated. Hearing the footsteps of his teacher, he held the pieces of the cup behind his back. When his teacher appeared the boy asked, "Why do people have to die?"
>
> "This is natural," explained the teacher, "everything has to die and has just so long to live."
>
> Then the boy produced the shattered cup and said, "It was time for your cup to die."[2]

Anna is describing herself as a cup breaker in the world of modern dance. Her choice of the metaphor of a shattered cup delineates, in bluntly functional and unromanticized terms, the literal task of an iconoclast, a breaker of icons. The teacups she has shattered are procedural, involving how a dance can be made, the role of personal history in shaping dance content, the role of spectators, and the degree to which the choreographer takes risks, experiments, and gives up control. This is what a teacher does—a radical teacher.

Although she comes decades later, Anna Halprin can be linked to the tradition of Isadora Duncan, Maude Allan, Loie Fuller, and Ruth St. Denis, women about whom the dance scholar Susan Foster once remarked, "They constructed of the stage a space where the self might unfold rather than a place where the self was depicted . . . they argued for an alignment of all of dance practice with the natural."[3] In deciphering Anna's work, one finds not a rarefied performer's body so much as a rarefied performer's *mind*, the performing of a social and confessional awareness as a way of aligning with the natural. The self that unfolds on her stage is plural—the routinized selves of everyday actions, encounters, exchanges. Anna's works resist the evolution of theatrical dance practice toward social diversion. She reverses this trend, reintroducing dance as a medium for social investigation and activism.

Anna Halprin's work opens a window on the interlocking histories of authenticity and the body shaping the cultural and aesthetic radicalisms of America in the second half of the twentieth century. In telling her story, I have been motivated by a desire to understand how experience becomes performance and how dances might change the people who witness and perform them. My perspective is intentionally two-sided—looking at both Anna's work in the context of twentieth-century American culture and at aspects of American culture through her dance.

Anna Halprin's story offers a vivid case study of modern dance in the process of redefinition in postwar America. Implicitly, I argue for dance as a rich medium of portraiture during moments of social unrest. The challenges in this undertaking are considerable—they require keeping the performing body at the center of analysis even when its actions are deliberately unscripted and the social body collapses into the performing body.

Anna Halprin: Experience as Dance explores what has given Anna's work the capacity to be emblematic of Beat culture in the 1950s, youth culture in the 1960s, multiracial culture in the 1970s, the culture of illness in the 1980s, and, subsequently, the culture of the aged from the 1990s to the present. This project traces the ways in which the pedagogical, artistic, psychological, and religious leaders Anna encountered shaped her regard for the role of performance in American culture. In the process she arrived at her own post-Freudian formulation of what it is that bodies need to express.[4]

I saw my first Anna Halprin dance in 1970, when she and her San Francisco Dancers' Workshop performed the undressing and paper-tearing sections of *Parades and Changes* to inaugurate the opening of the University Art Museum in Berkeley, California. I remember pressing to the edge of the spiraling ramps of the museum along with a mass of my fellow students to gaze down upon the ritualistic neutrality of the dancers' matter-of-fact nudity. The visual and emotional images were both startling and deeply memorable in their directness and simplicity. This seemed to me the perfect dance statement for this moment of body-against-the-machine anti-war demonstrations and quest for open disclosure and meaningful individual engagement.

In 1978 I encountered Anna's work again, this time as a young dance critic writing about performance for *ArtWeek*. I reviewed *Male and Female Rituals,* a dance presented in the grand fourth-floor rotunda of the San Francisco Museum of Modern Art. As soon as I took out my little critic's notebook, however, Anna approached me and informed me this was an audience participation dance and note taking was forbidden. Little about her dance, in either its form or its structure, seemed to invite a considered critical response. I wrote a dismissive review, noting what I perceived as her hostility to critics and *my* hostility to the loose and undisciplined nature of the join-along dancing. Apparently she didn't appreciate my review: several months later, when I interviewed her for an advance story about *Citydance* for the *San Francisco Chronicle,* she insisted on taping *me* and on having her assistant present for the full interview to be sure she was quoted accurately.

In 1986, now as the dance critic for the *Oakland Tribune,* I wrote about Anna Halprin again, this time by becoming a participant for the evening in one of the first Steps dance workshops she was leading for people living with HIV. I was interested in her leap from postmodern dance to performance rituals about healing and curious whether it represented a rupture or continuation of her work as a dance artist. It took me more than a decade to explore that question, and in the process I wrote another book, about Anna's teacher Margaret H'Doubler. That was far from a coincidental detour—for Anna's aesthetic is deeply pedagogical in conception, ambition, and scale. She is foremost a dance educator—primarily focused on others' responses to prompts that generate movement and, often, dances. In retrospect, my completion of *Anna Halprin: Experience as Dance,* more than twelve years after I started it, was aided by Anna's return to choreography and performing. In the last years of the twentieth century she began actively making and performing dances on public stages after a hiatus of nearly twenty years.

This book traces how the pedagogical methods Anna encountered, first as a student in elementary school, later through her work with H'Doubler in college, then as a spouse in the circle of Walter Gropius's classes at Harvard, and subsequently as a woman in postwar America helped shape her as an artist. Through each period of her life Anna steadily collected information about the relationships between the public display of bodily activity and the social categories of identity. Her work reveals some of the complex ways contemporary cultural information is shaped and relayed through that moving body.

In exploring how Anna Halprin has restructured spectatorship, redefined the dynamics of performer and audience, and activated the untrained body as a medium of discovery and expression, this book examines her dances as existing in a network of representations and identifications, and contingent on practices in modern dance history, performance theory, activist politics, popular culture, feminism, and education. Her work grapples with the prevalent mechanical, reductive view of bodies in Western culture, overwriting this with an understanding of the expressivity entropy and disintegration might allow.

"As your life experience deepened, your art experience would expand," Anna once promised.[5] This statement summarizes a major lesson of her more than six decades of making dances. Here is dance where the work is not primarily about what happens in the imaginary frame of the stage, but instead about what happens to the performers and spectators. Anna Halprin's work shows how dance, wed with moments of intense social and personal change, offers a starting point, a new beginning and permission, in the name of art, to explore. Experience. Perform.

ONE

Why She Danced

1920–1938

Biography is a novel that dare not speak its name.

ROLAND BARTHES

ONE SATURDAY MORNING in 1926, in a quiet Chicago suburb, a small girl peered through the wooden lattice that screened the women in the upstairs gallery of an old synagogue from the men below. At first she could see only a mass of black frocks and broad-brimmed black felt hats swaying subtly to the rumbling incantations. Then, as a group, the men beneath these hats, their long black side curls reaching the lapels of their coats, turned. They faced the two small narrow doors of the Ark, the cabinet that held the ornately wrapped scrolls of the Torah. Precisely on cue from their prayer books, they bent their knees and bowed their heads as one.

The girl held her breath in anticipation of the next moving prayer. "Shema Yisrael Adonai Eloheinu Adonai Echad . . . ," the rabbi intoned, and the full congregation joined in, the women softly from upstairs and the men more forcefully from below. This day, Simchat Torah, was the most jubilant Jewish holiday of the year, marking the changeover in the Torah reading cycle when the Book of Deuteronomy is concluded and the Book of Genesis is begun anew. The rabbi and the cantor carried the Torah scrolls around the synagogue as the boys and men sang and danced behind them in serpentine lines. Their arms flung upward and their feet stamped the ground as the rhythm of devotion, the physical passion of faith, rose up, sending their bodies into intoxicated action, echoing their joyful hosannas of communion with God.

Six-year-old Ann Schuman caught sight of her grandfather, Nathan Schuman, his head thrown back, his arms upraised, and his long white beard and long silky white hair swaying as he joined in ecstatic prayer. Years later she recalled, "I just thought this was the most beautiful dance I had ever seen. Not only that, but I thought he was God. He looked like God to me, and he acted like what I thought a God would act like. So I thought that God was a dancer."[1]

———

Nathan Schuman had been a prosperous tailor in Kreminlecz, a small town outside the old Russian port city of Odessa, which at that time had not yet been emptied of its Jewish population by emigration and a series of devastating pogroms. He had been born into as comfortable an existence as any Jewish resident in that area could hope to attain in the 1860s. At an early age Nathan learned from his father, a skilled and enterprising tailor, how to make finely fashioned clothing. As the eldest son of a prominent Orthodox Jewish family, Nathan was the only one of his parents' seven children permitted to attend the local school. There he learned Russian, a sign of begrudging social acceptance by the local government. When he was in his twenties, Nathan, who maintained his family's strict orthodoxy, married his stepsister Bertha, an equally devout young woman.

As Nathan's reputation for making fine-quality clothing grew, so did his clientele. By the mid-1880s, when his second-youngest son, Isadore (Ann's father), was born, Nathan had become the official tailor of the town's sizable Cossack regiment. Employing a number of assistants, Nathan made all the uniforms—long outer coats decorated with fur and braiding, close-fitting breeches, and side-buttoning shirts—for the Cossack soldiers. Since the 1840s, in villages around Odessa, the Cossacks had been burning and looting Jewish households, often killing their occupants. Sometimes the Cossacks abducted eight- or nine-year-old Jewish boys to serve twenty-five-year-long subscriptions in the Russian army in Siberia, where few survived the first year. Driven by the pogroms as well as the scarcity of economic opportunities, brutal despotism, and killings—all of which were frequently encouraged by a government confounded by the unwillingness of the Jews to assimilate and convert—the Jews of shtetl cities throughout Russia and Eastern Europe had begun a mass exodus. To stay was to face a government policy of "relentless butchery against the Jews."[2]

However, Nathan, along with his family and his growing business, was always spared during the Cossack purges. He may have been a Jew, but he was indispensable. In a macabre echo of the Passover tale, in which the Jews of ancient Egypt escaped the ordered killing of their firstborn sons by marking their doorposts so the angel of death would pass over them, Nathan and his family were saved by an identifying mark the Cossacks themselves put on their door indicating that the Jews who lived there were to be spared. Further, family legend has it that Bertha never learned to cook, because in Russia she never had to—the Cossacks kept Nathan's family supplied with servants as partial payment for their uniforms.

Yet Nathan knew that eventually his usefulness to the Cossacks would end and then he, his wife, and six children would all become victims. Placing his two oldest sons, Herman and Sam, in charge of the factory, Nathan, who spoke only Russian and Yiddish, left alone for an unknown future in America. He made his way to Chicago with its sizable community of German and Eastern European Jewish immigrants. The historian Irving Cutler has noted, "Between 1880 and 1925, over two million Jews left Eastern Europe, going mainly to American cities. In time eighty percent of the Jewish population of Chicago consisted of such emigrants and their descendants."[3] Nathan worked in the garment industry, the largest employer of Jewish men, women, and children. This industry was concentrated in the southern part of downtown Chicago, where many worked in crowded shops above storefronts. Workers usually labored twelve- and thirteen-hour days, six days a week, mostly doing piecework.[4] Nathan, who never really learned English, used to get to work by recognizing certain signs along the tram route. When the tram route changed one day, he was lost and frantic he would lose his job. He was eventually led back to where he was staying, and the next day a friend guided him to work, continuing to do so until Nathan recognized the new tram route.

Even within the Jewish communities of Chicago there were tensions, particularly between the more affluent and educated German Jews and the newly arrived and frequently illiterate Eastern European and Russian Jews like Nathan. The character of Chicago's Jewish community was changing, and by 1900 Eastern European Jews would outnumber German Jews by 50,000 to 20,000. According to Cutler, "The poverty of the Eastern European Jews"—like Nathan—"was much more desperate than the German Jewish poverty had ever been and their piety was generally much more intense."[5]

It took Nathan a number of years, laboring as a tailor's assistant, to earn enough to send for his wife and two daughters. The four boys were to be sent for later, once Nathan saved the money for their boat passage. Herman, as the eldest son, had been permitted to attend Russian schools, so he, like his father, had the advantage of being literate—a big help in the task that lay before him.

In the early part of 1898, Nathan arranged for Herman and Isadore's passage from London to Ellis Island. It was their responsibility, however, to get from Odessa to London, alone and on foot. With pieces of gold sewn inside their boots, the boys walked the hundreds of miles from Odessa to the Polish border. They wore coats with identification tags and, sewn inside, the itinerary of a network of sympathetic families who would aid them. At the Polish border they bribed the Russian guard on duty to permit them to enter, but as they ran across the border the guard suddenly changed his mind and fired in the air while pursuing them.

Herman and Isadore did make it to the Polish side, only to discover that the first link in their underground network had failed to show up. Terrified, they spent the night in the barn of a nearby farm, slipping in under cover of darkness, hastily eating the pieces of sausage and bread they had carried with them, and leaving again before daylight. Easily recognizable as Jews because of their short clipped hair with long side curls, white shirts, and black breeches with the tassels of their fringed prayer shawls hanging out, Herman and Isadore were soon spotted by a Polish Jew. Knowing how dangerous it was for two young Jewish boys to wander through Poland, which at the time shared Russia's official dislike of Jews, he helped the boys make it safely to their next contact. They then spent nearly one year, moving from one sympathetic family to the next, until they finally made it to Le Havre in France, from there across the English Channel to London, and finally, on steerage passage, to New York's Ellis Island. Years later, Isadore, weeping, would recount to his grown children how terrified he had been on that transcontinental crossing.

Isadore worked hard to become assimilated quickly. Soon after he arrived in Chicago, his father opened a clothing manufacturing business, and Isadore became a salesman there. His ability to read and write English remained minimal, however, and his guttural Yiddish accent stuck with him his entire life. As an affluent, self-made man, Isadore used to joke that he could get by without reading or writing; all he needed to do was purchase a rubber stamp with his name to deposit the checks that kept rolling in.[6]

By the time his daughter, Ann, witnessed her grandfather praying, the importance of religion in Isadore's life had greatly diminished. As was true for many Jewish families rushing to assimilate at the time, Isadore and his family expressed their Judaism privately, in their home, as part of their cultural heritage—usually just on major Jewish holidays. Instead of celebrating their coming of age at thirteen with a bar mitzvah, Ann's brothers were "confirmed" in a Reformed Jewish ceremony when they turned fifteen, and so was Ann. "We were so Reformed we were actually close to being Unitarian," Ann's brother Albert once quipped, noting that their synagogue's services were held on Sundays rather than Friday nights and Saturday mornings.[7] As Ann recalled years later:

> Being Jewish was more social to me than religious. It was a feeling of being part of a tribe. It was belonging. It was being able to tell jokes and know that they would understand. It was having certain intonations in your voice. It was having certain expressions that you would say and you would know that everybody would understand. It was the feeling of belonging more than it was any kind of religious connection.[8]

To fit in and be accepted rather than doggedly standing out as different was what Isadore and most other young Jewish immigrants in Chicago wanted. They had experienced the high price of being different in the old country. One link to his life in Russia that Isadore never forgot was his sympathy for the "little guy." "He was a staunch Democrat," his daughter remembered. "He had to be taken to the hospital when Nixon was elected. He got sick from the news he was so upset."[9]

Compared with her father, Isadore, her father's father, Nathan, seemed exotic and mysterious to the young Ann. This Orthodox Jew, who went to synagogue daily, davened, and spoke mostly Yiddish with a smattering of Russian, was a blood relation with the allure of a foreigner. In her rapt pleasure at Grandfather Nathan's "dancing," Ann discovered herself, responding to a love of movement wedded to ritualism. That Saturday morning in the synagogue Ann witnessed what Howard Eilberg-Schwartz has called the "savage" in Judaism.[10] This central ritual of worship for the Jewish male, with all its primal spiritualism, fascinated her. It offered a vivid contrast to the contained existence of her mother, aunts, and indeed all the adult women of her extended family, where there seemed to be no avenue for escape. Now Ann had seen an outlet for expression come from her staid grandfather—a man she could never talk to because of their language differences, but someone she already connected with almost intuitively, through touch, communicating more closely with him than any of his other grandchildren.[11]

> We would go and visit my grandfather and grandmother every week, and since he only spoke Yiddish he communicated with me by touching me.

So he touched me a lot. My father never touched me. So [with the grand-parents] there was a lot of touching, and Grandfather would pat me and he would stroke me and he would talk Yiddish to me, but he knew that I didn't really understand.[12]

Ann had seen her grandfather in the most sacred of places, the synagogue, expressing his fervor through dance. Here was a language she understood. For the young Ann, her grandfather's Hassidic dance helped initiate a process of learning about herself, and it lent support to her own nascent nonconformity. As she has stated:

I think that my connection to Judaism, the idea that you don't bow down before a golden idol, implied for me a sense of intellectual freedom, artistic freedom. It gave me the sense of being myself and acknowledging other people to be who they were. Not having expectations that there were dogmas to follow influenced me very much.[13]

Already at six, Ann loved dance—and now she had seen motion linked to the divine, to ritual, to some raw part of humanity's communication with the spiritual. Dance could be intoxicating by its honest ritualism and also important enough to be the ultimate avenue of ecstatic expression to God. It would be years before Ann would also discover that from that initial vivid childhood incident came another lasting lesson—through dance one can find an interior self. In her lifetime, all of Ann's art would, in some sense, be part of a larger search to find that hidden soul of herself.

Ann's mother, Ida Schiff Schuman, may not have understood all that dance would come to mean for her daughter, but she did sense its appeal. A warm, patient, benevolent woman, whom her children and family friends repeat-edly described as "angelic," Ida gave her only daughter dancing lessons be-ginning at age four, simply because she herself had always wanted to dance.[14] She assumed that Ann would, too.

Ida had been born in Chicago in 1893 to Samuel and Hannah Schiff, who had met in Chicago but had both emigrated, separately, from small towns in Lithuania a decade earlier. Ida enjoyed a comfortable, close-knit family climate at home. The push toward assimilation was there, as it had been with Isadore Schuman's family, but never at the expense of a harmonious family environment. Whereas excitability and the drive to get ahead were strong traits in the Schuman clan, in the Schiff household good deeds counted for everything. Samuel, who had learned his trade from his father, owned a small haberdashery in Chicago's South Side. He and Hannah quickly began their family. Always more comfortable in their mother tongue, Yiddish, than English, the couple accepted their American-born children's eagerness to embrace new American values—but only to a point. When two of their sons, Jack and Charlie, married non-Jewish girls, Samuel and Hannah disowned them and never spoke to them again. Hannah went into mourning and "sat shiva," the Jewish ritual when one mourns for someone who has died.

Ida, the last of seven children, was indulged by her two sisters and four brothers as the baby of the family. When her mother died in her fifties from what was likely diabetes, Ida, just fifteen at the time, was raised by her father and siblings. Four years later, on a family holiday to French Lick, a popular Jewish resort area in Indiana, Ida met Isadore Schuman, about seven years her senior, and they married shortly after her nineteenth birthday. Isadore, who had already worked his way up to a prominent position in the Chicago-based Schuman cloak and suit business, impressed her with his ambition and teasing sense of humor.

Ida and Isadore's firstborn, a much-desired daughter, Ruth, died a few days after birth, the victim of a too-violent forceps delivery. Then there were two boys, Stanton, born in 1914, and Albert, born in 1917. Three years later, on July 13, 1920, Hannah Dorothy Schuman, the long-awaited daughter, was born in the family's home at 623 Laurel Avenue, Wilmette, a lakeshore suburb forty-five miles north of Chicago. Named for Ida's mother, Hannah instantly assumed a special place in the family—an only girl with twelve male cousins and two older brothers. Ann, as she soon came to be called, was small and wiry like her father, with his intense blue-green eyes, but with the flaming, red frizzy hair of her mother. Ann stood out from the start.

Ida, like most middle-class women at the time, did not work outside the home, and Isadore saw to it that she always had plenty of household help. A full-time nanny helped with the children, a maid did the housework, and by the time Ann was seven, a full-time German chauffeur and gardener, Hugo, had been hired as well. Ida spent her days overseeing this household, cooking for the frequent social gatherings the Schumans hosted, and playing mah-jongg and bridge with other Jewish housewives. More than ever Ann became her focus, perhaps as a result of her own private restlessness in not having found an avenue of personal expression.

Always shrewd in business, Isadore began buying and selling property, eventually shifting from the clothing business into real estate. While Ann was growing up, he moved his family into various homes around Winnetka, the almost exclusively non-Jewish suburb of Chicago. Named after a Native American phrase meaning "beautiful land," Winnetka has been considered one of the most prestigious residential locations on Chicago's North Shore since the beginning of the twentieth century. By the time she was in high school, Ann's family had moved seven times, always within a few-mile radius. Ida dreaded the moves but said nothing. She just obediently gathered up the household and did as Isadore wanted. "Dearie," he would say, "we're moving." "It was a man's world and my mother had little to say," Ann recalled years later.. "So she never said a word. She just went along with it. I hated it. I had friends in the neighborhood, and it was always very disorienting to have to leave."[15] To Ann, moving seemed "repulsive"; indeed, since she and her husband built their home in Kentfield, California, in the early 1950s they have never moved, living in the same house for more than fifty years.

One of the Winnetka homes that the family moved into was an authentic Swedish farmhouse with thatched roof, secret compartments, beamed ceilings, and stenciled patterns along the windows. Miriam Raymer (now Bennett), a childhood friend of Ann's who lived four houses down the street, remembered the Swedish house as one of the most unusually beautiful in the neighborhood. To Isadore, however, it was primarily a good business investment. A few years later, as Isadore's wealth grew, he had a mansion custom-built three blocks from the Swedish home, on Tower Road, the most fashionable street in town. Situated on a spacious knoll, the two-story, Tudor-styled brick house had rooms of palatial proportions, including a huge bedroom for each child, and there was a pond that would freeze over, becoming a kind of private skating rink. When the stock market crash and depression hit in 1929, Isadore sold the Tower Road mansion and the family moved into a rental house. It was only a temporary setback, while he reorganized his finances. Not all the Schuman brothers were as resilient. In 1927, as the personal pressures among Isadore's brothers began to mount, Isadore's older brother, Herman, turned on the engine of the new car he had recently purchased—his first—and sat in the garage until he died of asphyxiation.

Perhaps because his reading comprehension was so limited, Isadore never trusted investments he could not wear, touch, walk on, or live in. When, after Herman's death, he turned the family wholesale clothing business over to his other brothers, Sam and Abe, he concentrated almost all his wealth in real estate rather than in stocks. As a result, he was hurt far less than many by the stock market crash. He got back on his feet quickly by using the property he did own as leverage. Isadore was learning how one's mastery of a new culture could be emblazoned through ownership of the urban landscape.

As an outward sign of success, Isadore loved clothes. Short, slender, with olive skin, blue-green eyes, and jet-black hair well into his eighties, Isadore was an impeccable dandy. His closet contained scores of hats, from straw ones for the summer to fine felt ones for the winter. All of his shirts were silk and prominently monogrammed. He had dozens of suits; jackets of every color, including custom-made gray and white silk ones, and a favorite gold tie. "My father wasn't parsimonious at all," Ann recalled. "If he needed one cashmere sweater he wouldn't get one of anything, he'd get six. He had a Cadillac because that was the best car."[16]

Isadore seemed to work all the time. "He was primarily a provider," Ann remembered. "He was never a pal or someone who would come to school or PTA meetings. He didn't enter into family life much."[17] Ann was twelve before the Schumans attempted their first (and only) family vacation. They drove to Northern California to visit Ida's brother, Jack, who lived in San Rafael. While Ann stayed with her parents at Uncle Jack's home, her two brothers hitchhiked to Los Angeles for a week to see the 1932 Olympic Games. What Ann remembers most about the whole vacation was the car ride. The car got several flat tires, and each time Isadore exploded in rage. The chatter of the restless kids in the backseat also infuriated him, and he would wheel his head around and bark in his heaviest Yiddish-inflected English, "Shut up or I'll trow my teeth at you!"[18]

Isadore did, however, have a playful side. "When he was alone with my mother he wasn't funny at all, he was very demanding," Ann later said. "But give him an audience and he was a funny man. He never told jokes: he was just funny. He had a comeback for everything anybody said. He had really Jewish, sarcastic humor. And when he talked he would gesture typical Jewish gestures. His face would be so expressive. Had he had a different upbringing I think he would have been a famous comedian, like the Marx Brothers."[19]

Early on Ann shared her father's gift for comedy, at first unwittingly. Ida recalled that when Ann was four she was laughed out of her first ballet class because she was so tiny, so cute, and so restless. Later, on Broadway in the Burl Ives musical *Sing Out, Sweet Land!* Ann did an unintentional comedic solo when the bloomers on her costume fell down and she kept trying to dance, prompting one critic to proclaim her "the Fanny Brice of dance."[20]

Isadore's irascibility, however, was sometimes more than the young Ann could take. At mealtimes, if Ida offered an unwanted suggestion, he might shout, "You crazy fool! You just stick with your pies and I'll take care of the business!" Ann began to get severe stomachaches whenever she sat down to a family dinner, and by age twelve she had a case of colitis so severe that she was put on a bland diet of broth, boiled chicken, and rice for a year.[21] Her brothers retreated too, Stanton by establishing close relations with Ida and Albert by becoming very quiet and introverted.[22]

Despite the emotional tension in the family, Ann recalled only one instance when tensions escalated into physical punishment. Stanton had done something that triggered Isadore, who grabbed the boy and a hairbrush and took him in the bathroom and spanked him. Ann was so upset that she stood outside the bathroom door sobbing.

For Ann, Ida and her side of the family always represented calm, stability, and infinite patience in the face of Isadore's and his siblings' edgy irritability.

> My mother's side of the family was very close-knit. They loved each other. They enjoyed being together. There was a loving kindness throughout that whole family. They were just delightful. Whereas, my father's side of the family—somebody was always fighting with someone. They were more high-strung. They were very dramatic and theatrical. There was always turmoil.[23]

The benevolent and the neurotic—Ann herself would vacillate between these two extremes of temperament as she attempted to balance what she wanted to be—an artist—and what she was raised to be—a wife and mother. For much of her life it would be an uneasy union.

When Ann's family left behind the religious and cultural familiarity of the Jewish community of Wilmette and moved to the predominantly non-Jewish suburb of Winnetka, they were drawn not only by the real estate opportunities, but also by the promise of the comprehensive reforms under way in the Winnetka public schools. The "Winnetka Plan," or "Individualized Learning," was an innovative Progressive curriculum designed by educator Carlton Washburne and implemented from 1919 into the late 1930s.[24] Although some critics labeled Washburne's program subversive, it grew out of a belief in individual learning. It belonged to a period when education was seen as the primary means for achieving societal repair and personal change, a perspective initiated by such intellectuals and educators as George Stanley Hall, John Dewey, and Edward L. Thorndike. These visionary thinkers implicitly linked pedagogy and social reform, a pairing that Ann would eventually echo in her dance work.

Ann spent her early life as a student exclusively in Washburne schools, beginning in 1926, when she entered first grade at the Hubbard Woods Elementary School, through 1934, when she graduated from Skokie Junior High School. The experience-based curriculum was ideally shaped to help Ann acquire the tools for becoming an artist and dance educator. Indeed, the reconceptualization of the individual in education paralleled a rethinking of the whole person in several arts disciplines at this time. The internal dimensions of humankind, our spiritual and psychological sides, became the subject matter of the visual and performing arts. In her dances of the late 1920s and early 1930s, for example, the choreographer Martha Graham revealed a new fascination with what she called "the interior landscape." Graham delved into the desires and motivations that shaped an individual's behavior, outlook, and capacity to make sense of the world.

Washburne's educational program promoted aesthetic understanding by heightening students' sensitivity to the world. He believed that processes can only be understood if they are based on experience and that a child's body and emotions, not just the mind, must be stimulated as facets of the whole individual. Washburne directly stated that he was cultivating "each child's special aptitudes" rather than genius in the arts or a particular subject.[25] As a Progressive, Washburne was unusual in his emphasis on the arts in education. His design allowed students to spend a substantial portion of each day engaged in painting, sculpture, drama, folk dance, music, or a combination of these disciplines. But even more unusual was how Washburne used the arts educationally. Instead of seeing classes in the arts as training for art making, he encouraged work in the arts as training for life, as a tool for learning about the world.

For Ann, the classroom experience provided support and encouragement, without the strain of competition with students fighting for the top grades. "There was never any homework," she recalled, and whenever the weather was decent, everybody carried the tables and chairs outside, so the class could be conducted outdoors for the whole day. Indeed, Washburne felt strongly that the spontaneous kinds of learning that take place outside the classroom are just as valid as those that happen within. He believed that students needed "time out of doors for gaining experience, for hobbies and explorations." Cultivating one's ability to attend to the world around may sound like a generic skill, but it is a key quality for an artist. Learning first to experience, then to understand, and finally to *represent* the particulars of experience as something vivid are prerequisites for an artist.

Although the curriculum broke boundaries, there were certainly religious and ethnic, if not class, separations among the students. Ann and her classmate friend Miriam Raymer (Bennett) recalled the extreme social isolation they felt as the only Jewish children in their class. As Ann put it:

> Knowing that I was different was sometimes very painful to me because I was discriminated against because of that difference. I wouldn't be invited to certain social events at school, and it took me a while to realize that was because I was Jewish. But all I knew as a kid was that I was different. My hair was bright red and very kinky. Everyone else in my school had blond hair and blue eyes, and the girls could swish their hair around. I would try and swish my head, and my hair would stand up and never come back down. So I knew that I looked different as well.[26]

They were always excluded from birthday parties, and the school seemed either ignorant or indifferent to this.

Stanton also remembered with painful vividness the outright hostility of the Winnetka community to Jews. "They built spite fences," he said in an interview in Winnetka in the 1990s as he pointed to eight-foot-high wooden fences that had been erected in the late 1920s by neighbors irate at having the Jewish Schuman family living next door, just a few blocks from Washburne's model school.[27] These early encounters with anti-Semitism would color Ann's approach to dance:

> Growing up and going to school in an anti-Semitic environment meant that having a Jewish extended family was very important to me. It gave me lots of security and a lot of loyalty. It did shape a lot of my attitude about dance because I felt a great injustice around this. I felt a great sense of loss and my dignity and self-esteem were very challenged. I really experienced being a minority person and had a lot of sadness around that. And a lot of resentment. I think that it did shape a lot of the directions that I ultimately went into.[28]

Although anti-Semitism made it difficult for Jewish students to make friends, Winnetka schools did foster a close relationship between all students and their teachers. Ann, like other students, at times brought her teacher home for lunch. On other occasions, teachers ate supper at students' homes in order to chat with the fathers just as they had with the mothers at lunch. Through this practice, one imagines, the teachers got a much richer sense of their students' interests and lives outside the classroom, perhaps helping them look more favorably on children like Ann, who did not excel in the traditional academic subjects, but developed a passion for the creative side of the curriculum. In her later work in dance Ann would often cap rehearsals and performances with communal meals as part of the social occasion where learning continued and teacher/student boundaries were bridged.

Ironically one of the most immediate identifying signs that marks Ann as a Winnetka alumna is that she cannot write cursive and is a poor speller. Part of Washburne's pragmatic approach to the curriculum was not to teach cursive writing. "Children learn manuscript [printed] writing more quickly than cursive," he said. "And the words look more like the words in books."[29]

This decision typifies Washburne's boldness in reassessing canonized aspects of the curriculum. More important, though, is the way Washburne's innovations challenged the authoritarian use of space and the disciplining of student bodies so central to educational institutions for centuries. As Michel Foucault shows in *Discipline and Punish: The Birth of the Prison,* the organization of classroom space "made possible the supervision of each individual and the simultaneous work of all. . . . It made the educational space function like a learning machine, but also as a machine for supervising, hierarchizing, rewarding." Foucault also discusses the control imposed by examinations and cursive writing: "Good handwriting, for example, presupposes a gymnastics—a whole routine whose code invests the body in its entirety, from the points of the feet to the tip of the index finger. . . . A disciplined body is the prerequisite of an efficient gesture."[30]

Foucault's argument suggests that Washburne's abandonment of cursive writing, tests, and the traditional classroom hierarchies liberated Ann in ways more profound than anyone knew at the time. Not until high school did Ann encounter the usual compulsory obedience to rules and subservience to the teacher signified through the student's "docile" body. For Washburne, it was much more important to give students time for creativity and self-expression than to burden them with rote "lessons." In his words:

Progressive schools, . . . are alive with the singing of folk songs and good music, with "rhythm bands" for little children (beating time on sticks and cymbals and triangles), and orchestras and bands for older children. They are colorful with the original painting of the youngsters. . . . There is dancing—folk dances, square dances, rhythms. There are "creative dramatics"—plays made up by the children themselves, the parts spoken spontaneously, not memorized. And there is "creative writing"—original stories and poems, often "published" in a fully illustrated room or school magazine or newspaper.[31]

Rather than cultivating exceptional talent in a few students, Washburne's program encouraged an artistic sensibility in every student. The connection between the Winnetka Plan's reliance on dramatics and the genre of personally confessional dance/theater that Ann would develop is striking. Washburne seemed to see the arts as important social tools for understanding oneself and the world. For Ann, it was not just that Washburne's ideas fostered artistry, but also that his focus on the social utility of art helped shape the kind of artist she would become. It prepared her to rethink the institutional structure of a dance company as well as the kind of dialogue with society she would have as an artist.

A dramatic example of Washburne's intended curriculum can be seen in the special projects at each grade level. Ann particularly remembered the time her class built an entire, full-scale Indian village on the school grounds. Her most vivid memory is of the several Native Americans who were invited to the village, where they wove baskets, cooked, and danced daily for a two-week period while the students observed them, asking questions and trying their hands at any of the various tasks they wished. Ann also recalled weekly field trips, such as the evening when her entire class assembled late at night to view stars through a telescope. Another time Ann's class visited an orphanage, and afterward they sent sandwiches each week to the children there. Occasionally, though, the emphasis on having a "real experience" could prove too much for some students. When Ann's elementary class visited the stockyards in Chicago, she became physically ill at the sight and smell of the slaughtered cattle.

For Ann, whose life work would involve how to represent publicly her inner experiences, being a student in Washburne's schools proved seminal. "The emphasis on the arts, on creating and the freedom of choice, the way we built together, acted as a group"—all these influenced her greatly. "The most important thing that I remember about school in Winnetka was that

I loved it," she said.[32] She and her friends didn't want to skip school at all, even when they were sick.

Ann always struggled academically. She called herself a "motor learner" to explain her lack of facility in math or academics. "I was in the slow learning class because I couldn't grasp concepts," she later commented. "I couldn't do math. Abstract thinking was very difficult for me. I excelled in motor learning."[33]

It was physical activity—a pick-up game of street baseball rather than playing paper dolls with Miriam Raymer and her friends—that interested Ann.

> I remember riding my bicycle and going down this big hill to go to school, and I remember going down that hill and feeling like a bird just flying, I wasn't riding the bike anymore, I was just relating to that moment of flying. It was a very powerful movement experience which gave me a feeling of freedom and liberation and ecstasy and a sense that I could immediately switch into the movement for its own sake rather than for a goal. I was no longer considering that I was going to school, I was really just in that moment.[34]

Always fiercely competitive, Ann was "an ultimate tomboy," as Robert Raymer, Miriam's brother, remembers it. "She wanted to excel at whatever her brothers were doing, whether it was swinging in a tree or participating in a neighborhood baseball game."[35] Ann's brothers, Albert and Stanton, excelled in both academics and athletics: Stanton became an honors student and star football lineman at the University of Michigan and went on to become a prominent real estate attorney in Chicago; Albert, an excellent swimmer, track man, and football player, eventually received a degree in engineering from Stanford University and became a businessman in Santa Barbara. Her brother Albert once remarked that part of the work ethic he, Stanton, and Ann were raised on emphasized two things: becoming a professional and becoming a person who did something that contributed to the world. "I only know two dirty seven-letter words," Albert quipped when he was in his late seventies, "Bastard and Retired."

Even as a young child, Ann used dance as her source of achievement. When Ann was laughed at in ballet class because she was "so funny-looking and so ridiculous," she recollected, "my mother was so insulted that she took me out of the ballet class and then decided that I needed something a little freer, so she enrolled me in an Isadora Duncan-type of class." This interpretive dance class was more tolerant of little Ann's energy. For the next two years, Ann studied creative movement at a local dance school in Winnetka, waving scarves up and down and tossing balloons in the air with the other young girls. She enjoyed skipping, galloping, and sensing in her body the pulsing piano rhythms the teacher played: "I just loved it. It was very free and I felt very comfortable in that kind of atmosphere."[36] For Ann, the experience may not have been of dance as art at this point, but it was one of raw physical motion and expression.

Ann's father did not always understand her desire to dance; instead, Isadore encouraged Ann, as well as her mother, Ida, to study the harp. The image of two women, mother and daughter no less, playing this celestial instrument fit right in with the neo-romantic trends of the time. This was after all the heyday of Maxfield Parrish's nostalgic portraits of an idealized American girlhood. Ida and Ann had no interest in learning to play the harp. But Ann did study piano for eight years, from the time she was ten until she left for college. She played the family's grand piano. "I had a hard time sticking with the piano because I didn't like the discipline of sight-reading and playing," she said. "I'd get on the piano and improvise. I liked that so much better. It was hard for me, but I was a good pianist for a long time. I'd play in concerts up until the time I went to college. After that I just lost touch."[37]

By the time Ann was in her early teens, Ida had discovered Alicia Pratt, a local dance school owner who brought in modern dancers from the Denishawn school founded by Ruth St. Denis and Ted Shawn to teach master classes and workshops. These classes consisted mostly of music visualizations, drapery manipulations, and decorative poses. "I loved it because it appealed to my fantasy," Ann recalled. "I could be an Indian, I could be a Nautch girl, I could be anything I wanted to be. They were very exotic."[38] St. Denis's dance notes of the time detail the kind of exercises that would lead up to these movement "fantasies." A typical set of instructions, according to St. Denis historian Suzanne Shelton, would read: "Walk forward—back through veil. Bend forward in pity. Hands in teaching attitude. Hands in prayer. Take veil in right hand, wrap around right wrist. Pose right hand then left."[39] A music visualization might have the students dancing to the first movement of one of Beethoven's compositions. One girl might take the part of leader, and the rest became members of a small army involved in a vague battle that ended in victory, but with casualties.

Ann digested everything she learned in these weekly dance classes by putting on impromptu recitals for her parents, brothers, and whoever else happened to be at home. Sometimes she would use her friends in the shows as well. The important thing was not so much what one did as that she had an audience. Albert remembered Ann dancing around the living room and the fact that his gentle teasing did not faze her in the least. From the start, Ann knew how to be comfortable in the limelight. By 1934 she had appeared in her first major public performance, at the Chicago World's Fair.

Ann's privileged place in her immediate family was amplified at big family get-togethers. Here she was the youngest girl, the fair-haired special one in a culture that traditionally gave women little voice, but at the same time stipulated that they were the ones with the power of passing on the Jewish heritage.[40] It was because she was still young that Ann's passion for dance was indulged, but no one in Ann's family really expected her to have a career. The family's goal for her was to get a good education so she could then make a good marriage to a nice Jewish boy.

Ann had other ideas, but at the same time she enjoyed her special status as a girl. "Girls were protected," Albert remembered. "She was spoiled by everybody. But then we were all brought up to make up our own minds about things and Ann certainly did. She's always been a *natural,* natural. She got started in that direction at age five and she just kept going."

By the time Ann arrived at Winnetka's New Trier High School, she was already living and breathing dance, and she rebelled angrily against this non-Washburne school's rules. In particular, she objected to taking the girls' soccer class in physical education—a requirement for graduation. She was one of the best female athletes in the school, so it was not playing soccer she objected to. What upset her was the idea that dance was not considered an equivalent physical activity. This enraged her. At lunchtime she often did not bother to eat, preferring to make up tap dance and soft-shoe routines with one of her black high school coaches. "I had absolutely no discrimination—as long as it was dance I really just loved it all," she said.[41] She finally made such a fuss that the school administration agreed to exempt her from soccer and let her substitute her outside modern dance classes for the PE requirement. She was the only student in the school permitted to do this. Like Isadore, Ann expected to get her own way. "She always objected to structure," according to her brother Albert.

The one place where Ann did employ structure was in the neighborhood classes she began teaching for her friends and their mothers when she was twelve years old. These classes consisted primarily of stretches and warm-up exercises as a prelude to improvisational situations. Ann wanted to give her students the same freedom she found so appealing in dance.

Ida agreeably took Ann to as many dance classes as she wanted, but it was modern dance that captured Ann's attention. "When I was introduced to modern dance, that's when the real dedication came," she later explained. "I was absolutely enamored with modern dance. It was physically challenging and it gave me a chance to begin to understand that it was OK for me to express my own creative life. That was a great turning point for me."[42]

> Although I'd been exploring all kinds of dance just for the love of it, it wasn't until I was an adolescent that I was exposed for the first time to the primary innovators of modern dance—Doris Humphrey, Charles Weidman, Martha Graham, and Hanya Holm. When I saw them a light went on. Here were dancers responding to political and social themes, using a freedom of movement I had never dreamed possible. It was Humphrey I was able to identify with most closely. I couldn't identify with Martha Graham at all, possibly because our body types were so different. Also she was so intensely dynamic it was overwhelming.[43]

By the time she was in high school, Ann was making weekly trips to Michigan Avenue in downtown Chicago to study with Frances Allis, a modern dance teacher who had studied with the ballet dancer Adolph Bolm and the German expressionist dancer Harald Kreutzberg. The trip was a two-hour train ride from Winnetka, and at least one other student in the class, Pearl Lang, took note of this level of dedication. Lang, who went on to a distinguished career with Martha Graham's dance company and then formed her own dance theater in 1954, remembered the unusual intensity Ann displayed in those classes and how it matched her own: "I do know we danced well. We were so enthusiastic. We worked day and night and we had a lot of energy at that time. The two of us were going to be dancers. There was no doubt." They both also decided early on which modern dancer they wanted to work with: "Ann said Doris Humphrey and I said Martha Graham," Lang recollected. "Ann had a very sparkling energy. She was interested in finding out and experimenting with movement."[44]

One day, inspired by a recent master class Doris Humphrey had taught at Northwestern University, near Chicago, fifteen-year-old Ann stripped her fancy bedroom bare in a gesture that also echoed the liberated spaces of the Washburne schools' classrooms. Ann's room, painted pale blue, had

had ruffled curtains, a canopy bed, and a big dresser with an oval mirror and frilly lampshades. Ann tossed all this out in the hallway, rolled up the rug, and set her mattress on the bare wood floor. She had decided she wanted to live in a dance studio.

Ann's tolerant and devoted mother took it all in stride. A short while later, she surprised Ann by inviting Tatiana Petroviana, who taught interpretive dance at the Alicia Pratt School in Winnetka, to live in the Schuman house. Ida gave Tatiana free room and board for the next year so that Ann could interact with someone equally interested in dance. Ann's two brothers were both away at college, so there was plenty of room in the house.

Tatiana was followed by Josephine Schwarz, a former dancer with Charles Weidman, who had also worked with Doris Humphrey. Josephine had been directing a dance school in Dayton, Ohio, with her sister, Hermene, but they were struggling financially, so Josephine, or "Jo" as Ann called her, came to teach at the Pratt School and lived with the Schumans for a year, playing four-hand piano with Ann in the evenings. Jo related to Ann as a big sister, taking her to see dance classes and all the major dance attractions in Chicago. It was with Jo that Ann first saw Doris Humphrey's dancers perform *Shakers* and the *New Dance* trilogy. "I remember being very impressed with *New Dance*," Ann recalled. "It challenged me. I kept wondering how did she do it? It was such a noble, philosophical statement, it stuck with me."[45] Many years later, in the year before Ida died, Ann asked her mother why she had taken those dance teachers into the house. "I did it just because you were so interested in dance," Ida replied simply.[46] Yet this was an incredibly radical thing to do in the mid-1930s. As Selma Jeanne Cohen, writing about Doris Humphrey and modern dance in 1935, noted:

At the beginning of 1935, the modern dance was anything but a household word to middle America. Few had heard of it; even fewer had actually seen it. Ballet was somewhat familiar, for Pavlova had toured in the 1920s and the Ballet Russe de Monte Carlo began its American travels in 1933. But Isadora Duncan had performed rarely in her own country, while the Denishawn tours had taken repertories of exotica, amply adorned with colorful sets, costumes, and picturesque paraphernalia. When audiences did see modern dance, even in its Broadway form, they didn't seem to recognize it.[47]

Petroviana and Schwarz shared more than their interest in dance with Ann; they provided her first up-close model of what it might be like to be a woman out in the world with a career in dance. Ann's study of dance flourished in this environment, and she began increasing her classes in Humphrey technique at the Pratt School to three times a week. In 1934 she had appeared in her first major public performance, dancing with a small student group at the Chicago World's Fair, where they performed Denishawn-style dance under Pratt's direction. What Ida and Isadore had not counted on was just how influential having dancers living in the house would be for Ann.

Ann, however, was not really aware of how financially tenuous the life of a modern dancer was in this period. The January 1935 concerts of the Humphrey-Weidman company that excited Ann were performed in the vast Chicago auditorium, which was only half-filled.[48] Dancers on a two-week tour of the Midwest with Humphrey in February 1936 reportedly received thirty-five dollars a week in wages, a significant improvement after months of unpaid rehearsals and teaching for a salary of two to five dollars a class. One collective dinner—a twenty-cent soup bone, water, and vegetables—was made to last for three days.[49] (It was a good thing Isadore did not know this. Robert Raymer remembers Isadore, in his old age, proudly boasting about his successful daughter by saying that Ann was in the studio "making lots of money." Of course she wasn't, but that was Isadore's only real way of understanding accomplishment.)

Rebellious and emboldened by having these older dancers in the house, the teenaged Ann began testing limits, but in a way that still allowed her parents to control her. For example, she started dating some of the older boys in the high school. Not only were these boys not Jewish (there were only two or three other Jewish families in the Winnetka schools then), but their families were snobbish and anti-Semitic as well. Moreover, Ann didn't like taking direction from any men at this time. Robert Raymer, a neighbor who was a year ahead of Ann, remembered catching a ride to high school with her every morning and shivering the whole way because Ann insisted on keeping her window wide open in the midst of January. She wanted "to maximize the fresh air."

At the beginning of her senior year, Ann did her first piece of choreography, a solo about nature entitled *Pastoral*. She performed the dance at the Evanston Women's Club and the Goodman Theatre in Chicago under the auspices of the Chicago Dance Council. In a note she wrote to herself about the dance a couple of years later, she remarked how the dance seemed to fall right into the form of the music by Poulenc. "I paralleled

the music exactly. The dance, like the music, was lyrical, gay and light. . . .
I did this because the music made me do it. I danced in no particular floor
pattern, although I was conscious of where I was traveling. I danced to
the audience."[50]

Toward the middle of her senior year, seventeen-year-old Ann entered
the annual high school talent show. This was going to be the first time she
would show her peers her own modern dance choreography. Remembering that modern dancers always had composers write music for their dances,
Ann asked a young musician to write some original music to accompany
her solo, earnestly titled *Saga of Youth*. She wore a rust-colored silk-crepe
dress with a cream-colored sharkskin slip. She noted the following about
the dance in 1941, when she began to compile a list of her choreography:

> The idea in this dance was one of struggle and growth. After the dance
> was finished I realized it was the story of Adolescence. I treated the ma-
> terial in a dramatic form. It was my form and not the form of the music
> for I had the music written after the dance was completed. The whole
> quality of the dance was serious, subjective, wild, terrifically spectacular
> (although I did not mean it to be) but most sincere. . . . [It] finally ended
> after a spectacular acrobatic tumbling to the floor, with me prostrated.[51]

The school assembled, and no sooner had she begun than the students
started snickering and then laughing loudly. "I was going through this dance
and hearing these people giggling, and what I was experiencing at that moment from the audience was so in contrast to what my experience was that
I was absolutely devastated. I was so embarrassed that I wouldn't go back
to school. I simply couldn't deal with facing my classmates because they apparently thought this dance I had done, was so weird. It was two weeks before I would go back to school, and during those weeks I kept thinking
about what had happened. I decided I would have to make better art, better dance."[52] Ida let her stay home. She recovered sufficiently to perform
the dance a few months later for the Chicago Council audition, where she
was commended for her "splendid technique."

Ida may have let Ann stay home from school for a couple of weeks, but
the real test of who was in charge came when Ann announced that she had
received an offer from Doris Humphrey to join her company. Humphrey,
impressed by Ann's musicality and high energy, invited Ann to come East
and dance with her in New York starting the week after her graduation from

high school. "To have Doris invite me to join the company was absolutely heaven," Ann recalled. "This is exactly what I wanted to do. But I had enough family obedience to not dare leave school. We all knew how much it meant to our parents for the three of us to get an education."[53] Ann rightly sensed that for Isadore and Ida this would have been one of her few requests they refused. So Ann prepared to apply to college. She began by searching for the school with the best dance program.

TWO

The Secret Garden of American Dance
1938–1942

The long infancy and childhood specific to the human species is an extended
training and rehearsal period for the successful performance of adult life.

RICHARD SCHECHNER
Performance Studies: An Introduction

NEW TRIER HIGH SCHOOL, which Ann attended, was known as one of
the best public high schools in the nation. Its top graduates could expect
to be admitted to any of the leading Ivy League universities. So it was with
considerable disappointment and shock that Ann opened a letter in the
spring of 1938, her senior year, from the one college to which she had applied, Bennington College in Vermont, and learned that she had not been
accepted. Ann had been confident that her grades easily equaled those of
the other applicants. What was different, she felt, was that she wrote "Jewish" on her application form when asked for her religion.

Jewish quotas at elite academic institutions in America had existed at least
since the 1920s, as had exclusion from certain neighborhoods. In the mid-
1930s, in line with the rise of Nazism in Germany, some Americans expressed
concern about the United States becoming a haven for Jews, so the college
quotas received reinforcement. With sad irony, just as the forced identification of Jews in Eastern Europe and Russia had reconnected them to Judaism, so too the label of "Jewish," which Ann felt Bennington's rejection
affixed to her, had the effect of strengthening what up until now had been
her fairly ambivalent cultural identity as a Jew.[1]

Jews were particularly resented in American higher education in part because they were viewed as highly competitive, eager to excel academically
and winning a disproportionate number of academic prizes. Harvard's pres-

ident, Abbott Lawrence Lowell, "was convinced that Harvard could only survive if the majority of its students came from old American stock."[2] In 1922 he proposed limiting the number of Jews at Harvard to no more than 15 percent, rationalizing that limits would prevent further anti-Semitism. "The anti-Semitic feeling among the students is increasing, and it grows in proportion to the increase in the number of Jews." Although the faculties at Princeton and Yale resisted, the administrations at these schools also imposed Jewish quotas. Indeed, most of the Ivy League schools kept the number of Jewish students at around 20 percent during the 1930s and 1940s, whether through explicit quotas or by other tactics, such as declaring a commitment to a nationally representative student body and thus limiting the number of students from such metropolitan centers as New York and Chicago, where the largest Jewish populations were. Another approach was to require photographs or personal interviews or to include application questions about changes in the family name and religion.[3]

Ann's parents were upset about her rejected application, but neither Ida, with only a high school education, nor Isadore, who had never attended school, knew how to advise Ann. They turned to their lawyer's wife, a family friend who was a graduate of the University of Chicago. She had recently heard of the dance program at the University of Wisconsin and suggested Ann apply there. Ann had no trouble being accepted by Wisconsin, but housing for a Jewish student in Madison would prove to be a challenge. Ann's most immediate focus, however, was on an intensive summer program, immersing her in modern dance.

Although Ann's application to Bennington College was rejected, she was accepted into the summer dance program held on its campus in rural Vermont. Founded in 1932, Bennington was the first college to offer a bachelor of arts degree with a concentration in dance, graduating its first three dance majors in 1936.[4] Both John Dewey and William Heard Kilpatrick of Teachers College at Columbia University had been among the Progressive educators involved in the planning of this college, which aimed to present the arts as equal to the other academic subjects.[5]

Bennington's emphasis on dance as a performing art was cemented with the inauguration, in 1934, of the Bennington School of the Dance, an innovative summer program, distinct from the regular academic curriculum. For the next nine years, until it was interrupted during the war years, the Bennington School of the Dance became the most intensive program of dance production and study in the nation. Its fifth summer, in 1938, was the largest and most ambitious yet, offering not only the usual four weeks of classes, lectures, and student demonstrations, but also a week of dance performances, August 4 to 10, in the Vermont State Armory. Some 3,800 people came from all over the country to attend the festival, and several hundred more had to be turned away for lack of space. For the first time, all four major modern choreographers—Martha Graham, Doris Humphrey, Charles Weidman, and Hanya Holm—were in residence at the same time with their companies, and they offered eleven premieres, including two works that would become emblematic of American modern dance: Humphrey's *Passacaglia in C Minor* and Graham's *American Document*, her first dance to employ a male, Erick Hawkins.[6]

Artistic edginess and competition among the "Big Four" choreographers were pronounced. Eleanor King, a Humphrey dancer and Bennington "fellow" (as the younger choreographers were called), recalled that Martha Graham's dancers "were forbidden to speak to other groups. . . . Clique-ishness and factionalism prevailed."[7] For some, the tensions were heightened by the new romance between Graham, age forty-six, and Hawkins, age thirty—the start of a relationship that would last until the early 1950s. Louis Horst, Graham's musical director, mentor, and former lover, continued to fulfill his usual duties including teaching his legendary dance composition class, which Ann took, but those close to him said that "inwardly he was seething with resentment and irritation."[8] Bennington faculty members gossiped about Graham and Hawkins, and the students probably knew something was going on as well. As Martha Hill, the director of the summer school, who stayed in the same faculty housing as Graham, reported, "Erick was around a lot. I'd hear noises in the kitchen at 3:00 A.M., go down to check, and find Erick and Martha having a cup of tea. This was a period of 'free love,' of course. You didn't get married."[9]

Although, for Ann, the focus was not on this budding romance but on the chance to learn from contemporary masters, still, implicitly, she would witness the juggling required to maintain one's personal and professional life in a relationship between two artists. Even though she was one of the youngest of the 180 participants in the Bennington School of the Dance that summer, Ann was very comfortable.[10] "I felt very self-confident and at home. I felt like this was my community," she said later.[11] Ann decided to audition for Eleanor King's dance, and King chose the perky Ann for the "Hoe-down" and "Hornpipe" sections of her three-part *American Folk Suite*. Ann also took Horst's challenging dance composition class. Although she found Horst "very bizarre with a dry and sarcastic sense of humor," Ann was relieved that he liked her and frequently picked her to demonstrate her solutions to his composition exercises.

To Jeanne Hayes (Beaman), who roomed across the hall from Ann in the Bennington dormitory that summer, Ann seemed lively and passionate, making up for what she may have lacked in rigorous technical training with an irrepressible appetite for dance. "She may not have had great turnout, but she was always musical in a way. She was wiry and with an articulate and just very alive body," Jeanne, who had a background in classical ballet, later said.[12] Jeanne went with Ann to the initial auditions to be in the dances by the young choreographers associated with Graham, Holm, and Humphrey. "Ann was watching my audition for Marian van Tuyl's piece," Jeanne recalled, "and we had to do a [Graham] back fall. When I finished, Ann said to me, 'Oh Jeanne, why did you hold your hands up in fifth position before you fell?'" Ann understood that "letting one's ballet show" in this era of a strict separation between ballet and modern dance was risky.[13] However, Jeanne did get the part, and at the end of the summer, Graham even invited her to New York, but she declined, preferring to join the San Francisco Ballet.

What Jeanne remembered most about Ann from that summer was her crazy sense of humor. "We were both in Louis's class and we both got along with him well," she recalled. "I remember one day Ann did a wonderful stylized little minuet. It was a very formal and severe thing [done for Horst's pre-classic dance composition assignment], but she managed to do it with some humor and an edge of parody to the refined movement. Ann was always a free spirit." Ann and Jeanne also engaged in a couple of minor escapades at Bennington. The first involved a ruse for getting more than the permitted single scoop of ice cream per day. Since they both loved ice cream, they quickly figured out that if they waited until the gallon ice cream tubs were nearing empty, they could pack their cones from the bottom to the top with all the remaining soft ice cream. This worked until one day the cook sternly suggested they stop stuffing their cones. Another incident was more audacious. Obliged to create a final student composition at the end of the summer, the two collaborated on a dance they titled "Reaction to Bennington." In this two- to three-minute duet, performed in silence, Ann and Jeanne crawled around aimlessly on the floor on all fours. "It was a comment on modern dance and what we had seen that summer at Bennington," Jeanne later explained. "We reacted to the idea that you had to follow these strictures in composition. So many of the choreographers were making works that were going to transform the world and uplift people. We were showing that we were not uplifted!" Their work was greeted with silence: "No one laughed. No one said anything."

One person who might have appreciated the girls' satirical movement commentary was Margaret H'Doubler, a guest lecturer at Bennington that summer. The founder and director of the dance program at the University of Wisconsin in Madison, and the nation's pioneering college dance educator, H'Doubler, a former phys ed teacher, was an anomalous choice for Bennington. Her philosophy differed markedly from the fast track to the professional dance world that Bennington championed. The dance program model Hill was creating at Bennington was on its way to becoming the major alternative to H'Doubler's approach to dance education. Hill, who had studied with H'Doubler in Madison in the summer of 1927, proudly distinguished her new program at Bennington:

> Taking dance out of the PE Department, from a sport to an art form, that was the big accomplishment of 1932. I was brought up to think that theater was something that nice people didn't do. There would be revivalist meetings where you could march up the isle and say you'd give up dance and drink. . . . So this was absolutely amazing that a New England college [like Bennington] would tolerate dance and the arts. . . . It was further unthinkable that dance, of all the arts, would be backed so thoroughly.[14]

In the brief six-week summer program at Bennington, Ann was already on her way to discovering a small voice in herself that countered the emerging modern dance mainstream. "Reaction to Bennington" might have been a prank, but it suggested a critique of some of early modern dance's often inflated, self-important qualities. In H'Doubler, who was about to become her mentor, Ann would discover a kindred spirit. More important, from H'Doubler she would gain a radically different conception of learning in the arts.

In late August Ann and Ida, accompanied by the young rabbi from their synagogue, set off for Wisconsin to find Ann a place to live in Madison. At the time Ann didn't question the rabbi's joining them for the trip; she thought this was just his usual level of concern for congregation members who were leaving for college. Soon, however, she realized he was in love with her and that his interest in listening to her talk about her dances was more an interest in her than in dance. Later, when he suggested coming to Madison to visit her, she began making excuses why she couldn't meet with him.

During those initial few days, however, the rabbi's presence provided a counterpoint to the religious intolerance that greeted Ida and Ann's attempts to find a room in one of the private homes renting to university students. At the first several homes they visited, Ann was asked her religion. When she said she was Jewish, she was bluntly told, "We don't mix." Finally, she found a room in a house close to Lathrop Hall, home of the university's dance program. Ida and the rabbi left. At last Ann was on her own.

The program that Ann enrolled in at the University of Wisconsin in the fall of 1938 was the oldest professional dance degree program in the nation. After starting in 1917 as a single summer class in interpretive dancing taught by H'Doubler, the Wisconsin program grew rapidly, offering the country's first BS degree with a major in dance by 1926. Two remarkable women were behind this achievement: H'Doubler and her boss, Blanche Trilling, the visionary chair of the women's physical education department.

By 1938 the forty-nine-year-old H'Doubler was on the cusp of national recognition as a pioneering dance educator. The story of her refashioning dance into an academic discipline for women is one of the stranger tales of early-twentieth-century cultural development in America. Never a dancer herself, H'Doubler avoided the established systems of classical, social, and concert dance training. Instead, she based her invention on short-term observations of dance teacher Alys Bentley's classes for children. H'Doubler had stumbled upon Bentley's private music and dance classes in New York while studying education and philosophy for a year at Teachers College, Columbia University, where she was greatly influenced by the pragmatic philosophy of one of the professors, John Dewey. Back in Madison, she adapted her impression of Bentley's classes into a college course suitable for propriety-conscious young women. Trilling helped give H'Doubler a direction for this achievement, framing her reduction of dance to its movement essentials as the way to make dance "something worth a university woman's time."[15]

From the start, H'Doubler emphasized training "the thinking dancer" rather than shaping students for careers in the professional dance world. Unlike the Bennington model, her thrust was on creating conditions for students to discover dance possibilities within their own bodies, not on conveying detailed and specific dance content. For H'Doubler, teaching, not performing, was the ultimate profession in dance. She once cheerily told Mary

Hinkson, a talented dance student who was confused about her professional performing career options, "You can always teach!"[16] H'Doubler valued dance for its capacity to foster the creative impulse independent of the stage. Her methods spurred students to question technical training in the arts and to conceive of education as broadly liberal, a preparation for life.

H'Doubler's approach echoed some of the same Deweyean principles behind Carlton Washburne's Winnetka schools, and the similarity was understandable. When in 1916–17, at Teachers College, H'Doubler took a seminar with John Dewey, the father of Progressive and experiential learning in higher education, she was profoundly affected by his new concepts of art as experience. Dewey's theories provided a rationale for H'Doubler's transformation of dance from a questionable social practice, particularly for women, into a valued educational one. Perhaps most critical for H'Doubler was Dewey's belief that the mind and body worked together, that bodily and mental activity were not separate.

Dewey posited that thinking is inquiry and that any act of inquiry begins with a problem and proceeds, through testing of possible solutions, to a resolution. What Dewey described was, in effect, the scientific method, which appealed to the scientist in H'Doubler, who had majored in biology. In her dance classroom she continually prodded her students to test the range of motion of each of the body's major joints and to improvise within the spatial, rhythmic, and stylistic parameters she set. Each student thus arrived, through personal experimentation, at movement solutions to the "problems" H'Doubler posed. If, for example, a student followed the impulse to curve her spine downward, she might find herself curling down lower and lower until she reached the floor. There she might find herself rolling over onto her back, eventually straightening her spine out once again, but this time stretched flat on the ground.

In Dewey's model, outlined in his landmark treatise *Art as Experience*, learning by experience was "art in germ," because the path of the student, through trial and error to understanding, paralleled that of the artist grasping for a resolution to a design problem.[17] What particularly attracted H'Doubler to these ideas of Dewey's, which he had ruminated on for years, was that this was an educational rather than a strictly aesthetic model, although decades later, in Ann's hands, it would become both. Interestingly, it was at the midpoint of Ann's tenure at Wisconsin, in 1940, that H'Doubler published *her* definitive book on the subject of dance education, *Dance: A Creative Art Experience*, articulating a vision of dance as a means for focusing on the development of self rather than performance.

H'Doubler saw dance as a rich democratic medium through which students', particularly women students', sense of their efficacy in the world could be transformed. Ann was captivated from the first class:

> When I arrived at the Lathrop Hall studio for my first class at the University of Wisconsin, I waited nervously in line with forty other bright-eyed students. I assumed our teacher would begin the class with exercises, the way a dance class usually began. Instead, H'Doubler arrived all breathless and enthusiastic. She greeted us warmly and, instead of taking her place in front of regimented lines of students, she invited us to gather informally around her in front of a skeleton. I was shocked. By the end of the day, I was so intellectually stimulated and creatively engaged that I could not wait for the next class.[18]

Ann understood immediately, on an intuitive level, that she was not expected to imitate H'Doubler (indeed, this would have been extremely difficult because H'Doubler never demonstrated). Rather, she was to learn how the human body was built for physical action. H'Doubler frequently started her movement classes by asking students to lie on the floor. Then she gently led them verbally through simple actions, such as the gradual shift of weight along the torso and legs as one slowly rolled from back to stomach.

Sometimes H'Doubler gave her students kneepads and instructed them to crawl at various tempi around the studio while paying attention to how their bodies adjusted. At other times she distributed blindfolds to encourage them to focus on their interior, felt sense of movement rather than thinking about dance from an external, observational standpoint. H'Doubler usually closed the curtains on the dance studio's mirrors so students could not watch themselves during these kinetic and sensory explorations. (Ann's dance studio, in which she has worked for more than fifty years, has also never had a mirror.) In some sense H'Doubler's students must have felt as if they were learning to walk again, so systematically did H'Doubler stress the rediscovery of natural movement patterns. Ann remembered this crawling exercise with awe and affection. "What other dancer at that time in history ever had anyone get down and crawl?" she wondered of H'Doubler. "Yet that action is such a vital movement because it deals with coordination. It's the whole thing."[19]

The young freshman from Winnetka was most startled by the real human skeleton H'Doubler kept suspended in a portable frame off to one side.

As already noted, H'Doubler was an empirical scientist at heart, who had not only majored in biology, but minored in chemistry and philosophy while a student at Wisconsin. She had chosen this path in part because there was no physical education major at the time, but also because, in spirit, her organizational approach to the world was one of systematic, sequential discovery. Her dance major curriculum came to require physiology, kinesiology, and a class in anatomy in which each student was part of a group of four who dissected a cadaver, exploring the layers of muscle fibers, tendons, and bones.

In every dance studio she created after leaving Wisconsin, Ann similarly set up a skeleton in the corner with charts of the body's muscles on the wall. These were the real diplomas of her college dance education. While teaching, Ann frequently referred to these props—showing her students, for example, just as H'Doubler had shown her, how the trapezius muscle connects the neck, spine, and shoulder blades through the activation of muscle fibers that stretch diagonally into the vertebrae. The idea, according to Ann, was to give you "a clear image of how the scapula supports your head and when you [got this] you would be working your body in the right way so it was very comfortable, natural and right."[20] Following her mentor, Ann built her dance vocabulary from the most fundamental kinetic logic of the body. Instead of teaching a movement technique, both H'Doubler and Ann encouraged a physical unpeeling of the body's habituated responses until one reached a core truth.

H'Doubler's attempt to draw out the distinctiveness inside each student resonated strongly with Ann's democratic impulses, especially in the wake of her recent experiences with anti-Semitism. As she later explained: "New York studio training was about imitating movement. It's like brainwashing you to respond automatically. H'Doubler always thought that one dancer imposing her movement on another was autocratic to the psyche. She fiercely defended the right of each person to have her own individual expression—that was the core of her philosophy."[21] While Ann's recollections always cast this quality of H'Doubler's teaching as an aesthetic value, her comments can just as easily be read as social.

———————

Although Ann may have initially felt isolated as a Jew in Madison, the University of Wisconsin had been a major destination for Jewish students since the mid-1920s. The campus was home to the nation's second-oldest Hillel Foundation, the Jewish organization for college students that began in 1923 at the University of Illinois in Champaign-Urbana. The University of Wisconsin's Hillel, founded in 1924, focused on providing opportunities for Jewish students to gather and engage in a variety of activities, from religious to cultural, social, and political. It offered, for example, weekly Shabbat dinners, celebrations of the Jewish holidays, and lectures on Zionism and the political situation in Palestine.

Initially, Ann went to Hillel for a pragmatic reason: she wanted to meet men. After a few weeks with only other women in Lathrop Hall, she realized the limitations of spending her days in the women's physical education building. "I wanted to socialize and meet Jewish guys," she explained. "The young people at Hillel were all very active—they had labor movement interests. It was a very exciting time."[22] Among the "guys" she met at Hillel were two who would become the most influential men in her professional, and personal, life.

At a time when Ann was becoming increasingly aware of anti-Semitism and its effect of contracting one's social space for self-expression, she was also discovering new ways of expressing her sense of who she was. Through H'Doubler she was learning that dance could be, *should be,* an arena for self-discovery. Self-*expression* would follow. Her high school paean to adolescence dance had flopped because, as often happens with young choreographers, it may have been more felt by her than communicated to the audience. In Hillel and its leader at the University of Wisconsin, Rabbi Max Kadushin, Ann found an arena of encouragement for expressing her sense of herself as Jewish. H'Doubler's classes promoted dance as an expression of the body's individuality, and now Ann was discovering that that individuality could have a name.

Kadushin, a prominent Conservative rabbi and scholar, had come to the University of Wisconsin Hillel in 1931, after serving a congregation in Chicago for five years and helping to found the Midwest Council of the Society for the Advancement of Judaism. Forty years old in 1938, he was a lively intellectual and cultural activist. He eagerly turned his Hillel into a place where being Jewish and doing "Jewish" activities were loosely defined—one could debate political policy or play basketball just as readily as participate in the annual Passover meal. He drew the line, however, at student radicalism, refusing to allow the young Communist league to meet at Hillel. The dean used to call Kadushin in whenever a Jewish student was in trouble because of his reasoned diplomatic outlook.

The year Ann started at Wisconsin, Kadushin had just published his second and most influential book, *Organic Thinking: A Study in Rabbinic*

Thought, in which he endeavored to demonstrate that rabbinic thinking presented a systematically structured worldview and that religious experience should be thought of as part of the ordinary course of daily life. Describing Judaism as an organic whole, Kadushin argued that rabbinic thinking may not seem logical in the philosophical sense of the word, but it is directed by an internal order. To erase an idea from the Jewish tradition, he contended, would be the equivalent of cutting a limb off the body—it would disrupt the inherent "organismic" pattern of rabbinic thought, which was all related, even though it might stretch over thousands of years.[23]

Kadushin led seminars at Hillel in which he discussed these ideas as well as his beliefs about the relation of the individual to society. Most important for Ann, he implied that one might balance the stabilization of society and the expression of the self with the making of art. As Kadushin later explained this: "A work of art, like a valuational situation, is a complete entity in itself and bears the imprint of the personality, which achieved it. To yield aesthetic satisfaction, any work of art—a painting, a piece of sculpture, a symphony, a lyric poem—must be a harmonious whole; and if it be such it will be charged with the personality of the artist who created it."[24]

Under Kadushin's direction, Hillel became a center of Jewish culture on campus, with a Jewish-themed theater group (the Hillel Players), a sports league, and a dance group, in which Ann would play a major role (she also belonged to Orchesis, a selective student-run dance group that offered regular concerts through the dance department). "Rabbi Kadushin encouraged me to dance my roots," Ann said of her shift to Jewish-themed dances. "It was at the University of Wisconsin that I really began to explore my roots on an artistic level and he helped me a great deal in getting me biblical references and encouraging that I continue to do this."[25]

Like the other students in Hillel, Ann was concerned about what was happening to the Jews in Germany. In her freshman year she learned through Hillel of Kristallnacht, the Night of Broken Glass, when on November 9, 1938, nearly two hundred synagogues were set on fire and numerous Jewish businesses and shops vandalized throughout Germany and Austria in a Nazi-orchestrated evening of violence. In the fall of 1939, for two of the early dances she created at Wisconsin, Ann reflected on the human cost of war. Her solo *Elegy, or Hymn to Dead Soldiers* was performed to a sparse percussion score in near-silence. "I was tremendously moved by the war situation and felt the deep tragedy of lives being taken by war death all over the world," Ann wrote about her inspiration for this dance. "I did not analyze any further but just danced my hymn. . . . The style was archaic as I walked within the path and twice I would break from this path and kneel over a dead body," she added, suggesting how much she had already absorbed the structural lessons of Louis Horst's summer class.[26] In *Song of Youth or Refugees*, a group piece, she used vocal accompaniment from the dancers to evoke the plight of those made homeless by war. Her notes on these dances include a few sentences about the audience reaction to each and her musings as to whether her intended feeling seemed to have reached the viewers. Even as a novice dance maker, Ann was sensitive to a possible breach between her impression of her work and that of her audience. Her notes suggest her realization that the content of these dances rallied support even if their form was shaky.

The Hillel Review published some glowing accounts of Ann's dancing, written by Ben Stephansky, a student Ann had met through Hillel and begun dating. In one long essay, he traced the history of Hillel's dance group, describing how it began in 1935, when at an informal Sunday evening get-together, while the group was singing a Yiddish parody, "Rose Blumkin, a student in the university dance department, arose to dance . . . [and] spontaneously synthesized her (and our) Hillel experience and the experience of her academic training in the art of dance." In the final sentence of the article Stephansky mentioned Ann and heralded her as "one of the most brilliant dancers in the history of the Wisconsin dance school."[27] Following Blumkin's lead, Ann was creating a bridge between the university's strong dance program and the responsiveness of the Hillel students and staff to contemporary dance done with a Jewish theme.

The summer of 1939, before her sophomore year, Ann had once again attended the Bennington School of the Dance summer program, which was held at Mills College in Oakland, California. Twenty-six Bennington faculty and staff members went West for the summer, including the "Big Four" choreographers. Through this program, Rosalind Cassidy, director of the Mills College summer session and chair of the physical education department, hoped that Bennington's School of the Dance would be "fundamentally affected by influences belonging inherently to the West" and that there would be "a new enrichment and strong consolidation of the whole field of the dance."[28] Ironically the short-term effect on the Bennington staff was the opposite: Doris Humphrey complained, "There is no view and there are no long stretches of space for the eye and the spirit on the campus . . . it all presses in too much." Martha Graham's teaching assistant, Ethel Butler, found the landscape equally stifling: "I couldn't breathe out there. . . . I needed to get somewhere where I could see out and beyond."

Ann didn't register any specific response to the California setting that summer, but eventually she would experience the western influences Cassidy outlined and, through her, they would radiate out, to the field as a whole. For her summer studies Ann again chose Humphrey's technique over Graham's, noting that "Doris's work came easy to me—she was friendlier. Martha was always putting on a show."[29] She also took Louis Horst's "Preclassic and Modern Forms" composition class and performed her dance *Exorcism* as one of the student pieces he showcased from his "Primitive Studies" assignment. What did impress Ann that summer was a slender young male student from the Cornish School in Seattle who had a remarkable jump. He dazzled everyone. His name was Mercier (Merce) Cunningham.

Ann had driven to California with Ida, but Ida had gone back to Chicago after a brief visit with her brother. For the return trip, Ann accepted an invitation from a new friend in the Mills workshop to accompany her and her family back to Chicago via the family's summer ranch in Santa Fe, New Mexico. Ann was particularly excited because the family had invited her to attend a big Native American dance festival in Gallup, New Mexico. It is possible that she had learned about this special showcase of Native American dance from Louis Horst, who attended the festival with his companion Nina Fontaroff and good friends Ruth and Norman Lloyd. Ann, however, never saw the dances. At the last moment, with no explanation, as she recalls, her hosts announced there was no room for her and left her at their ranch to take a horse ride while they went off to see the Indian dances. Furious, Ann checked herself into La Fonda, a hotel in Santa Fe, where she met a group of students who gave her a ride back to Chicago.[30]

Soon after her return to school, Ann began running the Hillel dance group, touring with them at the B'nai B'rith chapter at Sheboygan and fielding invitations from as far away as Chicago. *The Hillel Review* remarked: "Our Hillel Dancers, which originated this year under the guidance of Ann Schuman, has since become one of the most successful activities ever to originate at the [Hillel] Foundation."[31] In reviewing the Orchesis performances, the *Chicago Dancer,* the city's dance newsletter, described Ann as "outstanding by her range and power" and her *Three Pages from a Diary* as "one of the most coherent solo suites in contemporary dance."[32]

Ann was also proving herself very articulate verbally about dance. In a student-led lecture demonstration in the spring of 1940 Ann and four other Orchesis members presented the fundamentals of modern dance. Ann's introduction reads like an early manifesto of her goals for dance: "You see dance is like Democracy. It is a point of view—a concept. We do not have a code of movements that is standard step patterns. We do not have a dogmatic system of rules and regulations that sets a dancer as a cog in a machine. . . . The ultimate aim is . . . a perfection of the knowledge of our materials of dance and the nature of man."[33]

Ann's course work was going well—with the exception of Blanche Trilling's class on dance pedagogy for children. Preparing dance teachers for the public schools was an important part of the Wisconsin curriculum. The year Ann entered, the program included classes in "The Teaching of Rhythms to Children," "Dance Curriculum in Secondary Schools," and "Student Teaching." The thoroughness of Wisconsin's dance-teacher training was renowned—during Ann's first year at the university, forty-four dance graduates were already teaching in colleges and universities in twenty-three states, and each year the demand for dance teachers exceeded the supply.[34]

Ann, however, rebelled against Trilling's method, which was to have the college dancers teach dance classes for each other as if they were ten-year-olds, and they were supposed to react as if they were children. "I thought it was the silliest thing. It was just nonsense," Ann later said. "We were supposed to be elementary-age children, first grade to eighth grade. It was such a phony setup, I didn't give any credence whatsoever to that course. Trilling insisted we had to make lesson plans for every class according to a specific way of doing this, a grid system. So you wrote down every single activity and as much information about how you were going to present it, and why you were doing it."[35] Both the artificiality of the class and the overdetermined structure for teaching dance irked Ann. Trilling, a PE educator, was accustomed to teaching sports incrementally through repeating an action that eventually would become real—such as throwing an imaginary basketball repeatedly until finally one got to hold a real one. This method simply didn't work for dance, which in itself may have been instructive for Ann, for neither artificiality nor empty or excessive structure would ever be part of her teaching repertoire.

Ann found the required six months of teaching real children in Madison's public schools much more enjoyable. For her own classes in the Madison schools, Ann rejected Trilling's structure of having students imitate movement: "I just remember thinking it was so boring, but I didn't have any models other than the fact that I myself had danced all my life as a child. So I think my teaching of children came from what I would have liked if I had been a child. I taught what would have appealed to me."[36]

Although Ann had a special rapport with H'Doubler, not every student got along so well in the department. Attendance figures for H'Doubler's classes often settled into the single digits, and the attrition rate in freshman and sophomore classes was high.[37] At times, Ann sensed conflict between H'Doubler and other dance faculty whose approaches differed from her own. One of the most awkward instances was during Ann's junior year when Beatrice Hellebrandt, a former student who had received graduate degrees in music elsewhere, returned to teach in H'Doubler's program. Hellebrandt's new methods of music analysis and instruction as well as her more abrasive personal style conflicted with H'Doubler's approach. Once, when Ann was showing a dance she was choreographing to H'Doubler, who frequently would spend an hour or two watching and commenting on Ann's work, Hellebrandt joined in and disparaged work that H'Doubler had just praised. "H'Doubler was always positive and Hellebrandt was being very judgmental—I think because I wasn't somehow or other reflecting the modern dance imprint that was beginning to creep into the department. There was a lot of tension building up in the department," Ann recalled.[38] At the end of the academic year, Hellebrandt offered to resign and H'Doubler accepted immediately.

Overall, there seemed to be few shadows in Ann's life at Wisconsin, and as her self-assurance grew so did her personal aspirations. One evening while at Hillel during her sophomore year she noticed an older student holding a pipe and looking "very handsome and very sophisticated." That man was Lawrence (Larry) Halprin. As she remembers:

> I had come to Hillel to do a dance with a little group that I had formed in the dance department, and [Larry] was sitting there with his pipe, looking at the dance very carefully. Then he made some intelligent remark afterwards. He referred to people like Martha Graham and Doris Humphrey, and I was very impressed. Because nobody at Wisconsin knew about things like that. I was very impressed with his knowledge of the things that I was interested in—and the pipe.[39]

On his side, Larry says, "I remember this pretty thing coming into the room and she sat down in the back. She had this Grecian profile and I was rather intrigued by that. [She] did get up and cavort around a little bit and dance with a few other sylph-like ladies and I thought that was all very amusing and so I went over to see if I could make contact with her."[40]

That evening Larry succeeded in walking Ann home, being careful to avoid her boyfriend Ben Stephansky. Ann and Larry's paths crossed only at Hillel, so Ann began attending Hillel events more frequently. Soon Ann became part of the same Zionist Hillel group that Larry belonged to, doing folk dancing, attending lectures, and going on picnics in the surrounding countryside. Larry's attachment to Judaism was different from Ann's—he attended Hillel because of his commitment to the founding of a Jewish homeland. Everything about him was expansive, from the scale of his social activism to his range of experiences and concerns. From the start, Ann's and Larry's passions coincided on a number of levels even while their temperaments and sensibilities contrasted. As Ann explained, "Larry was my first real love. We had a lot in common. We shared similar attitudes about most everything. We enjoyed the arts. We enjoyed being in nature. So there was just a tremendous bonding from the get go. . . . [But] we were very opposite personalities, which I think was important for me, because I was very intuitive and spontaneous and he was always very intellectual."[41]

Four years older than Ann, Larry was considerably more worldly. He had arrived at the University of Wisconsin in the fall of 1939 as a graduate student researcher and teaching assistant in the department of horticulture. He had just graduated in June with a BS degree in plant sciences from the School of Agriculture at Cornell University in Ithaca, New York. While at Cornell, Larry had worked his way through school by washing dishes in a fraternity house, maintaining a newspaper route, and helping run a cooperative restaurant where he and his pals got their meals for free. He had also been very active in fighting social problems, marching on picket lines and traveling to Pennsylvania to help coal miners resist the mine owners' efforts to break the unions. "At one point," he recollected, "I was almost kicked out of Cornell because of my activities in support of the labor unions. I remember being hauled up in front of the president of the university after one particular escapade in which we went down to the Pennsylvania minefields, where people were starving. So I was very obsessed with social problems."[42]

Social activism was a cherished value in the Halprin family. Larry's father, Samuel W. Halprin, initially owned a wholesale women's clothing business but later became president of Landseas, a scientific-instruments export firm that traded between the United States and what was then the struggling Jewish population of Palestine. Rose Luria Halprin, Larry's mother, had begun working with the American women's Zionist organization Hadassah when Larry was thirteen years old. She served as its president from 1932 to 1934 and again from 1947 to 1952. After her first term she moved with Samuel and Larry to Jerusalem for five years to serve as a liaison during the construction of Hadassah's hospital complex on Mount Scopus, north of the city.

Larry's great-grandparents and grandparents had come from the same Eastern European roots as Ann's. His mother's family had come from a town in Russia called Radoshkovitz (now in Poland). His maternal grandfather, Philip Luria, was born in Kurenitz, a tiny town in Lithuania near the city of Vilnius. Luria, who was permitted to work outside the Jewish ghetto, bought and sold things. When he immigrated to America in 1881 at the age of seventeen, he opened a business that made silver objects. Larry's father's family, who came from the town of Halgrin in Germany, changed their name to "Halprin" when they arrived at Ellis Island. The two sides of the family were connected, and there was speculation that Larry's mother and father may have been second or third cousins.[43]

Larry's mother and father were both born in Harlem, which was then a Jewish neighborhood in Manhattan. Rose was born into an ardent Zionist family. Her parents, Philip and Rebecca Luria, taught her Hebrew as a child, and she became fluent in French, German, and Yiddish as well. She attended the Teachers Institute of the Jewish Theological Seminary of America and studied for two years at Hunter College before she met Samuel and dropped out to marry him at the age of eighteen. Larry proudly described Rose's parents as Jewish intellectuals: "They were literate and read the Yiddish newspapers and they attended the Yiddish theater. They were active Zionists as well."[44]

Although Samuel never attended college, he was a high school graduate, which was a respectable level of education for the time. Samuel's first business, selling women's clothing wholesale, was very successful, and at the age of thirty-five he retired as a millionaire. He decided to take the family, including twelve-year-old Larry and his five-year-old sister, Ruth, on a yearlong tour of Europe. The family intended to hire a governess to maintain the children's schooling while they traveled, but twenty-year-old Sydney, one of Larry's maternal uncles who was as close as a brother, offered his services instead. He still recalled that trip vividly, at the age of ninety-two:

In 1928 I learned that my brother-in-law, Larry's father, was selling his business. This was before the Great Depression. He and his wife (my sister) were taking a great trip abroad, and they were going to do it in style. There was no air travel in those days, so they were booking first-class accommodations on a great steamer. I learned that they were planning to take a governess with them . . . a kind of person who could keep [the children] up-to-date in their studies. When I heard about this, I couldn't believe that I was not the right person for that job![45]

Uncle Sydney got the job, after persuading his family and taking a leave from the City College of New York, where he was in his senior year. In December 1928 he set sail with the Halprin family on *The Europa.* "Oh, it was black tie every night," Sydney remembered. "It was first-class all the way. My sister had a steamer trunk [filled with clothes]. She never would be caught dead in a dress that she had worn the day before."

Once they arrived in Europe, they began sightseeing, spending time in the major cities, including a month in Paris. Samuel and Rose insisted that the children were Sydney's responsibility during the day. Dispensing with any traditional ideas about going through lesson plans in their hotel room, Sydney took them out to explore the city. Indirectly he gave young Larry an expansive sense of the environment as educator, of how the architecture and landscape of a city could be one's teacher, of how the stories of a culture could be written on the buildings and in the streets and walkways. One day Sydney decided to take the children to Versailles, and they spent the whole day wandering through the gardens and rooms of the palace. "I had to carry Ruth on my shoulders through the Hall of Mirrors," he recalled. "But the place was empty, and Larry was fascinated by everything that he saw. He wanted to move slowly through all of it to absorb it."

As they toured Paris on foot, Sydney noted that Larry kept "staring and looking at the city." Larry was "very easy to travel with as a young boy, not complaining . . . [but] looking, looking, looking." After their ship visited Naples, Sydney bought Larry some pads of drawing paper and gouache, and Larry began drawing everything he was seeing. It was then that Sydney became aware of Larry's artistic gift. They journeyed through Italy to Egypt and then to Palestine where, because of Rose's activity in Hadassah and Zionist affairs, they planned to stay for four months. Larry amused himself on the long train ride by looking out the window and drawing the endless desert with great interest. Under Sydney's tutelage, he was beginning to discover that his identity and the geography he found himself in could be linked.

The house the Halprins rented in Jerusalem was next door to several interesting families including that of the future Israeli political leader and archaeologist Yigal Yadin, who was Larry's age. The two became inseparable friends, going to school together and preparing for their bar mitzvahs, which they both had in Palestine that summer. It was an experience that would live on in Larry's imagination:

All of this was just a parade of fantasies, like from the *Arabian Nights,* in front of me at times. I fell in love for the first time, I can remember, with a beautiful Israeli girl. My family traveled all over the country. We went to Tel Aviv, where we saw some remarkable floats in a festival of Purim. Then we went up north and saw our first kibbutz. It all rubbed off on me in a profound way, and I'm sure that it has affected me for the rest of my life because it was so pure and so wonderful and without flaw. It was like I was in the middle of a living museum, a living archaeological museum, a museum without walls.[46]

Then suddenly the "parade of fantasies" ended. On October 29, 1929, as the Halprin family was returning to the United States on the steamer *Acquatania,* their holiday collapsed. With the crash of the New York Stock Exchange, all of Samuel's profits, which he had invested in the stock market, were wiped out. "On the way there my father was a millionaire; when we got off [the ship] my father was a pauper," Larry recollected. "The Crash happened and my father lost everything."[47] The family returned to Brooklyn, where Larry attended a leading local prep school, the Polytechnic Country Day School for Boys. Scraping together the tuition was difficult, but for the Halprins young Larry's education was the top priority. He remembers it as a great high school, and despite being one of only about twenty Jewish boys at the school, he didn't feel any religious bias. "I've never had a problem with anti-Semitism," he says. "My roommate once said something about Jews in general, and I swung on him, and he looked at me and said, 'Larry, for Christ's sake!' I was a Jewish WASP. I had what was either the good or bad fortune of being a top-notch athlete, so I was asked to belong to fraternities where no other Jew had ever even walked in the door."

The summer Larry graduated from prep school he left for Palestine, where he lived from 1933 to 1936. (His parents and sister moved to Jerusalem in 1935.) As he describes it: "I was going back to a place that I loved. I was looking for adventure. I worked in the building trade; I worked in gardens; I worked in a factory extracting potash from the Dead Sea. I worked in orange groves." He also helped found what would become Kibbutz Ein Hashofet, near Haifa, where he lived for several months, but most of the time he was on the move, eluding the British authorities because his two-month visitor's visa had long since expired. He remembers the cultural life in Palestine in particular as "intense": "There was folk dance every night. We'd do the hora. I lived with the Arabs and I learned Arabic and Arabic dances. I painted with an art group there." Not surprisingly, Larry was also very involved with Zionist activism: "I remember my mother and father were a little nervous about me going off, so they made me promise to come [back to the United States] and attend college."

Larry decided he would return to Palestine as soon as possible and live on a kibbutz, because he loved the life and the ideals he had seen there. First, however, he planned to gain useful skills by studying at Cornell's reputed agricultural school. Uncle Sydney, who had recently graduated from Harvard Law School and was practicing as an attorney in New York, served as Larry's guardian as he worked his way through college, receiving no financial support from his parents. While at Cornell, Larry pursued a full range of interests—becoming the championship pitcher on the varsity baseball team and doing research in biology, particularly about how plants adapted to natural environments. He also continued painting and joined Hillel, through which he was active in Zionist causes. "All Jewish kids in those days had social consciences," he recalled, noting that the apartment house he lived in at Cornell had "Zionists on the top floor, Trotskeyites on the second, and socialists and law [majors] on the first."[48]

In 1939, just as Larry was completing his degree at Cornell, one of his professors told him that a plant researcher at the University of Wisconsin needed help from someone who knew the kinds of things Larry had just been studying. So in the fall of 1939 he arrived in Madison prepared to pursue a Ph.D. in plant physiology, researching the influence of light on plants and their fruiting habits—and *then* return to Palestine. Decades later, Larry still wondered why he never did return to live on a kibbutz: "I've never worked that out in my head. It's a conflict and an inconsistency that I admit to," although he pointed out that the war intervened. Still, as he put it, "I'm quite introverted actually. I'm shy on a certain level. . . . And I'm not sure how I would have done. If I had gone back and worked in the kibbutz and lived there, I'm not sure how I would have survived."[49]

Within a few months of their meeting, Larry and Ann were sweethearts. In December of 1939, she went home with him to New York to meet his parents, who had returned to the United States when war loomed in Europe. Ann ostensibly traveled to New York to take a Christmas dance course, but only Hanya Holm was teaching. Ann had never been drawn to Holm's movement at Bennington, and after just one day of the workshop she told Holm she was not comfortable in the class. Holm was very understanding and let her withdraw. For the next two weeks Ann sampled classes at other dance studios in New York. She slept on the floor of the Halprins' apartment on East Seventy-fourth Street, between Second and Third Avenue. When Ann and Larry returned to Wisconsin for the winter semester, they moved in together, living in a room they rented in a professor's house. Larry took an avid interest in Ann's dancing, and on one occasion he obligingly played the corpse in a performance of *Lynchtown,* a famous anti-racism dance that Charles Weidman, the former partner of Doris Humphrey, staged on campus with student dancers. Soon after that, a real corpse prompted a far less aesthetic response from him: accompanying Ann to one of her anatomy classes where cadavers were being dissected, Larry promptly passed out.

During the summer of 1940, Larry spent time in Door County, in the northern Wisconsin lake country, where he tended experimental plots of cherry trees and other plants for the university's department of plant physiology and botany. "I had been away all summer running these horticulture experiments, and it was after I came back that I realized that three months away from [Ann] was a disaster," he later said.[50] Soon after he returned to Madison, Larry convinced Ann to take an evening hike with him to see the view from a tall structure on a steep hill that was a ski slope in the winter, overlooking Lake Monona. "I think we had been to the movies or something and I induced her to walk up to the top of this tower, and up on the top there was a small space, and so I had her trapped. I induced her to allow me my blandishments," Larry recalled. "I think it was at that moment that we finally realized this was more than a flirtation. She agreed to marry me."[51]

Larry's father and mother soon let it be known to the rest of the family "that there was this girl in Wisconsin who was very artistic and very nice, from a good family, a Jewish girl, that Larry was going to marry—and that he was madly in love," Sydney said. "I had not met her so I went out to Winnetka, and we became very friendly right away."

Ann and Larry were married on September 19, 1940, in the living room of the Schumans' Winnetka home. It was a small wedding, with just the immediate families and without any dancing. Because it was a traditional Jewish ceremony, the couple stood beneath a *chuppah* (wedding canopy) set up in front of a huge bay window that looked out over an expansive lawn and an adjacent, privately owned golf course. Rabbi Kadushin, who had come from Madison, read the marriage vows. At the end Larry smashed the traditional wineglass with his foot—its shards a symbol of the infinite years of happiness the young couple would, it was hoped, enjoy together. "They were so much alike," Ann's childhood friend Miriam Raymer (Bennett), who attended the wedding, recalled. "They even looked alike then. They were tall and slim with red curly hair. They were both arty, even in those days."[52]

The Schuman and Halprin families got along well together, particularly after Samuel Halprin and Isadore Schuman realized they knew each other. "At the wedding, Sam and my father looked at each other and said, 'Don't we know each other?'" Ann remembered. "It turned out that my father had sold to Larry's father when he used to go on the road as a salesman."[53] That broke the ice.

There was no honeymoon; Ann and Larry returned immediately to Madison. There is a photo of Ann and Larry taken in Madison a few weeks after the wedding. They stand gazing at each other in the midst of a meadow of knee-high grasses, each with one arm locked behind the other's waist. Larry, who wears crisp white pants and a white short-sleeved shirt, stands upright as Ann, in a full skirt, peasant blouse, and kerchief knotted over her hair, playfully leans away from him, her left arm bent at the elbow as if she were trying to coax him into an impromptu dance. In this image Larry, serious, looking with furrowed brow at a whimsically moving Ann, seems to anchor her as she prepares to take flight.

———————

Larry and Ann resumed their routine life as students, taking weekend trips around the Wisconsin countryside in an old car they had recently acquired. Sometimes they went to Door County, where they visited H'Doubler and her husband, Wayne Claxton, who had a weekend home there, just five miles from the university's agricultural plots. Larry got on well with H'Doubler and particularly Claxton, who was an artist and an architect. H'Doubler "was very emphatic about dance being part of biology and anatomy, and . . . an important part of life," Larry remembered. "She was very helpful to Ann, I knew that. It was evident immediately that the relationship between H'Doubler and Ann was very special. She had a very strong feeling, I think, that Ann was going to be a great artist."[54]

One afternoon Ann suggested the two of them go out to Spring Green, about thirty miles west of Madison, to see Taliesin, the home and studios of Frank Lloyd Wright. "Who the hell is that?" Larry asked.[55] Larry had never heard of Wright, the pre-eminent American architect, who by 1940 had created some of his most celebrated structures, including Fallingwater in Bear Run, Pennsylvania, and the Johnson Wax Building in Racine, Wisconsin. Ann had heard about Wright from H'Doubler, whose architect husband had likely visited Taliesen, and she may also have heard about him from Rabbi Kadushin. Since the mid-1930s, Kadushin and his wife, Professor Evelyn Kadushin, had preached to and befriended the apprentice architects and designers at Taliesen, which was regarded as an outstanding example of Wright's "organic architecture," a unified approach to the world akin to Kadushin's "organic thinking."[56] Later, angered by Wright's isolationist position on World War II and his apparent sympathy for Hitler, the Kadushins would break off relations and never speak with him again.

For the young horticulture student and dancer, the afternoon's visit proved a life-changing event. By 1940 Wright had purchased all of the six-hundred-acre valley land originally owned by his grandparents and their descendants. He named this property Taliesin, a Welsh word that translates as "shining" or "radiant brow," and he described the buildings he constructed there as wrapping around the brow of the hill. Testing new ideas about architecture at Taliesin, Wright explored compressing and expanding space to lend a quality of tension and release to his designs, while always respecting the natural beauty of the materials. In 1932, with his third wife, Olgivanna Lloyd Wright, he had begun the Taliesin Fellowship program, an arrangement in which young men and women lived with the Wrights at Taliesen and participated in every aspect of the life there, working on the buildings, in the fields and kitchens, on drawings and projects, and taking part in evening social events. To Larry it must have looked like an American kibbutz, with design rather than agriculture as its product.

"I'll never forget walking in and there was a banner headline across the lintel of Wright's studio. It said, 'What a man does, that he is,'" Larry remembered. "And then there was another one somewhere that said, 'Architecture is the mother art.' . . . I walked through the drafting room and by the end of two or three hours of being there, I said, 'Boy, this is what I really want to do.' It was just as simple as that."[57]

After spending the day at Taliesen, staying into the evening to attend a concert in the Wright-designed theater there, Larry and Ann drove home. That night, instead of studying, Larry raced to the main library on campus and looked up architecture. He found a short bookcase with what few books there were on that topic at the time. Under the heading "Landscape Architecture," he came across three books, one of them a classic by Christopher Tunnard on landscape architecture and the design of the environment that detailed how urban design should work at making cities wonderful places. "I thought, 'My God!' The bells starting ringing and I said, 'This is *really* what I want to do.'"[58]

The next day Larry found a listing for a small program in landscape architecture in the campus directory. He located a professor there and announced his desire to be in the department, explaining his sudden passion but also its link to his expertise in plants and design. The following day Larry was admitted to the department. Three weeks later, Larry was called into the professor's office. "You're a duck in water," he told the startled Larry. "We've gotten you a scholarship to Harvard."

Larry had only a few months left at Wisconsin, but Ann still had another year of school to complete. They discussed what to do. Ann was determined to be a dancer, but all of the models she knew—Graham, Humphrey, Holm—had put their careers before marriage. "I'd had a very traditional upbringing," she explained, "and marriage meant the woman stayed in the home and was domestic and the man went to work. That was my only model."[59] But here she was married at twenty, with her own career not yet started and with a new husband who was about to begin again as a student, unable to support her.

Somehow, intuitively at first, the couple made a decision that put in place the relationship between their lives as artists and their lives together that would remain for all the years to come. Each recognized the other's need for a creative life outside of the marriage. Perhaps because he came from a family with a model of a dynamic woman who worked outside the home, and also because he was an artist, Larry accepted Ann's commitment to her career and her art, as well as him. "Dance was so much a part of me that when he began to know me he knew me from the point of view as a dancer and somebody who was very serious and dedicated about my work. He was interested in it, so it didn't feel like there was any conflict. I felt there would be tremendous support and encouragement," Ann said of her realization that she could have both marriage and her life in dance.[60]

As things happened, however, the first critical test of support was Ann's for Larry. "The realistic expectation in those days was that I was supposed to support the family," Larry commented years later. "The idea that I would continue school was quite revolutionary." Even more unusual was that Larry would change his field and start school again in a whole new discipline. "That she encouraged me to change fields was, of course, the best thing she ever did," he said.[61]

Larry graduated from the University of Wisconsin in May 1941 with an MS degree in horticulture. He again spent the summer living in Door County and tending the university's horticulture experiments. This time, however, Ann lived with him, and the two spent a great deal of time visiting with H'Doubler and Claxton there. At the summer's end Larry left to begin Harvard University's Graduate School of Design.

Ann, who now went by the name Ann Schuman Halprin, continued her studies in the dance department at Wisconsin, but now, with the change in Larry's plans, her short-range dance career goals had suddenly shifted from performing to teaching. She rented an apartment with another student, and they lived downstairs from Lavinia Nielsen, a former member of the Jooss Ballet in Germany who had begun teaching in the dance department the previous year. Nielsen became close friends with Ann. Their friendship continued the rest of their lives, and when Nielsen married fellow Jooss dancer Lucas Hoving, he became part of that circle as well.

As her final project for the dance major, Ann submitted her senior thesis on May 11, 1942. This hundred-page, hand-printed treatise details the development of Jewish dance from biblical times to the present. Titled "Hebrews: A Dancing People," this passionate account, seemingly written in a fluid outpouring with almost no corrections, begins with dances as early as 2000 B.C.E. and concludes with a listing of contemporary Jewish dance figures, including Lincoln Kirstein, Andre Levinson, and Miriam Rambert. Its rousing final chapter carries an unmistakably Zionist call for "the settlement of a homeland for the establishment of a Jewish national center whereby the Jewish peoples can become a positive force in the world." Modern Jewish dance, she claims, "has great possibilities granted a land and freedom. This dance of the Jews should make significant contributions to the history of the dance of the world and to the history of human civilization."[62] This impassioned document neatly brings together all of the critical influences on Ann at Wisconsin—dance, Judaism, and, through Larry, Zionism.

Ann also presented a graduation concert of her own choreography in the main University of Wisconsin theater. Ruth Hatfield, a young dancer from Minneapolis who was in the audience, remembered, "Ann was very strong at that point. Her concert was based on the different stages in the life of a woman. It was like a biography."[63] Hatfield had been directed to see Ann's work by Gertrude Lippincott, a leading Minneapolis dance teacher who had seen Ann perform at one of the Bennington summer sessions.

Immediately after taking her last final, Ann left Madison, skipping her graduation because she was so eager to join Larry in Cambridge. The detour that four years earlier had led Ann to the University of Wisconsin had proved fortuitous. She now had the skills not only to dance but to teach dance, and thus earn a livelihood. More critically, however, through H'Doubler's classes she had discovered that one arrived at creative movement by attending to the biological logic of the body in motion. Embedded in this logic was a route to extraordinary freedom. Later this would be called improvisation, but H'Doubler didn't use that term, preferring instead that her students think of it as movement discovery. "Modern dance is a concept— a point of view and not a prescribed system," H'Doubler observed in an article published not long after Ann graduated. H'Doubler explained that "compositional form is no longer dependent on musical forms. Today dance is free to choose for its accompaniment from a variety of possibilities— speech, song, sound effects as well as music." She added, "The emphasis today is to know and experience dance as a creative art experience, expressing and communicating the dancer's emotional reactions to his impressions, as he evaluates them. The technical necessity is to train the body to become a strong, flexible, sensitive and well-coordinated instrument capable of responding to the exigencies of the expressive mind."[64]

H'Doubler's teachings had remade Ann's conception of where invention in dance begins. Ann would bring her own emphasis to H'Doubler's foundation, extending a revolutionary model of dance education that would help form the basis for the next generation's invention of postmodern dance. While the larger field of American dance built a divide between dance education and dance for the stage, Ann set about bridging that binary and demonstrating that radical pedagogy would be the springboard for the next wave of invention in dance.

In her four years at the University of Wisconsin, Ann had found three of the most critically influential people in her life—Margaret H'Doubler, Max Kadushin, and Lawrence Halprin. The first had given her a model for dance as an arena for self-discovery, the second had helped her find out who that self was, and the third was about to share with her a mutual exploration of how aesthetic, visionary, and social practices could be combined and made palpable, in space.

THREE

The Bauhaus and the Settlement House

1942–1945

Young people came . . . not to design correct lamps, but to participate
in a community that wanted to build a new man in a new environment
and to liberate the creative spontaneity in everybody.

WALTER GROPIUS

commenting on the original Bauhaus Manifesto

LARRY'S ENROLLMENT AT HARVARD, which had initially looked like such
a radical career leap, soon assumed the contours of an inevitable choice,
both for him and, just as important, for Ann. From this point forward,
their art, as well as their lives, became intertwined. Arriving in Cambridge,
Massachusetts, in the fall of 1941, Larry walked into the charged center of
a displaced European culture in the process of being transplanted to the
United States. Although Ann remained in Madison until the following summer, finishing her degree, they were in frequent communication as Larry
shared the excitement of the German design avant-garde he was discovering. "It was one of those wonderful periods in a school's life when the essence
and the core of creativity is present," he later said. "Not only were the professors wonderful, but I was in a class with a remarkable group of people:
Philip Johnson, I. M. Pei, Edward Larrabee Barnes, and Paul Rudolph, some
of the great architects of our time, were all classmates. I was surrounded by
students who were as excited about architecture as I was and through whom
I spent a remarkable period as an apprentice."[1]

As the situation in Europe worsened in the late 1930s, scores of writers and
visual artists fled to America, including Max Ernst, Fernand Léger, Piet Mondrian, Hans Hofmann, George Grosz, Hans Richter, and many designers

and architects from the Bauhaus, which had been closed by the Nazis in 1933. Among the prominent "Bauhauslers" were Josef and Anni Albers, László Moholy-Nagy, Ludwig Mies van der Rohe, Marcel Breuer, Lyonel Feininger, Herbert Bayer, and the director and mastermind of the Bauhaus from its 1919 inception in Weimar Germany, the distinguished architect Walter Gropius.

Gropius had arrived at Harvard in the spring of 1937, when he accepted the university's invitation to chair the architecture department. By the time Larry arrived with a scholarship in landscape architecture, Gropius's influence extended to all the departments in the School of Design. Every aspect of the program at Harvard—the students, the classes, and particularly the discovery of Gropius—delighted Larry. He had come wanting to study with the leading landscape architect of the time, Christopher Tunnard, whose book had captivated Larry when he discovered it at the library in Madison. Now, however, he realized that Tunnard's vision of interrelated nature and society fit into a much larger portrait of culture and community pioneered by Gropius.

In his book *Gardens in the Modern Landscape,* Tunnard characterizes contemporary garden design as "the last stronghold of Romanticism," claiming it is time to "face the task of creating a new landscape for the 20th century." Hinting at connections between social responsibility and design, Tunnard's book, which was published in 1938, in time for him to have known about the Bauhaus, reads more as a call for change than an actual blueprint. "I believe if we can gain a clearer picture of what a garden is, or should be, we shall be better equipped to evolve a technique of planning which will play a part in satisfying the complex needs of modern society," Tunnard writes.

> The fact that garden making is in part a science does not free it from the duty of performing an aesthetic function. It can no more be turned over to the horticulturist than architecture to an engineer. That it has a place beside the other arts is more than clear from a study of the past and that it still has a mission to fulfill. We need gardens for rest, recreation and aesthetic pleasure. How then can we neglect the art that makes [people] rational, economical, restful and comprehensible?[2]

Tunnard's call is for revisiting nature as an important moral and emotional force in citizens' lives. He redefines the landscape designer as an artist, one who works with colors and textures of living materials. For Larry, this notion of horticulture as an important aesthetic and cultural practice suggested how he might knit together the disparate parts of his intellectual life and marry romanticism to practicality. With the war intensifying, however, Tunnard, a Canadian citizen, left Harvard within a year of Larry's arrival to join the Canadian army.

Except for Tunnard, the department of landscape architecture did not have any distinguished landscape design specialists. So Larry approached Gropius and asked him for personal criticism of his work. Often Gropius told Larry, "Well, I can tell you what I think, but don't think that I know much about the landscape."[3] Larry also sought out comments from the architect Marcel Breuer, who also taught at Harvard. "I spent as much time or more studying architecture as I did landscape because there were so many more people in that department," Larry explained. "The big influence on me was really the architecture department, not the landscape school." Moholy-Nagy also occasionally lectured in Larry's classes: "On an American level, it was like being at the Bauhaus," Larry claimed.

Reportedly, Gropius's and Breuer's styles of offering comments to students differed significantly, so students often liked to hear from both men to get a sense of their progress. "Gropius was always in iron control of himself," his biographer Isaacs reported. "Sometimes his own perplexity was revealed by his finger-twisting, a curling of his right eyebrow, and an even more careful search for appropriate words. A balance was provided by Breuer's effervescence. He sometimes gave an artistic, light approach that, teamed with Gropius's fundamental and comprehensive one, offered the students an unforgettable experience."[4]

Gropius saw the School of Design as reflecting a conceptual, not just an administrative, unity. Even within classroom assignments, he would "encourage collaborative efforts, perhaps of two architects with a city planner and a landscape architect, selected freely by the students themselves."[5] An essential premise of Gropius's work at the Bauhaus had been to unify the practical arts—sculpture, painting, and crafts—under architecture and to erase the distinction between fine and applied arts, between the role of artist and craftsman. This was the basis for what Gropius called a "school that was the servant of the workshop."[6] Larry and Ann would eventually take this model of a fused production and educational environment into their respective fields and make the idea of a workshop, both in title and practice, central to their working processes. They were excited by the critical role of the human dimension in design, which was central to Gropius's concept. "The satisfaction of the human soul is just as important as the material," Gropius wrote when he began the Harvard program in 1937. "The intellectual achievement of a new spatial vision means more than structural economy and functional perfection."[7]

In the curriculum, this vision began with a general design course, modeled after one taught by Paul Klee at the Bauhaus. Larry called it the most significant class he ever took. As he explained, "The Bauhaus always started with a general course in design, which was painting and sculpture, and it wasn't the history of it, it was doing it—making drawings, building sculpture, and stuff like that. And it took me a great leap to the point where I understood the relationship of all the arts together. It was like somebody had opened a curtain and there was this great world of fantasy in front of me, with dancers and painters and set designers and music. That's what I saw all of a sudden. Up until then, on some level, I had been starved."[8] Throughout his first year at Harvard, Larry wrote regularly to Ann, reporting on his growing pleasure at having the disparate parts of his artistic, academic, and ethical life coalesce.

———

When Ann arrived in Cambridge, she walked into a small studio apartment that Larry had rented on Harvard Square. He had begun outfitting it with a few choice pieces of Bauhaus furniture, including a chair designed by Mies van der Rohe and a stool and table designed by Alvar Aalto. The rest of the furniture was makeshift student pieces, including a bed that doubled as the only couch and a bookcase made of boards sitting on bricks.

The intellectual life that Ann walked into, by contrast, was extraordinarily elegant, stimulating, and rich. Larry had become friends with Gropius, and soon after Ann's arrival Gropius and his wife, Ise, invited the couple to dinner. The Gropius house, now a landmark of early modernist architecture, was startling in its spare, white, rectangular simplicity. Built by Gropius immediately after his arrival in the United States and completed in the fall of 1938, the house was located in the Boston suburb of Lincoln. It was situated atop a rise and linked to its surroundings by a projecting entrance, terrace, screen porch, and vine-covered trellises. Reading a description of the Gropius's house, one can easily see why its flat-roofed novelty and austere design prompted the Federal Housing Authority to refuse to provide mortgage insurance, claiming that its design was unsuitable in a neighborhood of vintage colonial estates. It is equally easy to understand how the design dazzled the young Halprins:

> From within, large windows frame the landscape and expand the modest interior spaces. The subdued color scheme—throughout the house, a palette of whites, grays and earth tones sparked by occasional red

highlights—defers to the out of doors and modulates with the fluctuations of exterior light. The Gropiuses found that the house provided ideal growing conditions for houseplants, which became central to the decorating scheme, along with stones, shells, and branches. The house that is supposed to express reason in pure form has turned out to personify poetry as well.[9]

Ann was astounded not only by the house and its impressive modern art collection but also by the beauty of Ise Gropius. "I was very shy but very excited because all of this was so different from my background with H'Doubler. I felt I was really now in a community of artists," she later said.[10] At first Ann hadn't known who any of these Bauhaus artists were. She felt like "a hick from the Midwest" with her University of Wisconsin background in the midst of the artistic Harvard elite. Occasionally, she sat in on some of Larry's classes, including the general design seminar. She found the discussion of space in this class particularly stimulating to her own ideas about choreographic space: "It was an approach to dance and art that was totally new for me. My approach to dance at Wisconsin had been on a very scientific level because H'Doubler was a biologist, she wasn't a dancer. I didn't have any conception of the total scope of dance in relationship to theater, to space, and to architecture and all the other arts. . . . It was like looking at the whole universe and seeing dance in the perspective of a much broader context."[11]

As soon as she arrived in Cambridge, Ann contacted Winsor School, the most elite private school in town, to inquire if they needed a dance teacher. The former head of the PE program at Ann's old alma mater, New Trier High School, had recently been hired as the athletics director for Winsor. She not only remembered Ann, she hired her. "I was the first Jewish person ever to set foot in the school," Ann recalled. "I was teaching the children of the Boston Brahmins, the Cabots and the Lodges. The kids were exceptional. But I remember feeling very uncomfortable and out of place."[12]

For the next two years, Ann taught three or four days a week at the Winsor school, riding her bike, the Halprins' only form of transportation, from their little apartment, across town, and up the hill to the school:

It was an all-girls' school and they just did remarkably creative work, both in terms of their movement skills and their writing skills. I used writing, their poetry, and their stories, and the way they were able to make connections between what they were studying in their classrooms and bring that into their dances was just amazing—their sense of form and structure, their ability to work together and create dances as a team. They were the most superior group of kids I have ever worked with.

For Ann, the ease of teaching these girls translated into a heightened emphasis on creativity: "I was able to do much more with the creative process, and I was able to actually present more dance skills. The eighth graders were doing the same kind of movement skills that I would give to any adult class. I had them create their own dances and perform them for each other." In the program notes for a demonstration of student work on March 24, 1943, Ann explained that each of the nine dances was developed through rhythmic movement exercises that then suggested "a literal idea, a specific emotion, or a particular feeling state." This statement reveals much about what Ann valued most in her dance classroom. From the time she was a young child, her pleasure had always been creating new paths of personal expression.

Ann took care to mark the studio as a special space of transformation before her students even entered the room. She kept the children waiting outside until it was time for class to start. Then, each week she asked a different child to lead the others into the dancing room. "I made a very definite demarcation between outside and the dance space," she explained. "So the child who was the leader would set the movement and the floor pattern and all the rest of the children would be followers. It was like a ritual, and they would know the week before so they would be prepared."

If Ann had any illusions that teaching dance would always be this easy, she had only to look across town to the community of South End Boston, where she taught weekly dance classes in the South End Settlement House. Boston was home to five large settlement houses that had been opened in the 1890s in low-income immigrant communities. Essentially neighborhood welfare institutions, the settlement houses provided community services, classes, lending libraries, playgrounds, and educational programs for the urban poor. Ann found the settlement house the most challenging teaching situation she would ever encounter.

I remember coaching and helping them with basketball and stuff like that. I was just doing what was needed, but the dance classes that I taught—their attention span and their inability to focus—were very challenging. They came from extremely disturbed homes—alcoholic, violent. And I found this a very challenging and important experience because I realized for the first time what a protected environment I had been teaching in. I saw that there were kids that were the result of social disorder, and you saw it in their bodies and their minds. You saw it in their inability to express themselves in any other way than this constant chaos and frenzy and uproar. It was so disturbing to me.[13]

For a young dance teacher, it was an intense environment in which to discover the social uses of art, and for Ann it was eye-opening:

They would bring their babies and kid sisters because they would be baby-sitting, because their parents were working. I remember one little black girl who couldn't have been more than eight years old, and she was baby-sitting her little sister who couldn't have been more than two and a half. She was crawling all over the floor, and I remember she peed and made a big puddle. Her sister came over and whacked her across the face and then took her body and mopped up her pee with her body. I just stood there watching this, just appalled that she would have hit her for that and the humiliation of taking the kid and using her for a mop.

Ann was determined not only to teach dance but to deal with social issues. She may have at times seen teaching at the settlement house as "a horrendous experience," but she stuck with it for the full two years she was in Cambridge. "I had committed myself to something and I had to find a way to meet these requirements," she later said. "What I began to discover was that these children were a product of their environment and I had to create a different kind of environment for them to work in. They were so needy."

Remembering her own difficulties with freedom and structure in class when she was a child, Ann decided that the cure for the chaos of her classroom with the settlement kids was a different kind of freedom. She experimented with very concrete methods in her assignments. For example, one day she brought in a pile of cardboard cartons and set up a series of simple interactions between the kids and the boxes. First, she had the children do things in relation to the cartons, such as jump over them. Then paint them. Then move the painted boxes, depending on their colors, to different points in the room. "I started using very concrete techniques that would give them very clear definition and still promote movement activity," Ann explained. Next, she had the students gesture as if they were putting all of their angry feelings—the pushing, the shoving, and the banging into each other—into the boxes.

The demands of how to create structure and at the same time provide a climate that fostered the pleasures of unfettered dancing led her to other solutions that avoided labeling any behavior or action as "bad" or "wrong." She came to see the time the settlement house children had with her and with dance as "an oasis for them in their lives." "I remember being tough, but I avoided scolding them. I would handle them by saying, 'There are times when we move and the movement just takes over and we have no control of what we do. Now when I see that happening and when I think that somebody might get hurt, there's going to be a special place in this room where you can go and do something else until your body is able to help you.'"

"Uh-oh, your body needs some help," Ann would say when somebody got knocked down and started screaming. And she would direct the wild child to a section of the room she had outfitted with crayons and paper. The child had to stay there until Ann checked in and determined that his or her body was now back in control. Intuitively, Ann was reading back past the unruly child's actions to the emotional source that spoke through the uncontrolled movement. "They had so much hurt that it was coming out in this bombastic movement. How can you scold a kid for having all this anger because she comes from a really dysfunctional environment?"

Years later when she reflected on this early teaching experience, she underlined what the children had taught *her*. "I just think that [these] children sensitized me to the broader picture of life. I discovered you don't look at a child just when they come to dancing class. You really need to look at the child as a whole person. You really need to know what makes them tick, what creates the movements that they create. And this started for me, very poignantly, at the settlement house."

The desire to know more about the inner workings of her dancers may have started for Ann at the settlement house, but it did not end there. She began probing, first with the children, then with herself, and finally with other adults, not just what the intended meanings of the specific gestures were, but what the unanticipated patterns of their actions or poses might suggest when looked at from the outside vantage point of the audience. In particular, she was interested in how individual choices might suddenly look different if grouped together—more like a movement paragraph than a sentence.

One of the most popular dances she evolved in this way with her children's classes came to be called "The Cathy Dance." For years she repeated it whenever she taught children. The Cathy Dance emerged out of a basic, structured improvisation Ann did in class one day:

I had them spin and then I'd say "Stop!" And then: "Now move out of your frozen position." One time this one little girl froze and everybody else happened to be in a frozen position as if they were pointing towards her. So when I said, "Now just move from where you are," they all started making fun of her and they made her into a victim. They taunted her. This just came out accidentally, and then she suddenly shouted out, "Stop it!" and she said, "I turn you all into toads." So she became the bully and they became the victims. And they all became toads. "Now I turn you into this . . . Now I turn you into that . . . " The only thing I ever said in that whole dance was, "Well, Cathy, how would you like this dance to end?" And she just put her nose in the air and said, "And don't ever do that to me again!" and she walked out of the room.

The Cathy Dance became so popular that Ann had to do it again and again until everyone had a chance to be Cathy. What delighted her about the Cathy Dance was how true it was to the internal socialization process that all the children were experiencing at that time in their lives. They described a troubling problem and then, through movement improvisation, they uncovered a creative way to essentially rewind the scene and replay it with just the right witty comeback.

Ann rarely spoke with Larry about her teaching experiences at either the settlement house or Winsor. She had rented a small studio where on her days off she worked on her own choreography, creating a series of solos she eventually performed in a concert attended by several design students and faculty members from the Harvard program. The strongest link between Ann's daily experiences as a children's dance teacher and the stories of his Harvard classes Larry shared with her was a growing mutual awareness that the way in which a subject is taught can be as critical an educational experience as the subject matter itself.

This period in Boston confirmed for Ann that a revolution in design or art or dance is by necessity linked to a revolution in pedagogy. Through Larry's immersion in the School of Design program and her own attendance at public lectures, social gatherings, classes, and other events, she absorbed the spirit and challenge of Gropius's approach to teaching design. Ann was working in dance education and had been primed by H'Doubler to think of dance pedagogically, so it was logical that her absorption of the Bauhaus ideals and aesthetic was most vivid as a new educational model. Indeed, Gropius himself envisioned the Bauhaus fundamentally as an educational system—one that linked aesthetic production and social change.

Gropius's establishment of the Bauhaus curriculum at Harvard coincided with the U.S. government's first big and direct investment in culture as democracy. As part of Franklin Delano Roosevelt's New Deal, the country embarked on a massive employment relief program for artists in 1935, the Works Progress Administration. Created in the midst of the widespread unemployment of the Great Depression, the WPA redefined art as an important democratic and social activity. Projects were created that emphasized culture's interrelationship with every aspect of life. New academic theories and experiments were tried in an effort to address social and economic problems through education. Politically focused, collaborative art experiments were also regarded with new interest in the effort to address broad cultural goals through the arts. By the time it was officially terminated on June 30, 1943, the WPA had employed more than 8.5 million people on 1.41 million individual projects in writing, theater, dance, visual arts, history, and music.[14]

In many ways Larry and Ann rode the crest of this wave of cultural change, this redefinition of the role of art in American life. Moreover, at Harvard, they found themselves at the center of another revolution. Not only did the Bauhaus approach revolutionize design in America, but it also affected other art forms, suggesting new alliances between art and social utility, including art actions that echoed and perhaps even changed people's lives. In her own experiences at the settlement house and Winsor School, Ann was already discovering that there were appetites among the disenfranchised that art might fill and aptitudes among the privileged that it might stimulate. At other points in her life, Ann would again find herself shuttling between these two social extremes and attempting to address both, with compassion and curiosity, as vital arenas for making dance.

More immediately, however, Ann began shuttling between the art forms of dance and architecture. Just as Larry was finding his many disparate interests suddenly fitting together under the Bauhaus rubric of no segmentation in the arts, Ann started contemplating how she might play with architectural concepts like space through the medium of dance. Larry, too, began regarding her work in dance with new eyes. As he explained, "The Bauhaus itself in Dessau [the site of the school from 1925 to 1932] had included dance, theater, and costume design. So I was enveloped with the idea, which I still believe, that there are no pieces in the arts. That they are all one thing, and that all the arts are a way of creatively modifying and improving the world."[15]

In her own dance classes Ann began exploring the architectural concepts of space she had gleaned from Larry's general design class. She was able to implement this because a wealthy Chicago heiress and dance patron, Barbara Mettler, was impressed with Ann's teaching at the Winsor School in the spring of 1943. Mettler, who had studied at the Mary Wigman School in Germany, invited Ann to teach at her private residential summer program for dance teachers on her New Hampshire estate. Ann was given the freedom to teach whatever she wanted—and Ann chose the concept of "space," entitling her curriculum "Visual Design and Dance."

She led off the first week with an exercise that would become emblematic of her incorporation of the natural environment as a guide for creation in the arts. Specifically, she instructed the students to go out into the country and "bring back forms from nature they found exciting because of a design feeling. Bark, stone, twigs, foliage, fungi." Initially Ann had the students sketch these—probably a literal adaptation of a Bauhaus task. In a handwritten note on that first week's lesson plan, however, Ann indicated that the results were so unsatisfying that she felt discouraged. She then found an "improvement": "Instead of drawing objects asked them to dance or move as impressed by objects." She elaborated, "One by one each person began to show thru movement different ways of feeling space. We discovered that it was live substance. That we could act upon it and that it in turn could act upon our movements."[16] Here was a bedrock discovery of the nexus of space, form, and motion that would be the foundation of her dance teaching and performance for the rest of her life. Oskar Schlemmer's architechtonic space now had a link in American dance.

For the next two summers, Ann continued to teach and study dance in the big barn on Mettler's estate, living in one of the private cabins built to house the summer students. "It was a very serious course," Ann recollected. "It gave me a chance to begin to integrate what I had learned from the architects into dance. I was influenced by the way the designers worked, so first I did an analysis of space based on the influences of the Harvard School of Design, and then I designed this course for dancers. I would give them a problem and they would have to solve it. We might study planes in space, and then they would be required to design a dance in which they focused on the element of planes in space. Or I might ask, 'What is denseness and sparseness? The outside space, the inside space, open spaces and closed spaces?'"[17]

Since the bombing of Pearl Harbor in December 1941, Larry had entered a special accelerated program, designed to allow him to finish his degree in landscape architecture in two and a half years so he could then enroll in the navy. So Larry remained in Cambridge through the summer, taking courses. For Ann, the New Hampshire summer of dance on the Mettler estate was idyllic. It combined a secluded and spacious landscape, art making, the sensual pleasures of hearty group meals, and much time outdoors, presaging the model she would create at her California home two decades later. As she recalled:

> I arrived at Franklin station in New Hampshire along with a small group of girls from various parts of the country who came to study modern dance intensively at Barbara Mettler's school. We were met by the school's station wagon, which carried us ten miles out of town to the reconstructed farm where the school was located. The site was typical of New Hampshire, with hills and valleys on all sides, big clear spaces above, much earth, trees, and flowers below. When we first saw this magnificent country we wondered how one could ever ignore it long enough to work on dance. And yet at once we found we were affected differently, for each one of us became at one with the forces of the country, not merely a gasping spectator. We found that its beauty simply became an added stimulus to the creative process.[18]

When Ann returned to Cambridge in the fall of 1943, she decided to explore the overlap of dance and architecture from the opposite direction. She began offering dance classes for architecture and design students two evenings a week in the studio she rented. In her summer teaching, exploring space, Ann had discovered how space that was restricted affected not only what one could do physically but also how one felt. These evening classes were posed as problem-solving situations in which Ann asked the architects to use materials in the room—chairs, tables, whatever—to build an environment. Then she told them to "move" in the environment they had just constructed:

> We would continuously be working with creating these temporary environments and then moving in them. Because as architects, if you are building a house or a building, how is this going to affect the people living in it? How does this make them feel? What is the difference in feeling between designing something that goes around in one way or another? What does a curve feel like to experience in your body as op-

posed to an angle? So I translated what I understood about space into movement for the architects and into a conscious use of space for the dancers. It felt like we were pioneering.[19]

Several years later, when Ann and Larry began teaching joint summer workshops on the West Coast for architects, dancers, and artists, this would become one of their essential exercises. Whenever Larry later enumerated the central ideas he was exposed to during the Harvard years, this linking of space and form and the probing of the arts as an interdisciplinary investigation were paramount.

Ann remembers Gropius as being particularly supportive of her dance classes for the architects: "He was really pleased dance was going on." Certainly the incorporation of theater and performance with design were familiar concepts from Gropius's days at the Bauhaus, when Oskar Schlemmer created *The Triadic Ballet,* his famous 1922 study of form in motion, in which performers moved through different spatial environments in costumes that abstracted the body into geometric forms. Schlemmer described the stage as an "architectonic-spatial organism," in which all elements and activities exist in a spatially conditioned relationship.

Earlier, during her first year with Larry in Cambridge, Ann had, on one occasion, brought her presence as a dancer into the Harvard design circle. Since June 1937, three months after his arrival in the United States, Walter and Ise Gropius had been hosting parties at the end of the year for the graduate students in the School of Design. The alcohol flowed freely at these events, and the dancing and mood were wild. The first such party Ann attended was a costume party where everybody came dressed in Bauhaus-inspired attire. Two photographs from that party show Ann and Larry in costumes clearly inspired by *The Triadic Ballet.* Larry wears a hat sliced by stripes, which looks like a huge coiled snake on his head. Instead of a shirt he sports a huge cardboard shoulder pad, which protrudes over both arms, and a pair of dark tights with a spiral of ribbon running up one leg. Ann wears a black leotard and tights and a pair of shorts with a tutu-like skirt, made up not of fabric but of a network of thin strings. She gestures with a bent arm toward Larry. In the other photograph, a smiling Gropius presents Ann with a large bottle of champagne while an audience of other students, some in costume, looks on. Half of Ann's face is painted like a Picasso plate, and she looks poised and steadily in character as she stands in a doll-like ballet first position with her feet. Again, she gestures formally with a bent arm, this time pointing toward Gropius and the champagne. Larry built the costumes, but Ann performed them. She had never been to a party as sophisticated or as liberated as this, and she felt in over her head. Most of the time when she wasn't teaching, Ann spent working alone in her studio by herself. "I fended for myself at the parties," she later said. "I never drank. I was very shy, but I was a good performer at covering it up."[20]

When she was not pedaling off on her bicycle to teach children, Ann worked most of fall 1943 in her studio creating several solos. One of these, *The Lonely Ones*, emerged as her first major dance. Taking as its inspiration, and title, the book of cartoons published the previous year by the *New Yorker* cartoonist William Steig, Ann's dance is a humorous three-part meditation on the human condition. Each section—"Forgive Me I'm Only Human," "I Mind My Own Business," and "Very Few Understand My Works"—refers to a specific cartoon and character in Steig's book.

Steig was an astute and insightful social critic whose cartoons had been appearing in the *New Yorker* since 1930, but with the publication of *The Lonely Ones* he became an instant celebrity. His figures were hailed in the popular press as a new art form of symbolic, psychological drawing. Images from the book were reproduced on cocktail napkins, ashtrays, and greeting cards. Other artists in particular rallied around his satires of the human condition—the writer W. H. Auden compared his drawings to Goya's *Disasters of War*, and the photographer Walker Evans offered to loan Steig hundreds of photographs so he could study the faces.[21] Couching his social commentaries in psychological terms and relaying his criticism of the social order through the aesthetic means of popular culture gave Steig's work its edge.

Ann's initial attraction to Steig's work was more direct: "I thought I was getting boringly serious and that I had not developed any humor," she said. "I needed to develop a sense of humor in dance. So I started looking at cartoons."[22] Cartoons, like children's dances, can seem innocent and free initially, but some of the most memorable ones expose the foibles of daily life. Steig's drawings pushed cartooning in the direction of deliberate intellectual criticisms of the social order in which contemporary artists in more mainstream art media were engaging.

Through Larry, Ann was part of a sophisticated, almost exclusively male arts society at Harvard, but as a dancer and a woman, she was also outside of it. Her dance *The Lonely Ones* is a social commentary but also a self-portrait. All three of the Steig figures Ann chose are men, and each is lonely in his own way. "I Mind My Own Business" shows a smug little figure with closed eyes and pawlike hands held limply in front as he spins away on feet that whirl like propeller blades. Another cartoon, "Forgive Me I'm Only Human," depicts a dazed-looking little man, naked except for a pair of briefs and a fedora. He stares anxiously upward, his eyes shadowed by the rings of sleepless nights. In "Very Few Understand My Works" a regal figure sits icily atop a hill.

Ann feminized all three figures, dancing at first in an old dress covered with huge polka dots and a small, feathered, black hat. Although this figure does not match Steig's cartoons inside the book, it echoes an image he drew for the book's original cover, an image of a woman in a polka-dot dress and little black hat.[23] In the dance Ann's character is hunched and tentative in her gestures, her facial features twisted into an anxious and timid expression, as if just standing up straight were too bold a statement for her body to make. This image of loneliness also suggests the gestural pose of an old Yiddish theater caricature of a shtetl Jew. Everything about Ann's *The Lonely Ones*, from its inspiration to its tone to its cultural references, seems far from the cool Germanic modernism of the Bauhaus world. *The Lonely Ones* was Ann's own "Cathy Dance," as she grappled with how to find herself as a dancer, alone. In his introduction to the original edition of *The Lonely Ones*, Wolcott Gibbs makes the following observation about the Steig figures:

> In "The Lonely Ones," Mr. Steig offers us a series of impressions of people who have been set off from the rest of the world by certain private obsessions—usually it seems by a devotion to some particular disastrous cliché of thought or behavior. They are not necessarily unhappy—some of them, in fact, are obviously only too well pleased with themselves, and loneliness, or singularity, is, of course, by no means an unhappy state—they are simply not quite like the other girls and boys.[24]

In the fall of 1943 Ann premiered her new solos, including *The Lonely Ones*, which had a piano score by Norman Cazden, at two small gatherings: one for faculty and students at the School of Design and the other for the children and families from the South End Settlement House. There is no record of the reception, but well into the next decade Ann continued performing *The Lonely Ones* to warm critical acclaim.

For her opening pose, Ann copied literally the character's position in the Steig drawing; she then improvised nightly how that character might come to life. As already indicated, for "I Mind My Own Business" she became a hunched little old lady, very rigid and set in her ways; she looked almost motorized as she moved. With her white party dress covered with golf-ball-sized pink polka dots, a prissy expression, and a small-brimmed hat with an enormous tangle of feathers on top, she looked, in her own words, "somewhere between a little old lady and a parrot." The second character, while not specifically a man or a woman, was pitiful and dumb, a bedraggled clown who seemed to have lost her place not only in the performance but in life as well.

Between sections, Ann changed her costume by slipping quickly behind the onstage set piece of a cardboard cityscape. In the final segment she reentered wearing a long dark dress. Part fantasy, part mockery, this piece was danced to programmatic piano music, sometimes played live by Cazden. Seen by some as a thinly veiled comment on the modern artist's continual laments about not being understood, this last section climaxed with Ann "skillfully flipping her entire dress over her head so that she is transformed into a Mondrian-like abstraction."[25]

Writing many years later in an appreciation of Steig's book *The Lonely Ones,* Roger Angell commented, "The title sounds like a warning. Survival, we begin to understand, is the main event."[26] The same might be said of the way Ann was learning how to survive as a dancer independent of other dancers or a strictly dance environment. For the first time she, along with Larry, found herself belonging to a *mixed* community of artists working in diverse media and disciplines. This would be the kind of arts community they would continue to thrive in.

Larry was already familiar with moving through organized academic programs and being the one whose interests crossed over the neat boundaries. It was not so much that Larry was destined to be an architect as that, suddenly, architecture appeared as an arena in which he could address social, aesthetic, and community issues. Ann would draw many of the same lessons as Larry from the years at Harvard.[27] While Larry discovered that social problems and architecture were linked, Ann found dance could also be an important arena to effect social change, not just superficially as a topic, but by really blending the practice of dance with the lives of the people you wanted to help change. Larry learned that space and form were linked, and Ann discovered how to focus on the space around the movement, outdoors as well as indoors, as a critical partner in the dance. For Larry, the object was no longer an object; it had to be integrated into the landscape. For Ann, all objects in her dance came to have meaning and often the setting yielded the objects used in the dance. Both Larry and Ann recognized that the arts were not segmented. He discovered that there was no separation between draftsman and painter or the painter and the object painted. She discovered that everybody, every *body*, has a dance—both children and adults, dancers and non-dancers. For both, Halprins process would become more influential than the forms. Ann never called her working group of performers a dance company; instead, she had a dancers' workshop where everyone generated the material for performance.

With its witty mood of innocence and yet sophistication, *The Lonely Ones* revealed Ann's use of irony and humor as distancing devices to comment on social habits as well as her equally lonely status as an outsider to Larry's academic community. The work also suggested how much her children's dance classes could be useful as laboratories for her own choreography. Without a company and primed by H'Doubler to think proudly of herself as an educator first, Ann would make her classroom her most enduring site for creating and testing her choreographic ideas.

During the same period that Ann and Larry were assembling themselves as artists in the shadow of the Bauhaus at Harvard, another important center for Bauhaus influence in America was under way at Black Mountain College in North Carolina. Headed by Josef Albers, a student of Gropius's at the Bauhaus in 1920, Black Mountain College became the center of Bauhaus influence on the visual and performing arts, much as Harvard was for design and architecture. Gropius was part of the advisory board for Black Mountain, which existed from 1933 to 1956, and he acknowledged the success of Albers's approach.[28]

The Bauhaus also had an outpost in the Midwest, at the Chicago Institute of Design, which had opened in October 1937, under the name the New Bauhaus, just seven months after Gropius began teaching at Harvard. It was under the direction of László Moholy-Nagy, a close colleague of Gropius's and a frequent lecturer at Harvard who became a friend of the Halprins. At the same time Larry Halprin headed east for Harvard in the summer of 1941, the musician John Cage left California for the Chicago Institute of Design, where he had been invited to teach experimental music.[29] Cage would subsequently influence the other important modern dance innovator whose developing aesthetic intersected with Bauhaus ideas, Merce Cunningham.

Cage and Cunningham first met shortly before the 1938 Bennington summer program at Mills, when Cage began to accompany Bonnie Bird's modern dance classes at the Cornish School in Seattle. Cunningham was then nineteen, the same age Ann had been when she first met Larry. Cunningham's path would be different from Ann's, but both were affected by their early brushes with the Bauhaus.

Ann and Cunningham never formally met that summer at Mills, when their paths first literally crossed, but in the 1940s their paths again crossed—this time, conceptually—through their exposure to Bauhaus ideas. Although neither ever studied directly with Bauhaus teachers, they made work, experimented, and taught in this circle and climate. For Ann, the architectural end of the Bauhaus influence would be manifested in her spatial explorations of the body and the environments in which dance happens; for Cunningham, the Bauhaus impact was more about breaking from the synchronicity of gesture and sound. Two decades later, their separate paths would merge as influences in the Judson Church movement of the 1960s. Ann would give the next generation the ritual of daily tasks as a movement vocabulary, and Cunningham would introduce aleatoric structures for freeing dance from narrative. Both dancers would also create new models for using other artists collaboratively in their work, a more tangible aspect of the Bauhaus legacy in their work.

———

In December 1943 Larry enlisted in the navy. By the time his bachelor's degree in landscape architecture was conferred, in January 1944, he and Ann were already in Florida, where he had begun a two-month training program to be a fighter director officer on a destroyer. Ann stayed near the base in Florida during his training, and her childhood friend Miriam Raymer Bennett, whose husband was in the same program, joined her. In March 1944 Larry was sent out into the Pacific to join his ship, the USS *Morris VII*, at Hollandia in New Guinea.

Ann went to New York, where she planned to dance and live with Larry's family. She hoped finally to be able to dance with Doris Humphrey, a dream deferred from high school. Humphrey, however, was at the end of her performing career, in constant pain from her severely arthritic hip.

"New York was a curious place in the 1940s," Ann later said. "Things were in transition when I came." Among the "Big Four," Doris Humphrey and Charles Weidman were disbanding their company and going through a reorganization, Hanya Holm was moving in another direction, and Martha Graham was still going strong. "I came to join this great modern dance movement in New York [and] I ended up on Broadway," Ann noted. "It was a little unsettling because my expectations were set at one goal and I adjusted to another."[30]

At the end of the summer of 1944, Doris Humphrey and Charles Weidman announced they would be holding auditions for dancers for a new musical they were choreographing, *Sing Out, Sweet Land!*—a biography of the nation told through a string of popular and folk American tunes, held together by a sparse plot conceived and written by Walter Kerr, then a thirty-year-old beginning book writer for Broadway shows. Ann auditioned and was given a part among the large cast of dancers who provided the period background as the scenes moved from Puritan New England through the Civil War to the Jazz Age. The show, which opened on December 27, 1944, and ran for almost three months, featured folksinger Burl Ives singing "Big, Rock Candy Mountain." Ann was cast front and center for much of the dancing, and her expressive face added a comic edge to her character. The humor reached an unanticipated level one evening when, during the high-kicking Civil War number, the elastic waist on Ann's bloomers snapped and she continued trying to high-kick across the stage as the bloomers pooled around her ankles. One night a few weeks later she took on the part of the comedienne, who had called in ill. "It turned out that I had a great flair for comedy," Ann said.[31] She was subsequently approached to do other shows as a comedienne, but she turned these offers down.

Sing Out, Sweet Land! was a modest success, running for 102 performances before closing on March 24, 1945. Its run was undoubtedly affected by the fact that it had the bad fortune to open the day before the much longer-running dance musical *On the Town.* When the show's run ended, Ann continued to live in Rose and Samuel Halprin's apartment while she waited for news about Larry. She did not have to wait long. On April 6, 1945, she heard the news that a kamikaze pilot had hit Larry's ship. Forty-five of Larry's fellow seamen were killed and wounded, but he had survived. He was alive, and he was coming home.

The bombing of the USS *Morris VII* was a prelude to the battle of Okinawa, an invasion by land and sea that cost the Americans more causalities than almost any other single engagement of World War II. Larry served as an ensign on board the *Morris,* a flagship destroyer that saw extensive combat action in the Central Pacific. He was trained both as a fighter director officer, in charge of squadrons of attack airplanes, and as a radar officer, able to pilot navigational systems as well as surface and aircraft radar.

"I had both a wonderful time and a terrible time," Larry later said. "The terrible time wasn't the war, but it was being compressed into a small universe that I couldn't break out of." He underlined the "loneliness and boredom which any fighting ship [sailor] will tell you is difficult."[32]

On April 6, 1945, while the ship was on patrol escorting transports and cruisers, a kamikaze carrying a torpedo closed in on the ship. The destroyer's guns hit the plane, setting it afire, but they could not prevent it from crashing into the ship. Fires caused by the explosion spread rapidly. Several hours later, when the flames were under control, the *Morris* returned to harbor and the crew was evacuated. Larry had narrowly missed being killed:

> The guy who was sleeping in my bunk was killed by the kamikaze plane. He was a young fellow who [had recently been] badly injured on a coffee break. I [had] sent him out during an attack to get coffee, and he came back and there was a lurch in the ship and it spilled the coffee all over him and he was badly burned. So we put him in my bunk, and the next day that bunk got destroyed, with him in it.

It was a tragic coincidence that haunted Larry long afterward. Many other crew members also died in the explosion.

Larry was shipped back to the United States on survivor's leave in late April, arriving at Hunters Point Naval Shipyard in San Francisco, and quickly made his way to New York to visit Ann. There Larry and Ann went to see *Oklahoma!* (the show that *Sing Out, Sweet Land!* had been intended to challenge). Larry recalled catching a glimpse of Frank Lloyd Wright— flamboyant in his signature cape—in the audience. Soon afterward Ann and Larry spent a week at the Pennsylvania weekend home of Larry's Uncle Sydney. Larry loved this fifty-five-acre farm on the Delaware River, near the New Jersey–Pennsylvania border, and did many watercolor drawings there, giving Sydney some of these in appreciation.

Larry was then sent to Hawaii for a few weeks to teach his navigation radar duties on the destroyer. Then he returned to San Francisco. Ann had stayed on in New York for several weeks, continuing to live with Rose and Samuel in their apartment. A sense of providence and, in retrospect, inevitability framed the Halprins' arrival in San Francisco. Shortly before her journey west, Ann voiced her expectations in an exuberant note to a college friend:

> I'm off to meet Larry in San Francisco next month and we are going to stay there permanently—I hope hope. We are going to have a guest room

so you must come and visit us and see the wild open spaces—I'm so excited excited excited! . . . Now I'm glad I'm going to California—I want to be left alone, live a normal resourceful life with a connection to the soil and to the common pulse of ordinary people. I'm not interested in acclaim—I'm only interested in creating out of the soil and the people a healthy fresh dance that is alive and vital. I'm getting so sick and tired of New York dance—it's neurotic, eccentric and in many cases stale and in most cases uninspired. I'm not being smug—I don't say I can do better—but I do say New York itself breeds a warped kind of a dance.[33]

Ann's letter reads like an explorer's farewell and a challenger's manifesto. Its images of creating out of the soil hint at a the kibbutznic idealism she may well have heard from Larry or Rose Halprin. She already envisions life in the West as a purifying adventure and a spur to her own creativity. For her, New York represents the "neurotic, eccentric, . . . stale and in most cases uninspired" in life and art, while the "wild" West promises to be "alive and vital," "healthy" and "fresh."

Ann arrived at these sentiments in a remarkably short time. She had been in New York just over a year and already she was eager to leave for good. In consciously painting San Francisco as the social and aesthetic opposite of New York, Ann handily omitted the two communities' similar features. In fact, the Bay Area had its own emerging community of modern dancers who, at a meeting on October 29, 1944, had organized as the Dance League, a "non-profit cultural organization dedicated to the promotion of dance as a fine art."[34] By the mid-1940s California was already known in the dance world as the launching pad for two women who reshaped the field of American dance—Isadora Duncan and Martha Graham.

FOUR

Western Spaces
1945–1955

San Francisco is one of the easiest cities
in the world to live in. It is the easiest in America.

KENNETH REXROTH

1957

ANN AND LARRY HAD BEEN in San Francisco only a few months when
the war in Japan ended. They were living in one of the cramped and spare
Quonset huts hastily erected at the southern tip of the city, on the grounds
of Hunters Point Naval Shipyard, as temporary housing for military per-
sonnel, like Larry, who were out of combat on survivor's leave but expected
to return to active duty shortly.

One of Ann's most vivid early memories of San Francisco occurred late
in the afternoon, around 4 P.M., on August 14, 1945, when word reached
the West Coast that the Japanese government had unconditionally surren-
dered, five days after the dropping of the second atomic bomb, on Nagasaki.
As the news spread, Ann and Larry climbed up a hilltop on the naval base
and watched as the entire city exploded in a massive spontaneous celebration of the end of World War II. "We were all without words," she recalled,
describing how strangers embraced one another and cried with relief and
happiness. "Here I was, a young wife, unsure if Larry was going to be sent
back into combat—and suddenly I found myself in this ecstatic, exuberant moment."[1] Ann observed fireboats spraying water in the fading light
and, later that evening, saw flares and fireworks cascade over the bay.

Off the base, in the heart of the city's financial center, San Franciscans
celebrated the war's end wildly. In just the first twelve hours of the victory

celebrations, the *San Francisco Chronicle* reported, 6 local people died in related accidents; 624 were injured; 95 autos were stolen, burned, or wrecked; and scores of streetcars had their windows smashed by exuberant revelers.[2] Both the violence and the festivities continued. Although the war in Europe had ended in May, San Franciscans had not felt as celebratory then because enlisted men and women were still being sent from Bay Area naval bases into the Pacific theater. Now, however, they were ready. In the days following Victory over Japan (VJ) Day, the city's daily newspapers— the *San Francisco Chronicle,* the *Call Bulletin,* and the *Examiner*—ran huge photographs of the masses of people who swarmed onto Market Street and Van Ness Avenue, engulfing cars as they caroused, drank, and roamed.[3] At least four more people died in the next two days from "excessive partying" as roaming crowds of sailors and civilians looted and smashed windows along several blocks of Market Street.[4] Spontaneously, the streets became stages for performances of euphoria and anarchy. In 1945, then, the city celebrated the war's end with a huge impromptu performance. Within two decades, performances of war *protest* would be enacted in these same public arenas, and Ann would move from spectator to choreographer.

For a choreographer and a landscape architect, both on the dawn of their professional careers, these responses to VJ Day must have seemed like an inauguration of the performance potential of the city itself, making use of its public open spaces, its geography, its architecture, its citizens. In the decade ahead, these aspects of the city would become elements of a new theater of life for both Halprins. Years later, their daughter Daria would observe of these initial years, "They brought themselves out here and were part of creating what we now think of as California. Both its good aspects, as well as its faddish aspects. I think what California did was that it allowed them free rein to create their scene from scratch. [Ann] and Larry both needed that. They're both very big people. They needed the kind of space that California allowed them in that time to create their own stages. California was virgin land."[5]

Taking the grand scale of nature and the urban landscape of the West as their stage, and using the massive social and cultural changes under way in American society as their themes, Ann and Larry began to explore space and environment as critical silent partners in their arts. Indeed, thirty-two years later, in 1977, Ann orchestrated her own broadly scaled urban performance, *Citydance,* as a gesture of giving back to the city that had supplied her with so many formative experiences since 1945. This participatory day-long event channeled dancing participants along the very same stretch of Market Street as the VJ Day celebrations. Ann dubbed it "a gift to the people of San Francisco."[6]

The VJ Day image of the city imploding in drunken and chaotic improvisation proved a resonant visual metaphor, not just for San Francisco, but for California as a whole. As the cultural historian Richard Cándida Smith notes, during the mid-1940s "California transformed into one of the world's metropolitan centers." Like most Americans in the postwar period, Californians wrestled with complex, and at times contradictory, impulses between privacy and anonymity, between personal goals and a larger public responsibility to world culture.[7]

California's geography added to the sense of openness and possibility. As Larry recollected:

> I was terribly aware of being on the edge of the ocean. I was terribly aware of the mountains around Mount Tamalpais. The hillsides of Marin County, the foliage, the redwoods. It was just incredible. I can't remember any other place that was as beautiful in its natural environment. What I found also was the incompleteness of San Francisco, that it had a feeling like a forest with young seedlings growing up in the underbrush and that there was lots of change about to happen. San Francisco just seemed ripe for growth. Ripe for opportunity.[8]

That growth entailed a special responsibility to California's landscape was an idea that the Harvard philosopher George Santayana had suggested in a lecture in Berkeley many years earlier, in 1911. He pointed out that Californians are "surrounded by a virgin and prodigious world of mountains, forests, and sea." As a result, he argued, "You cannot feel that nature was made by you or for you. . . . You must feel, rather that you are an offshoot of her life; one brave little force among her immense forces."[9] Santayana's message to Californians was that their environment offered alternative ways of seeing nature and society and, most critically, our relationship to both—that we are not the center of the universe. The Halprins would come to learn this as well, and their work would posit a different dynamic between environment, artist, and art, in which the individual was no longer at the center of the world.

By the mid-1940s, with the specter of World War II's human and environmental devastation, Californians were becoming nostalgic for aspects of wild nature vanishing from their own landscape. Several environmental organizations and projects were by now firmly established. The oldest was the Sierra Club, founded in 1892, which had become an active force in purchasing and preserving the last untouched stand of redwoods in Marin County, Muir Woods, as well as the adjacent Mount Tamalpais, near the Halprins' future home. The rustic suburbia of Marin County, just across the Golden Gate Bridge from San Francisco, attracted the Halprins with its proximity to both nature and city life. In the nineteenth century the gold in California's streams and mountains had pulled people west, but now the streams and mountains themselves were coming to be regarded as golden treasures.[10]

The historian Kevin Starr has described the California landscape as "not a subtle drama, but a bold confrontation of flatland, mountain and valley. Topographically California had few secrets."[11] This sense of "full disclosure" in the geography is helpful in understanding Ann's work. Over the next two decades her dances pushed for psychological and physical candor in the geographies of the mind and body.

In the eyes of David Starr Jordan, the East Coast–bred first president of Stanford University, at the turn of the century, the California landscape "helped social and psychological imperatives." He asserted that "people in California minded their own business, tolerating everything except untruth and hypocrisy. With plenty of elbow room, traits of personality expanded in all directions."[12] The landscape seemed to invoke freedom and encourage expansion, as Larry observed in his description of San Francisco's "seedlings." For both Halprins, San Francisco offered an ideal place to begin their professions unencumbered by obligations to the past. It seemed to promise sweeping freedom and inspiration.

For Ann, the California landscape prompted the development of a new attitude to stage space, as well as to time and the performer's force—the basic materials of dance. The California outdoors, the expansive vistas of water and land, would soon be reflected in dances that used the body less as a vehicle of representation and discursive reason and more as a presence in the environment. Ann, like Larry, relished the privacy of the West. "There wasn't a dance movement in San Francisco and I liked that," she later said, suggesting it was a city of individual dancers not linked by any uniform stylistic traditions.

It gave me more space to develop my own point of view and my own vision. Although I wasn't appreciative of that in the beginning, I learned to appreciate the challenge. The isolation I put myself into required me to reinvestigate what dance was, what was the meaning of dance, what was the purpose of dance, why was I dancing, and so it put me through a kind of quest that was a very healthy experience to go through.[13]

Over the next decade both Halprins would explore the tensions between individual freedom, nature, and societal obligations by investigating the moving body's negotiations of space. Ann's work in particular hinged on her intuitive capacity to use dance as a way to foreground non-dancing bodies, or what the cultural theorist Susan Leigh Foster has called "bodies fashioned by other cultural pursuits."[14] Ann would not only have dancers use non-dancers' actions but also put non-dancers in the situation of dancers. For Ann, the imaginative rub of different kinds of bodies and bodily actions was as useful as a rehearsal strategy as a performance method.

For both Halprins, the conceptual, geographic, and aesthetic dimensions of space—whether space in nature, living or domestic space, theatrical space, or architectural space—would be lifelong concerns. Just as the painters Clyfford Still and Mark Rothko were bound together in what the art critic Dore Ashton has described as "their search for a new space for expressing emotion independent of discursive reason," Ann and Larry reconceived space as a dynamic partner not limited by conventional narrative.[15] A clearing of the ground in physical space has long been linked with pioneers in the West, but for Ann and Larry it was the poetic space of the cultural and aesthetic imagination that they surveyed most hungrily.

———————

Living in California at the birth of the postwar era, the Halprins found themselves in what was an enormously charged psychological climate for many artists. San Francisco avant-garde artists, like their New York counterparts, participated energetically in what Dore Ashton called the "postwar climate of rebellion fed by the release of dammed-up emotions and the inevitable hope for something fresh to come."[16] The Halprins, too, turned away from the classical and romantic traditions in their respective art forms, finding their new aesthetic community in the bohemian underground—with Beat poets and filmmakers, musique concrète musicians, and abstract expressionist painters. Ann would collaborate directly with the poets Michael McClure and James Broughton and the visual artist Bruce Conner, and both Ann and Larry collaborated conceptually with Hans Hofmann and Jackson Pollock.

The Halprins' developing aesthetics echoed the art critic Harold Rosenberg's pronouncement that for this generation of visual artists painting had become an encounter of material and direct activity without any preconceived image.[17] For Ann, this encounter involved the physical as well as psychological logic of the human body unmodified by training in specific dance techniques. For Larry, it meant emulating the implicit functionality and design of California's rugged environment.

For the visual artists Rosenberg described, painting became an act that was inseparable from the artist's biography and gestural actions. This aesthetic "permission" to make that which is immediately personal present in one's art must have felt particularly freeing for Ann, and at the same time curiously familiar. The task to discover the logic of one's own body through movement had been the mantra of Ann's college dance classes with Margaret H'Doubler. H'Doubler's pedagogy, however, stopped far short of exploring the dancer's emotional or psychological dimensions.

Although in moving west Ann had isolated herself from the East Coast modern dance world, she was able to insert herself into other influential aesthetic contexts. Her reinvestigation of dance became more of a radical repositioning of dance. Henceforth, dance for her would exist as a performance practice somewhere between the stage, the environment, and the home.

———————

The end of the war permitted Larry to finally start looking for a job as a landscape architect. Larry immediately contacted the distinguished architect William Wurster, with whom he and Ann had become friends at Harvard. Wurster, whose office was still based in San Francisco, had left the year before, in 1944, for the Massachusetts Institute of Technology, where he had been appointed dean of the School of Architecture. Wurster, a preeminent American residential architect, favored a style of regional modernism that looked for the affinity between architectural form, materials, and the needs of the client and setting. It was in this Bay Area tradition that Larry found his initial identity. Wurster stressed the unity of architecture and landscape architecture, calling the two disciplines "separated only as to materials and technique, not as to basic approach."[18] Indeed, Larry has at times described himself as more than a traditional landscape architect—as an environmental designer.

In the fall of 1945, at Wurster's suggestion, Larry joined the Bay Area landscape architecture firm of Thomas Church. Church, like his friend and lifelong associate Wurster, saw the house as a backdrop for private family life and the garden as the frame for the life outside. In this view the house served as a refuge from the "occasional" bad weather in California while the garden was the real center for living. Church extended this vision into an aesthetic that stressed the bond between indoors and outdoors among homes in the California landscape.[19]

"You know there are two important things you do: one is who you decide to marry or fall in love with, and the other is who you work for or apprentice to in your first job," Larry once remarked. "That's terribly important because inevitably working under a master influences your attitudes, your value systems, teaches you less about aesthetics than about how you approach life in your profession, and Tommy [Church] was wonderful at that. . . . He had such an incredible feeling about land and landscape . . . how to run roads up around hills without hurting them. . . . It was a remarkable experience."[20]

Church was linked to an earlier generation of Bay Area architects, foremost among them Bernard Maybeck, whose structures radiated a sense of modest efficiency, aesthetic simplicity, and reverence for nature. "There was a California attitude about the use of wood, the use of humility in architecture, the use of simplicity and plainness," Larry said of Maybeck's work. It was a model that deeply influenced Larry. As a result, he explained, "I had a kind of social concept of architecture in that I wasn't only interested in the aesthetics of architecture, which I was profoundly, but I also had a profound feeling that architecture and the design of the environment could affect social behavior."[21]

The field of architecture in America was less professionalized in this period. Good drafting skills, which Larry had in abundance, and an ability to learn on the job were critical. "Frank Lloyd Wright never had a degree in architecture, nor did Louis Sullivan," Larry remarked long afterward. "So I could have been fine. I would have apprenticed for a couple of years and been a good architect." Indeed, as he explained, after he left the navy he promptly found himself with job offers from the two top architectural firms in the Bay Area: "I went to Bill Wurster's office and they said, 'We'll hire you right away if you want, because Bill said to. But Tommy Church has dibs on you and he's downstairs.' Tommy said, 'I'll hire you tomorrow, if you'd like. In fact don't waste your time upstairs; come with me.' So I had to decide whether I wanted to be an architect or a landscape architect."[22]

Larry's involvement with Bay Area regional modernism would have an impact on Ann's work as well. A central tenet of this school—the belief that social trends needed to be interrelated with design, and that both needed to bow to the natural influences of nature in order to create an architecture that acknowledged its time and place—would find an echo in Ann's radical repositioning of dance. She would try to forge a new relationship between her art and nature and society, envisioning dance as a performance practice existing somewhere between the stage, the environment, and the home.

Before the end of 1945, the Halprins had rented a duplex apartment in Marin City, an undeveloped suburb of San Francisco at the time. Although the Golden Gate Bridge, connecting the rural communities of Marin County to San Francisco, was completed in May of 1937, it didn't become a major thoroughfare until after the war. After a few months the Halprins moved into public housing in a project built expressly for navy families. As Larry recalled, the navy housing was "beautifully designed by one of the best of the architects here [in San Francisco] at the time. They were temporary buildings made out of wood, and very nice."[23] For the Halprins, this housing held another advantage, beyond its affordability and attractiveness: it brought them closer to Ann's Uncle Jack Schiff, her mother's oldest brother, who lived in nearby San Rafael with his wife. (Uncle Jack was the brother who had been disowned by his parents when he married a non-Jewish woman.)

The Halprins lived in the naval housing for a little over a year before purchasing a small house in Strawberry, another rural community in Marin. Larry remembers the house, which had originally been built for workers from the nearby shipyards of Sausalito, as sweet and little (only nine hundred square feet), with two bedrooms, a bath, and a living room. They converted the garage into a workspace for Ann. (Eventually they would hire a live-in nanny to care for their firstborn, and she would live in this space.) Larry also promptly began creating a small backyard garden, which came to be featured in *Sunset,* the leading western home and garden magazine, as a key example of how design can enhance people's lives—in this instance by retooling a functional wartime home into an aesthetic and pleasurable postwar domicile.[24]

The article that appeared in the July 1947 issue of *Sunset* was both written and illustrated by Larry, and prophetically subtitled "Good Theater in the Garden." The introductory remarks describe how Larry began with "a GI house on a 50'×150' lot in a typical subdivision north of San Francisco" and, in what sounds like a fairy-tale narrative of transformation, "'kissed' a toadlike house on a muddy lot into a thing of beauty." Larry then suggests how to create an inviting and stimulating exterior scenic design by using carefully thought-out lighting, ambient sounds from nature, and the choreographed motion of water, birds, and people. "When you set the stage for entertaining in the garden—or just plain living—there is nothing dishonest in following a few ideas that make for good theater," Larry writes while showing a sketch of a garden illuminated at night by dramatic spotlighting.[25]

Over the next two years *House Beautiful, Living Magazine,* and the *Los Angeles Times* also published features on the Halprins' first home. The *Los Angeles Times* article celebrated Larry's economical recycling of fence and lawn materials as much as the spacious illusionism in his curved and angled designs for lawns, a badminton court, and paving.[26] Already in his early projects, Larry built part of his design around "found" objects—in this case, existing materials in the yard.

In an eight-page feature in *House Beautiful* Larry and his coauthor, Thomas Church, prompted homeowners to "discover the gold mine on your property"—their backyard. The first of the "buried riches" that they list is privacy. "Everyone needs a place he can go to shut out the world," they write. "Your backyard should be one of these places. You should be able to rest, play or entertain in your yard without sharing the time with idlers. . . . Privacy doesn't mean isolation, and you needn't own a big lot. But you do need to cut off the view of those outside your yard. Then you can wear what you please, romp with the children and the family pets, or spend the afternoon asleep in a hammock."[27] This idea of the backyard as a sanctuary from the public gaze, a site where one could retreat from the neighbors' gaze and gossip, occurs repeatedly in Larry's articles of this time. It suggests how desirable a space outside of the public gaze had become for the Halprins, and how idealized the garden was as a sanctuary for personal expression and candor.

Early in 1948, his third year with Church's office, Larry had collaborated with Church on a garden design for Mr. and Mrs. Dewey Donnell in Sonoma, California. This garden, for which Larry was named as associate designer, is regarded as one of the landmarks of American landscape architecture. Combining a bold statement with stark simplicity, it is remarkable for the breathless balance it strikes between the huge cantilevered terrace and pool and the surrounding vistas. [28] In this dramatic dialogue between garden, architecture, and greater landscape, the deck daringly juts into the air, appearing to float over the wetlands, creek, and bay in the vista beyond.

In its own way the Donnell terrace anticipates Larry's most important work of dance architecture, the dance deck that he and Arch Lauterer would make for Ann in 1954. Both structures are filled with motion, force, and energy—the key elements of dance. They offer a vantage point from which to view the natural surroundings, giving the illusion of nestling in nature. Yet at the same time they are clearly man-made sites, boldly challenging nature as they lunge outward off the hillsides, anchoring air to ground. Larry remarked of the Donnell project: "That was a beginning of trying to do ecological design in the sense that you formulate the form that you're doing based on the natural configuration of the landscape around it. . . . It has actually always influenced what I've done ever since."[29] For Larry the environment came to function as both a collaborator and a teacher. Nature's contrasts of form, color, texture, and scale served as aesthetic templates that could be echoed or "cited" in his environmental designs.

After four years of working with Thomas Church, Larry decided to set up his own private practice. "I got a wonderful apprenticeship with Tommy Church," Larry said, but he realized that he was essentially a socially minded loner. "Tommy was not basically interested in social problems. I was interested in public spaces more than private gardens," he said. "I was interested in communities and the building of communities. I was interested in how you take vast areas and develop parks and networks of open space. I felt the need to expand and look at the total landscape, the total environment with architecture in it for the public."[30]

On September 1, 1949, Larry opened his own office at 802 Montgomery Street in San Francisco. "For the practice of landscape architecture," his announcement read, "Lawrence Halprin—Landscape Architect." That same year Larry intensified his apprenticeship with the natural environment of the Bay Area. During the summer he had made his first visit to Phoenix Lake in Marin County, a place where he would spend many hours over the next four decades hiking, sketching, and observing nature.[31] Over the next several decades he would also spend weeks hiking and sketching in the Sierras, teaching himself to see nature's aesthetic dimensions and design forms.

――――――――――

The apprenticeship in dance that Ann set up for herself in the Bay Area had strong parallels to the model Larry was creating for himself in landscape architecture. Both artists arrived in the West steeped in the formal training of their respective disciplines yet open to California itself as a unique form of postdoctoral education. For both, living in the West brought a certain isolation from more established communities of dancers and architects, but it allowed them easy access to nature and involved them in interdisciplinary communities of artists and cultural activists. It also immersed them in the practical realities of how to make a living from their art. Just as Larry felt the need to apprentice with an established firm before striking out on his own, Ann spent years teaching children and adults of mixed ability before settling into an ensemble with which she could create challenging group work. They did not consider this wasted time. They were discovering how art intersects with daily lives and how those lives shape art.

Determined to continue the exploration of her body's natural movement that she had begun in Cambridge, Ann began renting a small studio in late 1945. There Ann embarked on the dancer's equivalent of quieting and teaching herself to sense the natural world by spending hours working by herself. She shared the studio with a group of folk dancers, but they used it only in the evenings and allowed Ann to use it by herself during the day in exchange for cleaning and maintaining it. The studio was in North Beach, San Francisco's old Italian neighborhood and an emerging center of bohemian life in the late 1940s.

Initially, Ann used the studio to prepare for her December 1945 performance in the audition winners' concert at the Ninety-second Street Y in New York. Encouraged by Doris Humphrey, who had been hired as director of the Y's dance center earlier that year, Ann auditioned in the spring of 1945, shortly before leaving to meet Larry in San Francisco. That summer she learned that she had been named an audition winner and was invited back to perform on a December 30 afternoon program. Ann flew back for the concert, sharing the program in the Y's Theresa L. Kaufmann Auditorium with Ethel Winter, Yuriko, Miriam Pandor, and Helaine Blok. Ann performed her comic solo *The Lonely Ones,* which was enthusiastically received, and a new solo about the Holocaust that she had created for the occasion. Titled *Bitter Herbs,* it had an original piano score by Norman Cazden. It was not well received, and Ann never performed it again.

A few months later, in spring 1946, Ann took a fortuitous afternoon break from her studio work and went to the nearby Washington Square Park in North Beach, where she struck up a conversation with a man who happened to be the dancer Welland Lathrop, who was sitting on a bench near her. Lathrop, who had initially trained in San Francisco, had gone on to teach at the Cornish School in Seattle, where he served as chair of the dance department, and had then taught at the Neighborhood Playhouse School in New York. He had danced with Martha Graham's touring company and in his own concert group, as well as in Broadway productions.[32] Experienced not only as a dancer but also as a designer of costumes and sets, Lathrop was teaching design at the Rudolph Schafer School in North Beach when he met Ann. In his own choreography Lathrop remained loyal to Graham's angular and dramatic movement style, and he tended toward biblical and mythic narratives as in Graham's early works.

Ann and Welland made for an unlikely partnership, with little to connect them other than their substantial training in modern dance. But the community of highly trained dancers in the Bay Area was tiny at the time, and the financial risks for a single teacher with her own studio as well as production costs for a solo concert were high. By the fall of 1946, Ann and Welland joined forces to rent an old Victorian-era building at 1831 Union Street in Cow Hollow, near North Beach, turning it into one of the first modern dance training centers in San Francisco. The space was ideal for their purposes. The ground floor had a spacious parquet wood floor ready to dance on, as well as a small foyer that easily served as a lobby. There was also a small raised stage area with curtains and a small garden behind the building. Upstairs there was a spacious apartment, which Lathrop immediately occupied. For the next eight years, the Halprin-Lathrop School became the center of Ann and Welland's shared teaching, choreographing, and performing. John Graham, an actor who studied dance there, recalled that the studio accommodated only ten to fifteen students comfortably, but no one ever described it as too small.[33]

That Ann and Welland were an odd team aesthetically as well as temperamentally is attested to by Nina Lathrop, who met Welland in 1955, just as his studio partnership with Ann was breaking up, and who married him in 1960, at which point Ann and Welland had long since parted ways. Nina, a Russian-born psychotherapist who was forty-five when she began dating Welland, was ten years older than Ann, and her clipped comments decades later suggest she saw Ann as an emotional as well as a romantic rival. "I had the feeling that they didn't see eye to eye," she said. "I remember that a couple of years after they got together, I heard Ann announce on some occasion that she was tired of dancing; she wasn't going to dance anymore. She was more interested in social problems than she was in dance at the time. Welland was interested in social problems, but they never took precedence over dance." Although Nina admired Ann's "gift for comedy," indicating that Ann "could be extremely funny," she stressed, "I was never impressed with her movement quality. The thing that impressed me about Welland was the movement part. There was never a gesture or movement that was not quite enough or too much."[34]

Reviewers also saw differences between the two dancers' styles, contrasting Welland's earnest narrative dramas with Ann's lively, often humorous, and always lushly movement-based works. When they gave a recital at the California Palace of the Legion of Honor under the auspices of the San Francisco Dance League on October 26, 1947, Alfred Frankenstein, San Francisco's leading art, music, and dance critic, reported:

> Miss Halprin, as these columns have repeatedly noted, is particularly fortunate in her vivid and compelling personality. She was born for the theater, and would have made an excellent actress if she had not chosen to be a dancer instead. She has a thorough command of all dance techniques, and uses them brilliantly in the service of intelligent, important, and at times highly entertaining ideas. . . . Most of Mr. Lathrop's pieces seemed to be much less well realized except for his "Three Characters for a Passion Play," wherein the emotional atmosphere of three medieval types was beautifully set forth in movement.[35]

In another review from 1947, for a different program sponsored by the San Francisco Dance League, Frankenstein wrote:

> Miss Halprin has a superb choreographic and theatrical sense, and she used them splendidly both in her dramatic solo, entitled "Entombment," and in her satire on the ordinary events of daily life called "People Unaware." The several works of Welland Lathrop which were presented were, I thought, excellent in idea, but somewhat static and relatively uninteresting in realization.[36]

Another critic, with the unlikely name of Spencer Barefoot, had a similar response to this program:

> The work of Miss Halprin was the better integrated, and the more dramatically and choreographically forceful of the two. Mr. Lathrop's dances suffered at times, as they have in the past, from a failure to project with complete conviction the elements of story, movement and emotion on which the dances are based. This failure seems at least in part to be a result of movement that is not always meaningful and necessary and of a choreographic structure that does not always allow for proper climaxes and dramatic development.[37]

These reviews suggest that, even in this early work, Ann commented ironically on the ponderously dramatic and self-consciously meaningful nature of much contemporary modern dance. While this delighted the critics, it may have distanced her further from Lathrop, particularly when her buoyant little comedies were performed side by side with Lathrop's ambitious and weighty works like *Hamlet*. Perhaps in response to Ann's success with her humorous dances, Lathrop dabbled in comedy—with mixed results. Here too his meaning did not seem to read clearly through the movement, and for the critics the result was disappointing. About Lathrop's *Drawing Room Comedy*, Barefoot wrote: "Mr. Lathrop had an excellent idea, but a certain diffuseness of movement kept it from achieving the desired results."[38]

In her classes as well as her performances Ann offered an alternative to established modern dance. She used her background in education to shape dance experiences for her students that encouraged cognitive and technical growth rather than specifically preparing them for performing or requiring the absorption of a defined body of material. In keeping with John Dewey's notions of Progressive education that she had absorbed from H'Doubler, Ann challenged behavioral conformity and what Dewey had identified as the "fundamental authoritarianism" of existing educational models.[39] Instead, she offered a "student-centered curriculum" in which her young dancers took an active role in choosing and designing their dances, costumes, music, and stories. Gale Randall Chrisman, who in 1948, at age seven, began studying with Ann, describes this experience as a "transforming influence" on her life:

> I fell in love with the dance classes. I would get on the bus on Saturday with a hard knot of excitement in the pit of my stomach. The studio was like all dance studios, wooden-floored with a piano in one corner, mirrors along one wall. One area, with curtains, was raised up a few steps and it could function as a primitive performance space. There were changing rooms in a corridor behind. Facing the main studio area was a small railed-off area where parents could sit and watch the classes and wait for their children to finish. . . .
>
> I think Ann was a very highly gifted dance teacher of children. She wanted children to love movement, to explore and extend their pleasure and joy as dancers. I also think that as a dancer (and I could see this even as a young child) she herself was riveting, compelling. She moved with a feline grace and confidence, totally comfortable with her body and her technique, which was not virtuosic, but somehow just right.[40]

"I don't recall anything being tense in Ann's classes," Chrisman recollects. "Ann was a smiling, encouraging presence. The rehearsals and performances were casual, open-house events, as I recall. Lightly costumed. More a chance for parents to see what classes consisted of."[41] A photograph taken by Chrisman's parents at a 1949 student demonstration at Ann's studio shows five boys and five girls, one of whom is African American, messily but enthusiastically galloping at full force across the studio while Ann stands to one side, supporting their actions with the simple beat of her clapping hands.[42] She seems to be discreetly shaping, but not dominating, the children's excitement. They are all but oblivious to her presence, so engrossed are they in flying across the studio. In another photograph the group sits sprawled on the floor, avidly watching a classmate in a silly hat who brandishes a handmade sword as he energetically gestures toward his classmates with a lifted foot and upraised arm. All of the children are barefoot; the boys wear t-shirts and slacks, the girls blouses and skirts—routine playclothes of the time. The message is clear—the dancing body is also the everyday body. It transforms into an expressive art medium in a special space with sound, light, and the dancers' concentration.

In the most revealing photograph Ann, dressed in a leotard, tights, and a long wrap-around dance skirt, holds a baton in her hand as she faces a row of seven ten- to eleven-year-olds, each of whom pounds vigorously, and completely out of unison, on a long row of lacquered Japanese drums. Behind the children, some squiggly line drawings are pinned to the wall, visual footprints of the movement paths of dances they have made. In all the photographs Ann remains on the sideline while the children are the active ones, with each child unselfconsciously immersed in his or her task as dancer, musician, or audience. The blending of technique, improvisation, composition, and visual art into a sweeping dance experience comes across in Chrisman's description of Ann's teaching:

> Classes began with a bit of tumbling work (somersaults, cartwheels). I don't remember how much technical training was incorporated into the work we did as young children. But I remember it involved floor stretches to develop flexibility (soles of the feet together, head down, bounces) and quite a bit of cross floor movement (runs, gallops, leaps). Ann accompanied her classes with drum, a gong, and she had us working with percussive instruments as well. The emphasis, for the young children, was on developing creativity. Each class ended with us drawing to music. We also were encouraged to make up our own dances. I remember one performance based upon a circus theme.[43]

Just how unusual Ann's approach was is clear when one compares photographs and descriptions of San Francisco's other leading creative dance studio of the era, the Peters Wright School of Dancing, headed by Lenore Peters Job. In a 1946 photograph, a class of ten preadolescent girls, all white and all in leotards, their hair neatly clipped back or braided, sit on the floor grouped evenly around Job's raised figure, on her chair. The air is formal and reverential, suggesting a teacher-centered classroom that Job's description of the workshop's signature dance, *The Picnic,* confirms:

> In quaint costumes three pairs of children are discovered downstage right, back to the audience facing an imaginary rowboat. The music says, "Get in, get in, get in, sit down," and in turn they do just that: six children and a chaperone. She sits facing them in the prow of the boat and they row and wave to the shore. Next, having arrived at their destination, they "Get out, get out, get out" upstage. Then they look around for a good place to settle in, find it and run to the upper right stage and sit down. The next strain of the music is legato when they eat their lunch supervised by the chaperone.[44]

There was definitely competition between the two studios. Job's daughter, a dancer, teacher, and eventually director at the school, once commented that when Ann arrived in town she seemed to dry up all the resources. Chrisman confirmed the edginess, recalling once having attended a concert of Lenore Job's work with Ann. "It included an anti–Joe McCarthy dance called, I think, *The Informer,*" Chrisman said. "It was full of ugly, pointing movements, slithering, snakelike movements. Ann was quite dismissive of the political content of the dance."[45]

Over the school's first three years more than two hundred adults and children had enrolled in classes at the Halprin-Lathrop studio. This figure included a sizable number of recreational dancers, an emphasis Ann deliberately brought to the studio. "Dancing is a way of life," she claimed in a feature in the *San Francisco Chronicle,* which lauded Ann as "one of a group of young artists throughout the country with a new and vital approach to the dance—a conception of it as something belonging to everyone, not alone to highly trained virtuosos."[46] As in her children's classes, Ann welcomed students of different races in her adult classes. Ruth Beckford, an African American dancer whose modern dance teacher at the University of California at Berkeley sent her to study with Ann and Welland, explained: "Everywhere we went people weren't prepared for a black dancer and they gasped. It was courageous for them to open the door to an African American dancer back then."[47]

Beckford also commented on Ann's and Welland's different teaching styles, noting that "Welland would say, 'You have to pull up!' He had kids running out of the room crying. Ann was strict, but kind. They were both good people." Lathrop, who was gifted as a designer, began to offer classes in costume design as well as Labanotation and Graham-based modern dance. Ann veered off in another direction, teaching classes in the Humphrey-Weidman technique and a new area that rapidly became her signature—improvisation, for both adults and children. Before long her hugely popular children's' classes were supporting the rest of the studio.

Almost from the start the studio had offered a special six-week summer session. The 1948 summer session, for example, included classes in rhythmic analysis, design, composition, contemporary dance technique, and ballet for adults; children's classes; and a seminar for teachers of children. During the 1948 summer session the students and faculty decided to begin a dance magazine. *Impulse Magazine* (later shortened to *Impulse*) debuted in the fall of 1948 as a thirty-eight-page hand-typed journal edited by Murray Louis, a student in the adult classes at the time. The inaugural issue, which had a dramatic photo of Ann in profile, included articles by Louis, Jim (James) Waring, and Ann as well as commentaries by students, witty sketches by Larry, and photographs of a concert and the students. Its goal was "to erase some of the cloudy mysticism that generally surrounds modern dance" and "to communicate to the community the activities in a dance school."[48] Ann also tried to involve her students directly in the community, requiring that those in her teacher training program do practice teaching of dance in local schools, echoing the model she had experienced at the University of Wisconsin. One of Ann's advanced students, Jenny Hunter Groat, later clarified the philosophy behind this practice: "Ann told us to read theory. We read [John] Dewey, Herbert Read. Ann mentioned H'Doubler all the time."[49]

More and more, Ann was turning to improvisation as a major part of her approach to teaching, using it to heighten students' movement invention. She took H'Doubler's fundamental kinesthetic exercises and explorations of the actions of individual limbs and recontoured them into ways of investigating internal emotional states. In doing so, she was consciously reconfiguring H'Doubler's movement investigations into devices for accessing fresh movement material. The beginning point for improvisation, then, was always an exploration of the body's natural movement tendencies. "My training [was] in anatomy so it was easy for me to go into the bone and muscle structure and to work like a kinesiologist," Ann told Yvonne Rainer in a 1965 interview. "When we improvised we were finding out what our bodies could do, not learning somebody else's pattern or technique. We would improvise with rotation or flexion or other anatomical structures."[50]

John Graham, who began taking classes at the Union Street studio in 1947 while a freshman at San Francisco State, was immediately captivated by Ann's experiments with improvisation. He had been taking Lathrop's classes regularly when he became intrigued by Ann and her interest in dance as education. "I was fascinated by the kinds of things she would do with young people," Graham said. "She used ropes and stones and bells." When she offered an hour-long improvisation class for anyone who could stay after the usual classes, Graham decided to try it. "The first instruction Ann gave us was to curl one of our fingers and follow it," he recalled. The structure of this movement investigation resembles H'Doubler's approach, but H'Doubler's directives generally focused on the actions of big joints. The idea of using a single finger to lead the entire body into movement carried Ann's unmistakable stamp, in both its whimsy and air of earnest questioning. Even years later, Graham was enchanted by the novelty and simplicity of Ann's instruction. "To me that was the basis of all of Ann's work— that attitude to make it simple, possible and available. And she made you feel that you were such a success at it. . . . The whole process was about discovering things for yourself."[51]

Ann's high-velocity personality was also an important part of her draw as a teacher. "Ann had this incredible magnetism—physical, personal," Hunter Groat said, drawing a vivid verbal portrait of Ann as a dancer in her early thirties. "She was an enormously charismatic person. . . . She was gorgeous and willowy, with a beautiful body. She was long-waisted, flexible, with a closely knit body and her hair was frizzy and full. Her arms, her hands, and the sensitivity of her toes and feet were extraordinary. When she did whole body movements she was totally in command."

Ann shaped her experiments in improvisation into what she called "organic choreography," in contrast to the "representational choreography" of most modern dance.[52] Critical to her use of improvisation was her view of it as a compositional and physical training device as well as an ideational one. In almost the reverse process of Merce Cunningham's aleatoric methods, Ann stepped outside of an approach to dance that put the conscious shaping of the mind first, before gradually addressing the body. Instead, she asked her dancers to first move and then think, edit, and shape their material, progressing from raw improvised action into dance with an emotional resonance. Ann carefully qualified the nature of this emotion, insisting that "emotion in art must become impersonal," not so much immediately felt as broadly represented.[53] In the postwar conservatism of the time this was a critical sequencing, leading the dancers gently into the radical act of dancing about oneself.

In a lengthy essay published in the 1948 *Impulse* Ann recounted an anecdote about how teaching children at the studio led her deeper into improvisation:

> The children had arrived early as usual, and started to play with the instruments and tumble on the mats in the studio. A few moments later an excited youngster came running in the back patio to find me and breathlessly ask me to come and help them with a dance. Apparently they had come across a record of a Prokofiev classical symphony and had started to play it on the record machine. The children had started, almost involuntarily, to dance around the room. Their movements were completely undisciplined and disorganized. Although they felt a deep desire to dance to the music, they had soon realized that they had exhausted their own possibilities and needed help.
>
> What these children had experienced in this first complete free period of reaction was the basic springboard which all creative artists experience. No matter what the age or the art medium may be, there is always a strong compulsive urge towards improvisation as a result of a specific stimuli.
>
> I immediately realized the challenge this placed before me as a teacher. I had to preserve the spontaneity and the high enthusiasm that these children-artists were bubbling with, and at the same time I had to channel it and give them the sense of organization they felt they needed. Only in this way could they feel a sense of progress and accomplishment.[54]

In lauding the innocent wisdom of children as a source for her own invention and at the same time acknowledging the way structure contrasts so productively with freedom in art, Ann echoed the sentiments of other contemporary visual and literary artists who were looking to "innocent" sources—non-Western cultures, precolonial tribes, and children—for fresh inspiration in their own work.

In a 1949 essay for *Impulse,* Ann described how her children's dance class progressed from follow-the-leader locomotor explorations, strongly reminiscent of H'Doubler's approach, to leading her students into assembling short movement phrases as the kinetic translation of visual images or sounds and finally into imaginary trips, which each child narrated silently through a vocabulary of movement gestures. This experience seems very full for the child and incredibly demanding of the teacher. At the same time the child is learning various paths into a rich improvisatory experience, the teacher, Ann, must improvise the "tasks" that will keep engaging the children.

> It is important that the child's everyday experience be brought into focus by the teacher in the dance class. It is also an enhancement that the teacher add to whatever is lacking in the child's realm of experience. The teacher can bring this approach to his class by knowing the child's age level characteristic, being aware of his background influences and keeping up with subjects he is learning at school. The teacher must also have established a friendly and sympathetic atmosphere in the classroom so that the children are free to respond. From the response of the children the teacher can get his cue whether to dance about fairies and flowers or fire engines and scribble houses, or just a wiggly movement with a sudden stop. Teaching this way you never know what will happen in advance of a class.[55]

Ann's essay also warns that "the teacher must not let the children merely pantomime a story but rather guide them to give simple form in pure movement to their own creative imagination. The teacher should also cultivate good motor skills and develop pattern to an otherwise bedlam of noise and uncontrolled activity."[56]

In the 1955 issue of *Impulse*, Ann offers further thoughts on improvisation, stressing it now as "a means of execution and a way for releasing the free flow of intuitive intelligence."

> The basic method in improvisation is twofold. The first and most important is that the dancer must have no other factor but the kinesthetic sense to rely on in the process of improvising. The second requirement is that there be absolutely no preconceived notion to direct the action. . . . He must be a craftsman as he uses his kinesthetic sense, and a creator as he thinks with it. He will improvise as a way of unleashing inner experiences, and will shape and define this experience with his creative intelligence.[57]

In order to make improvisation a serious choreographic method, Ann consciously bled it of spontaneous messiness. She shaped it as discovery within parameters where movements originated in an intuitive union of feelings with actions. It was also great fun, particularly for the children, most of whom had few outlets offering this kind of freedom.

The dance training Ann favored, as she explained in a 1957 essay in *Im-*

pulse, was one that "integrates technique with expression at every level of the child's growth [in order to] bring forth a child who dances with spontaneity, a freshness and a vitality with the expressive mind flowing through the muscles and nerves." To encourage children (and adults) to move "with grace and freedom," she reconceptualized dance as "training for expression" rather than "senseless activity and a needless waste of time and energy that will only end in stifling their creative impulse by exhausting it with frustrated effort."[58]

Although the value of improvisation was well recognized by jazz musicians, who had always associated it with a special kind of virtuosity, improvisation in dance training was almost unheard of when Ann started using it. Most children's dance teaching of the time focused on structured warm-up exercises and movement pantomimes of poems and simple stories— just the kind of thing Ann said exhausted children's creativity. That Ann directed her young charges, as well as her adult students, to really move with great abandon and invention was radical.

———————

Ann's belief in the value of improvisation received critical support from Doris Dennison, an accomplished musician who became the music director and accompanist at the Halprin-Lathrop School. Dennison, a graduate of a two-year program at the Dalcroze School of Eurythmics in London, had met Lathrop at Seattle's Cornish School, where she taught from 1938 to 1940 under the head of the dance department, the former Graham dancer Bonnie Bird. A young musician named John Cage was Bird's accompanist and Dennison was quickly enlisted as a second. "I was helping John play the piano," Dennison said years later. "I'd play one hand and John would play the other."[59]

In the summer of 1940 Cage was invited to give a percussion concert at Mills College in Oakland, and he brought Dennison and another musician from the Cornish School with him. Dennison had a great time at Mills and the following year she relocated to the Bay Area, taking a job accompanying movement classes at a gym in Alameda. Then, in the fall of 1941, the dance accompanist at Mills left and Dennison was hired, remaining at Mills for thirty years. She started accompanying classes at the Halprin-Lathrop studio in 1946.

"I thought she was very good," Dennison later said of Ann. "Ann had fire. You watched her. But her and Welland's approach to dance was so different. I had some troubles with her classes. She did beautiful free classes for children. But as far as her work with adults or in composition—there was a lot of improvisation. She had created such an atmosphere of freedom that little kids would come into the studio before class and just start moving without a word. They would just get in there and improvise and I'd do the same [on my instruments]."[60] For Dennison, improvisation seemed okay to use for children's dance or as a musical accompaniment, but an entire adult dance class of improvisation was taking things too far.

Elaborating her views on improvisation and musical accompaniment in a short essay for the inaugural 1948 issue of *Impulse,* she underlines the intimate physical responsiveness an accompanist must have to a dance teacher. Perhaps reflecting her early association with Cage, she also suggests silence as a useful feature of accompaniment at certain moments in a dance.

The dictionary defines improvisation as a process of playing or doing without preparation, and that is what must be constantly kept in mind. There must be no preconceived idea limiting or in any way blocking the unity between the pianist and the dancer. This policy is of course varied to the instructions of the teacher, but in almost any case the fluctuating ability of the musician must always be present. Often when a rhythm has been established the accompanist will find himself in the position of being unnecessary to the students moving across the floor, in which case he may stop playing and let the dancers continue their own counting, but he must remain so much a part of the entire movement that the moment the tempo falters or slackens, he can enter the picture and support the class.[61]

Ann's experiments with adult improvisation in the late 1940s may not have profoundly impressed Dennison, but they influenced an important quartet of adult dancers—Murray Louis, James Waring, Richard Ford, and Nancy Cronenwelt Meehan—at a significant moment in the beginning of their careers. Ann's effectiveness as an improvisation teacher for adults lay in her ability to inspire her students with the infectiousness of her own high energy and then to give them just enough direction to set them in motion but not so much as to foreclose their own invention or overdetermine the outcome.

Murray Louis arrived at the Halprin-Lathrop studio in the late spring of 1946, soon after he was discharged from the navy in San Francisco. A native of Brooklyn, Louis had been drafted in 1942 at the age of eighteen. His sisters, both modern dancers, had studied with the Jewish dancer Benjamin Zemiach, a 1920s Russian émigré from the Habima Theater in Moscow, and at sixteen Louis had turned the pages for a pianist at one of Helen Tamiris's concerts.[62] So Louis knew about modern dance, and he had made up his mind that he too was going to dance after he was discharged. "I knew I was going to dance, I was a natural dancer," he recollected. "So I went to see the Halprin-Lathrop studio on Union Street. The little arts community in San Francisco knew about her."[63]

Initially, Louis took technique classes with Lathrop. "They were agony for my body," he recalled of those Graham-based lessons. "I also decided I wasn't going to be a ballet dancer because I didn't like those Russian shoes you had to wear where you rocked on a slab of leather." Then he found Ann:

> What I discovered with Ann was an improvisation class. I just gravitated to it. She was high energy. Everything about her was vital. The way she moved. The way she talked. She contacted on an energy level that was my level, and it was vital for me. With Ann it was a free experience of being in the movement. It all dealt with experience, and later when I discovered John Dewey I recognized it.
>
> I responded to Ann's vitality—all the people she attracted responded to that vitality. James Waring was in that class, and Doris did the percussion. With Welland I stepped on the brakes, but with Ann it was releasing my energy. She taught me to step on the gas. It was in her improvisation classes that I decided I would be a dancer.[64]

Ann remembered Louis with equal affection: "Murray was a very lively student. Very bright and he loved the work. He and I just hit it off. He was there for about three years and I really enjoyed him. He was a very upbeat guy and he was certainly talented. With Murray the work we did together was an entranceway for him to work with Nik [Alwin Nikolais]. I was delighted they found each other."[65]

After meeting Nikolais in Hanya Holm's summer dance program in Colorado in 1949, Louis moved to New York and began developing the children's dance program at the Henry Street Playhouse, where Nikolais's work was based. Louis immediately began incorporating what he had learned from Ann, and improvisation became a central element of his classes. As he later explained to Jennifer Dunning of the *New York Times,* "We'd improvise with the arms or feet, all of the things an arm or foot can do. This became a way of exploring the body and strengthening it, of giving the children a taste for the range of movement rather than the limitation that a technique class imposes."[66]

James Waring, like Louis, studied improvisation with Ann in the first few years of the Halprin-Lathrop studio and then took that experience with him to New York in 1949. The dance critic Mindy Aloff once described Waring as "a teacher of classical ballet known for his highly individual and often fantastical dances of the 1950s and 1960s, works which influenced the founders of the Judson Dance Theater."[67] Unlike Louis, however, Waring did not tend to credit his study at the Halprin-Lathrop studio as influencing his later life as a choreographer.

It wasn't Waring's dancing so much as his physical presence that made a vivid impression on Ann. "Waring was very frail and thin and delicate and very introverted," she recalled. She knew he had been a ballet dancer and that now he wanted to experience modern dance. "I was such a purist that I didn't take him seriously," she said. "I thought, 'How can you be a ballet dancer *and* a modern dancer?'"[68]

Waring, however, was determined to study both dance forms. In an article for the 1948 issue of *Impulse,* he ruminated on the ideal technical preparation for a dancer. He concluded that, with the exception of "a great genius" like Isadora Duncan, who "has no need of technique at all," it is "imperative for a professional dancer to equip himself with at least two different conceptions of dance movement—classic ballet and contemporary dance."[69] Waring was sampling dance styles, and while improvisation was not on his list, Ann must have presented her approach to movement invention with enough rigor to make him willing to include it in his repertoire of dance forms that year.

Although Waring didn't have any money, Ann invited him to take the improvisation class for free rather than watch it, as he initially requested. Because her movement approach was radical at the time, she worried that anyone simply observing it wouldn't understand it. "I was a little embarrassed to have people watch," she confessed. "Perhaps I thought it might have looked chaotic because at that time I was drawn to children's freedom. I was looking for something more. I wanted to free things up."[70] Waring stayed at the studio for a year, teaching ballet for Lathrop while he studied with both teachers and watched Ann develop her methods for teaching improvisation. In the late 1940s Jim Waring left for New York.

Louis and Waring both filtered what they had learned from Ann's improvisation classes into their own choreography and teaching, but Richard Ford took his experiences in her classes into the highly visible arena of public television. Ford, who arrived at the Halprin-Lathrop studio the year it opened, was soon performing in Ann's and Lathrop's dances and subsequently taught at the Marin Children's Dance Cooperative Ann started in 1948. Tall, with the lanky grace of Dick Van Dyke, a popular actor at the time, Ford parlayed his knowledge of improvisational dance for children into *Hop, Skip and Dance,* a popular half-hour program on San Francisco's public television station, KQED. The director of KQED had initially approached Ann, asking her if she might be interested in creating a television show out of her children's improvisation classes. Although she thought it was a great idea, she said it would be nice to have a male dance teacher because it might help to draw young boys into dance. What Ford taught was Ann's approach to dance improvisation. Even the title of the show reflected Ann's approach of sliding gently into movement improvisation as just another step in an easy progression from play and games to dance.

In a 1953 article for *Impulse,* Ford echoed Ann's emphasis on the importance of having a male dance teacher model: "I feel that, if possible, boys should have a man teacher for their introduction to dance because, for the boys' safety, physical strength is necessary in teaching tumbling feats, and, more important, the leadership of a man gives a masculine model. There is such a fear of being considered a 'sissy' that even the wearing of shorts in class has been on occasion a stumbling block." Ironically, while lamenting traditional biases against men in dance, Ford tacitly confirms some of them in his insistence in presenting himself as a "non-sissy" dancing male who uses masculine props and sports games to ease boys into creative dance and improvisation.[71]

Among the female dancers Ann influenced was Nancy Cronenwelt Meehan, who began taking classes at the Halprin-Lathrop studio in the summer of 1953, right after graduating from the University of California, Berkeley, with a BA in sociology. Meehan's real passion was not sociology, but the arts, and she was already an accomplished pianist and had trained as a dancer at the San Francisco Ballet School before arriving at the Union Street studio. "When I first came to the studio, Welland was teaching and he immediately offered me a scholarship and welcomed me so wonderfully that I fell in love with being there," Meehan recollected.[72] Within a few weeks she discovered Ann's Wednesday night adult improvisation class, and for the next three years she regularly took evening and weekend classes, studying Graham technique and Louis Horst's approach to composition with Lathrop and improvisation with Ann. "Both of them had commitments to dance that were so strong, positive, and generous; it was very inspiring,"

Meehan remembered. "They created a whole atmosphere that was like a total world of art and theater and dance. It wasn't just technique. There was this feeling that it was a whole part of your life, and everybody pitched in. We all helped with everything, making the costumes, etc. It was really quite idyllic in a way."

According to Meehan, H'Doubler's influence was pronounced in Ann's improvisation class in that the emphasis was on self-discovery. "It didn't have an end in sight that I could specifically see," she recalled. "It was about freeing you up and getting you to sense what you were doing, rather than just copying an external form." It was while she was at the Halprin-Lathrop studio that Meehan began choreographing, premiering her first work on a program that Ann arranged.

While Ann was influencing young dancers like Louis, Waring, Ford, and Meehan, she herself continued to be influenced by others. One such influence was the dance educator and anthropologist Franziska Boas, who became a guest teacher at the Halprin-Lathrop School during the summer of 1953. Boas, a graduate of Barnard College, was the daughter of the famous German Jewish anthropologist Franz Boas, an expert on the Northwest Coast Indians and the pioneer of American anthropology. A.A. Leath, who joined Ann as an assistant that summer, remembers, "Boas's accompaniment was from her primitive self and Ann picked up on this," using it later in her improvisation classes for interested adults.[73] Gertrude Lippincott, an influential Midwest dance educator, head of the Modern Dance Center in Minneapolis, also taught in the 1953 summer program at the studio.

One of the most important influences on Ann, not only while she was running the studio with Lathrop but throughout her career, was her husband, Larry. In their early years together, the Halprins were very open about the stimulation and insight each gained from the other's work. In 1949 Larry wrote a contemporary fable about the theatrical nature of gardens over time, illustrating it with his own whimsical Steig-like line drawings:

> Our lives have changed over the years. So have our dances, and our gardens. We are no longer content to sit stiffly in the garden in our best Sunday clothes, protected from the sun by a frilled umbrella. Our gardens have become more dynamic and should be designed with the moving person in mind. Our garden space has become a framework within which

activities of all sorts take place. . . . As a framework for movement activities the garden can influence our lives tremendously . . . it can influence people's movement patterns through its spaces taking on the fine sense of dance.[74]

His vision of a garden here is of a space whose design has a rhythm that is visual as well as kinesthetic. Landscape is choreography in the model of design Larry describes. He concludes his essay with the promise that a well-designed environment has the capacity to "give our lives the continuous sense of dance." The full implications of that are still a few years away, yet his essay gives a sense of the capacity of space to animate actions and emotions and for dance to stand as the ideal model of the body deployed harmoniously, and yet socially responsively, in the world.

For both Larry and Ann, their artistic careers were interwoven with their life together. Ann, for instance, continued teaching until just a few days before giving birth to their first child, Daria Lurie Halprin, on December 30, 1948. And she resumed teaching two weeks later. The birth announcement Larry designed is a jaunty line drawing showing an elaborately costumed clown ceremoniously drawing back a curtain to reveal the text: "Daria Halprin, Dec. 30 1948, Ann, Larry." Although parenting would be a major collaborative production for Ann and Larry, it would not slow their developing artistic careers.

Four months after Daria's birth, on April 30, 1949, Ann, Lathrop, and Ford presented a full-length dance concert, which sold out, at San Francisco's Marines Memorial Theater. A few days later they reprised it in Southern California at Royce Hall Auditorium on the University of California, Los Angeles, campus, under the sponsorship of the university and the physical education department. Ann performed in five of the eight dances presented, including her solos *The Lonely Ones* and *The Prophetess*. If she had once worried that motherhood would end her career as a dancer, she seemed determined to demonstrate emphatically that it would not. In fact, it seemed to accelerate it.

For Larry, the year following Daria's birth was also a productive one, with the opening of his office on Montgomery Street in September 1949. Before the year was out he designed his first major garden in collaboration with the architect William Wurster. The clients were Mr. and Mrs. Isadore Schuman (Ann's parents), who had moved to California in order to be near Ann and Larry and their new family. Working on four level acres in Woodside, not far from San Francisco, Larry created a huge meadow of golden poppies as the centerpiece of the garden. In a March 1955 feature in *Sunset* on the Schuman garden, Larry said that it was "conceived as a space for movement—movement of people, and of birds, rabbits and other wildlife."[75] He made several home movies of Ann and her dancers performing Jewish-themed dances in the dense meadow as if it were the promised land.

Interestingly, just when Ann was about to become a mother herself, she increased her involvement in teaching dance to children. Early in 1948, soon after she became pregnant with Daria, Ann was asked by the parents of a co-op nursery school in Marin to teach some creative dance classes for the children. The classes proved very successful, and within a few months Ann joined a group of liberal mothers to organize a new cooperative that would focus exclusively on creative dance for children. Incorporated as a nonprofit community organization, this dance co-op had strict rules—drafted by the parents as part of its by-laws. Mothers and fathers were asked to participate with their child, and at least twice a semester parents were required to assist in the dance classes, escorting children to the bathroom, tending to the injured, and helping the dance teacher demonstrate movement games like "floppy flop." Within a few years the program grew to include more than eight hundred boys and girls between the ages of three and sixteen studying modern dance at six sites throughout Marin County.

"I was captivated by the unpredictability of what the kids would do," Ann later said of the open-structured movement exercises she designed for this program. "I was interested in getting the children to be present. I might say something like 'Skip' and then I would close that direction by saying 'backwards,' 'faster,' 'smaller.' I was most interested in just generating an idea."[76] As with her own work Ann preferred that movement have its own meaning rather than stand as a symbol for something else. And the way one arrived at this meaning was through guided improvisatory work. "I cannot approach art symbolically or literally with any enthusiasm," Ann would write in a letter to the parents of her young students in 1960, "and therefore I cannot teach this way. The most rewarding part of teaching children is that the child's art is one of complete immediacy. It is impossible to bottle it up into the art labels of adulthood."[77]

A.A. Leath remembered these improvisation classes as being a complete revelation for him when he arrived in San Francisco in August 1953. Ann had asked H'Doubler for help in finding a good teacher to assist with her booming children's classes, both in Marin and in the city, and H'Doubler responded by sending Leath, a doctoral student in biology who had been auditing her dance classes at the University of Wisconsin. Compact, muscular, and delightfully unpredictable as a dancer, Leath connected instantly to Halprin's improvisation classes.

Teaching children served Ann both as an educator and as an artist. Indeed, Leath always insisted that he and Ann were educators first. "The dance productions were, in a sense, by-products of our discoveries of teaching and making the development of one's creativity possible," he said.[78] The creation of conditions in which learning could take place would prove to be one of Ann's steadiest gifts as a dance maker. Her first choreographic goal was never just generating the movements themselves, but rather imparting to dancers the tools for unlocking movements within themselves and learning to read their environment for movement scores.

In linking her children's dance classes with the beginning of her own family, Ann was also probably acknowledging the conflicting tensions of the time, which saw satisfaction for women largely tied to the fulfillment of their duties as wives and mothers. Ann had already opted for a personal life over a strictly professional one when she left the East Coast for the Bay Area. The Marin Children's Dance Cooperative, although it eventually proved profitable and artistically inspirational for Ann, was, in its early years, a means of keeping the two halves of her life—the domestic and the artistic—connected.[79]

Ann worked with the Marin Children's Dance Cooperative for twenty-two years, until 1970, the year her second daughter, Rana, graduated from high school. "My whole concept in working with children was to have them appreciate their aliveness," Ann later said. "I wanted to give them a sense of believing in themselves so they weren't worried about being right or wrong. It takes a lot of self-confidence to be a dancer because you are totally exposed all the time. It takes the most courage [of any performing art]. Kids have to grow up believing they are just fine the way they are. I did this through improvisation because with improvisation you aren't right or wrong, you just are."[80]

"Improvisation was a tool, the most important tool, I used with the children's dance collective," Ann emphasized. And she used this tool to link movement to other arts. As she stated in *Dance Magazine* in 1957:

All co-op teachers share [my] underlying conviction about the importance of imbuing and maintaining in the children a genuine pleasure for discovering dance ideas in all their experiences. The primary motivation is to encourage each child to realize and understand the basic values of creative movement. He is instructed in percussion and singing, so that dance becomes an integrated art experience. Classes draw upon the multiple stimuli of poetry, drama, painting and sculpture.[81]

A fragment of black-and-white film footage dating from 1957 or 1958 gives a sense of these early children's classes in improvisation and their strong ensemble quality. Shot by Larry with a hand-held camera, this film unfolds as a slice of spontaneous play. It begins with a chain of little girls, led by Ann's daughter Daria, dashing downhill across the stairs that led to Ann's outdoor dance deck. Like nymphs from the woods come to frolic in a forest glade, they skip wildly around the gnarled madrone trees that poke through the dance deck, each child a study in the naturalistic beauty of simple skips, jumps, and running turns.

Next, faces serene and bodies blissfully limp, the children lie on the deck and take turns relaxing and letting each other gently lift and rotate their arms and legs in a sequence Ann called "floppy flop." One little girl in a black leotard lies on the floor, looking as if she were dreamily floating, while another child softly tugs her limp arms and legs until her whole body flops over in a sleepy roll. One of the most touching passages is between Ann's oldest daughter, Daria, about nine years old, and a younger child whom she tenderly pulls to standing. There is an air of intense investment in the immediate task that Daria conveys as she leans back to get more leverage on the soft body she is tugging. Her concentration is both focused and affectionate. She is performing a task, yet one is also aware of how the trusting little child gives Daria complete authority to shape her body. (One can imagine the attraction this kind of meditative focus must have held for adult performers a few years later, in the 1960s, when "being present" was such an important social as well as aesthetic goal.)

Ann's belief in improvisation as a serious tool of dance invention is most apparent, ironically, in the way she frames it as something for which the body must be physically and emotionally prepared. The "floppy flop" exercise would become a staple of Ann's teaching and a means for attending to the first murmurings of the conversation with one's body that improvisation initiates. She also developed lucid warm-ups designed to prepare the body for improvisation that were later codified into a form she called movement ritual. This movement practice is "about coming back to feeling the body and feeling the integration of yourself," she explains. "It's a basic identification of how you are as a dancer."[82]

The final few minutes of the dance co-op film footage show three girls in a pose that echoes the twisted lines of the large madrone branch that lies next to them on the dance floor. One by one they propel themselves around the branch, echoing the form of its smaller branches with reaching arms and stretched legs. What is most captivating about this section of film is not its fascination as a performance product, which even Ann would probably agree is negligible, but what it reveals about the dancers' attention to their environment. These girls are looking seriously at the branch, feeling its linearity, its stiffness, and the arabesques of its curving wood. It seems that a first step in finding out what is inside is to acknowledge and respond to the forces of the surrounding world that impinge on our protected interior.

In the late 1950s, in an address she gave before the annual recital of her Marin Children's Dance Cooperative, Ann noted: "We are children once in a lifetime of art. The way we experience [art] in our youth may open its world of seeing, enjoying, creating for the rest of our lives."[83] So here is another key attraction improvisation held for Ann: it is about a process of discovery, of engagement with the world that, once revealed, can become a path and a process to be visited again and again. For Ann, improvisation and its discoveries are a way of being in the world and of fashioning reliable paths through its complexities.

This view of improvisation as a way of discovering the world comes across in a second film of her Marin Children's Cooperative Dance classes, dating from the early 1960s, which documents an indoor end-of-the-year festival. The dancers range from toddlers with their mothers to teenagers, and for each age group the reality of their moment now in the world is also the text of their dance. This is particularly evident in a curious exchange between two adolescents, a dark-haired boy and a long-haired blond girl. Facing each other, they stare for a long moment into one another's eyes and then the boy dodges as the girl lunges for him, their play fraught with the awkwardness of budding sexual attraction.

Ann was on a mission to foster creative vision by letting her students be themselves. "I had begun to realize that a class didn't have to be orderly, that it wasn't so bad if a class was unstructured," she remarked. "If a certain amount of chaos didn't bother the children, why should it bother me?"[84] She did, however, worry that the term *improvisation* might be misunderstood, as the word was too often associated with casualness, a casualness antithetical to what she saw as the real purpose of her children's dance classes. For her the classes entailed the serious task of enhancing a child's natural awareness while, in her own words, "providing a method of training that would let the child grow, develop, and mature."[85]

As she explored the uses of improvisation, Ann kept returning to H'Doubler's model. In class H'Doubler had spent hours having students explore the motion of various joints of the body as the wellspring of movement invention. For Ann, this notion of discovery within the body's own set parameters was a way to find oneself without relinquishing total control; it offered a structure for learning about one's own potential for creative movement. "I [wanted] structures I could use that told each child *what* but not *how*," Ann said. "As a guide I had to be open and flexible."[86]

In the end teaching dance to children helped Ann find an open-structured form of movement pedagogy for adults. "She had a real gift for teaching children," her daughter Daria remarked years later. "She just set up an absolute playground, a fantasy stage. In a way she was such a child herself. [She] was working with the imagination and play and speaking to the essence of what it means to be a child."[87]

Although the Marin Children's Dance Cooperative represented a step toward combining Ann's domestic and artistic life, there were conflicts. Ann still needed space both for rehearsing and for her teaching of adults, so she continued to share the studio with Lathrop. In the fall of 1950, *Mademoiselle* magazine ran a feature on jobs and futures for college dance majors, noting the financial hardships of a career in dance. Included among the five college graduates in dance was Ann, the only one who was married and had a child. "She teaches about half her working time, spends the rest practicing for concerts or choreographing new dances," the article stated, noting that dancers had to teach if they wanted to earn a livelihood.[88]

In 1951, however, a change in the Halprins' domestic world altered this picture, giving Ann an opportunity to rejuggle her three-part balancing act between teaching, choreographing, and caring for her family. The Halprins hired the architectural firm of Wurster, Bernardi and Emmons to design a simple, compact redwood and glass home for them on a dramatic three-acre site Larry had picked out on the bayside flank of Mount Tamalpais. The home was completed in the winter of 1952, and late that year Larry and Ann moved into it, with Daria and their infant daughter, Rana Ida, who had been born that June.

In addition to offering a panoramic vista of the San Francisco Bay and marshes, the hillside site was surrounded by redwood and madrone trees. As Larry described it:

The site is steep and covered with madrone, redwood, bay, California live oak, and tanbark oak trees. Undergrowth is bracken fern, some sword fern and wild blackberry. The views are south to the 300-ft. peak of Mt. Tamalpais and eastward across San Francisco Bay to Berkeley. We are at the end of a narrow road which has no other houses and winds down the cliff's edge to a turn-around. One parks outside the fence and walking through the low entrance gate sees the house for the first time ahead. This entrance garden is a space confined on three sides by walls formed by the fence at the entrance, a 25 foot vertical-cut bank on the left, and the two-story element of the house ahead. But the space explodes outward to the view on the downhill side—it is in effect, an outward room opening across a broad expanse of treetops forming a green, almost level carpet to the view. This entrance garden is paved in red brick and the trunks of birch form a sequence of space markers along its edge. The house has much the same space configurations [as the garden]. You enter by the front door into a low-ceilinged, confined entrance under the stair and, to the right, the glass-enclosed living room extends out into the view with a high ceiling which moves the space vertically as well. . . . I attempted in my design to make the most of all these relationships, these elements; to use the site to the fullest capacity; to put on the land what would enhance it, and in that way to enrich the living environment of my family.[89]

The Halprin home and garden become in this description a stage set with strongly determining influences on the kinds of "freedoms" one enjoys there. What it invites is a structured improvisation. One is both in the midst of the woods and observing them from the glass walls of the house's main rooms.

In this house Larry and Ann would find the most extreme privacy one could imagine in an urban setting. More than fifty years later the home remains almost as secluded, remote, and secret as when it was built. The setting is so private that the design of the house can be extraordinarily open and revealing. And it seems interesting that, as he had done with their first home, Larry took this intensely private house and presented it to an audience of unknown viewers in his May 1958 cover story for *Progressive Architecture,* the architectural magazine with the biggest circulation in the world. In doing this, Larry was playing with the tension between the seclusion of his daily domestic life and the broadly public presentation of the discoveries it allowed. Just as Larry began designing intensely private domestic environments and landscapes that he proudly revealed to huge audiences in numerous drawings, photographs, and articles, Ann would make public art about private issues germinated in the privacy of her home dance studio.

The need for a home dance studio came to the fore with the birth of Rana, as Ann began to find commuting from Kentfield to San Francisco increasingly burdensome. Now that Larry had his own architectural firm he was feeling new financial pressures. Not only was the rent on the Union Street studio a steady expense, but few, if any, of Ann and Welland's concerts made money and the costs of production and theater rental were high. Moreover, Ann had problems with the caregivers she engaged to help her with the girls. One afternoon she was hurriedly summoned home by neighbors when the woman caring for little Rana passed out in a drunken stupor on the sofa and started a small fire with her lit cigarette. Although no one was hurt, Ann always felt uneasy afterward, wondering about the level of care her daughters received in her absence.

Late in 1953 Larry engaged the respected theater architect and designer Arch Lauterer to work with him in designing an outdoor dance studio for Ann. The bringing together of their two areas of design expertise, Lauterer's with theaters and Larry's with outdoor "rooms," would result in the creation of one of the most legendary dance spaces in contemporary dance. This outdoor dance deck would materialize physical and imaginary space simultaneously, turning presentational space into a site of poetic transformation. In a 1954 essay he wrote for a Canadian architectural journal, Larry argued for a new conception of garden design as "an art of shelter" and of gardens as powerful utilitarian environments that enrich the lives of people who live in them. "In the final analysis, the garden is simply one of the most wonderful aspects of environment we can design and control. It is our total environment and all the parts of it which we must transform through design into a rich and varied work of art," Larry wrote.[90]

One senses in his writing the growing enthusiasm of a man who is passionate about environmental design and determined to move it from the fringes of daily life into the center of socially and aesthetically useful practices. The idea for the dance deck may have come in part from a commission Larry had completed the previous year, in 1953. In one of only a few projects in which he designed the building as well as the landscape, Larry created a modular glass, stucco, and plywood building for the Red Hill Nursery in San Anselmo. A feature about the project in *Sunset* suggests Larry created the building because it was a nursery filled with plants and hence close to landscape architecture. Another reason may have been that its similarity to the Halprin property permitted him to build a prototype deck on a steep slope before he tackled the considerably larger deck he would build for Ann's dance classes and performances.

The nursery was set on hillside that sloped steeply down to a creek. To increase the site's usability, Larry extended a deck out over the creek, blending indoor and outdoor elements. When Larry and Lauterer built the dance deck on the Halprin's similarly steep acreage, the blending of indoor and outdoor was also a feature, albeit more subtly attenuated on the dance deck. In Red Hill the indoor building and outdoor deck were contiguous, while the Halprin house and outdoor deck were linked conceptually rather than physically. The oddly shaped dance deck was designed by Larry to echo the angular pattern of the house, which is some fifty feet up the hill.

Within a few months of its completion, in the spring of 1954, the dance deck, as this outdoor studio was called, not only transformed Ann's life, it profoundly changed her art. "Arch Lauterer and Larry have designed a magnificently beautiful and straightforward dance deck in our own woods that can also be used as an outdoor theater!" Ann wrote to her former student Gale Randall Chrisman. "I feel my dance life is about to begin just at a point when I was most unhappy feeling it was all over."[91]

The dance deck creates theatrical space in the midst of raw nature. Walls are replaced by trees, the ceiling is a canopy of trees and the sky, and the sounds of this space are the muted calls of birds, the fluttering of leaves, the hum of insects. Ann has described the smell of the deck as "fresh foliage and the deep sweet smell of leaf mold."[92] Like the house above, with its simple glass pavilion that functioned as the living room looking out into the woods and a screened gazebo that serves as an outdoor dining room in the summer, the deck is not architecture as a statement so much as architecture as response.

Reflecting on the significance of the dance deck years later, Larry observed, "The deck was not an object, it did not become an object in the landscape. It became part of the landscape and that is very different. The fact of its free form, which moves around responding to the trees and to the mountain views and other things, has been a premise of mine ever since. So it was a place that affected [Ann's] work and also affected mine as a role model for the future."[93]

In several newspaper and magazine articles of the time, the deck was described variously as "a flying deck," "an outdoor stage," and a studio in the woods. Indeed, supported by hidden wooden beams, the dance deck does appear to soar out into free, wooded space. One approaches it by following a steep spiral of steps down the hillside to the floating performance island below. Sitting just above it on the hillside are five angled tiers of benches that seat a total of one hundred fifty. This spectators' gallery looks out over the deck, across a cluster of live oak, redwood, and madrone trees, which, when the deck was new, framed a vista of San Francisco Bay and the majestic Mount Tamalpais rising to the right.

The deck was originally situated so that a pair of madrone trees formed a natural proscenium arch and two others grew straight up through the broad Douglas fir boards of the deck. Lauterer was envisioning a new theater that would be literally transparent. "In contrast," he later wrote, "virtually every theater since the fifteenth century has been opaque, presenting a series of narrow pictures on a box-like stage hemmed in by scenery. In this theater we are not attempting to present pictures. We're trying to create dramatic images out of movement."[94] Lauterer reportedly yearned to make the place a stage as mobile and volatile as the dance it sought to contain. "He labored to create, in effect, a two-fold dance in which the potential of stage-space—its capacity to vibrate in a frame like a painter's pigments or a poet's rhetoric—could penetrate the dancer's invention and accompany its progressions."[95]

In one of his descriptions of the design concept, Larry makes it sound as if the deck were dancing with the woods:

> The form of the deck responds to the site—it meanders to avoid tree clumps, it reaches out to open spaces—it elongates to include trees as anchor points and finally it returns to the hill. The deck is a level platform floating above the ground where it almost touches earth. It is half a foot from ground level—at its highest point it stands 30 feet above the sloping ground.
>
> The deck floats above the ground but the trees anchor it in its space. Along the East face it is closed by a grove of redwoods which form a backdrop and sound reflector. Downstage two great madrones pierce the deck and form a 35 foot proscenium arch. Upstage a third madrone forms the apex of a tree triangle.[96]

As Larry's remarks suggest, the deck is a highly theatrical space, not just because its nonrectangular form invites movement, but also because of the way it is situated in the environment to reflect the changing nature surrounding it. It is a primed canvas in a setting of shifting lights, sounds, colors, and temperatures. Larry, with his painter's sensibility, noticed this immediately.

There is great change on the deck. The light moves through the trees and various parts of the deck shift from sun to flickering shade to deep shade. The seasons change and the madrone sheds first its bark and then its flowers and finally its fruit on the boards. . . . The shifting light on the deck and the varying degrees of heat and coolness in the air give another dimension of stage movement.[97]

One senses in Larry's comments his delight as an architect in discovering how every design consideration he made in fashioning the dance deck has such a direct impact on the thoughts, actions, and interactions of the dancers working on it. Somewhat more than a year after the deck's completion Ann made the following observations about its effect on her work:

I find much less need for constant sound as background and am much more content with silence. Simple sounds work well within this frame-work. . . . Since there is ever changing form and texture and light around you, a certain drive develops toward constant experimentation and change in dance itself. There develops a certain sense of exchange between oneself and one's environment and movement develops which must be organic or it seems false. Movement within a moving space, I have found, is different than movement within a static cube.[98]

The dance deck would prove to be Ann and Larry's most enduring and complete collaboration. Space, presence, the environment, and time were fundamental and constitutive of both of their art forms, and now the over-lap had been made material.

On a July evening in 1957, on a date that happened to be Ann's thirty-seventh birthday, Merce Cunningham presented a lecture demonstration on the dance deck. Unaccustomed to the foggy chill of summer evenings in the Bay Area, he opened his lecture by joking about the weather. Later he questioned the outdoor setting of Ann's dance studio, asking, "But where do you live in the winter?" as if a habitation this intertwined with nature could only be seasonal.[99] Ann, in fact, was learning to work in all kinds of outdoor climates. "I became almost animal-like in that I could adapt my body temperature to work in all kinds of weather," she said later. "Some-times I would be dancing with mittens on or with shoes on. I even got so that when it rained I would accept the rain as being part of the environ-ment." This marked the beginning for Ann of redefining movement to ac-cord with nature and her manner of operation. "I began to simply shed all of my old patterns, and I had to start anew with new ideas of what is the nature within me and how did that nature and my nature interface. That's where I began to develop a new approach to movement."[100]

It is tantalizing to imagine Cunningham's presentation on the dance deck that evening, because the typewritten rough draft of his text, which Ann saved, reveals he was searching for the same kind of balance between the man-made and the natural that Ann was exploring. "Dance is an act of concentration taking visible form in a way that cannot be done otherwise," Cunningham said at the opening of his talk. "It is its own necessity. It is an old art, and it is a manifestation of man's activity. It has changed as man has inhabited the world, and as man's habits have changed. Yet of course it remains the same. It is a realistic approach . . . done with the belief and full conviction that man is part of nature and society and that he inhabits his art actions with himself."[101]

Here Cunningham distills his quest for a theater dance that could be "like nature in her manner of operation." Ann, however, was looking to the natural world of her immediate environment for direction. And the deck on which Cunningham was standing that evening was the very lab where Ann's daily experiments were unfolding.

Cunningham was not the only distinguished visitor to the dance deck. In August 1954, a few months after the dance deck was completed, Ann welcomed Martha Graham to her theater without walls. Graham and her company were on the West Coast to perform at Mills College in Oakland, but Graham and Baroness Bethesbee de Rothschild were also canvassing in San Francisco for emerging choreographers whose work they could present in the invitational three-week American Dance Festival series at the American National Theatre and Academy (ANTA) in New York the following spring, which Rothschild was sponsoring. This search for new choreographers was not a total surprise to Ann. Doris Humphrey had written Ann in the fall of 1953 about the upcoming festival and encouraged her to apply:

> There was a meeting at which I offered a number of suggestions, one of which was to explore the possibility of presenting dancers [at the American Dance Festival] from other areas than NYC, and I commended you. They wouldn't take you sight unseen of course (there is, or will be, an artistic committee on which I will serve). So I got to thinking how you might manage to get here on the assumption that you want to. . . .

Whether it's right or not N.Y. is still the place that offers the recognition, the most intelligent audiences and the largest, the two best critics, etc. You know all that. . . . Reading between the lines and getting the "feel" of your things, I gather that Welland's dancers are not so good, but that he would expect to share equally in any such endeavor. I hope this is not the mill-stone around your neck. I can well imagine if this should be so that you might find the Rothschild committee saying, "We'll take her, but not him," then what?[102]

A few days before Graham visited Ann's deck, Graham, along with the baroness, and the baroness's assistant, Malka Kenyan, had all come to the Union Street studio, with the intention of seeing Lathrop's work. Ann had promised to be there out of friendship for Lathrop, who was very excited about showing his work to Graham and needed Ann to perform the small part of Rachel in his *Jacob*, an ambitious but convoluted allegorical tale about man and his progress toward wisdom presented in the style of a folk play. To showcase another side of his dramatic ability as a dancer, he had asked if they could also perform Ann's own biblical tale from 1953, *Daughter of the Voice*, the story of a pagan king (danced by Lathrop) who forces a mother to sacrifice her seven sons.

After the studio showing the baroness and Graham simply thanked the dancers and quickly left the studio. Ann felt slightly foolish; her role in *Jacob* basically consisted of melodramatic acting gestures. She had never thought it was a particularly good dance; it was decorative and stylized and borrowed too heavily from Graham's own style, she thought, but she said nothing to Lathrop. Apparently, though, Ann's *Daughter of the Voice* intrigued them, as did her presence in *Jacob*. Humphrey's enthusiastic endorsement of Ann was also probably important.

That evening Ann received an unexpected telephone call from Malka Kenyan. Did Ann have any other dances, a solo perhaps, that she could show Rothschild and Graham? Ann thought quickly. She mentioned the solo she had created a few years earlier, *The Prophetess*. A showing was arranged for the following Saturday. Graham, Rothschild, and Kenyan would drive across the Golden Gate Bridge to the Halprins' mountainside studio and home for an afternoon demonstration of Ann's solo followed by dinner.

The Prophetess, created in 1947, was the first major dance Ann made in the West. It told the story of the fearless biblical heroine Deborah. This work was not just personal, but resolutely autobiographical, both privately and culturally. It represented a distillation of the broad Jewish themes of her earlier work, as encouraged by Rabbi Kadushin, into deeper personal ones. In dance one can always find the traces of the choreographer's body in the work, indirectly through the predilection to certain gestures and ways of linking movement phrases together, and intuitively through the manner in which the choreographer intertwines or uncouples dance and music, dance and narrative, and fits images of movement expression to the physical capabilities and limits of her or his own body. These same choices also reveal autobiographical narratives of the artist. This was the case in Ann's *The Prophetess,* where the subject of the dance became the immediate ethnic history of the dancer—an Eastern European Jewess, exotic to mainstream America, yet in reality so acculturated that she had to reinvent pieces of the shtetl culture her parents left behind.

In the visual arts during this period, a similar impulse toward autobiography was resulting in an emphasis on the process of making an artwork. For example, in the abstract expressionist painters' canvases, as Dore Ashton has noted, "the process was becoming so important that the act of making a work of art could interest the artist psychologically almost as much as the final product." While this might be read as an anti-materialist posture, it is also "a gesture of heightened self value, suggesting even one's tentative actions in making an object are worthy of a framing and considered regard by viewers."[103] This concern with the processes of creation, and particularly the spontaneous moment of invention, would become very important to Ann and other West Coast artists and performers. As Richard Cándida Smith noted, for this generation of Bay Area painters, following the lead of the New York abstract expressionists, painting became an "encounter of material and direct activity without any preconceived image [which] led to a 'painting that is an act inseparable from the biography of the artist.'"[104] This focus on biography as process had immediate and profound implications for Ann's work, particularly as it played out in the new explorations with improvisation that marked her early work in the West.

As Ann rehearsed her solo *The Prophetess* on the dance deck for the command performance for Graham, she went through the entire dance, beginning with the dizzying opening spin. She kept her gaze inward and her feet paddling in pumping steps as her body revolved and her head snapped around like a wobbly beacon in a lighthouse. Her goal in putting this spin in the opening section of the dance was to actually alter her state of mind. She let the act of spinning transport her into a vortex of discovery, into "Inner Conviction," the first of what she called the dance's three "moods." This was how Ann thrust herself into the character of Deborah, the Old

Testament prophetess who helped the Israelites free themselves from tyranny, and the woman for whom Ann had been given her middle name.

Ann slammed her bare feet into the wooden deck. Then, as she envisioned the Israelites being attacked, she thrust her arms outward on rigid diagonals for the "Proclamation" section. Next her arms snapped inward sharply from the elbow as she swung one leg up with the force of a flag bearer raising his pole to lead a regiment into battle. Bold and commanding, Ann's actions were large enough to stand as both the harbinger of danger and a symbolic enactment of the advancing battalions of warring soldiers. Hearing the two-piano score of Alan Hovhaness's music, its sharp percussive tones a sonorous echo of her vengeance and determination, Ann saw herself launching into the final section of the dance, "Victory."

Splaying her fingers in the spiky pose of a seer about to utter a prophecy, Ann began gesturing violently, her torso twisting with tension and her legs and arms moving urgently. As if summoning the Israelites in big lunging and gathering gestures, she directed her invisible army to assemble for the final attack. Ann later reflected on how she drew this part of the choreography from her adolescent memories of the mystical hand motions her family rabbi made when he blessed the Torah or offered a Shabbat blessing over the bread and wine.[105] She was not so much interested in the religious roots of these actions as simply hungry for movement that was outside the traditional modern dance vocabularies. So Ann plumbed these actions as something fresh and new to her purposes. It would be nearly ten years before ordinary gesture and movement tasks would be a part of the American modern dance vocabulary.

In the last section of the dance Ann slowly pulled herself to standing. Here was where she used her facial features, eyes glaring, lips slightly parted as if calling out. She was consciously trying to get away from the "mask look," the frozen features she disliked in other modern dancers, including Martha Graham.

Saturday afternoon, when Graham, Rothschild, and Kenyan arrived, Ann greeted them at the door, wearing the long, blue, high-necked rayon dress with its flared skirt and the tall blue and white headdress and wide Israeli metal bracelet that was her costume for *The Prophetess*. She quickly ushered them through the house and down to the wooden benches overlooking the dance deck, the woods, and the shimmering San Francisco Bay beyond. Ann then began to dance. As she had hoped, once she began to spin she slipped into the role so completely it was almost like going into a trance. As usually happened to her when she performed, Ann felt no nervousness, only the deep and reassuring sense of refocusing her attention on the immediate demands of the choreography.

Two weeks later, Ann learned she had been chosen to perform in the ANTA festival. She was asked to bring *The Prophetess* and one other contrasting short solo. Rothschild was wealthy, but she was also financially careful. Humphrey had already warned Ann that it was preferable if both her dances were without sets, because, given the strict union rules at the ANTA theater, all sets had to be made by union members. Any music would have to be played live, but orchestrated for no more than a twenty-two-piece orchestra because that is what came with the rental of the theater.[106]

Ann arranged to arrive in New York a week before the May 7, 1955, opening night of the festival. She asked Jenny Hunter Groat, who was studying and performing with Ann at the Union Street studio, to take over her classes for the two weeks she would be in New York. To save money she stayed with Larry's parents, Sam and Rose, in their apartment on East Seventy-fourth Street. She spent the first week rehearsing daily by herself in a spacious practice studio Graham had arranged for her to use. It was located in the elegant three-story building at 316 East Sixty-third Street that Rothschild had recently purchased for Graham. The building, which had previously been a school for children, had three studios, a garden, two small kitchens, and a dressing room and rest space.

Honored by the special treatment Graham accorded her, Ann was surprised when Graham herself walked into the studio one day, watched for a few minutes, and then motioned for Ann to follow her. Graham led Ann to a costume room filled with boxes of all kinds of material and decorative ornaments for costumes. Ann was thrilled. As she watched, Graham dug into a box and pulled out a long length of glittering silver rope. She then began wrapping the rope around Ann's torso and across her shoulders in a design that simultaneously suggested military braid and the breastplate of a heroic goddess. "It covered my whole body," Ann said. "It was amazing. It took a drab and ordinary dress and turned it into something elegant and meaningful. It made such a difference." Graham then disappeared as quickly as she had come.[107]

Ann also received welcome assistance from Lavinia Nielsen, one of her teachers from the University of Wisconsin (with whom she had roomed) and now a dancer in the José Limón Company. Nielsen's husband, Lucas Hoving, was also a dancer with Limón. Nielsen watched Ann rehearse her second piece—*The Lonely Ones,* with its three witty character studies based on characters in William Steig's cartoons—and offered suggestions about the dance's comic timing and dramatic shaping.

Ann performed *The Lonely Ones* only once in New York, but *The Prophetess* received three performances, alternating slots with works by the other invited soloists—Paul Draper, Pauline Koner, Daniel Nagrin, Janet Collins, and Iris Mabry. Ann was in serious company and she knew it. The festival was in many respects a midstream retrospective of the major masterpieces of Martha Graham, Doris Humphrey, José Limón, and Anna Sokolow, with performances of Graham's *Diversion of Angels, Seraphic Dialogue, Appalachian Spring, Night Journey,* and *Deaths and Entrances;* Humphrey's *Day on Earth;* Limón's *The Moor's Pavane* and *The Traitor;* and Sokolow's *Rooms.* Ann attended every concert, watching from the wings on the evenings she was performing.

Each morning after a concert she would sit with her mother-in-law over a cup of coffee and discuss the works she had seen, and each day she realized she was growing increasingly disillusioned. It had been eight years since Ann had left New York. She was shocked to see how similar all the younger choreographers' works seemed to those of their mentors and how little room there seemed to be for voices that challenged this domination.

Ann felt extremely out of place because there was so little traditional modern dance technique in her dances. She also felt odd because her device of drawing from her own cultural heritage in *The Prophetess* seemed out of place next to the grandly elegiac and broadly humanistic themes of many of the other works. In addition, no one—not even the droll dance humorist Charles Weidman—had presented anything as irreverently light as *The Lonely Ones.*

Ann was harder on herself than the critics were. Reviewers in San Francisco had always enjoyed *The Lonely Ones,* praising the dance for neatly capturing the bittersweet truth of Steig's portraits. Even the usually reserved *New York Times* critic John Martin had lauded *The Lonely Ones.* He had written Ann a personal note when she presented the Steig suite in New York in 1947, praising the "wonderful sense of the grotesque it demonstrated without losing its relation to life."[108] Now Martin praised *The Prophetess,* writing: "From the West Coast came Ann Halprin to give us a solo, *The Prophetess,* which showed her to be a dancer of genuine authority who knows how to make a dance as well as to dance it."[109]

While the ANTA festival may have been a public success, Ann returned home complaining bitterly to Larry that she was greatly depressed by what she had seen. "I went away feeling that I never wanted to dance again," she remarked later.

It seemed as if there was no connection between my life or what was real, and the dances I'd seen. Even my own work seemed abstract and preachy. The whole aura in the theater was so annoying in its self-centeredness; there was no graciousness between people. I kept asking myself, "Why do all the dancers in the Graham troupe look exactly like Martha? Why do all the performers in this company look like Hanya Holm? Why are all these dancers just like Doris Humphrey?" This isn't for me. Where is their individuality? Where are their differences? I felt as if I had gone into a world I was no longer part of.[110]

Ann returned in a markedly different state of mind than when she had left. Not only was she profoundly disturbed by what she had seen, she was, perhaps just as importantly, unsettled by what she hadn't seen. It would be ten years before she returned to New York with a new evening-long dance, *Parades and Changes,* that would prompt rumors that the police were about to issue a warrant for her arrest on charges of public indecency. Between her departure in 1955, however, and her sensational return in 1965 lay a decade of introspection, experimentation, and rejections.

Within a matter of weeks after her return to the West Coast, Ann severed her partnership with Lathrop, closing down all but the children's classes she taught at the studio. According to Hunter Groat, "Welland suffered [from Graham's selection of Ann over him]. The hurt was deep and I'm sure he felt a sense of betrayal. It was probably a life disappointment for him. They didn't belong together after that, and Ann just started to offer classes at her studio on the deck."[111] A.A. Leath also remembered Lathrop's deep disappointment at being passed over by Graham. "It's sad that Welland didn't make the grade," Leath said. "His loyalty to Martha was there in his own teaching in the school. I'm sure he was hurt that he wasn't gifted in the sense that he could be a Martha Graham dancer. Ann was being born again. She was saying good-bye to all her training; she had all that ballet as a girl; and then she had all that New York stuff. By 1954 she was ready for something."[112]

In a strangely prophetic coincidence, several years earlier, in 1951, the San Francisco filmmaker and poet James Broughton had cast both Ann and Welland in two of the four short film poems he made for *Four in the Afternoon: A Quartet for Poems Moving,* which grew out of *Musical Chairs,* his book of whimsical poems. Each vignette, filmed in a different cinematic style, focused on a different age and stage of life. Ann was featured in the third segment, "Princess Printemps," about "a woman of 30," according to a note Broughton wrote.[113] In this episode, done in the style of a turn-of-the-century mime or variety show, Ann appears as a slightly loony maiden tripping along with filigreed baroque dance footwork as she loops around the plants and huge columns of San Francisco's Palace of Fine Arts. Ann's whole body seems a comic platform for rising and crashing expectations as she first pursues and then evades John Graham, who, dressed like a court jester, chases her around the pillars in the manner of a silent comedian. Ann hunches over and scampers away, rabbitlike, from Graham, who springs in place, futilely pedaling his legs after her. The primary accompaniment for "Princess Printemps" is Broughton reading his poem. His slightly singsong, nasal delivery is actually as humorous as the text. And the wit of Ann's portrayal is that she seems to be simultaneously capturing and satirizing the comic sweetness of Broughton's prose. She is a natural comedienne, her features plastic and her timing crisp.

The scherzo tempo of "Princess Printemps" is followed by the lento movement of "The Aging Balletomane," a solo reverie danced by Welland Lathrop, which is the final poem in the film quartet. Film critics consider this the finest section of the film because of its fusion of auditory and visual action. As P. Adams Sitney put it, "This film is a crucial case of the fusion of verse and film within the American avant-garde."[114] There is far less dancing here than in Ann's segment, with most of Lathrop's movement being restricted to rocking sadly in a rocking chair and occasionally lurching forward into a post on the porch where he sits. Wearing a string tie and turn-of-the-century black suit, Lathrop's aging balletomane temperamentally seems styled as a cross between the stern preacher and the quietly wise matriarch from Martha Graham's *Appalachian Spring,* with a nod to designer Isamu Noguchi's rocking chair from the work's spare set. Earnest and seriously dramatic, without the irony that marks Ann's performance, Lathrop's portrayal seems more poignantly autobiographical than either he or Broughton intended. Lathrop is depicted as looking backward at a life in dance, and to underline this Broughton reverses the projected image so that the illusionistic ballerina Lathrop's mind conjures arrives in a backward leap.

After *Four in the Afternoon* Lathrop never again worked with Broughton, but Ann's friendship with Broughton drew her into a vibrant new artistic group, the Beats, with whom he was associated. *Four in the Afternoon* marked the beginning of several delightful collaborations with Broughton.

When Ann left the Union Street studio, she invited a few of her longtime students—Graham, Leath, and Hunter Groat—to begin working with her on her dance deck as she searched for a new, more immediately meaningful reason to make dances. "I was consciously making a break from modern dance," she later said. On the heels of her ANTA experience, she was on the threshold of discovering the relative isolation of the Bay Area from New York dance circles an advantage. For the first time since she had moved West, Ann was ready to heed what California historian Kevin Starr has called "the region's call to pleasure and to the enhancement of life."[115] The simple fact of being outdoors was leading her toward a new contentment with silence, toward increased movement experimentation, and an enhanced sense of self.

FIVE

Instantaneous Experience, Lucy, and Beat Culture

1955–1960

The magic of image-making is that the spectacularly thin layers—almost merely layers of concepts—evoke in the observers of the image the whole spread of human emotions. It is hard to believe that such powerful responses are coming from such frail, delicate and inherently evanescent stimuli.

EDWIN H. LAND

ONE DAY IN THE EARLY 1950s, Larry came home with a new camera he had just purchased. Called the Polaroid Land Camera, it created instant photographs, processing them inside the camera just seconds after the shutter was clicked. This 1947 invention by the scientist Edwin Land revolutionized perception and brought serious regard to swiftly composed or spontaneous images. Instant gratification could now be an art value. Art photographers like Ansel Adams lauded the Polaroid for its capacity to "free intuition," allowing artists to take risks and experiment, as they could see results immediately.[1]

Larry had always carried a notebook with him to record images in the landscape, a moment in one of Ann's dances, or just the postures of people around him, yet this new camera offered more than just an accelerated means of documentation. It seemed instantaneously to increase and heighten one's power of perception. One got immediate feedback on how life might look framed as art and how art could be snipped out of life. Lauded by Land as "a new eye, a secret memory," a device that "enhances the art of seeing," the instant camera revolutionized the image-making process.[2]

For Ann, a dance artist steeped in a quest for lightly mediated authenticity, the possibility of instantaneous images offered a provocative model for live performance and a validation of her own interest in shaped improvisation. By the mid-1950s Ann was stretching toward an "instant" sensibility in dance, searching, like the photographer with a Polaroid, for a way to observe her work and her subject nearly simultaneously. Her dances were about capturing the commonplace, quickly and with a minimum of alteration, like an instant photograph.

Years later, what Ann remembered most about that first Polaroid camera Larry brought home is that the photographs didn't last.[3] Over time early Polaroids darkened into black rectangles and the moment they had captured receded back into memory. For the dancer, however, the aesthetic value of the instant has always mattered more than the longevity of the afterimage. Within a few years, Ann was using the terms *instant theater* and *immediate dance* to describe her improvisatory dance performances.

Like a new Polaroid owner scanning her surroundings for subjects for instant photography, Ann began looking for new environments that could be sets for her instant dance theater. Soon the environment became more than a set; it served as a "score," giving direction for a dance. Ann also began collaborating with non-dance artists, with poets, musicians, architects, and painters, as well as a handful of dancers. One of the dancers, Jenny Hunter Groat, recalled, "She surrounded herself with artists. Ann always wanted to be avant-garde and in the lead."[4] At times ideas from other art forms inspired Ann to explore parallels in dance. Ann began doing with people what she did with the environment—studying how these non-dancers moved, looking at their contours, proclivities, and interests as potential sources for dance. She noticed that non-dancers tended to approach movement functionally, and this directed her attention to tasks as generators of movement. "I was trying to get away from movement based on one dancer's personality and what that personality felt was evocative or beautiful. I was trying to open up the possibility that movement came from a more functional basis," Ann later remarked about her turn toward task performance.[5]

One of the non-dance artists Ann collaborated with was the filmmaker and poet James Broughton. He had no experience in dance when, in 1951, he made his first film of Ann, performing her "Princess Printemps" solo. Broughton had first seen Ann's dancing in early 1947, at a concert of *The Steig Pieces* at Herbst Theatre in San Francisco. "I was absolutely bowled over by Ann," he recalled. "I was entranced with this performer, this incredible clown . . . she was absolutely hilarious. It was deadpan comedy and this is such a rare thing in the dance world." Broughton, a connoisseur of comedy in his own poetry and films, quickly became close friends with Ann and Larry, often stopping by the Union Street studio to visit. "She never herself valued her comic gift as much as I think she should have," Broughton said. "But that's because it was so easy and such a natural thing for her to do."[6]

In those days, Broughton commented, "San Francisco was still a very small place, so everybody in the arts knew everybody else and the same people would go to everything, all the openings, the performances and the parties."[7] Influences easily ran across disciplines. As Broughton once observed, "I have learned more about the writing of poetry from music than from literature. And more about the making of films from dance than from cinema."[8]

The tie to dance can be seen in Broughton's best-known color film, *The Bed* (1968), a twenty-minute romp in which a string of individuals play on a double bed, set, like a miniature outdoor stage, in the midst of a rolling meadow. Broughton's friends, lovers, and fellow artists spill, one by one or in pairs, across the bed, enacting brief, silent rites of repose or chaste passion. Emotional entanglements become physical intertwinings in this dance of life. The stream begins with a pair of Ann's nude dancers, John Graham and Jani Novak, who embrace then teasingly flee from one another in slow cascading runs like giant Picasso bathers dashing along the beach. Ann's frequent musical collaborator, Warner Jepson, provided the music for *The Bed,* which has no words. Choreographically, the film resembles one of Ann's structured improvisations of the time, only here the bed is the environment to which each performer must spontaneously respond.

In the last film Broughton made with Ann, *The Golden Positions* (1970), the structure stems entirely from movement and dramatic possibilities of three body positions: lying down, standing, and running. For her solo in *The Golden Positions,* filmed in the Divisadero Street space she was then using as a studio in San Francisco, Ann slips, slides, or crashes into a fall, all with deadpan calm as she repeatedly tries, and fails, to remain standing. In the final moments of the dance, she strips off her shoes, shirt, and workman's overalls. Then, crouching nude behind her shoes, neatly stretches herself out on the floor and disappears behind her shoes, a little mound of defeated flesh. Broughton said he had to persuade Ann to perform this comic dance for the camera, but after her initial resistance she was "very pleased to see herself being silly."[9]

"Ann always wanted to do what nobody else was doing, and I think that was our great sympathetic core," Broughton recollected. His appreciation for her talent as a comedienne is interesting because in dance, as in film, comedy is dependent on two critical skills—timing and the capacity to give the illusion that one is totally immersed in the present moment and oblivious to the disaster around the corner. This quality of knowing when to draw things out and when to deliver a physical punchline, as well as how to be so consumed with the present instant that spectators are drawn in with you, was critical to Ann's contribution to experimental dance.

––––––––––

Ann seemed to follow intuitively in the footsteps of another curly-haired, red-headed comedienne—Lucille Ball, who emerged as the most popular public woman of the 1950s. Like Ball, Ann situated her performances in the comic dilemmas of the distaff side. Although she generally stayed within traditional gender roles in her dances of the 1950s and early 1960s, Ann and her dancers (some of whom were gay) played at the edges of mainstream heterosexual tensions between women's struggle for autonomy and their "caretaking" responsibilities to family and society.[10] In at least five dances—her "Princess Printemps" solo (1951), *Rites of Women* (1959), *Trunk Dance* (1959), *Mr. and Mrs. Mouse* (1959), and *Apartment 6* (1965)—Ann took an ironic view of the wife's expected domesticity. Through these dances, she was moving toward defusing the contradictions between the values placed on women's work inside and outside the home.

While Ann's dances didn't repudiate the dominant social model of female domesticity, artistically they broke new ground. Women modern dancers in the 1950s were a serious group, and, with the exception of Katherine Litz's gently humorous little dances, their work tended to reflect this. Domestic tales were generally framed as grand mythic opuses, as in the works of Martha Graham, or weighty social portraits, as in the dances of Doris Humphrey. Ann's family stories, in contrast, were scaled to daily life, representing the real uncertainties of women's place and women's power.

Adopting an approach she would embrace for her entire career, Ann grounded her art making in the everyday. She would use a piece of her daily world as a score, recycling her offstage life with Larry, Daria, and Rana. At the same time, she developed a style of choreographic bricolage, drawing on what she saw others around her doing as a means for her own invention. "It wasn't so much that Anna was an innovator," the visual designer Jo Landor recalled affectionately. "It's [that] whatever was innovative Anna would grab. She comes in at the crest of the wave and grabs it in her inimitable fashion and works it."[11]

As she tried to find a way to blend career and family, Ann must have been aware of Lucille Ball's "solution." "I was aware of Lucy because she was so very, very funny," Ann has acknowledged. "Unconsciously I must have identified with her strongly. I've always had a huge interest in people who were funny."[12] From October 1951 to April 1960, Ball's television program, *I Love Lucy*, played with the story of the homebound American woman in the postwar period. It showcased Ball's apparent success at combining career, marriage, and family by paralleling her "real life" with the "fiction" of the television series.[13] In much the same way Ann blurred her family life with the mediated "reality" of her dances.

Like Lucille Ball, Ann cultivated the spillover between her private domestic life offstage and her public life as a performing artist. Both women did this in part as a way of legitimizing the fact that they were mothers and professional women. Being a "screwball" undercut the perceived unfemininity of the career woman. Ann, like Ball, seemed to define herself as a wife and mother at heart at a time when mainstream thinking linked femininity to women's roles in the home and women thus had to exercise their power covertly.[14] The public perception was that neither Ann nor Ball abandoned their kids at home when they worked; instead, they brought them with them onto the dance deck or into the television studio and, most important, into the narratives of their art.

Ball's television husband, Desi Arnaz, was also her real-life husband, and when she became pregnant, her pregnancy and her new baby, Desi Jr., were written into the show. Ball became the first openly pregnant woman to perform on television at a time when public representations of pregnancy were considered improper.[15] In January 1953 Ball gave birth, virtually simultaneously, in her real life and in her television life. Ann also worked well into her pregnancy. Yet she never performed when pregnant with either child; instead, she focused on her teaching. And, as Doris Humphrey had done, she returned to performing within a few weeks of the births of her two daughters, Daria and Rana.

The Halprin daughters would become frequent participants and performers in Ann's dances and workshops throughout the 1950s and 1960s. While Ann made several dances in which Daria and Rana played themselves, she always disguised their relationship to her in the program, listing them by different names. Daria became Daria Lurie (from Larry's mother's name) and Rana went by Ann's maiden name as Rana Schuman.

Daria later remembered the lived daily experience of this intertwining of art and life as often quite intense. She praised her mother as a "pre-feminist," noting how unusual it was at the time to be both "an innovative artist and a woman at home." "I don't think she wanted to have to choose between her art and her life as a wife and mother," Daria said, describing how Ann's dance associates would frequently overflow from the studio into the home. "She felt the only way for her to do it was to bring her work home," Daria added. "And the whole atmosphere became permeated with this kind of culture—which was much more challenging and disturbing to my father, my sister, and me than she could understand. Our family life became infused by the fact that her work was going on literally in the landscape of our family. It wasn't an intellectual inquiry, but a lived reality on a daily basis."[16]

Larry never performed with Ann outside of their joint workshops, but his presence hovers noticeably over at least one of Ann's dances from this era, *Apartment 6*. In this work, Ann plays a frazzled housewife desperate to please her indifferent spouse by preparing the perfect pancake breakfast for him as he sits immersed in reading the morning paper. The harder she tries to make the perfect pancake for him, the further from the mark she goes until she is maniacally tossing the failed pancakes out the window in a scene that might come right out of *I Love Lucy*. But it wasn't the pancakes that irritated her own Larry. Rather, he was growing increasingly frustrated at finding his Kentfield home filled with Ann's dancers. Simone Forti, one of Ann's dancers at the time, reflected, "I think Anna liked having everybody eating around her, and liked having all the kids, the students, really hanging out. And I think Larry would have liked a little more privacy and a little more time as a family."[17] Jo Landor recalled a time in 1963 when Larry returned from a trip to find the living area overflowing with dancers eating and talking noisily. He loudly told Ann that he was fed up with all these people in his house and announced that he was leaving. "Ann went out and slashed all the tires so he couldn't go," Landor recollected. "It was high drama. I know it was difficult on Larry."[18] It was also difficult on the children. Daria and Rana pleaded for a normal home life as well. Daria recounted that while Ann was deflating Larry's tires, she and her sister "stood in our pajamas crying. For us it was our family. It wasn't a performance anymore. We wanted the people down in the living room to leave. What we wanted was our father, not the crazy workshop people dancing in the living room. The two of us, Rana and I, stood at the top of the stairs in our pajamas weeping."[19]

For some young dancers in her workshops, Ann's juggling of her life as a wife and mother and her life as an artist was radically inspirational. Meredith Monk, who was twenty-two when she took a summer workshop with Ann in 1965, recalled how Ann "impressed me most because she was striving to be so many things. To be true as a mother, artist, wife. There were no other women then doing that."[20] Although she never read Betty Friedan's *The Feminine Mystique* (1963), Ann intuitively embraced its warnings that frustration rather than fulfillment would be the lot of women who tried to find their satisfactions and identity in suburban domesticity or traditional female jobs.[21] Coming on the heels of the massive recruitment of women into the workforce during World War II, the 1950s emphasis on the woman's role as homemaker was a paradoxical and confusing turnaround. As historian Susan Hartmann notes, "World War II did not redefine gender roles in American society so much as it temporarily legitimized women's nontraditional activities as a wartime necessity."[22]

The social architects may have felt the redefining of women's "place" was temporary, but Ann, as well as many women who came of age during the period of the war, did not. She found a way to step outside the boundaries separating art from female domesticity. Using comedy as her tool, Ann gained license to be both physical and outrageous as a performer without appearing overly serious about the whole business of being an avant-garde artist. Which is not to say she wasn't serious about her art.

Ann has often been described as a quirky outsider and cultural provocateur in the West. However, it seems more accurate to say she belonged to a group of postwar American artists who consciously didn't belong—to those who rejected the idea of developing "a style," undermining the belief that an artist has a single voice or vision that gradually becomes more unified.

Ann was one of just three dancers, and the only female one, mentioned in Steven Watson's comprehensive sociogram in the catalogue for the 1996 Whitney exhibition "Beat Culture and the New America 1950–1965."[23] Her inclusion reveals much about the impact of Beat culture on postmodern dance, especially when compared with the other two dancers Watson cited: Merce Cunningham and James Waring.[24] Ann's dance embodied the raw, funky, strangely improvisational ethos of Beat art far more than the cool, disciplined and structured work of Cunningham or the ballet-trained, if quirky, Waring did. On every front—geographic, aesthetic, political, and personal—the links between Ann and the Beats are tangible and persuasive.

What Ann responded to in the Beats was their discourse of authenticity. The poet Lawrence Ferlinghetti, cofounder of the City Lights bookstore in San Francisco, wrote in the spring 1958 issue of the *Chicago Review:* "The [Beat] poetry which has been making itself heard here of late is what should be called street poetry. . . . It amounts to getting poetry back into the street where it once was, out of the classroom, out of the speech department and in fact—off the printed page."[25] The Beats' aversion to conformity and emphasis on individual choice resonated with Ann's work, even though their heightened masculinity myths tended to devalue women.[26] "What we were all after was to have our art be more reflective of real life issues and to do this we all tried to break down the aesthetic barriers we had inherited," Ann remarked years later. "And since movement was my medium, out of that came a new kind of realism."[27]

It does not matter if Ann was highly visible in the North Beach Beat scene. "We *were* part of that Beat culture," Forti insisted. "But we were so busy doing what we were doing that we weren't much in touch with the others."[28] Although Ann did work with four recognized Beat artists—the filmmaker and poet James Broughton, the poets Michael McClure and Richard Brautigan, and the visual artist Bruce Conner—she wasn't present at many of the "main events." She did not attend Allen Ginsberg's landmark reading of *Howl* on October 13, 1955, at the Six Gallery in San Francisco, the West Coast event that began Beat poetry readings. She missed Lenny Bruce's scandalous stand-up comedy routines at the Hungry i. And she didn't frequent the City Lights bookstore or live the hardscrabble life of most Beat artists. Still, her sensibility as an artist links her to Beat literature and the Funk style in the visual arts.

Although their point of departure differed, the Beat writers were, like Ann, propelled by an interest in improvisation and in using the immediate body as the medium and at times subject of their art. And the Beats took pleasure in enacting publicly what the cultural historian Richard Cándida Smith has called "interior conflicts" over the limits of freedom—particularly in relation to hedonism and chastity—something Ann would exuberantly do in her dance works, especially in the 1960s.[29]

Almost all of the landmark Beat events seem to be remembered as one kind of a performance or another. There were the readings themselves, the cross-country rides, the all-night writing binges, and, in the case of the comic Lenny Bruce's three obscenity trials, his performances of the legal responses to his performances. The firsthand accounts of some of the most momentous of these events cloak them in metaphors of participatory theater that sound at once like call-and-response jazz scores and Ann's later participatory dance events. The most notable is, of course, the story of Ginsberg's first reading of *Howl* at the Six Gallery, where Jack Kerouac collected donations from the audience to buy wine and everyone drank and listened while Kerouac shouted "Go!" between the lines as Ginsberg read. One year later, when Ginsberg read *Howl* again, his presentation reportedly had become even more dramatic—he took off his clothes and challenged a heckler to do the same. As Michael McClure noted about the initial reading of *Howl,* "It left us standing in wonder, or cheering and wondering but knowing at the deepest level that a barrier had been broken, that a human voice and body had been hurled against the harsh wall of America and its supporting armies and navies and academies and institutions and ownership systems and power support bases."[30] (That this act of rebellion came from someone who, like Ann, was a first-generation American born of Eastern European Jews is of interest. Ginsberg once quipped that half the Beats were Jewish and the other half were Catholic.)

Within these performances was what might be called the Beat body. It is a body charged with risk and daring, a body that is also intensely immediate, spontaneous, personal, and nonvirtuosic. All these qualities permeate Ann's dances. She shows how the Beat aesthetic combining alienation and total experience can be articulated, explored, "riffed on" through dance.[31]

Allen Ginsberg openly acknowledged the importance of an embodied presence for the Beat poets. He observed that "whatever really great poetry I wrote like 'Howl' or 'Kaddish,' I was actually able to chant and use my whole body whereas in lesser poetry I just talk it."[32] Body and soul come together in the work of several Beat writers, unifying "into a single conscious entity," allowing hidden truths to slip out.[33] Ginsberg once called *Howl* his "coming out of the closet," adding that it was "a public statement of feelings and emotions and attitudes that I would not have wanted my father or family to see." For him, the Beat scene created "a social place for the soul to exist manifested in *this* world," allowing aesthetic forms to contain what up until now had been private emotions.[34] In a culture where spontaneity was lauded, individual experience was coming to be looked to as a better guide to reality than social conventions. And, as Ann was discovering, severing personal insights from a stylistic ideology and predetermined form left the artist with few old rules intact. By the mid-1960s she would come to digest a lesson of Ginsberg's public readings of *Howl,* namely that what happens on the stage is less important than the emotional release the action inspires in the spectators.

All this emphasis on personal freedom was, as Cándida Smith explains, "a response to the insecurity caused by the war." In his words, "Americans believed they were free citizens in a democratic society, but the war showed that free citizens had very little control over the forces that influenced their lives." Art offered an arena for addressing the resulting postwar search for personal freedom.[35]

Reflecting back on the Beat period, Ann commented, "San Francisco was a small town then and all of the artists essentially knew each other. Those of us who were the avant-garde sought each other out. In those days of the fifties I was an isolated nut doing my own thing [as far as the dance world was concerned], but with the Beat artists there was a constant interchange. We were all looking for new ways of inventing compositional forms and building continuity between words, sounds and movements."[36]

As much as she flirted with alternative lifestyles, Ann never relinquished the stability and comfort of her middle-class existence as fully as the Beats did. Yet in the same way that the Beats derived a certain force and focus from what they were reacting against, Ann rebelled most strongly against the lifestyle of the studio, eventually replacing the regimen of indoor classes and drill for formal performances with informal workshops outdoors in nature with clothing-optional attire and communal improvisations as fuel for art.

Like the early Beats in San Francisco, Ann began to assemble a small community of interesting dancers, designers, and musicians around her as part of her initial efforts to create an environment for modern dance in the city. Her dance deck in the woods served much the same role as City Lights bookstore. It effectively institutionalized her and Larry's bohemian existence so that Ann's life as an artist and homemaker were now contiguous.

The Halprin home and outdoor studio became a gathering point for a number of artists from various disciplines, including actors, dancers, architects, musicians, and writers. There they socialized, gave readings, saw dance showings, and participated in workshops and events in the environment. "Ann had this incredible magnetism—physical, personal," Hunter Groat remembered. "She was able to go out and talk to other artists and the studio became the center for all kinds of things."[37] Fellow artists in other disciplines, including some Beats, like Conner, Brautigan, and Broughton, were frequent guests at evening "salons" in the Halprin home. Like the Beats, Ann made the geographical distance of the West from New York a way, and eventually a mandate, to find her own voice.

Essential to her newfound voice was Ann's ability to be deeply immersed in the present, something she learned from observing nature. "Spontaneity in nature interested me particularly," Ann said. "It led me to be aware and responsive to the movement and that is what led me to improvisation."[38] This lesson greatly impressed Simone Forti, who became one of Ann's students in the mid-1950s (when she was known by her married name, Simone Morris). By reading the world of nature as a model for how art might be structured, Ann began to extend her improvisatory discovery well beyond H'Doubler's methods. "One of the most important tools Ann gave me was how to work from nature," Forti recalled. "She taught the process of going into the woods and observing something for a period of time, and then coming back and somehow working from those impressions. We were not judging what kind of movement we wanted. We were hoping for awareness and the freedom to just use any movement quality. Stiffness, heaviness, speed, fluidity—anything."[39]

Anything in the surroundings became a potential source for constructing a dance. As Forti explained, "You might look at how a plant sits still, but your eye can follow so many edges on it. And then you notice how your eye moves very differently along the snakeplant than it does on the pot that it sits in. Your eye can still move along it, and you still have a somatic response when you look at the pot. So she led us to this awareness of somatic sensations in response to perceptions outside so that the inside and outside of each of us would be working together."

Starting with anatomical explorations, like those from H'Doubler, Ann might point out a limb or joint in an anatomy book or on her studio skeleton, and then ask her students to explore that area while moving the whole body. She particularly wanted them to notice how gravity affected their movement. She effectively extended H'Doubler's trial-and-error process of discovering the joints' range of motion into attending to the laws of nature, especially gravity, as guidelines for movement.

Already in May 1953, a few months before her dance deck was built, she had tested her ideas about natural forces in her first outdoor public improvisation, *People on a Slant*. Performed near the Union Street studio, on one of San Francisco's almost vertical streets, Ann, A.A. Leath, and Jenny Hunter Groat simply walked, struggling to keep their bodies "straight as a board" against the fierce incline of the hill. Costumed in long overcoats, they played with contrasts in force and direction as Leath strode uphill against Hunter Groat and Ann, who inched stiffly downward. "I was trying to break down patterned movement, to find actions uncontaminated with dance," Ann later explained. "I thought about it the way a painter might do a lot of cartoons before starting a painting."[40]

Ann was not yet ready, however, to make a clean break from tradition. In spring 1953 she made *Daughter of the Voice,* a Jewish-themed dance about a biblical heroine, like *The Prophetess.*[41] In a section of film that still exists of *Daughter of the Voice,* Ann, costumed in a black headscarf and full-length jersey dress, huddles over eight-year-old Avril Weber, whom she comforts and admonishes to fight the evil Haman (danced by Welland Lathrop), hovering menacingly above them brandishing a long spear. The movement here alternates between the emotive density of early modern dance and the more pedestrian, everyday vocabulary that Ann had begun to investigate in pieces like *People on a Slant.* Both the child and Ann dash forward and back in little runs of indecision, their movements fluid and naturalistically shaped. The scale of the emotion is not exaggerated and the theatricality of their delivery is scaled back. "The runs were natural," Ann said later, " because working with a child there is no way it could be dramaticized."[42]

In the summer of 1954 Ann began teaching two-week summer workshops on her dance deck, inviting a small group of dancers to work with her "improvising to find out what our bodies could do, not learning somebody else's pattern or technique."[43] John Graham, A.A. Leath, Jenny Hunter Groat, and Simone Forti all participated in these early dance deck workshops. Forti remembered being recruited by Leath after class one day at the Union Street studio. "Look, you're an improviser," Leath told the surprised Forti. "Ann is starting this dancers' workshop in Marin; you've got to come . . . check this out."[44] Built like a gymnast with a compact frame and strong, well-developed upper body, Leath both taught and performed in Ann's workshops. The dancers were all very fond of him and admired the inventiveness of his movements in dramatic situations, as well as his crazy wit on and off the stage. Indeed, it was Leath's enthusiasm that had led many of them to Ann's deck. "One of the fascinating things about being out there on the deck," Leath recalled, "was that we were separated from everything that was going on in New York. Much of what we did and how we did it was due to being out in nature. We were only one step from wilderness, on the dance deck. We had Mount Tamalpais's main peak rising up before us. Everything we did evolved out of what happened in improvisation."[45]

Both Forti and Hunter Groat reported being exhilarated but also at times frustrated by the experience on the dance deck. It seemed like the most open and liberated approach to dance invention imaginable, yet some rules did emerge. Sometimes Ann "would give an assignment and I would find the most direct and crudest, in the sense of raw, way to fulfill the assignment," Forti reflected. "Once in the *Branch Dance* I crawled across the deck, and I remember Ann wanted me to keep some tension in my feet or formalize my feet somehow and I said no, that I was just crawling. Ann would feel that the movement should be somewhat refined or aestheticized."[46] But Forti had a clear sense of why she wanted to deviate from Ann's instructions, so after some discussion Ann accepted her version of the crawl. Hunter Groat, however, found the competition from Ann's intentions overwhelming. "The [deck] space was so inviting," Hunter Groat remembered. "I thought, 'Just turn me loose!' But Ann had the attitude that if you weren't doing what she was doing, it wasn't good. So I told people, 'Go,' but don't believe all the promises." Indeed, Hunter Groat's observations have been echoed by several of Ann's associates over the years who recognize what can be the genius of her eclecticism but also chafe at its pragmatism. "She had an eclectic attitude. She used people up," Hunter Groat said sadly. "By 1957 I had gotten so frustrated that I had to leave to form my own group and do my own work."[47]

In her classes and workshops, Ann assimilated influences from the people and environments around her, at times, it seemed, unknowingly. This method of working in response to what was going on around her was critical to her aesthetic. In the years ahead it would work greatly to her advantage, giving her work its topicality and tone of contemporaneity. Essentially, however, Ann was just continuing to read the environment—not only geographically but also socially, culturally, and politically. At first glance this approach seemed totally free, but on closer inspection it was predicated on a set of implicit understandings about the outer limits of possibility. Ann was pragmatic—not everything was possible. Frictions would arise, as they had with Hunter Groat, when a dancer's hopes and Ann's expectations or sense of limits didn't coincide.

Ann's move from the traditional indoor dance studio on Union Street to the expanse of her dance deck in the woods obviously enlarged the whole frame around her experimentation. Now, day-long workshops on the dance deck, often lasting until late into the night in the summer, replaced the strict sixty-minute studio class. "I remember dancing till midnight," Forti said. She recalled overhearing Ann being interviewed by a newspaper reporter, who asked what she did when it rained. "Well, the rain runs down between the cracks of the deck," Ann replied, as if it were obvious that they continued dancing.[48]

Living *with* nature was very much part of the Halprin family style. In the summer of 1954 Larry began the first of a decade of annual four-week backpacking trips to the Sierras, first with Daria and later with Rana as well. "My parents did stuff with us during our childhood that was quite important, wonderful and valuable," Daria pointed out. "My father took me up to the high Sierras starting when I was six years old. I started on a pack horse because I wasn't old enough or strong enough to make the extraordinary trek in."[49]

Ann often sought out novel environments in order to witness the kinds of improvisational dialogues dancers might initiate with a locale. She encouraged her teachers and students to look for unusual environments as well. One weekend Norma Leistiko, a dancer with Ann, along with Leistiko's boyfriend, Jacques Overhoff, explored the construction site of a huge United Airlines cargo hangar being built at the San Francisco Airport. (At the time Leistiko was working as a receptionist for Skidmore, Owings and Merrill, the architects for the hangar.) Ann had glimpsed this site from the freeway and also been intrigued.

As Overhoff, a structural engineer and sculptor, walked around the deserted site, Leistiko started playfully hanging from the metal frames, improvising a little dance. Intrigued, Overhoff called a friend that evening, the filmmaker William R. (Bill) Heick, who was a neighbor of the Halprins, and invited Heick to film a dance improvisation at the hangar the following weekend, provided Ann agreed. She did, asking Forti, Graham, Hunter Groat, and Leath to join her and Leistiko. That weekend three cars, whose inhabitants included Overhoff, Heick, Halprin, and the five dancers, drove to the site. Heick, who was familiar with construction sites from documenting the Bechtel Corporation's international projects, shot three hours of film as he followed the dancers through the site. A couple of hours into the improvisation, Heick recalled, a security guard arrived and ordered the dancers to leave. One of the women dancers, however, had just stepped on a rusty nail, so the guard was pressed into service speedily driving her to get first aid. The rest of the dancers continued dancing and Heick kept filming until the guard returned a half-hour later, when they were finally forced to stop. A few days later, Overhoff borrowed Heick's camera and persuaded a friend who flew over architectural sites, photographing them from the air, to make several passes over the hangar so Overhoff could get shots zooming into and away from the hangar by air. Heick and Overhoff worked on and off over the next four months editing the film into a tight seven-minute short, an edgy improvisational dialogue between the dancers, the filmmakers, and the steel skeleton. Heick, who had ties to San Francisco's Beat scene, helped lend *Hangar* its hip aesthetic.[50]

The film shows the dancers working quickly and quietly, mindful that they are trespassing without permission in a dangerous construction zone. They begin their improvisation on the rocky dirt field adjacent to the half-built hangar. Crouching, reaching, gesturing both toward the hangar and, in geometrical semiphoric arm movements, away from it, Ann and her five dancers start to echo in their bodies and their actions the visual rhythms of the three-story orange steel skeleton of the hangar. "Reading" the hangar as if it were the "score" for their improvisation, they seem to be communicating with the hangar in full-body sign language.

The dancers charge toward the hangar, and the next image we see is of them positioned inside the grids formed by the massive I-beams, the repetitive squares and rectangles of the hangar's open gridwork of skeletal walls and floors. In Ann's own improvisation, there is perpetual interplay between improvising with an eye toward the look of the movement and performing actual physical investigations such as testing just how far a dancer can safely lean off a beam, which may result later in performable movement.

The improvisation in *Hangar* is bounded by just a few preliminary decisions—like the choice to have vertical movements predominate. And yet the freedom given to the dancers to design their own actions doesn't guarantee that they'll enjoy the performing experience. Decades later, when Forti watched the film of *Hangar,* she remembered instantly how much she had disliked doing the dance: "I hated being there. I was so uncomfortable on those I-beams. I remember feeling it was dangerous. It was physically uncomfortable and it wasn't kinesthetically satisfying to me. It was very design oriented, in ways that didn't especially interest me."[51] As far as anyone recalls, *Hangar* was only screened once, in June of 1964 at the Playhouse in San Francisco, at an evening of short films by Heick and David Myers.[52]

Forti's memories of the discomfort of the work point to an interesting paradox. In the film the dancers performing on the I-beams several stories above ground seem coolly dispassionate and extremely controlled, displaying rigid geometric postures atop these perilous perches. Yet if Forti's memory of her discomfort is accurate, then in its formal drama *Hangar* violates Ann's own credo that the dance should arise from the performers' honest interaction with their environment. Aside from the opening moments of the film, where the dancers spill across the rocky field, advancing toward the hangar as if it were a deity-like monolithic presence, the improvisation *Hangar* showcases is relatively static, focusing on a series of slow postural changes, pliés, and crouches that lead one back to noticing the anchored stability of the hangar's form.

More than any conscious dance reference, it is this aesthetic of cool containment in the face of peril, combined with spontaneous art making, that suggests the link between Ann and the Beat musicians, writers, and visual artists of this era. In 1957 the Beats and Beat "style" were in full swing in San Francisco, so that even the women dancers' black leotards and the men's tights might be perceived as part of a Beat uniform. Heick, with his photographer's eye, found the contrast between these black leotards and the brilliant orange structural beams particularly vivid.[53] Rhythmically, *Hangar* bristles with the late swing era rhythms and emotional energy of tenor saxophonist Lester Young, which Allen Ginsberg described as pulsing through his *Howl.*

Although a sparse sound score of wind instruments was later added to the film of *Hangar,* it is cool jazz that seems to drive the dancers. Each dancer presents a very private mien as they freeze their bodies in a huge "X" atop a beam, some holding still while others crouch and change levels with an air of understatement and detachment. The improvisation here is of the sort jazz scholar Paul Berliner has called "in the moment" improvisation, a jazz form based on heightened immediacy to what one feels at that instant.[54] *Hangar* offers a parallel "in the moment" dance improvisation.

Although they never returned to the hangar, Ann and her dancers continued to explore through dance a variety of unusual environmental sites, from small caves on Mount Tamalpais to a steep embankment or a jumble of huge rocks on the Halprin property. They would work at the chosen site for an afternoon, improvising a relationship to each other, the environment, and objects from nature. The purpose of these exercises, Forti said, was to prompt each dancer to develop his or her own instrument without letting particular steps or stylistic patterns get ingrained. That same intention carried through to other exercises on the dance deck. As Forti recalled:

In the 1950s [Ann] was exploring what she felt were natural group processes. She'd have us start walking in a circle, let's say clockwise. And she'd just tell us to keep going, and that we didn't have to worry about staying single file, that we could just continue. And she'd have us go for maybe three hours nonstop. She'd sit there on the steps [above the dance deck] and just be there. And we would accelerate. We'd get to running very fast, and then we'd get tired and slow down, and then we'd start to speed up again. At the beginning she'd tell us not to think about taking any initiative, not to get interesting. And then she'd just watch this unfold. And I think we'd end up just collapsed on the floor.[55]

For Ann, even a simple movement task, like repetitive walking, could become exciting to observe. There was no telling where it might lead if it were allowed to unfold naturally, free from anxieties about making it look interesting to an audience. Forti underlined that Ann's approach "was absolutely breakaway from the dominant modern dance approach of the time, where you would learn certain movements and you would learn a technique that would give you a certain style. It was radical in terms of what dance could be. What movement could be dance and how was the dancer really owning his or her exploration and discovery of movement? In that way I think it was also political."[56]

———————

Ann's insistence on this kind of independent thinking and the way Ann used chance and spontaneity in these exercises, as well as in *Hangar* and the fourteen other dances she created in this period, clearly align her with the Beats. In 1951, for instance, Kerouac started to practice spontaneous writing as a way of sliding loosely into his prose. Similarly, Ann discovered automatic drawing in the early 1950s and spontaneously sketched visualizations as steady tools to lead children and adult dancers deeper into what she once called "a concern with movement rather than how movement is composed."[57]

Rather than focusing on chaotic unrestraint, however, Ann was interested in seeing what would happen if a group of dancers and actors played together with sufficient skill and communication so that each could make his or her own decisions, mindful of the others and selecting appropriate constraints in the course of the work. For Ann, as for the Beats, such a loose structure allowed one to state feelings and reactions directly rather than carefully mediating them through the constraints of deliberate form.

Hangar represents a liberating of dance, much as the Beats were already freeing poetry and other art forms from traditional styles. While the Beat poets declaimed on street corners and in coffeehouses or nightclubs, taking art out of the academies and museums, Ann took dance and presented it, often unedited, in woods, vacant lots, and construction zones, outside the theater and studio. She placed it in the midst of the disorder and danger of life. Ginsberg once stated that he was interested in using emotional improvisation over rational reflection, in making poetry "a graph of the mind." "The body is where we must begin," he insisted.[58] Ann amplified that, making dance a graph of the individual, in the world. Soon Ann would begin including audiences in her improvisatory recipes for art making. In her opening remarks before a wholly improvised performance she gave with dancers and musicians on the dance deck in 1957, she said:

> If you are ready and willing, it is possible that your mind can turn the accidental into a meaningful event—when this happens, you have begun to participate in our experiment. As the performers get under way various facets of improvisation will take place between dancers and musicians. By improvisation we mean literally making up music and dance completely spontaneously. Nothing that happens tonight has ever happened before, nor are we concerned at this time with preservation of the finished product.[59]

Like Ann, the Beat artists insisted on creating a somatic experience of their art for audiences. Performance was more than an ancillary practice for them; it was a model for their poetry. In contrast to academic poets, the Beats claimed their work could only be fully apprehended *in* the performance space, where the bodies of the spectators were as immediate as that of the performer.[60] They initiated a culture of orality focused more on a process of remembrance than memorialization.

Ann, too, highlighted memory, charted through the kinesthetic system, rather than memorialization, which in dance usually takes the form of a repeatable technique and repertory. In early 1958 she and A.A. Leath created *Duet*, a ten-minute improvisation that presages the kind of task-oriented work that would become a signature of the Judson Church dance experimentalists in the early 1960s. During *Duet* Ann and Leath together held a harmonica, and as one blew out, into the instrument, the other inhaled its vibrating hum. Accompanied by the sound of their "harmonica-ized" breathing, the two dancers tried to move with as much energy as they could in the rest of their bodies while keeping their heads stuck together, clinging to the harmonica. Ann, like her Beat counterparts, was aiming for a presentation of the performing body as a unity of the physical and emotional presence of the dancer.

More tellingly for dance, she was defining another road into movement, a disarming "back door," where the focus on an object and the task at hand of "working" it, replaced an overriding concern with choreography and the "look" of the dance. Yet, although Ann did not really realize this at the time, the emphasis on a task did not eliminate narrative or sexuality. As in much of 1950s behavior, the erotic was present if not openly acknowledged. Indeed, decades later Ann said if she were to retitle *Duet* she would call it *Kiss*.

Around this time language and vocal sounds entered into Ann's movement investigations. John Graham remembered Ann responding to his own interest in the spoken word and vocalizations, which originated in his training as an actor:

> Ann had enthusiasm and a commitment to say "let's try it." She had the ability to read whatever you did, feel it, read it and use it. When we would do our improvisations, Ann left it wide open for me. I would make sounds and say words and Simone [Forti] was willing to try anything. We'd start talking as part of the movement. That's how we started to use voice. In the beginning Ann would go over to a corner, she'd watch what was going on. She has a combination that's very interesting. She has a very strong nature, she has a strong sense of something she's got to do in this life. She's also a little naive. It seemed to work quite well for her, and us.[61]

In much the same spirit of experimentation, Ann began using costumes unconventionally, as a way to direct the performers' actions rather than having them assume a specific character role or enact set steps. She scavenged junk and antique shops for outdated clothing, artifacts of personality and identity she and her dancers could layer on themselves. Without making any modifications in what she found, Ann simply handed each dancer in her piece *Trunk Dance* some used or vintage clothing. The dancers were then asked to let the clothing inform the kind of movement choices they made. For Simone Forti, who performed this dance with Ann and A.A. Leath, the nonsensical and random manner in which movement and narrative were combined gave the performance a comic and surreal thrust. In yet another variation of her method of selecting an outside object or setting to dictate the form of the dance, Ann did a solo improvisation based on the actions of birds and insects overhead—she instructed herself not to move until she saw a bird or insect fly by, and then the animal's motion determined the direction of her own actions.

Ann's courting of random order in some ways paralleled Merce Cunningham's and John Cage's experiments with chance procedures, but her work had a different resonance. Ann used as her starting point objects with dramatic and emotional content. "My concern is form in nature, like the structure of a plant. Not in its outer appearance, but in its internal growth process. This form I speak of is a spontaneous naturalistic phenomenon—not paralleling nature but in its manner of operation," Ann said.[62] When Cage and Cunningham spoke of following nature in its "manner of operation," however, they meant finding a more global and neutral relationship of parts to the whole. For Ann, this phrase signified a more sentimental subservience to the organic structure and order of life forms.

Having a man and a woman alternately blow into the same harmonica, or giving an old train conductor's cap and black leather jacket to a sturdily built man, as she did with A.A. Leath in *Trunk Dance,* lends a certain dadaist edge to the results because neither the actions nor the costumes connect to any coherent narrative. "We didn't push for comic effects, but people laughed," Forti later said.[63] She described how at one performance Leath, in his black jacket and cap, made his entrance crawling backward until he collided with the backdrop, when he rolled into a fetal position and stopped. Graham burst on the stage next, skittering wildly across the space, flinging his arms around and turning swiftly in different directions as he chattered nonsensically about trains, buttons, and sneezes. Then came Forti, slowing pushing the trunk onto the stage. As soon as Forti positioned it in the center of the stage, Ann dashed in, flung the trunk open, climbed into it, and closed the lid. From there the dance progressed into a vaudeville-like shtick with the dancers searching for Ann while she shouted back to them from inside the trunk, "I'm here, I'm in here!" The audience laughed with pleasure at being the only ones who saw the whole story as Ann and her dancers kept not hearing and not seeing each other. "I wouldn't say we pushed for comic effects," Forti said. "But it was a form of comedy."[64]

Although the outcome might seem planned, it was something that developed by chance, through just letting the dance emerge, in the moment of improvisation. And just as one impulse might push the dancers toward the comic, another might lead to a moment of great poignancy. As Forti described it, in one very emotional scene Leath was balanced with his back stiffly against the trunk and his feet in the air as he froze in a shoulder stand while Ann sat on the trunk, her head covered by a veil. With subtle movements Leath managed to rock slightly back and forth, while Ann began moving slowly, maintaining close contact with the trunk and thus with Leath. Eventually Ann lay down on the trunk and Leath assumed various positions, trying to see her face from different angles like a desperate man courting an indifferent woman.

The kind of improvisatory storytelling that emerged in *Trunk Dance* found an echo eleven years later, in 1970, in the performances of Grand Union, a collective of New York choreographer-performers that included two alumni of Ann's summer workshops—Yvonne Rainer and Trisha Brown. Forti claimed that as soon as she saw Grand Union she recognized Ann's work as the antecedent:

> The way Grand Union was working with movement and narrative was very much like Ann and A.A. and John and I had done. But Ann's improvisation didn't come from concept as Robert Dunn's workshop assignments did. It came from impulse, kinesthetic awareness and impulse—and then the idea of an outside eye. So that you are following your impulses, but seeing how things are developing and doing some editing as you go.[65]

Yet, for all the seeming freedom Ann gave her dancers to explore what might happen, she did not abandon all control. All of the dancers who worked with Ann during the mid- to late 1950s mention her need to be the leader and arbiter of whatever dance theater material the group created.[66] "Anybody who was a leader and needed to be in control had no future with Ann," Leath commented. "I was never interested in being a leader or forming a production group. I'm just a good little boy who goes along with what mother says."[67]

Paradoxically, despite her controlling tendencies, Ann was unusually accepting of what might be called mistakes in a more rigid creative environment. Had *Trunk Dance,* for example, not been the product of committed improvisation, Ann and her dancers might well have rejected certain movements as too corny and literal. Yet because these movements just "happened," through improvisation, they were believed to carry a special authenticity. Ann didn't seem to mind whether the results of her experiments were prosaic, as in *Trunk Dance,* or radically unexpected, as in *Duet.* Her focus was steadily on how to generate movement from a source beyond conscious and deliberate control and yet remain true to the physical logic of the body. If one honored this, then whatever resulted was within the bounds of acceptability for her. "Everything we did evolved out of what happened in improvisation," Leath emphasized.[68] Improvisation was the technique.

As Forti described it, Ann might ask a group of dancers to simply walk in a circular path as a group on the dance deck, being careful not to let anyone stand out as an individual or consciously initiate a change. As Ann sat silently watching from the sidelines, the dancers shifted imperceptibly from walking to running and back, going from a slow walk to an easy jog and vice versa or from a dawdling aimlessness into urgency and anxiousness. They did this all in absolute silence, with only the language of their bodies as cues, like a flock of migrating birds changing course. Through exercises like this, Ann was inventing a way to *work* in dance rather than just inventing dances. Forti explained that Ann found improvisation to be "sort of like hitting a billiard ball and once you've hit it you have to let it go. Either she was going to direct for a certain effect, or she was going to get us improvising and just accept what happened."[69] Most often she chose the latter.

Ann found a compatible model for shaping her open and conversational approach among San Francisco poets in the late 1950s. She began collaborating with Richard Brautigan, a young poet fifteen years her junior, known for the laconic, some said self-indulgently coy, tone to his poems, which scan like carefully constructed sentences more than lines of poetry.[70] His works have been described as focusing on "a certain restricted range of experience: low-key, private sensations and ephemeral, minor constituents of the world."[71] Brautigan's sensibility, sometimes called "aesthetic primitivism" for deliberately ignoring traditional poetry, paralleled Ann's search for a new kind of dance, "not just to clear the ground [in modern dance] but to widen it as well."[72] Ann was looking for "another layer to give [a new piece] some spice and imagination. Brautigan's poetry was so simple but combining it with [this piece's] movements gave it a twist that was engaging."[73]

The piece in which Ann and Brautigan first linked their art was the 1959 dance *Flowerburger,* named for one of the three Brautigan poems that lace through it. Ann subtitled *Flowerburger* a "Dance Dialogue for 3 People" and pointed to "indeterminacy [as] the basic principle underlying this dance." As she explained in a program note: "I like working on this dance this way because I like being surprised, amused or astonished by relationships that I could never have pre-conceived."[74] Performed by Ann, Leath, and Graham, *Flowerburger* called on the dancers to make choices as they were performing in regard to sound and movement, as well as the associations between the two. Their movement choices were restricted to sitting, standing, and falling down, while for sound used text drawn from Brautigan's three poems, which could be spoken either by each dancer individually, by a pair, or by all three at once.

Reviews from several performances suggest just how provocative *Flowerburger* was for the audience. It always began with the three dancers entering through the audience: Ann, dressed in an orange dress and pink jacket, lugged in an old suitcase; Graham, in a peaked cap and loose overcoat, staggered in like a noisy drunk; and Leath just stood up from where he had been sitting unnoticed among the audience. Once in motion their activity built until they all raced madly toward the stage, pushing and shouting, climbing over empty chairs, sometimes even stepping on people's feet. Once onstage they dragged some chairs from the wings and proceeded to climb on, over, and through these chairs while noisily knocking them around. In the process their limbs became as entangled as the chairs until they were jointly sharing coats and jackets. The audience at times responded by taking action. Some people left the theater, while others yelled and jeered at the dancers, who retaliated by sinking into listless postures and staring back at the audience.

How did the critics respond? Writing in *Arts and Architecture*, Peter Yates found the work tedious in parts but concluded positively:

> I was particularly impressed by the ability of Ann Halprin and her two companions to perform, easily and offhand, feats of physical and dramatic dexterity which gave theatrical weight to what they were doing. 'Wait' also in the punning sense, because they were able to set and hold their pace, not forcing the action, to avoid trying for laughs, and quite simply sit out a long burst of audience reaction—munching their apples and banana.[75]

An alternative San Francisco journal, the *Open City Press,* praised *Flowerburger* as "madcap enough to delight the students and gain their immediate interest but also containing some profound and bitter observations, free-associational recollections of a world outside the auditorium much madder than the one within."[76] Ann seemed to resist this attempt to read social statements into *Flowerburger,* and in a lengthy program essay for a 1960 performance, she pointedly underlined the "in the moment" nature of this piece:

> The dance that you will see on the program tonite will be seen for the first time, and then can never be repeated in the same way. The dance is happening on the spot as the dancers and musicians improvise their own parts. In this departure the choreographer has constructed a framework open to a series of unpredictable possibilities and chance relationships.[77]

Ann took Brautigan's objective narration and turned it into a kind of kinesthetic realism, where happenings, with all their discontinuity and improbability, governed her aesthetic. It isn't that the content is unimportant, but rather that it is constructed in the heat of performance, where the body speaks and the mind listens.

A different kind of collaboration emerged in *Mr. and Mrs. Mouse,* which premiered as part of the larger *Rites of Women,* in late 1959. It used the poetry of James Broughton as its narrative and the music of Terry Riley as its sound score. Described as a "light little satire on the antics and tribulations of mice . . . with a torch song quality," the piece featured Ann as Mrs. Mouse and Leath as Mr. Mouse.[78] For her costume, Ann shopped the secondhand stores, where she found a long-sleeved black velvet gown that she shortened to three inches above her knees. Most of the dance takes place on an old (secondhand) Victorian settee, upon which Ann sits in a variety of odd positions—sideways, upside down—as Leath scoots along the floor behind her, occasionally tossing out a word from the Broughton poem that gave the dance its name.

"I thought she was wonderful because she was so forthright," Broughton said later of Ann. "She was always on the edge of growing into something, she never had fixed ideas and I always like that quality that any visions she had, any dance idea, she always was exploring. She would call me up early in the morning and say 'I have another idea. Why don't you come over and we'll try it?'"[79]

In 1960 Ann created three new dances, *Still Point, Visions,* and *Birds of America, or Gardens Without Walls.* Each work pushed in a different direction— one played with narrative abstraction and another abstracted the form of the body itself. Improvisation was still a basic part of all the dancers' technique, but now Ann was moving toward severing the link between cause and effect in her dances. *Still Point* and *Visions,* with a sound score by Terry Riley and La Monte Young, were experiments in a series of solo movement directions using objects and props and space in what Ann called "a deterministic way."[80] In *Visions,* for example, one dancer was restricted to dancing only alongside the railing of the dance deck, and all the dancers' bodies were curiously transformed by fantastical headdresses and big clumps of wadded-up fabric stuffed into their leotards and tights.

Over a three-month period Ann pulled together the previous two years' experiments in improvisation to present her first long work, the fifty-minute

Birds of America, or Gardens Without Walls. She chose Young's *Trio for Strings*, a score that has become known as the first piece of musical mini-malism,[81] to accompany *Birds*, which was structured as a series of seven directives for five dancers (Ann, Leath, Graham, and her daughters, Daria and Rana). A large chart Ann made listed the tasklike actions each section was to encompass, which dancers were to perform them, and the encumbering props to be paired with these actions. In this chart Ann designated the dancers by age and size. The youngest and smallest, eight-year-old Rana, was assigned tasks like kicking and carrying beach balls on and off the stage. One part of the dance was later filmed. Characterized as "Child and Tall Man, Lifting and Carrying," this section features eleven-year-old Daria and Graham, who at six and a half feet was the tallest of the dancers. In this section of the dance, despite the prosaic functionality of Ann's instructions— "lie down, stand, sit, be lifted, roll, still"—the dancers' interactions evoke a palpably sensual mood. It is easy to read emotional surrender into the swooning collapse of Daria as Graham stands over her and repeatedly swishes her limp body on the floor, gently swinging her first by one arm and then the other. He then cradles her balled-up form, and, standing hunched over, his legs spread wide, he swings her as if she were his tiny primate offspring. Again and again, Graham tugs the reclining Daria to standing, pulling her arms as her head hangs limply backward and her body crumples lifelessly toward him.

This posture of relaxation is so complete that it borders on erotic submission, an interpretation Ann at the time seemed unaware of, but one that is impossible to escape when viewing the film of it today. Daria looks like a large doll in Graham's arms, and he manipulates her with a gentle but persistent forcefulness. Remarkable in its single-minded investigation of what a big and little person can do together, both on and off balance, this section of *Birds* is also memorable for its naïveté. There is no deliberate eroticism here, only frank physical facts about performers' sizes and the physical reality of the adjustments one body has to make to lift another.

In a 1962 interview with Yvonne Rainer, Ann recounted how, just before the premiere of *Birds of America*, she made one last addition to the improvisatory tasks: she handed each dancer a ten-foot pole. "By chance I happened to become very aware of the space in the theater, the stage. I just didn't like it, it bothered me and I didn't know what to do," she said. "I got this flash: just before the performance, I put a bamboo pole in everybody's hands, including mine, and we had to do the dance we'd always done, holding these bamboo poles."[82] A series of still photographs of this performance suggests that, in addition to amplifying the dancers' presence in space, the poles encouraged a surprisingly aggressive narrative, as the dancers make spearlike gestures.[83] This was a curious change to make at the last moment because it did not simply tweak a design element of the dance, but it displaced the dancers' complacency in the scale of their bodies onstage. It was a "what if?" experimentation more typically found in the workshop rather than the performance phase of a dance.

Ann's openness to experimentation was apparent not only in her dance inventions but also in her choice of music. The music for *Birds of America* was composed by the twenty-five-year-old La Monte Young. Young, an alto saxophonist since the age of seven, had recently graduated from the University of California at Los Angeles with a BA in music and had arrived in 1958 in the music department at the University of California at Berkeley to begin a Woodrow Wilson Fellowship. In the summer of 1959 Young had traveled to the Darmstadt Festival for New Music in Germany to take the composition seminar of Karlheinz Stockhausen. In addition to an immersion in Stockhausen's music, Young got his most thorough exposure to the work of John Cage through lectures by Stockhausen and performances given by David Tudor while in residence at the festival. He returned to Berkeley inspired to continue exploring sustained and continuous frequencies as modal music forms as well as chance procedures. He also began to correspond with Cage and to perform Cage's work at Berkeley, learning, to his surprise, that "everybody there still considered him an out-and-out charlatan. I had to really fight to get him on the program."[84]

One person who didn't consider Cage a charlatan was fellow musician Terry Riley. Riley, a gifted pianist who started the MA program in music at Berkeley in 1959, had known about Cage and his prepared piano since he was a high school student. At Berkeley he was drawn to Young, whom he considered "definitely the most radical of all the composers there,"[85] and the two would soon collaborate jointly with Ann.

In early January 1960 Cage wrote in the margin of a letter to Young: "Hope you can get in touch with dancer Ann Halprin." And on February 7, 1960, Young wrote back: "I did get in touch with Ann Halprin, at your suggestion, and plan to meet her soon. I am told she does beautiful dances."[86] As Young remembered it, "I played her some of my music, including my Trio for Strings, which had been recently recorded for me by Dennis Johnson for a performance called Avalanche No. 1 at UCLA. I don't exactly recall the details but she became interested in my work and my ideas and invited me to become the Musical Director." Within a couple of months

Young was eagerly recommending Ann's work to other artists: "If at all possible attend Ann's concert at UCLA. She is probably the best American? Dancer? (although Merce Cunningham seems more athletic). I have been working with her for several months now and it has been a marvelous experience. . . . We improvise and Terry and I make sounds even better than electronic sounds. Live sounds (no tapes, on the spot)."[87] Young would later recall this work with Ann as "central to his development in offering such a free avenue of sound experimentation."

Ann in turn was excited by the new sound possibilities that Young and Riley introduced. She always welcomed change, and the implications of introducing her dancers, through Young, to Cage's music would be considerable. Warner Jepson, the musician who had composed the score for one of Ann's earlier dances, *Rites of Women,* and who had been providing improvised accompaniment for her workshops with another musician, Bill Spencer, remembered arriving one day, expecting to play for the workshop as usual. He was startled to find two new musicians—Young and Riley—there.

> Everything was on the spur of the moment it seemed. We arrived and Riley
> and Young are in position and they both have mirrors on the floor and
> coffee cans, and they are scraping them on the . . . you know, the fingernail
> down the blackboard? Well, it was worse. And that was their music. And
> Ann was all excited. And she greeted us, "This is what we're going to do
> today!" I responded, "No, this is not what *we're* going to do today." She
> just announces that they're there in our place. She was just excited about
> what she was doing, about what was happening. And she figured, well,
> maybe we would like to see it to, you know, incorporate us.[88]

It would be some time before Jepson, who was also a photographer, would work with Ann again.

Young would leave for New York in late 1960 and Riley for Europe in February 1962, but until then, their musical aesthetic dominated the sound environment for Ann's workshops and work. The sounds they provided "were ancestors of the wild sounds—natural sounds abstract sounds—interesting material juxtapositions such as metal on glass, metal on metal," Young later said. "Terry and I started making incredible sounds; they were very long and very live, and we'd really go inside of them, because they filled up the entire room of the studio."[89] The same climate of freedom and license to experiment within the loose boundaries of the avant-garde that Ann was carving out for her dancers extended to her musicians, Young and Riley.

Left: Isadore and Ida Schuman, Chicago, 1910s.

Right: Ann Schuman, Lake Michigan Shore, 1920s.

Above: Ann Schuman in her bedroom/dance studio, 1930s. Winnetka, Illinois.

Below: Ann Schuman in publicity photograph for the Hillel Dance Group, University of Wisconsin–Madison, 1942. Photo: Danny Yanow.

Lawrence Halprin and Ann soon after they were married, 1940.

Portrait of Ann Schuman Halprin, Chicago, 1942. Photo: László Moholy-Nagy, by permission of Hattula Moholy-Nagy.

Ann Halprin with Walter Gropius at a costume ball, Harvard University Graduate School of Design, Cambridge, Massachusetts, 1943.

Ann Halprin in *The Lonely Ones,* 1944. Photo: Lawrence Halprin.

Ann Halprin in *The Prophetess,* 1947. Photos: Imogen
Cunningham, © The Imogen Cunningham Trust.

Ann Halprin and Welland Lathrop in the 1831 Union Street studio, San Francisco, 1949. Photo: Philip Fein.

Ann Halprin, Welland Lathrop, and Avril Weber in *Daughter of the Voice,* Veterans'
Memorial Auditorium, San Francisco, 1953. Photo: Philip Fein.

Below: Jenny Hunter Groat, Ann Halprin, and A.A. Leath performing *People on a Slant,* outside the 1831 Union Street studio, San Francisco, 1953.

Above opposite: A.A. Leath, Ann Halprin, and Simone Forti improvising with a branch on the dance deck, Kentfield, California, 1954. Photo © Warner Jepson.

Below opposite: Merce Cunningham on the dance deck, Kentfield, California, 1957. Photo: Lawrence Halprin.

Above: Ann Halprin and dancers performing *Hangar,* on an airplane hangar under construction at the San Francisco airport, 1957. Photo: William Heick.

Above opposite: Ann Halprin with children of the Marin children's dance co-op. Photo: Ernest Braun.

Below opposite: Ann Halprin and Simone Forti in *Trunk Dance,* The Playhouse, San Francisco, 1959.

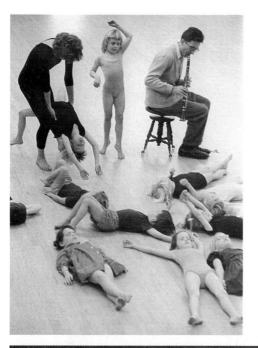

Above: 1960 Summer Workshop participants on the dance deck in Kentfield, California: Shirley Ririe, June Ekman, Sunni Bloland, Ann Halprin, Lisa Strauss, Paul Pera, Trisha Brown, Jerrie Glover, Ruth Emerson, Simone Forti, Yvonne Rainer, A.A. Leath, unknown, Willis Ward, unknown, John Graham. Photo: Lawrence Halprin.

Below: John Graham and Rana Halprin in *Birds of America, or Gardens without Walls,* International Avant-Garde Festival, Vancouver, British Columbia, 1960. Photo: Chester Kessler.

A.A. Leath and Ann Halprin in *Apartment 6,* The Playhouse, San Francisco, 1965.

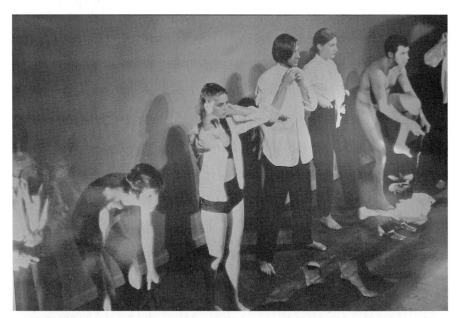

Above: San Francisco Dancers' Workshop performing the undressing and dressing section from *Parades and Changes,* 1965.

Below: Multiracial group from the San Francisco Dancers' Workshop performing the paper-tearing section of *Parades and Changes,* University Art Museum, Berkeley, 1968. Photo © Paul Fusco/Magnum Photos.

"Working with Ann at that time was very influential for our work," Riley remembered. "Because she was working in such a free form and intuitive way, without intellectual planning. It was amazing to see how things could develop with just a few simple materials. I really liked swimming around in that way."[90] While the specifics of *Still Point* and *Visions* (the first two dances for which he and Young collaborated on the music) blur together in Riley's memory, what remains clear is the risk he and Young took in improvising on the spot. "I think there was a question if we'd gone too far," Riley recalled, recounting how he and Young arrived at UCLA's Schoenberg Hall the day of the concert and "just looked around for what we could find in the way of improvised percussion instruments." In Ann's studio they had become accustomed to picking up some of the many percussion instruments she had lying around, reminiscent of the kinds of instruments she had seen in H'Doubler's classroom twenty years earlier. For the UCLA concert Riley and Young's instruments of choice turned out to be empty metal garbage cans and lids, which they relentlessly dragged and tossed down the cement corridors and stairs bordering the stage and audience. Riley remembered that the effect was extremely violent and threatening and seriously distressing to some of the people present, although not Ann. The sounds Young and Riley made were certainly the most radical music that had ever been played in Schoenberg Hall. The audience was so upset that they rioted, shouting out and making a ruckus. Young's parents left in tears.[91] Afterward, there was some discussion between Ann and the musicians, but she never censored what they did.[92]

In the spring of 1960, when *Birds of America* was having its premiere, three young dancers on the East Coast were beginning to share ideas about improvisation. Yvonne Rainer, Simone Forti (who had danced with Ann until she left for New York in 1959), and Nancy Cronenwelt Meehan (who had studied at the Halprin-Lathrop studio from 1953 to 1956 and was now a dancer at the Graham School) had begun meeting once a week to improvise and talk.[93] In late 1959 Rainer had started taking classes at the Cunningham studio and had met Forti soon after that through Meehan. Rainer took Cunningham's June 1960 intensive course, and then, persuaded by Forti to take Ann's summer workshop, she left for San Francisco in mid-July, driving across the country with Forti and Forti's husband, the artist Robert Morris.

Fifteen dancers took Halprin's workshop that summer: Rainer, Forti,

Shirley Ririe, June Ekman, Sunni Bloland, Lisa Strauss, Paul Pera, Trisha Brown, Jerrie Glover, Ruth Emerson, Willis Ward, A.A. Leath, John Graham, and two others whose names have been lost.[94] Rainer was particularly excited by La Monte Young's afternoon sessions, when Ann became a participant. His presence, she felt, "pushed the work in the direction of Cage's ideas: the aleatory, the task, sounds and actions outside of the traditional art nexus, the gap between art and life, what came to be known as Fluxus ideas."[95] In fact, Halprin had already begun working at the boundaries of this art/life nexus, but Young's infusion of Cage's aesthetic seemed to legitimize her own investigations and give her license to ground them more fully in movement and theater. Young himself would influence the coterie of conceptual artists that became known in 1963 as the Fluxus group in New York, and he linked Ann into this as well, including her in the little art books and postcards they mailed to one another throughout the 1960s.

In an afternoon lecture that summer on the dance deck, Young told Ann's students about his *Composition 1960 #2* and *Composition 1960 #5*, two works he had composed a few months earlier and which both, at least conceptually, involved as much movement as sound. Reading from prepared notes, he presented their scores, each one scripting a series of simple tasks. The first, *Composition 1960 #2*, involves constructing a fire in the performance space. The instructions recommend using wood, but other materials are allowed. The fire may be as large or small as the builder likes, although it should not be connected to an object like a candle. The performance space can be dark, without lighting other than the fire. After the fire is lit, the builder is invited to sit gazing at it for the remainder of the performance—as long as the audience's view is not blocked. There is no time limit for this composition.

The second score, *Composition 1960 #5*, is one of Young's most famous works from this period. In this composition the performer is instructed to let go of one or more butterflies, allowing them to fly freely. (It is suggested that any windows be opened.) Again, the composition has no time limit. If there are no restrictions on time, the composition may last until the final butterfly has made its way outside.[96]

In their attention to the environment and the inherent order and sequence in nature, Young's scores #2 and #5 are evocative of the choreographic method Ann was using in her workshop, where she prompted the students to attend to nature for compositional lessons. While Young called these two compositions musical scores, they might just have easily been called dances, given their emphasis on the perception of framed movement, be it of a fire or a butterfly, in a specified locale, for a designated period of time—which is just what dance involves. In both Ann's dances and Young's compositions of this period, the goal is to fuse visual aesthetics with the semiotics of contemporary reality and the natural world. The result is an art *of* the world, situated *in* the world, where the critical factor is the frame. Its boundaries determine which slice of life is being held up specifically for our aesthetic regard.

Young said his butterfly piece, which is dated June 8, 1960, was conceived one afternoon on a special outing he made to Mount Tamalpais with the Beat poet Diane Wakoski.[97] It was important, Young later explained, that "a person should listen to what he ordinarily just looks at, or look at things he would ordinarily just hear."[98] His premise here of using nature as the model for an aleatoric structure echoes Ann as much as Cage. The butterfly piece also involves the performance of a task, but instead of attending to the actions of taking the jar, opening it, and releasing the butterflies, Young made the visual a synecdoche for the auditory—how could such a rush of motion from the escaping butterflies possibly be silent?

"Our ideas all overlapped," Ann reflected years later. "All of us were looking for new ways to approach dance. Both Merce [Cunningham] and I were looking how to break up cause and effect. La Monte Young and Terry Riley [were so diligent about this that] they used to accompany us with their backs to the dancers so they wouldn't even be tempted to match their sounds to the dancers' actions."[99]

That Ann led movement sessions in the morning and Young music sessions in the afternoon does not seem to have dichotomized the art forms so much as reinforced the cross-disciplinary possibilities of improvisatory and chance procedures. At this time Young was extending his lessons in chance procedure into his spoken texts, and that summer he delivered "Lecture 1960," a talk comprised of aphoristic anecdotes, rather like the Cage text for Cunningham's *How to Pass, Kick, Fall, and Run*. His stringing together of several little vignettes seems to have been an important model for Ann, whose subsequent works played similarly with short movement narratives.[100] Young was also experimenting at this time with long, sustained notes rather than traditional melody. As he later commented, "When the sounds are very long, as many of those we made at Ann Halprin's were, it can be easier to get inside of them. I began to feel the parts and motions of the sound more."[101]

There seemed to be a constant give-and-take between Ann, Young, and Riley, as Ann's open experimentation with her dancers encouraged Young and Riley to push traditional boundaries in their musical accompaniment and vice versa. Their sensibilities paired up well. While Young and Riley were moving on a path that would lead in a few years to music minimalism, Ann was unhinging dance from traditional narrative logic, not so much in a quest for minimalism as for a stripped-down, functional realism. She was trying to break free of a tight cause-and-effect, predictable logic in her dance gestures and situations, as well as in the sounds that accompanied them. For his part, Young once described his *Trio for Strings*, which was used with Ann's *Birds of America* (a dance of simple tasklike manipulations of one dancer to another, independent of plot and character), as "a series of single sounds, each surrounded by silence and produced independently of melody."[102] Riley commented, "We talked a lot about that [breaking free from tight cause-and-effect logic in the relation between movement and music] after each performance. How to create a separate medium."[103]

For Ann's month-long August workshop, Young and Riley continued improvising as the dancers pursued their investigations of tasklike activity. Riley called what they were doing "going along with their spirit," as he and Young dragged metal objects along the plate glass windows of the indoor studio (built a few years after the dance deck) to create friction sounds or rolled steel ball bearings across the sound board of the little upright spinet piano Ann kept in the studio. "She was a perfect collaborator for us," Riley reminisced. "She was a little older than we were and she was very connected with the avant-garde. I was very inexperienced when I started with her, but it seemed we were all getting a lot."[104]

It is indicative of the profoundly experimental quality of Ann's collaborations with artists of all media that Young served as a conduit for Cage's ideas into her workshop and she in turn gave Young and Riley a forum of essentially absolute freedom and a room full of ready collaborators.[105] It was this quality, teamed with the rugged and remote beauty of the setting of the dance deck, that figured prominently in the buzz that drew dancers and artists to come study with Ann that summer.

What was the experience like for the dancers, like Rainer and Forti, who drove three thousand miles to attend this workshop? Rainer "was surprised to discover that in the morning sessions Ann led us through some floor exercises that resembled Graham technique," but there was also time for individual exploration. As Rainer described it:

> Ann also had us explore something that might be called structured improvisation, assigning tasks for voice and body. I remember Trisha

Brown flying around with a long-handled broom. I did an improvisation using my voice to utter fragments of words while emptying the contents of my bag, including a tampon and other personal items. (I remember this because years later Trisha told me how shocked she was to see the tampon.)[106]

The image of personal disclosure, of unpacking intimate aspects of oneself, functions as a neat metaphor for the special permissiveness and quick intimacy the summer work on the dance deck invited. It was not just the deck's seclusion, the warmth of the California summer air, or the immersion into hedonistic languor that working in a leotard-clad body on this platform in the woods invited. The workshop seems to have provided a unique space in the summer of 1960 for experiencing dance as a deeply educational and at the same time wildly radical enterprise. It was H'Doubler Meets the Beats, with Ann at the apex of this triangle.

Rainer, Brown, and Robert Morris have each confided separately that what surprised them the most was the discovery of how comparatively traditional Ann's finished dances appeared after the richness of all this open process. "Various things were tried out in the workshops in a fairly open, non-judgmental way," according to Morris, who, although not an official workshop student, was around that summer with Forti. "The materials explored in those improvisations involving language, sound, objects and movement seemed to be unearthing very fresh and surprising intersections between these things. But my recollection is that the concerts tended to hold onto only remnants of these discoveries and to eliminate the rawness and edge of uneasiness the workshops set in motion."[107]

Brown, who met Rainer, Forti, and Morris for the first time that summer, had come to Ann's workshop after two years of teaching dance at Reed College in Portland, Oregon. A 1958 graduate from Mills College in Oakland, California, Brown had been cautioned by her Mills dance teachers, Marian van Tuyl and Eleanor Lauer, to avoid two things during her years there—ballet and Ann. "Ann Halprin was considered outside the realm of modern dance for what she was doing," Brown recollected. What drew her to Ann that summer was her desperate search for some way to teach dance to her Reed students. While still a student at Mills, she had seen a performance with Ann, Leath, Graham, and Lisa Strauss that astounded her with the wit and inventiveness of the improvisations and the structures that generated them. "I was working with a lot of untrained dancers [at Reed] and these students didn't fall into the categories of dance I had been taught at

Mills," she explained. "I needed to give them a dance experience without having to rely on these kinds of techniques and I had begun to work in improvisation, so that's why I went to Ann."[108]

Although Ann would likely have bristled at being called a dance educator at this period of her life, that is in fact what she consistently excelled at doing, and precisely what Brown enrolled in her workshop for. "It was a most volatile experience," Brown later said. "The actual experiences I kept having I kept putting a lid on because I didn't want anyone to know that I thought they were all half-mad. . . . There were movement explorations, and she told us to MOVE! And they were extraordinary and we went for hours. There was no end to it." Brown found this extraordinariness was soon tempered by her growing frustration at the inconclusiveness and apparent lack of goals of the workshop exercises. "I didn't have a sense that there was a curriculum, or a structure or a sequence in the classes that [was] intending to lead to something, some understanding of what we could do through improvisation. Ann may have had a game plan, but I wasn't informed of it. If I said to one of my professors at Mills, 'I don't understand this point of choreography,' they had an answer for me, and I remember the answers. But I don't remember the answers from Ann."

One device Ann used was to give each student "a job" as a way of prompting him or her to find movement. "Mine was with the broom and it was to sweep the deck," Brown recalled. "I swept the floor for hours and I went totally out of my mind. I was obsessively involved with my job. I never really swept the floor. I guess I just took it as a dance structure, and action structure, and I held it." It was in the midst of this exercise that Rainer chanced to look over and saw Brown fly up and off the dance deck as she held onto the broom handle and propelled herself forward.

"I wanted to make dances," Brown said of her experience that summer. "It bothered me that all this material was going into the ether." Brown was equally frustrated that there was no system for critical feedback or discussion. "Ann persisted in communicating with us through letters at the end of the day, and I recall writing and asking that we make dances! Her response to me was that she didn't feel like the group was ready to do that, and so I felt thwarted. These improvisations were so rich and so wild and went through so much material. I had a sense of being lost, of not knowing where any of this was going."

Ironically, earlier that summer, in a prepared text delivered to an audience at a performance on the dance deck, Ann had offered reassurance for the lack of conventional signposts in her dances, implicitly acknowledging the lack of customary structures in her work. It is a disclaimer that applies equally to her pedagogy:

> I hope that what I will say will prevent you from looking in vain for that which will not happen. Usually in a dance program the audience views a product. By that, I mean a dance or demonstration which has been worked over and fixed into a static form. This program has a new form. The form is not a static product but is a form to be found in the process. This focus demands a different way of viewing dance.[109]

In part Ann was practicing an aesthetic of erasure, a partial peeling back so that the messiness of making the dance was as much in view as the finished work. Fueled by an abundance of raw material from the dance deck, her approach as a creative artist was to find rather than impose structure to eclipse some of her authority as decision-maker. Like many of the narratives of divesting authority that surround readings of social relations of this early 1960s period, an ambiguously defined notion of liberation shadows Ann's actions. A studio filled with fifteen dancers freely inventing movement may have been enormously stimulating for a choreographer observing it, but for the student on a four-week mission to learn how to make dances, it might well have felt as if he or she were a hungry person foraging for food someone else would eat.

Ann's interest did not lie in developing a cohesive onstage presence through the technical or stylistic uniformity of traditional modern dance. She wanted to create the conditions for each dancer to find his or her own presence, not by "making up movements," but by responding to an external natural order. She was looking for something "new." As she wrote in January 1961 to the critic Jack Anderson, who was preparing an article about her:

> I would like all my dances to be a complete surprise each time I do one. If I can say to myself as a dance begins to take hold, "How extraordinary, I never would have thought of that," then I am truly interested in proceeding with that dance. I would hope that the audience would enjoy with me the sharing of this surprise in a spirit of inquiry, involvement and delight.[110]

This invocation of surprise as a choreographic goal raises questions of what the consequences of surprise are both in the general spirit of the decade and as a primary objective for art. A choreographer who focuses on surprising herself has no assurance the audience will find the points of surprise still intact once the work has been rehearsed to the point of a public performance. Ann hinted at a response to this in a lecture demonstration she gave in February 1961 at the University of British Columbia in Vancouver. She explained that she was looking for a kind of friendship with the audience when she danced. "It's too bad [that] this doesn't always happen," she noted. "Perhaps we fail to play skillfully, or the audience fails to listen skillfully."[111] Ann herself, it should be added, had a marked charisma onstage, which stemmed from her cannily intuitive and intensely energetic and ambitious presence—and this was something that was not directly transferable or teachable. Instead of making dances like hers, dancers acquired the tools for mapping out experiments that would lead to their own.

Ann could exist comfortably in the improvisational present without knowing where it was going, or at least not worrying about it until she got closer to a performance date. This may have come from her early experience with H'Doubler, where actions like testing the range of motion of a specific joint, or slowly and deliberately crawling, could be the focus of hours of work in the studio. Ann modified this somewhat by using functional, everyday tasks, bled of their context, as the improvisational prompts for the workshop dancers. These tasks served as ideas for how the dancers might generate movement material. Effectively, Ann made her dances in reverse: she began with tasks instead of choreography.

For Rainer, the most salient lesson of that summer was "finding ways of generating movement outside of the body."

> That summer workshop was where I was first exposed to movement in
> relation to objects. Sometimes it was something you held in your hand,
> or devised little psychodrama or task-like activity around. I remember
> exploring moving through space while carrying some object. Ann preferred
> tree branches; I was later to use industrial objects, like gears. [Ann] was
> certainly an inspiration and energizing force. I knew even then, however,
> that the nature-and-dance combo was not for me, a bias that the women's
> movement of a decade later would only confirm.[112]

One dance Rainer created that summer was a piece for screen door (sound), flashlight (light), and dancer (motion). She also adapted at least one of Ann's signature images of nature-inspired dance, improvising with branches. To Rainer, Ann seemed "very present and dynamic and initiating" as she conducted discussions and introduced ideas. Rainer pinpointed

Ann's contribution, indicating, "She didn't represent a style of dancing; she was interested in exploration. She is a great educator, that is undeniable." As Rainer remembered it, "Her workshop situation was one where anything could be explored."[113]

Rainer didn't see Ann's work in performance until several years later, when *Parades and Changes* premiered in Stockholm in 1965. "When I actually did see a performance I was surprised at the theatricality of the work and I realized that the way she worked was always a preparation for finding material that could be transformed into a more theatrical kind of genre," Rainer later observed.[114] In the work Rainer herself would begin doing in Robert Dunn's workshop and at the Judson Church in 1961, she would make use of the pre-performance stage she encountered in Ann's workshop. She began taking the exercises involving the unadorned execution of movement tasks as finished performance material. Rainer's signature dance work from 1966, *The Mind Is a Muscle, Part I* (later called *Trio A*), celebrates the cool functional minimalism of those dance deck tasks, deliberately stripped of accents, attacks, and pandering to the audience. Viewers simply observe Rainer doing the functional work of dance actions. "I think the physical experience of the action being executed was more important than the look of it," Rainer said of Ann's workshop—a statement that illuminates with equal clarity *Trio A*.[115]

Like Brown and Rainer, Forti felt that at the end of the workshop she needed to take the content she had found there through improvisation and give it a form. "I think that improvisation was really beginning to pain me," Forti later noted. "I can remember saying that my inner ear could no longer take those limitless seas. There just seemed to be all this turmoil and turning of image upon image."[116] "The intensity of steady improvisation was so great," she said, "I felt like I was overdosing on staying in the state of mind that came up with so many images. The images just seemed to be writhing around. There were times when I'd wake myself up at night because I'd be dancing, I'd be improvising and pounding my arm on the floor."[117]

Forti credited Ann with teaching her "how to achieve a state of receptivity in which the stream of consciousness could spill out unhampered."[118] This climate of freedom was in some ways deceptive, for when a boundary was breached Ann recognized it and called a halt. Ann would sit up on the steps overlooking the dance deck and watch an improvisation, calling out to Forti to stop initiating interesting things. She wanted to see how a moving group would behave and Forti's intentional shaping was interrupting the natural flow.[119] Indeed, several workshop participants remembered Forti and Ann arguing repeatedly that summer.

Although Forti had her criticisms, she indicated that what made Ann exceptional as a teacher was her ability to create assignments that stimulated dancers to learn from their own movement explorations and "to really trust the body, its intelligence and how it wants to move."[120] Ann, however, would qualify this, commenting, "I didn't really have anything to teach that wasn't already there, and it was really up to them to get it."[121]

Ann loosened a great deal of creativity in that 1960 summer workshop for Rainer, Brown, Forti, and others, but the critical next step, how to distill the flood of ideas "going into the ether" into choreography and performances, would happen elsewhere. At the conclusion of Ann's summer workshop, Rainer, Morris, and Forti drove back to New York and Brown headed east as well. Rainer and Brown would reconnect several weeks later when both became part of the inaugural class of five in Robert Dunn's new choreography course beginning at the Merce Cunningham studio, and Forti and Morris would soon become participants in performances there as well as at Judson Church.[122]

Dunn, who was not a dancer or choreographer but rather an accompanist with a knowledge of contemporary dance, had deliberately set his class up as a liberating antidote to the composition classes given by Louis Horst, Martha Graham's music director, who believed in strict adherence to preclassic and modern musical forms.[123] Dunn also shaped his class as a corrective to what, as a student, he had felt as the "lag in productivity" in John Cage's 1956–60 class at the New School for Social Research, "Composition of Experimental Music." In contrast to Ann's workshop, Dunn's class pointedly focused on the production of dances. His weekly assignments stressed the structures one might use in constructing a dance, and there was a regular deadline of presenting it at the following class. A typical assignment might deal with abstract time constraints—for instance, to "make a five-minute dance in half an hour"—while the subject matter was usually of much less concern to Dunn. This flipping of priorities from Ann's workshop appealed especially to all of the dancers who had taken her summer workshop. "Bob Dunn asked us to be very specific about our parameters and to invent new ones," Forti said appreciatively. "Dunn's [workshops] seemed more academic in form," Morris agreed.[124]

Yet Ann's influence was still present in these classes. "Ann gave me my first permissions to use my body and imagination," Rainer explained. "And because she was into so many different kinds of things, the workshop provided a quite varied and expansive palette from which to start shaping and channeling my own future directions. . . . I would use my voice in my first solo using a chance procedure from Cage's 'Fontana Mix,' made in Dunn's class, but in many ways beholden to having attended Ann's workshop."[125] Even those in Dunn's workshop who had never met Ann recognized her impact on the Dunn classwork. "Simone [Forti] brought certain ideas from Ann Halprin into a situation of extreme discipline," Marni Mahaffay, one of the dancers in Dunn's inaugural class, noted. "The effect of those very simple elements was thrilling. I was so moved by the simplicity and strength of it: the comfortable, clean, expansive run, the quietness of the stepping."[126]

Within two years Dunn's workshop would evolve into the Judson Dance Theatre, a series of concerts offered between July 1962 and the summer of 1964 at the Judson Memorial Church in Greenwich Village, showcasing many of the dances composed for Dunn's choreography class. In her book on the Judson group, Sally Banes offers this impression of some of the individual choreographic styles: "Yvonne Rainer's dialectical work, mixing ordinary or grotesque movement with traditional dance technique, pushing the body's operations and coordination to the limits, and testing extremes of freedom and control in the choreographic process; Robert Morris's task dances, using objects to focus the attention of both performer and audience . . . [and] Trisha Brown's improvisations and flyaway movements."[127] For all three, these movement discoveries had been awakened in that summer of working with Ann. Her 1960 summer workshop created the educational context for these dancers to find themselves, the content of their dances, and to reach toward a new definition of the performing body that was highly individualistic, attentive, responsive, and resilient. The body in this model has its own intelligence, and the self emerges as each dancer physically negotiates her or his relationship to objects, other dancers, and the encumbrances of the assigned tasks. As in contact improvisation, which would develop a decade later out of work done by Steve Paxton, Nancy Stark Smith, Lisa Nelson, and other members of the Judson dance circles, one learned why to move, rather than absorbing a set vocabulary of actions.[128]

In Ann's workshops the instantaneous image became a new starting point for dance. Dunn's class led these sensitized bodies to find structure, limits, and form.

SIX

Urban Rituals
1961–1967

I am interested in ceremonies of the present. What is ceremonious and curious
and commonplace will be legendary.

DIANE ARBUS, *1962*

People call me a sick comic, but it's society that's sick, and I'm the doctor.

LENNY BRUCE, *1962*

IN JANUARY 1961, with the inauguration of John Fitzgerald Kennedy,
America celebrated an end to the cold war mentality of the 1950s and a new
era of exhilaration and confidence began. Ann was in step with this shift,
pushing ahead on the new path she was defining for American dance. Her
critique of dance convention focused on the reframing of dance performance, grounding in the ordinary the images it created, and, most significantly, the content it put forward. She did not want to train dancers to enact a script where their bodies functioned as instruments of someone else's
grandly scaled expression. In Ann's theater the desired subject of the dance
was emerging as the peculiar moment-to-moment lived reality of each
dancer her- or himself. In the early 1960s this emphasis on the self was not
yet the therapeutic cliché it would become; rather, it was a radical and dangerous creative enterprise.

The man who would become Ann's mentor during this decade, the Ger-
man-born psychotherapist Fritz Perls, made his first visit to California in
1959, staying for several months with a family in Northern California while
he consulted at Mendocino State Hospital. When his funding ran out in
late 1960, Perls left for Los Angeles.[1] Perls would not be lured back to what
would become his permanent California home, the Esalen Institute in Big

Sur, until late 1963, at which point his path would cross with Ann's for the first time. In the interim they each worked in their separate disciplines, pursuing work that would eventually converge. Perls was developing his Gestalt therapy by focusing on reading feelings through bodies and their movements. Ann was progressing in an inverse direction, mining her own and her dancers' feelings as a means of generating images and shaping movement toward a new realism in dance theater. Both Perls and Ann operated at the intersection of the creative process with its psychic costs and physical manifestations. Their explorations would prove to be deeply sincere and ultimately more intuitive than those of analytical researchers of the human landscape.

Immediately after the conclusion of the 1960 summer workshop, Ann, A.A. Leath, John Graham, and Lynne Palmer began rehearsals for Ann's first evening-length dance made up entirely of task performance. For years Ann had been preoccupied with the movement qualities created when a person just did a routine task, but now she edged toward an interest in the task itself. She and her dancers experimented with how to sequence a series of disconnected physical tasks while layering them in the performance space to create an inherent theatricality. The result was a dance theater piece that emerged initially as *The Four-Legged Stool* in the spring of 1961 and then, after a poor reception and a year of reworking, reappeared as *The Five-Legged Stool* in the spring of 1962, opening at the Playhouse repertory theater in the North Beach area of San Francisco. Designed as a sensory experience without deliberate meaning or continuity, the content was whatever the audience saw.

On opening night, Ann and Leath began the show by each standing in frozen postures on the audience side of the footlights as people slowly filtered into their seats. For the next twenty minutes, until the formal start of the show, Ann and Leath kept shifting their positions imperceptibly so that one had the sense that they had moved without ever seeing when it had happened. As their movements brought them into sight of each other, their features gradually broadened into silent expressions of recognition.

Leath, wearing a white shirt, black pants, and a safari hat and with a long spyglass hung around his neck, was positioned in one of the boxes. Ann, dressed in the thrift shop finery of a beaded 1920s flapper dress, stood on the apron of the stage at the opposite side of the house. Her red hair was fashioned into a towering mass, back-combed into an absurd exaggeration of the fashionable bouffant hairstyle of the time. "In those days people were ratting their hair and doing these tall things," Palmer recollected. "Ann and I had extreme hairdos. We had a hairdresser friend make our hair go as high as possible. When the light would go through it—it was really beautiful to look at, and also funny."[2] This costuming extreme introduced an Albee-like element of social farce to the performance.

The buildup of this little drama between Ann and Leath faded out without ever resolving, and other solo events began to unfold on the stage. For instance, Graham kept passing swiftly by, repeatedly lunging across a darkened space hung with strips of shiny black oilcloth. A dozen feet above the stage, in a small suspended balcony framed with an oval opening cut in oilcloth, Palmer sat at a dressing table eating grapes and combing the thick hair of a waist-length black wig she had pinned to her head. Occasionally, gazing through a hand-held mirror, she slowly surveyed the scene below. Meanwhile, on the floor below, a bicycle wheel spun across the stage; then, seconds later, Leath, now pant-less and with the tails of his white dress shirt trailing, dashed after the wheel. No sooner did he catch it and throw it off than he repeated this surreal sequence of chasing/catching/throwing, chasing/catching/throwing, again and again. Later, Ann, having exchanged her flapper costume for a flesh leotard draped with a floor-length, embroidered and fringed, red Victorian shawl, very rigidly and slowly descended a tall staircase on the side of the stage, only to ascend backward as soon as she reached the ground. This action too was repeated to a point past boredom until, because of its extreme monotony, it once again became interesting.

The two-act ninety-minute work was filled with more than a dozen vignettes like these. Composer Morton Subotnick's score added what Stanley Eichelbaum in the *San Francisco Examiner* described as "a bedlam of taped and live noises—jet engines, yelping dogs, crashing piano chords and ambient voices."[3] One of the most written-about actions involved Ann systematically gathering one hundred empty wine bottles from the wings and then, as she stood on a four-legged stool, stealthily handing them up, one by one, to a disembodied hand that reached down from the rafters. Palmer remembers Ann resembling a praying mantis as she stretched her torso, legs, and arms as long as possible to gather the bottles and then stretching long again as she handed them upward. The most climactic moment in the dance came when Leath, who had been lying in a recessed area at the back of the stage, suddenly did a full-bodied fish dive to standing and lunged at Ann as she stood atop the stool. He clutched her thigh and bellowed in a wordless wail as Ann responded with a similar guttural cry, somewhere between pain and passion, full of both effort and impotency.

In the final moments of the dance, all the labor of Ann's bottle passing was poignantly reversed as a giant cloud of white feathers noiselessly wafted down onto the stage just where she had so tirelessly cleared the bottles. Arts critic Alfred Frankenstein declared, "The final episode of the piece, wherein, to the sound of silence, feathers drop from the ceiling to the floor of the stage, is worth the price of admission in itself. Each one of those feathers had a personality all its own. This, I suspect, we should *not* see if our sensibilities had not been sharpened by watching the rest of *The Five-Legged Stool*."[4]

Ann's use of repetition and parallelism tied into the Theater of the Absurd dramatists' efforts to communicate the fallibility of communication. There was nothing clearly narrative or specific in any of the actions in *Stool*, yet they seemed clearly to be about the desperation and agony of communication and partnerships and the impossibility, at times, of having both. Later, when Ann saw Samuel Beckett's *Waiting for Godot* (1953) for the first time, she immediately understood *The Five-Legged Stool* lived in the same existential territory.[5] (Curiously, Ann reported that she knew nothing of the legendary *Godot* production her studio neighbor, the San Francisco Actors Workshop, under the direction of Herbert Blau, had staged in November 1957 at San Quentin Prison, just across the freeway from her home in Marin.)

Even though the dancers' actions seem disconnected, without a clear narrative, one might describe *The Five-Legged Stool* as presenting a domestic ritual of alienation and absurdity in keeping with the political and social climate of America in 1962. On October 13, 1962, a scant six months after Ann's piece premiered, Edward Albee's abrasively realistic and absurdist nuclear-age drama *Who's Afraid of Virginia Woolf?* opened on Broadway. Albee's play and Ann's dance both live in a once-sacred landscape where the American dream of family, happiness, and meaning is imploding. Through similar theatrical devices of repetition, parallelism, farce, wit, failed communication, violence, and shattered relationships, both works evoke the hollowness of lives without purpose, lives with traditions so bled of meaning they have become vacant rituals that numbly reproduce the urban condition.

Altogether, *The Five-Legged Stool* signaled a radical break in the customary use of ritual in modern dance. Instead of invoking ritual as a spectacle of decorative and highly theatrical entertainment, as Martha Graham, Ruth St. Denis, and Ted Shawn had done, Ann wanted to use ritualized tasks to initiate a perceptual awakening to the mundane for both the performers and the audience. Ann was theatricalizing task, linking it back to preparation for the stage in the same spirit that she had contemporized H'Doubler's 1920s exercises into the avant-garde task performance of the 1960s. While others from the 1960 summer workshop pushed task into an avant-garde dialogue with minimalist music and visual art. Ann's use of task might be better compared to Larry's exploration of rituals of human behavior through his urban designs in public spaces. As Ann has explained, "Dances that change and transform our lives can be called rituals in the way I am using this word. A way to create ritual is to invest the objects of our daily lives with new significance. Ritual and ceremony can happen anywhere at any time."[6] With this definition Ann was claiming the capacity for contemporary Western life to create its own rituals.

Ann's working definition of ritual both embraces and contradicts traditional anthropological definitions; at the same time it locates her dance events as being different from simply a theater performance. The anthropologist Roy A. Rappaport demarcates five attributes of ritual, and three of these are found in Ann's work: (1) "Ritual is performance. If there is no performance there is no ritual"; (2) "In ritual performance transmitters are always among the most important receivers of their own messages"; and (3) "In ritual the transmitter, receiver and message become fused in the participant."[7] Effectively Ann was beginning to move personal experiences across the boundary of contemporary performance. Instead of just aesthetic enjoyment, she had begun to manipulate not just objects and actions but also space, time, and spectatorship ritualistically.

Ann defines ritual in a nested relationship to sensory life. In Ann's words: "The symbol of people's myth is their own body. How people experience their body is their story. That story is their myth and how they perform it is their ritual. Everybody has a personal ritual."[8] This belief in writing the experience of the body through performance expands on Ann's lifelong essentialist belief in the body as a fount of deep knowledge that can be nudged into expression and made available, through dance.

The Five-Legged Stool presents a movement account of how rituals are rooted in our bodily experience of even the most mundane parts of daily life. As the performers engage in quotidian tasks, stripped of purposeful meaning, the audience members are invited to construct a meaning, shaping their own mini-myths. By prompting audiences to participate in this intensification of the prosaic, Ann hoped to nurture new perceptual skills. She wanted to take both audiences and performers to that "strange liminal space in all of us," identified by the Scottish-born anthropologist Victor Turner, where "life discloses itself at a depth inaccessible to observation, reflection and theory."[9] Ann's *Five-Legged Stool* aimed, initially awkwardly, at this sensorial territory where ritual heightens our consciousness of what is normally inaccessible to observation and reason.

Ann also used ritualistic actions in *The Five-Legged Stool* to rewrite the cold war hierarchy of the senses. The kinesthetic rather than the analytical is posited as being truth bearing, like the visual, and the ambiguity of relationships is celebrated rather than hidden or feared. There is a hint of irony as well as defiance in staging this message in San Francisco, a city that just two years earlier had been the site of a demonstration against the House Un-American Activities Committee, which was holding hearings to investigate disloyalty and subversion in the Bay Area. On Friday, May 13, 1960, later dubbed "Black Friday," two hundred anti-HUAC protesters gathered in front of City Hall, only to be beaten by the police and sprayed with fire hoses. The nosiest demonstrators were flung one by one down the steps and then flushed onto the street by the torrents of water.[10] For the police, one might imagine that this was a metaphoric cleansing and casting out of sinners (although it is unlikely the police would have phrased it this way). For the radicals, the injured and soaked protesters became martyrs. When the Michigan student activist Tom Hayden hitchhiked to California a few weeks later, inspired by reading Jack Kerouac's Beat narrative *On the Road* (1957), he came to the Bay Area in particular to see the site of this confrontation, the "stage" of this coercive performance.[11]

Actions would not just prove louder and more persuasive than words at this moment in American social history, but also be deemed by many to be more trustworthy. These Bay Area activists' belief in physical engagement over rhetoric paralleled Ann's own bypassing dialogue in favor of a more immediate, sensory conversion of her audiences in *The Five-Legged Stool*. "This theater event is meant to appeal directly to the senses and primarily the kinesthetic sense," Ann wrote of her intentions with the initial 1961 version of *Stool*. "Anything stirring up the mind would only serve to build up walls of pre-conceived ideas, of habits of perception. The point of reference here is in the tensions of muscles, nerves and the total human responsive intelligence." In keeping with this belief, Ann did not want programs to be distributed to the audience "unless the program can be treated as an independent, poetic event of its own." As she explained further:

The customary program with academic verbalization explaining the drama would serve only as a distraction. . . . Ideally the role of the audience is that of a group member of the composition. They are given the freedom to discover and select out of a series of possible combinations of relationships. A single center of focus is never imposed on them. They are participants in the very act of composition. The elements of indeterminacy utilized in the composition make this possible, the non-fixed spaces, and the open implications and associations. Choice is a freedom built into the composition for the benefit of the spectator. This involvement is the audience role.[12]

This is a remarkable declaration of Ann's application of chance as a perceptual method and of her dance theater as a ritual practice. It aligns with similar emerging sentiments in the visual arts and in Merce Cunningham's and John Cage's experimental dance and music work in New York.

When Cunningham had visited the Halprins at their home four years earlier (see chapter 4), he had remarked on how her dance deck might affect the dancer's performing consciousness. "Ordinarily," he explained, "the dancer deals with a fixed space set by outside convention, the dimension a box with a view from one side. But here on the dance deck there is a totally different situation. Aside from the obvious openness in the architectural arrangement there is another freedom for the dancer. There is no necessity to face front, to limit the focus to one side."[13] Rebellion against modernist hierarchy had led Cunningham to his use of the stage as a flexible frame where the dance within it held no specific front or back and viewing it from any angle was an aesthetic choice. Yet here was Ann arriving at the same discovery of the openness of the performing arena with the California environment as her teacher.

For *The Five-Legged Stool* Ann took what she had learned in her outside space into the formal environment of the theater and probed that spatial setting as if it were an architectural playground. *The Five-Legged Stool* opens with an incursion into the viewer's space and time, as actions, sounds, and events unfold at curious paces and in odd places within the theater. Ann deliberately tried to get her performers to use the whole space of the theater, from the balcony to the aisles to the lobby. Lynne Palmer remembered that throughout the performance John Graham repeatedly strolled from the lobby to the stage, walking straight through the audience while carrying a portable radio tuned to a local station with the volume all the way up. "John's role was all about entering and exiting through the audience,"

Palmer recalled. "It felt almost like he was a deliveryman."[14] At another point Palmer and Graham ran through the audience with flashlights. Later they stood in the aisles and screamed. At one point a chorus of people Ann scattered throughout the theater began singing "A Mighty Fortress Is Our God," and the audience spontaneously joined in the hymn. Ann was using a broad range of devices to bluntly bridge the divide between performer and spectator.

In *The Five-Legged Stool* Ann essentially took the theoretical work of John Dewey and Margaret H'Doubler to its theatrical conclusion. If the aims of education and art are to help us become more human and whole by reflecting on experiences and using this reflection to illuminate life, how might this process be enhanced by dance, with its capacity to allow an interpenetrating of the physical and the mental? Dewey was known to abhor dualisms, and in this piece Ann functioned as a distant disciple, invoking ritual to triumph over the dualisms of perception and representation, of creation and reception. It was here that her work met its greatest challenge.

Ann discovered that just designating the whole theater a performing site was not sufficient to give the audience tools for real engagement. She had built her myths and rituals collectively with the performers, recognizing implicitly that group collaborative performances can themselves be a species of rhetoric. They involve debate, deliberation, and compromise, and in the process they create the illusion of cultural uniformity and consensus. But she had not yet thought to prepare the audience similarly. Several weeks of rehearsals could achieve this for the performers, but what about the viewer who arrives at the theater without such preparation? She, after all, refused to distribute programs.

Writing in the Sunday edition of the *San Francisco Chronicle,* the same week that *The Five-Legged Stool* opened, Larry Halprin endeavored to set up an informed reception for Ann's dance theater piece, which had been trounced by the critics and public the previous year in its first incarnation, *The Four-Legged Stool.* He discussed the reconstituted piece, with the additional work symbolized by the fifth leg in the title, as inaugurating a new relationship between an art event and its audience—a relationship both ancient and innovative. Ann was taking her art back toward ritual as a social model and at the same time propelling it forward by deploying ritual as a contemporary aesthetic strategy. Her goal was to reengage the gestural vocabulary of everyday life as art and to cast the spectator as a more active participant.

This last point had been the site of the most serious miscalculation of *The Four-Legged Stool.* When Larry cited the work's capacity to take art back to its "ritualistic beginnings," when "art was only a sharpened expression of life,"[15] he overlooked that in ancient times there was a knowledgeable audience receptive to the communal experience being offered and comfortable with the role prepared for them. This critical element was lacking for Ann's work. Instead, the public reacted to Ann's initial version with hostility and anger. People jeered, walked out, and, at couple of performances, hurled verbal insults and objects at the performers onstage. Concerned that this might happen again, Ann coached her dancers:

> If this theater piece is performed for the general public it is important for the performers to be aware that many members of the audience will be uncomfortable and confused. They are apt to manifest this state by making audible irrelevant remarks, by giggling nervously or leaving the theater. This cannot be avoided and the entire cast must develop the skill to maintain concentration and continue giving as strong a performance as possible.[16]

Ann believed that it was the absence of the traditional performance anchors of gestural narrative and logic that distressed the audience. "We were just scrambling, that's all, just scrambling things up," Ann said. "Sometimes in rehearsal we'd try to scramble things up so that we'd do everything backwards and we'd start at the end instead of the beginning. We were trying to break this habit of cause-and-effect predictability, which is in a way what collages did. And the first part of this dance was really, visually, just like a collage."[17]

In his article Larry pointed out how the work was grounded in everyday life and our basic humanity: "She is making theater out of physical images in ordinary life, of simple occurrences and the most deeply rooted relationships between people. . . . She wants most, I think, to create an environment—a landscape, if you will, within which both audience and performers are part of the cast and the events are common to them both." His reference to Ann's dance as aiming for a kind of landscape involving both audience and performers reveals a connection to his own evolving architectural vision, in which he saw the natural world as the ideal model for art. Art, in turn, he defined as "only a sharpened expression of life."[18]

In 1962 Larry was beginning work as the landscape architect for the conversion of San Francisco's Ghirardelli Square from a nineteenth-century chocolate factory into a development of terraced plazas, fountains, court-yards, shops, and restaurants. Integrated into this plan was his desire to "choreograph" people's movement through ramped and winding staircases, past fountains, and onto tiered platforms and balconies that offered views of San Francisco Bay, Alcatraz Island, and Aquatic Park. At its completion, six years later, Ghirardelli Square would be lauded as one of Larry's "finest examples of creating space as theater."[19] The Playhouse theater, where Ann created and performed *The Four-Legged Stool,* was a few blocks away in the same San Francisco neighborhood.

At the same time Larry was embarking on designs for the Sea Ranch development on the Sonoma Coast of Northern California. As the land-scape architect for this project, his challenge was how to preserve the char-acter of the land if a relatively dense development was built on it. He suggested clustering condominium units and individual houses in a way that offered views and privacy while providing maximum open space as com-mon area for the entire community. This design solution had social as well as aesthetic and theatrical resonance. Like his wife and the playwright Ed-ward Albee, Larry was commenting through his medium on the postwar state of American domestic life and offering an alternative arrangement, where the individual could engage with nature and a community of like-minded neighbors. For Larry, "community" included the environmental as well as personal relationships, and he marked his ideas about social re-design on the landscape and its edifices. It was a solution Gropius would have applauded.

Larry's interest in community came through in his *San Francisco Chron-icle* essay on *The Five-Legged Stool.* He championed Ann's art for its imme-diacy and capacity to resurrect theater as a communal event of "supreme im-portance" in people's lives, "to speak to people in a language which they can understand through all their senses."[20] Almost all of the dozen or so attri-butes of his wife's art that Larry enumerated are qualities associated with this notion of art as "a sharpened expression of life," as a slice of ordinary expe-rience, framed, intensified, and set out for aesthetic regard—ritual as art.

By invoking ritual, Ann enhanced the desire Susan Sontag once identified as a characteristic of modernity—that people like to feel they can antici-pate their own experience.[21] Avant-garde ritual packs the dual satisfaction of being new as art and yet comfortably familiar as an experience because of its patterns of repetition. Like spectatorship in the visual arts, Ann's the-ater set up a relationship where the audience did not lose consciousness of self, where visual meanings dominated over linear narratives, and where the capacity to anticipate experience was made vital. Yet there is an irony here, for it seems that the more like life avant-garde art becomes, the smaller its audience. True realism rarely equates with accessibility.

In *The Five-Legged Stool*, then, little truths about one's body, about one's daily actions and interactions, one's social rubbing up against others, became the building blocks of Ann's urban ritual. In the same way that Richard Schechner would later speak of "performance consciousness" as a transformation of being or consciousness that activates alternatives,[22] Ann added the term "ritual consciousness" to her conception of "body consciousness" to denote the conceptual shift that accompanied her regard of behaviors as ritualistic. She would come to define ritual consciousness as "a way of shifting awareness from an automatic, habitual way of living your life to one of active awareness and to using dance with [a] purpose."[23] Increasingly, Ann would identify this as healing, and over the years the scale of this healing would grow from private emotional ceremonies, to public ceremonies such as *Citydance* (1976–77) in response to the murder of San Francisco's mayor George Moscone, to the massively scaled *Circle the Earth* for groups of people confronting life-threatening illnesses, and finally to international rituals advocating world peace. "Ritual and ceremony can happen anywhere at any time," Ann later wrote in her manual for people with cancer. "Creating dances that change and transform our lives can be called rituals in the way I am using this word."[24]

In the audience for *The Five-Legged Stool* was the man widely considered the leading Italian composer of his generation, Luciano Berio. Berio, who was guest-teaching at Mills College in Oakland, had first met Ann on a visit a few years earlier, when Doris Dennison had taken him to see a performance of Ann's children's dance co-op. Berio had been ecstatic about the children's performance and had also liked a piece he saw Ann perform, but a plan to collaborate did not materialize.[25] After seeing *The Five-Legged Stool*, however, Berio was again captivated, praising it as the "most interesting and alive approach to the theater today."[26] Berio himself was composing in a parallel style of aural collage—suturing spoken and sung text with live and recorded, natural and synthetic sounds, run through tape machines and live performers. He soon contacted Ann and invited her to provide the dance portion of an experimental opera score that he was writing for an April 18 premiere at the 1963 Venice International Festival of Contemporary Music. Early on, as he explained in an interview in July 1962, he envisioned the plot as "an endless journey," providing a loose-enough frame to encompass anything Ann and he might produce in this collaboration and yet still lending it an air of intentionality and cohesion:

[This work] will not be an opera or a ballet, but an improvised stream-of-consciousness procession of actions and sounds . . . a continuous polyphony of almost independent developments in action, situations, words and sounds. There will be no story but rather an indefatigable assemblage of situations suggesting different levels of meaning. The most obvious and general meaning will be one of continuous search, of an endless journey, of a very meaningful exodus; but the purpose, cause and scope of this exodus will be left an open question in the minds of the public.

Berio added that he hoped the audience would react to this work where "there is not a story but rather an indefatigable assemblage of situations. . . . The most obvious and general meaning will be that one of a continuous search," of an endless journey with the audience being "put in the condition of being unable to decide whether Ann Halprin and her Group are dancers, actors, mimes, acrobats, or singers."[27]

Over the next ten months Berio and Ann exchanged numerous letters as they proceeded with the long-distance planning of this work, titled *Esposizione* ("Exposition"). Beginning in January 1963, Berio, who was in Milan, began trying to secure several days of rehearsal for Ann and her dancers in Teatro la Fenice, the Venice opera house, prior to the work's opening. In a letter to Ann, he outlined a simultaneous double opening for the work, with performers in the grand Renaissance square in front of Teatro la Fenice as well as on the stage of the ornate horseshoe auditorium indoors. "I will use musically 2 boy sopranos from Milano's Duomo Choir, 1 clarinet (Morton Subotnick) and 2 trombones. They will walk toward the orchestra pit (where something else has already begun) through marble staircase and audience, inviting with captivating and endearing charm the latecomers to our terrible *Esposizione*."[28]

For the *Chronicle*'s critic Alfred Frankenstein, Berio's inclusion of Ann was "the biggest thing that has happened, internationally speaking, to a local theater group since the tours of the San Francisco Ballet and the Actors' Workshop," and he urged the community to help with funds to make her participation possible. In various editorials and articles Frankenstein and Kenneth Rexroth stressed the honor this invitation conferred upon the city, as well as the shame when it was revealed that the city was not helping this particular artist. A longtime supporter of Ann's work, Frankenstein was likely the author of an unsigned editorial that appeared in the *Chronicle* calling on city officials to rise to this important opportunity to "demonstrate to the world something of the cultural vigor of San Francisco" and proudly support Ann as the only American dance or theater artist invited to the festival.[29] Her work might be challenging for locals and her audiences at home small, but—the editorial contended—this was a unique San Francisco art product, and if the European avant-garde found it interesting, then the city should proudly claim it. They didn't.

On the opposite coast, a debate about Ann's influence was also unfolding. In August 1962 *The Floating Bear,* a New York literary and performance newsletter edited by the poets Diane Di Prima and LeRoi Jones, contained a column by Di Prima commenting on the Judson Memorial Church dance concert of July 6. Yvonne Rainer had premiered her *Ordinary Dance,* a work Di Prima praised as one "that will probably become a classic." As Di Prima described it, this dance, which was accompanied by Rainer's recitation of a poetic autobiography that included every address where she had lived in San Francisco, Berkeley, Chicago, and New York, involved "naming streets of her past, moving in her inimitable manner, pausing and twitching, lyric and wooden, a system of dante's hell in dance, personal as any hell, but terrifyingly clear to the observer."[30] Parts of *Ordinary Dance* call to mind the ordinary actions of Ann's task assignments, as well as Ann's verbal experiments with the blunt use of language and prosaic autobiographical details as the impetus for movement narratives, all of which Rainer would have encountered in the summer workshop. In speaking about *Ordinary Dance,* Rainer said she created the dance "mainly thru dealing with fragments of observed behavior in different kinds of people—a ballerina demonstrating classical movements, a woman hallucinating on the subway."[31] It is tempting to read this, as well as her pairing of what the dance scholar and historian Sally Banes describes as "unrelated, unthematic phrases, some with repetition," with the live spoken words of the performer talking about her own life, as an urban adaptation of Ann's injunctions to her students to anatomize nature and themselves for direction in their dance making.[32]

One person who recognized Ann behind this work was the poet Diane Wakoski. After reading Di Prima's column, Wakoski wrote to the editor:

Being a West coaster (from California) I am aware that Miss Rainer's methods of dance composition, while delightful and engaging in the way that she uses them, are not original with her. The idea she uses for constructing dances through an improvisatory and associative manner, using her own voice as an instrument, is a technique which was developed in the Ann Halprin Dance Company (San Francisco, California) and which was really most extensively used and elaborated on by a dancer named Simone [Forti] Morris.

Now do not get me wrong. I approve of Yvonne Rainer's dancing— very much. Like it. Admire it. But like any good Californian hate to see credit given where it is not due/and of course feel wretched when it is not given to those who deserve it.[33]

Wakoski was closer to the source than her letter admitted. During the early 1960s, when La Monte Young was teaching for Ann, Wakoski was close to him, and she saw Ann's work firsthand.[34]

James Waring also joined in the debate over the provenance of Rainer's improvisatory methods. Without mentioning that he too had studied improvisation with Ann in San Francisco, he set out to correct what he called the mistakes and misconclusions of Wakoski's letter. "The idea of constructing dances, or any other art form, by means of an improvisatory and associative manner is not something begun by either Ann Halprin or Simone Morris," he stated, insisting that, in fact, Ann could only have drawn her inspiration from "[Isadora] Duncan, [Harald] Kreutzberg, [Mary] Wigman and [Ruth] St. Denis." And he concluded, "As for Simone Morris, she is not a dancer at all. She has studied little in the usual dance techniques, nor has she wanted to."[35]

Even in these small inner circles of dance experimentation, the trail of Ann's contribution was difficult to pin down. Certainly Simone Forti (Morris) was an early disciple/colleague and a source of bringing Ann's approach to creating movement to New York. But, as described earlier, unlike many important artists in modern dance, Ann seemed to be someone with whom it was possible to study for a short time and still take away a new perspective on how bodies make choices based on connections between daily routines and spontaneous motions. She was teaching people how to throw away externally based power in performance and replace it with a new belief in the abundant kinetic impulses of monitoring oneself. Remy Charlip, who danced with Merce Cunningham's company in its early years and who knew both Ann's and Cunningham's work well, saw Ann's influence as very significant for the Judson artists: "Although the first work the students of Robert Dunn presented at Judson Church was influenced by John Cage, it seemed to me that Ann's work was just as influential. Yvonne, Simone, and

Trisha [Brown] had studied with Ann, and David Gordon was a student of that wonderful, quirky choreographer James Waring, who had also studied with Ann."[36]

In late November 1962 Ann offered the first of a series of in-progress open rehearsals, at which she both solicited funds from individual donors for *Esposizione* and sampled audience reactions. William Roth donated one thousand dollars plus the use of a large loft in San Francisco for the dancers to rehearse in; he also paid for a professional fundraiser for the group. Ann insisted on purchasing two cargo nets, shipping one to Italy months in advance of the performance as she continued to rehearse on the second one. She also shipped a massive eucalyptus tree trunk to be used with a cargo net in addition to Charles Ross's sculptural set, only realizing later that the freight charges far exceeded the cost of purchasing several cut trees in Italy. With its three thousand seats, Teatro la Fenice would be the biggest public venue, and the first foreign stage, in which she and her company had performed. She insisted on having a three-week rehearsal period in La Fenice prior to the opera's single performance.

Ann's dance making was not about a distinctive movement or choreographic style, but about creating an event out of the dancers' response to a specific environment and real situations. To do this in the intensely formal and highly theatrical space of the 225-year-old La Fenice meant tossing away the conventions of theatrical transformation and illusionism.[37] Instead, Ann saw this remarkable space as a frame for the unremarkable, for the deliberate functionality of realism (one critic labeled it "super naturalism"). Early on she described the performers as "a family" and the stage in La Fenice as "someone's fireplace in a large room." In her mind she was rescaling the theater as a domestic space and neutralizing its grandeur and associations with class, privilege, and high art. Fourteen-year-old Melinda West, one of the dancers, recalled how, during the days of rehearsal prior to opening, the Italian theater crew became increasingly worried about what these wild Americans might do, climbing over the opera house's tiers of gold-leafed boxes and glittering chandeliers, so they started removing the pieces of crystal from the chandeliers lest the dancers smash them.[38]

By 1962 this kind of raw engagement with the environment had become one of Ann's regular methods for making art, an approach from which there was no easy retreat or halfway point. She was treating the theatrical space of the stage much as the artist Robert Rauschenberg had treated painting's "space" several years earlier, when he shocked the visual arts world with *Bed* (1955), mounting a pillow, sheets, and a quilt in a frame and splashing paint on top. Here was a work that, like Ann's *Esposizione,* redefined the space of art making, in this instance by breaking the confinement of painting to a canvas on the wall and extending its surface not only into the surrounding space but also into ordinary life.

The talented but very disparate group of performers Ann had gathered would have looked foolish trying to do conventional modern dance or steps in unison, confined to the traditional space of the proscenium stage. They were primed to answer the questions Ann was asking in *Esposizione,* such as "How does the body react when going downhill? Uphill? What happens when it is carrying many objects and doing this?"[39] Her dancers were charged with navigating, voyaging across and through, the spaces of La Fenice, with its baroque exterior, ornate lobby, and five tiers of boxes. Effectively she was anatomizing one of the most basic tasks of the performing artist—how to get into and out of the theater.

In exploring this task, Ann allowed the choreography of the piece to keep evolving. Berio's letters to her shifted from warm support to growing anxiety as she continued to make changes and "explore the process" into the final weeks before the performance. Finally, he wrote to her in exasperation and desperation: "Please, please, please Ann stay in the scheme we established and work on that: don't change it anymore. There is still everything to do or polish within that scheme. I am working like mad to write music for you according to our decisions: I am not making chewing gum. Ann, dear Ann, you are my love and my despair!"[40]

The La Fenice program opened with John Graham and Rana performing the duet from *Birds of America,* followed by the premiere of Ann's solo *Visage,* in which Ann lay on the stage covered with a painted canvas by Jo Landor and rolled about under the stiff material as Berio's wife, Cathy Berberian, sang his score of vocalized cries and gurgling. As with *Esposizione,* Ann was concerned how to make an intimately scaled work play in a large theater. In a note to Berio she revealed just how mindful she was of manipulating scale so her smallness becomes a conscious theatrical choice. "I think of Beckett's play with the lady buried in the mound, 'Happy Days,' and for three hours all you see is her from her waist up, then in the second act from her head up. . . . I plan to confer with Herb Blau, Actors' Workshop Director, and find out how I stand on this."[41]

During the intermission, in full view of the audience, a crew of twenty workmen in blue overalls unloaded the huge eucalyptus tree from a barge docked at the rear of the theater at the old gondola entrance. As the audience watched, the tree and one end of the cargo net were anchored to the flies over the stage and the other end of the net was stretched out onto the apron of the stage on the other side of the proscenium arch. Intuitively, perhaps, Ann exaggerated the ragged roughness of her presence in the opera house by restricting the choreography to the blunt actions of transporting the detritus of modern life. The first of what Ann called the ninety-minute dance's three "episodes" or "acts" begins with the dancers emerging from the orchestra pit like an enormous pile of "moving, breathing, plowing shapes." As she described it, "We are all six of us pressed together as one and we each carry large sacks, boxes, umbrellas and so much litter that none of it is separable but together it makes a monstrous, ridiculous, sculpture."[42]

The second act starts after a blackout. As the lights come up, several figures are seen moving up the net. The dancers drag large bundles of rags, hampers of tennis balls, rolled-up newspapers, and old tires into the theater, across the audience and stage, and up the massive cargo net. "I am thinking about the vertical feeling in the space and the formality of it that we want to change," Ann explained.[43] "The rhythm is one of going and going and going," she told Berio. "There are times when Rana is carried, or Daria slides and falls, or John swings out into space on a single strand of rope and is revolving upside down between heaven and earth. At the end the figures hang like fruit off a tree, just hang and drop onto the floor beneath the net and the net becomes a house. The figures draw together and regroup again into a mound . . . like a quiet, still, enormous rock. We again are lost as individuals and only become a breathing shape."[44] This "episode" contains images of beauty as well as risk. At one particularly breathtaking moment Daria suddenly drops, as if falling from the top of the net, only to roll swiftly down its length and catch herself before spilling onto the floor. The realism of the performance is heightened by the way the dancers' costumes of thrift store chic rip and shred as they climb, crawl, and lug themselves up, across, and over the cargo net. "We look like we've been through a monumental experience, and we have," Ann noted at one point. Later, in a diaristic entry about the performance, she wrote, "It is fascinating, though not altogether surprising, that many people are sure our opera concerns the struggles of refugees from war-torn Nazi Germany."[45]

The final act is performed in darkness. The figures in the mound move out into a wide horizontal line, and they each hold a flashlight as they walk quietly away, occasionally illuminating another dancer "like passing cars on the highway" as they recede up the aisles and out into the plaza and the night. Rather than defining a style or making a statement *through* dance, Ann was allowing her dance to become its own statement. In the narrative-driven context of an opera house this might be seen as a grave act of kinesthetic disobedience.

The twenty-five-foot-high cargo net did much to dwarf the Italian theater's enormous stage and counter the formality of its space with Ann's countercultural California style. How did Ann arrive at this image? At one of her open rehearsal showings in California, Ann told the audience that the idea came to her while driving along San Francisco's waterfront and seeing "a huge cargo net on a ship and men moving packages up it."[46] The cargo net also suggests the influence of Larry's architectural eye, especially as Ann described it to Berio as "a mountain, a landscape, a house, a desert," whose repeating squares reiterate the structure of the plaza and the rectangular boxes and balconies inside the opera house.[47]

Critical reaction to *Esposizione* was mixed and divided on whether Ann's or Berio's contributions were more distressing. One admirer was the Stockholm critic Jan Bark, who thought Berio's music—performed by a full orchestra and choir, with a special Latin text that Graham spoke while dancing—disappeared next to Ann's dance. "Ann Halprin teaches us something about the paradoxical congruence between the ugly and the beautiful," Bark wrote, assuming Ann exercised a conscious aesthetic control over the impression her work generated. "She does not try to deny the miserable things of our existence, but she gives a higher light to ugly things. . . . The public, after this stormy introduction, felt as if they had been stripped. They had been raped in the nastiest way, and they had let it happen. . . . *Esposizione* could not have got a better reception. Ann had succeeded in activating the public. . . . She had prevented apathy and condescension."[48] Bark's tongue-in-cheek comment about the "better reception" was in keeping with Ann's own belief that anger and outrage are part of a continuum of engaged responses from an audience. Irritation and annoyance as aesthetic responses never bothered Ann; indeed, they fell within her personal objective for the performance, that of activating the viewers' senses rather than forcing on them a ready-made experience and response. This was Ann the artist/educator making the theater a classroom for not just her dancers but audiences as well.

After the performances in Venice, Ann's company traveled to Rome, where they performed *The Five-Legged Stool,* as well as Graham and Rana's duet from *Birds of America* and Ann's solo *Visage,* at the Teatro Eliseo. The response she recalled most often from the Rome performance came not from a critic but an ordinary man in the audience. He became so incensed at the section of the performance where Ann systematically carries one hundred empty wine bottles out onto the stage, one by one, that as she entered with the sixtieth bottle, he charged onto the stage and, facing his fellow audience members, shouted in Italian, "For this, Columbus had to discover America?" before storming out of the theater.[49]

On May 10 and 11, 1963, Ann and her group performed in the Yugoslavian capital of Zagreb, where they had been invited by the Muzicki Biennale Zagreb, a new music festival. There audiences and critics were so perplexed by the two works they presented, *The Five-Legged Stool* and *Visage,* that the festival director, Josip Stojanovic, asked Ann and the dancers to remain a few days for a hastily assembled press conference "because we have never had such a controversy over the merits or demerits of any performing group."[50] This meeting was televised throughout Yugoslavia, with a simultaneous radio broadcast throughout Europe. After considerable debate, the one hundred fifty critics and drama and music teachers at the press conference resolved that either Ann's work was the greatest artistic achievement in years or the performers were groping among art forms they didn't understand. Ann was delighted with the controversy: "Whether we were liked or disliked, booed, cheered, misunderstood or understood, we were never taken lightly. . . . In every case, there was a thirst for information, a thirst for insight into what we were after, that somehow made every reaction an acceptable one."[51]

Vera Maletic, a young Yugoslavian choreographer who was fluent in English, was recruited to help Ann and the company in Zagreb. The experience changed her life. "I was stirred up by *The Five-Legged Stool,"* she said years later. "It was so new. It was like when you meet a new paradigm, it upsets your sense of the norm. The use of the everyday movement wasn't like anything known to our dance theater audience before."[52] Two years later, Maletic, who later became a professor in dance at Ohio State University, came to New York to study at Juilliard, and she made a pilgrimage west to visit Ann at her home in Marin County to thank her.

Back in California, without the glamour of being a foreign artist, Ann found little had changed in regard to her local reception. For several months the San Francisco Opera considered presenting the American premiere of Berio's opera with Ann's choreography as part of their 1964 spring season. But in December 1963, when Ann called James Schwabacher at the opera about a scheduled meeting to listen to Berio's tape, she learned that the opera had decided not to go ahead with the project because of the expense and concerns about the work's marketability and controversy. "How discouraging to come home to this," Ann lamented to her dancers, informing them of the rejection.[53] Ann continued, however, to use the cargo net as a climbing structure on the hillside adjacent to her dance deck, frequently inviting students in workshops to explore it as a vertical stage.

About this time Ann decided that, in addition to her dance deck, she wanted a presence back in the city of San Francisco again. This time she would be in the center of the youthful activism of the 1960s—on the edge of Haight-Ashbury. In the fall of 1963, she accepted an invitation from the musician Ramon Sender, cofounder with Morton Subotnick of the San Francisco Tape Music Center, a loose coalition of Bay Area new music composers, to join this group in the spacious three-story Victorian building Sender had just rented at 321 Divisadero Street in San Francisco. (The public radio station KPFA also shared this space.) Sender had been interested in Ann's work since his arrival in San Francisco in 1960, and two of her dancers, John Graham and Lynne Palmer, often improvised on the concert series titled "Sonics" that Sender, Subotnick, and Pauline Oliveros produced at the San Francisco Conservatory during 1961–62. "I was very enthused about Ann's work," Sender recollected, also noting that the building's main studio could seat seventy-five, which was just right for the center's experimental music concerts as well as Ann's dance events.[54] Later, in 1967, when the Tape Music Center moved to Mills College in Oakland and KPFA consolidated its operation in Berkeley, Ann took over the lease and her company, the San Francisco Dancers' Workshop, stretched out to occupy the entire building. (The name of her company was Ann's translation of the German *Bauhaus* ["workhouse"], because for her it denoted both a communal relationship and an emphasis on process.)

Ann's next local public performance was on May 4, 1964, when she presented *Yellow Cab*, an odd surrealist solo developed out of *Visage* from the European tour the previous fall—set to a signature score of babbling, sighs, coughs, and brief fragments of conventional melody written by Luciano Berio.[55] The piece flummoxed the local critics who covered it. "Miss Halprin was the solo performer, although it was not easy to find her under the mobile mess of paint-stained fabric that first covered her and under the subhuman, drippy dressing of her ogre-like make-up and costume," wrote Alexander Fried in the *San Francisco Examiner*. "When the ogre put on sunglasses, brushed its teeth and lit a cigarette, the expressive value of the performance caved in." Berio's sound collage using the human voice paralleled the physical collages of human actions and relations Ann was exploring. As Fried described it, the score involved "agonizedly frustrated stammerings over guttural syllables that gradually emerged into freer sounds including laughter, sobs and chatter in an unknown language."[56]

This would be the final time Ann performed a Berio score and the only occasion on which she paired his serious modernist music with her zany comedic side. Berio had originally intended Ann to perform this score, which featured his wife in a challenging display of vocalism, in Venice, but he did not like Ann's solo or its premise of offering a movement visualization of the persona of the voice. He suggested she simply roll around under a tarp—an idea that did not appeal to Ann. The piece, which never was performed in Venice, became such a point of contention between Ann and Berio that Morton Subotnick stepped in as an intermediary to negotiate its only performance, at the Tape Music Center. Ann had a tendency to tip unwittingly into parody when she pushed past the limits of invention with certain material, so after the extended collaboration with Berio on *Esposizione, Yellow Cab* may have served simply as a brief, perhaps unconsciously motivated, moment of comic relief. In envisioning the kind of creature who might inhabit Berio's disembodied vocalizations, she and Landor teasingly yoked the most experimental music and dance together in the most traditional model of musical interpretation.

In early 1964 Ann was introduced to Fritz Perls through Paul Baum, who had studied at the Halprin-Lathrop School starting in 1948 and later taught children's classes for Ann in Marin County. Baum, who was now completing his Ph.D. in psychology at the University of California, Berkeley, was meeting informally with a group of therapists in Berkeley who were pioneering an approach to psychology as personal growth for everyday people. There Baum had met Perls during one of the German psychotherapist's visits to the Bay Area. Baum told Ann that Perls was someone she ought to get to know.

Ann was discovering that the more she used structured improvisation to free herself and her students from habits of moving, the more her students would occasionally, and unpredictably, erupt emotionally, crying and becoming distraught in a way that perplexed her and left her feeling helpless.[57] Yet she persisted in trying to make dances whose raison d'être was to follow one's physical impulses, not one's thoughts. When Yvonne Rainer commented on Ann's use of task as simply a way to get at "the movement or the kinesthetic thing that the task brought about," Ann acknowledged this but also explained that she was moving toward selecting tasks so com-

pelling that just executing them would occupy the performer's fu..
cal and emotional attention.[58]

Intuitively, Ann was pursuing a Zen-like approach, sensing that natu.
was the best model for human behavior and that people, if freed from ar-
bitrary external rules and conventions, can more easily achieve a harmonious integration of themselves with the world. Perls's work, which stemmed
from a fascination with Zen, also aimed at directing people to live totally
in the here-and-now.[59] In his later years, Perls jokingly referred to himself
as "Zen Jewish," because of the fusion of his German Jewish cultural heritage with this adopted philosophy of harmony and acceptance.[60]

Ann would discover both a model and a mentor in the sixty-nine-year-
old, short, rotund, bearded, balding, chain-smoking, drug-taking, sex-
chasing psychotherapist. After starting out as a classically trained European
psychoanalyst, Perls had spent the next thirty years radically challenging
the assumptions of Sigmund Freud and psychoanalysis. In 1964 Perls's
approach—focusing attention on the present moment as a means of curing people of their preoccupations and encouraging the free display of emotions and desires—was both radical and supremely simple. Two fundamental tenets of his brand of Gestalt therapy—that it was not therapy and
that it was nonanalytic—secured its appeal to Ann.

Ann never forgot her first meeting with Perls. Baum had arranged for
Ann and three of her dancers, A.A. Leath, John Graham, and Norma Leistiko, to attend a group therapy session Perls was leading at the home of the
Berkeley therapist John Rinne. Ann arrived in a combative mood. She was
still deeply stung by the San Francisco Opera's peremptory rejection of *Esposizione* and already weary at the prospect of trying to fund-raise for another European tour. In her words:

> I remember the day I came. I was really hurt. Because I felt I knew what
> we were doing and I couldn't understand why the critics didn't and why
> we weren't getting more support. I was feeling pretty upset and brazen
> and sort of furious with the world. We were all waiting for Fritz to come
> and I was sitting next to this man who was wearing a black suit, white
> shirt and a tie and black shiny shoes and black silk stockings. And he was
> sitting sort of upright in his chair.
>
> Something about the look of that man sitting there like that, wearing
> those kind of clothes, just freaked me. All my resentments about not
> being understood just triggered me off. So I stood up in front of this man
> (John Enright, whom I have since learned to love and appreciate), and I
> started to rip my clothes off. I was just staring him in the eyes as I pulled

this off and that off until I stood in front of him stark naked. I stood there very brazenly and then I sat down and crossed my legs. Humph![61]

Ann hadn't noticed that Perls had arrived at the start of her spontaneous undressing, and he watched her improvisation unfold from the doorway as he stood smoking a cigarette. As Ann flung off her final piece of clothing, Enright began to sob, tears pouring down his face. This made Ann even angrier. She had expected him to at least shout at her to stop but never to react with such passivity. Then Perls entered the room, gave the group a slow, relaxed look of appraisal, and finally, looking over at Ann, he said, "*Nu?* [Yiddish for "Well?"] So why have you got your legs crossed?"

Ann felt belittled and at the same time charged with admiration. In a single sentence Perls had identified her aesthetic goal, her personal inhibitions, and the inconsistency in her performance. If this was an impromptu dance of full disclosure, then why was she hiding her crotch? "All I could think was oh, my God, he's just totally busted me! It was terrific!" Ann later said. "I was inspired, he was just so right on!" That evening began a six-year friendship between the therapist and the dancer, one in which the congruence between the task of psychotherapy and the capacity of art to remake the maker became manifest. Perls had understood immediately what Ann had been trying to do, and he told her bluntly how she had failed. It was the cruelest, and most useful, piece of criticism she could have received at that moment.

"Anybody who can see the connection between movement and another dimension of what's really going on, who you really are—that's part of art," she later commented. "I wasn't thinking of that as therapy. I was thinking of it as theater. You've got to be totally open and honest and true to be a performer."[62] Perls believed that one had to cultivate a similar pleasure and openness to the immediate present to be awake as a person. His "Gestalt prayer," which in turn became the mantra of the human potential movement of the 1960s and 1970s, was a do-your-own-thing endorsement set to loosely metered rhyme:

I do my thing, and you do your thing.
I am not in this world to live up to your expectations.
And you are not in this world to live up to mine.
You are you, and I am I,
And if by chance we find each other, it's beautiful.
If not, it can't be helped.[63]

Several years before Susan Sontag wrote her famous essay "Against Interpretation," Perls was championing Gestalt therapy as a noninterpretive approach to experience. Ann too was looking to define a space where individuals could experiment with how to perform their immediate present and be in the here-and-now, but in a theatrical rather than a therapeutic context. Ann's stage and Perls's therapy office were joined by their interests in not only cultivating an awareness of the immediate present but also in consistently denying a mind/body split.

Ann's sharp criticism of previous modern dance centered on her sense that it operated by opposing creativity and human nature. It presumed that rules were necessary to produce art and the present always needed to be masked. As she explained, "Martha Graham was always interpreting. The modern dancers were not really dealing with real issues. They were always on the outside, portraying, not being. Well, this was different. This was being. And I didn't have any models."[64]

Long before he met Ann, as an adolescent in Berlin, Perls had been fascinated by the theater, serving as an extra at the Royal Theater in a crowd scene or chorus. While still an adolescent, Perls began studying with the director Max Reinhardt, who was known as brilliant but a harsh disciplinarian. Reinhardt demanded a new realism, free of the heavy melodrama then in vogue. In particular, Reinhardt wanted his actors to project their emotions on a more realistic scale using more convincing physical demonstrations and vocal inflections or tones to accompany reactions like pain or laughter. In Reinhardt's theater elaborate sets were discarded in favor of more realistic settings that allowed the drama to focus on the tension between the characters and the audience. Perls's biographer Martin Shepard attributes the therapist's awareness of the importance of body language and his ability to read psychological truths on bodies to this early apprenticeship with Reinhardt.[65] In New York in the late 1950s Perls had been introduced to Julian Beck and Judith Malina, the founders and directors of the Living Theater, who advocated blunt honesty between actors and the audience. Perls soon began attending rehearsals and performances and socializing with the actors. "He had something in mind that was half-way between the kind of performances we were doing and therapeutic sessions," Beck recalled.[66]

Within a short time Ann and her dancers were working with Perls whenever he was in town. He led encounter sessions in which they probed their performing relationships. Ann recalled how in one early session Perls "busted" everyone—moving through the group and identifying each person's emotional weakness through a physical trait. He told Ann that she had a dishonestly stiff upper lip and Leath that he had furtive eyes, reading these as physical signs of the emotional landscape underneath. Again, Ann found herself feeling both resentful of and impressed by Perls's comments, which followed his Gestalt mandate of "paying attention to the obvious and to the utmost surface."[67]

Ann also had individual sessions with Perls in the six years before his death in March 1970. During these sessions Ann explored a dream she had had in one of the early group sessions with her dancers:

> We were, again, in a circle. A.A. was there, John was there, Norma was there. And he [Perls] looked at me and said, "Now, let's work on something." And I was very frustrated and I said, "God, Fritz, I don't know, I don't have anything." And he said, "What are you doing?" I said, "Oh, I'm pulling my hair." "Where are you pulling your hair from?" "Top of my head." And he said, "Get down on the floor with me." And he put his legs down in a kneeling position and he said, "Start pushing your head through my legs." And I had to start pushing my head through his legs, and as I struggled through, he said, "Now what's happening?" And I said, "Nothing. Everything is black. I'm in a void." And he said, "Good! Now stay there." And he said, "Just wait, just stay there and wait. Some picture will come."[68]

The picture did come, and it was of Ann's childhood home when she was five years old. For the next four hours of a marathon session, Perls coached Ann through entering the house and beginning a tour of the rooms starting with the library, where she took the Bible off the shelf and began reading Genesis. The next time they met, Ann went into the second room, and each subsequent time she explored a different room. "It was just so creative!" Ann later said. "And he'd have me move the dream. So I wasn't just talking about it. I would move it."

> The last dream I had, I said, "Oh Fritz, all the rooms are just . . . all the walls in the room are just melting away, and it's just turning into one big room!" And he said, "Where in your body are those walls?" And I said, "Right here." So he had me just make a sound, just like an outburst of sound, to break through the diaphragm. And as the walls opened up . . . I just made this . . . it wasn't like I was shouting, it was just making a bursting sound of an opening. And then I said, "Oh, there's a door leading out into the woods. I have to go out into the natural world now. And

you know what, Fritz? I h⌁
you now."

alone. So I have to say goodbye to

Perls's relationship to Ann in these guided ⌁
director coaching a performer on where to ta⌁ ⌁ons is like that of a stage
she is developing—but the "character" in develop⌁cular character he or
self and the script is written on her bodily postures, her ⌁ere is Ann's "true"
self ⌁ ⌁ her presence.

In 1968 Perls permitted a camera crew to film several o⌁ ⌁estalt therapy sessions at the Esalen Institute, a retreat near Big Sur or⌁ ⌁ California coast, where he lived and conducted workshops from 1964 until ⌁ death
in 1970.[69] These remarkable unedited documents provide one of th⌁ ⌁ew
visual records of what actually went on in his Gestalt therapy encounters.
They offer proof of just how intensely theatrical and shaped with an eye
toward an audience these sessions were. In one segment titled "Birth of the
Composer," Perls sits in a chair at the front of a room, barefoot and smoking cigarettes, as he and the nineteen other workshop participants silently
watch a woman rotate through three roles in one of her dreams: she play-
acts talking on the phone to her complaining mother, being a waitress who
is conducting a dismal-sounding orchestra, and then snickering as a critical member of the audience. In a voiceover Perls explains that he is letting
her play every part in her dream because he considers each part a facet of
a split-up personality, the disintegrated self she is seeking to integrate. The
metaphor of her playlet is obvious—the orchestra that she is struggling to
make harmonious and melodic, the conductor she wants to be effective,
and the audience whom she wants to appreciate all these efforts are each a
part of the self she needs to accept and unite to become "authentic" in the
Gestalt sense. "A person who has this ability to become something else is a
really good actor," Perls concludes, using the word *actor* with approval.[70]

What is most significant about the sequence is just how public and performed this identity testing is. The whole sequence is entertaining—like
amateur stand-up comedy, with moments of tearful despair. The others in
the room laugh heartily and often at the woman's statements. As Perls di-
rects the woman, telling her when to switch chairs (signifying a different
character) or when to extend or repeat a hypothetical interaction, his focus
seems curiously trained on affecting the woman's performance. At times he
prompts her to repeat sections that ring false until some kind of emotional
bedrock is reached. Implicitly it seems that if it's fresh and deeply personal,
it's also affecting theater.

Ann saw working with Per[
the Jungian analyst Joseph
stand visualization from
me [Perls] was what S[
parison underlines [
physical actions [
them. Paul Bar[
access to an[
called art[
Trish [
1964[
th[

[...] for her dance, but she turned to [...] "for dream analysis and to understand [...] point of view."[71] In Ann's words: "For [...] probably was for a lot of actors." Her comparison [...] identity as a director, as the person who shapes [...] primed emotions can surge up like a spring to fill them. [...] Ann as "trying to visit that place therapy usually has [...] it back as art."[72] If so, then Perls was visiting the place [...] pulling it back as therapy.

[...]own, who had returned to guest-teach at Mills College for the 1964 [...] academic year while her husband pursued a master's degree in dance therapy in the Bay Area, attended some of Ann's weekend classes with her husband during this period. She was surprised to see how different the work had become since her summer workshop with Ann four years earlier. "She had changed completely," Brown recollected. "She'd become involved in catharsis, expression. There were these early dance therapy people there and she was completely involved with that. It was not my idea of a dance class."[73]

Brown happened to attend one of Ann's weekend events that was led by Eugene Sagan, a psychotherapist trained at the University of Chicago who had been working with Perls since 1960 and who had taken Ann's dance workshops. A.A. Leath believed Sagan, a diagnosed manic-depressive, sought out dance because he thought it might help his illness.[74] Brown and others were distressed with Sagan's aggressive encounter style as he pushed a distraught Holocaust survivor to painful limits in playing out her experience. "He kept going, pressing, going, pressing. I just recall feeling too young and inadequate to witness or participate in this. It was big stuff," Brown commented.[75]

Soon Sagan, a specialist in cognitive behavior techniques, became a regular at the rehearsals and summer workshops of the San Francisco Dancers' Workshop, and he began subtly, and then overtly, exerting control over the individual participants and their work. "He was crazy," Ann later admitted. "Things got violent and physically dangerous."[76] She recalled one time when Sagan pushed Graham so hard to work at the edge of physical rage that he swung at Ann's face, nearly breaking her nose. Sagan, who was institutionalized several times for his own mental illness and was banned from Perls's psychotherapy circles at Esalen, eventually jumped off the Golden Gate Bridge to his death in 1974. Several people who were present at Sagan-led events at the San Francisco Dancers' Workshop described him as physically and emotionally abusive, a Svengali-like character who induced

people to ...
he bid. Carla ...
when she attende... ...tionally and then manipulated them to do as
being relieved that sh... ...ecent graduate of Sarah Lawrence College
with Sagan one afternoon. ... 1965 summer workshops, remembered
of the personal growth movem... ...oup Ann sent to work individually
times did more harm than good a... dark underside of the early years
proaches to individual therapy. ...nia, when practitioners some-
...mented with aggressive ap-
Ann's workshops, however, were not solely...
mer of 1965, Meredith Monk, a 1964 graduate h... ...n therapy. In the sum-
a week on a Greyhound bus from New York to San... Lawrence, spent
study with Ann. Monk, who had already premiered *Brea*...co in order to
environmental work in an urban setting, had heard about An...), her own
firsthand from two other dancers affiliated with Sarah Lawrence: Carla...lank
and Jani Novak, a dance major there who was dancing with Ann. Like Rainer
and Brown before her, Monk found the descriptions of Ann's improvisational work, outdoors in the California sunshine, an alluring antidote to
the more formal, indoor East Coast dance training. "I felt I needed to get
away in nature. All that working outside and not being in a studio was wonderful. It made me think a lot about artistic identity," Monk recalled, although she acknowledged that an implicit, and at times elitist, California
body-beautiful ethos underlay much of the nude work on the deck. "I loved
some of the warm-ups and the physical exercises were very beautiful," Monk
added, explaining that she felt intuitively that Ann's work related to her
own explorations with transformational and mythic images in city environments. "She was working from the bone and there was a lot of release,
alignment, and slowing down. She was doing something very ahead of its
time."[78] In Monk's assessment: "She really looked at the set of habits of
dance and tried to open them up to what it was to be a human being who
moved. The beauty of the way she worked was that it was encouragement
to find your own way."[79] Monk recalled Ann asking the workshop students
to play with tearing rolls of butcher paper (from a section of a new piece
Ann was working on, *Parades and Changes*) and to work on climbing the
cargo net from *Esposizione*. "I thought her scoring was brilliant, how she took
one concept and stuck with it," Monk reflected. "There was a plasticity in
the way she worked with tactile objects like paper and the net. Big forms
with movement and texture." To the twenty-two-year-old Monk, Ann
seemed to be able to do it all—exist as a serious artist, a wife, and a mother:
"There were very few women doing that then."[80]

Soon after moving into the two lar... second floor of 321 Divisadero Street, Ann began work ─────ajor European commission,
a full-evening work for the St...emporary Music Festival. This
dance, scheduled to premie...work 5, 6, and 7, 1965, would become
the signature statement o...rformance choreography and her last
work in this mode bef...ned fully toward the emotional territory
of Gestalt therapy i...*ent 6. Parades and Changes* is a valedictory to
her initial movem...ed approach to dance and the point of departure
for her emergi...est in challenging the dancers' and the audience's passive spectat...as a means to instigate change.

Early...process of creating *Parades and Changes,* Ann explained to
the...ce at an informal showing how the entire ninety minutes were
base...on three simple attitudes: (1) the dance form evolves from the very
processes—the tasks set by Ann—that form it; (2) the objects in the performance are as real as the actions; and (3) time is compressed, so instead
of depth one gets an accelerated view of everyday life.[81] There is a Perls-
meets-Ann quality to each premise. Instead of a task serving as a means of
discovering kinesthetic logic, it now serves as a physical Rorschach for the
body, so physical confrontation with external and environmental limits
prompts the dance. At the same time Ann, like Perls, exerts a subtle control over everyone's "free" actions. Her identity is etched in quiet clarity
over all their physical choices and responses.

The dance, as its title implies, is a parade of changes in which the task
of theater becomes the creation, rather than the *depiction,* of a life situation. This attitude would stay with Ann her entire career, and only very
rarely, even in workshop situations, would she offer analytic or interpretive
criticism of a dance. She was abandoning a purely formalist approach to
task in favor of a more Gestalt relationship—investing each action and response to an object on stage with an intense sense of the present. According to Ann, Perls used to tell the dancers, "I don't want you to rehearse. I
don't want you to think about this. Whatever we do, we do what's present
right now. No rehearsing, no planning, no trying to figure out, no analysis. Just deal and express what's there right now."[82]

By the spring of 1965 the Dancers' Workshop was ready to give two pre-
view showings of *Parades and Changes,* in Fresno and in San Francisco. The
centerpiece, which would become the most legendary part of *Parades and
Changes,* was a seven-minute section in which the full cast serenely undressed, dressed, and undressed while coolly locking eyes with someone in

the audience. Although this section derived directly from that spontaneous striptease she had done the first day of Perls's workshop, Ann now revisited removing one's clothes as a statement of art rather than of anger. It had become a post-Gestalt strip, where taking off meant inviting in, uncovering meant peeling back to the skin of the emotions. Reflecting on her initial experience with Perls, Ann explained:

> Yes, that was the beginning of *Parades and Changes*. That was the beginning of dressing and undressing, because what I learned from that was that my attitude was just totally off. There is a way of removing your clothes and appearing totally vulnerable—open and vulnerable—without this attitude. I needed to learn how to be an extension of nature, and not impose this self-righteous attitude. I had been so self-righteous, standing in front of this man and judging him and saying, "You think you're free? Look at Me!" So that's what inspired me to make *Parades and Changes*.[83]

The original cast of *Parades and Changes* consisted of only three adults (Ann, A.A. Leath, and John Graham), as well as six adolescents (Ann's two daughters, seventeen-year-old Daria and fourteen-year-old Rana; college-age Jani Novak; eighteen-year-old Kim Hahn; and two veterans from Ann's children's dance co-op, fourteen-year-old Paul Goldsmith and sixteen-year-old Larri Goldsmith, who came along mostly to help unload props but also performed some).[84] Morton Subotnick created the music score, Patric Hickey the lighting, Jo Landor the costumes and staging, and sculptor Charles Ross fashioned the scenic environment out of backstage objects, including a tall scaffold used to change lights.

Everyone who was in the September 1965 premiere of *Parades and Changes* remembers a different dance and no one can say with certainty, least of all Ann, what opening night or the subsequent two evenings actually looked like. The reasons for this are many—not the least of which is structural. Ann was ritualizing spontaneity, and this often made for a stronger memory of motivations than stage pictures. "There was no chance in *Parades and Changes*," Subotnick recalled. "Everything was done by choice, but there was a freedom in choice. We did everything independently first, working on different attitudes of space. Then we'd look at ways of putting each section together. It was a real collaboration."[85]

Each element of the dance—lighting, sound score, props, and choreography—was divided into six discrete units that could be combined in various orders or relationships. The choreographic sections were (1) stomping (which the dancers did wearing oversized unisex clothes and heavy men's shoes); (2) unrolling sheets of plastic down the aisles, exploring them with flashlights, and then dragging them up onstage to drape over a scaffold and play as an instrument; (3) talking in the audience; (4) dressing up from rows of props laid out for each dancer in a line on the floor; (5) a slow ritual of undressing and dressing repeated three times, each with a different focus, until the dancers took off their clothes a fourth time, when, instead of getting dressed again, they walked over to begin (6) the paper-tearing section, where the functional action of tearing created the dancers' movements.

For the three Stockholm performances, Ann stood backstage twenty minutes before each performance and shuffled index cards containing the names of the dance's sections. At the same time the lighting designer and the musician (in this case, Folke Rabe, a Swedish musician who had been studying with Subotnick and took his place for the Stockholm performances) shuffled their own six cards. These cards were then posted. The correspondences between the music and the dance, as well as the lighting, were thus changed every evening so that one night the undressing and dressing section might be paired with the part of Subotnick's score that called for a radio to be turned on to whatever was playing and the next night it was totally different. Subotnick had initiated this concept of "scoring" all facets of the event, borrowing a method of musical scoring he had pioneered a few years earlier at the Tape Music Center.

What one watched was not so much the individual performer but the process of watching theater being made in response to a changing stage environment. The actual look of *Parades and Changes* from moment to moment during those September evenings is all but impossible to reconstruct. However, it's real raison d'être was to set up certain structures to allow for spontaneously vital, what Ann called "unarmored," moments. Each of the six sections was designed as a set of instructions containing parameters rather than the specifics of stage behavior. "We weren't using our emotions," Graham recalled. "Instead, we were looking at them."[86]

In the undressing section the dancers were instructed to undress in a smooth, slow, uninflected manner, stacking their clothes neatly in front of them as they disrobed. They stood in a line facing the audience, maintaining eye contact with a member of the audience as they began to remove their clothes. "We wanted there to be an extraordinarily smooth rhythm throughout the line," Landor recalled, "so that your eye was constantly going to objects, seeing the bodies as interesting shapes rather than only men and women."[87] Hahn, however, noted that on opening night at least one man persisted in seeing it the other way—he sat squarely in the front row flourishing a pair of binoculars.[88] Still, Ann believed that in this sequence the nude body was not an object of display or desire, but rather that the task of unedited undressing substituted for Perls's "hot seat," as a psychological peeling away. "It was a ceremony of trust," Ann explained. "It was as if each one of us were saying, 'Here I am, look at me and see who I am. Trust me.'"[89] Earlier, during her 1965 summer workshop, Ann had experimented with various styles and paths of undressing. Carla Blank remembered an evening when Ann divided the dancers into two groups and asked one to travel around the circumference of the room on a small ledge three or four feet off the ground. The other group, which Blank performed with, walked parallel lines on an imaginary grid on the floor of the studio, with instructions to change lanes only at the beginning or end of each imaginary parallel line. As they traveled they could pick up or discard objects or clothing that was within their reach. In the process, Blank said, they went through moments of nudity. "It was the first time I was performing nude in public, and I suddenly realized I was inches away from Robert Morris, who had come to watch the dance."[90]

Throughout *Parades and Changes* the dancers' actions in each section were the consequences of making onstage choices within the limits defined by offstage parameters. It was like a democracy with a good government or post-Gestalt therapy living. Ann also gave some thought to how to script the audience into the dance. In the opening sequence, the dancers entered through the aisles of the theater carrying huge bouquets of lighted flashlights through the darkened house, and in the final moments of the dance the dancers returned with the flashlights, passing them to people on the aisles who in turn passed them to others, until the entire theater was filled with hundreds of traveling points of light. The edge of stridency and indifference to the audience that seemed to anger the Italian spectators of *The Five-Legged Stool* is softened in *Parades and Changes,* where there is a more elaborated relationship between audience, performer, and the essential material of dance—movement.

In *Parades and Changes* Ann and her collaborators tried to strike a balance between radicalism and popular entertainment using movement to construct social and emotional associations. Perls's Gestalt processes colored much of this work. At the same time *Parades and Changes* was a dance about formally framing task performance and the functional exchanges of people and objects on stage as the actual material of performance. The dance assembled several of Ann's key devices for "getting real" and making art out of this stripped-down approach to theater. "Being an artist for me is allowing yourself to be open to unexpected outcomes, about removing the armor from your movement and yourself," Ann explained. "And I find that very connected to life. Otherwise it's as if you are trying to control what's uncontrollable. Process is the center of dance, but not the whole performance."[91]

Before opening night, Ann and her collaborators had engaged in intense debates as they struggled with how to produce aesthetically an alternative social space. How could they best use the unique features of this Swedish theater as a design element in the performance? And how might they manage transitions between the six randomly ordered sections of the dance? Their discussions often turned into heated shouting matches as Ann, Ross, Landor, Hickey, Rabe, and occasionally a dancer or two addressed the form of the work and how it might best identify and display the plurality of experience that was at its root. Hahn, who left to start college at Oberlin immediately after the three Stockholm performances, remembers these discussions becoming so acrimonious at times that Graham or Larry would suddenly announce he was taking the "kids" out for lunch or a walk, in order to get them away. When he wasn't helping cool things off, Larry spent days walking around neighboring Swedish towns, strongly influenced by the economy of the Scandinavian transportation systems and the designs of the city parks (he also took a trip to see the Tivoli Gardens in Copenhagen at this time).[92]

Well before arriving in Sweden, Ann had peppered Rabe with questions about technical and rehearsal needs, and he relayed her concerns to the theater staff. One major worry she voiced involved the Swedish laws regarding performing nude. Rabe responded casually, at the end of a long letter, "They told me that there are no laws in Sweden forbidding it. I told Bengt about your idea about naked bodies in the [transparent sheets of] plastic and he thought it would be great. He said that it is also perfectly all right with uncovered nudes on the stage. It is not necessary with any 'hiding angles' and it makes no difference with sexes." He concluded with magic words for Ann: "You can do absolutely anything you like."[93]

When *Parades and Changes* opened in Stockholm, it was part of a festival that, under the direction of Carl Albert Anderson, was aggressively embracing the new. This eighteen-day blitz of music, dance, theater, opera, vocal recitals, and film showings throughout the capital city also featured performances of Peter Weiss's *Marat/Sade*, Dario Fo's *Isabella*, and Yvonne Rainer and Robert Morris's *Tape Music*, as well as more traditional fare. Rainer, who had not seen Ann's work for five years, was surprised at how theatrical it had become and how divergent from her own use of Ann's task material. "I realized," Rainer later commented, "that the way she worked in these exploratory modes was always a preparation for finding material that could be transformed into a more theatrical kind of genre, and I guess what was revelatory to me was the task itself."[94]

The Swedes seemed primed to observe Ann with open minds. Rabe had been interviewed about Ann in Stockholm's major daily newspaper, and he perceptively described Ann's aesthetic goals in the festival program notes: "In the compositions of the Dancers' Workshop there is no pathetic protest nor deep-philosophical symbolism (except what everybody himself desires to explore or invent). Instead it is a question of vegetative ('growing') human constructivism; an attempt to present direct sensations and feelings and the possibilities of expression of everyday objects and situations."[95] In his contribution to the program notes for the festival, Bengt Hager, the curator of the Stockholm Dance Museum, equated Ann's work with Happenings, but with a difference. Noting that she "aims high in her art," he quoted another Swedish critic, Jan Bark, who said of Ann, "She desires not only to go beyond the limits of her spectators' reactions, but she seeks a new level of experience, a new instrument with which to observe everyday life."[96] In Sweden the implication was that life was the subject rather than a veiled critique of society. "The fact that Ann and her dancers use improvisation doesn't mean they can do whatever they like," the Swedish critic Ryman wrote. "You have the same freedom when you cross the street. It can take 10 or 20 steps to cross it, but you can't just throw yourself up on a car that is passing."[97]

A television crew filmed segments of *Parades and Changes* for broadcast in Sweden, bringing images of Ann's work to a larger public (this is also the only film document of the original dance). Ann herself was more pleased when her work affected the common viewer than the sophisticated theatergoer. One of her favorite fan letters came from Sven Kyberg, a Swedish farmer who saw the television broadcast produced by Arne Arnbom. Arnbom had insisted that the nude scene could not be cut from the program and that if anything had to be changed for television, the whole show would be canceled. "The dance impressed me very deeply," Kyberg wrote the television station. "At first I was very skeptical, because a lot of modern art seems to me to be much too egocentric and without humanity or humility. But in the taking off of clothes and the rolling out of paper . . . I saw the naked human animal slowly and unafraid and shy and clean, just like one of my own newborn cattle or lambs, approaching, going near and near, something unknown . . . I felt cleansed and washed and shaken."[98]

It was an effect that would resonate for Swedish dance and theater for a significant time. Hager called it "one of the most remarkable events in contemporary American art."[99] Madeline Kats, the dance critic of the largest Scandinavian daily, *Expressen,* claimed, "Ann Halprin's performance is 90 concentrated minutes of pure theater."[100] Even the leading dissenting voice, that of Bengt Jahnsson, the drama critic of the liberal *Dagens Nyheter,* saw clearly what Ann was doing; his objection was primarily that she should be doing something else. "I found the undressing scenes to be indifferent and impotent, lacking all eroticism," he wrote, describing how they belonged inside the frame of task, not eroticism.[101]

———

Along with *Parades and Changes* Ann prepared another evening-long work, *Apartment 6,* for her European tour, as well as a revival of *The Five-Legged Stool. Apartment 6* opened on March 19, 1965, at the Playhouse in San Francisco. This tight little domestic drama was performed by Ann, Graham, and Leath while sculptor Charles Ross simultaneously constructed a sculpture on stage and Patric Hickey worked the lights. Created in a single month of intense daily rehearsals in the Playhouse, *Apartment 6* was a physical drama about the Gestalt-driven social interactions between people, using their bodies as their most articulate medium. One critic called it "absolute reality for two hours. *Heightened* reality, actually."[102]

The participants in *Apartment 6* disrupted and bent expectations about choreographic and dramatic structure in an effort to open up new possibilities of theatrical realism and meaning. Largely improvised and played on a set that looked like a real apartment, the choreographic intention in *Apartment 6* was multilayered, presenting a live theater of the moment where Ann, Graham, and Leath endeavored to "perform" their offstage identities onstage. Their actions were spontaneous, within the set Jo Landor and they had devised, and their instructions to themselves were to explore rather than suppress their true feelings. "The subject of *Apartment 6* is ourselves," Ann explained in an advance article for the Sunday *San Francisco Chronicle*. "All the while the play will be real. That is, there will be no play."[103] The prose style may have sounded like Samuel Beckett, but the dramatic effect was pure Gestalt. Instead of paring back emotions and interactions to their bare essence, Ann's theater of the moment was earthy, chaotic, unpredictable, and lush with sentiments expressed with simple immediacy. It was a high-wire act with a net. Ideas, situations, and movement interactions splashed across the stage with no more time for development or shaping than the episode actually took in real life. It was reality drama, long before the genre was coined by television, at a time when Americans were still cautious and edgy about any kind of unmediated intimate disclosure.

What made this dance, according to Ann, was the fullness of the bodily responses the three performers brought to their exchanges. Ann recalled a vivid moment in a rehearsal, just before opening, "when Graham was seated at the kitchen table, peeling a potato. Leath was reading a newspaper. Graham asked Leath, tensely, 'Please get me the salt.'" Leath's response was ferocious. He dashed across the room, searching everywhere and flinging things into the air and onto the floor as he rummaged like an animal for the salt. He even knocked Graham out of his chair, although Graham calmly continued peeling his potato. Then, as if it had only been an instant, Leath was back in his chair, reading the paper and commenting evenly, "I don't know where it is."[104]

Apartment 6 was as close as Ann would come to staging a pure Gestalt session onstage. "We wanted to simply have two hours on stage . . . in which you as a performer and you as a person were completely the same thing," Ann later said.[105] Perls actually watched rehearsals and offered suggestions, but Ann and her collaborators shaped the starting premises and theatrical parameters of the piece. They began by identifying and then exaggerating just slightly each of their natural proclivities in interpersonal situations. Graham had as his prime action the manipulation of household objects—lamps, a radio, chairs, a typewriter, and food. He recalled of one performance, "I had A.A. lying out on the table. I don't know how I got him there, but there he was. I put an orange on his chest and I cut through the orange [here he grimaced in anger] as though I was cutting through A.A."[106] Leath concentrated on externalizing his feelings, and Ann, apparently with an ironic nod, focused on compulsive tasks. As if on a continual Gestalt "hot seat," they spent the evening on the wobbly edge between real and "restored" behavior, the term Richard Schechner has coined to describe a piece of behavior that is independent of the causal system that created it (in this case, the causal system has been displaced).[107]

The work was performed three times a week for a month, and each evening the performers invested their interactions with the gravity and levity of a real exchange. "We'll listen to the radio, read the newspaper, eat, talk. We may shout or argue, cajole or tease or just sit quietly," Ann wrote in a program note. "The reality of being. The reality of feeling. The reality of imagining. To play the reality of whatever is happening. Because we are people, something will develop between us. Because we are artists by training and instinct, something will get built."[108] Leath later indicated that this reality-based approach originated in a 1953 summer workshop in improvisation taught by Franziska Boas at the Halprin-Lathrop studio. "That workshop," he claimed, "was what led the then non-existent Dancers' Workshop onto the road of developing the skill not only of structured improvs, but also free improvs. From these improvs came out dance concerts and theater events both in a theater building and outside in the public world."[109]

Most nights the three dancers tangled in a domestic tragicomedy. They listened to whatever was playing on the radio, they talked, and they argued. The gender roles were deeply traditional, more so even than Ann lived in her home life. As the two men relaxed, Ann worked in a fully outfitted kitchen, complete with a *real* window that opened onto the street. She actually cooked onstage, frenziedly struggling to make the perfect pancake for her demanding partner—the lanky Graham, who was known offstage for his love of food. If she failed, she hastily flung her ruined pancakes out the window, literally onto the street. If the pancake looked promising, she ran it over to Graham on an outstretched spatula while it was still sizzling hot. If the pancake met his approval, Ann would "balance [it] on the spatula and do a dance with John clapping, singing, and getting the audience enthusiastic so the whole theater would be joining in the responsive clapping and stomping as the pancake would be marched over to the table. . . . A few times John responded with such overwhelming love and affection that we both cried. By now, the audience was hard put to tell what was real and what was being played. We surely had never set any demarcations in these terms."[110] Each night Graham responded differently, sometimes displaying irritation. On one occasion, as the *Chronicle*'s critic noted with amusement, Graham carefully fixed Ann's perfect pancake to a dartboard on the wall.[111]

While all this was going on, Ross, in an action that echoed Robert Rauschenberg's building of an assemblage during the premiere of Merce Cunningham's *Story* in 1963, steadily constructed a sculpture from newspaper and tissue paper. Working persistently and quietly in a deep alcove at the back of the stage, he built a different huge animal each night, considering the work complete just at the moment the dancers stopped. Everything about this piece was done in real time. Even its title had a real-time function—it came from the made-up room number they gave whenever they ordered food delivered during a rehearsal. (The room they were using in the theater had no number, so one day someone taped a handwritten sign with the number *6* to the door and henceforth they asked for orders to be delivered to "Apartment 6.")

For Ann, *Apartment 6* existed precipitously between dance and psychodrama. "Relationship exploration" was what Ann called it. Although in real life she rarely drank, she had a gin and tonic placed on her little table onstage at every performance, so she could take the edge off her feelings of vulnerability.[112] In keeping with the process of realism of *Apartment 6,* she didn't drink before going onstage; instead, her onstage persona sipped the drink, and the audience watched her become a little tipsy.

Ann admittedly found it exhausting to invent herself afresh for each performance, and she counted on Landor to bring in new props and set pieces as a way of revivifying the environment to which she and the other performers were responding. But there were also constants. The set always included a real bed, where Ann, Graham, and Leath appeared together in the last of the three acts. Ann usually lay in bed caressing Graham as she stared past him across the room at Leath and said repeatedly, "I love you, I love you."[113] As Ann explained in her program notes, the subject of *Apartment 6* "is ourselves." She underlined its realness—"except that we are in a theatre and are limited by space and time and the need to organize irrationality."[114] The play then encompassed different levels of reality—doing, feeling, and imagining.

Apartment 6, with its demanding nightly improvisations focused on the dancers' relationships, took a toll on the group. The European tour that fall added the tensions of traveling as a group, plus there was always the issue of tight finances. Soon after the Dancers' Workshop returned to San Francisco from Europe in early October, Graham and Leath announced to Ann that they wanted to do more psychodramatic dance with the therapist Eugene Sagan as their director. While Ann enjoyed performing in this exposed style for the San Francisco engagement, as well as on the European tour, where *Apartment 6* alternated with *Parades and Changes,* she knew that she did not want to pursue this direction exclusively. Ann spoke with Perls regarding her worries over Sagan's aggressive use of therapy in workshops with dancers, and Perls advised her to tell Sagan to keep away. It was too late to salvage her company, however. Graham, Leath, and Novak all left Ann to work with Sagan and his wife Juanita at the Institute for Creative and Artistic Development they opened in nearby El Cerrito. Ann was devastated at the departure of Graham and Leath, and it would be years before they spoke again. Concerned that Sagan might use Leath's and Graham's keys to 321 Divisadero to gain access to her studios, she had the locks changed.

Ann spent the next year rebuilding her company, drawing on a new group of dancers a generation younger than she and Graham and Leath. In early spring 1967 she received a call from the director of the theater at Hunter College, part of the City University of New York, asking if she could bring *Parades and Changes* for a weekend of performances there, after the modern dancer Sybil Shearer canceled an engagement in the college's performing arts series. Ann accepted and quickly began reshaping *Parades and Changes* to reflect a new cast. She visited New York several weeks before the opening and had dinner with Jack Anderson, whom she had known when he was dance critic for the *Oakland Tribune,* and dance writer George Dorris. Ann, in a jovial mood, imitated her father's Yiddish pronouncements of horror at viewing the kind of contemporary work she was now doing. She imagined him walking out muttering, during the middle of the performance: "I pay for my daughter to have dancing lessons and everything, and what does she do? Shit!"[115] Anderson and Dorris responded by offering to host a party for Ann to celebrate the New York debut of her company.

The *Parades and Changes* that debuted on the Hunter College stage on April 21, 1967, was very different from the Stockholm performance. Only the undressing and dressing and paper-tearing sections remained similar. Ann was very conscious that she was now more than twice the age of her dancers, so she developed new material to reflect what she called a "multigenerational" company. "The dance became very symbolic of what I was appreciating of these young hippies," she said of the organizing theme of her changes. This time *Parades and Changes* began with the undressing task, performed by a group Ann called her "flower children"—Daria, Karen Auberg, Kathy Peterson, Nancy Peterson, Michael Katz, Morris Kelley, Joseph Schlicter, and the young dancer Peter Weiss—most of whom she had recruited from San Francisco State University, where she had presented at in-progress showing of the work in 1965.[116]

Instead of undressing with the dancers, Ann created a separate section for herself in which, dressed in a clown costume and accompanied by a man playing a harmonica, she performed a mock soft-shoe in front of a live goat and then carried the animal up the ladder of a scaffold to a platform at the top. "I wanted to capture their spirit of being so contrary to everything," she explained.[117] It was there, as the scaffold was slowly wheeled across the stage, that Ann performed her undressing as a solo, bathing herself from a bowl of water in an image she intended to stand for a return to the natural and a shedding of the material encumbrances of life. The goat watched.

"The work was beautiful," Dorris reflected decades later. "It had a purity that still stands out in the memory. The kids were so beautiful that watching them undress, dress, undress and just stand there had no prurience but only an awed astonishment. The same, of course, for Ann at the end."[118] Anderson also recalled this "nude scene" as stunning: "It's sculptural, and it has great textures of movement and it is implicitly tactile, great appeal to the senses."[119]

Long before opening night a buzz began in the New York dance circles about the nudity in *Parades and Changes*. It was rumored that the New York Police Department was ready to arrest Ann and stop the performance for lewdness if the dancers took their clothes off. "A warrant was indeed issued then for Ann's arrest," Dorris later indicated. "If I remember the story correctly, knowing that nudity would be involved, the two main daily critics, Clive Barnes on *The [New York] Times* and Walter Terry on *The Herald-Tribune*, went into collusion, ensuring that their reviews would not appear until the following Monday, when the company would be on its way."[120] Reportedly, during the undressing section, one audience member was overheard saying, "They're not going to . . . oh—they are. My God, they did it!" At the conclusion of the performance the audience gave the dancers a standing ovation, presumably as much for the boldness of the gesture as its aesthetic merits.

Overall, reactions to the performance were strong and divided. Guests jammed into the promised post-production party hosted by Dorris and Anderson.[121] But Clive Barnes, who lived in the same building and had been invited, did not appear (earlier he had explained that he would go to the party if he liked the performance). His review, headlined "Dance: The Ultimate in Bare Stages," was not exactly favorable. He zeroed in on the nudity, the only sections of the dance he detailed. "They undress. I mean they remove every last stitch of clothing, and boys and girls together are as rip-roaring naked as berries," he wrote. But then his dismissive sarcasm gave way to surprise as he described the paper-tearing sequence that followed: "Fantastic shapes evolve, paper sculptures mingling fascinatingly with nude bodies. The result is not only beautiful but somehow liberating as well. It is all so unexpected and uncoy: and the sight of these very attractive kids all aggressively bare and blissfully unconcerned about it, churning their way through great mounds of brown paper was enormously effective."[122]

At Hunter College Norman Singer, the director of the concert bureau, received a phone call from the college president warning him to be prepared for a communication from the chair of the Board of Higher Education over the uproar about *Parades and Changes*. Ann, on the other hand, received a telegram from the New York gallery director Lee Nordness thanking her for "one of the most exciting nights in the history of New York dance theater" and inviting her and Jo Landor to Sunday brunch with the ballet choreographer Antony Tudor, who had also seen the performance and was eager to meet Ann.[123] (Ann, preoccupied with leaving New York as quickly as possible lest she be arrested, had to decline.) The theater directors Richard Schechner and Joseph Chaikin, who both saw *Parades and Changes* at Hunter College, were significantly affected by the work. Schechner, who would found the Performance Group the following year, would invite Ann to work with his theater group.

Theater director Jacques Levy was also in the audience for Ann's performance, as was Remy Charlip. Several months after the concert, Levy contacted Charlip and asked him if he would audition dancers and then choreograph some nude dances for an off-Broadway production of ten brief plays the British theater critic Kenneth Tynan was stringing together and calling *Oh! Calcutta!* Charlip decided that it was not enough to ask prospective actors simply to drop their clothes; instead, he wanted them to pretend they were preparing to go into a warm pond while composing a letter in their minds telling someone they had just had a book manuscript accepted. Charlip, who clearly had understood the nature of the nudity in Ann's dance, said this audition was one of the most moving theatrical experiences he ever had—"it was very real."[124] Levy, however, had a different kind of nudity in mind and Charlip turned down the project. Instead, it was the choreography of Margo Sappington, who also performed in the original cast, that was on display when the show opened in New York on June 17, 1969. *Oh! Calcutta!* began with the cast peeling off their terrycloth bathrobes to reveal their nudity with a show-business salesmanship that was the antithesis of Ann's staging of undressing.

Much of what Ann originally said she intended the undressing in *Parades and Changes* to stand for endured over the years. At a 1997 performance of this section that Ann staged when she received the Samuel H. Scripps American Dance Festival Award in Durham, North Carolina, the chaste simplicity of this gesture of disclosure, which she has resolutely refused to call a striptease, remained poetic and affecting. In 2004 the undressing and paper-tearing sections would be the hit of her debut in France at the Centre Pompidou.

Already in 1967, however, Ann was shifting into what would be the new dynamic of her interaction with her dancers, who would now always be considerably younger than she. She was beginning to function as what the critic Marcia Siegel labeled "a permissive mama" with a bunch of "big, boisterous kids."[125] For her daughter Daria, however, there was an awkward disingenuousness in this dynamic, especially in relation to how Ann parsed the life/art divide in her work and in her family life. "She made art a safe place to experiment and life very dangerous," Daria noted with painful irony. Daria recalled that while she was preparing to perform in the Stockholm premiere of *Parades and Changes,* she disclosed to her mother that she and her childhood sweetheart, the son of the Halprins' closest family friends, were lovers and Ann "became hysterical." In Daria's recollection: "It was one of the most disturbing explosions between us. Here my mother had me performing and workshopping and dancing naked at a time when I was just moving into adolescence. That seems to me a delicate time to use a teenager in that way. There were times when it was very provocative and on-the-edge and uncomfortable."[126]

Incidents like this reveal how for Ann blurring the divide between the real and the mediated onstage was very different from eliminating all boundaries between living one's life and making art. Yet it was this illusion that gave her work in the 1960s both its immediacy and its allure. While Daria intimates a certain hypocrisy in this stance, in fact the work's containment as art and its enactment in the context of a stage—real or metaphoric—were crucial to putting this idea forward as a cultural statement. Remy Charlip and other dance and performance artists who came after her would speak of the prosaic, functional actions of daily life, *in* daily life, as art—but Ann's demarcation of these activities between life and art was a critical intermediary step.

———————

Back in San Francisco, Ann tried taking her dance into larger popular venues. Early in October 1967 she accepted an invitation from the Straight Theater, a rock ballroom on Haight Street, just around the corner from her Divisadero Street studio. The Straight Theater asked Ann to help bridge from the passive audiences to the rock music and light shows by introducing a community rock dance. Ann and members of her Dancers' Workshop were supposed to help spontaneously transform each Friday and Saturday night concert into "a festive gathering, a joyous celebration," according to a press release that carefully describes her role in the process: "The focus of this mutual creation will be the members of the audience. Ann Halprin will act as a catalyst, not as an authoritarian or exhibitionistic teacher. She will help all those present create together from their immediate personal needs and desires a sensuous, heightened awareness."[127] Ann intended to do with the rock music crowd what she did with dancers in her studio a few blocks away. But the planned series fizzled after the first weekend. Despite the disclaimers in the press release that Ann's guidance would be offered rather than imposed, there was still an implication that Ann, who was billed on a poster for the first night as a "kinetic catalyst," would structure the event's unfolding in keeping with her own aesthetic. Apparently, what looked radical and spontaneous for dance felt like imposed structure to concert-goers who just wanted to groove on their own.

Soon afterward, at the invitation of Bill Graham, Ann performed with her dancers at his Fillmore Auditorium, where she directed the loose gyrations of the crowd as people moved to the beat of the Charlatans, the Congress of Wonders, Janis Joplin, and the Grateful Dead. Using her dancers as catalysts, Ann staged an entrance over the top balcony so that her dancers literally descended on the dance floor. Illuminated by a pulsating light show, they balanced on one another's shoulders and offered more varied examples of spontaneous physical partnering to the delighted crowd. "I liked working with these large groups of people," Ann later said. "I'd have the men hold women on their shoulders and we'd work toward configurations that formed a sense of community because everyone seemed so isolated and into themselves."[128] Ironically, Ann seemed not to have noticed that these rock palaces were in many respects consciously shaped as sites for solipsistic retreat into oneself. With their dark interiors, cloudscape light shows, and music so highly amplified that all one could do was listen, drop acid, and trip, the Straight Theater and Fillmore were sites for an introverted contemplation antithetical to the engaged group experiences Ann delivered.

Parades and Changes continued to exercise a strong attraction for the performing and visual arts world. In 1970 Peter Selz, director of the new $4.8 million art museum at the University of California, Berkeley, asked Ann to perform an excerpt of *Parades and Changes* as part of the grand opening of the modernist concrete museum. Selz however, was anxious about the nudity and tried to convince Ann to put the dancers in leotards. She refused. He then suggested dimming the lights. Ann replied that, like the leotards, it would only make the dance look like something that should be hidden. Finally, Ann told Selz if he got into any trouble for the performance, he could simply say Ann had ignored his orders not to perform nude. That resolved the discussion. Ann gathered a new multiracial group of young dancers and taught them just the two nude sections of the dance, the undressing/dressing and paper-tearing parts, which they performed, along with a new, brief, improvisatory piece, to great acclaim at the museum's opening.

A filmed fragment of the event shows the dancers in ordinary street clothes of the era—one woman wears a miniskirt and boots while the men wear tight bell-bottoms and leather vests. Because the audience is several floors above, the dancers lock eyes with each other as they undress. The miniskirted woman stretches out on the ground to tug off her panties, making the undressing horizontal since the audience unfolds above her so vertically. The ritual of undressing and dressing here suggests itself as a postmodern citation to the opening of George Balanchine's *Serenade* (1934), where the body is seen transforming from a prosaic working body into a performing body and back again.

The pairing of performance and social analysis in *Parades and Changes* echoed that in the work of another Bay Area Jewish artist-activist at this time, the comic Lenny Bruce. Much as Ann used frank nudity, Bruce built his comic monologues at the Hungry i nightclub in San Francisco and the Café au Go Go in New York's Greenwich Village by speaking the unspeakable on the forbidden subject of sex and bodily pleasures.[129] Credited with turning stand-up comedy into social commentary, he championed an edgy humor filled with scatological words and ethnic slurs. Bruce, like Ann, worked through exploratory improvisation, feeling his way into an audience's confidence as he presented himself as a subversively hip satirist. In equal measure brilliant and shocking, Bruce offered humorously autobiographical rhythmic riffs on the boundaries between his onstage and offstage identities.

At the 1964 New York trial that resulted in his obscenity conviction, the license inspector Herbert G. Ruhe, who had been sent by the Manhattan district attorney to covertly see Bruce's act, recounted in a monotone what Bruce had said. Bruce, who was in the courtroom, was heard saying in a stage whisper: "This guy's bombing and I'm going to jail for it."[130] Bruce's career was marked by drug arrests and charges of obscene performances in Chicago and Los Angeles in addition to San Francisco and New York. He was arrested several times for lewdness and obscenity because of his open discussion of sex and the body, racism, and religion in his comedy routines. To a far greater degree than Ann, Bruce found himself a cultural lightning rod for his performative anecdotes that blended the sublime and the earthy and in so doing questioned the norms of behavior. Both artists used and enjoyed San Francisco's increasing visibility as a center for transgressive social expression.

After he was arrested in mid-performance for obscenity on October 4, 1961, at the Jazz Workshop in San Francisco, Bruce began basing his stand-up routines on verbatim readings from the transcripts in his legal battle (he was ultimately acquitted of this charge in March 1962).[131] In August 1965 (one year before his death from a morphine overdose), and at the same time Ann was finalizing *Parades and Changes* for its Stockholm premiere, Bruce engaged a film crew to document one of his performances at a San Francisco nightclub as evidence for his continuing legal appeals of his obscenity convictions. The result is both a re-creation and an actual presentation of the very text, sounds, and actions for which he had been convicted of obscenity and against which he was now defending himself to the audience. In the film, as Bruce reads from his trial transcripts, he defines a liminal space for uttering the unspeakable in the guise of "performing" it. In the final minutes of the film he opens a door at the rear of the stage and calls out to passersby on the street, asking them about his innocence or guilt.

Three years earlier Ann had concluded *The Five-Legged Stool*, in a theater a couple of miles away, by similarly opening the backstage door and letting the chill night air off San Francisco Bay blow through the audience.[132] In opening the stage door, Ann and Bruce both mark the instant in American culture when the permeability of the stage wall and the door between art and the world around were linked in a struggle over standards of behavior and cultural expression.

Three thousand miles away, on the East Coast, the photographer Diane Arbus was working toward the same ends through the medium of photography. In her 1962 application to the John Simon Guggenheim Foundation for a fellowship, Arbus described her goal as a photographer as being a documentarian of "ceremonies of the present." She wrote, "What is ceremonious, and curious and commonplace will be legendary," explaining that she was endeavoring "further elucidation and description of these rites," the rites of daily suburban life. Arbus received her fellowship and in the process, with her stark photographs of the freakish in the everyday, joined this same valorization of the ordinary that Bruce was delimiting in comedy and Halprin in dance. Halprin, Arbus, and Bruce never met, but from their separate corners and disparate media, they each worked to illuminate, define, and frame for our contemplation parts of early 1960s American culture that many would have preferred remain invisible.

SEVEN

From Spectator to Participant
1967–1968

I think the *Ten Myths* were my first really intentional pieces about audiences. What happened is that people had begun responding so violently to my work, throwing things at us and getting up and stomping out. This was so surprising to us, particularly me, because it wasn't my intention. It wasn't like the Living Theater, where they wanted to provoke an audience. I didn't want to. So that's when I became aware of the power an audience had.

ANN HALPRIN

ON APRIL 5, 1967, the Gray Line Bus Company initiated its two-hour "Hippie Hop" tour of the Haight-Ashbury district in San Francisco. Five days a week, the large commercial buses lumbered past the Dancers' Workshop studio on Divisadero Street, taking gawking tourists with cameras on what was touted in the brochure as "the only foreign tour within the continental limits of the United States." Passengers were given a "Glossary of Hippie Terms," and on the first day a TV crew joined the riders.[1]

The sarcastic framing of daily life in this San Francisco neighborhood as a "foreign" practice not only imposed the role of tourist-spectators of another lifestyle on the bus riders, but it also reconstituted the daily actions of the denizens of Haight-Ashbury as ritualistic, quasi-religious performances. The intimation was that the youths outside the bus windows were practitioners of behaviors and beliefs so far apart from the acceptable boundaries of American culture, so novel, that it was worth journeying to stare at them as one might view the Golden Gate Bridge or Alcatraz Island. This irony was not lost on the denizens of the Haight, who on one occasion commandeered the bus and announced to all the passengers, "You're all free!" Quickly, however, the mood began to change. By mid-April 1967, some Haight-Ashbury residents walked alongside the bus holding mirrors to reflect back to the tourists their own faces.[2] The spectator-performer divide no longer seems clear; as this action suggests, the act of spectating could be a performance in itself, and *of* oneself.

There are strong parallels between this performance device and the theory of reader-response that emerged in the literary world in the late 1960s. Reader-response theory, like the politics of this period, reflected an attempt to shift power from a central authority to a more egalitarian model. As in Ann's participatory theater, this approach to making meaning from words frames the reader herself as playing the crucial role in making sense of a text.[3] This approach echoed the new validity being given to personal and intuitive knowledge, self-knowledge, of precisely the kind that Fritz Perls's Gestalt therapy was trying to build.

The opening speech of the Hippie Hop tour guide parodied some of the more prevalent shortcut methods to getting this knowledge of self by referring sarcastically to drugs, meditation, and making music. At the same time it reinforced the expectation of glimpsing aberrant practices by detailing behaviors that included illegal drug use, social protest, discussions about the need for social change, and improvisatory expression in the performing arts. The following is an excerpt from the opening remarks the Hippie Hop tour guide would recite as his bus began its trip into "The Haight," the place where the concept of a trip was redefined into travel inward, the nonphysical tourism of one's emotional and psychological landscape.

> We are now entering the largest Hippie colony in the world and the very heart and fountainhead of the Hippie subculture. We are passing through the "Bearded Curtain" and will journey down Haight Street, the very nerve center of the city within a city. . . . Marijuana, of course, is a household staple here, enjoyed by the natives to stimulate their senses. . . . Among the favorite pastimes of the Hippies, besides taking drugs, and parading and demonstrating: seminars and group discussions about what's wrong with the status quo; malingering; plus the ever-present preoccupation with the soul, reality, and self-expression, such as strumming guitars, piping flutes, and banging bongos.[4]

By reading this description as a catalogue of *un*acceptable behaviors, a sharp view of what was acceptable emerges—that is, *not* questioning society, *not* thinking and talking about social change in small groups, and *not* daring to create spontaneous music on instruments. This cold war conservatism was what both Ann and the hippies were reacting against. From their perspective, it was the mainstream world that needed a fresh vision and a relaxing of limits to become *more* democratically American. The guide's description of "passing through the 'Bearded Curtain'" suggests entering a performance space, as *beaded* curtains were frequently used as fanciful room dividers in the counterculture; it is also a punning reference to the Beatniks, who were known for their beards. Although the term *hippie*, first used by journalist Michael Fallon in a September 6, 1965, story in the *San Francisco Examiner*, had come into more frequent use by the establishment press by 1967, it was still easy to confuse these two groups of social outcasts.[5] The Beats and the hippies were, of course, linked in more nuanced ways than beards and outlaw behaviors. But both populations became the focus of spectatorship in San Francisco. The hippies, however, became increasingly hostile about the Gray Line tours, and on May 15, little more than a month after they began, the tours were discontinued.

While the tourists were eyeing the "tripping" hippies as an ethnographic spectacle, Ann was working toward framing a number of mundane practices—taking a bath, cleaning up the litter on downtown streets, eating lunch—as art spectacles. Much as Marcel Duchamp had transformed everyday objects into art, Ann created "found" dances, "ready-made" collections of movements that served as a prefabricated rather than customized choreography. Ann was, as the art historian Wanda Corn has noted of Duchamp, "questioning every inherited boundary of art making, especially those hierarchical categories that declared what was and what was not art—or what was and was not beautiful."[6]

Ann was "finding" not just the finished product, but also the means for generating it. By 1967 she had absorbed the teachings of Fritz Perls, turning his Gestalt psychology methods of being on the "hot seat" into her own rubric for generating movement situations in workshop settings. She had also reached a complacency about the use of nudity in her work, so that having students or performers take off their clothes was becoming just another aesthetic and psychological training tactic for her. The Hunter College scandal sparked by the undressing and dressing section of *Parades and Changes* had helped bring her to this point of equanimity. Now, in 1967, Ann turned her self-actualizing gaze on the spectator. She was about to prompt and prod the audience in a way that was more confrontational than the eye contact in *Parades and Changes*. In the process she would become a student herself and a mythmaker. She was fluidly changing roles, like Carolee Schneemann and other contemporary women artists who were endeavoring to write their own story through the medium of the body. In her work she would invite a deliberate confusion between what the performance scholar-theorist Peggy Phelan has noted in "ordeal art" as the divide between presence and representation.[7]

For Ann this shift in her work had been years in the making, and it came more from a ritualistic than an experimental theater focus:

> I've always longed for that sense of tribal belonging and that sense of a complete life where all aspects of one's life can come together and can be expressed tribally or community-wise. This is something that was very important to me and it's been translated into the relationship of audience to performer. I have resisted (this separation) for many years and one of the first breakthroughs I made, I made it spatially. I broke through the proscenium arch and then I began to deal with audience participation and then to create dances for audiences.[8]

A key transitional piece in Ann's new conception of the spectator was *The Bath*, a group event in which Ann cast the audience as a collective voyeur. Voyeurism can be seen as a stage of partial embodiment for the spectator. The spectator of sensual or sexual material is at once lost in the traditional role of yearning to be the fully embodied performer, yet also more sharply conscious of herself as someone who is looking on at the scene before her. This dual attentiveness means that she only partially loses herself and at the same time partially becomes acutely aware of herself watching.

The Bath selects a set of physical gestures from the same room in which Duchamp found his urinal, the bathroom, and puts them on public display. As with Duchamp's *Fountain* (1917), there is an inescapable eroticism to transporting such a private practice into a public space. The fact that Ann picked sensual content for *The Bath* wasn't coincidental; by its nature the material compelled the audience into the role of voyeur, a halfway point on the road to the full audience participation she would initiate within a few months.

Most immediately, *The Bath* focused on ritualizing the commonplace, on generating a dance through task performance. Early in the summer of 1966 Ann was invited to create a work for a performance the following February at the Wadsworth Atheneum in Hartford, Connecticut. "I was shown the theater space at the museum," she wrote at the time. "But the fountain [in the courtyard, with its ornate, figurative marble statue] interested me much more. It is an environment we can extend, enliven and make relevant by performing a simple task, bathing."[9] For the next several months, Ann and her dancers met weekly, exploring bathing in a different way each time, depending on their mood and inclination that day.

> I start by bringing bowls of water and having us wash our hands. You wouldn't believe all the different ways we washed ourselves. . . . The effect is terrorizing. Each performer pours into the simple act his whole essence. There it comes out in the way he bathes, and he is super-conscious of it because it is a performance. He says, "I didn't know that about myself." The performance of the simple action, the natural action, objectifies what is really going on inside the performer's self. It is the same with the spectator. The spectator's interpretation of what is there says more about himself than it does about the performance.[10]

For Ann this kind of improvisation using basic tasks was becoming a means of "clarifying relationships through a focus on ordinary actions." She noted excitedly, "It says how we feel about each other."[11]

To prepare for the Hartford performance, Ann staged a public showing of the piece at her San Francisco studio after just ten weeks of development, after which the dancers continued to revise their bathing sequences. When Ann and her dancers finally arrived in Hartford a day before their performance, they spent the afternoon "becoming attuned with the environment." In this new setting, her dancers spontaneously drew on their repertoires of bath dances, reimagining the water collecting below the fountain sculpture as a river or stream. Daria began by lying—at the fountain's edge, in the water, at the feet of one of the statues' figures—and later she bathed the statue. Morris Kelley "put his head in a bowl of water and kept it there until he began to drown"; Nancy Peterson balanced a tiny bowl of water on her head, ritualistically dipping her fingers into it to wash patches of her skin.[12]

What could be more commonplace than the daily use of water to wash and bathe, and what could be a more natural costume for doing this than nudity? This final level of realism, however, so upset the Hartford sponsors that Ann consented to flesh-colored leotards for the women and briefs for the men. According to Ann, she decided to forgo nudity in the Hartford performance of *The Bath* because she knew that she and her dancers would be arrested, and she didn't want to risk this immediately before their next stop, New York's Hunter College, where they were giving the first U.S. performance of *Parades and Changes,* with its undressing and dressing sequence. Moreover, the person at the Atheneum who was responsible for their visit, Vladimir Hubernack, told Ann he would lose his job if the dancers took off their clothes.[13]

Ann decided instead to amplify the act of *dressing*. As if enacting the inverse of a tape loop of a never-ending striptease, Ann created a processional preamble to *The Bath*. First she arranged a path of clothes and various objects winding through several galleries of the Atheneum. The performers were then instructed to each take three different items and put these on their bodies, walk for one minute, then take the things off and repeat this process with the new materials ahead on the pathway. "So you were supposed to see this progression of images," Ann said, noting that "it was open if the audience wanted to join in."

Indeed, that is what happened during a parade of costumed performers that went on in one of the museum's interior medieval galleries while *The Bath* was being performed in the courtyard. The audience in this gallery quickly dispensed with spectatorship and joined in, donning costumes and walking in the parade. One audience member, Judson Church dancer Deborah Hay, also tried to join in the bathing sequence. Ann, who didn't know who Hay was at the time, remembered vividly how Hay climbed to the top of the fountain's statue. But climbing on the antique statue was something Ann had been warned not to do, so Ann regretfully sent someone to ask Hay to leave. It wasn't until she arrived in New York the following week that Ann learned who Hay was.[14]

Ann's growing interest in the audience's involvement in the performance comes across in this comment about *The Bath:* "The people were amazed to see a space they took for granted transformed and used with such simplicity. . . . In this way the spectator is changed to see an accustomed surrounding stretched, extended, and bent by an ordinary activity."[15] It is an insight that is as much architectural as choreographic. And, indeed, there was an architectural connection. Just before rehearsals for *The Bath* began, Ann finished teaching the first "Experiments in Environment" summer workshop with Larry. The 1966 workshop had emphasized the "continuing search for new approaches to creativity," asking its thirty participants to solve a series of tasklike exercises about relationships between people and their environment.[16] This focus on locales and the people who inhabit them had an immediate impact on how Ann related to the fountain environment of the Atheneum. Much as one of Larry's landscape architect associates might study how people navigate an urban plaza, sitting here to eat lunch and there to sunbathe, so too Ann seemed to regard the site for this next commissioned dance as a tacit collaborator and the source of the themes and gestures for her dance.

Larry himself had begun to regard an environment as a series of constraints that prompted "Happening-like" events. In a series of notes and sketches that he made while planning for the summer workshop, Larry mused on the relationship between theater and the environment. He drew nine movement studies, progressing from a dancer lying relaxed on the floor, through her moving her body along the floor and noticing the space between the body and the floor, until she is interacting with the other dancers, the walls, the space, and the rhythm. "An environment is in fact simply a theater for action and interaction to occur," Larry wrote. "One can [also] take the theater as a mirror image of environment design in that the classical theater has a programmatic structure of events."[17]

During the 1966 summer workshop Larry and Ann, along with the architect Charles Moore, who was designing the Sea Ranch development with Larry at the time, asked participants to build a city on the beach out of driftwood, an exercise that would become a staple of Ann's Sea Ranch workshops for decades. Like an architectural Rorschach, the design solutions that emerged gave, as Larry noted, "enormous insight into each person's interior desires and personality, his interests and attitudes." He concluded, "The restrictions create the form."[18]

Ann's work with her dancers on the dance deck, however, steadily moved away from framing habituated behavior in the manner that architectural design tended to, in favor of instigating actions that were novel because of the unexpectedness of displaying them in the public sphere. This put her at odds not just with Larry's interest in letting restrictions create the form, but more importantly with the customary progression of most theatrical rehearsals. Instead of cementing movement sequences and phrases in a dancer's head, Ann encouraged her dancers to move past the easiest and more predictable responses. She moved from closure to increasing openness, whereas most dance performances of the time went in the opposite direction. Her thinking was that if she could get her performers to take a bath by acting out clichés in rehearsal, they would move on to even fresher material for the actual performance.

The Bath seemed to play provocatively with the nature of voyeurism and spectatorship by deliberately blurring the fine line between the two. Moreover, bathing in itself is usually a very private act, and to offer it up publicly to a paying audience makes the private act not only public, but also commodifies it. In so doing Ann introduced commodification as a framing device for turning quotidian acts into theater. The person who pays and the one who receives payment parallel the spectator/ performer divide, establishing who will watch and who is embodied.

As a dance event *The Bath* might have been forgotten quickly, except that on September 14, 1967, the photographer Irving Penn came to the Bay Area to do a photo essay on hippies for a special issue of *Look,* the first one devoted entirely to the arts. Penn rented a photographer's studio in Sausalito and ordered a cement wall, which he textured himself, to be built as background. One by one emblematic figures of West Coast counterculture— including the Grateful Dead, Big Brother and the Holding Company, and the Hell's Angels motorcycle gang—appeared before Penn's camera. Finally, it was time for the San Francisco Dancers' Workshop to be photographed. Ann recalled that as the dancers entered the room, the Hell's Angels, whom Penn had just finished photographing, all walked to the windows, raised them, and urinated out onto the street below as their way of acknowledging Ann and her dancers.[19]

"The situation was extremely tense to begin with," Ann recalled. "Irving Penn did not know us and we did not like the idea that was assigned— to paint each other in couples."[20] Ann persuaded Penn to let the dancers begin with a warm-up period, in which they would divide into couples and give each other a bath. So the dancers undressed, performing *The Bath* nude for Penn. Then, ingeniously, Penn suggested first the water bowls, then the towels, then the pitcher of water—all of the props—be removed. "We were left with the absolute purity of a boy and girl relating to each other in the most magical, mysterious way, and yet it seemed real. What [the dancers] were left with was creating the essence of the bath, but it had nothing to do with actual bathing anymore."[21] In Ann's words, it had turned into a strange combination of "exquisite poetry and sculpture and yet dance and drama too."[22] Looking at the contact sheets from that photo shoot eighteen years later, Penn spoke of the chaste naturalness of the dancers:

What I remember is the purity of relationship of these young people and an innocence so different from today's. As I look at these pictures, how the dancers touch each other, how they embrace, because the pictures are primarily of embraces, a boy and a girl, boy and girl, boy and girl, beautiful and touching. Here they are without clothes, there's love, the gestures are tenderly erotic but certainly not pornographic. And there's a serenity that as a photographer I'm not used to. I didn't know Ann Halprin at all, but I know from these pictures, I tell you, I like her very much.[23]

As the photographer, Penn created the images as much as his subjects did: he effectively edited the dance as one would a film, telling the dancers when to start moving, when to shift into another relationship as they improvised, and when to pause while he made an exposure, freezing the moment that he wanted. Penn responded to the capacity of Ann's work to transform the presenters, to make their investment in the direct task of what they were doing transcend exterior concerns about vanity, appearances, and consciously "performing." Ironically, the *Look* editors could only appreciate such a cultural move in consciously theatrical terms, not as a matter of practical, innocent nudity. Tellingly for the time, they were also the only photographs from the session that *Look* refused to publish because of the untheatrical frankness of the dancers' nudity. (Nearly thirty-five years later, in the spring of 2002, Penn opened an exhibit at New York's Metropolitan Museum of Art of a series of awesomely frank nude photographs of worn and overweight women that he had photographed in the late 1940s and only now was displaying for the first time. These nudes, beautiful in their candor and unromanticized documentation of the female body, are the precursors to the kind of looking Penn immortalized in his photographs of *The Bath* that afternoon.)

In the lead editorial for this issue of *Look*, "Culture: The New Joy," William K. Zinsser pays lip service to the cultural winds of change, lauding precisely what the magazine did not publish: "I detect an underground rumble which says that we must redefine 'culture' to make it far more embracing, less an exclusive club for the fortunate few, closer to life as it is lived every day. It means staying loose. It means that joy and celebration are proper lubricants of art and of the national spirit."[24] In censuring Penn's photographs, the magazine's editorial staff probably felt uneasy because these images are confessional studies of what the art historian John Berger would call *naked* people, distinctive individuals being themselves rather than artful nudes, posing without clothes.[25] In fact, the *Look* issue contained several images of nudes—Marilyn Monroe partially wrapped in satin bedsheets, a woman on the beach with her nude backside turned to the camera—but none showed full frontal nudity, nor did they offer the candid, unassuming exposure of one's private self that *The Bath* plays with as its central theme. The dance is also, implicitly, about task performance, the execution of prosaic actions offered as something one might regard with the same aesthetic attentiveness one does classical dance movements. Ironically, the *Look* staff found it acceptable to print consciously seductive, partially clothed bodies as agreeable but banned the more chaste yet complete nudes in Penn's photographs.

Of all the photographs he took for that *Look* shoot, Penn believes the ones of Ann's dancers may "live" the longest.[26] As if to confirm this assessment, in a 1999 exhibition of Penn's work at the Maison Européenne de la Photographie in Paris, his photographs of *The Bath* were presented as emblematic of the mid-1960s moment in America. In the catalogue introduction Edmonde Charles-Roux describes these photographs as "anthropological," noting that they do not represent the exact choreography, but rather a "free interpretation of the movements of the dancers, mise-en-scène, uniquely captured in the medium of photography." Speaking generally about Penn's work, Charles-Roux observes that "never before had people seen such a desire for truth or such a spare, uncluttered style." This is particularly true of his *Bath* photographs, where truthfulness and spareness are also qualities of the improvised performance. *The Bath* photos reflect a photographer and a choreographer who met on the same common aesthetic ground, territory expressive of a nascent moment in American culture, one filled with "the melancholy grace of young, nude couples—their gentle gestures—their timid looks— at the same time capturing the pleasure of bathing together."[27]

———————

On Thursday evening, October 19, 1967, Ann followed *The Bath* with the opening of *Ten Myths,* an event that took spectatorship and embodiment in dance to a further frontier. This event, which took place on ten Thursday evenings, scattered over several months, at the Divisadero Street studio, was initially announced to the public by a postcard, mailed in late September and written by John Rockwell, then a young arts critic as well as a graduate student in German studies at the University of California, Berkeley. Basing his text on discussions with Ann about her goals for this daring series of audience participation events, Rockwell wrote:

> "Myths" are experimental. The performers, members of the Dancers' Workshop Company and participants in Ann Halprin's Advanced Dance Seminar, are unrehearsed. What unfolds is a spontaneous exploration of theater ideas.
> "Myths" are meant to evoke our long buried and half forgotten selves. Each evening will explore a different relationship between the audience and performers, and between our awareness, our bodies, and our environments. The audience should not be bound by accustomed passivity, by static self images, or by restricted clothing. "Myths" are your myths. They are an experiment in mutual creation.[28]

Provocative in tone and word choice, the postcard seemed to script in advance an enticing parameter of loosened behaviors. "Experimental," "unrehearsed," and "spontaneous"—these words, appearing in the first three sentences, carry a sexual innuendo that is amplified by subsequent promises to "evoke long buried and half forgotten selves" and "explore a different relationship between . . . our bodies." Participants seem invited to approach a precipice of behavioral norms and then, with the final sentences, to jump off : "The audience should not be bound by accustomed passivity, by static self images or by restricted clothing." It is interesting that the *inverses* of Rockwell's words are all markers of a performing body—activity, dynamic self images, and unrestrictive clothing. The implication is that a truer, sexual, physical, *performative* self lies beneath each person's socially constrained one. There is also the suggestion that the dancing body gives out special, often sexual, truths.

Participation in *Myths* is proffered as a way of entering a newly permissive space, where the realization of the freshly liberated self will be possible. The emphasis is more on shedding behavioral encumbrances than on what specifically participants are supposed to create. Only the last sentence addresses this, and it is tempered by a reminder about group behavior: these events "are an experiment in mutual creation." Rockwell's words underline Ann's way of working. The very choice of the word *creation*—rather than *performance, work, piece,* or *event* (the more customary nouns used to denote a dance product)—signaled this was a process rather than a set piece of choreography. Ann has never been particularly interested in creating individual choreographers or even in being a traditional I-made-every-movement-up-by-myself director; rather, her most comfortable role, and one that is clearly apparent in *Myths,* is as a director/facilitator. She likes to set up the conditions for a dance or performance to happen (the set, environment, context, and larger metaphoric themes) and then have people collectively begin to find their own movement answers to the theatrical questions these elements pose.

There are clear liabilities to working this way. It is one of the ironies of improvisational dance that, while it may be intensely real in the moment it is invented and performed, it usually fades quickly from memory—both the performers' and the audience's. Without the traditional memory anchors of repetition, choreography, rehearsals, staged ensemble passages, plot, and a set musical accompaniment, even trained dancers have difficulty re-creating what a particular evening's improvisation looks like. This problem of recall is, of course, intensified for novice performers. So there is hardly any documentation of what a full evening of one of the *Myths* looked like.

Participants among the San Francisco Dancers' Workshop members, who acted as initiators in the first two sessions and knowing participants in the subsequent ones, recall mostly isolated moments and images, as well as "things that went wrong." Although Ann has described her ambitions for each evening and the environments her collaborators, lighting and environment designer Patric Hickey, drummer Casey Sonnabend, and sculptor Seymour Locks, created,[29] the actual bodily movements and incidental choreographic patterns have vanished, except in some still photographs of the evenings. For the historian this is both frustrating and instructive—the focus each night was really on the process of personal transformation from a heightened sense of oneself as an individual to a more muted sense of oneself as part of a collective social body. This kind of process often leads to personal epiphanies and insights, things that are felt more than performed. It is about *experience,* not the communication of a set text or the production of an artifact of performance. "The whole reason for doing these *Myths,*" Ann explained, "[was] that I wanted to find out what people . . . what ordinary people would do, and how they would react. So I was doing it to study audiences. This was like research for me."[30]

The first myth took as its focus "Creation." For this opening event Hickey filled the studio with sixty opened folding chairs, which he hung from the walls at eight- and twelve-foot elevations. On the ground he placed a series of platforms, eight, four, and two feet high, with lights illuminating them. Since the chairs were too high to sit on, the audience members seated themselves in the pools of light, either on the floor or on one of the platforms. No instructions were given before the first myth began. Once the fifty or so attendees had paid their $2.50 admission and found a place to sit, the Dancers' Workshop dancers entered and seated themselves in a circle on the floor. The performance was under way.

(Throughout the *Myths* series Ann steadily collected an admission fee from those who showed up to participate. Charging admission in this context seems to exist as a vestige of a traditional performance, where a prepared spectacle is "sold" and delivered to the audience. The other common dance occasions when one pays a fee to participate are workshops or classes, where one will learn some skills, have an experience, be changed by an encounter with a master teacher. The *Myths* hover at the margins of these two events. It is meaningful that Ann initially staged all of the *Myths* in her Dancers' Workshop studio, a space used for performances as well as daily classes and workshops and at times as a communal home by several of her dancers. Already, then, this was a space that blended the "real" of training work and daily life with the "not real" of performance, the same states Ann would commingle in her dances.[31])

The first evening formally commenced when one of Ann's Dancers' Workshop dancers was asked to step forward, stand in the center, close her eyes, and wait. Then another dancer was asked to stand behind this person and slap her up and down the spine, progressing over the shoulders, arms, hips, and legs, through the entire body. The drums began to sound, and eventually all of Ann's dancers were slapped into sensory alertness and set in motion. As Ann later explained:

> A dance began with audience becoming performers, the original performers acting as catalysts. The physical environment, originally meant for seating, became the stage. The director began to work with responses in movement, guiding them, shaping them, and adding new ideas until everyone was actively participating in "mutual creation." As the energy spread through the studio, the idea of the original circle with its unconsciously perceived powers kept reappearing.[32]

Clearly, in this interpreted and editorialized account, Ann, as director, infers her own cultural reading of archetypal patterns and significance into the spatial patterns of the performers. The "mutual creation" becomes simultaneously a public exploration of oneself.

The most detailed artifact remaining of this evening is a diagrammatic drawing with an elaborate key depicting the "score" and just where in the space the platforms, performers, lights, and drum player were situated. Photographs of this first myth yield little choreographic information. One shows a group of six figures in shadowy light: two are crawling on the floor, two are seated, and a pair of men stand together as one walks his hands down the curled back of the other, who hangs over limply. This photograph suggests that the performers were engaged in their own private exploration of the space around them and their movement colleagues. Perhaps most important, they seem transported by the heady freedom of regarding their actions as ends in themselves rather than as rehearsed utilitarian motions for another function. They seem focused, serious, and they do not appear to be performing for show.

A few weeks after this gentle beginning, the second myth, "Atonement," abruptly changed the tone, offering an emotionally and physically hostile environment. Hickey had covered every inch of the studio's floor, ceiling, and walls with newspapers, actually the same identical page. As Ann later described the "ordeal":

> After being briefed on the floor of a small room, and deciding whether to participate in this "ordeal," the audience entered the studio one at a time. They stood facing the wall, looking into blinding spotlights placed around the perimeter and ceilings of the room. They selected a position, minimally altered some pieces of their clothing, and remained still and silent for one hour. A deafeningly loud continuous roll on a snare drum was played by Casey Sonnabend seated in the center of the room.[33]

Ann concluded this assault to the senses with a debriefing in the small studio, where the "survivors" were asked to think of two words that best described their experience and relate them to each other in small groups. Although she never spoke of it as such, "Atonement" had the quality of an initiation rite, a passage to test the lengths to which the spectators would go in dutifully following and silently enduring whatever challenges, or abuse, Ann and Hickey tossed at them. The docility of this behavior, particularly in the face of such an assault to the senses, makes it seem like a hazing rite. Years later Ann said that her intent was to evoke the Holocaust from the position of the inmates.[34] If this was indeed a reference to World War II, then another reading is possible. Instead of being the victims, the participants in "Atonement" could also be seen as willing executioners, the "good Germans." Equally poignantly, they could have been feeling lost and manipulated, like Dustin Hoffman's character from that year's film *The Graduate*.

The subsequent eight Thursday evening events, which stretched into February of 1968, dealt with progressively more interactive and sensual material.[35] The third myth, "Trails," and the seventh, "Carry," for example, both invited touching and other physical contact that lapped at the boundaries of publicly permissible behavior. At the same time all the events had an instructional quality, as if they were "lessons" in human experience. The fourth myth, "Totem," for example, gave the audience a chair- and costume-filled space to explore for two hours. Afterward, coffee was served and the poet and filmmaker James Broughton talked about the relationship of totems to myths and about historical and cultural traditions of sitting. Only one myth, the ninth one, "Story Telling," used the spoken word. Here participants walked one by one around the interior of a large circle formed by the other participants and told a childhood story, a story no one had ever heard before. The storyteller held a candle and then passed this candle on, signaling another person's turn to begin her story. People then gathered in small groups, with the remaining storytellers recounting their tales to the person seated next to them. At the end the words stopped and all the participants danced slowly together, each holding a lighted candle.

According to Ann, there was no grand plan at the outset of *Myths,* other than to find a way to bridge the gap between audience and performers and to channel any potential hostility viewers might feel at the nontraditional nature of her work. For Ann, the dance is discovered by attending closely to simple biological truths—like the range of rotation possible in a shoulder or hip joint. Different movements can evoke different emotional states, which in turn can inform one's physical actions. From the mid-1960s forward, this was really the only kind of dance Ann trusted. Viewed from a dance historical perspective, it also positions her in direct opposition to the intense focus on individuality through dance that the previous generation of modern dancers had championed. The individual voice of each participant, like each student, is loosened and encouraged in *Ten Myths,* but only temporarily as a step on the way to re-forming a collective group identity. On the performance evenings Ann effectively turned the theater into a classroom and a kind of behavioral psychology laboratory. To prepare the *Myths* audiences to be performers, Ann drew on the kinds of group body exploration warm-ups she had learned from Margaret H'Doubler—attending to one's breathing patterns, noticing how one's muscles and joints moved as one executed a simple action. Like H'Doubler, Ann worked like a conductor, gently orchestrating the group's focus and energy.[36]

The exercises helped loosen and encourage the individual voice of each participant as a step on the way to re-forming a collective group identity. As the evening progressed, Ann watched from the sidelines as various kinds of movement material and different interactions among participants were tried on and accepted or rejected. What happened was arrived at in the moment and then shaped and pushed forward by Ann. In all this, *Ten Myths* foregrounds Ann's skills as a teacher rather than showcasing her choreographic prowess, the more customary function of an evening of a dance artist's work. Ironically, in one sense, she becomes even more of an authority figure than the traditional choreographer, because she roams the performance space during the actual performance, editing, encouraging, and prompting the dance into being at each moment. Authority and power become making people move. While in *Ten Myths* these were people whose mantra was absolute freedom, the dynamic of the environment Ann set up suggests something more complex. The dance studio became a safe and contained place to be wild, to go crazy within reassuring boundaries and never for longer than the two-hour duration of the event.

As a press release issued partway through the *Myths* series explained:

> On any given evening, varying slightly according to the central idea of the night, there was remarkably little passive observation. A few people left. But the vast majority stayed, participated, even participated ecstatically. Some people, those who left on any given night or who lasted one evening, dropped out. But they were more than replaced by a continually swelling influx of new people, attracted, one assumed by word of mouth. And many came regularly, making MYTHS a part of their weekly schedule.[37]

"What I was trying to do was to design scores for the audience to do," Ann later said. "So at the beginning, for the first few Myths, we had a company who would engage the audience. That was the first step. They would do things like demonstrate. But then later on, as we moved into the fourth and fifth myth, we didn't have that catalyst at all. They just met in one studio. They were given a score, and they were told, 'If you would like to do this score you can come in and we'll do it. If you don't want to do it, you don't have to, and we've had a little warm-up, and thank-you and goodbye.'"[38]

There is an unspoken myth referred to here—that of primitivism, the natural man/woman who waits dormant inside of our compliant social selves. Yet instead of freeing the "uptight" in ordinary people, Ann may have simply attracted *un*constrained individuals from the general population at the outset. By the fourth myth in early December, Ann discovered that the audience, many of whom had become regulars, had taken over the show. No longer occasional or part-time participants, they were "on" from the moment they entered the studio, sometimes constructively and at times destructively. "In *Myths* the audience actually did the scores [mapping out the performance]," Ann recalled. "I was giving the audience choices of how close they wanted to be, or how they wanted to distance themselves. And to be able to make those choices during the performance, because they wouldn't know before they started what was going to happen."[39]

Who was this audience? According to Ann's press release, "the 'audiences' were, by and large, neither homogeneous nor an 'in-group.' They were a fascinating mixture of hippies, student groups from the San Francisco Art Institute, all types of businessmen, dance students and professionals, architects, city planners, encounter groups, psycho-therapists, casual visitors to the city, and even occasionally, people lured by the Workshop's reputation for nude performances."[40] The working class is essentially absent here. This is an audience of generally affluent Bay Area residents—students, professionals, the hip, the artistic—people who may even have been practiced in readily letting their social guard down for the duration of an evening.

After each event Ann and her dancers discussed what had happened for days and sometimes weeks. "We learned how things worked, and then we based our next myth on something that did not work but could have," Ann later explained.[41] "Not working" meant that the participants had not become meaningfully engaged with the evening's tasks, or they had deviated from the implicit intention of Ann's score and instead become captive to an expression of their personal desires.

Almost as if the process were ethnographic fieldwork, Ann used audience questionnaires and post-performance "coffee klatches" to solicit feedback:

We quickly noticed that we had to evolve structures that were free enough to allow everyone to become involved in his own way, avoiding any feeling of manipulation, but simultaneously we had to set up boundaries, so that the inclusion of so many people wouldn't lead to complete chaos. It was touchy, balancing these polarities. It meant avoiding the use of words and relying on the materials to create stimuli and multiple choices—verbal explanations are either interpreted a hundred different ways or simply forgotten.[42]

Ann's abiding belief in "body wisdom" being more infallible than words and, more important, in what Victor Turner calls "spontaneous communitas," generated the rules of the game.[43] While Ann had a distinct idea for each evening—ranging from sensuality to conflict, aggression, play, bewilderment, and the sharing of tragedy—she was wary of overdetermining the event. "We can no longer depend on our masterminds," she explained, elaborating, in what can be read as a sociopolitical statement: "There is too much for one mind to master. It's more enjoyable and more unpredictable to let things happen that just let everybody be, and it's wonderful to see what comes about when you release people's resources."[44]

This kind of spontaneity has been strongly criticized by Richard Schechner, who sees it, in direct opposition to Ann, as the "weakness" of "group creativity." He cautions that "outside of a culturally defined theatrical system participants tend to fall back on their own sincerity, their own personal truth . . . all too often a combination of clichés of intimacy, unexamined cultural fact and romantic distortions of pre-industrial religious experience."[45] Judged by standard performance criteria Schechner is right; spontaneity does not necessarily make for a transporting experience for the spectator. Yet viewed from the perspective of an *educator*, which might more accurately define Ann's role in *Ten Myths*, spontaneity can be a rich pedagogic starting point, a way of generating a strong connection between "preparer" and "partaker." Ultimately, spontaneity becomes an active form of participant enjoyment. The test of whether this approach can work as theater depends on where one goes from there.

Like a costume party for personal emotions and behaviors, *Ten Myths* was a forum for sampling various social ways of being. Ann said that in *Ten Myths* the overall ideas she was exploring were "intimacy, sensuality, and trust, as opposed to sexuality."[46] Ann's third myth, "Trails," focused on touch between strangers. When the audience entered the studio, they were directed to a small platform at one end, where they discovered chairs arranged close together. After sitting down, they were told to relax into the chair, letting out whatever sounds flowed from their breathing. The group sound eventually grew into a shout and then quieted into a prolonged humming. Ann's dancers then blindfolded the audience members, who were instructed to grasp someone's hand and form a line.[47] Then the last person in the line was told to move to the front by feeling his or her way along the row of strangers. The long line was then split up into four or five shorter lines, which Ann called "trails," and again the last person in each moved to the front. After repeating this action in silence for an hour and a half, people pulled off their blindfolds and just gazed at each other "for a long time."[48] This concluding "cool-down" stage, which Ann usually included in her participatory dances of the time, allows for processing of what has been learned. Whether through a post-experience discussion or ritual, or both, time is allowed for the performers to return to the ordinary sphere of existence from which they began.[49]

With *Ten Myths* Ann seemed to trust in, as she still does today, a natural state of innocence in people. It is difficult not to think of the risks of taking a group of fifty men and women, including anyone who walked in off the street, and having them remain blindfolded as they touch their way across each other's bodies. Ann reveals this trust in a curious exchange with three of her dancers who performed in *Myths* and who voiced a clear uneasiness with the tenor of several interactions with the non-dancer participants:

ANN: Because they [the audience participants] have no pre-set physical habits, the things they do have tremendous authenticity. . . .

DANCER 2: I don't think that's true. They are more frightened than we are by the intensity that can be reached.

DANCER 3: [agreeing] When you are working with dancers there is always care and love for the body. Even if you're mad and use your greatest energy, a dancer won't break your bones, because he knows about the body. "Carry" would have stopped much earlier if it had been in a class. At first it was beautiful when I was carried, but it went on and on, and I felt I was being used. They forgot that it was me, the person.

ANN: Watching, I had the exact opposite feeling—that these people were involved in a gift-giving ritual.

DANCER 3: [protesting] They said, "Turn her around in a somersault," and they were hurting me. . . .

DANCER 2: I find it hard to be really open with guys from the outside. They were kind of horny. They got me up-tight.

ANN: They usually get horny when the lights go off. There is tremendous starvation for the opportunity to touch. If they had had more experience they could balance it. . . .

DANCER 3: I think it's frightening to see all those people who are not sensitized yet, having their first sensual experience of not only touching but moving. I go through with it because I believe the man on the street can learn, but it takes a great deal of humility on my part to look at it.[50]

As much as Ann embraced spontaneity, she also had an impulse to control, or at least edit, people's reactions to her work, and it seems telling that this exchange was omitted from the collection of her writings *Moving toward Life*, published in 1995. The dialogue documents the dangers inherent in activating the audience in *Ten Myths*. The three dancers speaking here point to the predictability and safety of working with a trained partner and the riskiness and potential violence of being manipulated by untrained strangers. This interchange also reveals the sexual resonance of *Ten Myths* as well as how swiftly the audiences positioned themselves as performing equals with the dancers. Instead of mentors, the dancers simply served as better-equipped bodies to play with. Ann's dancers suggest that they felt they were in the odd position of dancing with theatrically *unsocialized* people. The social anthropologist Erving Goffman has used the phrase "merchants of morality" to discuss how people in everyday life may market themselves as obeying moral concerns when in reality they are play-acting as they pursue their own, not always moral, ends.[51] For some people, "becoming authentic" in Ann's *Myths* may have allowed a similar illusion, giving them license to abandon certain norms of behavior and instead pursue their private ends, charging ahead with whatever felt good. It seems clear that even in audience-participation works, including fairly chaotic and thematically prosaic ones, the stage must have its own code of morality and behavioral order, and Ann would swiftly learn to build this into her scores. In the meantime she enjoyed leading audiences to the edge of promiscuity and back.

> We really didn't have a progression in mind, in the sequence of *Myths* from "Creation" to "Trails." I think that we just got ideas as they came. "Trails" was very interesting, because we were dealing with intimacy and sensuality and trust, as opposed to sexuality. Because everybody was blindfolded the person at the end of the line had to find his way to the front, and the only way they could do that was by feeling their way down the line. So you had to be touching people and had to be being touched. And there was no time to linger to get involved in the touch. It would just happen, and then you'd go on. They could touch you on your breast or your genitals or your face—you just had no way of knowing. . . . I wanted the audience to have that experience so that they would appreciate that touching was more than sex.[52]

Ann's three dancers' comments suggest, however, that for some touch became sex, or at least foreplay. The seventh myth, "Carry," tipped the balance between sensuality and sexuality. The evening began with the participants entering the performing area and climbing up to seats on two risers at opposite ends of the room. For a long time they all sat watching each other, accompanied by steady drumming from below. Finally, Ann stepped forward and asked for someone to choose another person and carry that person across the room to the opposite riser. As Ann recounted, "After a pause a man jumped down, selected a girl, and very simply carried her, and the drumming rhythm, the lights, and the carrying action began to work together." Soon Ann broadened her instructions to include "Will two people carry one person?" and "Will five people carry two people?" and "Will those of you who want to be carried stand in the passage [between the risers] and wait?" In her words, the evening soon resembled "a Bacchanalia [and] was suffused with a ritualistic quality."[53] As Rockwell recalled with clear amusement thirty-two years later:

The idea [in "Carry"] was that you would go across to the other side, take a person who was sitting on the other side, and carry them back to your first side, and then go back to their side. Well, you know, given the general musky vibes hanging in the area, there was a lot of sexuality to this. I mean, you were going over to strange people (most people did it heterosexually) and you'd go to your regular partner or to a new person or something so there was trust involved, but there was also sexuality involved. Anyway, one couple got into it, and started fucking in the middle between the two rows. There were . . . nineteen people watching this couple. What was so funny to me about it was that Ann, this great avatar of free sexuality, was utterly flummoxed by this, did not know what to do, and didn't like it! Because it wasn't part of the drill, right? And here they were, fucking away, and all Ann could do—she must have said this about five times—she would say over and over, after about a fifteen-second pause each time, she'd say, "Will the people who have finished the activity please move to the side of the room?"[54]

Like Duchamp's dramatic gesture of submitting R. Mutt's *Fountain* to the 1917 show of the Society of Independent Artists in New York, Ann's use of real-life activity was dependent on its being presented in the context of art, and it needed this contrast to give it resonance, meaning, and value as "art." A main reason Ann objected to sexual intercourse in the midst of "Carry" was that it broke the frame and evaporated this aesthetic opposition. It also deviated from the intended focus—on the task of carrying—and disrupted a deeper exploration of this prosaic act by letting immediate personal desires take over. (Ann was also sensitive to the fact that at the time nude performances were illegal in San Francisco.)

A man and a woman simply coupling with one another in public lacks the sophistication of art and also the complexity of having a theatrically articulate body suddenly start speaking "vernacular." As Sally Banes has noted, the performing arts of the 1960s came suddenly to "embody" democracy by blending artistic and social radicalism, and this radicalism was often enacted through "new aesthetics that could be incarnated several times in several decades."[55] Ann and the San Francisco dance community, however, didn't have the artists and critics of the Judson Dance Theater performances of 1962–64 to provide an art reference for the significance of task performance in postwar modern dance. Although Ann introduced this in the late 1950s summer workshops and was using it extensively by the 1960 summer workshop, on the West Coast there wasn't enough sense of dance history for local dancers or the public to appreciate the daring and aesthetic meaning.

Outside of *Ten Myths,* the overt performance of "love" was widespread in San Francisco in 1967. *Ten Myths* followed the much publicized "Summer of Love," and public lovemaking was not unheard of at the huge love-ins in Golden Gate Park. Kathelin Gray recalls a Death of Mr. Hippie Passover event at the time, where unison lovemaking was part of the untraditional seder ceremony.[56] The topless clubs of North Beach had also initiated nude "love acts" as floor shows with amateur performers, and on occasion some of Ann's moonlighting dancers joined them. Rockwell and Gray recalled that one afternoon in 1967, "just for the hell of it," they joined two Halprin dancers who regularly performed in the North Beach clubs, simulating intercourse. "[We] just went and cavorted around one afternoon . . . before an audience consisting of ten old guys in raincoats," Rockwell remembered. "I took off my shirt and kept on my jeans while the women were topless and wore g-strings."[57] Others who studied with Ann reported embarking on similar experiences. Sex, marketing, and "love" without entanglements intertwined in curious ways. Publicly showcasing one's ease with sex seemed to connote emotional and physical candor of the sort that Fritz Perls's Gestalt workshops aimed for on a psychological level.

An indirect consequence of Ann's audience participation experiment in *Myths* was to make the boundary between performative behavior and real-life action permeable for the dancers and highly confused for the nondancers. As Goffman has noted, a special kind of intimacy exists among people engaged in group physical activity, like teammates, but this is "intimacy without warmth" or "dramaturgical co-operation."[58] Ann's audiences could quickly become fairly intimate when asked to perform actions like touching or carrying, but did they need to be educated about the virtual nature of imagery, emotionality, and theatrical intimacy in dance? Over the next few years Ann would, in fact, elect to keep the reality of using nondancers and their actions authentic. Instead, she would shift the frame of her theater to highlight these unmediated undertakings as "art."

At the outset of *Myths,* however, Ann's goals were different. In a press release issued in the midst of *Ten Myths,* Ann said every evening was about answering a different human need or desire and then testing the audience on the kind of commitment it takes to be a performer. In this way the public could gain respect for work that puzzled them or which they disliked. Ann later explained:

I felt that a performer has to make an incredible commitment to perform. The commitment is on so many different levels. It's on a physical level, the training for that performance, the rehearsing, the building the body to be able to physically do the piece. And then to become vulnerable and place yourself in front of an audience who are all judging you, and critics who are going to make decisions about whether this is a good or bad piece.[59]

Almost as if she were treating each evening's audience as a huge collective performer, Ann deliberately prodded these crowds into vulnerability, testing the commitment she saw as essential for a performer to stand in front of an audience. Viewed from this perspective, Ann's emerging idea of audience participation concerns transforming the audience into a participating perceiver sensitized with the vulnerability and humility of a performer.

While Jerzy Grotowski, Herbert Blau, and the Living Theater, as well as Allan Kaprow and other artists involved with Happenings, were experimenting with forms of audience participation in the 1960s, none rethought audience participation so systematically in dance. In an interview she gave several months before *Myths* began, Ann acknowledged the intertwining of educational objectives and theater in her approach to art making. These objectives can be in tension in the same way that art and politics frequently are—one is about creating iconoclastic images and the other is socially normative.

Since I've been working simultaneously in education and theater all my life, it's hard for me to know the source for an idea. But I do know that in the theater experiences, I want very much to deal with people on that stage who are identifying with very real experiences in life, in such a way that the audiences can identify themselves with the so-called performers. Rather than just looking at somebody doing something very unusual, I want the audience to be able to identify and realize that this is a person more than he is a dancer, a person who identifies with very real things.[60]

Here Ann candidly reveals her desire to demythologize the acts of both spectating and performing and to elicit a new sympathy of one for the other. She is not striving to create illusionistic theater, but rather to emphasize the everyday reality of her performers as people. While other choreographers would work in this direction by making bluntly functional costumes and choreography for their dancers, Ann simply invited the prosaic and everyday folk onto the stage. In this way she did not dissolve the audience so much as reconstitute their role into that of "witnesses."

Indeed, Ann has said of this period: "I began to stop thinking of an audience as an audience and to think of them as witnesses. I tried more and more to break down separations, whether it was separations between audience and performer or whether it was separations between people within the performance. [I wanted] a sense of gathering together to appreciate our differences and then to find our commonalties."[61] This notion of the audience as witness gave Ann a new conception of what kind of engagement she wanted her dances to initiate and what kind of viewers she wanted her audience to be when they weren't participating. "My idea of witness rather than audience is that a witness has to have a commitment," she indicated, "that they're there for you, that they are supporting you in some way."[62]

In Ann's mind, one major influence that pushed her from the idea of spectator to that of witness was the creation of her dance deck in 1954. As she explained, "When we started showing some of the work the audience was right there. They were practically in the same area we were dancing in. And I think that the separation between audience and performer began to be diminished when we were doing those early works."[63] A few years after *Ten Myths,* Ann's budding ideas about active spectatorship gained reinforcement from a performance of the Mandan Sun Dance that she and her husband attended at the newly opened Native American D-Q University outside of Davis, California, in 1971. The Halprins stood in the circle facing the young men who had gathered around a large cottonwood tree. They watched as each man had the skin on his chest pierced by a bear claw, which was then attached by rope to the top of the tree. Each initiate then tried to break loose by letting the hook tear through his chest skin—a bloody and painful task. Unhooking by hand is not permitted; instead, the performers repeatedly circled the tree, trying to get the hook to tear through their skin. After several hours of watching the young men's agony, Larry suddenly passed out. As Ann stooped to help him, she felt a sharp pain as a branch was whipped across her shin. "The dancer needs your help," an elderly Native American woman seated next to her reprimanded her. "Your husband will be fine; keep your focus on the dancer, your role is to help him by being a witness."[64]

Ann later said this experience dramatized for her the concept of witnessing. It underlined how crucial the viewer is in supporting the performer. In much the same way that Larry was seeking design models of organic unity in the California landscape at the time, Ann began looking to Native American ritual practices as ideals for performances that engaged viewers and performers equally and also held special social potency. As she increasingly incorporated this more engaged posture of witnessing into her dances, disrupting the traditional role of the spectator, all other parts of her performances also shifted. She was looking for ways to make her performances as instructive for spectators as her workshops were for the performers. Ann's whole dance began to take on more of the ceremonial qualities of a ritual, with active audience "witnessing" as one of these.

––––––––––

One of the most direct, and implicitly ironic, references Ann made to her heritage as an American modern dancer in *Ten Myths* was through her simple choice of the word *myths* as her title. In the 1940s and 1950s Martha Graham had initiated the widespread dance theater use of myth with dances that drew on Greek mythology and Native American rituals from the Southwest. In what were generally highly theatrical, meticulously structured, and emotionally dramatic pieces, Graham retold, in her rigorous dance vocabulary, archetypal tales of the human psyche. She tended to use myths metaphorically, as parables for intensely emotional and private material couched as a heroic figure's story. In this she was strongly influenced by Carl Jung's theorizing on the relationship between the workings of the psyche and the images that stream out of the subconscious through dreams. Jung believed that by observing preindustrial cultures, people in modern Western culture could glimpse essences of their own rational existence.[65] Generating myths was seen as a psychological process, a form of living religion that bubbled up from the subconscious.

Ann's concept of myth, however, was considerably different from Graham's. Rather than creating a modern work of art around an ancient parable of human behavior as Graham did, Ann envisioned myth as a much more intimately scaled movement expression that was immediately functional. Ann's sense of myth was more consonant with aspects of Joseph Campbell's interpretation, which sees myth as the fuel for everyday life experience, a narrative we generate that gives a logic and aesthetic shape to our "life journey." When asked about Campbell's influence, however, Ann said, "I didn't connect strongly to Joseph Campbell because he was talking about myths that relate to certain cultures and I saw myth as something that people make out of their ordinary lives."[66]

It is interesting that Campbell, who was married to the choreographer and former Graham dancer Jean Erdman, believed the artist is our closest contemporary equivalent to the great heroes of antiquity.[67] The artist is the one who shapes expressions of individual experience into a new mythology, a ritualistic story, for our time. For Campbell, rituals are the means through which individuals learn the myths of their communities and become members of these groups, a type of contemporary tribe. He warned of the social dangers of abandoning myths, cautioning that youths may become destructive without rituals (myths) to induct them into their community-tribes. The absence of a rite of passage from childhood to adulthood in modern society, according to Campbell, leaves a vacuum that can only be filled through release—sometimes sexual, sometimes violent—to simulate a ritual. The artistic process, in his view, offers a model for a ritual passage, allowing for discovery and re-creation of the self through the particular material the artist chooses to work with.

Campbell's dicta can in some ways be seen as a blueprint for *Ten Myths*, in which Ann functioned as an "artist-shaman," creating the context for her audience's public invention and discovery of a ritual for the evening. In her press release for *Ten Myths*, Ann spoke of "a theater of movement and involvement" and "a seminal theater of community." She indicated, "The central factor in the initial planning [of *Ten Myths*], in the search for something which would release people's buried creativity, was a commitment to ritual, to ceremony, to rites, to initiation."[68] Instead of going "from ritual to theater," as Victor Turner proposed in a book by that title, Ann was taking theater "back" to ritual. Turner described how, as an actor in a ritual performance, "one learns through performing, then performs the understandings so gained"—a statement that might apply equally well to Ann's impromptu dancer/spectators.[69]

The communal myths created each evening during the *Myths* series grew out of the audience's performance, fabricated by the San Francisco Dancers' Workshop dancers and initially shaped by Ann. Unlike Graham, Ann was not interested in using historic myths as ancient narrative structures to showcase contemporary dance dramas; rather, she wanted to have her audiences create their own spontaneous links between their psyches and an invented vocabulary of movement symbols. Her goal was resolutely on emotional change for the participant. While Ann kept her gaze steadily on altering the spectator's role and engagement, the whole dynamic of her theater became reconfigured as well. Over the course of each evening, as the participants explored that evening's topic, their "myths" became contemporary mini-rituals, what Campbell would have called "spontaneous productions of the psyche" rather than the "manufactured symbols" of theater.[70]

A decade later Richard Schechner would draw a theoretical distinction between ritual and theater that may serve as a measure of Ann's success. He recast this divide as one between "efficacy and entertainment," and he coined the term *transformance* to describe performances that "do something" in the way rituals do. In a transformation, as in a ritual, efficacy becomes an essential criterion for judging the success of the event.[71] Sincerity, experiencing the requisite feelings, thoughts, or intentions, creating the appropriate mood and atmosphere, and staying within the proper boundaries were all signifiers of a well-working ritual. Just as equally, they were standards of success for *Myths*.

For the mainstream media at the time it was unclear what standard to use in measuring the success of *Myths*. Was it a licentious "hippie" escapade or an attempt at art? Reviewers for the local papers seemed uncertain whether to adopt an inside (participant) or outside (critic) vantage point and whether to let the licentiousness emerge on its own or impose it in their reporting. The suggestion was that licentiousness exists in opposition to art. In part because the erasure of a spectator's viewpoint was one of the work's objectives, the reviewers seemed to have had a difficult time figuring out where to situate themselves as traditional critical spectators in relation to the work. They roundly failed *Myths* as traditional dance, but they sensed it might be working on some other level. Ritualistic? Therapeutic? Prelude to a love-in? They could not quite identify it. "Things were getting friendlier and friendlier all the time, but I had had it," Heuwell Tircuit, a conservative opera and music critic for the *San Francisco Chronicle*, wrote, adding: "One could easily be upset, considering this a childish or even a dirty event, but the dominant aesthetic was one of overwhelming innocence. Here lies Ann's power—that one leaves feeling bothered by not being able to like it."[72] This reaction to Ann's work as being affecting as a process yet unpersuasive as art was a frequent one at the time.

The *San Francisco Examiner* critic William Gilkerson actually quizzed Ann about whether there would be any nudity in the *Myth* performance he planned to attend. He reported that she responded with "a giggle" and the statement: "Everybody wants to see nudies now," going on to explain that nudity is erotic only if it is presented as a performance spectacle. This was a time when feeling casually intimate with strangers, without being compelled to actually *be* intimate, may have come as a welcome relief. The Sunday before *Ten Myths* opened the city's conservative music critic Arthur Bloomfield had written a surprisingly supportive feature about nudity, describing a controversial performance in Ann's studio. Choreographed by some of her dancers, this concert had at one point involved a nude dancer painting her body. Apparently it was more risqué in the recounting than the viewing. "It would have taken a pretty puritanical mind to see anything crassly pornographic in the evening's entertainment," Bloomfield wrote. "The nudity was incidental and natural, not a parading of voluptuousness." He concluded by citing Ann's response to nudity: "She doesn't see the bareness as rebellion but simply an affirmation of the body as a part of nature. In the highest sense, she feels a performance involving bare facts can make for an honest situation re-enforcing the idea of a communion between audience and performers."[73]

Gilkerson came to realize that the *Myths* programs "were not performances as such. They were rather heightened forms of life experience, open to the general public, intended to do away with an audience as a passive factor. Everyone participates."[74] Throughout his article Gilkerson flickered between the perspectives of voyeurism, traditional spectatorship, and would-be participant as he searched for the right vantage point for *Myths*. In the end he took a sympathetic tone, understanding the performance as a game, as "an exceptionally intimate kind of blind man's bluff." And he quoted Ann on how she judged the success of each "myth": "As long as I'm discovering new things I'm successful. I use [Marshall] McLuhan's definition: He says a Myth is simply an audience turn-on." Although Gilkerson seemed to interpret this as a sexual turn-on, for Ann the turn-on could be in many other realms.

Beyond describing a performance, critics often want to clarify what the piece "means." But for *Myths* this question was not easy to answer. In abandoning text-based theater in *Myths* and in valorizing the spontaneous while devalorizing the choreographed, Ann had placed her work firmly in the tradition initiated by Antonin Artaud—that of regarding theater as an open field: "I maintain that the stage is a tangible physical place that needs to be filled and it ought to be allowed to speak its own concrete language."[75] However, the ambiguity of the performers' relationship to the material they were performing in *Myths* and their divergent understandings of what it all meant invited confusion. As the historian Gay McNulty has noted, even in the most controlled situations, performance is radically unstable in the meanings it generates and the activities it engages because it is an event rather than an object.[76] Gilkerson hinted at the mix of metaphors when he described the actions of one man who enthusiastically removed his shirt while "moving like a strange caterpillar" and later began bellowing excitedly "like a bull rhino." In effect, Gilkerson and Tircuit could find no fixed meanings in *Myths* because Ann deferred transmitting meaning in favor of letting each performer "give or make an offering of his or her presence,"[77] a position that echoes Artaud's metaphorical redefinition of theater:

> It is a theater which eliminates the author in favor of what we would call, in our Occidental theater jargon, the director; but a director who has become a kind of manager of magic, a master of sacred ceremonies. And the material on which he works, the themes he brings to throbbing life are derived not from him but from the gods. They come, it seems, from elemental interconnections of Nature which a double Spirit has fostered.[78]

Artaud's faith in the magic of author-less theater being a conduit to the gods escaped the journalists who wrote about *Myths*. In January 1969 *Time* magazine depicted Ann's *Myths* as some tawdry and vulgar practice of a lost tribe known as San Francisco's hippies. While skeptical of Ann's large-scale claims toward "releasing people's creativity," the writer was clearly charmed by the sincerity of the performers. Intuitively this writer sensed one of the dilemmas of performance—that what is presented is always both real theatrically and not real practically. "Her workshop activities are as much anthropologic as choreographic. . . . By encouraging her audiences to act out their anxieties in terms of free-moving myths, Ann is providing not only a therapeutic outlet but an artistic one as well."[79] The irony for critics was that the more "real life" details Ann added, through audience participation and individuals' generation of their own actions and stories, the less the sense of a theatrical reality *Myths* generated.

A related but different approach to blurring the boundaries between theater and reality can be seen in the work of Julian Beck and Judith Malina's Living Theater, whose radical performance model was overtly political from the start. Like Ann they were interested in generating a community of artists through collaborative works of non-naturalistic theater, but, as Sally Banes chronicles, by the early 1960s "their concern with community had shifted . . . to organizing, through art, in the larger community—rousing both actors and audiences to political consciousness and action, in particular against the Bomb and for world peace."[80] In 1968, after four years in exile in Europe for failure to pay taxes, the troupe returned to the United States to begin a nationwide tour. In the spring of 1969 the troupe reached the Bay Area, where they performed their disorderly and aggressive call for nonviolent social revolution, *Paradise Now*. This work ended with the full cast, joined by the audience, streaming off the stage and into the streets outside the theater, ready to begin the new order, but more often into the arms of police officers waiting to arrest any nude performers for indecent exposure. "Even within the Movement they were controversial for their anarchism," Banes notes.[81]

Beck and Malina contacted Ann before their arrival in the Bay Area and arranged to "work out" in her studio. "I think Julian and Judith considered us fellow revolutionaries and anarchists because we would disrobe," Ann later said.[82] More directly, Ann's warm-up exercises had become part of the Living Theater's movement regimen when Peter Weiss and Karen Auberg, two of Ann's dancers who had appeared in the 1967 Hunter College performance of *Parades and Changes,* joined the Living Theater.[83] Yet the Living Theater's anarchist path of social engagement was very different from what Ann envisioned for her small Dancers' Workshop company. "I thought they were amazing and bold, but visually messy," Ann recalled. "I admired them very much. I don't know any other artists who were that committed." Ann worked her dancers and her dancing audiences more gently and more apolitically, much as H'Doubler had led her classes of young women at the University of Wisconsin in the early decades of the century. What the dance looked like and whether it entertained the audience and moved them to political activism mattered little to Ann. For her, the most important thing was how the experience of embodiment changed each person who shared the performance space with her that evening. So far the myths that Ann had explored were gently universal in theme, with the people performing them feeling their way through the dark to express small personal truths. In the months ahead her canvas, and her goals, would broaden considerably.

———

The most immediate context surrounding *Ten Myths* was not aesthetic but social. By the mid-1960s in America, disengagement was out; it was not longer enough to watch passively from the sidelines or to just finger-point. The common use of the term *activist* at this time underlines the emphasis placed on "doing something." Even the shorthand "the Movement," for the coalition of activists who were gathering to protest the war and other issues, reflected a premium on action. Mario Savio's 1964 speech that galvanized Berkeley's Free Speech Movement called for political engagement via bodily commitment—putting your body against the machinery of the state. By the later 1960s, as the protests against the Vietnam War escalated, the call was growing for draftees to register their protest by withholding their bodies from the military.

Throughout San Francisco in 1967 people were grappling with ways to awaken, address, and control the social body. One feature in a local paper commented on a new light show Glenn McKay and his Headlights team premiered at Bill Graham's rock concert hall, the Fillmore Auditorium, where multiple projection devices "composed the entire room in one vast abstraction, constantly in motion, bathing the walls in an unending wash of liquid color." The writer speculated: "You felt that the young people who were there wanted to telescope time and swallow all of experience in one immense gulp; hence music and light and dance together, and hence also the overwhelming volume at which the music blasted out of the speakers onstage."[84] This kind of sensory inundation suggests a visceral rather than a gentle intellectual engagement. "Tune in, turn on and drop out" of socially constrained behaviors, the mantra of the cultural left, might well have been the subtitle for *Myths*.

Be-ins, love-ins, rock concerts, and antiwar vigils—all were indirectly exploring the boundaries of participant/spectator, because just showing up at these events implicated one as a participant. In San Francisco the year had begun with the January 14 "Human Be-In" in Golden Gate Park. This all-day celebration of self, involving twenty thousand young people, featured antiwar speeches by countercultural celebrities including Allen Ginsberg, Timothy Leary, and Gary Snyder; Jerry Rubin's pleas for bail money for draft resisters; and performances by the Jefferson Airplane and other rock bands. Anyone who attended was asked to bring food to share, flowers, beads, costumes and feathers to wear, bells and cymbals to play, and flags to wave. Marijuana joints were passed from stranger to stranger, and thousands of tablets of high-quality LSD were distributed free to the crowd. Viewed from the perspective of a performance, it was a spectacle, with chemical inducements shaping the audience's perceptual state. It was not a traditional formula for art, but it certainly offered one model for how to mass-produce a specific state of receptivity among spectators as an integral part of a public event. The social historian Todd Gitlin writes of a prevalent utopian fantasy of this time as "the hippie as communard: the idea of a social bond that could bring all hurt, yearning souls into sweet collectivity, beyond the realm of scarcity and the resulting pettiness and aggression." He explains, "The counterculture thus devised institutions in which hip collectivity and the cultivation of individual experience could cohabit."[85]

Participation in free festivities like this was a way, of course, to keep protesters motivated and involved, and social protests cast a broad performance frame over daily life. Over the next few months several other mass participatory spectacles were staged in San Francisco: On March 5 a "rockdance-environment happening" benefit was staged in honor of the CIA (Citizens for Interplanetary Activity). On April 15 one hundred thousand people gathered for an antiwar protest in Kezar Stadium in Golden Gate Park. On June 2, for a Magic Mountain Music Festival on Mount Tamalpais, "Trans-Love Buslines" ferried participants from the parking lots to the festival. June 16 saw the International Monterey Pop Festival, August 27 the start of the Peace Torch's hand-carried trip from San Francisco to Washington, DC, and finally October 6 the massive demonstration "The Death of Hip" at the intersection of Haight and Ashbury Streets.[86] Less than two weeks later Ann opened *Ten Myths*.

———

In the 1960s one didn't even have to be a participant to become a performer. Just being a spectator, even at a nontheatrical event, could thrust someone into the role of performer through the framing device of the media lens. Onlookers at an antiwar rally, for example, might see themselves in footage broadcast on the evening TV news or in a newspaper photograph the next day. From rock music, to protests against the war, to general displays of mellowness (love-ins and be-ins), group activities in the streets, parks, and outdoor stadiums were becoming ways to add a political charge to the narrowing gap between obedient actions and new socially challenging postures.

As a variety of audience members at different art and political events discovered what it felt like to cross over from spectating to doing, they were indirectly structuring a space for confounding culture by being both consumers and producers of their own art. In disrupting the categories of doer and looker, they echoed a crisis between activist and pacifist roles that resonated throughout the Vietnam War. How might one perform social estrangement and disengagement? In *Ten Myths* these would become aesthetic as well as political categories.

The disruption between the categories of observer and participant was not just happening on the radical fringe. Within popular culture, photo booths and the television program *Candid Camera* reveal a fascination with disrupting the categories of observer and participant, framing the nonperforming person on the street as an ironic performer. The divide between voluntary and involuntary participation in a performance was blurred. In an almost Duchampian gesture, *Candid Camera* stretched the definition of a performer to include anyone who performs a functional activity that, because it is given the frame of an accidental performance, becomes "art."

One's body is freed to be regarded as a site of cultural projection without one's even being aware of it.

Photo booths, prevalent in arcades and drugstores in 1950s and 1960s America, were little curtained stalls—mini-theaters actually. There, for about a dollar, anyone could sit on a small bench before an automatic camera and discreetly strike four quick poses. Three minutes later, a strip of those arrested moments of improvised performance emerged from a tray outside the stall. The result was that one was framed as a performer, a short-term star, a closet celebrity, in a show of one's own impromptu design. Then, just as quickly as one emerged from the booth, all the facial and bodily projections of "cutting loose" ceased, one returned to one's controlled public self and retrieved the documentation of oneself as a recondite performer.

With *Candid Camera*, the creation of a former Yale psychology major, Allen Funt, hidden cameras were trained on unsuspecting people as they found themselves in the middle of bizarre scenarios that had been secretly staged. The scenarios were designed to catch them "in the act," usually in the act of being themselves. The understanding was that being oneself was an act, an act based on assumptions about controlling who one was in public and who in private. Of course, once the footage was broadcast, the private and the public were turned upside down. Funt was a follower of Kurt Lewin, a founder of modern social psychology who used experimentation to test hypotheses, particularly those related to group dynamics and how people behaved in social situations. Funt's *Candid Camera* moments "freeze" the psychology behind attitude changes and social influence. They show the situational causes of behavior—how situations can have such powerful effects on behavior and thought that they override personality differences.[87]

One classic *Candid Camera* vignette showed bowlers waiting for their bowling balls to plop out of the return chute, only to discover that suddenly the balls had no holes. In another, a trio of men mimed carrying a massive pane of glass; as they staggered back and forth across a huge sidewalk with their imaginary load, passersby had to decide whether to walk around or through them. Another episode featured an actress soliciting passersby to help her lift a heavy suitcase, which was secretly locked to the ground. In each of these scenes, the hidden camera invites a massive crowd to witness the "drama" without being seen. These unseen spectators turn people's puzzled examination of hole-less bowling balls or frustration at finding the entire sidewalk blocked by three men carrying something impossible to see into humorous entertainment, where a realistic emotional response to a deceptively unreal situation becomes a comic performance. One might compare this to a forced method-acting exercise, in which an authentic affective response is elicited by an acted event in a real-life setting far outside the theater or the television studio.

A spectator's pleasure in watching *Candid Camera* comes in part from a sadistic voyeurism, from relief at seeing someone else embarrassed and at times humiliated. Yet the captivation also comes from the delight of seeing the ordinary suddenly thrown into relief as the theatrical. The show wrests an individual from the anonymity of daily life into the focused spotlight of a performer. Instead of celebrating nonconformity, as much experimental and street performance does, *Candid Camera* at first tacitly ridicules anyone who does not conform. Yet this haven of conformity is short-lived, because once the ruse is up and the hidden camera revealed, the person feels even a bigger fool for having participated. It turns out that the frame of conformity is outside the situation one participated in—for example, one shouldn't have crossed the sidewalk to avoid the invisible pane of glass; instead, one should have trusted one's own sense that there was nothing there and walked on through. There is an added irony because, in the context of *Candid Camera*, willing participation in the skit makes one an object of humiliation for the television audiences at home. The interesting thing about *Candid Camera* was that both the audiences and those caught as unwitting performers loved this coercive performativity.

As much as Ann may have been trying to frame the ordinary as art in *Ten Myths*, it involved a kind of compulsory performing, and the potential for being humiliated and intimidated through that performing, that was in the spirit of *Candid Camera*. With *Ten Myths*, however, the climate of slightly coercive participation pushed participants into individuality. Even when the focus was on creating a group identity, it was a group of individuals, with room to celebrate standing out. With Ann's work, the safety for individual performance was knowing that everyone was doing it and no one was watching. With *Candid Camera* it was not knowing that anyone was watching, although, in fact, millions were.

How we "present" ourselves on and off "stage" (or on- and off-camera) was the focus of Erving Goffman's influential 1956 book, *The Presentation of Self in Everyday Life*. In his reading of daily living as performance, Goffman spoke of perception, as well as behavior, as a form of communication. "If we see perception as a form of contact and communion, then control over what is perceived is control over contact that is made," he wrote.[88] In other words, what we let others see helps determine our relationships to others. We are always both performing and watching others perform. What Goffman's text offers is a way of reframing our quotidian acts in a new context. He referred to his book as a "report" that can serve as a "sort of handbook detailing one sociological perspective from which social life can be studied." The perspective Goffman chooses is that of a theatrical performance. Although Ann had not read Goffman's work, she too was interrogating the performer/spectator relationship with an eye to highlighting the spectator's engagement, to making explicit the transformations and perceptual shifts theater traditionally prompts in a viewer.

Goffman's use of theater as a metaphor for human behavior and interactions in a sense turns the question posed by Duchamp's *Fountain* on its head. Instead of asking whether an object becomes a work of art because an artist makes us see it differently by choosing it and placing it in a gallery, with Goffman's work we are left wondering: could art be an ordinary event, chosen by an artist but not placed in a gallery? Having put the frame of theater around life in this way, Goffman's insights might well have indirectly influenced Ann to play with this framing device in other contexts. In *Ten Myths* she moved the frame of the theatrical from the stage to the entire environs of the theater space. In this way, as in Goffman's model of a generic society, everyone inside the space becomes a player—the house staff, ticket takers, lighting technicians, and, of course, the audience. Ann's ends were not only aesthetic but also practical and social; she allowed the spectator's fantasy of having the kind of embodied and authentic experience usually reserved for the performer to become a reality.

———————

At the time she began her *Myths* Ann was aware of the work of Antonin Artaud, whose influential call for a reassessment of theatrical structure, *The Theatre and Its Double*, first published in French in 1938, had been published in its first English translation in 1958. In this collection of essays, Artaud argues that the Western tradition of literary theater had reached a dead end and that theater should abandon the word and return to more Eastern conceptions of ritualistic spectacle and an intimate performer-audience relationship. Artaud advocated enticing the audience to become participants in the theatrical process, a strategy he borrowed from ritual theater.[89] Ann learned about Artaud indirectly, after the critic Kenneth Rexroth referred to Eugene Ionesco in his review of *Apartment 6.* "I wanted to find out who Ionesco was," Ann recalled, "and so that led me to Beckett and then Artaud."[90]

It is tempting to draw parallels between the social moment in mid-1930s

France, when Artaud penned his reflections on theater and culture, and Ann's own moment in 1960s America, which prompted her to push for a similar immediacy in her dance works. The analogy works to an extent. Both these artists were working in periods of great political uncertainty, with the likelihood of a great war in the instance of Artaud and with an expanded (unpopular) one in the instance of Ann. In his first essay in the collection, "The Theater and the Plague," Artaud deliberately linked his aspirations for art to social aspirations: "And the question we must now ask is whether, in this slippery world which is committing suicide without noticing it, there can be found a nucleus of men capable of imposing this superior notion of the theater, men who will restore to all of us the natural and magic equivalent of the dogmas in which we no longer believe?"[91] It is a question with which Ann could agree. Politically, however, Ann's and Artaud's social moments were quite different. The "slippery world committing suicide" that Artaud referred to was Europe in the grip of rising totalitarian regimes in Spain, Germany, and Italy and the threat of World War II. Ann's *Ten Myths,* in contrast, sought a new set of natural behavioral codes to replace cold war America's emphasis on containment, blind obedience to the government, and a materialist, middle-class life.

By 1967 Ann was also aware of the work of the other leading theater rebel of the time, Jerzy Grotowski, and his Polish Laboratory Theater. Ann and Grotowski had planned to meet in Poland in 1965, one of the stops on the Dancers' Workshop's European tour with *Parades and Changes,* but at the last minute an airline strike prevented them from connecting. Indeed, Ann had not yet had a chance to see Grotowski's work (relatively few people outside of Poland had), but his exercises and descriptions of his work had appeared in the *Tulane Drama Review.* One parallel between Grotowski, as well as Artaud, and Ann lies in their concept of creating a new "myth" for the contemporary moment through audience participation pieces. Grotowski uses the word *myth* repeatedly in his writings, recasting it as the "equation of personal, individual truth with universal truth," a kind of knowledge that we "put on like an ill-fitting skin" to look at life.[92]

More important, like Ann, Grotowski sought to dissolve the audience-spectator dichotomy, although he approached the problem from the standpoint of a theater director. As he explained in his influential book *Towards a Poor Theatre:*

[An] infinite variation of performer-audience relationships is possible. The actors can play among the spectators, directly contacting the audience and giving it a passive role in the drama. . . . The elimination of stage-auditorium dichotomy is not the important thing—that simply creates a bare laboratory situation, an appropriate area for investigation. The essential concern is finding the proper spectator-actor relationship for each type of performance and embodying the decision in physical arrangements.[93]

Implicit in Grotowski's vision for theater here is that the relationship of performer and spectator should be rethought for each performance along with the physical design of the performance space—just what Ann was doing in *Ten Myths*. Grotowski called this new performance form "poverty in theater," a model that abandons what he derisively referred to in an industrial metaphor as "the stage-and-auditorium plant" of traditional theater.

The first major work in which Grotowski challenged the actor/spectator division was his production of Adam Mickiewicz's *Dziady* (1961), where he abolished conventional staging, vowing that he would never return to it. In this piece Grotowski treated viewers as silent and stationary actors, structuring their presence in the performing space so that they effectively performed the act of "spectating," watching the action around them, while in turn being watched by other audience members. Like a frame within a frame, this setup highlighted the idea of the drama as a spectacle specifically for the viewer, and it also invited a regard for the act of spectating as a performance of "paying attention."[94] The fact that *Dziady* was a classic patriotic tale of Poland as a victim of foreign powers added an important emotional bond between the original actors and spectators, but there did remain a divide between who was active and vocal and who was passive. The following year, with *Kordian*, Grotowski stepped up his level of audience involvement. Once again he placed the spectators amid the action, in chairs or seated on the props of hospital beds; this time, however, they were designated as patients or inmates of the asylum that was the setting for the play. As Richard Schechner has noted, it was with *Constant Prince* (1965)—where Grotowski had the audience peer over a fence built around the performing area to see what was happening to the prince—that Grotowski first called the audience "witnesses," because this play is not complete unless it is actively seen. "So I think possibly Ann took that term from Grotowski or maybe they discovered it simultaneously," Schechner said. "Most importantly with Ann," Schechner continued, "I would say [that] rather than making the spectator obsolete, she put holes in the boundary on the walls separating the spectator from the performer . . . [to show us that] in life we are constantly participating and spectating at the same time."[95]

Interestingly, in his later works, rather than progressing to full audience participation, Grotowski shifted his attention more and more to the actor. By 1968 he would state: "Gradually we abandoned a manipulation of the audience and all the struggles to provoke a reaction in the spectator, or to use him as a guinea pig. We preferred to forget the spectator, forget his existence. We began to concentrate our complete attention and activity on, above all, the art of the actor."[96]

By forcing her audience to move, to dance, Ann circumvented the challenge of how to provoke a distanced emotional reaction; she simply orchestrated a visceral one. Grotowski, in contrast, perhaps because participation in his work entailed the professional delivery of rehearsed text, confined his audience confrontations to the physical level, herding people onto the set so that they were on view as spectators wherever one tried to watch an actor. Yet it is curious that however aggressively Grotowski forced the integration of the theater space, he remained respectful of the audience's ultimate passivity. Ann, in contrast, invited participation, and then once she secured the spectators' commitment she pushed hard to their limits.

The visual artist Allan Kaprow had also been pushing the boundaries of passive spectatorship, beginning with his *Eighteen Happenings in Six Parts* (1959). Like Grotowski, Kaprow at times scattered the audience throughout the performance space, but his intent seems mainly to have been to play with the vantage point of the viewer. As he explained about Happenings in general:

The Happenings were presented to small, intimate gatherings of people in lofts, classrooms, gymnasiums, and some of the offbeat galleries, where a clearing was made for the activities. The watchers sat very close to what took place, with the artists and their friends acting along with assembled environment constructions. The audience occasionally changed seats as in a game of musical chairs, turned around to see something behind it, or stood without seats in tight but informal clusters. Sometimes, too, the event moved in and amongst the rows, which produced some movement on the latter's part. But however flexible these techniques were in practice, there was always an audience in one (usually static) space and a show given in another.[97]

Kaprow admitted that performing his Happenings in gallery spaces invited an unfavorable comparison with theater. In comparison he understood

his Happenings might look like "a 'crude' version of the avant-garde Theater of the Absurd . . . night club acts, side shows, cock fights and bunk-
house skits." Once audiences caught these "unintended" allusions, he cautioned, they would take the Happenings for "charming diversions, but
hardly for art or even purposive activity."[98]

It is a curious irony that spectators are accustomed to be mobile when
viewing the static art of a gallery and static when viewing the mobile art of
performance. Kaprow, as a visual artist presenting what he called little performed "acts" in the nightclub sense of the word, confounded these categories when he asked his audience to be static to view quasi-static acts. The
other challenging border that Kaprow straddled was that between what
Michael Kirby called "the genuinely primitive and the merely amateurish."[99]
For the most part, Kaprow used performance novices: non-professionals from
the visual arts world and occasionally amateurs from the performing arts.

Writing in the mid-1960s, after Happenings had become a cottage industry among visual artists, Kaprow spoke out against the presence, or even
the existence, of an audience:

> . . . the audience should be eliminated entirely. All the elements—people,
> space, the particular materials and character of the environment, time—
> can in this way be integrated. And the last shred of theatrical convention
> disappears. For anyone once involved in the painter's problem of unifying
> a field of divergent phenomena, a group of inactive people in the space of
> a Happening is just dead space. It is no different from a dead area of red
> paint on a canvas. . . . A Happening with only an empathetic response on
> the part of a seated audience is not a happening, but stage theater.[100]

Kaprow lobbies instead for what he calls "knowing participation" as a way
to circumvent this. "I think that it is a mark of mutual respect that all persons involved in a happening be willing and committed participants who
have a clear idea what they are to do. . . . The best participants have been
persons not normally engaged in art or performance, but who are moved
to take part in an activity that is at once meaningful to them in its ideas,
yet natural in its methods."[101]

Although Ann shared Kaprow's interest in absorbing the audience in the
performance, she didn't agree with the chaos of his performance, any more
than she did with the aleatoric methods of Cunningham and Cage. "I
thought with Merce and John it's so odd to throw the dice or I Ching to
make a decision—why torture it?" she asked rhetorically. "All you have to

do is sit on my deck and feel nature. I never wanted to call events Happenings like Kaprow. I wanted whatever I did to be organic, not clever. I really like Allan Kaprow as a person, but his Happenings were nonsensical to me. I thought, why are we doing this?"[102]

_____

Not since the dadaists had decried the devastation of World War I and nationalistic hypocrisy had theatricalized public spectacles been such a popular medium of registering social protest as they were during the mid-1960s. This social context, with its emphasis on civic engagement, likely provided a supportive push for Ann's audience members to cross over and become performers in her works. Of course, there were ancient precedents for this kind of theatrical modeling of civic responsibility. In the fifth century B.C. Greek drama had been used to coach Athenian citizens in democracy by portraying moral, legal, and social dilemmas theatrically in ways that challenged notions of citizenship and justice. The Greek theater scholar Rush Rehm calls it "a theater of, by and for the _polis_ ('city'), the social institution that bound Greeks together as a human community. . . . Athens [was] a _performance culture,_ one in which the theater stood alongside other public forums as a place to confront matters of import and moment."[103] This regard for the value of theater was not nearly as pervasive in America in the 1960s, yet within a subset of the alternative community—the marginalized youth of draft age—the public participatory events of the 1960s had the allure of institutional subversions, serving as ways to define a disenfranchised subculture.

Although the social agenda for Ann's _Ten Myths_ was deliberately loose, the exercises—whether in "Creation," "Atonement," "Carry," or another myth—could be seen as practice sessions for acting collectively. Indeed, loose organization rather than tight sophistication was a trademark of many 1960s social protests. Since prime targets of antiwar and Free Speech Movement protesters were the "military-industrial complex" and regimented democracy, their opposites—spontaneity, loose organization, and an easy ("mellow"), accepting manner—were virtues to be cultivated. And these were the performance attributes showcased in _Ten Myths_. As Herbert Blau noted of this era in regard to performance: "When we think of the state of awareness required to live consciously in this world, we're not entirely sure, in the illusory passage of current events, whether we are spectators or participants. It is a confusion out of which we tried to make theater."[104]

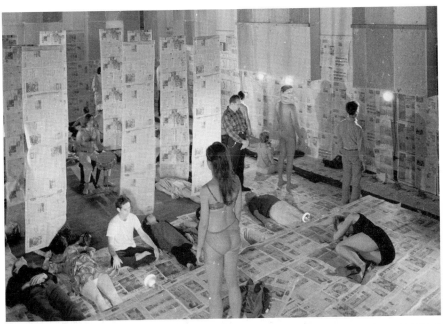

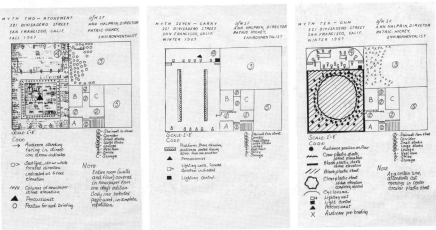

San Francisco Dancers' Workshop and audience members performing Myth 2 (Atonement) from *Ten Myths,* SFDW Studio, 321 Divisadero Street, San Francisco, 1967. Scores for Myths 2, 7, and 10. Photo: Casey Sonnabend.

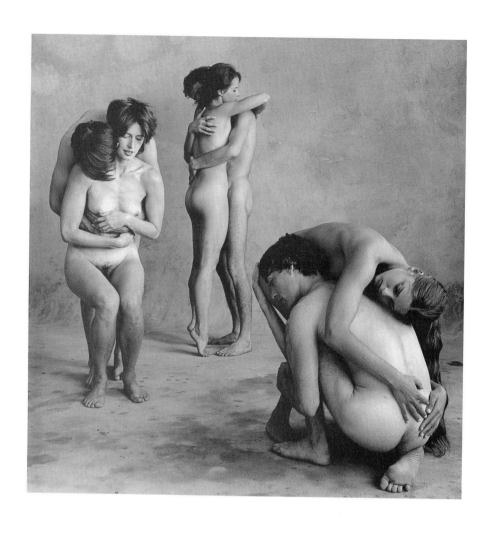

San Francisco Dancers' Workshop in studies from *The Bath,* Sausalito, California, 1967. Both photos © Irving Penn.

John Rockwell and Ann Halprin with San Francisco Dancers' Workshop in *Blank Placard Dance,* Market Street, San Francisco, 1968. Photo: Lawrence Halprin.

Architects and dancers performing *Automobile Event,* part of the "Experiments in Environments" Workshop, in a parking lot at 1620 Montgomery Street, San Francisco 1968. Photo: Rudy Bender.

Below: Ann Halprin, Norma Leistiko, Gary Hartford, and Larry Reed in *Lunch,* Hilton Hotel, San Francisco, 1968. Photo: Michael Alexander.

Above opposite: Annie Hallett and Sir Lawrence Washington with other San Francisco Dancers' Workshop members working through a disagreement in the workshop for *Ceremony of Us,* 321 Divisadero Street, San Francisco, 1969. Photo: Tion Barea.

Below opposite: Ann Halprin and Margaret H'Doubler, her teacher from the University of Wisconsin, in the Halprin home, Kentfield, California, 1970s. Photo: Coni Beeson.

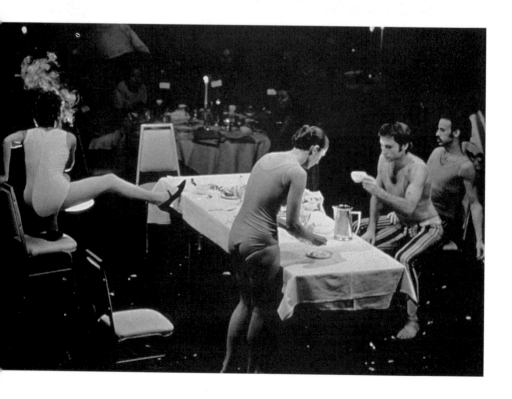

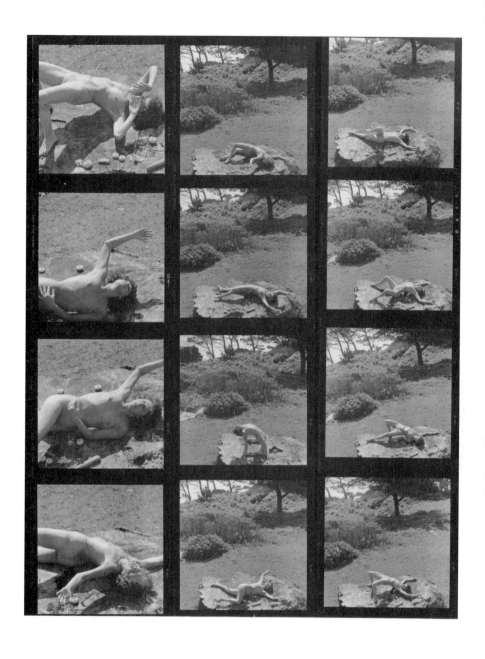

Ann Halprin doing outdoor improvisation at Sea Ranch, California, 1970s.
Photos: Coni Beeson.

Closure of a *Trance Dance*, 1970. Photo: William Vorpe.

Above: Ann Halprin dancing the positive side of her self-portrait with cancer.

Below: Ann Halprin and students on the dance deck, Kentfield, California, 1970s. Photo: Peter Larson.

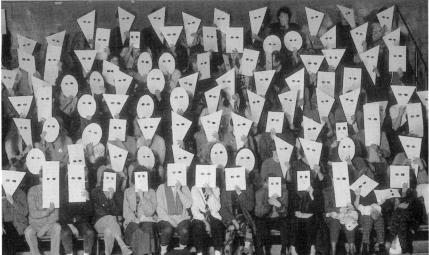

"The Monster Dance" from *Circle the Earth,* Redwood High School gym, Larkspur, California, 1989. Anna Halprin and participants *(above);* witnesses participate by donning masks to protect themselves from the monsters *(below).* Both photos © Paul Fusco/Magnum Photos.

Anna Halprin in *Still Dance with Anna Halprin* by Eeo Stubblefield, 1998.
Photo © Eeo Stubblefield.

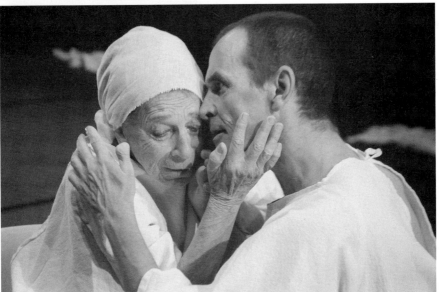

Above: Anna Halprin in *The Grandfather Dance,* Southside Theatre, Fort Mason, San Francisco, 1995. Photo: Coni Beeson.

Below: Anna Halprin and David Greenaway in *Intensive Care: Reflections on Death and Dying,* Paris, 2004. Photo © Rick Chapman.

Above: Score for *Planetary Dance,* showing outer circle (vigorous run), middle circle (moderate run), inner circle (easy steps), and center, where runners can rest by standing around musicians. Graphic design by Stephen Grossberg.

Below: Planetary Dance, Santos Meadow, Mount Tamalpais, California, 2002. Photo © Sue Heinemann.

Seniors Rocking, Marin Civic Center, San Rafael, California, 2005.
Photo © John Kokoska.

Lawrence and Anna Halprin, at their home in Sea Ranch, California, 2005.
Photo © Rick Chapman.

Ann often claimed that the experience of having an agitated audience member charge down the aisle onto the stage during a performance of *Parades and Changes* on the University of California, Berkeley, campus in early 1966 challenged her to rethink her assumptions about the passive viewer. "There was one woman in the theater who seemed to become unglued by the performance," Ann recalled. "She rushed onto the stage and smashed the sole kerosene light we were using for illumination, cutting Daria's legs and stunning the cast, who abruptly ended the performance."[105] The woman banged furiously against the theater doors as she fled out into the night, with such dramatic rage that many in the audience assumed it was a planned part of the performance. Ann, already shocked at the level of anger her work had elicited on her 1964 and 1965 European tours, decided to address the audience directly, and so in designing *Ten Myths* she gave it not just tasks to do, but an actual role in creating the performance. By virtue of its participation, the audience was essentially swallowed into the performance.

Ann found herself asking: if audiences were going to be active, how could she frame and channel that activity, threading it back into the performance? Contrary to the literary theorist Hans Ulrich Gumbrecht's suggestion that the active performer and passive spectator work in opposition—that authentic experiences for the subject are offset and enabled by the triviality of spectacles for the passive viewer—Ann's impulse in her dance works of the mid-1960s was to shift the notion of an authentic experience to the viewer as well. This meant that the assumption of passivity would have to be abandoned, a move that was both practical as well as strategic, since emerging models of performance as social activism suggested that a truly passive viewer was an oxymoron. This was true not just in the performing arts, but in other arts as well. Writers in particular were working with different literary structures that forced readers to collaborate in creating meaning. It was a time of what the literary scholar Marjorie Perloff has called "making rather than taking" meaning.[106]

Ann had begun penetrating the space of the spectator well before *Ten Myths*. *Parades and Changes* and *Esposizione* both instructed the performers to enter the stage through the audience at various points and to perform certain tasks in the theater aisles or off the balconies. Penetrating the viewer's space in this way not only disrupts theatrical conventions and the safety of the viewer's passivity, but it aggressively integrates the feminizing space of being on view on stage with the masculine role of the observer in the audience.[107] Curiously, the effect is to make everyone feel observed, under the interrogating gaze of another. The convention of the stage as the site where individuals and their actions are on display spills into the theater, so everyone and all actions suddenly come under a different type of regard. This democratizing of the roles of spectator and performer reflected other binaries that were also being breached. As faith in the objectivity of the artwork becomes increasingly questioned, so too does the necessity of technique training and the divide between high and low art practices.

Gumbrecht contends that spectacular shows compensate the viewers for their state of disembodied inaction with a virtual or illusory full-bodiedness in the performers.[108] If this is so, then might the converse also be true—that nonspectacular events, those that offer limited scopophilic rewards, need to compel a more embodied and active response? If satisfaction does not reside in the role of the viewer, or it is diminished, then Gumbrecht's claim suggests a new equilibrium can be achieved by giving the spectator a more active, engaged, participatory role.

In *Ten Myths* Ann's larger subject was what cultural theorists Hans Ulrich Gumbrecht, Erving Goffman, and Barbara Freedman have explored in other contexts as the dialectical relationship between performing and embodiment on the one hand and spectatorship and disembodiment on the other. Yet Ann did not start out with any sense of theory guiding her. Rather, she set out to learn intuitively through practice how a dance created in this period of intensive questioning in American society could offer a fluid new canvas linking the performers' and spectators' bodies. Ironically, in order to challenge her audiences Ann began by effectively eliminating the performance as it was customarily defined in the Western dance traditions.

Gumbrecht, Goffman, and Freedman have all implied a perilous and potentially politically charged balance between being a watcher and being a doer. Theoretically, in Gumbrecht's terms, the one who engages in physical performance action is represented as having an "authentic" experience, while the one who watches has a "trivial," passive or inauthentic experience. The person who acts becomes embodied, while the viewer slides toward disembodiment. The pleasure of spectatorship is that it offers this passive viewer the illusion of embodiment, albeit at the price of disembodiment. Spectator sports offer a good example. There is an old joke about the definition of a televised professional football game being twenty-two men desperately in need of rest being watched by thousands desperately in need of exercise—a simplification Gumbrecht's model supports.[109]

Freedman also indicates that the self-presence spectatorship creates is illusionistic.[110] She points out that human captivation with corporeal images in particular lies at the heart of the spectator's identification with a performer. Gender too plays an important part in this identification, as feminist theorists like Ann Daly and Laura Mulvey have pointed out.[111] Building on Mulvey's formulations on the male gaze in film, feminist readings of the performing body have emphasized the pleasures of specular engagement as a gender-based negotiation of power, objectification, and desire.[112] But that does not mean the performer is without agency. As the feminist theorist Elizabeth Dempster explains, "Social and political values are not simply placed or grafted onto a neutral body-object like so many old or new clothes. On the contrary, ideologies are systematically deposited and constructed on an anatomical plane, i.e., in the neuro-musculature of the dancer's body."[113] This assertion supports the dance historian Susan Foster's claim that each dancer constructs a performing body that not only encompasses her personal identity, her physical limits, and the dance styles that have shaped her movement, but also serves as an evolving document of the expressive vehicle she is struggling to invent out of herself.[114]

After tracing what "intellectuals" who view performances do with their bodies, Gumbrecht concludes, "As authentic subjective experiences of the body, today's intellectuals stick to those body experiences that go the limit . . . to those limits where the experiencing of the body turns into an expansion of consciousness. Perhaps this obsession with 'experiencing limits' is an indication of how difficult it has become for them to be in their bodies at all."[115] (Gumbrecht's supposition suggests an interesting parallel with twentieth-century dance, where events with the most physical virtuosity, like classical ballet, garner the largest audiences, and those with the most prosaic bodies or audience participation, like much of Ann's work, attract some of the smallest.) Gumbrecht complicates this challenge of how to be in one's body while lusting after the virtuoso "other" of an athlete or dancer by suggesting that one of spectatorship's lures is the pleasure of a vicarious embodiment. Nested within these observations seems to be the belief that (to paraphrase Walter Pater) all spectators aspire to the condition of the participant. Ironically, it is an aspiration that looms as continually attractive in part because it is never realized. Seeing is generally positioned as more pleasurable than doing, and there is a special satisfaction in denial. *Wanting to* perform can often be more satisfying than actually performing.

Goffman has observed that the audience de facto disappears as a third party when the event portrayed moves from theater to real life.[116] Instead of existing separately as spectators, the audience is now embodied in each "player." Yet even in real life, Goffman notes, the role of the spectator does not completely vanish; instead, it is absorbed and traded between individuals as they alternately act and attend. What they are playing with is the possibility of moving from the mode of apprehension as a spectator to the state of authenticity as a performer. This is not just a change in vantage points. It is an actual change in perceptual states and embodiment, a shift in the way one focuses one's attention on, and attends to, information within and without oneself and one's body, one's world.

Dance is the art form that deals most vividly with these kinds of shifts between being embodied (performing) and disembodied (spectating). For a moment in the mid-1960s American dance bridged the traditional divide between performer and audience to become an authentically participatory event for the viewer, and Ann was at the vanguard of this crossover. Coming from a background steeped in experiential education, and mindful of the links between female physicality and American culture that had been the implicit lesson of Margaret H'Doubler's dance instruction at the University of Wisconsin, she was prompted to explore how motor (physical) involvement could stimulate a more intense aesthetic engagement, a compassionate regard for others, and perhaps, ultimately, a changed awareness of the world outside the stage for her spectators. Three decades earlier in H'Doubler's classroom, Ann had learned that one could quest for a moral and democratic ideal via the dancing body. Every day in class she had experienced the subtle interconnectedness between emotions, the body, the mind, and moral behaviors. Now she was attempting to make this model accessible to both dancers and non-dancers, performers and audience members.

Early in March 1968, after almost five months of *Myths* performances in San Francisco, Ann took her new formula for audience participation on the road, when she and her dancers visited the University of Oregon in Eugene. She decided to adapt her tenth and final myth, "Ome," for a larger audience. Originally, this myth had been a calming group meditation, which began with breathing exercises and gradually grew louder into an effortless exhalation of the sound *om*. After thirty minutes, a drumbeat started and, one by one, the participants entered a central area, framed by a hanging plastic sheet, where they performed a simple movement, rolling, stretching, or rocking. At one point the movements intensified, only to quiet into another meditative chanting of the sound *om*. As Ann described it, "These people were no longer an audience but were by now a community."[117]

For the Oregon performance, Ann began by instructing the seated audience to chant *om* as a vocal warm-up and way of resonating sound through their bodies. Then she asked everybody to stand and begin dancing in a line up and down the aisles of the theater. Here Ann was consciously trying to forge links between the mutuality that emerges in an audience responding to an affecting performance and the individually transforming experience of a workshop. She had found a way to merge spectatorship with embodiment, at least for an evening. With her next investigation, she would take the aesthetic potential of this new collective performance process more clearly into the social area, tackling the difficult issue of race.

EIGHT

Ceremony of Memory
1968–1971

In habitual memory the past is, as it were, sedimented in the body.

PAUL CONNERTON
How Societies Remember

Improvisation is an act of collective memory as well as invention.

JOSEPH ROACH
Cities of the Dead: Circum-Atlantic Performance

ON A LATE AUTUMN DAY in 1968 Daria Halprin, a sophomore at the University of California, Berkeley, was in the ceramics studio in Lower Sproul Plaza throwing pots when she was called to the telephone. The Italian film director Michelangelo Antonioni was on the phone and wanted to speak with her. Daria, sure it was a prank, discovered it was not. The director of the avant-garde film *Blow Up* wanted her to take a screen test for a part in his next feature film. He had glimpsed her dancing with her mother's San Francisco Dancers' Workshop in *Revolution,* an underground film about hippie street life in 1967 San Francisco, made by Jack O'Connell, a former associate of Antonioni. Already at nineteen Daria was strikingly beautiful, with thick, straight brown hair that hung well below her waist and smoky green eyes. She had the long legs and slim hips of her father and a cool, self-assured manner.

In *Revolution* Daria makes only a brief appearance, as one of six nude dancers whose bare torsos are repeatedly offered to the camera as living canvases for spiraling light projections of tie-dye-like patterns. Only the women's torsos are shown full-on, usually headless, like one of California sculptor Robert Graham's detailed miniature female bronzes. Daria's long hair shrouds her face and breasts as she repeatedly steals across the narrow and darkened stage in front of the projections. There is a wild-child quality to her determined crouching walks, but she never says a word or appears in full light or face. Clearly Antonioni must have been responding to a "look," a fantasy, here. All of the dancers in this film sequence improvise freely, presenting their bodies as undulating and curving surfaces for the lights to dance across. Their bodies look shaped by dance training, but more to achieve control than stylization. The visual impact is one of physically sophisticated and trained performers moving with the ease and open unselfconsciousness associated with the theatricalized "natural" of nude performance.

Daria flew to Los Angeles and took the screen test for Antonioni. Within two months she found herself on location in Death Valley as the lead in Antonioni's *Zabriskie Point,* a meditation on 1960s American youth, racial tensions, and violence. Antonioni put Daria opposite another non-actor, Mark Frechette, whom Antonioni had discovered standing at a bus stop in Boston, where Frechette was screaming angrily at a stranger in an apartment window across the street.[1] Media accounts of the time noted the life-imitating-art coincidences of this casting, since in *Zabriskie Point* both Daria and Mark use their own names and portray individuals similar to their real-life personas. Daria plays a middle-class hippie (*Look* called Daria "a bratty, free, earth child" whom Antonioni didn't try to change)[2] and Mark a sensitive lower-class guy who is radicalized and drops out of college.

Zabriskie Point offers a cinematic world of modernist fictions in which characters do not have elaborate psyches or pasts, reality is fluid, and a certain one-dimensional characterization is fine. Mark joins, half-heartedly at first, with students protesting for a black studies department on campus. Suddenly he seems to get swept up in the cause, murdering a policeman and then stealing a private plane to escape. But then he quickly forgets about this cause as he encounters Daria in Death Valley and his flight turns into a kind of joy ride. Antonioni tends to keep his distance not just from the events in the film, in a sense underdramatizing the dramatic, but also from the people, giving us only the outlines of Mark and Daria as two disconnected kids with no real commitment to social or personal causes.[3]

The way Antonioni does *not* cinematically amplify the scope and the directness of Daria's (or Mark's) actions, mood changes, and emotional expression offers a pure sample of Ann's performing ideal of the time. In this way the film offers a rare window onto what one of Ann's performers looked like at this moment and suggests the quality of untheatrical, privately scaled projection and presence in Ann's work of the late 1960s. Only a movie situation like *Zabriskie Point,* where Antonioni deliberately recruited Daria as she was, could do this. Rather like the fossil of an ancient animal accidentally trapped in tar, Daria's celluloid image preserves intact the Halprin dancer at the end of the 1960s.

Both Daria and Frechette were inexperienced as actors, but their presence in front of the camera differs. Frechette's lack of any performing background shows in his acting, which tends to be more wooden than naturalistic. He fails to convey either a theatrical or a real attraction to Daria; instead, his character dissolves into his surroundings and feels as shallow as the indifferent police and corporate executives, who are deliberately shaped as one-dimensional establishment figures. Daria, in contrast, seems more realistically scaled, so that she seems to perform an untheatricalized self-portrait.

At the time, having Daria cast in *Zabriskie Point* seemed the perfect fulfillment of the hybridity between life and art that the Halprins were promoting, and both Larry and Ann were proud of Antonioni's choice of her. A contemporary newspaper account suggests that not only did Daria idealize American youth for Antonioni, but that his direction of her was a sparse variation on the "be yourself" directive that reverberated through much of the Dancers' Workshop work.[4] As in the summer workshops Larry and Ann were conducting at the time, in *Zabriskie Point* authenticity is positioned as something arrived at by stripping away the sediment of civilization and socialization from oneself. Yet, however much Antonioni's open directing style was reminiscent of her mother's work, film proved to be a less forgiving medium than live performance for Daria, one that demanded a special amplification and performativity about emotions in order to register it as natural. Playing oneself has a different edge when it involves a professionally trained actor (or dancer) letting go and throwing away technique for the moment than it does when someone, like Daria, has no acting tradition to discard. As Daria later explained:.

This unexpected branching out [as the female lead in *Zabriskie Point*] from my home environment, my involvement with dance, my community of friends, was the beginning of a seven year period in my life which challenged me in ways I'd never expected, and exposed me to a life style which was radically different from the one I'd known. I was unprepared! Although I'd been a performer and "lived" in the theater since childhood, acting in films required another set of skills and an awareness which I didn't have.

After *Zabriskie Point* I joined the Lee Strasberg School in Los Angeles, feeling that if acting was what I was going to do, I'd better start learning how to do it! I found method acting to have close similarities with the movement-theater approach I was familiar with and the orientation of being present and authentic within a character.[5]

Daria's lack of experience in the artifices of acting may have effectively ended her film career, for even Antonioni would later opt for illusionistic naturalness, not the raw, unmediated real thing. Still, in watching Daria in *Zabriskie Point,* one realizes how radically Ann rethought not just the nature of the actions inside her dance, but also the framing concept of theater and spectatorship around it. Performers could be realistically scaled in her theater because the frame was about exposing the individual's emotional self, not inventing a new one. Additionally, in live performance spatial and sensory information registers more meaningfully than in film, so observers in real life pull meanings out of a range of stimuli that are never consciously shaped.

What Antonioni's film allows us to see through Daria's performance is the direct and unaffected Dancers' Workshop manner of wedding emotions to actions while biasing the nonverbal. In *Zabriskie Point* Daria knows how to be present, but there is no history or future to her representation of character. What we see is the Daria of Irving Penn's photographs of *The Bath,* a young woman who is naturally, rather than theatrically, sexy. Her actions are scaled to daily life rather than cinema or the traditional stage. In the film's big lovemaking scene in the desert, she is far more natural than her partner, Frechette, planting real kisses on his lips and tumbling over him as her loosened hair envelops them both. She also seems unabashedly indifferent about being seen, focusing instead on what she is feeling at the time about her partner.

Daria's experience in *Zabriskie Point* reveals some of the liabilities of the climate of candor and easy creativity the Halprins' work during this period offered. The on-camera romance between Daria and Frechette spilled into an offstage affair, so that by the time the shooting was finished Daria had dropped out of college and was living with Frechette in his commune in Boston. They split up soon afterward. Then in 1975 Frechette was arrested and jailed for robbing a bank. He was found murdered a short while later in the prison gym, a violent end eerily presaged by *Zabriskie Point,* where his character is shot to death by police.

The similarities between Antonioni's method and Ann's go beyond their respective use of non-actors and non-dancers. Antonioni's narrative in the film is comparable to Ann's impressionistic style of storytelling, particularly in the way he spills narratives across a spatial field. *Zabriskie Point* begins with a naive addressing of the social issues of race in the form of a student-led revolt, but then the discussion of race is soon forgotten and the film instead becomes the story of disconnected sex among the parched earth ruins wrought by the violence of American culture in the 1960s. The one sex scene in *Zabriskie Point* is staged like a great neo-romantic ballet, where suddenly Daria and Mark's nude coupling is echoed by a dozen other nude long-haired young women and men kissing and embracing on the sand dunes around them.

Most important, the themes of racial tension and sex in Antonioni's film would be central to Ann's next dance event, *Ceremony of Us*, which was created at about the same time. Specifically, *Zabriskie Point* modeled how a white artist's focus could slide from issues of race into sex and violence—three issues that were often linked in the late 1960s. The African American studies scholar Calvin C. Hernton, for example, devoted his 1971 book, *Coming Together: Black Power, White Hatred and Sexual Hang-ups*, to the complex tensions, prohibitions, and desires surrounding sex and race in 1960s America.[6] As the feminist scholar bell hooks has observed, "Race and sex have always been overlapping discourses in the United States."[7] A 2001 study reported how often fiction has linked ideas about the civil rights movement and social change in the 1960s with interracial sex, communicating the larger social issues through small-scaled stories of personal relationships across the color line.[8] Tales of interracial couples became a means for authors, including Alice Walker in *Meridian* and Lanford Wilson in "The Gingham Dog," to explore the push for racial equality through metaphors of intimacy. As Tommy, one of the lead characters in *Meridian,* taunts a black man married to a young white Jewish woman, "Black men get preferential treatment, man, to make up for all we been denied. She ain't been fucking you, she's been atoning for her sins."[9]

For Antonioni, the subjects of civil rights and racism in America served not as a focus, but as the cultural background for his film. For Ann, these topics would be treated as background mythology for her collaborative performance about race, *Ceremony of Us,* in which she began making participatory theater out of conscious and subconscious engagement.

In July 1968, a few months before Daria received her call from Antonioni, Ann and Larry held their second "Experiments and Environment" workshop, for forty architects, designers, city planners, dancers, and students. They collaborated with Jim Burns, a former senior editor of *Progressive Architecture*, and Paul Baum, the psychologist who had introduced Ann to Fritz Perls and who served as an on-site consulting therapist. As the interpersonal issues in these workshops heated up, his role would become increasingly critical.

Larry intended for this second summer workshop, subtitled "Communities," to explore the links between "meaningful urban design and the right process of bringing together disparate elements and experiences that make up an urban environment."[10] Most radically, he aimed to maximize creativity and innovation in design work by prompting people to use the "intuitive modes of perception of bodily and kinesthetic awareness" when they were placed in different natural settings. As he later commented:

> The 1968 workshop was the [most] seminal workshop that I ever did and I think it was for Ann too. Its idea stemmed from 1966 when Ann had done some workshops before and I had seen what she did. Most design studios in architecture deal with the intellect, almost completely, or did at that time . . . and I thought that, having watched Ann, some of the same attitudes that dancers have and which were revealed in music and in drawing and movement might be something that we could apply to architecture as well.[11]

In *Ten Myths* Ann had worked in the reverse, mapping a method that was equally novel for the dance world by creating an artificial environment and rules, and then letting people loose to see the behaviors these environments evoked.

Shortly before the 1968 workshop Larry had completed a design study for the City of New York that was "the first major proposal stressing the importance of having citizens participate in what happens to, and in, their own environment."[12] This 119-page report, with its proposals for six urban renewal projects in New York and its redefining of open space in the urban environment, attracted significant public attention, particularly because it called for treating the black inhabitants of the Morningside neighborhood around Columbia University as equals with university officials in redesigning their community. Indeed, the report would earn Larry the 1968 Smithsonian Institution Industrial Design Award of Excellence and the Municipal Art Society of New York Certificate of Merit for its pathbreaking approach to having citizens actively help plan the uses of space in their community. Larry's study argued repeatedly against the "mindless imposition of open spaces in dense crowded city spaces." Instead, as Douglas Davis, the architecture critic for *Newsweek* noted, Larry's plan "sees the city as an excuse to enjoy many options rather than just a few and it keeps open a multiplicity of options for the citizens—work, play, rest, repose, tension."[13] This reenvisioning of the city as an array of sites evoking different "performances" is evocative of Ann's participatory theater pieces. In the realm of architecture Larry was seeking the same thing Ann was in theater—to create an avenue for participatory fieldwork.[14]

Starting with the building blocks of a community—families—Larry and Ann now wanted to script a series of situations in which it would be possible to observe how family and community relationships develop and evolve. They hoped to create a performance site that generated a working process, bridging civic and artistic arenas. The model they chose—a large group workshop—was not surprising. Conceived and led collectively by the Halprins, Burns, and Baum, this workshop sought to both model and inspire collective creativity as a social and design solution to contemporary problems. Over the three weeks of the workshop, participants engaged in a variety of exercises designed to sensitize them to their environment, their bodies, and each other, many of which—like a blindfolded environmental walk and a group partner massage on the deck—were familiar exercises from Ann's dance classes. Yet the degree of interchangeability in the way these core exercises might be framed by each leader (they took turns facilitating sessions) to highlight architectural, choreographic, or psychological problems and solutions was remarkable.

The workshop was documented in 1974 when MIT Press published *Taking Part: A Workshop Approach to Collective Creativity,* a thick handbook replete with the messy exuberance of images, ideas, and ambitions that must have characterized the actual experience of being in the workshop. The digital media artist Chip Lord, who participated in the workshop, coming to it directly from architectural school, and went on to cofound the art collective Ant Farm five months after the workshop ended, felt it was a very strong influence, particularly the movement sessions on touch with Ann. "It has all stayed with me and I really think that is valuable," he later said. "It probably translates into a video-camera, looking through it. The way you frame, the way you look at a person's body. A sense of movement when you're recording something or when you're framing something."[15]

In his introduction to *Taking Part,* which includes a day-by-day description of the 1968 workshop, Larry draws a direct link between a soci-

ety of engaged and diverse citizens—individuals animated by active listening, attentiveness to body language, and the pleasures of play—and a
political structure free of chaos and dictators. The tone of the book is en-
ergized and innocently optimistic about viewing each person as a "contributing artist" whose objectives are "personal growth," "artistic expression,"
and "recycling the experiences of the workshop back into life."[16] In linking the artist with the engaged citizen and making this link available to others
through the 1968 workshop, the Halprins enhance the function of both.
They suggest that creation is not reserved exclusively for the professional,
nor is it frivolous, but instead a critical dimension of civic life for all.

One of the signature exercises of the 1968 summer workshop involved
blindfolding all the participants and instructing them to stand in line with
a hand on the shoulder of the person in front. Then, holding onto each
other, they had to walk "blindly" over wooded paths, uphill, downhill, and
through cascading water. The goal of these "environmental awareness
walks" was to prompt people to experience their surroundings using senses
other than sight. As the participants would inevitably discover, these other
senses—smell, taste, touch, and hearing—when attended to, put one more
deeply in touch with the corporeal, which in the climate of the late 1960s
also immediately meant the sensual. Underlying this exercise was also the
belief that in muting our strongest sense, the visual, the competencies of
our other senses can be heightened.

Since the furor over the dressing and undressing sequence in *Parades and
Changes,* nudity had become *de rigueur* in Ann's summer workshops. Burns,
who participated in both the 1966 and the 1968 July workshops, recalled
how matter-of-fact Ann was about advocating nudity as an important way
of "building community" and trust:

> I think it was about midway through the [1968] workshop and Ann led
> an all-afternoon session on the dance deck in Kentfield. . . . It was a very
> long session, but it was very relaxed and nondemanding. I was one of the
> last persons to take off my Fruit of the Looms. But Annie was very good
> at that. She just stood there and looked at me until I said, "This is ridicu-
> lous," and "Why don't I take off my shorts?"
>
> There was one guy, an architect, who practically lost his mind because
> he had to miss that session because he had a family thing back in the East.
> And he came out just at the end of it, and he looked down on the dance
> deck and everyone was naked as a jaybird. He cried, "I've missed it! I've
> missed it!" As if he'd missed his whole life opportunity. Obviously no one
> had to do it, but eventually everyone went along, most of them happily. It

was a kind of bond between everyone in the group. So much so that the very next day . . . we decided to have a celebration lunch and to take an official class photo.

So we took the photo and then someone said, "Okay now we have to take a photo that shows the end of the process," and so we all took off our clothes and got back in the same pose and no one had any problem doing that at all. It was just immediately clothes hitting the ground all over the place.[17]

As Larry and Burns explained in *Taking Part,* the point of this kind of nudity is "not how naked people can get, but how confident they can feel with their own bodies and how trusting and non up-tight they can become with the group."[18]

The nudity "score" started off with the participants pairing off and taking turns massaging each other's body. Framing this partner massage as a form of psychological research, Larry and Burns assert, "The operative question concerning nudity was: 'What are your objections to removing your clothes for a massage?'" This sounds like more of a challenge or a rhetorical inquiry than a neutral question. Yet Larry and Burns continue: "This approach, not demanding but asking, puts the responsibility for being clothed or nude on the person instead of behind a stalking-horse of societal moralism."[19] Their description suggests, in the prevalent spirit of naive innocence of the time, that physically exposing oneself is linked to psychological candor, that taking off one's clothes might have a social and moral resonance—rather like the undressing in *Parades and Changes.*

The final day of the 1968 workshop was devoted to seven scored events, beginning with a movement session led by Ann in which the participants were instructed to "isolate, then reassemble, different parts of your body." Moving through basic explorations of the sort H'Doubler might have used, the participants tested possibilities of lifting, supporting, cantilevering their bodies as if they were construction materials for a building. Then, prior to lunch, the men and the women were divided into separate groups and asked to make a performance of what the leaders had identified as "women castrating men by defusing and diverting all process discussions and men letting it happen." (No mention was made that three of the four leaders were male.) Photos of this show the women in a close cluster, wearing underpants and bras, their long hair loose, as they embrace one another. On the opposite page the men, shirtless and wearing pants and shorts, are standing with arms solidly linked as one ring of men stand on the others' shoulders. Read decades later, these images that must have seemed so natural and spontaneous in the 1960s now look markedly shaped by essentialist clichés about gender roles and behaviors.[20]

During lunch it was decided to take two photos of the whole group—a before and an after, presumably to show how the changes of the twenty-four-day workshop registered on the participants' bodies. Here too there is a strong sense of people performing the roles of counterculture rebels, recording, through what they are willing to take off, how much they have taken in. In the first, "before" version, the participants and instructors pose on the back balcony, stairs, and patio of the Halprins' Kentfield home. Everyone is dressed in casual clothes—mostly cut-off jeans and shirts. They are packed in close to one another, almost all facing the camera, looking relaxed and smiling broadly with their arms resting affectionately on each other's shoulders or knees. In the second, "clothes-off" version, everything is the same, but everything is also very different. Although everyone is in more or less the same position as before, they all seem to be laughing self-consciously and only a few people look directly toward the camera. There is unease in this disclosure of a complex history of bodies, particularly the women's bodies, whose tan lines suggest a history of sunbathing in bikinis.[21]

This emphasis on nudity, heightened by the prominence of these two full-page photographs in the book, loomed disproportionately large in the workshop's legacy. Years later Larry put this bit of spontaneous play into the broader context of the workshop's objectives:

I am concerned about the emphasis about nudity as if this [were] the major emphasis of the workshop. It certainly was *not* my intention. Mine was particularly for the architects to urge them to realize that architecture/landscape architecture is largely a sensory art as well as intellectual and that sensory implies the sense other than the visual, which is the usual way it is taught, i.e., through the use of paintings as vehicles for plans! My emphasis then is on sound, smell, touch, movement through space, kinesthetics (which for Anna leads to the body). For that reason we did do a score for body which involved removing clothing.[22]

For Larry, the 1968 workshop was a turning point, crystallizing his conception of what he called an "RSVP" feedback loop, an approach to the creative process that Ann soon found crucial to her work as well. This way of addressing and solving design problems involves four components: an assessment of resources (R), the formulation of a plan or score (S), an evaluation (V), and a performance (P).[23] Larry's involvement in drafting the performance blueprints for *Ten Myths* may have prompted him to think about how one might plan for flexible participation in creating an event where the goal was to promote perceptual acuity and to foster change rather than to control a theatrical situation. According to Larry, "My own interest in participation stems from early experiments in scoring . . . scoring meaning the energizing of processes over time such as in musical scoring. . . . I first became involved many years ago through my need to develop choreographic notations for the new theater of my wife."[24]

Indeed, the 1960s was the period when Ann and Larry collaborated most harmoniously and profoundly using their respective art forms of dance and environmental design. This was the decade during which they each forged signature identities in their respective fields precisely because of the hybridity their interactions prompted. While Larry was gaining a new sense of how to include interactivity, bodily awareness, and group participation in his architectural projects through Ann's influence, Ann was applying spatial, design, and architectural insights to her choreographic problems. "The lessons learned in the 1966 and 1968 workshops gave rise to the conviction that people in communities could become important influences on how those communities evolve," Burns later wrote.

Later in 1968 Ann would wed these lessons in community with her expressionistic performance methods and work with the performer's genuine subjective responses to deal with an urgent social agenda. She had already been reacting against the pretense of fictional narratives in dance, just as Jerzy Grotowski and Joseph Chaikin were attempting to eliminate the social mask from the actor in drama. Ann had begun doing this in dance through her use of task performance, because tasks did not create a fictional illusion of character and they existed in an actual, not imaginary, time and place. (These were some of the same benefits the Living Theater was gaining from using *task acting* in its mid-1960s pieces.) With *Ten Myths,* however, Ann had advanced further into identity realism by using not stripped-down actors, but confessional audience members and workshop participants as her performers. More and more she was focusing on the group rather than the individual as the important identity, a facet of what Theodore Shank calls the "We" rather than the "I" theatrical idealism of the mid-1960s.[25]

Ann found her art dramatically challenged by Larry's concern with how to include urban voices of varying classes and social roles in his design solutions. While working on his New York study, Larry had detailed in his personal notebook his fantasy of setting up a weekend encounter group to study the real needs of cities. He described the site as "in the environment" and the participants as "housewife, cop or fuzz, pusher, kids, druggist, . . . pool hall hustler, designer, beurocrat [sic]."²⁶ Within a year Ann would bring together a somewhat different grouping of urban denizens to create a dance out of a city crisis.

By 1968, as violence and hard drugs displaced the earlier innocence of the Haight-Ashbury district, serious social problems began to intrude on the idyllic notions of community Ann's work had championed. Both Halprins sensed the urgency of finding new means and new communities to assist them in addressing social problems through their art. Ann did not have to look far for her new community and wider context. Turning her aesthetic gaze away from Haight-Ashbury and its hippies, she now looked four blocks north of her Divisadero Street studio, to the center of San Francisco's oldest black community, a neighborhood called the Western Addition. Since the period immediately after the 1906 earthquake, the city's African American community had been centered in this area of several blocks, which formally located its cultural center, the Booker T. Washington Community Center, on Divisadero at Bush Street in the 1940s. As Ann later recalled:

> I had just finished teaching the twenty-four-day July workshop with Larry and Paul, and I was asking, "Where are the black members of our community?" I felt that we were not getting an accurate response to our design problems because we weren't using the real mix of people in the real world. I had gone as far as I could exploring *boundaries* of audiences and theater. Now I wanted to go into the next phase, *who* the audience was. If we were creating for the urban world then shouldn't ALL the variety of people who live in a city be part of the design process too? Where were the black members of our community?²⁷

In *Ten Myths* and *The Bath* Ann had focused on the distinction between passive spectatorship and active performance and the implicit divide between public and private behaviors. Now she wanted to address the incendiary divide of the 1960s—race. What had been in the background would be brought sharply into the foreground as she struggled to find a performance form that could both recover and actualize the mnemonic reserves in the bodies of two very different groups of performers—working-class

African Americans (from Watts, as it turned out, not the nearby Western Addition) and the middle-class white students of the Dancers' Workshop. The dance that would result would be a performative slice of that period, an artist's living document of these bodies and of what the cultural historian Paul Connerton has called the bodily practices of social memory.[28] Rather than an interpreted statement of these two populations' responses to their moment, Ann would create a structure, a container, into which both groups could sift their viewpoints and imaginings. Yet any hope she might have had for a smoothly collective, non-messy theater was illusory. No position in regard to race, particularly in a dance theater made with black and white bodies, could be neutral. As Toni Morrison cautions in *Playing in the Dark:* "The habit of ignoring race is understood to be a graceful, even generous, liberal gesture. To notice is to recognize an already discredited difference . . . [so] every well-bred instinct argues *against noticing.*"[29] Ann's struggle would be how to both notice and respond, and in responding to actively cancel out the habit of "not noticing" to which Morrison refers. She needed to figure out how to push for the visibility of race while at the same time curtailing her own interpretation so that the performers might be both visible, vocal, and noticed on their own terms. The work she would begin creating in the summer of 1968 would activate the racial American imagination of its participants and audiences, embodying and replacing the dichotomy of race with an image of social love, harmony, and an "us" group identity.

Civil rights marches, sit-ins, and riots were some of the contested forms of spontaneous expression different groups of Americans had already employed in response to the racial divide. Ann, however, wanted to pioneer an atmosphere in which the content grew out of the personal issues of the participants in her theater, so that together they might generate a dialogue in art. She was hoping to express the elusive shape of racism by embodying, and perhaps defusing, it through the language of participatory theater. The risk was, as Morrison has noted, that the subject being imagined cannot be free of the person imagining it.[30] Much of what would happen in Ann's work with these two groups of performers would directly reflect her own tacit, white, middle-class myths about sexuality and race.

Ann had already begun incorporating a form-generates-content approach in *Ten Myths.* But making a theatrical event out of contained improvisations with real-life objects, performers, audiences, and impromptu environments, as *Ten Myths* did, and actually letting an environment generate its own art form, as the summer workshops had done, were two different things. The dance project she was about to embark on would do both and serve as her first foray into the social topography of race.

In working toward a truly participatory dance, Ann has acknowledged that she was inspired by Larry's steady insistence on finding the group's common experience and paying attention to the feeling as well as the content of people's statements and design goals. In eliciting felt responses to racial divides Ann would tap parts of a cultural and physical memory—something the performance theorist Joseph Roach explores in his idea of a "kinesthetic imagination" as a form of historical memory that each individual holds as a muscular artifact of the past.[31] Larry and Ann focused on how to take this embodied memory forward, into a deeper understanding of the intersection between human movements and how civic behaviors become sedimented in the body. They were aware that both urban design and postmodern dance, however much they might have emphasized openness and bringing the voices of the real world into the decision-making process, had effectively ignored one arena of deeply ingrained habits: that of a racial dichotomy.

Already in 1967, in his work with Paul Baum on mediating the dispute between Columbia University and the surrounding black neighborhood over the development of Morningside Park, Larry had found a way to defuse tensions considerably by giving people a way to map their own short-term destiny. While Ann had not been part of that project directly, the lessons about how one's place in society determines one's perception and capacity to call for change were not lost on her. By the summer of 1968, in the months following Martin Luther King Jr.'s assassination, she, like other leading liberal artists, was calling for more black participation in work for mainstream audiences.

Although Ann was not familiar with them at the time, several revolutionary models of theater for the dispossessed were already being explored. The Free Southern Theater, for example, had formed five years earlier, in 1963, in Tougaloo, Mississippi, with the goal of using theater to call for integration. Created by John O'Neal and Gilbert Moses, two writers working in the civil rights movement, and including the actor Eric Weinberger (a veteran of the Living Theater), the Free Southern Theater was envisioned as a means for "fortifying in the rural Southern Negro the sense of pride in his heritage from which a new way of life would be built."[32] In 1964 Richard Schechner, then a professor of drama at Tulane University in New Orleans, accepted an invitation to work with Free Southern Theater as a director, creating another direct link between the theater avant-garde and political action. The Brazilian theater director Augusto Boal's Theater of the Oppressed also emerged during this time with the goal of using theater to foster critical thinking among outcasts as a first step toward political action.

Ann's theater, however, differed from the Free Southern Theater and the Theater of the Oppressed because it was less didactic in content and much more focused on change for the performers rather than the audience. Perhaps most dissimilar was that Ann rarely knew going into a new piece just what its specific political aims and messages would be. What Ann did share with these groups was an emphasis on participatory theater, which is essentially rooted in the call-and-response tradition of African culture. The Kenyan social activist Ngũgĩ wa Thiong'o has lauded this tradition as the ideal pedagogical form of theater, because through call and response the drive toward change becomes a community effort.[33] Admittedly, Ann did not arrive at this way of working from theory as much as from being a perceptive observer of African American cultural practices around her. Her dance theater was not true call and response so much as a "try it, you'll like it" form of theater where the options are open and the stakes not so high. But an enriched sense of community was indeed one of its goals.

The political roots of the changes that led to Ann's investigation of race began three years earlier, on August 11, 1965, in the area of South Central Los Angeles known as Watts.[34] It was a hot and muggy evening when Lee Minkus, a California Highway Patrol officer, responded to a tip from a motorist, who had complained about a car that was speeding and weaving in and out of traffic. After pulling twenty-one-year-old Marquette Frye over, Minkus stepped off his motorcycle and began to fill in an arrest citation for drunk driving. A small crowd quickly gathered to watch with amusement as Frye humorously responded to the field sobriety test. It was 7 P.M. and already Frye and his brother, Ronald, had consumed several screwdrivers in celebration of Ronald's release from military service and his return home. Following procedure, Minkus radioed for backup and for a tow truck. The backup officer, tow truck, and Frye's mother, who had been summoned by a friend, all arrived within a few minutes, and the tone of the gathering shifted. Frye became belligerent, the officers swung at him with their riot batons, and issued a code 1199—Officer Needs Help—over the radio. Frye's brother, Ronald, and mother were both arrested as they tried to help him.

By now the crowd, growing angrier by the moment, had swelled to more than a hundred people. Continuing to follow the prescribed procedures for dealing with such a situation, officers poured into the area, sirens screaming. Advised to go home, the crowd began to disperse, when suddenly one of the police officers felt someone spit on him. He and another officer rushed the crowd and dragged out a young woman in a barber's smock, resembling a maternity dress, and threw her into a police car. Upon seeing this the crowd became enraged, and rocks, bottles, and bricks were thrown at the departing police vehicles. The Watts riot had begun. According to Larry Reed, a San Francisco participant in Ann's Dancers' Workshop, one of the members of the angry crowd that day reportedly was the mother of Xavier and Jasmine Nash, two Watts teens who would soon become leading teachers and performers with the Dancers' Workshop.[35]

The Watts riot lasted six days. In that time 34 people were killed (all but 2 of them African American), 1,034 people injured, 3,952 arrested, and 1,000 buildings burned. At least 31,000 African Americans were believed to have actively participated in the rioting. The strictest military curfew in fifty years for a domestic crisis was imposed on an area of forty-six and a half square miles (larger than the city of San Francisco).

In retrospect, the riot would come to be seen as a protest against a social system that many saw as broken, as an enactment of what analysts have called "the politics of violence" and "the politics of despair." Scores of studies and commissions investigated why this riot, a watershed event for American race relations, happened in the midst of a major national civil rights effort, with passage of the 1964 Civil Rights Act and the 1965 Voting Rights Act to support enforcement of the Fifteenth Amendment. The conclusion was that Los Angeles may have been the first, but it would certainly not be the last city rocked by the collision of a rapidly changing African American population with an indifferent white population controlling the institutions.[36] Indeed, for three years after the Watts riot other violent protests shook such cities as Chicago, Newark, Detroit, and Cleveland.

Within Watts itself, the riot was followed by a boom in projects and organizations rooted in the community, and in outside money to sustain them. One project, the Studio Watts School of the Arts, was actually started a few months before the riot by a group of nine artists, including a young theater artist, James Woods. This laboratory for art and theater exploration offered free classes in the visual arts (including ceramics), music, and theater, targeting young high school dropouts as its main population. Woods, the director, wanted to use the arts to help young people take leadership roles.

In June 1968 Woods was introduced to Ann's work when he happened to see a performance of *Lunch* by the Dancers' Workshop in San Francisco. He was attending a meeting of the Associated Council of the Arts at the Hilton Hotel as the guest of theater director Howard Adams, and Ann had been commissioned to perform during the lunch hour. Her piece *Lunch*, a one-time event held in the hotel's banquet room, had echoes of the call-and-response tradition in the recondite dialogue it set up between the audience and the performers. It was also an actively subversive form of theater because it offered a prototype for how to wrest power from those in control and claim it for oneself, at least for the duration of the lunch hour. During *Lunch* the spectators were prompted to become conscious of themselves as a community for the day, a community that had the ability to acknowledge itself as a powerful group.[37] This must have resonated as a vision of the future for Woods.

When Ann was asked to perform for the conference, she asked if the dancers might also eat with the attendees. "'Certainly,' was the reply," she later reported. "I didn't hint we'd be doing both simultaneously."[38] Letting the banquet hall venue set their theme, Ann and her dancers proceeded to dissect the "act" of eating lunch, using this act as the score for their dance. Just what did the physical act of eating lunch involve? According to Norma Leistiko, Ann decided this could be reduced to sitting down, picking up a fork, moving it to your mouth, and so on. "Ann then did variations on this theme, playing with tempi and spacing," Leistiko said.[39] The intention was to encourage the audience to identify with the performers by noticing that they too were eating, just like the dancers. Each performer was asked to eat in a particular style: one might always steal food from the other plates, while another might keep spilling things. Like the mirrors the hippies had held up to the tourists in the Gray Line buses the summer before, the treatment of eating as a slow-motion dance of fork raising and water sipping flirted with role reversal, turning the Hilton's grand ballroom lunch crowd into a giggly participatory audience.

On a raised platform in the center of the room where the eight hundred delegates were being served lunch, a spotlit table was set with white tablecloth, cloth napkins, silverware, and dishes identical to those on all the lunch tables in the room. Ann's leotard-clad dancers sat around this table, each posed at first in a frozen attitude of vacant concentration. Norma Leistiko crouched on top of the table staring down at the food like a half-wild, half-domesticated animal ruled by hunger and unsure of the proper social decorum in such an environment. Patric Hickey, billed as the performance's "environmental design expert," arranged candles on each of the tables and set up his lighting equipment at the sides so that the dancers' actions could be seen very clearly.

The commencement of the real lunch being served in the ballroom triggered the beginning of the performed *Lunch,* although not all the guests noticed this right away. Woods, for one, remembers asking his friend Adams when Ann's performance was going to begin. He was at first startled and then delighted when Adams explained that the dance was already well under way, that the people eating lunch in slow motion on the dais in the center of the ballroom *were* the dancers!

> I was kind of stunned by the fact that I had been midway through the lunch waiting for her dance presentation and then I realized it had already started. . . . I thought it was just the preparation and I said, "Well, when are the dancers coming?" And my friend said, "Well, you have been in the concert!" And I was stunned because I was affected by them. The process of perfection the dancers described in the act of eating made you think of the way you yourself were consuming food and the way you too were in the process of eating. I said, "This is really something else. I really want to get to know that person."[40]

As the delegates ate, the dancers echoed their actions in excruciatingly slow motion. "It was like watching living sculptures," William Glatkin, reviewing the performance for the *Sacramento Bee,* wrote.[41] Beneath this surface of docility and naive simplicity, however, the performance carried an edge; *Lunch* resonated with social satire, providing an acid commentary on the overdone social ritual of the business luncheon, in contrast to people's simple need to take in midday nourishment.

With his musical score for *Lunch,* Charles Amirkhanian (who had been with the Tape Music Center upstairs from Ann's Divisadero Street studio) helped to heighten the audience's awareness of the slowed-down eating:

> I worked with the audio technician John Payne, and we created a quizzical mix of Muzak-like radio station music broadcast recordings which were piped into the room from time to time, fading up for a few minutes, then down and out for a few minutes. This way we found we could choreograph the heads of the diners in the room. When they heard the odd Muzak, they'd turn toward the center of the banquet room where Ann and her dancers were, moving in slow motion, as if eating their lunches in a standing position. Lots of the motion had to do with lifting a fork

high over the head and stabbing an imaginary steak down at foot level on the tabletop, then slowly moving the fork toward the mouth. I am still amazed at the ability to turn heads of the guests by raising the sound up and down.[42]

It was not just the volume but more importantly the rhythm of the music—from Chopin to *Porgy and Bess* to rock-and-roll—that influenced the pace of the eating.

The establishment, even an arts-administration establishment, was accustomed to being the butt of public jokes, so it was likely in this spirit that they gave Ann what Leistiko described as a "cheering ovation." While fully aware that they were the target of her satire, they must have been relieved that their participatory roles had been so painless, inadvertent, and (unlike those on *Candid Camera*) nonhumiliating. Besides, Ann's method of working at this point seemed safely innocent of any overt social agenda. She focused on formal experimentation—in this case, the task of eating and its various forms, patterns, vocabulary—leaving the meanings to converge between the comfortably ambiguous and personally intimate (eating is a bodily function people don't generally like to be observed doing). Ann trusted that one's values radiated through one's work and that to be overtly political, as in the guerrilla theater of this time, resulted too often in statements that were as weak artistically as they were strident politically. She was never deliberately a politician, but she was often an astute artist-activist. The embodiment of performance for her intersected and overlapped therapeutic probings into the self. "We wanted to stimulate in the audience a sense of community by . . . pointing up that we are all performers in the 'performing' of our normal activities," Ann wrote soon after the event.[43]

Half a year earlier, in the fall of 1967, two of the most flamboyant antiwar activists, Jerry Rubin and Abbie Hoffman, in a purely political gesture, had created a public event that shared a spirit of confrontation cloaked in humor similar to that of Ann's *Lunch*. Under the guise of responding to an announcement by the Washington police that they were ready to use a new stinging, temporarily blinding spray called Mace, Hoffman and Rubin announced a new drug of their own, "Lace." Lace, they said, when squirted onto the skin or clothes, quickly penetrates to the bloodstream, causing the subject to disrobe and get sexually aroused. As Todd Gitlin describes it, "Before bemused reporters, two couples sprayed each other with water pistols full of a fluid . . . called *Schwartz Disappear-O!* imported from Taiwan, which was as good as its name: it made purple stains and then disappeared. The couples proceeded to tear off their clothes and make love, not war."[44]

Here, as in Ann's *Lunch*, the object was to illuminate reality by satirizing a business-as-usual practice and hold it up for public scrutiny. In *Lunch* the performance exposed the hypocrisy of the business lunch, where taking in sustenance is one of the least significant goals. In Hoffman and Rubin's demonstration, the notion of a new "street" weapon that would cause individuals to make love not war neatly turned the table on the escalating aggression of the time. What if we performed art three times a day instead of just eating a meal? What if police sprayed affection instead of discomfort over the crowds of disenfranchised students? A revolution could start here.

Theatricalizing the act of eating, while on the surface an innocuous and even whimsical gesture, actually taps into significant issues about social discipline, memory, class, and even race. Perhaps what Woods responded to was the tacit social and class critique in *Lunch*, tacit even to Ann. Paul Connerton argues that a mnemonic and ceremonial display of bodily control is often vividly enacted through the etiquette for eating. Ann seems here to have intuitively gravitated toward a gesture that was simple on the surface yet profound in its interior implications. This was one of the steadiest lessons and most frequent epiphanies of her theater—that standing outside a practice allows one to notice how performing authorizes a new set of symbolic meanings to be assigned to actions. By focusing on what is there in a ritual practice, like sitting still on chairs at a table and manipulating utensils to eat, one can see what isn't there, the invisible "rules" behind these actions. Manipulating these rules can then become the basis for turning life actions into performance gestures.

> The implements used at the Western table are not implements with obvious purposes and evident uses. Over the course of centuries . . . their functions were gradually defined, their forms consolidated, and the values attached to those functions and forms slowly inculcated. The way in which knife, fork and spoon are held and moved was standardized step by step; the practice of using a fork was acquired slowly, as was the habit of taking liquid only with a spoon . . . they are technical skills imbued with moral values. . . . What is being remembered is a set of rules for defining 'proper' behaviour; the control of appetite in the most literal sense is part of a much wider process which will appear, depending upon our vantage point, either as a structure of feeling or as a pattern of institutional control.[45]

With *Lunch,* Ann was responding intuitively to this relationship between behavior and social and institutional control. This is a relationship in which the body is the "point of linkage," to use Connerton's terminology.

Critiquing an institution from within the institution can be both mischievous and dangerous, and this is what made Ann's work such a flashpoint for both social and artistic activists of the 1960s. "Everything she does is prophetic," Amirkhanian said about Ann. "Where we see barriers, she sees possibilities."[46] Ann's work could stand as easy satire or trenchant social critique. *Lunch* exaggerates the internalized constraints that rule us in as common a practice as eating, and in this way brings out important nuances about the lines between our public and private lives and civility and the cultured control of appetites. Through table manners we see how rules of consumption get remembered in the body.

———

Ann may not have focused directly on the political situation in her work to this point, but she was living in a time of accelerating political and social awareness, not only in the nation as a whole but in the Bay Area in particular. Beginning in 1965, as the first American combat troops landed in Vietnam, antiwar protests erupted at UC Berkeley, followed by huge public demonstrations against the draft at the induction center in Oakland. The assassination of Malcolm X in February 1965 drew attention to his call for black nationalism, while the Watts riots underlined African Americans' anger at ongoing inequities. In the fall of 1966 Huey P. Newton and Bobby Seale founded the Black Panther Party for Self-Defense in Oakland, which soon gained national attention. The year 1968 brought increasing turmoil. Martin Luther King Jr. was assassinated in April and Robert Kennedy in June. The United Farm Workers' grape boycott went national, and women's liberation groups started as part of the women's movement that had been growing since the 1966 founding of the National Organization for Women.

There was both an expansive and a theatrical quality to many of the protest events of the time—as if social conflict were suddenly being played out on a scale designed to capture the attention of the media and the hearts and sentiments of the nation. An event had to be big enough to make large numbers feel it was their community issue, yet personalized enough to make one care on an emotional level. Costuming was part of the political package. The identifiable look of the Black Panthers, for example, heightened the impact of their message. As Bobby Seale recalled, the Black Panthers' all-black uniform of pants, leather jacket, turtleneck, sunglasses, and beret was inspired in part by an old movie on the French underground that he, Eldridge Cleaver, and Huey Newton watched one evening on television.[47]

Just as theater was becoming the means of politics, so too were political issues becoming the stuff of theater, particularly in the Bay Area. In the fall of 1965 members of the San Francisco Mime Troupe, a fledgling street theater group, were arrested for using obscenity in *Il Candelaio,* a free play staged in Golden Gate Park. The troupe's young manager immediately arranged a benefit for the arrested actors. At the benefit, the manager, Bill Graham, discovered rock music, simultaneously launching his career as a presenter and the Bay Area's reputation as America's center of rock music. "San Francisco created the sound for the revolution," Wavy Gravy has said about the era.[48] Ann created the dance.

Indeed, the pulsing, pumping beat of rock and colorful, amorphous splashes of light shows seemed to underscore the salient subjects of the time—sex, a new body awareness, and a focus on inward experience as a precursor to external, social action. For anyone living and working in the Bay Area at the time, the words and the pulse of this music revolution were inescapable. "The lyrics of rock and roll and the music made a lot of white people do what most of them had never done before—move pelvically, publicly," Bill Graham wryly observed. It was an insight not lost on Ann, who also, in response to the era's loosening attitudes about sexuality and physical expression, was working to broaden her performance vocabulary with movement and improvisatory situations, including nudity and more openly sensual and potentially erotic situations.

Another undercurrent of these times was the romance between liberal Jewish artists and black political causes.[49] While the Dancers' Workshop performers and audiences may have been predominantly white, just the act of setting up shop in the predominantly black Western Addition neighborhood was a significant gesture of interracial support in the 1960s. The Fillmore Auditorium, Graham's landmark venue for his weekly rock concerts by groups that included the Grateful Dead, the Jefferson Airplane, and Country Joe McDonald and the Fish, was located a couple of miles away from Ann's studio on the other side of the Western Addition neighborhood. More than just inexpensive rent, there was a certain political idealism at the time that prompted Jewish Americans like Ann and Graham, who had emigrated from Poland just before World War II, to locate their music and dance centers in San Francisco's black community. (By 1971, however, Graham would close the Fillmore Ballroom, and Ann would follow suit two years later, moving most of her operations from Divisadero to San

Francisco's Fort Mason for two years and then to her home studio in Kentfield.)

———————

James Woods called Ann in late July 1968 to ask her to create a work like *Lunch* with his group of young theater people in Watts. "I wanted her to come in as a teacher and to work with African Americans in Watts," Woods recollected. "And out of that action would occur a piece that would be a statement of that process, a statement of the involvement of a master dancer with apprentices. That's what I was attracted to, and that's the experience I wanted to commission an original work about."[50]

According to Ann, "When James Woods called I recognized from his voice and his way of talking that I was talking to a black man. But he never said anything about that; then when he said he was from Studio Watts I put the two together." She listened to his proposal, but she immediately began rewriting the assignment: "I remember thinking to myself, 'Now this is a great opportunity!' He was shocked when he asked me if I would do it and I said, 'Absolutely no!' Then I followed up by telling him what I wanted to do was develop an all-black company at Studio Watts. 'Can you make this possible?' [I] asked."[51] What Ann had in mind was eventually to see what would happen if a group of black dancers from Watts came together with her all-white San Francisco company. The negotiations, tensions, and realities of that encounter would become the basis for a performance embracing audience participation as well.

It took awhile to hammer out the details, but in late September Ann began commuting weekly to Watts. She was to be paid a total of two thousand dollars, most of it coming from money Woods had raised from private sources. For the next five months Ann flew down to Los Angeles early every Saturday morning at her own expense. She spent the full day, from 9 A.M. to 6 P.M. with an hour-long lunch break, in an intensive workshop session with eleven Studio Watts performers before returning to the Bay Area at night. It seemed to Ann she did little else during that period except work on the Watts performance, either planning for each Saturday marathon or working with the San Francisco contingent. Patric Hickey was overseeing a repeat of some of the previous year's successful *Myths* performances at the Divisadero studio; Ann was involved, but her priority was to pull the Watts project together.

From the first, "fascinating" day, Woods remembered, Ann made a strong impression. The Studio Watts performers "were impressed with her because

Ann is a very dynamic woman." According to Woods, she told them she hoped they would be able to explore their interactions and "to work out their own energies and myths and directions."

According to one of the Studio Watts participants, Wanda Coleman, Ann conducted auditions for the Watts performers by watching them interact with one another and sort through "power dynamics" as they set up relationships in improvisatory exercises. Coleman said she was selected as the "symbolic earth mother" of the group: "I was the biggest. I weighed about one hundred sixty pounds at the time. So I was heavy. I was probably the least physically attractive in the sense that the dominant culture understands beauty or defines it."[52]

Ann did not have any technical requirements for the group. "None of them were trained dancers or movers per se," she recalled, "but Jim Woods had been doing interesting things with them so I just basically took whoever he had."[53] In total, seven men and four women were selected for the Watts group.

Soon after Ann started working with the Watts group, she began shaping a counterpart group of eleven dancers in San Francisco. She soon had eight women (many of whom, including her daughters, had already performed with the Dancers' Workshop), but to create more of a gender balance she added three men between the ages of eighteen and twenty-five whom she auditioned in San Francisco in late October specifically for the Watts performance.[54] She began rehearsing this group every afternoon, from 4 to 6 P.M., on the dance deck. Larry Reed, one of the men selected from the audition, recalled the climate of intensity and experimentation with its emphasis on what the dancers were feeling: "I think this was one of the transition projects for Ann, where she went from being performance oriented to being therapy oriented. She was very excited about Fritz Perls at the time and that whole movement, the Gestalt thing. And she really went from wanting to be an avant-garde theater person to wanting to be a therapeutic dance person. And this was on the way to that."[55]

Rather than turning outward in an effort to make a large political statement, Ann seems to have been catalyzed by the social moment to turn more deeply inward. Her work in Watts would change the scale of her artistic imagining. Decades later she reflected that in bringing together the all-black Watts and all-white San Francisco groups, she attempted "to use my experience with Gestalt therapy to integrate emotional responses through an art process instead of therapy. I wanted the dancer to be a whole person."[56] Unlike *Ten Myths,* in which she had to create the situation to induce emotions and then explore those emotions through movement, the Watts performers already had a reserve of strong emotions. Reed noticed this as well, remarking on the difference when the two groups came together: "I think the challenge there [was] to direct these hippie feelings of sort of vague, all-encompassing love, and then these ghetto feelings that are very much more directed, and to make a mix of them all—that required each of us to really become someone else, to open up, to be more than we had been."

Coleman, who would become an accomplished poet but who at the time was on welfare with two young children and a marriage that would soon break up, pinpointed one difference. She recalled that the Watts performers responded to the opportunity to work with Ann with an enthusiasm approaching desperation: "You have to remember that all these carrots of opportunity were being held out to young blacks at that time and I was snatching for the carrots just like everybody else. We saw this as a real possibility. All the black members of that troupe felt this was a beginning, that this was going to take us to great heights."

Ann herself entered into the project charged with the excitement of embarking on a new undertaking, one redolent of social discovery and emotional change. For her the first shock was the setting of Watts itself. "I was not so much surprised as touched," Ann said of that first visit to Watts. "In those days to see that kind of poverty was shocking. And it reinforced the sense I had of the polarization in our community and our society. It was much more of a ghetto than anything I had ever seen in San Francisco. You really didn't see any white people at all. I was the only white person in sight."[57]

The thing that struck Ann most about the initial rehearsals was that there was little room for make-believe in the gestural language of these performers: "The intensity was mind-boggling. It was like nothing I'd ever experienced before. I remember at one point having them share weight by taking partners, holding hands and pulling gently back and forth. I started to demonstrate with John Hopkins, and I realized as I started doing it that they were not abstract about movement at all. It immediately triggered off a sense of challenge and competition, and it suddenly became a black man and a white woman pulling." The rest of the performers gathered around and watched with growing interest as Ann planted her feet, realizing she had walked into a drama larger than both of them. For Ann, that one movement turned into a dance metaphor for the struggle between African American men and white women, a public testing of her mettle as the workshop leader. It was an exchange that would be played out repeatedly in the months ahead, prophetic of both the politics and the sexual territory the Watts project would explore.

The dancers dubbed Ann "Blue-Eyed Soul Mama Number One" as an affectionate tribute to her grit and sincerity. "We loved that woman down to her dirty drawers, as they say in the ghetto," Coleman laughed. "In fact, we loved Jim Woods too. I don't think there are two people I've known in my experience in an artistic arena that were more loved, with no reservation."

Soon after the initial challenge to her determination, Ann decided to introduce an exercise drawn from the "Experiments in Environment" workshop. She was working hard to define the Studio Watts performers as a cohesive community, a community that trusted her direction enough to follow her into the risky territory of personal exploration. The assignment Ann planned was for the performers to each blindfold themselves securely and then join hands while she led them on a serpentine walk through the neighborhood surrounding Studio Watts. The idea was that with the sense of sight closed to all but Ann, the performers would be dependent on her vision and their own hard-working other four senses to experience the environment. They were effectively "blinding" themselves in order to "see."

As it happened, however, Ann's plane was fogged in at the San Francisco airport the morning the walk was scheduled. So an assistant of Woods, a young white woman with no particular experience doing this sort of thing, took Ann's place as leader of the line. For Coleman, it proved a disastrous substitution. A few minutes into the exercise, as Coleman clutched the hand of Xavier Nash and moaned that she had a strong premonition that something bad was going to happen if she continued to walk blindfolded, her upturned face smacked into a lamppost and the metal pole shattered her right front tooth. She became hysterical and had to be carried back to the studio by three men, bringing that experiment in trust to an abrupt end. Woods saw that Coleman got a false tooth made, and the next week she was back in rehearsal, wary but determined to make this opportunity work for her.

After that mishap the rehearsals in Watts continued relatively uneventfully, with Woods a steady presence in the studio. He participated mostly from the sidelines, assisting with administrative details and watching, as he called it, each performer embarking on a personal "healing process"— "healing his sense of who he was."

In late January 1969 Ann brought the two groups together for the first time for an intensive ten-day joint rehearsal period before they performed together in Los Angeles. The dance now had a title, *Ceremony of Us,* but no cohesive order had been set, nor had a specific body of material to be included in the performance been chosen. Ann was trusting the interaction of the two groups to generate the shape and focus of the event. The black group and the white group now both had a voice in movement; the charge was to create a physical conversation for the stage.

For Ann, the intensity of that first meeting, which was held in her San Francisco studio, was both electrifying and frightening. She decided to designate the Watts group as "hosts" for the day, and they gathered outside the studio door, preparing their entrance, with the white dancers sitting inside as their audience and "blind date" partners. Pepe Hill then led the Watts dancers in a serpentine line around and through the large studio. The impact of the Watts group's opening was extraordinary. It was as if that snaking line of eleven people, linked hands to hips, contained a distillation of the Watts performers' aspirations and trepidation. As they passed the stream of movement down the line, the dancers' weight was firmly into the ground, and the action rippled through their spines, into their pelvises, and ended in eleven pairs of feet slamming as one into the floor. The men exhaled a guttural "HA!" with a volume and intensity that left the white men in Dancers' Workshop bracing themselves for a power challenge. Melinda West, a twenty-year-old member of the Dancers' Workshop group at the time, recalled crying at the raw expression of rage the stamping line of Watts performers generated.[58]

The white dancers responded to the black group's dance of introduction with their own line dance of open, expansive, and consciously shaped gestures. Ann sat on the sidelines, anxiously wondering, "How are these two groups ever going to move with any kind of cohesion?" The answer came as the two lines of dancers sinuously curved paths through the studio, the blacks trying to "steal" dancers from the white line and the whites trying to steer away from the building confrontation. A pair of drummers— one a virtuoso black musician, Billy C. Jackson, and the other a young white one, Casey Sonnabend—played congas in the corner, and Ann and Woods watched silently as the dancers worked toward finding their own resolution.

"Life is being now, not yesterday," Ann's voice intones at the start of the film *Right On!* which Seth Hill made of the initial days of the joint workshop, as the two groups began to explore one another and intense emotions seemed to coat every exchange. "Now is something you don't know, you have to discover it."[59] Rather than starting out with a preconception of the final performance, Ann was willing to let the dancers discover their dance through their encounters with each other. As much an opportunity for redefinition as healing, the rehearsals offered all participants the chance to examine and possibly begin to re-create not just themselves but the racial attitudes of their society. The concrete poet Liam O'Gallagher, who assisted in the workshops once the two groups came together, explained: "We were all there for various reasons, but we were intent on proving that we could and would use each other as a bridge. The object was not to make something that was aesthetically pure but to create something that was real and would prove itself over time."[60] Through dance, Ann was offering the possibility of reconstituting the world, at least temporarily, within the confines of the studio. This in fact would become the emphasis of the Watts piece. Not so much a dance as a lived experiment in attempting to erase boundaries, prohibitions, and taboos, *Ceremony of Us* would turn out to be in equal measure both daring and timid, both a challenge to the status quo of racial stereotypes and an unwitting reinforcement of the sexual and class myths embedded in them.

In a "cut-up" poem that he created based on what he saw and tape-recorded of the dancers' experiences, O'Gallagher offers a distillation of the *Ceremony of Us* workshop experience. The splash of one-word impressions suggests a chaotic, emotionally intense climate, where personal revelation and sexual tensions dominated. In the poem the biggest and boldest fonts are reserved for the words "naked," "love," "reality," "risk," and "intensity."[61] As O'Gallagher later commented, "Rehearsals were highly charged emotional encounters. They would last from two to three hours. My job was to help Ann resolve not only borders, but barriers and boundaries of centuries of fear, mistrust, and hate due to inequality and ignorance. It was painful. The nice thing, of course, was there was a maximum allowance for improvising, and I think this was Ann's greatest contribution to modern dance. She allowed the form to emerge rather than imposing it."

Initially, Ann used many of the same tasks for generating movement and allowing a form to emerge that she had used in other rehearsal and workshop situations. As Ann has described it, "[We used] body exercises, massages, psychic-stress movement, improvisations to break through an individual or group impasse, drawings, self-portraits, and group portraits. We modeled ourselves in clay, we wrote about the ways we identified with our workshop experience, we spent time breathing in and out of each other with our bodies; vocalizing, singing, touching, looking, leading and following with our eyes closed, acting out dreams, fantasizing with dress-up costumes, acting out roles on street corners with pedestrians as audience.

When things got too heavy, we'd play tag, have horse races, do red light–green light, construct pyramids with our bodies, etc."[62] For Ann, such childhood games were a favorite device for generating movement because not only were they disarming in their simplicity but they suggested, deceptively, that the content was light and playful. "I used games to offer a container and focus for placing the intensity of conflict and competition into fun and play," Ann observed later. "But even then we had plenty of explosions. I wanted to find some balance."[63] Ann may also have been thinking of her early success at generating creativity by using games in her children's classes during the 1940s and 1950s, and she may have been influenced by a resurgence of these games' popularity in the mid-1960s.[64]

The games provided straightforward scores. For example, if the direction was to play follow-the-leader, one person would lead off with a movement, which a line of people would then copy, one at a time. For red light–green light, the focus turned from making movements to one's speed in secretly sprinting up behind a designated leader and trying to overtake that person before she or he turned around and yelled, "Red light!" Abstract movement itself was rarely what interested Ann in introducing these games; rather, she was trying to wipe away preconceptions about proper dance actions. "I was working to establish a common language between the black and white groups," Ann said later. "I wanted to show that a value system was being created mutually and that I was there simply to set the tone, to generate creativity but not to write the score." It was an aesthetic as well as pragmatic choice: "Working with a group of black people in Watts who mistrusted the white culture and had felt unheard, not listened to, not paid attention to— this in retrospect was the only way I could imagine I could have worked and that they could have accepted me. It took everything I had just to be alert every minute."[65] It is curious, however, that Ann chose children's games that play with testing authority as the bedrock of building a new value system with the Watts and San Francisco performers. Children's games can be fiercely competitive and hierarchical, reinforcing rather than repudiating power structures.

The two groups found they had a lot to negotiate in ten days of rehearsal together before the performance in Los Angeles. Reed recalled feeling on edge throughout the process: "I do remember that we became very intensely involved with each other and that it was threatening to a lot of people. There was nothing monolithic about it at all. Every kind of emotion that you could imagine came up, and some of it was positive and some of it really wasn't, except that through Ann's coaching, we kept going and kept trying to trust the process basically."

Ann's way of working involved a kind of psychological nudity that proved a lot more risky than the physical nudity of the "Experiments in the Environment" workshops. Without consciously aiming to do so, Ann had arrived at the threshold of many of the tensions and myths of racism. Bolstered in part by her work with Fritz Perls, she knew how to probe and loosen emotions in the art-making process. What she wasn't equipped for, and eventually would choose to ignore, were the larger implications of social tensions and societal racism. Up to this point her art had never been deliberately about grand issues, only personal and immediate ones that by honest exploration could become so transparent they became universal. Now she was trying to translate this onto a big screen. As Larry Reed expressed it:

> We were trying to do something that was much talked about and very little accomplished at the time, which was to work together between the two races. There were a few music groups that achieved that. And very little else. So there was a lot of talk about integration and very little action on it. And we just went right into it. I guess it was a psychically dangerous area to go into, for everybody involved. And the fact that we could, and that we could come through it, and that we could do something with it, I think, was hugely significant.

Ann counted on therapeutic means and a trusting relationship like that between a therapist and client to select the information and then the instinct of a performer to shift focus to deliver this information to an audience.[66] What made this method particularly incendiary with the Watts project was that Ann did not mute this confrontational aspect of her process even as she moved into race as her topic. Rana Halprin, who was sixteen at the time, recalled that from her perspective, the Watts cast didn't seem dramatically different than other groups of artists her mother had worked with. When Rana stopped by the studio one afternoon after high school and joined in the workshop, she felt that the tensions in the room could be bridged by innocently and intuitively employing the mirroring movement skills she had learned from Ann, skills that years later she dubbed "empathetic bonding." In her words:

> I walked in the studio one afternoon, [and] people were in the midst of confrontation and shouting—trying to find resolution in Perls's Gestalt

style, which I was not into. There was one male participant in the Watts group who was on the floor, weeping. No one knew what to do—so my mother asked me to go in. I went in and simply got down next to him and curled up into a ball mirroring his position on the floor. I reached out and held his hands and stayed present with him until he stopped crying. After a while he shifted, tears turned into some sort of release, because he jumped up and put me on his shoulders and went into the street with me still riding on his shoulders. After that the male participants in the Watts group were all very, very protective of me because of the way I chose to relate.[67]

Other participants, however, had a different perspective. Wanda Coleman felt that Ann and Woods deliberately steered away from looking at the core of the Watts experience—the 1965 riot and racism. To her, racism was the implicit, but never satisfactorily addressed, subject in *Ceremony of Us:*

It's complex. Racism is the largest part of it because it was a black and white statement and you could not ignore that. But if we were truly going to function on the level that they said we were going to, then we had to come to a certain understanding. [But] there was a sort of naiveté on Ann's part. That we could get eleven black kids together and eleven white kids together and make this wonderful racial statement. Well, they made one all right. It is not a simplistic thing that all is peace and love and light and candles. All that stuff was nice. But it had nothing to do with what is the ugliness and nastiness of what racism really is. Until you get down to the root you ain't going nowhere. And as artists, the minute they got close to that they started running scared.

Here Coleman might have referred to the words of Richard Wright, who, in a radio broadcast in Paris in September 1960, said: "Our life is still invisible to whites. It remains outside the pale of whites' preoccupations. I'd like to hurl words in my novels in order to arouse whites to the fact that there is someone here with us. Negroes, a human presence."[68] In Coleman's view there was a lot more at stake than simply bringing black and white dancers together to create a performance:

You see I was passing through. But these people I knew [the other dancers in the Watts group], they were investing everything in that experience. What went wrong . . . was racism. They did not understand, neither Ann nor Jim, what they were doing. And they did not understand the dynamics of racism. They didn't really understand how deep it went and how people would respond to it.

It had never been Ann's interest or method to seek social engagement directly. Her focus was always pointedly on the *individual's* experience. What came out of that she mediated through scores, prescriptions for acting out in the safe environment of theater. But for her the glimpse of strained fury that the Watts workshop brought was tantalizing.

Ann would later call *Ceremony of Us* absolutely pivotal in her work, illuminating for her the possibility of using "real people dealing with their real life issues" as art. "You can separate your life from your art, but it is so exciting and full of creative possibilities if you don't," she said. She acknowledged that she had no real plan for what *Ceremony of Us* would look like. "Wherever we were at the end of ten days would be our statement about who we are in relationship to blacks and whites," she said. "I didn't know what the outcome would be. It might not be very pleasant or it might be very hopeful. I was after a microcosm and it was very risky."[69]

That riskiness came out in the ways issues around, and distinctions between, sensuousness, sexuality, and intimacy played out along racial and gender divides. "When these white people saw these [Watts] guys coming in doing these movements, they were blown away," Ann recalled. "They'd never seen anything like it in their lives. The way black people move, the way street people move. It was totally raw and direct and had all the intensity and solidity and openness of street dance. There they were out there with their bodies and so sensuous!"[70] Melinda West had a somewhat different take: she recalled, "I remember wondering what it would be like to get to know these people. Then the arguing started, and this whole dynamic came out, and I got kind of scared, especially when I heard that some of these black men had never even touched a white person before." For most, the sensual subtext was hard to ignore. Coleman noted: "As we worked, the intimacies of sweat and smell unraveled tension. By the end of the day we knew each other as well as it is possible to know another's body sans sexual intercourse."[71]

Ann tried to ground the emotions that came up more in the realm of the sensual than the erotic. In the *Right On!* film she demonstrates an exercise, working with two black men clad in brief swim trunks. She prompts them, using touch and words, to release the pelvis and buttocks to increase openness in the hips. Her level of ease at touching the bare skin of men's bodies, especially in a region near their genitals, seems very progressive for the time. Squatting down, she cups her hands under the buttocks of one of the black men and models what she calls "a respectful, scientific, and not sexual way of relating to the body."[72] Ann's mother, then seventy-six, was not so sure about this distinction. When Ida Schuman received a postcard announcement for the film broadcast, she expressed shock that Ann would allow such "cheap" filming of intimacies between the dancers. In a reply to her mother, Ann explained, "To read intimacy as trust, warmth and openness between young people of conflicting race differences is quite different than if it is being read as 'cheap.' What I see in Hollywood movies is cheap because relationships are shallow and of no particular humanistic desire for improving understanding between people."[73]

Ann's use of bodies in the film is paradoxically chaste yet intensely physical in a way that invites the spectator to begin to construct her or his own narrative of memory. These seem to be bodies with private, yet immediately accessible, personal histories. As the dancers tenderly stroke water along the skin of their partners and then stroke them dry with towels, or as they stare at the mirrored reflection of their partner and say, "I see the tip of a gold zipper on the top of your shorts," they are enacting complex visual seductions with one another. Ann later said her intention with this exercise had been to lead the dancers to distinguish between what was "real" and what was a fantasy projection, the kind of behavior she thought might lead to racial prejudice.[74]

One of the most pointed elements of risk involved the tensions between black women and white women that saturated many of the workshop exchanges. In the liminal space between society and art opened up in the process of creating *Ceremony of Us,* desire and suspicion—polarized emotions that can be especially frightening across racial lines—had a chance to be aired and acted on within parameters of safety. Coleman later wrote a poem about the workshop, "A War of Eyes," in which she depicts some of the tensions that arose through the metaphor of an intense, theatricalized battle between herself and a white woman.[75] In the poem Coleman's dislike builds to such a fury that she is about to inflict serious physical injury on a white woman in the workshop under the guise of following one of Ann's directives. Although the Dancers' Workshop members were familiar with how Ann used the real emotions that emerged, improvising with them to create performative, narrative material, the performers from Watts didn't have the same training history with Ann, so for them the feelings elicited may have hovered much closer to the real than the metaphoric. "The point of the piece was to work with tension and reconciliation metaphorically," Daria explained, underlining that "this was a radical and brave work coming right after the Watts riots."[76] Ann believed so deeply in the salutary capacity of dance metaphors that she seemed not to have worried about the dangers of the literal anger and hostility that had fueled the Watts riots and still simmered in many of the exchanges between these white and black youths.

During the *Ceremony of Us* era, Daria later noted, "it was more about letting it all hang out than letting it all hang out for the purpose of putting it back together in a way that was healthy." She explained that, for Ann, "the main thrust was, and still is, to let it all hang out as artistically as possible. If it gets put back together, that's a booby prize." It was only later, Daria indicated, that Ann learned through her work with psychotherapists, as did Daria (who later became a movement therapist), that "one has to be very careful because this [process] can be detrimental and dangerous, and I think it has been."[77]

Ann did try to defuse the tensions, asking Berkeley psychologist Paul Baum to lead a group session with the performers. Indeed, Baum had already been meeting with Ann for several months about her difficulties around this performance. As he later remarked to James Woods, "Ann has had to confront some issues in her life that she has avoided with an incredible tenacity. I am sure it is true that any artist confronts himself in the process of creation."[78] When Baum came into the group as a "human relations consultant," he said, somewhat cryptically, "Things had gotten very, very wild and wooly." As he reported it, "I don't know that I helped at all. But apparently my presence was helpful because I still [decades later] hear about it."[79]

To a great degree the "wild and wooly" scene that Baum described centered on sexual tensions. Hidden power relations were seen as tainting many exchanges between blacks and whites at the time, particularly sexual exchanges. Black Panther Eldridge Cleaver's *Soul on Ice,* published in March 1968, was being widely read at the time, particularly its most provocative essays, which painted a complex picture of sexual relations as the archetype of black oppression. The black man, Cleaver charged, had been emasculated because the white woman, symbol of his oppression, was taboo.[80] The charged couplings between some of the *Ceremony of Us* performers may have seemed to refute that taboo, but they still upheld the traditional power dynamics of gender. Moreover, Coleman pointed out, "that myth about love being able to overcome all turned out to be a myth"—most of the romantic liaisons in the workshop were short-lived.

At one point tensions between the men and the women intensified to a boiling point, so Ann separated the sexes for two days, sending all the men into the large studio and the women into the smaller one. At the end of the second day they came together to share the dances they had created. The men, black and white, formed a line and like a flank of warriors performed a furious stomping dance in tight unison as they surged forward.[81] The women offered a parallel essentialization of gender roles by enacting a childbirth scene. Coleman was selected by the group to give birth to a white woman dancer. The other women crouched in front of Coleman and in unison pulled her first to one side and then the other while she moaned as if in labor. Ann viewed these dances as critical turning points where sexuality as a tool for power and domination softened into intimacy and trust between the sexes, and they became incorporated into the final performance.[82] For Coleman, the "birthing" dance was a particularly memorable experience. During a later rehearsal, while embracing the "baby," she began spontaneously singing the lullaby "All the Pretty Little Horses" a cappella in her strong, husky voice. When she did this in the actual performance, the audience told her to keep singing after she finished the song, and she did. "I will never forget it," she recalled twenty-five years later. "It was like the audience was one mind, like this beast out there who said you haven't sung enough, sing more. It was the most electrifying audience I've ever had."

The material in the performance on February 27, 1969, at the Mark Taper Forum at the new Los Angeles Music Center complex served as a metaphorical refrain of the discoveries made in the workshop process. The performance was framed with an opening and closing sequence of gentle audience participation. At the start, borrowing from an incident during the joint rehearsal period, Ann had all the Studio Watts performers line up along one aisle leading into the theater and all the Dancers' Workshop performers along the other. The entering audience was thus faced with the choice of walking down a corridor of either black or white performers. And the audience for this single performance was as racially mixed as the performers were. Woods, who was chairman of the Second Annual Los Angeles Festival of the Arts, of which this performance was a featured part, had bussed in scores of blacks from Watts. So what happened was that the entire audience spontaneously divided according to color.

As they walked down their respective lines, the performers made the audience the focus of another workshop task—holding up small mirrors in front of various audience members, the performers briefly described three vistas as they looked at the individual audience members: "this is what I see," "this is what I imagine I see," and "this is what I want to see." Ann remembered that the black members of the audience immediately got into the spirit and responded back, while the whites for the most part walked in embarrassed silence to their seats.

The performers then moved to the stage platform, stopping at the edge to take off their everyday clothing, stripping down to briefs and leotards.[83] They had all previously recorded their own reactions to looking at each other, and these became the starting point for the performance, as they began gazing at and touching each other. Then the dancers split into two groups—black and white—snaking in a line behind a leader as they confronted each other in different ways. Eventually the men in both groups split apart into a "contest" of masculinity before the women. The women then performed their "birthing ritual," after which the men and women danced together and finally paired off for a ceremonial washing of each other. Taking their bowls of water and towels, the performers then moved out to gently bathe the hands of several members of the audience. This ritualistic cleansing was intended by Ann as a task performance of metaphorically washing away surface differences of skin color. It concluded the first half of the program, called "Starting Point." As Jim Burns later described this opening half, "Almost no one in the performance of 'Starting Point' lost his own identity, although the entire effect was a beautiful microcosm of people struggling together and against each other not only to survive but to *be*."[84]

Following an intermission, the second section, "Continuing," began with Norma Leistiko functioning as an onstage director. She pointed to a huge chart at the rear of the stage, where a variety of activities were written on sheets of butcher paper. Among the "choices" were such traditional children's games as red light–green light and tug-of-war, as well as new "games," invented for the performance, and more tasklike options, such as "carry." Whatever activity Leistiko pointed to, the performers had to execute it, continuing full-out until she suddenly shifted to another instruction. Neither winning/losing nor accuracy in following directions was the focus here. Rather, these were the structures for getting this radical assortment of performers (radical for 1969 in its mixing of blacks and whites) to move *together* in an atmosphere of mutual discovery.

The performance concluded with the dancers moving through the aisles, inviting the audience to join in a processional out into the courtyard outside the theater. There *Ceremony of Us* participants met the exiting audiences from the two adjacent theaters. For the performers it was an incredible event. "We were so happy, we were swinging from the trees outside," Coleman recalled. But after the euphoric premiere, *Ceremony of Us* lived on only in a couple of local performances and on film. The line between the real and the acted, between art and life, as portrayed in the film of the workshop sessions and the memories of the performers, looms thin.

Indeed, underlying tensions surfaced as soon as the day after the performance, at a lunchtime "seminar" held at Studio Watts to "review the entire concept of the Festival and to forecast the Festival for 1970."[85] Led by Woods, Ann, and Baum, the meeting began with a heated discussion by the performers, who were angry that their names had not been included in the printed program but had instead been listed on a mimeographed insert, where they were arranged alphabetically in two columns—one for the white performers and one for the black performers, including black drummer Billy C. Jackson. In the partial transcript that exists of this meeting the performers' argument rages for several pages with both the white and the black dancers passionately explaining how hurt they felt by this oversight, particularly since they had spent the previous five months creating this dance piece. Baum later summarized the larger issues behind this dispute:

> It seemed remarkable and fitting to me that the issues [that came up] so closely paralleled the issues being raised by minority groups in all phases of society. Here we were faced with the problem in a group that had just completed a performance of a dance which supposedly had made some statement to the issues that are dividing our society. The active, vocal minority was saying "we want in, we want to be included, we want a piece of the action, we want self determination, we want a share of the profits." The Establishment, in this case represented by Jim and Ann, was stating, "We know what's best for you and we'll run things benevolently, but we run them."[86]

As Baum explained, this issue was further complicated by the fact that Ann, although ostensibly asking the performers if they wanted to perform *Ceremony of Us* in San Francisco, had already placed an option on a theater, and the Dilexi Gallery Foundation was to privately produce a record using tapes of some of the workshop discussions. Charles Amirkhanian, who created the electronic tape score for *Ceremony of Us* and worked on the record, described the studio atmosphere as one of "combustion": "Ann felt she could bring the [Watts] dancers to San Francisco, have them work with upper middle class white kids, and somehow change their picture. But what we all learned was that there are certain psychological imprints that are embedded in our psyches and it's very hard to change."[87]

The rage about the program listing was probably heightened by a divisive conflict that had arisen earlier when late one afternoon, after a particularly rigorous rehearsal, Ann distributed a piece of paper to all twenty-two performers and asked them to sign it. According to Coleman, all but one Watts performer, John Hopkins, or Black John as he was called, signed the paper without even reading it. John, however, balked. The piece of paper turned out to be a consent form for the making of a documentary about the workshop process. Ann, who was one of eleven Bay Area artists to receive a five-hundred-dollar grant to make a film of their work, chose to film the Watts project. As she customarily did with grants, she turned the money over to the Dancers' Workshop fund, which distributed money to members of the San Francisco group (excluding Daria and Rana) to help toward covering the costs of their performing in Los Angeles. The specter of inequity had been loosened. As Coleman indicated later, rumors started circulating among the black performers that they were getting "ripped off" by the whites, who were "rich anyway and didn't need the money." Although things were eventually smoothed over enough for the performance to proceed, an important breach of trust had occurred. Several of the Watts performers felt their worst suspicions of being exploited had been confirmed. When these feelings came up at the post-performance seminar, Ann countered by trying to drag the discussion from status, power, and money back to art:

> Do you want to continue as artists? It's one thing to continue and another to work towards a specific goal, which we did. What happened last night has never happened on any stage in the world. That's the reason we're all feeling so intense, we all know this, and we could effect tremendous change through artistic and social change. It's another problem to know if you can stretch yourselves in your personal lives. That's the answer I came here to get.[88]

Baum, however, sensed a limitation in Ann's answer when he remarked: "I felt a certain shallowness [in the performance] which I attribute to an avoidance of those issues which appeared at that meeting the next day."[89] In seeking to escape the painful binary of being either invisible because of race or *too* visible because of it, the Studio Watts performers found that art practices have their own rules of power and authority. Invisibility of one-self and one's issues can be achieved inadvertently, just when one thinks one is proceeding toward visibility. In *Ceremony of Us,* crafting a theater piece about race and personal empowerment resulted in the individual rad-icalized identities of the performers being erased and their authority being subsumed in the established power structure of the theater. Moreover, there was a difference in expectations. As Coleman pointed out, the Studio Watts performers were looking to *Ceremony of Us* as "their ticket out of the ghetto." "We were all fixing to go to New York," she said. "We thought, 'Oh, Broadway is the next stop!'"

Much as *Ceremony of Us* drew criticism from its performers, it also re-ceived a mixed reaction from reviewers. Many people, including Ann, Baum, and the critics, expected more in the way of an art event. *Ceremony of Us* had turned out to be a dance about the process of uncovering rather than arrival at a well-formed statement. Martin Bernheimer, who reviewed the performance in the *Los Angeles Times,* derided it as "pretentious" and at best "mildly entertaining." Bernheimer suggested that Ann had aban-doned her traditional modern dance training in favor of shallow philoso-phizing through physical actions. "Thursday's overriding impression had something to do with happy goings-on at a co-ed gymnasium, one where the participants take their private religions very seriously," Bernheimer wrote. "The artistic validity of the evening is difficult to evaluate, since the producers pretended to be more concerned with sociology than with art. Miss Halprin long ago gave up conventional dance formalities and turned her back on her Humphrey-Weidman-Margaret H'Doubler training. She concerned herself instead with the expression and solution of philosophic problems in symbolic, physical terms."[90]

The review that stung Ann the most was that written by her former as-sociate and student John Rockwell. Writing in the *Oakland Tribune* as mu-sic critic, Rockwell sensitively described the gap between what he felt the intentions of the dance were and the ways in which it failed to reach those goals. He criticized the evening for having "too many parts [that] went on far too long" or that were "crippled by a kind of terribly earnest, self-indulgent pretension." In particular, Rockwell noted the audience partici-pation was "qualitatively and quantitatively on a low level." He wrote that Ann "hasn't figured out yet how to combine a performance situation and this kind of audience-generated theater experience," referring directly to the tension that would plague much of Ann's work from this moment forward—how to create an experience that was as captivating for the spectators as it was transformative for the performers: "The art did not succeed in projecting the full intensity of the things I am sure Halprin wanted to get across: the two groups, the roles of the various strong and weak members within the groups, the simple fact of racial and human interaction. Far too often *Ceremony of Us* was neither natural nor artful."[91]

When Ann communicated to Rockwell how upset she was with his review, he wrote her a two-page note of apology and explanation. Rockwell gently tried to explain how his understanding of her work made him a perceptive, but not necessarily a reflexively sympathetic, viewer. "Being a critic is a complicated thing," he noted. "Sometimes I feel, in true D/W [Dancers' Workshop] manner, that I should just dig things. But I, and the D/W for that matter, am more complicated than that!"[92] Rockwell was striving to broaden Ann's conception of criticism and the critic's role while acknowledging that much in his perceptual training was rooted in his experience of doing her work. As often happened with the more accomplished people she gathered around her, Rockwell wanted to push Ann to face the limits as well as the bounty of her methods. By this point, however, Ann was so deeply inside the climate of candor and confession that she had worked to build in the *Ceremony of Us* workshop that she knew more how the piece felt than how it read externally as an independent work of art.

In Ann's attempts to converge the ideological and the aesthetic, the aesthetic lost out in *Ceremony of Us*. Success in the world of the studio's reality—a frank performance of tasks, for example—doesn't automatically equate with success on the public stage. In addition, Ann's efforts at making social morality the score for the piece had confused theatrical performance and ritual.[93] Even though Ann was creating a theatrical work out of the real emotions and encounters of her two groups of dancers in *Ceremony of Us*, the performers' attempts to substitute a theatrical presence for a real-life one were necessarily incomplete and ambivalent. Being oneself on stage—or, as Daria had discovered, in front of a camera—is different from being oneself in daily life, and the context changes the expectations of the spectator.

In the wake of all the criticism, Ann's focus went more deeply into the studio and away from the stage. The experiences and lessons of *Ceremony of Us* took hold on the microperformance level, in Ann's daily studio practice. If this piece failed as art, that mattered less than whether it succeeded as an experience. Working intuitively, Ann would turn increasingly to the experience of change as the goal rather than a performance per se.[94]

The value of the workshop experience was suggested in an article that

John Rockwell wrote based on his direct observations. Even though he criticized the final performance, he recognized: "The Watts sessions, both in each separate group and especially when the two are combined, have been absolutely extraordinary in their intensity. Not only are the personal changes marked, but their expression in artistic terms is transparently clear." Although others might have disagreed, for him the prevailing tension in these workshops was "not a racial tension, really, but an artistic and human tension." He indicated, "All of what Ann Halprin had been doing over the last 10 years seemed to coalesce in these sessions."[95]

As a way of continuing the interracial workshop experience, Ann invited several of the Watts performers to San Francisco to join her group, and three of the men—Xavier Nash, Melvin Garrett, and John Hopkins—came. *Ceremony of Us,* however, was not performed again with the full cast, although there was one performance in the gymnasium at Oakland's Laney College. In late March 1969, a month after the Taper performance, Ann and several of the Studio Watts and Dancers' Workshop dancers presented an abbreviated version, "Event in a Chapel," at the University of the Pacific in Stockton, California, at the invitation of the university chaplain. A newspaper account contains the by-now customary mix of derision, curiosity, and dismissal. "It might have been better described as 'The Big Turn-On,'" the reporter said, describing a series of conga lines, pat-a-cake, and red light–green light games that came directly from *Ceremony of Us.*[96] "We were idealistic. We wanted everyone to love each other," Annie Hallett, one of the San Francisco dancers, said years later, ascribing a chaste innocence to the affection. "Everyone was smiling and hugging—it was the sixties."[97]

The five months of the *Ceremony of Us* workshop gave Ann a fresh understanding of just how complex and layered the interweavings of each individual's political, racial, and cultural history are in the performance work the group fashions. This realization prompted Ann to rethink how to prepare individuals to perform and how to lead them to discover, within their own lives, the material for their performances. She spent the summer of 1969 tracing how the personal might evolve into the political and social for herself as well as her dancers. In July Ann held the first of dozens of multiracial workshops in which she probed these issues and tested means for doing what she now felt was her raison d'être as an artist—"trying to connect dance to people's lives."[98] She also began her Reach Out program, a multiracial ensemble of dancers, funded by the National Endowment for the Arts' Expansion Arts Program.[99] This innovative program would continue for the next twelve years, until the government funding ended in the mid-1980s with the Reagan administration's cuts.

In a letter written in late August 1969, at the end of her first multicultural summer workshop, Ann reported to the people who had donated money to support it that the twenty-six participants, all in their twenties, included ten African Americans, one Asian American, two Latinos, and thirteen Caucasians. Calling the work they did together "a natural theater of life" and "humanistic art as social action," she posited the workshop as a critical social intervention, a laboratory, and a model for new solutions to social problems:

> Staff and administration were all white (but this will soon alter as a result of the workshop training). The extreme polarities that were manifested in our group [were] a microcosm of our present society. We were black/white; rich/poor; ivy league education to ghetto streets; the mystic drug oriented hippie to the hard core realist. Breaking down barriers that have separated us for too long and building a common trust became the task of this group. Using the media of movement and the arts, we explored and discovered new ways to meet the staggering challenge of these differences that affect us all.[100]

The Reach Out program extended the efforts in the summer workshop. This outreach program (its title an inadvertent tribute to Ann's humorous penchant for malapropisms) aimed both to recruit minority students and to place these students as teachers and administrators. As if returning to her own roots in H'Doubler's program for developing dance educators, Ann began a teacher training program for the minority dance students she recruited. The year-long Reach Out training and apprenticeship began with students assisting Ann for six months in her dance studio teaching. Then, for two months, teams of two students shared the teaching of a whole class while a third one watched and commented afterward as an evaluator. Each student was given $50 weekly for expenses and free housing was provided. The staff used the old Victorian Phelps House (now a San Francisco landmark) behind 321 Divisadero, which the Dancers' Workshop rented for $275 a month. (Ann had a room there as well for times when it was more convenient to stay there than to drive back to Marin.) Others associated with the studio lived, sometimes with their partners, in another house down the street. These living situations were practical, since the rental houses were next to the studios. Most of the black dancers who began working with Ann were men, and some of them paired off with white women from the studio, so the arrangements came to be ideological and romantic as well. The spillover from life inside the studio to life outside underlines just how theatrically unmediated the physical and emotional material was that Ann was drawing out of these performers.

As Ann explained the program, "I was training these minority dancers so they could go out into their own communities to teach and network with community groups to spread dance back into their own neighborhoods." At the end of the apprenticeship program, Ann helped the trainees find jobs with community groups and correctional centers. In terms of the classes she offered, Ann said, "I always wanted to invest in people's own creating. I never allowed people to imitate me." When choosing the stylistic forms for her curriculum, Ann noted, "I wanted them to stay in the black tradition." Ann also arranged for the black dancers to take classes with Ruth Beckford, a former student of Katherine Dunham who was the only black dancer teaching in the Bay Area at the time and who had stayed in touch with Ann since performing with her in the late 1950s.

Several of the students who were particularly good at street dance, including Jasmine Nash, Xavier's sister, began teaching classes in street dance at the studio. "Ann had been inviting me to come over [to the Dancers' Workshop studio] and share some of the dances that I knew and I hadn't done that," Jasmine said. Then one day she peeked through the door at Ann's class and decided she was intrigued enough by what she saw to give it a try. "So I began teaching these dances that young people, teenagers and younger, create all the time in high school and junior high school and at home, but they weren't valued. And it really wasn't until I met Ann that I got in touch with the value myself and was able to teach that and translate it."[101] Through Jasmine Nash and others, Ann offered classes in street dance for white dancers decades before hip-hop made it into modern dance schools. She was finding not just art, but dance culture where no one else had looked.

While the traditional dance world may have been skeptical about Ann's work at this time, the funding community embraced her enthusiastically. In May 1970 she hosted a press conference at the Dancers' Workshop studios to announce the receipt of a $25,000 matching grant from the San Francisco Foundation to support what she was now calling her "humanistic theater" and "working studies in racial harmony through dance."[102] She told the assembled press that an anonymous donor in the East had already matched the foundation money with a $25,000 private donation.[103] Ann explained to the assembled journalists that the newest binary she was working to shatter was that between "a professional company and a training school situation," and that her target population of performers was now "Blacks, Whites and Asians."[104] After setting up a miniature mazelike environment in her studio for the bewildered press to negotiate, the dancers served them a lunch of "Chinese meat buns, fried chicken à la Midwest, potato salad with a touch of kosher pickle and peach cobbler à la Soul." Just as in *Ceremony of Us* and *Lunch,* Ann freely traversed the fresh and the curiously clichéd as she mined cultural memories in her quest for a socially relevant aesthetic framework.

As Ann's multicultural training program developed, she turned her focus in performance to the larger topic of social justice, creating four consciously activist works in quick succession: *The Bust* (1969), *Blank Placard Dance* (1970*), New Time Shuffle* (1970), and *Kadosh* (1971). *The Bust* (which got its title only later) was a curious event. It began as an improvisatory street happening, what Ann described as a "St. Vitus Day Parade" project of the student composition class. It was performed by twelve members of Ann's new multiracial company. Paul Ryan, a friend of Ann's, filmed the event by closely following the dancers as they skipped, crawled, and rolled down Haight Street on the afternoon of December 17, 1969. In the twenty-minute film there are glimpses of Ann wearing a black cape over her shirt and pants, at times with sunglasses and a scarf over her Afro-like "natural" hair. But it is the white women who are the most raucous performers. They bellow, claw at the air, and swing their limbs wildly while the three black men repeatedly attempt to swaddle them in lengths of brown butcher paper. As the white women dancers throw themselves to the sidewalk and crawl on all fours across the busy Haight Street intersections, biting the lengths of paper like leashes held in their mouths, the black men alternately bind them in the paper and roughly herd them around. The film thus presents a strange vision of racialized victimization and willing white female subjugation to black males that is paradoxically made less distressing by the presence of the men with cameras (who are included in the film). This act of documenting the making of the film also puts the frame of performance around the actions of the dancers and immediately signals that their actions and cries are performative, not actual, and that this is art, not unmediated abuse. The role of spectatorship is thus modeled for the viewer and cast as a prepared part of the performance. The presence of the men documenting the work suggests the manner in which viewers should react to this scene, as well as signaling that this craziness is virtual and theatrically deliberate.

At several points in the film the camera pans past the drivers and passengers in the cars and buses traveling along the busy boulevard and captures their reactions. Their expressions mostly register surprise and amusement, but in one instance a black woman with a small child quickly locks the car doors, seemingly in fear. In the final minutes of the film, an additional layer of spectatorship is added as uniformed members of the San Francisco Police Department Tactical Squad arrive and begin assisting the women performers to their feet. Two of the men and one of the women are then put into a police wagon to be driven to the station for booking. Throughout the police roundup, Ann stands calmly outside the action, occasionally stepping up to an officer to explain a few things to him and then respectfully stepping back. Sergeant Donald Goad later reported that he responded to reports that a crowd of people were "exposing themselves" and found that "two of the girls were rolling around on the ground on their backs very slowly as if under the influence of drugs."[105] Two weeks after the arrests, on New Year's Eve, Ann staged a benefit party at the Divisadero Street studio to earn back the $2,265 bail charges paid for the three "busted" dancers.[106]

Paradoxically, in the film, which goes by the title *The Bust,* everything seems chaotic, in visual and emotional disorder, until the spectacle ceases to be the performance and becomes the arrest, when the "event" becomes most tightly focused and scripted. The arrest seems a matter-of-fact consequence of and yet an extreme reaction to the infraction of creating a public theater improvisation or, as Ann explains in the film, "doing a little street theater downstairs." (Years later Ann acknowledged that the easiest reference people could make when they saw this performance was the uncontrolled behavior of stoned kids in the Haight-Ashbury area. "The police decided we must be freaking out on drugs and arrested us," she said.[107]) As the film shows, the final "performance"—a spontaneous collaboration between Dancers' Workshop and the Tactical Squad—drew an ad hoc cluster of black residents from the neighborhood, who gathered to watch the curious spectacle of these young folks nonchalantly inviting arrest. The spectators' expressions are inquisitive and amused. What kind of decadence is it for middle-class whites to do something so crazy as to deliberately court arrest by this kind of art making? As the police drive off with her dancers, Ann turns to the camera and explains that this is part of a "class presentation dealing with the community" and "a theatrical protest against all the killings in the world today." She says simply, "We were interested in how the community would respond."

A more stylized protest, created in early 1970 and referred to simply as *Blank Placard Dance,* was Ann's performance riposte to the arrest filmed in *The Bust.* As a gesture, it was pure 1960s in its simultaneously active and passive posture. Ann and her dancers, all dressed in white, marched through several downtown streets in San Francisco carrying placards. It looked like a typical protest march. Yet as soon as one looked at their placards, the ordinariness gave way to puzzlement. There was no message on any of the placards they waved in the air. One is conditioned to reading such white rectangles as spaces for blunt warnings, not the ruminative ambiguities of art.[108] Everything and nothing might be protested here. Ann captures a classic cyclical 1960s attitude—provoke authority and then wait for a reaction and react to that.

In *Blank Placard Dance* it is possible to see the intersection of a number of Ann's concerns about memory, performance, and community behaviors. Happenings and street theater are the most closely related performance genres, but the kind of socially activist art initiated by *Ceremony of Us* is also evident. Layered on that is a questioning of behaviors framed as if a psychologist or social scientist were setting up a research project. The marchers in *Blank Placard Dance* stay the requisite ten feet apart, so they do not constitute a demonstration as defined by the law, and thus avoid being arrested again. "My idea," Ann has said, "was that there were so many protests going on and this way each person watching us could just imagine whatever protest slogan they wanted on the placards."[109] Ann's dance thus became a performed statement about both those who protested through public demonstration and the institutional practices that controlled them.

Interestingly, on February 21, 1965, five years before Ann created *Blank Placard Dance, Candid Camera* aired a vignette called "Picketing Against Everything with Nothing." Filmed in the Bronx, New York, this episode featured three men in suits and overcoats walking in a small circle on a sidewalk in front of a huge snow-covered empty lot. The circling men carried big placards, all blank, while a fourth distributed blank handbills to passersby and pleaded with them to please join the picket line. *Candid Camera* director Allen Funt's concern here was to activate social science rather than aesthetic strategies, but viewed side by side with Ann's dance it is curious how these issues overlap. As the psychologist Stanley Milgram has noted, this and other *Candid Camera* episodes do several things that mark them as participating in the methodology of the social sciences.[110] Most relevant to Ann's work is the technique of focusing on a behavior embedded in the stream of everyday life and then, by disrupting the setting for this behavior, revealing our habits of vision. Whereas Funt is interested in revealing (and ridiculing) human behaviors and the desire to conform and not stand out, Ann's work champions the nonconformist impulse and allows individuals to feel comfortable being iconoclasts and standing out for the right (art) reasons. By thrusting blank handbills into the hands of passersby and recruiting people, huckster-style, off the street to walk the picket line, Funt orchestrates a complex ruse to coerce people into looking foolish by tricking them into obedience. This could be a recipe for totalitarianism whereas Ann's use of these same props becomes, in the best instance, a rehearsal for democracy.

Several months after *Blank Placard,* Ann turned to what can be seen as a middle piece in a trilogy that includes *Ceremony of Us* and *Kadosh,* works she identifies as focusing on the "relationship of the individual body to the collective body, and the interrelationship of communities."[111] In early June 1970 Ann received a letter from a black inmate in Northern California's Soledad State Prison, a heavy security prison known during that period for its racial trouble and tensions between guards and prisoners. The writer, Stanley Goree, had read an article in the *Oakland Tribune* about Ann's multiracial company, and he wanted to invite Ann to perform in the prison as the guest of a newly formed group of black men organizing for more options for educational skills:

> I dig the things your dance group is doing, and as I read the article I was thinking how beautiful and realistic it would be if you could do a show for us here in one of the state's tightest iron boxes. There has never been anything hip here, ever. Would you consider bringing your dancers here to entertain us? And simply to visit with us? To do a show for the Black, Brown and White inmates (scratch inmates and insert humans) who believe in unity and brotherhood against a common enemy.[112]

Ann was delighted with the invitation. She saw in it the opportunity to extend the notion of performing about racial communities that she had begun with *Ceremony of Us.* Her personal writing from this period indicates that rather than slowing her down, the Watts conflicts had only inspired her to take on with more urgency the cause of addressing racial and social tensions through dance. The possibility of pursuing this in the high-risk environment of a men's prison excited her. As she wrote in a diary about her performances around that time:

> No performance has taken place at Soledad without the prisoners themselves being seated in the hall in a segregated fashion, Black, Chicanos, Whites in their own territories. No performance has taken place at Soledad in which the prisoners have not walked out in large numbers during the performance. We were shown special exit doors to use in case of a riot during the performance for our own safety.[113]

The idea of wresting a social success out of this climate of hopelessness reinforced Ann's belief in the power of her art. In August Ann's managing director, Ken Margolis, signed a contract to perform the work Ann was calling *New Time Shuffle* on October 3 in the prison. For the Soledad experiment Ann was joined by several new minority dancers she had recruited from Watts and Oakland.

The racial polarization in the prison was intense, so Ann commenced *New Time Shuffle* by addressing the sharply segregated units in the hall. She mirrored on stage the divisions and then amplified the distinctive racial identities through improvised songs, rhythms, and movements. Even her account slips into the rhythm and slang of the various groups as she describes them:

> The black guys in the group do a black rap and jive that sends the black inmates howling. Alicia, a [Chicana], carries on a dialogue in Spanish with the Chicano prisoners, Pamela does an Asian song and a white dude comes across as a hippie type. The experience is less a performance than a confrontation between our two communities—the workshop community and the prison community.[114]

After addressing the racial groups in the hall in their individual performance style, the room as a whole was coaxed into a collective clapping and singing jam as the Dancers' Workshop dared to come out into the audience. As Ann described the experience to Margaret H'Doubler, when her mentor from Wisconsin came to California to teach master classes at Mills College later that year, in *New Time Shuffle* her formula for dancing (and singing) across racial divides worked, and by the performance's end the prison hall was a changed place. The result, Ann reported, was hailed as "the inmates' first positive interaction with each other." It was also a learning experience for Ann. "I was the only white person [among the female performers]," Ann told H'Doubler. "And I can't say I'm white because I'm Jewish," Ann continued in a reference to the way she had begun to consciously cultivate *her* ethnic identity. "White middle class society is so secure. I just have a little inkling of what it is to be a minority in this society, and in very subtle ways to not conform to White Anglo Saxon culture."[115]

After one additional workshop at a women's correctional facility on the East Coast, Ann would never again work with incarcerated populations, yet she would take this belief in the communally curative force of dance into marginalized and at-risk groups in other ways. "We are saying by our rhythm and movement and the way we inter-relate: 'Look, we can get it together and have a good time; you can too, and look what is possible on the outside. Life doesn't have to be a nightmare.'"[116]

About two months after *New Time Shuffle,* in early December 1970, Ann was visited by the fine arts committee from Temple Sinai in Oakland. Under the leadership of Rabbi Samuel Broude, the adventuresome head of this Reform synagogue, Temple Sinai had begun to include monthly performing arts performances as part of its Friday night Shabbat services, in place of the customary Sabbath sermon. After watching a rehearsal of the multiracial group the committee decided to commission its first dance work for the synagogue from her. "The fact that this was an integrated group was a plus," Broude remembered, "because in addition to expressing the Sabbath we were saying here's a social motivation."[117] For the next two months Rabbi Broude made weekly visits to Ann's studio, where he would offer impromptu explanations of the meaning and background of the Jewish prayers that were part of the Friday night services.

During this period Ann seemed to be reidentifying with her Jewish heritage as a cultural tradition, just as she had prompted the black, Asian, and Latino dancers in her group to do with their heritages. Jasmine Nash recalled with amusement that at the same time that Ann was generously sponsoring her multicultural dancers in Werner Erhard's est training seminar for minorities, she tried to talk her way into this large group awareness program as a minority—Jewish.[118] The est staff was not convinced. "It became very apparent to me that dance had been dominated by an Anglo-Saxon culture," Ann later told an interviewer. "I was just astonished at the prejudices that I didn't even know I had. I didn't know a damn about this scope of movement on an ethnic level," said Ann, who had let her own curly red hair grow into a soft, full Jewish "Afro."[119]

In *Kadosh* Ann brought her focus on prompting dialogues among communities home to her own Jewish background. She was trying to use dance aggressively to bridge cultural differences and to foster an empathetic understanding of others' feelings by physically trying on their gestures, rhythms, and rituals. *Kadosh* began with Ann and her dancers davening, moving in the rhythmic swaying characteristic of Eastern European Jews, like Ann's grandfather, deep in prayer. The dancers streamed down the aisles of the sanctuary toward the raised *bima,* where the rabbi and cantor stood. The dancers then began hurling a litany of unanswerable questions at the rabbi, demanding to know how it is possible to celebrate Sabbath joy when there is so much pain and suffering in the world, and why people are afraid to touch one another, and why six million Jews were murdered in the Holocaust. Then the dancers tore their clothes and fell to the ground in violent twisted gestures of broken limbs, extinguishing the lit candles they held as they collapsed. Rabbi Broude said he cried at this portion of the service, because the visualization of the text that he knew so well was made freshly vivid with this enactment.

In the darkened sanctuary the rabbi began to recite the Kaddish, the Hebrew prayer for the dead, and the dancers gradually stood up. Each one lit a Sabbath candle, and their gestures and their mood began to escalate into joyfulness. "Little by little it crescendoed to where it was very joyous," the rabbi recalled. "We had an elderly couple from the congregation, Ed and Amelia Kushner. They came in from the entrance to the sanctuary and down the middle aisle with myrtle branches, a sign of life and renewal. So the dancers started dancing around because by this time their joy had led them up on the bima." Then, in a gesture echoing the conclusion of *Ceremony of Us,* the dancers joined hands with willing members of the congregation and led them up the aisles and out into the street in a weaving line dance that continued around the corner and into the social hall next door.

Neither fully symbolic nor fully literal, *Kadosh* showcased Ann's fusion of the real and the imagined as an artifact of cultural memory. When asked if he thought Ann's goal was to actually move the congregation to social action, the rabbi demurred. "I think the idea was to enable us to get into this spiritual place, to have a taste of the messianic." Rabbi Broude said that for him the only surprise was how emotionally moved he was by the performance. About half the congregation was equally moved, while the other half was outraged. "I don't know if anybody was neutral," Broude said. "Half thought it was fantastic, and half thought it was terrible!"

The subsequent issue of the Temple Sinai newsletter printed several impassioned reactions to the dance—members who were upset that shirtless men had danced on the bima and others who were touched to see a black man repeating the words of a Hebrew prayer over and over with real passion. "I am stirred by this new way of expressing brotherhood," member Susi Oppenheimer wrote. "As an aftertaste it left me with the feeling of being part of the community of all men. So wasn't it worth having?"[120] The aesthetic impact of Ann's socially conscious dances reverberated beyond the performance, publicly constructing allegories that might literally reveal the relational nature of all communities.

Throughout the late 1960s and early 1970s Ann was gesturing toward making her art more inclusive by broadening the categories of who performed it and by drafting, initially fleetingly, spectators as participants. She was moving beyond simply espousing the idealism of democracy through the implied egalitarian narratives of her dance events, something that had a prior history in American modern dance between the wars. Rather, she was moving toward creating dance that could be performed by hundreds of nondancers. Her increased social activism was only one aspect of this shift. Another came from the unlikely arena of the human potential movement and her earlier work with Fritz Perls. Decades later Ann commented that for her the most profound idea of the sixties was: therapy isn't just for "crazy" people. She effectively came to rewrite that as: dance isn't just for dancers. Her favorite Gestalt aphorism was "emotions are facts." Ann wanted to integrate these "facts" of the common person's emotions into dance. Not because she was doing therapy, she insisted, "but because it was a necessity in the art process."[121] Real emotions, just like real bodies and identities, had been ignored for too long.

During this late 1960s and early 1970s period Ann was recruited by George Leonard, vice president of Esalen, to help him orchestrate the opening group improvisations at several weekend workshops conducted by Esalen around the United States. "She was a very important person in the field," Leonard later said, describing how he and Ann directed the hundreds of workshop participants who gathered in hotel ballrooms in Texas, Nebraska, and Hawaii to sample the Esalen approach. "She brought dancing and the whole somatics movement" into the human potential movement, Leonard indicated. "She had great spirit and energy and showed that the body has a wisdom and is not a dumb mechanism."[122] In turn, for Ann, the crowds at these gatherings opened the possibilities for orchestrating mass movement that was individualistic and social without being uniform or fascistic.

At the same time that Ann was pushing for the formation of new, integrated communities, she discovered firsthand that there could be a dark side to all this openness. The incident, which occurred at the end of 1970, would eventually help lead Ann into a focus on healing, both physically and emotionally. It involved Sir Lawrence Washington, a young football player at Merritt College in Oakland whom Ann had seen in a dance class and recruited to join her Reach Out group. "I had never known a white person before the Halprins," Washington recalled. "And here she was inviting me into her school and home. They [Ann and Larry] were the first white people I trusted. I loved them both."[123] At the end of 1970, in a workshop, Washington had drawn a portrait of himself with a large helmet on his head and his body bleeding and pierced by arrows. He depicted half of himself as a dead tree with an arm and a leg chained to the edge of the paper. Later that evening, when the workshop held a New Year's Eve party in the Divisadero Street studio, a rowdy group tried to crash the party. As they climbed the stairs to the studio, Washington and two other Reach Out dancers tried to turn them back. Washington was hit on the head with a wooden table leg that had a long screw protruding from it and was knocked unconscious. He underwent emergency surgery and spent the next several weeks in the hospital, paralyzed in his right arm and leg, the same ones he had drawn in chains earlier. It was months before he recovered, and during that time Ann visited him regularly in the hospital. She continued to be troubled by the strangely prescient quality of his self-portrait. During one visit to his hospital room, Ann brought Washington's self-portrait and asked him to indicate to her what she should do to modify the image. He gestured for her to sever his chains. "I did and after that, he began to improve," Ann said. "[Soon] he was dancing with the multiracial company on its first tour to the East Coast."[124]

In the summer of 1971 Ann appeared for the first time as a guest artist at the American Dance Festival. The festival, held at Connecticut College in New London, was the successor to the Bennington summer program and the most distinguished summer center for modern dance in the nation. Ann's performance was scheduled for the last weekend of the six-week festival. She led up to it by conducting two parallel workshops, one in San Francisco with her Reach Out company and one in New London with the festival students, modeled on her approach to *Ceremony of Us* almost three years earlier. Ann brought the two groups together in New London the week before the performance to explore jointly a series of improvisatory situations around the idea of an East Coast and a West Coast pack of animals.

John Muto, a Dancers' Workshop staff member, designed an elaborate score, printed in the program, that detailed the progression over the evening from random and individual placement in space through meetings at a watering hole, hunting, courtship, and fighting, into a resolution with the formation of a unified herd.

Ann approached the animal imagery with sincerity, believing it could be a path into what she called "the emotional body" of each individual. She was trying to find a bedrock issue that each performer could respond to as intensively as the *Ceremony of Us* dancers had addressed race. The resulting dance, called alternately *Animal Ritual* or *West/East Stereo,* was based on Ann's belief that group situations provided a special reality where the self-imposed limits of physical and emotional blocks could be surmounted. She saw this as an aesthetic goal, although it could just as readily have been perceived as a therapeutic one. And that is where some took issue with *Animal Ritual,* calling it a public exercise in sensitivity training and an encounter group rather than art. Ann steadfastly insisted she was engaged in an experiment to find out what this work could accomplish in the way of individual and social change, and she deliberately chose the term *ritual* as a way of sidestepping the view of art and therapy as mutually exclusive categories. Throughout her career she has always shunned the appellation *therapy* or *therapeutic* in conjunction with her work.[125]

On a personal level, Ann was working at this time with different therapists, trying to push past her own physical and emotional limits in private sessions with the psychotherapist John Rinn and the physiotherapist Ida Rolf. Rinn, a student of Ann's who was married to Mills College dance instructor Rebecca Fuller, collaborated with Ann on relating to sexuality, sensuality, and intimacy, and negotiating the distinctions between them.[126] They worked together on creating sound and movement exercises to push past physical behaviors, releasing feelings along with muscles. Much of this was focused on interior changes, the kinds of alterations that felt more dramatic, and interesting, than they looked. With Ida Rolf, Ann underwent the intense and often very painful process of "Rolfing," a deep massage of the fascia muscles of her body intended to recenter and better align her in relation to gravity. Ann later said this work "alters the body drastically, but in so doing, also alters your capacity to feel and increase[s] energy. Obviously, such increased capacities are invaluable to the performer."[127]

In performance, *Animal Ritual* seemed to hover between dance and a salutary rite, without becoming particularly compelling as a spectator event.

Several East Coast dance critics remarked on this, puzzling aloud about what frame to use when looking at Ann's dance. Marcia Siegel, writing for the *Boston Herald Traveler*, wondered if the work should even be reviewed since it seemed shaped so much more for participation than audience consumption in any traditional sense:

> What's really going on here, I kept wanting to know. I suspect the animal imitations were the *least* real thing about the piece, serving as a convenient disguise for the displays of power, hostility and perhaps exhibitionism that almost all the participants were engaged in.
>
> Ann Halprin seems caught somewhere between art and therapy, and what she needs for herself is probably different from what she intends for the members of her company. *West/East Stereo* [or *Animal Ritual*] made me wonder if the artist has the right to expose a real therapeutic situation to an audience, of if the therapist has the right to interfere with the therapeutic process in the interest of effective theater, or indeed whether a therapeutic change can take place at all in the presence of spectators. If Ann Halprin gets a consistent answer to these questions, she may really come up with something.[128]

The *Animal Ritual* Siegel describes teeters on the edge of uncontrol, an *Apartment 6* without the complexity of developed relationships or the formal bracing of a clear structure for the improvisation. Hostility and exhibitionism may become placeholders for ideas, or they may appear simply as unmediated emotions tapped, but not reimagined or reshaped, for performance.

Robert Pierce, another critic who was in the New London audience, voiced a different impression of the piece: "Although the action on stage was similar to what you might find in a jungle, Ann's interest was in basic human reactions, instincts and rituals. . . . While they were portraying animals, the dancers reacted to each other in ways not permitted in a civilized, highly socialized and restrictive society."[129] Indeed, the animal behaviors were a frame within the frame of performance, sanctioning essentially whatever aggression, sexuality, hostility, and mock fornication the performers brought forth—and they brought forth a lot. No one seemed to notice the paradox of a "natural" human dance based on make-believe about what other species might do, perhaps because it was so transparently just a device for sanctioning "liberated" (unsocialized) behaviors.

Ann's strategy here was collective memory as invention or, as Siegel saw it, an event "caught somewhere between therapy and art." Ann's *Apartment 6* had, of course, already grafted intense therapeutic-type exchanges onto the stage, and therapeutic change as a spectator event had been pioneered in Fritz Perls's group Gestalt sessions. What *Animal Ritual* revealed as much as anything was both how stubbornly Ann clung to a path of exploration and how unabashed she was in allowing both the trials and the failures of her work to unfold in full public view. Perhaps the dance deck had given her a falsely cloistered sense of public space and the seemingly infinite possibility of trying and discarding performance material. Much of her work of this period was performed on this high wire of constant and full exposure, and the missteps, like *Animal Ritual,* could be embarrassingly public.

Ann and her company of African American males, which is essentially what Reach Out became as the women dancers left one by one, also presented a participatory *Animal Ritual* downstairs at New York's City Center as part of their trip east. Larry's uncle Sydney Luria, his wife Lucille, and the dance writers Jack Anderson and George Dorris were among those who attended a workshop Ann also gave in the Open Center in New York, a New Age space. All four came away perplexed. Uncle Sydney and Lucille had gamely come with a cardboard box, since the performance announcement specified that participants were to bring an object to help carry out the theme of the evening—the creation of an environment. Others arrived with a range of amusing and dangerous objects, from armfuls of tennis balls to a board covered with sharp nails that would shred the foot of anyone who stepped on it. Ann instructed the men and women to retreat to separate rooms and decide collectively what they wanted to do to carry out the evening's theme. The men created a dense tunnel-like structure, which they instructed the women to crawl through. After this Ann, speaking through a megaphone, instructed the fifty participants to take off as much of their clothing as they felt comfortable removing. "Then we did some rolling on the floor, but not with the person you came with. I said to my wife later that if a client had been there I would have had no [law] practice left!" Sydney, a prominent attorney, laughed.[130]

Jack Anderson and George Dorris recalled watching the evening unhinge when a group of the participants, men and women, charged in and smashed and ripped apart the whole carefully constructed environment made by the others. The next day Anderson ran into Ann, who confided that, unannounced, a psychotherapist had sent his encounter group into the workshop without telling her about the psychological disorders of his patients.[131] She was very upset by what happened, but powerless to do more in the midst of the workshop than try to contain the damage and keep things going. She certainly had limits in mind, even if no one else could see them.

The era of simple faith of the early 1960s had already ended for her, as it had for the nation, with the assassination of John Kennedy, followed five years later by the murders of Martin Luther King Jr. and Robert Kennedy, killings that shook the national trust in individuals' ability to self-regulate in an open democracy. The Death of Mr. Hippie, carried out in a flashy mock funeral in the Haight-Ashbury district in October 1968, a few blocks from Ann's studio, had buried innocence along with the effigy. Now the increasing violence and aggression, evidenced by the party and workshop crashings in San Francisco and New York, were shattering the freedom of Ann's stage and her allegiance to the idea that collective action led to collective good.

NINE

Illness as Performance

1972–1991

> Illness is the night-side of life, a more onerous citizenship. Everyone who is
> born holds dual citizenship, in the kingdom of the well and in the kingdom
> of the sick. Although we all prefer to use only the good passport, sooner
> or later each of us is obliged, at least for a spell, to identify ourselves as
> citizens of that other place.
>
> SUSAN SONTAG
>
> *Illness as Metaphor*

DANCE, MORE THAN ANY OTHER art form, is weighted toward showcasing the kingdom of the well. Both those who create and those who perform dances are presumed to be healthy, the carriers of what Susan Sontag
calls "the good passport." Using the body as an art medium usually depends
on physical control and stamina—signifiers of wellness. The more visible
the body, as in athletes or dancers, the more developed and refined this control tends to be, conveying an impression of underlying health. The kingdom of the sick is hidden, and for certain types of illness it is a kingdom
of the shamed.

As 1972 began, Ann continued to map psychological well-being and health
through choreography. This was generally as close as contemporary dance
had come to portraying the kingdom of the sick. For dance, the psychological was the most comfortable dimension of the unwell because "illnesses" of the mind rarely disfigure the body the way other diseases can.
Ann was finding her way by using the investigative and therapeutic tools
she had learned from Fritz Perls and other alternative therapists to track
psychological behaviors into performance states. Since the symptoms of
psychological disturbance often play out as exaggerated behaviors by bodies that are otherwise unmarked, they are well suited for expression in dance.

Physical sickness, in contrast, marks the body, often making it too vulnerable, too uncontrollable, too inscribed to be neutral as a medium for performance. What the body in disease performs relentlessly is its own citizenship in the kingdom of the sick.

For Ann, the year 1972 would deepen her notions of how dance can affect bodies in both sickness and health, physically and emotionally. But before she turned to explore "the night-side of life," she helped her daughter Daria prepare for one of the biggest traditional celebrations of wellness: marriage—to the actor Dennis Hopper. In the early 1970s Daria had met Hopper at the Belgrade Film Festival; soon he began actively courting her and they moved in together in Taos, New Mexico.[1] Their wedding was planned for May 16, 1972. Drawing on Ann's sense of theater and Larry's sensitivity to shaping individuals' encounters with space, Daria and her parents designed a muted ritual on the dance deck, more notable for who was there and the rustic location than for any scripted performances.

The marriage ceremony, a freely adapted Jewish rite of betrothal, was described by a reporter from the *Washington Post* as "one of the most unusual weddings we could witness in America" in an article headlined "Captain America Weds."[2] (Actually it was Peter Fonda who wore the "Captain America" motorcycle jacket in the 1969 film *Easy Rider*, in which Hopper not only starred but made his directorial debut.) The *Post* reporter elaborated that the celebrity-studded wedding commenced with the sounding of a trumpet. On this cue Larry took Daria's arm and, holding it high in the air, led her very slowly down the curving steps from the house to the dance deck as the guests, assembled as an audience, sat on the benches overlooking the vista of San Francisco Bay. Ann and the rabbi were waiting on the deck under an elaborate chuppah hung with an old prayer shawl from Larry's family. After the wedding vows were exchanged, the guests scattered to load their plates with food from the tables that ringed the deck. Most unusual, as Larry's Uncle Sydney recalled, was that there was no dancing.[3]

Seven months later, in December 1972, Daria gave birth to Ruthanna, Larry and Ann's first grandchild. By 1974, however, Daria would leave Hopper and return to the San Francisco Bay Area with her daughter. "I was in a lot of trouble, very close to burnout. I just got through by the skin of my teeth," Daria later told *Parade Magazine*, somewhat cryptically, of that period in her life. "It took me a long time to find my way again."[4] In some ways Daria was the first person to really inhabit the liminal qualities of Halprin's art made at the boundary of life, and she spoke with honesty about how ill-equipped a life in her mother's art had made her for a life outside.[5]

Within a few months of the wedding, Ann, who had inexplicably begun losing weight, would encounter the most serious health crisis of her life. Dancing and a reinvention of ritual would be critical to her response. Already, with her increasingly frank use of race, nudity, and sexual politics in her male and female dance rites, Ann had been extending the aesthetic use of ritual for rediscovery. Now, however, her work would gain new impetus from her personal experience of life-threatening illness. Urgency and desperation would propel her out of the "normative conditions of urban life" into the state of "homelessness" that Marianna Torgovnick identifies as "producing primitivism in its most acute modern forms."[6] Her dual citizenship was activated, embracing not only the kingdom of the well, but also the kingdom of the sick.

Ann had launched her career in the postwar period by repudiating Martha Graham's formalized dance vocabulary, rendering herself stylistically homeless as a dancer in much the same way Merce Cunningham had. However, Cunningham remained in a consistently adversarial artistic dialogue with Graham's work, whereas Ann's work resonated with certain aspects of Graham's ritualism. Roger Copeland refers to Cunningham as having "modernized modern dance by repudiating its primitivist heritage."[7] Ann also modernized modern dance, but she did this by *contemporizing* its primitivist heritage rather than disavowing it. More important, Ann's later work would do the same for postmodern dance, essentially remodernizing it by recuperating primitivism as a response to the aesthetics of indifference. She recast dance as a vital agent for community expression and social change. For Ann, primitivism would serve as what Torgovnick describes as a frame whose presence allows us to "recontextualize modernity."[8] Ann was drafting a contemporary urban variation of the primitive through dance and in the process she was about to reveal to the West some of its own most deeply worked metaphors of illness.

Over the previous four decades, Ann had traced a path from investigations of the structural logic of movement, to task performance, to ritualized group encounters, in which she began experimenting with dance as a way of healing society. In all her explorations, teaching was inseparable from performance, and the pleasures of discovery in one linked with the satisfactions of presentation in the other. Her workshops led her to the subject and content of her dances. She continued to care about the end product, a dance, and she would fuss with it when a performance was imminent, adjusting costumes, spacing, and performance tone. But her initial interest lay in the early broad discovery phase and the personalized response of the individual dancers. Here the lessons from H'Doubler's classroom were contemporized and writ large, giving Ann an antidote to what she had long decried as the *anti*-individualism of modern dance.

In building her approach to choreography on what she did not want to happen (lockstep duplication), as much as what she did (personalized solutions), Ann was pushing dance making toward the realm of the remedial. In the period following the Kennedy and King assassinations, this took on the added valence of social honesty through allowing each individual to tell her or his own story. Most critically, Ann was increasingly working this way not so much because it made better art for audiences, but because it made for a deeper and more salutary experience for the performer. In Ann's theater of the 1970s, performers could disclose that they were something other than robust, tireless, and perfectly formed. It would be a short step from this to a broader agenda of using dance to heal.

For several years Ann had favored starting her workshops by guiding her adult students through a "visualization" process, asking them to draw life-sized self-portraits as a first step in recovering their stories.[9] In Ann's formula, visually displaying one's beliefs about oneself leads to physical responses. The direct path into one's body/mind is through the senses and one's emotional reactions. The drawn visualizations serve as the maps for this journey. Much more than just a visual approximation of oneself, the self-portrait drawing is intended as a site plan of the psyche, synecdoche of the anxious soul, splayed graphically across the paper. In Ann's process, this drawing is a critical first step in externalizing sentiment and sensation before they can be given kinesthetic form and danced as art.

The blank piece of paper Ann presented her students with for the "psychokinesthetic visualizations" had much the same function as the empty chair Perls used in his psychodrama therapy sessions.[10] From their recitations of dreams, Perls often encouraged his patients to produce characters, split-off parts of the self, which they could place in an empty chair and then interrogate and confront. Instead of serving as a seat on which to project one's feelings toward the unresolved part of oneself, Ann's blank paper offered a two-dimensional stage on which to visualize this hidden and unassimilated aspect of oneself. After the visualization, the critical part was the process the student/patient used to assimilate his or her insights. Ann encouraged these encounters with unassimilated corners of one's identity to unfold through movement rather than spoken words. She prompted her students to "move" what they imagined to be the emotional state of the drawn "other self." Like Perls, she was aiming at a cathartic experience of insight, achieved by improvising the movement of the character in the self-portrait. Ann had intuitively recast this part of Perls's Gestalt therapy into a tool for dance and a script for choreography.

Indeed, since the 1940s, when she first introduced drawing in the dance studio as a way of helping preliterate children script plots for their dances, Ann had trusted in a romanticized link between the heart and the hand. She saw drawing as a way to uncover danceable subjects and content, and she used it extensively in the Watts workshops as well as in her summer sessions on the deck. In their drawings students found task movement, gestural improvisations, and gentle insights. Now, however, Ann was about to discover, firsthand, that perhaps these images could have diagnostic and treatment uses as well. Perhaps the aesthetic could be remedial and curative.

One afternoon in the fall of 1972 Ann was leading the Reach Out performers in a collectively drawn group self-portrait, in which each person took a turn adding to one large drawing. When her turn came, she was surprised to find herself drawing a dark circle the size of a tennis ball in the pelvic area of the crayon figure, then putting an "X" through it. At first she told herself this was just a symbolic embryo to which she was giving birth. The image troubled her, however, because earlier in the workshop, when everyone had drawn individual self-portraits, she had drawn a similar dark circle in her pelvis. In the future she would often recount how her drawing this image twice both surprised and frightened her. The first time she dismissed the image:

> I drew a rear view of my body with an "X" going through it, slashing it. In the region corresponding to the pelvis—where the two lines of the "X" met, I drew a circle like "X" marks the spot. I remember hesitating to take the group's time to dance my self-portrait. Then finally, with time running short, and being the workshop leader, I allowed my personal needs to slip by.[11]

When the dark circle with the "X" through it appeared the second time, Ann responded differently. As with the ritualistic two stumbles that condemned the virgin to death in Vaslav Nijinksy's *Rite of Spring,* an event that occurs twice loses its spontaneity and takes on the force of something fated. With her second drawing Ann dismissed her original rationalization of the circle being an embryo and instead recalled how Sir Lawrence Washington's self-portrait two years earlier, using this same psychokinetic visualization process, had presaged his health crisis, and she was troubled. Ann viewed what she called this "imagistic language" of the self-portrait as a way of "receiving messages from an intelligence within the body, an intelligence deeper and more unpredictable than anything I could understand through rational thought."[12] Specifically, Ann later explained:

> Now the reappearance of the dark area in the group's collective portrait left me feeling uneasy, and reminded me of my earlier drawing. The next day I went to the doctor and asked him to examine my pelvic region. He did so and found a malignant tumor of the same size and shape as the one I'd drawn the previous day—and in the same place.[13]

Actually, the critical piece for Ann was not the drawing's deformity but rather *her inability to dance* this image of a figure with a mass in its abdomen. She said later, "It was because I couldn't put the drawing into motion that I felt blocked."[14] For her, giving shape to a feeling or understanding through movement was how she metabolized experience. If it couldn't be danced, it hadn't been truly experienced.

The tumor her physician found led to a diagnosis of advanced colorectal cancer. At age fifty-two Ann plunged into Susan Sontag's kingdom of the sick. In the 1970s, as Sontag describes in *Illness as Metaphor,* a horrible fear and dread accompanied any diagnosis of cancer, for the disease was thought to be uncontrollable, intractable, and incurable. "Cancer is the disease that doesn't knock before it enters. It fills the role of an illness experienced as a ruthless, secret invasion," Sontag cautions.[15] As Sontag explains, at the time cancer was seen in terms of a metaphoric battle waged inside one's own body, a fight against a sickness known for attacking parts of the body that were the most embarrassing to acknowledge—breasts, prostate, liver, colon, and, at the pinnacle of the hierarchy of shame, the rectum.

Adding to the cancer's assault on her body was the fact that the only cure was mutilating surgery. Ten days after she received her diagnosis Ann had a length of her lower intestine removed as well as one ovary. She came out of surgery with a colostomy, what is described in medical literature as "an artificial anus on the abdomen."[16] At Ann's request, her physician used her navel as the new exit point for her colon rather than opening a new incision in her abdomen—a practice that has since become routine in this kind of cancer surgery.

Ann remained in the hospital for three weeks following her operation. Not only was she was in considerable pain, but she was frail, having lost twenty-five pounds, and her spirits were low. As she later wrote, she wanted to get out of her body, to crawl out of her skin, the room, the hospital, the world. She raged silently in her mind against Fritz Perls, angered that he was no longer alive to help her through this. Then one afternoon Ann's mother, Ida, came to visit. She sat simply and quietly by Ann's bedside, holding her daughter's hand as Ann sobbed. "Connecting again to my feelings of love was the beginning of my restoration," Ann said of the epiphany this quiet act of handholding brought her.[17]

Ann's body had been irreparably changed, as had her relationship to it. Several months after the cancer surgery, she began to work with Robert Hall, a Gestalt therapist who had been a protégé of Perls, in order to focus on the emotional residue from her operation. One day she recounted to Hall a dream in which she was back on the operating table and a team of six faceless physicians were mechanically cutting away at her body, removing hunks of her anatomy. "Please don't harm my body. Dear God, please don't harm my body," she screamed furiously as they continued cutting. "This is my dancer's body and if you harm it, what will become of me?"[18] She railed against this fate as she had raged against Perls's absence. Ann was realizing just how deeply set in her body her identity as an artist was and how any strategy to reclaim it would have to be physically based as well.

For the rest of her life, Ann now needed to monitor carefully what and when she ate and drank as well as to irrigate her remaining colon daily. She never complained about this routine, but she was dismayed that the surgery had severed part of her psoas muscle, critical for abdominal strength. Two or three times a year she suffered painful spasms that usually resulted in her being rushed to the hospital to have a blockage opened. Her main regret was that she hadn't insisted on a reversible colostomy, which would have made the rerouting of her colon through her abdomen only temporary, as became the practice soon after her surgery.

Once Ann had recovered from the surgery, her doctor informed her that she could dance again and that if the cancer did not recur within the next five years she could consider herself healed. To mark her return to health, Ann now changed her name to Anna, as a way of returning closer to her given name of Hannah. Within a few weeks she returned to teaching, but it would be nearly twenty years before she took to the stage again publicly as a performer. As her strength returned, Anna studied her students' self-portraits, and now she noticed how the images tended to polarize into a dark side and a light side, the repressed and the accepted halves of oneself. Intuitively, she was now beginning to search for a means to link dance to rejuvenation and to unify the body severed by disease.

Three years after her surgery, in 1975, while on an individual retreat at the oceanfront weekend home and studio she and Larry maintained at Sea Ranch, Anna once again drew an image of herself that she was unable to dance. This time, however, what blocked Anna was that the portrait was too young and too healthy. "When I looked at the picture after drawing it," she later explained, "I knew I couldn't even begin to dance it; it just didn't feel like me. I turned the paper over and furiously began to draw another image of myself. It was black and angular and angry and violent. I knew that this back-side image of me was the dance I had to do."[19]

As Anna was drawing this "shadow side" of herself on the back of the paper, she became aware that she had begun bleeding internally, one of the emergency signs of the cancer's return. She returned to Kentfield and called her doctor, who asked her to come in immediately. She asked him if she could wait one more month before undergoing another colonoscopy. Now, she decided, she needed to dance.

On a quiet afternoon in 1975, after summoning a small group that included Larry, other family members, students, and friends, she ushered them into the big empty studio at 321 Divisadero Street and shut the door. Anna then commenced what would come to be known as her "Dark Side" or "Exorcism" dance. Wearing a loose and flowing tie-dyed caftan covered by a full-length, hooded black cape, she stood in front of her life-sized sketch of herself, with her back to her ten witnesses, and danced. The number of viewers was a *minyan,* the minimum required for a Jewish prayer session, the number necessary to get God's attention.

At the last minute Anna asked her friend the filmmaker Coni Beeson to document the dance. The resulting film opens with an image of Anna, shrouded in her hooded cape, standing before her drawing of a towering monster woman, who is nude except for black corset-like armor, high black boots, and bikini panties. It is not difficult to read a highly eroticized female into the image of a dominatrix-like woman Anna has drawn, someone who scripts and choreographs dangerous sexual encounters. In the film Anna crouches in front of this drawing and raises her hands upward as she emits a strange guttural groan that grows louder as it rises from deep inside her. As she battles with her malevolent and repressed side in her "Dark Side" dance, Anna literalizes the common metaphor that cancer is a fight waged inside one's own body. Unleashing waves of pent-up feelings, her dance seems to echo Sontag's conceptualization of cancer as a disease that is the result of repression.

The film is difficult to watch as Anna howls, shrieks, and sobs at her own image while intoning Kaddish, the Jews' ancient Aramaic prayer for the dead. In essence, the one praying in Kaddish is holding an audience with God, and at the conclusion of the prayer one is supposed to step back respectfully, signaling an end to this act of holding God's attention as a witness. Anna's emotional outpouring is raw and unmediated. As she recites the sacred prayer text of Jewish funeral services, asking God to remember and hold dear the departed, her hands claw desperately at the air. The funeral here seems to be for her "dark side"—for ego satisfaction, carnal pleasures, and vanity—anguish overtakes her as she tries symbolically to flush this part of her character and the cancer out of her body. "When I did it I was overwhelmed by the release of rage and anger. I kept stabbing at myself and howling like a wounded animal," Anna wrote later. "Witnesses said it sounded like I spoke in tongues," as if she were channeling a side that had not been allowed to speak.[20]

Anna's cancer had presented her with the ultimate challenge to her faith in the body as the basis of performance truth. By detonating her emotions in her dance, Anna hoped to purge herself of her disease itself, in line with beliefs at the time that cancer stemmed from "insufficient passion" and "the wages of repression."[21] Releasing emotions, especially anger, had also been seen as an important stage of healing in Fritz Perls's Gestalt sessions. Anna recalled how he had often pretended to fall asleep in the midst of a therapy session with a patient specifically to provoke the patient's anger. Perls saw anger as a necessary step toward liberating emotions, and he could be creative, even theatrical, in prodding patients toward this liberation.[22]

In unlocking patients' suppressed emotions, Perls had urged them to move through a range of actions, as though they were both victim and victimizer. Anna, who had been very influenced by Perls's concept of polarities, knew she had to find the other part of her self-image—what Perls sometimes called the mother and father parts.[23] She did not end her dance with the "dark side." She turned her portrait over, removed her black cape, and began to dance the "healthy" side. Borrowing from a wide range of aesthetic and therapeutic traditions, she imagined the cancerous part of her body cleansed by the flowing "waters" of her movements and her breath. As she explained, "I had an image of water cascading over the mountains near my home, and that the water flowed through me and out to the endless vastness of the sea, taking with it my illness."[24] When Anna finished dancing, she felt drained and also strangely purified.

After the dance Anna went to see her doctor, who ran several tests and determined that the bleeding had stopped. In 1977, after two more years without symptoms, she was pronounced cancer-free. From her personal experience, Anna had discovered both the performative and the salubrious qualities of dancing *near* death. Her cancer went into spontaneous remission, spurred, she believed, by this intensive process of visualization and physical enactment of the images. The supposed incurability of colorectal cancer made her dance-activated remission all the more remarkable.

For Anna, her battle with cancer was about more than her own healing. "The experience of cancer shook me up philosophically," she said later. "If I was devoting my whole life to doing this work was it just an ego trip or was it connected to life?"[25] Her sense of anguish grew as she thought of the six million Jews lost in the Holocaust. This survivor guilt for a globally scaled horror would become a springboard for Anna's next body of work—the massively scaled *Citydance, In and On the Mountain* and its sequels, including *Circle the Earth* and the *Planetary Dance*. On a much broader level than before, she began not only including non-dancers and non-dance elements, but also deploying emotions in a way that ruptured the traditional social frames used to hide them.

Most important, Anna's emotional journey to her own heart of darkness signaled an important aesthetic breakthrough. In her "Dark Side" dance, she had envisioned and performed her vulnerable self, the monstrous side that is usually repressed in each of us. Margaret Shildrick, a leading bioethicist and theorist of the body, has identified this contact with the liminal in each individual as "embodying the monster," a practice of acknowledging the insecurity of the borders that frame normative identity. "Monsters evoke opposition to the paradigms of a humanity that is marked by self possession," Shildrick explains. "The monster is not just abhorrent, it is also enticing, a figure that calls to us and invites recognition."[26]

As Anna's dream about the operating table expressed, for a dancer, the monstrous is associated with physical disfigurement and illness, changes to the corporeal self the dancer cannot control in a life premised on willful physical control. Anna's self-portrait dance sought to emotionally exorcise the malevolent half of herself by actually performing with her surgically disfigured body. Through dance, she confronted the transformation of her once healthy body into one that was diseased, damaged, broken. As

Shildrick cautions, the diseased or damaged body forces itself into our consciousness, our perception, as "other," and this is compounded by the fact that, historically, moral deficiency has been linked with non-normative bodies.[27] One of the realities of Anna's post-colostomy body was the possibility of real leakiness, a term that has strong metaphorical associations with bodily degradation and vulnerability. By addressing her "dark side" directly, Anna reversed this shaming process. She faced her monster within and all the enticement of its open sexuality. Through a spontaneous choreography of the grotesque, she reclaimed new moral strength in her dramatically altered form.

For Anna, the extreme challenge of a life-threatening illness became additional corporeal knowledge to be assimilated into her conception of dance teaching and performance. Through her "Exorcism" dance, she inaugurated a radical practice that would eventually grow into the major concern of her remaining career—the acceptance of a different body, the body recontoured by disease, as the subject, the medium, and the messenger of her dance.

As she began to expand her own personal experience with illness into healing dances for larger communities, Anna was certainly aware of Larry's evolving work with collective creativity. In 1976 he closed his large office practice, Lawrence Halprin and Associates, which had grown to nearly sixty members after more than twenty-five years of continuous operation. Larry and Sue Yung Li Ikeda, a fellow architect from his office, established RoundHouse, described as "a studio/thinktank," with the mission of exploring modes of collective creativity and collaborative processes by which individuals from different fields could jointly discover solutions to significant urban problems through workshops, films, and designs.[28] With the assistance of a grant from the National Endowment for the Arts, Larry went to film school in his quest to explore new areas of design and communication. Then, on behalf of RoundHouse, Larry and Ikeda traveled to Cadaques, Spain, where they made a surrealist film about Salvador Dalí, *Le Pink Grapefruit* (1976), as preparation for Larry's design of a proposed museum in Cleveland, Ohio, to house Dalí's work. In 1978, however, Larry and Ikeda dissolved RoundHouse, as the developer Gerson Bakar had wooed Larry back to landscape architecture, inviting him to do the site work and gardens for Levi Strauss's San Francisco headquarters.

Larry was restlessly searching for new models of collaborative design, on a scale that could ensure his hands-on, day-to-day creative involvement.

In sampling alternative approaches to linking individuals and their environments, Larry taught a ten-day workshop in 1977 for twenty-eight students from the University of California, Berkeley, College of Environmental Design at sites in San Francisco and Sea Ranch. He discovered what he saw as archetypal design themes in the gendered spaces the workshop members created—womblike hollows on the beach by the women and a high lookout by the men—architectural forms that were in many way counterparts to the movement designs the dancers in Anna's workshops were generating in the same environment.

Larry was also involved in another major design project. In 1976, after fifteen years of work, full of intense controversy and fierce competition, he had been officially commissioned as the designer of a national memorial for Franklin Delano Roosevelt in Washington, DC. This project would be the major work of his career, a massively scaled design experience that brings nature back into a park in the midst of a densely urban setting and turns spectators into performers crossing the landscape as they wind their way through the four magnificent outdoor "rooms" of the memorial. Here American history and the achievements of an American hero are displayed as a geography of texture, light, sound, and motion stretching over a seven-and-a-half-acre site along the Tidal Basin and the Cherry Walk. The critic Phyllis Tuchman described the memorial design as "creating a spatial experience in the landscape."[29] Although nearly twenty more years would pass before the FDR memorial project received enough funding to be built, Larry's selection as its designer in 1976 assured the scale of his legacy as an artist, not to mention the indelibility of his gestural writing with bodies on landscapes. In this grandly scaled work he succeeded in embracing both ends of the continuum on which all of his work, and to a great extent Anna's work as well, was located—between the majesty of secular public space and the sacredness of memorial space. The manner in which Larry's plan for the FDR memorial actually orchestrated a slow-paced contemplative experience for the spectator suggested a hybrid art genre of processional choreography and landscape as both a historical and an experiential text.

Larry's involvement with moving people through urban spaces had an immediate impact on Anna, who was about to launch her own grand-scaled artwork for a metropolis, *Citydance* (1976–77). In name as well as scale, *Citydance* would evoke Larry's "City Spirit" program from 1974, a project to encourage and stimulate community organizations to create open forums on the uses of art as a creative force in their communities. Even earlier Larry had created two much more specifically choreographic city-scaled·

scores for workshops in San Francisco. "City Map," from 1968, is a set of written and visual instructions for events around the city filling the first day of a twenty-four-day workshop. As Larry discussed this, "It was a score designed to sensitize people to a given environment and to other people's activities within it." In 1969 Larry planned "September 1970," an event intended to "use the entire city of San Francisco and its population as an art medium."[30]

Citydance, which began with workshops in 1976 and was performed in the summer of 1977, was the largest dance of Anna's career to this point.[31] In addition to Larry's scores, a distant precedent may have been the 1962 *City Scale,* a big environmental happening in San Francisco by Ken Dewey, Anthony Martin, and Ramon Sender of the Tape Music Center, which began at the center's original home on Russian Hill and spilled across the city with numerous scripted events.[32] Anna vaguely remembered having attended it because two of her dancers, John Graham and Lynne Palmer, reappeared at various times during the evening as a man giving a woman driving lessons in a crowded intersection. This was task performance on an automotive scale. In another scene, a car ballet, cars with colored gels on their headlights, as well as two pairs of lovers stationed at different points on the neighborhood streets, could be seen by the audience from a small park overlooking North Beach. The audience then was driven in two trucks to a book-returning ceremony at City Lights and a viewing of a bullfight movie through a lens that distorted all the figures. Finally (by now it was close to midnight), the audience was trucked to a park at the top of Potrero Hill, where two large weather balloons awaited their playful involvement. Their screaming arrival seemed to break up an imminent rumble between two teenage gangs.[33]

 Citydance was a more individually open performance that turned the entire city into a conceptual stage on July 24, 1977, from 5:30 A.M. to 6:00 P.M. The city's inhabitants, prompted by a core of Anna's dancers and students, became the dancers for this performance. In her notes for *Citydance,* Anna described it as three layers of simultaneous performances: The first involved the journey along the miles-long path from the start at sunrise atop Twin Peaks, through various designated sites in the city, to the waterfront finale at Embarcadero Plaza. The second was the enactment of the "scored" activities at each of the nine stopping points on the journey, and the third encompassed the individual dances each person performed within these two larger circles of activities.[34] This triple framing ensured that no matter what one was doing, it could be constituted as performing. As Anna later reported, "Children play-performed at South Park; a healer enacted a ritual at Twin Peaks; a poet created a thread throughout—reading at every episode; bums and crazies joined in at Market Street; dancers from the Mobilus group gave performances at the cemetery; and individual dancers and actors appeared in masks and costumes, contributing their individual pieces of theatre unexpectedly and effectively."[35]

Anna called *Citydance* her bicentennial gift to the people of San Francisco, and she led up to it with nine free monthly evening workshops at the San Francisco Museum of Modern Art. In these workshops she offered a redefined role for spectators, recruiting them as "witnesses," which she outlined as "observers who ratify and confirm our desires, or energies and successes and failures. By witnessing our successes as well as failures [they see that] both are the same . . . for we learn by what we were not able to accomplish as much as we learned from what we were able to do."[36] These two roles of witness and participant were also available at the performance itself as some citizens spontaneously joined in the passing parade of dancers and others watched them from sidewalks as the dance wound its way through the city's various neighborhoods.

Citydance was the inverse of how architects and designers work with space. Instead of building structures, paths, and environments and then waiting for passersby to animate them, *Citydance* claimed the city as a "found" stage in the Duchampian sense of the term, and its residents' actions immediately became "found" choreography, which was enhanced as they negotiated their way through a day in their life in the city. However, it was not the aesthetic references that interested Anna in *Citydance* as much as the ritualistic and communal possibilities. She focused on the dance's capacity to suture art more closely to daily life and awaken people to their connections to one another as inhabitants of the same city.

The Citydance events may be experienced on many levels, including recreation and entertainment. In addition, they are artistic experiences—changing our perspectives toward our environment and selves. We experience ourselves as dancers through awareness of our movements, and our city through awareness of our movements within it. The events may be used to facilitate self-study, recognizing that we reveal ourselves through our movements and they may also be viewed as a spiritual experience, viewing the ritual as an historical community means of integrating self with community and environment.[37]

Citydance invited people to find collectively their own path through an urban stage/environment. Earlier in her career Anna had taken small tasks from daily life and asked performers to explore these little actions as dance. Now in *Citydance* the tasks involved hours and miles of walking, carrying, holding, and watching. Hundreds of performers enacted these tasks, and thousands of people saw them. Anna increased the scale of her work in *Citydance* in part because this was a way to increase the reach and impact of dance. Instead of waiting for audiences to come to her, she was bringing the dance to them, so that by virtue of going about their daily lives, they became both her viewers and her performers.

In the 1960s and 1970s the customary reason large groups of people gathered and marched in the city's public spaces was for social protest. Anna's goals in *Citydance* were less overt, but she did have a purpose in having people move together. "All the folks in our city, as in all places in the country and the world at large, have the capacity to experience their lives as a dance," she said in a prepared statement she read at one of the workshops leading up to the event. "I think dance, in its seminal beginnings, was meant to have a purpose, and the purpose was a direct link and tie-in with the life of the individual, the life of the family, the life of the community. My concern is to renew and reaffirm these seminal purposes of dance . . . to give greater harmony and wholeness to our lives."[38] Because *Citydance* took place soon after the assassinations of San Francisco mayor George Moscone and supervisor Harvey Milk, Anna's intent was also to help reunite a city that was angry and divided over these murders. "I wanted to bring back a sense of trust and enjoyment to the city," she later said.[39]

Anna had embarked on a changed path in dance now that she was back from her brush with death. She was spurred by a new spirit of *Tzedakh*, the Jewish tradition of doing good deeds by giving to others, as part of living a righteous and thankful life, and her dance had grown significantly more inclusive in the process.[40] When she was convalescing from her cancer surgery, Anna had had a spiritual experience. She was lying in her bed overlooking the redwood trees in her yard when a black raven flew in and sat on her bed. In Jewish legend this bird is the herald of death, and Anna, feeling that he had come to take her, began to protest. She insisted that she still had work to do and the bird agreed to let her stay if she devoted herself to using dance to promote personal, social, and environmental harmony.[41] Initially, she channeled her relief at surviving into *Citydance,* as a big, fun, participatory event for anyone who wanted to join in, drawing on the experience she had gained with the Esalen workshops with George

Leonard. By 1981 she had begun an annual public healing rite that would come to be called *Circle the Earth* as her gift for having her life spared.

Most critically, Anna had recovered a meaning in life through this bargain she made with death's messenger, the crow. While physicians' viewpoints and popular belief divulge widely on the role visualization and optimism play in healing, the one point on which they agree is that those who manage an illness like cancer most successfully do so by using it to find meaning in their lives. Anna used her cancer to find meaning in her dance as well. *Citydance* was the first installment of that reconnaissance. It would be another five years before Anna found a social issue around which she was again compelled to construct a public dance.

———

During her three-year experience with cancer, Anna had read about alternative medical and healing practices, both ancient and contemporary, across a wide range of cultures. She now saw her role as an instigator of communal rites and her work as community ritual. With Daria she cofounded the Tamalpa Institute in Kentfield in 1978 with the goal of creating a nonprofit research and educational arm of the San Francisco Dancers' Workshop and offering training in a creative process integrating psychology, body therapies, and education with dance, art, and drama, as a path toward healing and resolving social conflict. They initially assembled a group of twenty-eight students and staff for a new, condensed ten-week intensive training program. Participants in the training program met for eight hours a day, five days a week, at Anna's Kentfield studio and dance deck. Classes continued on Yom Kippur and Thanksgiving, with special prayer and food rituals incorporated into the activities on these days. Not just the time, but also the content of the program was intense. Anna, Daria, Jasmine Nash, Norma Leistiko, and G. Hoffman Soto took turns leading the participants through scoring, visualizations, warrior dances, and more, moving from a concern with self to relationships and finally groups. Daria describes the Tamalpa training as providing a stronger structure for the emotional and psychological elements stirred up by Anna's dance teaching of the mid-1970s. As Daria explains:

> I felt so strongly that the ways in which the work had been so provocative needed to be reframed. There needed to be a more conscientious responsibility taken for the places participants were being taken. There were aspects of Anna's work that others of us like Norma Leistiko, G. Hoff-

man Soto, and Jasmine Nash, who had been teachers in Dancers' Workshop, were modifying and adding to. So Tamalpa Institute was a coming together of two quite different perspectives and orientations. The result, which took many years of tumultuous confrontations and transformations, was a real training program and a successful "grounding" of Anna's absolutely unique experimental work. Tamalpa led to the reconciliation and "proper" bridging between life and art that was Anna's original vision and hope.[42]

Anna's teaching practice, begun some thirty years earlier as an anti-establishment gesture, was now institutionalized.

One morning, in the middle of the fifth week of the intensive training program, Anna announced that her theme for the day would be "Relationships through Looking at Bodies." After the group assembled at 10 A.M. she stepped forward matter-of-factly, removed her clothes, and showed everyone the colostomy opening in her navel. She asked Peter Land, the resident photographer for the workshop, to take a close-up of it. "Don't feel sorry for me," she told some of the more squeamish ones, "it doesn't hurt."[43] Although she no longer had pain from her surgery, Anna was still in the process of reclaiming her injured body as her medium of teaching, and this full disclosure of its external wounds was as much for her acceptance of her new self as for giving her students a new way to regard *their* bodies as unmarked canvases for their art. She was reversing the practice of keeping the diseased or mutilated body hidden and making it instead a focus of spectatorship, and thus an art medium once again. At the same time she was trying to invite a regard for the body that wasn't always sexual. "I wanted to create a more trusting environment for the women and men," Anna said later. "I especially wanted to make the women feel they were not sex objects."[44]

Anna turned to the group and asked the students to undress and find a partner. She then led them on a tour, at first visual and then tactile, of each other's bodies. "The objective is not to get into your feelings," she cautioned those who started hugging. "It is to look at your feelings. Notice them, and then go on." In her notes on the training, the Reverend Sandy Park, one of the participants, recorded the curious bluntness of Anna's instructions for this body survey. "Don't stroke. Touch objectively," Anna commanded. "Select a hairy spot, or a rough spot. Touch. Hold. Let go. Absorb. Breathe into your rib cage if you're anxious. . . . Your hand is like a stethoscope. Palm gives information. Take your time. Look at some place you've avoided.

Touch there. Guys, if you've got a hard-on that's fine."[45] Anna's instructions carried an est-like edge of confrontation, as well as a teasing interrogation of some of the body's most private recesses.

Next came a curious piece of choreography emphasizing the spectatorship of body parts. Anna ordered the men to line up "according to penis size" and the women to "move down the line looking at each penis." Sounding like a drill sergeant, she said, "OK guys, stop chattering. This is an initiation. You won't get this opportunity again. This is a trust opportunity. Don't miss it." The women were then instructed to line up according to "boob size" and it became the men's turn to eye them and then touch three places on each woman's body. "You've performed a beautiful ritual. Give yourselves a hand," Anna told everyone at the conclusion of the exercise.

Reminded of this episode in her eighties, Anna laughed with rare embarrassment. "I was trying to disengage personal sexual response and to free people to work with the body without censoring. I wanted them to begin to appreciate the body objectively. I wanted to neutralize the body," she explained. "I wanted to say, 'Look, if *I* can accept [my colostomy]—you can accept *your* bodies.'"[46]

The exercise's concluding acts of self-exposure closed the circle that had begun with Anna's displaying her "new" rectum. She had long sought emotional health through dance and now, she was suggesting, a physically repaired body might also be claimed, virtually, through dance. The quest for health, individual and collective, and the acceptance of a diminished body had already been launched as a topic of Anna's work and now it was part of her workshop pedagogy as well. It would become, in one way or another, the subject of every dance she would make for the remainder of her career.

Drawing on her own desperate and spontaneous reaction to her illness and systematizing this experience, Anna developed a method for dealing with emotions and real-life crises like terminal illness. She began working with a five-part process she developed with Daria to aid others in "looking at their dark side." First, using movement, visualization, and free-association writing, people *identify* their issues, their shadow side. Then, with movement and sound, people *confront* this material, exploring it. As they express the issues they have identified and visualized through physical movement, they *release* destructive patterns and open up for new creative possibilities. After release comes *change*, as people tap into their energetic forces and redirect these forces for healing. Finally, in a stage of *integration*, people take their experience in this process and apply it to their lives. They can repeat this process whenever necessary to look at a new or old issue that surfaces.[47]

With this process, Anna essentially recycled her own "exorcism" dance into a patterned process others could trace.[48] By emphasizing the dimension of healing, she expanded the integration of life and art at the core of her earlier Reach Out workshops. As she later described this way of working: "When our dances are connected to our real life issues in this manner, it is called the Life/Art Process. This method of working with dance seeks to access the life story of each person, and then use this life story as the ground for creating art. This is based upon the principle that *as life experience deepens, personal art expression expands, and as art expression expands, life experiences deepen.*"[49]

In the spring of 1981 Anna gave the first performance of a communal dance that would evolve into *Circle the Earth,* her signature statement about the dancer in everyone, collectivity, and health. In this work Anna inaugurated a new kind of tourism of the kingdom of the ill. She began to make dances whose content concerns critical social issues and which collectively constitute audiences as witnesses, students of information whose presence serves the performers and, by extension, gives a civic dimension to their issues. This undoes the customary relationship in which the performers provide scopophilic pleasures to the audience. As Anna later explained to Richard Schechner: "I don't want spectators. Spectators imply a spectacle that takes place to entertain and amuse and perhaps stimulate them. I want witnesses who realize that we are dancing for a purpose—to accomplish something in ourselves and in our world. . . . The role of the witness is to understand the dance and support the dancers who have undertaken the challenge of performing. Spectators often come with their own personal aesthetics. They sit back and watch and judge to see if what is done lives up to their preconceived notion of a particular, very culture-bound idea of a certain kind of 'art.'"[50]

In 1980–81 Anna and Larry had taught six joint workshops, called "Search for Living Myths and Rituals through Dance and the Environment," at the College of Marin. They wanted to involve residents of Marin in an exploration of movement combined with environmental awareness, leading to an artistic statement about their common vision through performance. Curiously, when asked to draw during the workshop process, the participants repeatedly came up with images of Mount Tamalpais, the central mountain in Marin. At the time the mountain, which towers over the Marin landscape, was closed to the public because since 1979 seven women had been murdered on its trails and the murderer, dubbed the "trailside killer" by the media, was still at large. As Anna later explained, "When we noticed this recurring image we knew we had found the myth we were searching for."[51] The focus among the workshop participants then became the enactment of a ritual to reclaim the mountain.

On April 10, 1981, the workshop participants, including several Tamalpa trainees, presented a two-day ceremony/performance called *In and On the Mountain*. It began in the College of Marin theater in the evening with ritual enactments of the murders, as family members of the dead women and others from the community watched as witnesses from the audience. The frame of a formal proscenium theater was a strange setting for this event, which was visually chaotic and scaled more as an intimate exchange than as a large-scale statement for spectators. Pieces of the performance clearly echoed Anna's earlier works—a "water dance" by the women resembled the original improvisatory structure of *The Bath,* the animal dances of the *Male and Female Ritual* resurfaced as the dancers enacted the creatures living on the mountain, and the rolling scaffold from *Parades and Changes* was pressed into service as a sliding stage for various dances evoking the elements of wind, fire, and earth. Although a proscenium stage served as the venue for the first segment of *In and On the Mountain,* Anna was already shifting into a mode where the real recipients of the dance experience were the performers themselves. As if confirming this, the performance continued throughout the night, long after the audience left, as the participants slept in a "dream wheel" formation, with all their feet pointing toward the center of an imaginary wheel and their heads positioned outward. The suggestion was that they continued dancing in their sleep, or that the act of sleeping itself could be framed as a section of the performance, as their involuntary sleep movements within the larger frame of this formalized arrangement of their sleeping bodies.

The next morning, after a brief "sunrise ceremony," the performers and audience members (or witnesses) were bussed to the top of the mountain and began walking down the trails, leaving offerings at the site of each murder. Someone brought a tree to plant, another brought poetry about the mountain to read, and several members of the Pomo Indian tribe as well as local families with children joined in the free-form dancing downhill. Because the killer was still at large, the police and sheriff's deputies were on the ground and helicopters kept watch from the air, stretching the scale of the performance into aerial space (and including the criminal justice system). Circumstances soon suggested that it swelled into community space as well.

Thirty-six hours after the performance, an anonymous phone call helped police pinpoint the killer, and three days later he was caught.[52] Without this final act, Anna's *In and On the Mountain* might have remained just a broad dramatic gesture. But she found it difficult to dismiss the suggestion of a causal link between the dance, the tip, and the capture. "I have never said we caught the killer," Anna clarified, acknowledging it wasn't that the dance had magical qualities, but rather that "the dance focused the mental intention of the community toward solving the problem."[53] From the unsolved murders of several strangers, Anna would move toward a focus on individuals' own impending death, creating collective dances that harnessed this deep attention as a means of healing. Soon she would turn this energy inward on a microscopic level toward visions of cellular battles with cancer and AIDS.

Later that summer, when Don José Mitsuwa, a 106-year-old Huichol Indian shaman, visited Tamalpa Institute to present a deer dance, Anna asked him about a possible link between the dance and the capture of the murderer. Mitsuwa told Anna there was a connection and that mountains were among the most sacred places on earth, but that the rite she and her students had done needed to be repeated for five years in order to complete the purification. Anna complied, and the repeat performances—*Thanksgiving* (1982), *Return to the Mountain* (1983), *Run to the Mountain* (1984), and *Circle the Mountain* (1985)—each focused on the theme of life against death and each did so by enacting outdoors the big emotions of loss, recovery, and reconciliation.

Anna did not end the rite with the fifth year. Instead, she continued with *Circle the Earth* through 1991, conducting a week-long workshop each year that culminated with a performance on Mount Tamalpais. Gradually she shifted the scale and ambitions of her ritual from returning peace to the mountain to reestablishing harmony to the individual participants and their communities, and eventually to easing global tensions. By 1987 Anna's students would effectively universalize this "peace dance," calling it the *Planetary Dance,* as they organized local performances of the "Earth Run," a segment of the old *Circle the Earth* ritual, in countries from Australia and Japan to Germany and England. In 2005 Anna celebrated the twenty-fifth anniversary of the *Planetary Dance,* tracing its beginnings to the original *In and On the Mountain* performance.

Yet the all-inclusive rhetoric surrounding these group experiences can mask the genuine set of standards and expectations Anna brings to the work. The challenge of peeling back to what she calls the "unarmored" performer is substantial. The critical element for her has been how to collectivize the performers' sensibilities so that they learn how to express themselves as one person. A case in point was the *Planetary Dance* held on Sunday, April 30, 2000, at Santos Meadows, near Muir Woods, in Northern California. About 130 people gathered in an open grassy field, most of them graying fifty-year-olds who participated enthusiastically but with little initial sense of how deliberately structured even the loosest-appearing of Anna's community dance rituals are. As the participants half-walked, half-jogged around the circular path marked off in the meadow, embracing the four directions of north, south, east, and west, Anna cast a critical eye on the circling performers, waiting for what she calls their "self-expression to burn off." "This is a rare opportunity to express ourselves as one person," she told the group. "Let's seize this!" When a man asked how they could all become one body, Anna answered, "It's simple—just pay attention. Pay attention to all of your senses. Look at the person in front of you and behind you. Listen to the drum beat, and you merge with all of that." One man then ran the circle holding his baby aloft, and Anna commented on how sweet it was. "Can't we dance for the child within us?" he asked. "No," she responded, "that's still dancing for yourself." Anna assigns herself the role of Koshare, the person in Native American culture who tells performers when they are standing out too much as individuals. As Anna told her crowd, their quest was to become one body as Native people do and to do this they needed to get back into the spirit of the dance: "Where people dance for hours . . . there is another force that becomes alive so you dance for all people."[54]

"I dealt with my cancer privately in my training program for ten years and then came out with *In and On the Mountain,* which I didn't like," Anna confided several years after its performance. "I liked what I was trying to do, but I didn't like the way I did it."[55] After the fifth-year performance on the mountain, Anna reflected: "As a choreographer who has been making dances most of my life, this has become my challenge and personal criterion: to make it simpler and simpler for people to experience the fullness of their own nature, the humanity in the movement."[56] For Jamie McHugh, who served as Anna's assistant from 1986 to 1991, it was precisely this simplicity and its attendant satisfactions that drew him to her work from his background in modern dance. "[Her] simplicity honors the complexity of each person's individual experience while also connecting them to the power of the group," he explained.[57] The "power of the group" here refers to what Richard Schechner has defined as "the experience of group solidarity, usually short-lived, generated during ritual."[58]

Although she had been using the word *ritual* for decades, it wasn't until *Circle the Earth,* immediately following the Mount Tamalpais performances, that Anna finally found a balance between efficacy and entertainment, the critical dyad Schechner identifies as the polarity on which ritual and the performing arts are constituted. The more Anna articulated the purpose of *Circle the Earth* as functional change, the more her means of generating movement aligned with the kinds of attributes Schechner has associated with ritual, including providing a link to the transcendent, a sense of timeless time (an eternal present), a trancelike experience for the performer, a downplaying of virtuosity and an enhancement of the possibility for self-transformation, audience participation, and collective creativity.[59] Yet as she has clarified for Schechner, "The people enact in ritual what they want to have happen in their lives. . . . Efficacy in this sense is not cause and effect. The purpose is to awaken people to peace [or another issue] and move them to action."[60] Later, in her manual for people with cancer, *Dance as a Healing Art,* Anna refined her conception of ritual: "Ritual is another word that needs a new definition. . . . Ritual, as I use the term, refers to an artistic process by which people gather and unify themselves in order to confront the challenges of their existence."[61] McHugh has elaborated: "*Circle the Earth* is not a substitute for direct action in the world. . . . How people apply this experience in their lives becomes the acid test of its success."[62] Both Anna and McHugh have described the performance of this ritual dance as a "prayer," underlining its spiritual dimension. From her earlier work in stripping movement down to simple task performance, Anna has evolved toward a way of bringing the sacred back into the everyday. With *Circle the Earth* and the *Planetary Dance,* using a deliberately accessible movement vocabulary, often as simple as walking or running, she invited anyone to enter into what she has called "the magical and transforming power" of dance.[63]

In her workshops during the late 1970s and 1980s, Anna had begun taking her personally desperate and spontaneous reaction to her own cancer and recycling it into a patterned process others could trace. In the later 1980s she would draw increasingly on her credentials as a shaman for people in life-threatening situations. Anna shifted from using untrained dancers from the general population in her collective dances to a focus on a less visible segment of society—the ill—and she shaped the movement vocabulary around the task of recovering health. Two different workshop experiences—

with cancer and HIV-positive patients—ensured Anna's continued allegiance to what she understood as bodily wisdom, and particularly the power of the communal body she constituted through performance, in combating challenges.

In 1987 Anna was invited to work with the Cancer Support and Education Center, a support facility for individuals with cancer in Menlo Park, a suburb some thirty miles south of San Francisco. Magdalen (Maggie) Creighton, one of Anna's former students from the late 1960s, had founded the center in 1982 and she ran the program there. Twice a month Anna would commute to the center, traveling about one hundred miles round-trip, to work for half a day with a group of patients. For two years she did this regularly, often visiting her mother at her home in nearby Woodside on her way to the afternoon cancer workshop.

At the center Anna would lead cancer patients through a series of body awareness exercises and then ask them to draw their images of themselves, including the "dark side," just as she had done in confronting her cancer when it returned. Systematizing her own intuitively shaped response, Anna led them into finding movement tools for expelling some of their anger and fear about having cancer and for visualizing their body's resistance. "We were working on the core issue with Anna," Creighton explained. "People were surprised when we wanted them to act things out, to actualize their energy toward healing. But Anna helped them so much in being able to become aware of how they blocked energy."[64] Anna persuaded each person, no matter how restricted their physical ability, to move in some way, even if only while seated in a wheelchair, so that the body's capacity for shaping, rather than just being shaped by illness, was activated. "Words didn't do it—moving it out did," Creighton noted. "The patients were actually imagining that they were their white cells assertively destroying cancer."[65] Anna had come to view her psychokinetic visualization process as a contemporary way for people to identify, delineate, and then purge anxieties about critical illness. She encouraged the cancer patients to release their fears in order to make themselves emotionally available to "the healing power of the flip side of the destructive force."[66] Face death, but choose life was the implicit but steady message.

In one session at the center, for example, Anna focused on the participants' taking passive or active roles in a relationship as a means of prompting them to see how relationship or old family issues might be reflected in their feelings about their illness. After each participant took a turn at being led with eyes closed by a partner around the room or doing the leading (with eyes open), she asked the class to make a drawing of what the exercise had been like for them. As Anna described in her manual *Dance as a Healing Art:*

> Virginia has been struggling with cancer in the bridge of her nose and has suffered terrible headaches and eye problems for several years. Her drawing was a large face with closed eyes and an open mouth with the word "AH" coming out of it. She also drew clouds floating across her forehead. After the exercise she said she felt so released, tranquil and soft. She loved being led with her eyes closed and had not felt so good in years. Her partner, Janice, drew a picture of two figures. One was a frail young girl with a large red heart for a torso dripping drops of blood. She called this figure "bleeding heart." The second figure had wings. She called her "guardian angel." . . . Janice could feel on a deep movement level that she was being led by a guardian angel.[67]

In another session, Anna guided participants in a series of movement explorations; then, after a break, she asked participants to clear their minds and draw an image. Next they were to "write a poem, a chant, a single word, or a sentence" and share that with a partner. Then they took the image into improvised movement and finally recounted their experience. Dennis, a father of two young boys, was having a difficult time with his cancer, which had spread throughout his body. Yet the word he had written was "gratitude," and his dance conveyed a deep sense of reverence and gentleness. In both instances Anna's focus was to help people bring awareness back to their bodies and to resensitize them to the manner in which movement sutures sensing to feeling and emotions.

A year after Anna began teaching in Menlo Park, the center started a new program, "Moving toward Life," created for Bay Area people who were HIV-positive. The staff at the center invited Anna to work with this new population, and in late 1988 Anna began a ten-week pilot movement program just for men and women who were HIV-positive, or who had AIDS or ARC (AIDS-Related Complex). Not only were the health issues different, but the population of the HIV-positive contrasted dramatically with the cancer patients at the center. Instead of mostly older and middle-aged white women, the AIDS group, which soon became known as the Steps Theater group, was made up almost exclusively of attractive, fit-looking young men from various racial backgrounds. Most were in their twenties and thirties. For a choreographer, even one as untraditional as Anna, young men were usually the most enticing, but most elusive, population to work with, and now men were suddenly calling, begging to work with her.[68] After her first workshop with HIV-positive people Anna noted another quality that made this work so rewarding for a dancemaker: "I have found in these groups something I have never found before—100% commitments."[69] She had also found a social issue that needed no justification about its importance.

Influenced by her work with the AIDS group at the center, Anna decided to change *Circle the Earth* in 1989 into a public ritual by and about individuals with AIDS and cancer. The event *Circle the Earth: Dancing with Life on the Line* was born. Participants have remarked on the uncanny correspondence that emerged between feelings and forms in the movement images the group spontaneously generated. Describing what became known as the "Monster Dance" score, McHugh said:

> We were to hold up our partner's drawing of their monster as they advanced toward us in their dance of ugliness, anger, rage and darkness, and then comfort and restore them after this confrontation. As I held my partner in the aftermath, amidst the tears and sobbing, I felt myself slipping back through time, back through all the many battlefields in history. I imagined the wailing and keening of women the world over, grieving for dead sons and lovers and fathers and brothers. . . . That all of this would emerge through a simple movement structure was very new and exciting for me.[70]

McHugh, impressed by the "chillingly strong archetype" that emerged, saw *Circle the Earth* as a ritual that re-created a dual sense of tribal and dance experience, re-forming "ancient consciousness in a contemporary being."

When the "Monster Dance" was performed publicly, each member of the audience was instructed to take a simple white cardboard mask from under their seat and to hold it up to their face as a means of protecting themselves against the dangerous things being cast off by the performers. The effect on the spectators was immediate, because it not only became very difficult to actually see the dance, but they too became performers with roles and "costumes" so specific that one was fearful of disobeying.

One of the hundred participants in the nine-day workshop leading up to the 1989 *Circle the Earth* performance commented, "The score for the week shakes up each person's feelings to a fizz, throws us into more intimacy than we would choose on our own, and uses the pressure of a scheduled performance to help us loose our individual self-importance and focus on our common goal while still honoring our own feelings."[71] On the most fundamental level, the workshops leading up to this and other *Circle the Earth* performances not only erased the isolation and loneliness of terminal illness but turned a state of hiding into a moment of bold public declaration. As Anna recalled, at the 1989 performance, held in the Redwood High School gymnasium in Marin County, several parents present in the audience learned for the first time that their sons had HIV when they saw them step forward at the opening and shout: "I want to live!"[72] AIDS was still a relatively hidden issue in 1989, and Anna's presentation of a performance by people with AIDS confronting their disease was one of the first in a genre historian David Gere has come to call AIDS dance.[73]

Anna decided to deepen her work with HIV-positive performers. Her program at the Menlo Park center was so successful that by the summer of 1989, twenty-four men from the workshop accepted Anna's invitation to continue the project. In the fall of 1989, under the direction of Anna, these men formed the first all-HIV-positive dance group. They named it Positive Motion.

At about this time Anna learned that Allan Stinson, a local black actor who had studied with her in the mid-1970s but had then moved to New York, had been diagnosed as HIV-positive. "When I moved to New York in 1980, Anna and I kept up our relationship. We wrote back and forth all the time," Stinson recalled shortly before his death from AIDS in 1993. He described how Anna, in trying to adapt her cancer workshop model to encompass AIDS, came to invite him back to the Bay Area to work with her on this project.

> She didn't know anything about AIDS and HIV. She had no reason to because it had never crossed her life or affected her family. But she began to try to find out things and to understand it because I had it. And she found out that it was around her more than she realized. . . . She was getting attention, media attention, phone calls, inquiries. . . . AIDS was hot in the therapeutic sense and so she was pushed, guided, and led to it by those kinds of things.[74]

Stinson, with his serene presence and resonant, trained voice, became an important link between Anna's 1970s work about individuals marginalized because of race to this new population marginalized because of AIDS. Anna would eventually form an all-women's group of AIDS patients, most of whom were young and had become infected through drug use or bisexual partners. She called the women's group "Women with Wings." With both groups it was the larger frame of disease that was her primary focus rather than its identity as a critical issue for gay men. "I find it ironic," she once remarked, "that physical closeness and touch are usually part of what goes on when one contracts AIDS, yet the minute you are diagnosed they are the first things you lose."[75]

On June 16, 1990, after nine months of weekly evening classes, Positive Motion made its debut at San Francisco's Theater Artaud, a small alternative space in a renovated warehouse. The fourteen men in the group, supported by musicians Jules Beckman and Norman Rutherford, offered an hour-long performance, *Carry Me Home*. This dance developed out of the men's workshop experiences of their struggle to come to terms with death in their twenties. In his forty-minute documentary video of the rehearsals and performance, Andy Abrahams Wilson chronicles the journey of this group of articulate, impassioned men from residents of bodies in crisis to compatriots in a new community of hope. Anna guides the men through her customary sequence of voicing, drawing, and moving their feelings, focusing specifically on their sentiments about having the AIDS virus. Over the first seven months of the workshop, which the video records, many of the men become progressively weaker and Anna gently accommodates them. At one session she teaches the entire evening-long workshop with the men all lying flat on the floor, their interactions quieted to slow sliding on their backs as she instructs them to connect and move past each other "like water over a stone."[76] For Anna, there is dance in any movement, and virtuosity resides in the depth of the performer's candor in acknowledging what his body can't do rather than straining past what it can.

Wilson documents the first time the men of Positive Motion move their sessions into Theater Artaud. Anna goes into a spontaneous "rant," crying out to the men assembled around her and to the cavernous space of the empty stage behind them:

I thought I got rid of all the decorations and all the bullshit and tiddly-winks that went with this goddam type of theater. I'm very angry. And I didn't know I felt like that. And I don't know how to transform this. So it's up to you and it's up to you and it's up to you. To be so goddamn good. To be so real—real. To be so together. And to be so what it is you are here for. And what it is you have to do for yourself. And what it is you have to say to someone else. And what it is that you feel. And what it is that you think. And what it is your spirit tells you. That we're just going to bust this fucking place wide open and make it alive with some kind of fucking life! I can't stand this black box![77]

While Anna was clearly angered at the sterile neutrality of the black-draped space, she was also, intuitively or deliberately, modeling for the men precisely the kind of authenticity-in-the-moment she wanted them to display. Particularly with a disease with as many social prohibitions and containment strategies as AIDS, teaching people how to peel back to the layer of true feelings and then to disclose this publicly required an enormous leap. She was showing them that she could jump first.

This moment marked one of Anna's rare returns to the formal constraints of traditional theatrical space in these middle decades of her career, and it was not an easy fit. In particular, she must have felt the irony that she was back in the theater now only because the subject of men with AIDS performing was radical for the venue—whereas in the past she had used sites that made the venue radical for her subjects. As a work of dance theater, *Carry Me Home* never really transcended the hard facts of its subject—the men themselves and their insurmountable life-and-death health issues. Instead, it inaugurated a theater of illness where being present and watching made one a witness whose presence allowed public confession rather the spectatorship of judgment. Anna's 1960s experiments with participatory spectatorship were coming full circle. The participants now arrived with the issues that needed to be addressed and Anna's task was to shape a movement theater that allowed this.

In her work of the 1980s Anna had become a guide to the kingdom of the sick, a specialist in a performance category of her own invention, one that might be called "the tourism of sickness." Reshaping her own path from illness into remission as the detailed itinerary for a journey anyone could take, and that all would eventually make, Anna's *Circle the Earth* became the most often performed dance of her career, with *Parades and Changes* a distant second. Each year, starting with the Mount Tamalpais healings in 1980 and continuing as *Circle the Earth* from the mid-1980s through 1991, Anna had offered free preparatory workshops to the public, inviting large groups of individuals to design a community myth, which they filled out through drawing, writing, talking, and dancing individually, with partners, and as a group. The results were highly individual and idiosyncratic, so it is not possible to designate any one occasion as a typical performance. Yet the scores setting the process in motion remained remarkably constant from year to year. As Anna has described this dance aimed at bringing peace to individuals and communities: "*Circle the Earth* is a series of ceremonies and prayers expressed through movement in the tradition of a dance ritual. It is comprised of eleven little scores, each with its own intention, props, and vocabulary of actions. PREPARATION . . . Peace Meditation coming into mutual alignment. I AM THE EARTH . . . we birth ourselves. I WANT TO LIVE . . . confronting death. VORTEX dance . . . we create a group identity. MONSTER DANCE . . . we evoke and confront the destructive forces within us. RESTORATION . . . we heal our wounds and restore our lives. BRIDGES AND PASSAGEWAYS . . . we create a pathway to Peace. THE EARTH RUN . . . we offer the planet our commitment to Peace. PEACE WHEELS . . . we create a wheel of harmony. BIRD TRANSFORMATION . . . we send word of what we have learned and created to the whole planet. PEACE BIRD AND COMMITMENT . . . Celebration. Performers and Witnesses join."[78]

Many performing artists had commuted from the realm of the therapeutic to that of the artistic, but with *Circle the Earth* Anna transported the exotic cargo of illness into the center of the postmodern dance tradition. Anna's tools remained resolutely pedagogical in this regard. Like her mentor Margaret H'Doubler, she wrote numerous statements about her process, the majority of them manuals for how to teach these public rituals.[79] Anna's lessons were designed to lead participants through the physical, emotional, and imaginal landscape of the body. The destinations were understanding, acceptance, possibly even remission, and the means was performance.

Schechner, a longtime friend of Anna's, once challenged her about this causal linking of dance with recovery. In an interview he said to her, "But I want to know when you ask people to come together, is it in order to enjoy dancing, making dances, or is it to 'change the world'?" Anna replied, "I don't know the answer to this question yet. We are engaged in an experiment and we are by no means finished with it."[80]

In conversation several years later, Schechner expanded on this issue: "It becomes suspect when you think individual actions can change structural action. Certain artists want to make the world better. When you make the world better through art, you change individuals, but you can't make these big claims." The more defensible contribution Anna made through her work around performance and disease, Schechner suggested, is the way in which it questions and challenges the idea that there is a required body for dance. "She helped shift the focus from the body to the person," he said. "Every person has a body and uses it. In ballet you choreograph onto the body. There is no agency. Anna made the whole person the basis of choreography."[81] Anna had pursued a transformation of the dancing body into the prosaic body and looped it back into a new possibility of what could constitute a performing body. At the same time, in recasting the audience as witnesses, she forced open the insularity of her subject, disease and death, and demanded a different kind of engaged participation from the viewers. "Why perform?" she had asked in her manual "Circle the Earth." Her answer? "We needed the attention of the witnesses to know that we weren't talking just to ourselves, that we dance in relation to our larger community."[82] Scripted in relation to this one dance, this is a mission statement that holds equally well for all of her work of this period and, indeed, her career.

TEN

Choreographing Disappearance: Dances of Aging
1992–2006

The disappearance of the object is fundamental to performance; it rehearses and repeats the disappearance of the subject who longs always to be remembered.

PEGGY PHELAN
Unmarked

Dying is an art.

SYLVIA PLATH
"Lady Lazarus"

ANNA'S LAST LIVING PARENT, her mother, Ida, died in the summer of 1992, and one and a half years later, in the winter of 1994, Anna broke her twenty-two-year absence from the stage with the premiere of her solo *The Grandfather Dance.* She had continued dancing in her classes and workshops, but 1972 had been her last professional appearance on stage. Now, as she approached her mid-seventies, Anna began looking at her own aging, addressing this subject obliquely at first by invoking her late grandfather from her remembered impressions as a little girl.

People sometimes speak of first grasping their own mortality when the last generation of family members before them passes away, and they realize they are next. Anna's mother died four days before her ninety-ninth birthday. (Anna's father, Isadore, had died in the autumn of 1980.) In the final moments of Ida's life, Anna crawled into bed with her mother and effectively enacted a duet of stillness in the environment of the hospital bed. Like a parent, she cradled *her* parent as Ida's breath faded. At the same time this "dance" that Anna improvised in the hospital bed in the dwindling moments of her mother's life suggested the image of a child communicating silently with a beloved elder, a relationship that *The Grandfather Dance* would explore. Her "duet of stillness" also curiously presaged her participation in Eeo Stubblefield's *Still Dance,* a series of photographs through which Anna would "rehearse" her own aging and impending death in relation to nature. The performance scholars Peggy Phelan and Heidi Gilpin have both connected this kind of repetition in live performance to Freud's exploration of the psychic process of repetition and its links to the trauma of disappearance. "A child's *fort-da* [peekaboo-like] game of disappearance and return (mimicking the disappearance and return of the child's mother) exposed for Freud how an individual, through the repetition of a traumatic experience, could take on an 'active part' in relation to that traumatic event," Gilpin notes. She concludes, "The act of recollecting is a substitute for repetition."[1] Anna's late-career dances are performance recollections, an attempt to access a memory of a trauma yet to happen to her specifically, but already scripted in many respects through her observation of the passing of her parents.

Taken together, the dances Anna began to create and perform when she was in her mid-seventies offer a series of gradually enlarging close-ups of her psychological preparation for her own death. Her candor in delineating the tensions of this confrontation and her attempts at honestly depicting female old age are remarkable. Anna's position as a key forerunner of American postmodern dance makes her charting of her own journey through her seventies into her eighties a model that forces us to consider issues of identity and disappearance in live art.

Anna's works at the end of the twentieth century chart her ambivalence toward the use of her own body as what some performance theorists would call a "colonized" product of the times.[2] She challenges not only the ways in which social mores construct her body, hiding its age, but also the conventions of live performance, which both courts and then evades the disappearance of its product and performer. Anna implicitly resists many of the silent "rules" of live art—that old women don't dance, that elderly females should remain an invisible presence in society, that the fixation on youth should be unchallenged in dance.

In her early work Anna questioned, and often changed, the nature of dance. Who can be a dancer? she asked. What does dance look like? Where does it happen? What is its attitude toward everyday life? What is the role of the viewer? And what is the relation of one's work to one's emotional and physical environment? These same questions led her inextricably into the revelations of her late-career performances. Throughout her career she has explored what a body knows at different stages of life.

Intuitively, Anna has built her investigation on the other side of what the writer Naomi Wolf identified, simplistically, as the paradox of *The Beauty Myth:* "Women's craving for 'perfection' is fired by the widespread belief that their bodies are inferior to men's—second-rate matter that ages faster."[3] Through these dances it is possible to glimpse many of the complex social tensions surrounding older women and the performing body in late-twentieth-century America. At the same time Anna's dances allow for a recasting of the condition of age in the performing artist, and particularly the female dancer, as what the performance artist Rachel Rosenthal once affectionately, if euphemistically, called "ripening" in defiance of mechanical logic.

Implicitly Anna's dances of the past decade can be seen as rehearsals, providing a slowly accumulating vocabulary of movements and images, for a dance of death. At the same time Anna is drafting her valedictory to contemporary dance. Her RSVP approach to art making receives the ultimate test here, as she attempts to "score" the one "performance" we can never "valuact" (evaluate and then decide on a new action). Having come to this art form in the early 1930s, as dance ushered in new images of women's equality through the redefined physical force and social presence of the female body, Anna closes out the century with images that suggest how a path of transcendence might be charted through the representation of decline. Her subtext is now aging, and particularly how to draft the complex public narrative of a woman performer's aging.

The aging dancer choreographing dances for herself is locked in a difficult economy of disappearance and a self-portraiture of decay. The dancer spends her entire life trying not to "let her body go," a Sisyphean task, and then she finds herself on the edge of having to "let it go" for all eternity. While the desire to be remembered is a fundamental feature of performance, as Peggy Phelan has observed, so too is disappearance. For the aged dancer who continues to make and perform new work herself, rather than accumulate and recycle repertory, this commerce with disappearance becomes particularly fierce. Her medium, her changing body, relentlessly charts its own decline regardless of her efforts to wrest time and expressiveness from it. Having spent a lifetime accommodating to the evanescence of her art, the aging dancer faces a new tension—a medium whose temporality ironically grows more salient each time she creates a new work, enlarging her inventory of (vanishing) dances. The dancer who continues to work into old age, then, struggles with a triple disappearance: the first is the impermanence of the object she creates, the dance; the second is her ephemeral medium, her own living body, which ages and then vanishes with her death; and the third, and most immediate, is with her control over the narratives she still wants that diminishing medium to tell.

Inside this struggle against disappearance an aged dancer's work thus tells a double story—one is the conscious statement she constructs in her choreography, and the other is the spectral narrative her aging body spins independently as it quietly discloses its softening form, stiffening joints, and waning strength and range. As it ages, the dancer's body sheds a professional lifetime of the assumed narratives it has, and might have, expressed. In their place is an authentic narrative that grows increasingly vivid with the passing years—the performance of aging.

Dance is an art form that is particularly anxious about age because its physical deteriorations impose themselves on the medium of dance, the dancer's body, so irrefutably. Not only do the presence and effects of age evade concealment in the dancing body, but their very opposite—youth, physical power, and stamina—are the attributes on which the art form is constituted. It is little wonder, then, that in most Western theatrical dance forms a performer is considered "old" at thirty-five and generally "finished," outside of character or mime roles, after the early forties. To continue dancing even into one's fifties is a rarity, into one's sixties is practically unheard of. To dance about one's immediate experience in one's eighties is nearly unimaginable.

Anna is working within a Western performance tradition that has almost no history of the elderly performing or of decay being showcased. In contrast, in the Japanese tradition of Butoh, old age is routinely depicted. The great Butoh master Kazuo Ohno was legendary for performing into his eighties.[4] His performances offered layerings of strangely blurred gender and age personas. Through costuming and dense makeup he would seem to assume the form of a young girl, an ancient woman, an elderly man, or a cooing infant, sometimes in such quick succession that the identities seemed simultaneous. Despite his declining robustness, Ohno remained very much a performer in these works, layering on personas rather than peeling them away as Anna does. Yet in a 1986 interview with Richard Schechner, Ohno was asked, "When you finish a really good performance . . . what do you do? How do you cool down?" Ohno laughed. "At the age of 80 there is no more 'stage' and 'daily life,'" he said. Eiko, a Butoh-trained dancer half Ohno's age who was serving as his translator, explained simply, "He doesn't commute."[5]

If Anna "commutes" as a performer at all in her late-career dances, her journey is to interior psychological spaces rather than parallel performing presences. She makes her path by stripping away rather than accretion. For a woman in a Western dance tradition, her bold statement is to stay in her true identity. One myth that Anna implicitly rewrites with her late-in-life dances is what the feminist sports historian Patricia Vertinsky refers to as "the familiar master narrative of [physical] decline."[6] In its place her works posit high endurance, risk, and a dynamic concept of aging as not so exceptional. Implicitly they lobby for the active aged woman's body as an icon of physical and performance prowess that belongs in the public gaze.

Simone de Beauvoir's pioneering book *The Coming of Age,* which first appeared in English in 1972, inaugurated a discussion about how, in Western culture, age and aging are conceptualized more negatively in regard to women than men. At that time de Beauvoir observed, "I have never come across a single woman, either in life or in books, who has looked upon her old age cheerfully. In the same way no one ever speaks of a beautiful old woman."[7] While the cultural possibilities for women have expanded dramatically in the last few decades, this negative conception of aged women remains as a final piece of the identity baggage Anna's generation still needs to redress. As an artist, Anna, with her dances of old age, offers a dramatic physical image as a visual riposte to this neglect. So not only is Anna working within an art form and a cultural tradition that valorize youth, and a medium that demands it, but she belongs to the gender whose associations with age are the most negative and the least nuanced culturally. "Of course men don't age any better physically," Naomi Wolf says. "They age better only in terms of social status. We misperceive in this way since our eyes are trained to see time as a flaw on women's faces where it is a mark of character on men's."[8]

De Beauvoir catalogues a number of great artists who have created self-portraits in their old age—Leonardo da Vinci, Goya, Monet, and Rembrandt, and not only are all of them male, but their self-portraits tend to be, like that of da Vinci, "extraordinary allegories of old age . . . with features chiseled by experience and knowledge—they are those of a man who has reached the highest point of his intellectual powers."[9] These portraits valorize aged males in terms of the good that time has etched in their characters, as it is revealed on their bodies, primarily from the neck up. If one positions Anna's last dances, particularly her performances in Eeo Stubblefield's *Still Dance* from 1998 to 2002, in this tradition of male painters making grand consummatory self-portraits at the end of their lives, they become fascinating studies of Anna's attempts to depict her own old age. Like the late-nineteenth-century Countess de Castiglione, whose futile struggle to author her own image through staged photographs has been chronicled by Abigail Solomon-Godeau, Anna is grappling in *Still Dance* with drafting a bluntly candid image of her aged self as she presents herself to the camera.[10] This is relatively unmapped terrain, particularly for a female dancer.

Arguing as an advocate for aging women in sports, Patricia Vertinsky has called for a new, active concept of aging as "self-narrated experience."[11] Instead of treating the aging woman's body as a fiction, hidden reality, or curiosity, Anna's dances reinscribe it in the public sphere as part of an "aesthetics of expressivity" rather than an "aesthetics of effacement."[12]

Writing about live performance, Heidi Gilpin observes, "Indeed, we must begin not only to let the body go, but also to revel in its absence, and in the traces engendered by its passage from presence to absence."[13] It is these traces that Anna's late dances seem to be deliberating as she herself considers the many levels of that passage from presence to absence, as the will battles entropy. The line between traces of her presence in the end of her performance and the end of her life is permeable.

Ida's death was still very much on Anna's mind when the dancer Nina Wise, who had been working with A Traveling Jewish Theater, asked her if she would create a "Jewish" dance for the theater group's festival of Jewish artists. *The Grandfather Dance* premiered at the Fort Mason Theater in San Francisco on February 2, 1994. For this dance, Anna wears a pair of her father's black silk pajamas along with her own lace-up mountain boots and a long white tasseled scarf, which she uses as a prayer shawl. She begins by chatting casually with the audience from the stage. She uses a first-person narrative to frame the dance as intimate and personal, while at the same time shaping it as a theatrically informal disclosure. "My daughters had some chance to connect to the Yiddish culture, but my grandchildren, they missed it all," she comments, explaining that this dance is for them. As the faint sound of a klezmer band is heard, Anna slides into a tipsy, joyous stomping dance, her arms lifted up imploringly and her head tilted quizzically to one side in a theatrically "Jewish" pose that might come directly from *Fiddler on the Roof*.

Anna appears before us as her grandfather, but the voice of her character becomes that of herself as a little girl in awe of this devout and bearded old man. "All my life I've been searching for a dance that would move me as much as my grandfather's dance moved him," she says. This is her first pass at portraying old age, and she does it indirectly. Instead of representing the women in her family, she identifies with the male legacy, masking her gender. So she presents herself visually as the right age but the wrong gender. (The fact that gender disappears in some sense in old age becomes perhaps liberating, or at least aesthetically useful, for Anna.) At the same time, through her voice, she presents herself as the right gender but the wrong age. She seems to be casting about for how to situate herself somewhere between the performer and the spectator of her own senescence. This is negotiating the balance between representing and inhabiting.

By approaching the subject of age obliquely, and through the male gender in whom age is equated positively with wisdom and insight, Anna seems to be wresting a corresponding regard for her own old age as a woman performer. But it isn't her old age she is performing, yet, and it also isn't her real self she is dancing about. As a lifelong performer, it is Anna's body as much as her mind that holds her knowledge. By wearing her father's sheer silk bedclothes she seems almost to be trying to climb into his skin, and her grandfather's as well, as if "trying on" an elder relative's old age before she can address her own.

Late in the summer of 1998 Anna found herself confronting a health crisis with Larry that brought the subject of age and death into much more immediate proximity to her own life. On Monday, August 24, Larry went into a San Francisco hospital for a minor elective surgical procedure on his arthritic hip. His physician said he did four hundred of these procedures a year and that Larry should be out and on his way by the next morning. However, Larry had been taking large amounts of aspirin for his arthritis and had not been informed to stop prior to surgery. As a result, in surgery he began to hemorrhage profusely, suffering a blood clot and two major strokes that left him in intensive care on a ventilator, temporarily paralyzed and battling pneumonia. It was a month before he was taken off the ventilator (leaving his voice with a permanent huskiness) and transferred to Marin General Hospital, closer to Anna and their daughters and their families.

During the two months of Larry's hospitalization, Anna shuttled between home and hospital, attending to him as his mobility gradually returned. It was a profound immersion for her in the links between mobility and life and in the body's capacity to give birth to ambitions in the midst of a struggle against death. One Sunday evening in early September Anna staged a healing with a few friends, and later, in October, she sat by Larry's bedside and led him through a movement meditation to help him sleep. It worked after one and a half hours, until a male nurse barged in and turned on the lights to take Larry's vital signs. Anna was frustrated, but when the nurse left, Larry said he thought he could do it himself if she just massaged his feet. She did and he was asleep in ten minutes. With a resilience and resourcefulness that paralleled her own, Larry began to investigate how to use a computer mouse to be able to draw and design in case he didn't regain full use of his hands. He also asked Anna to contact friends who were in wheelchairs so he could discuss with them how to get around that way should he need to. He seemed to swiftly accept the possibility of his disability and figure out how to accommodate to it in order to keep his creative productivity going. Like Anna, he viewed life experiences like this as setbacks to be overcome or adjusted to while his work as a creative artist continued. Fortunately, within a few months he returned to full health and mobility.

Prophetically, Anna had taught a workshop in early October for a meeting of the California Dance Educators Association at San Francisco State University, which she titled "Regaining the Passion of Dance." "So many teachers get burned out after years of teaching," she said, explaining that her focus was on "getting them to reconnect with why they became interested in dance in the first place."[14] This is an internal conversation that has fueled her own creative work in dance for decades, and one that she was in the process of revisiting with new immediacy in the wake of Larry's medical emergency. Movement performance as a mechanism for survival was not just theory but deeply embedded practice for her.

Anna's next dance, *From 5 to 110,* was performed at San Francisco's Theater Artaud on November 7, 1999, as part of a shared bill with three other aging dancers, infelicitously named "*Still* Moving." At seventy-eight, Anna was the oldest in the group. She received the only standing ovation of the evening for her performance, and in the question-and-answer session that followed she displayed a sharp humor and a focused intelligence that suggested her cognitive dexterity easily matched her physical adroitness. The scale of her presentation was theatrical but the scope of her concerns was intimate.

From 5 to 110, a solo, is Anna's second attempt at depicting her own old age. It opens with her striding in boldly to center stage from an upstage corner, wearing a long gray knit skirt, boots, a suede vest, a loose-sleeved white blouse, and a fringed scarf over her shoulder. "I don't see my birds," she says. "I don't feel the ground under me. I feel lonely in this big black box." This lament for nature is a familiar anti-proscenium stance she has taken before in traditional theater spaces, but here it serves to disassociate her actions from "performing." Additionally, what is arresting about it as a beginning is that she is, intuitively, expressing a lamentation for the dislocation of the elderly. We suddenly realize that as spectators of an aged performer we are worried that the elderly on stage are going to lose their sense of place and that in their journey of transformation they will forget the way back. For most of us, the theater is by definition a deeply unfamiliar place, where location is continually redefined. For someone with Anna's duration as a performer, however, the theater is extremely familiar and its paths well mapped.

From her opening "confession" Anna slides imperceptibly into the dance, punctuating each of her statements with a brief gesture. "When I was five years old I danced for the fun of it. When I was a teenager I danced to rebel." She makes a fisted gesture to wistful violin music. "When I was half a hundred I danced for peace and justice. God of longevity, grant me the time. For I have so many dances to do. Grant me the time. When I am one hundred and nine I will dance as things really are." (It was at this point that the audience rose in a spontaneous standing ovation.)

In *From 5 to 110,* as in *The Grandfather Dance,* Anna is still backing into a portrayal of herself as aged. The marker of age she starts with is an image of herself as a child. The remaining reference points of age are all on the other extreme of aged—even the one middle-aged reference is framed in terms of its relationship to old age: "when I was half a hundred," not just "fifty." In fixating on the two extremes—the start and the finish of her life, the middle decades of Anna's existence as a dancer are made to seem mere stations on the road to the present. Her body's history reverberates with each cultural epoch she has lived and danced through, and the culminating point is where she is at this moment. More typically, dancers view their performing life as a tragic march away from this middle period.

In the post-performance discussion, Anna paraphrased an old Mae West joke about the essentials of life: "For the first eighteen years, you need good parents. Then from eighteen to thirty, good looks. Then from thirty to fifty, good genes. Then from fifty on, just money." She continued, "'Art serves my life' is not my motto so much as 'life serves my art.' With eighty staring you in the face it's enlightenment at gunpoint."[15] With these comments, Anna begins to inhabit her age publicly. In her subsequent work, she will rewrite Mae West's recipe, making the cultivated capacity of the performing artist's body to reflect her lived, and immediate, life, the dancer's equivalent of "money."

During the autumn of 1998, as Larry convalesced, Anna asked Eeo Stubblefield, a performance artist who had studied with her in the late 1970s, if she could participate in a site-specific form of environmental performance art Stubblefield had developed called *Still Dance*.[16] Since the early 1980s Stubblefield had been staging and performing her pieces from *Still Dance* in nature, and she had taught this form of dance at Anna's Sea Ranch workshops. Stubblefield's process relates to the genre of "staged photography" that emerged in the 1980s, in which photographers created scenes specifically for the camera, constructing "real" visual narratives and assuming the roles of director, set and costume designer, and often even actor in their own scenery. In *Still Dance* performance, body art, photography, and the particularity of a place in the environment are woven together. Aesthetically, *Still Dance* is situated between environmental theater, performance art, feminist body art of the 1970s, and massive earthworks.

For years, both on her dance deck in Kentfield and during her summer retreats at Sea Ranch, Anna had been exploring dance in relation to specific locales in nature, so this way of working was not new to her. As she explains:

> I collaborate with my environments because I have a strong attitude about the body not being an object. It is part of a total environment in space. That is influenced by Larry's work. You can see it in that our house is in and out of space.
>
> I also believe philosophically that humans are not the center of the universe. . . . My physical body is what I relate to on one level. But then what I am most concerned about is related beyond to the environment, and that is my holistic body. One reason I'm attached to the natural environment is it emphasizes for me my whole environment. That's also one reason I like doing *Still Dance*, because that brings me into direct contact with my personal body in relation to my collective body. I don't focus just on my personal body. In our culture we tend to think of our

body as the center. Our social body is our body in relation to others. The body in the environment, that's the collective body.[17]

In collaborating on Stubblefield's series of photographs *Still Dance with Anna Halprin,* Anna placed herself in a position of trust, allowing Stubblefield to select the environments and costuming, establishing the setting for Anna's dance. When they began the project, Stubblefield, sensing Anna's concern and anxiousness over her husband's health, chose a locale that would allow Anna to work with these feelings. Stubblefield took Anna to the beach at the Marin Headlands, across the Golden Gate Bridge from San Francisco. As if literalizing the emotional weight and helplessness Anna was feeling, Stubblefield asked Anna to strip nude and then buried her in a cold, wet hole, four feet deep, in the sand at the ocean's edge. Stubblefield arranged Anna so that she could move only from the ribs up; the rest of her body was encased in sand, paralyzed in a cement-like prison. Her breasts, arms, shoulders, neck, hair, and face were painted as well as caked with wet sand, stuck firmly to her body with a sticky coating of molasses. Her eyes eventually became red and swollen from sand that blew into them.

With Stubblefield directing and photographing her, a shivering Anna began to improvise from her sandy cell. In Stubblefield's photographs of this performance, the "Rock Series," Anna seems to be already buried, like a figure sinking in quicksand. With her skin and hair painted to match the rust and gray tones of the huge beach rocks behind her, Anna looks like a half-buried pewter and rock sculpture. She seems to be both receding into the earth and being extruded from it. In her dance for this work Anna physicalized in her own body what she imagined her husband to be feeling with his legs immobilized from paralysis and his hands frozen in stiff claws. In the process Anna discovered, in her body, her capacity to dance death. She had begun to choreograph disappearance. She was now ready to start physicalizing loss and demise. The process of taking on the form of these emotions also allowed her to discover their affective qualities. "It was like a living death," she later reported. "I confronted my anguish in that dance."[18] In her last corpus of works, and particularly *Still Dance,* Anna abandons a focus on the mind's understanding of death in order to listen to the body's. Her focus as the performer in this *Still Dance* piece is not on demonstrating an idea about death; it is about the body feeling buried, replanted in the earth, and the mind coming to terms with this purely through the body. Working collaboratively with Stubblefield, Anna performed in twenty-one *Still Dance* locales, with the resulting photographs often named for their location. For these meditative works, often of near stasis, set deep in rugged natural settings, Anna danced nude and alone, with Stubblefield and her camera the only witnesses. With her body coated by Stubblefield with mud, molasses, straw, dry grasses, clays, plants, bark, or body paint, Anna uses performance in these works to envision her own eventual return to the earth.

An image from the "Mud Series" of 1999, for example, captures Anna seated at the edge of a muddy pit, her body, head, and hair entirely coated with a crust of deep brown mud. Anna's arms are upraised, and in the fist of each hand she holds a clump of mud-covered grasses, which look just like handfuls of her own matted and sticky hair. We see Anna only from the back, but the image is startling because, although her pose resembles that of a female bather in a Degas pastel, instead of cleaning her body, she is smearing herself with wet dirt. The effect is that of first recognizing this as a classic image of a female nude on display and then feeling one's power as a spectator undercut because Anna's mud play seems a ritual as much for herself as for us.

Another sequence, the "Old Woman Series," shows Anna facing the camera in a kneeling position, covered with mud over her face and body. The darkness of the wet mud might make one think of the blackface of minstrelsy, but because Anna's entire face, including both her lips and her eyes, is coated with the same mud veneer, so the facial features are not exaggerated as in minstrelsy, this reference doesn't stick. Another reference that might seem to resonate through this and other mud studies of *Still Dance* is the chocolate-smeared body of the performance artist Karen Finley in her 1989 monologue *We Keep Our Victims Ready*. But the mud on Anna is not a conscious stand-in for excrement and defilement as Finley's body smearing was. There is no aura of seduction or spectatorial display about her simple actions in Stubblefield's tableaux.

Although Anna's consciousness of her Jewish heritage is more cultural than religious, numerous elements of Jewish burial traditions are at play in the *Still Dance* series. The fundamental Jewish law shaping burial is to have the body returned to the earth quickly, within twenty-four hours of death.[19] According to Jewish tradition, the body is prepared for the grave with the utmost simplicity. The body is cleaned, and no attempt is made to preserve or prettify it. Everyone, regardless of gender, age, or wealth, is buried alike, in a plain wooden coffin and wearing nothing but a simple, white shroud (a garment that, in fact, is the only article of clothing Stubblefield uses on Anna in any *Still Dance*). Cremation and embalming are strictly forbidden in Orthodox Judaism because they are seen as repudiations of the natural pace of the body's decomposition. The emphasis is on supporting the natural breakdown of the flesh so that the body is returned swiftly to the earth, the source of life. Since the Holocaust, images of ovens, chimneys, and the charred remains of Jewish bodies have lent additional negative associations to cremation.

It is possible to infer many other references, deliberate as well as unconscious, in *Still Dance*. These range from the visual arts—including Ana Mendieta's earth-body sculptures, Carolee Schneemann's use of her body as material, and Kazuo Shiraga's *Challenging Mud* body actions—to ecofeminist and ecopsychological concepts of personal and "planetary" well-being, to Larry's grand revisionings of nature as a charted landscape for the moving figure in his urban designs. All of these flicker through *Still Dance*. Most notably, the manner in which Stubblefield represents Anna as both image and medium in *Still Dance* evokes Mendieta's *Silueta* series (1973–80). While Mendieta as a visual artist in her twenties used images of the silhouette of her body emblazoned into the earth to suggest metaphoric associations between soil and the fecund female body, Anna's body in *Still Dance* creates narratives of the fragile, fleeting existence and contradictory meanings of an old female body.[20] Like Mendieta's works, *Still Dance* contains essentialist associations of the earth as a maternal link to ancestry, as both a burial site and a site of rebirth. Depending on the place in nature where she is performing a particular *Still Dance*, Anna appears alternately durable or frail, a form that seems to have just crawled out of the earth and may slide back in at any moment.

Visual artists like Auguste Rodin have revealed decrepit and tortured bodies as simply another side of nature the artist can depict. But in *Still Dance* we see not just nature mapped onto the body, but the body in turn being mapped onto nature. In the 1998 "Driftwood Series," Stubblefield has Anna, encased in a sheer white shroud, crawl along the cold damp sand at the ocean's edge, as if she were a giant thread of mucus coughed up on the shore. In the 1999 "Log Series," Anna rolls in the hollow of a rotting redwood, burying herself in a deep bed of compost and dead leaves. Thus Stubblefield shapes Anna to render what is customarily thought of as the least theatrical stage of life, old age, as an intensely performative state.

"As a dance artist I am propelled towards the natural world by three beliefs," Anna has said of her outlook in *Still Dance*. "One is the notion that the human body is a microcosm of the earth; the second is that the processes of nature are guidelines to my aesthetics; and the third is that nature is a healer. Rather than imitate the outward forms of nature or use nature as a stage set, I identify with its basic processes. The work is reflective, and attempts to understand how the natural world and human experience reflect each other."[21]

The *Still Dance* images convey the rapport Anna feels with the environment as a text and a partner. Anna is the only figure in these images, yet it would not be an exaggeration to say they are all duets, pas de deux between an old woman and the landscape. The environments with which she dances are expansive stretches of nature—the Northern California shoreline; a deep redwood grove; a cavernous watery grotto in "Underworld Series," where she sits as a small sky-blue figure huddled at the water's edge; or acres of hay fields in "Straw Series," where she cavorts at sunset, transformed into an ambulating haystack by the huge tufts of straw affixed to her body. Each of these environments introduces a different dialogue, framing a different portrait of the same image, that of Anna's body as a tiny figure in a dramatic, desolate setting in nature. Her form is at once a figure of force as well as one of extreme repose.

As Stubblefield explains, "*Still Dance* is not a process of forcing the land to serve as a metaphor for an internal human state. Nor is the land used as a backdrop for an abstract set of aesthetic principles. . . . The place does reflect our inner world, but the dancer explores that reflection through chosen movements so that the outer world influences and shapes the dance."[22] Stubblefield further clarifies: "My use of color and texture (body paint, mud, grasses) emerges from the interplay of both the character of the story and the direct observation of the land. This body art helps prepare the performer to move out of the ordinary realm, and also gives the viewer the chance to go with her. My hope is to refine and extend the senses, triggering memories deep within the body."[23]

Ana Mendieta once remarked about her *Silueta* series that "I use the earth as my canvas and my soul as my tools."[24] This is a statement that Anna and Stubblefield might just as easily have made about *Still Dance,* where, as in Mendieta's work, the aggressiveness of nature is not only present but palpably performed on Anna's body. In making this work, Anna's aging, female body is analogized within the most ritualistic, and final, frame we come to inhabit—the moist embrace of soft earth.

By December 1999, a little more than a year after Larry's ordeal, Anna was deep into creating a major new dance, *Intensive Care,* a twenty-five-minute piece based on her experiences at his hospital bedside. Here she focuses directly on the prelude to death. While she draws on her husband's illness and brush with death, it is significant that she stages it on her own body. Dressed in white hospital smocks that gape open in the back, revealing the naked backside of each performer, Anna and three younger dancers move through a slow tableau of postures of pain, suffering, terror, outrage, and finally acceptance. This litany of movements is structured on the five-part process Anna initially developed in her work with dance and illness twenty-five years earlier. Now she brings it full circle to buttress a stage dance *about* illness.

In the months of rehearsal leading up to the premiere of *Intensive Care,* the four performers each try to find their own point of engagement with the subjects of death and dying. The actor David Greenaway, for instance, had done hospice work in San Francisco's AIDS community; Lakshmi Aysola had studied Butoh with Min Tanaka in Japan; Jeff Rehg was battling both AIDS and cancer. (Rehg died in September 2001, a little over a year after the work's premiere in June 2000.) It is their private reality Anna is asking her dancers to perform in *Intensive Care* as she searches for hers. This is a dance about death, and it's on her body, but still it is not yet her own death she is dancing about.

With each performer drawing on her or his own storehouse of experiences, the result is a performance that hovers between rawness and realism, making viewing it at times both uncomfortable and engrossing. One critic said of its premiere that "it was hard to look at but impossible to look away."[25] That reaction curiously parallels aspects of Anna's own response to Larry's illness. "I was so frightened with Larry in intensive care that I would just come to the studio and dance," Anna recalled of the genesis of *Intensive Care.* "So it grew from a very personal thing. It started as a solo, but I wanted to expand the idea of the dance so it wasn't so personal and to explore our differences around the theme of death and dying to find our commonalities."[26]

In the years since its premiere in 2000, Anna has continued to rework *Intensive Care,* drawing on the contributions of new performers. She has added a new ending, using Meredith Monk's breathy and ethereal "Gotham Lullaby." The four dying figures slowly advance toward the audience, swooning into a final series of painterly stations of death, arms swinging vacantly against their chests and mouths shaping silent cries as black-garbed attendants support the fading individuals.

The June 2000 premiere of *Intensive Care* took place at the Cowell Theater in San Francisco, as part of an evening-long concert to celebrate Anna's upcoming eightieth birthday (in July). For this program Anna revived the undressing and re-dressing section of *Parades and Changes,* and the juxtaposition with *Intensive Care* illuminated how this earlier body, with its defiant youthfulness and prowess, captured with such vividness by Anna in the 1960s, had now given way to a worn and corpselike body of old age, riddled with anxieties about death. For the same program, she also paired *The Grandfather Dance* and *From 5 to 110* with two new dances in a selection she called *Memories from My Closet.* The two new dances were *Gratitude,* a short monologue about her male and female ancestors, and *The Courtesan and the Crone,* a short solo. In his review of this concert John Rockwell wrote:

> Like all her work, and the work of many of the artists with whom she has collaborated, these dances could easily be dismissed as New Age California dippiness. "I'm accused of being touchy-feely," she once said. "Well, I am." But what made these retrospective performances so moving was her ability, enriched by a lifetime of desire and human drama, to refocus her experience back into art.[27]

The Courtesan and the Crone, like *The Grandfather Dance* and *From 5 to 110,* is a dance about two extremes of identity—in this instance, sexual and gender identities—that frame Anna. Wearing an elaborate Venetian carnival mask of a beautiful young woman, which one of her daughters had brought her as a gift from Venice years earlier, and a long gold cape, which she originally bought for a White House reception she attended with her husband, Anna repeatedly flip-flops from the gestures of a coy seductress to those of a finger-jabbing old crone. As she shifts her mask, her body seems to gain and lose years as well. As the courtesan, Anna strokes her breasts and thighs inviting the spectator's touch. As the crone, she curves her spine forward, hunches her back, and stares menacingly at the audience. In this brief snapshot the seductiveness of beauty and the fear of age are portrayed as opposite sides of the same feminine coin.

The crone is the real archetype Anna is closing in on, an archetypal figure of matriarchal power. Historically, the crone has been seen as the embodiment of wisdom and the final figure in the three stages of a woman's life—virgin, mother, and crone. The counterpart to the "death-dealing" crone is the "life-giving" virgin. Even if today, as the feminist writer Barbara Walker indicates, "the law doesn't murder witches any longer . . . modern society does eliminate older women in a sense. They are made invisible." Walker directly links this denial of the crone to our society's abhorrence of death: "In their anxiety to deny the crone archetype through religious imagery, patriarchal societies even denied the fact of death itself. The crone was the one who took the soul through the dark spaces of nonbeing. She represented the kind of death that our culture wished to conceal, making it invisible as old women are invisible." Indeed, as Walker argues, the permitted images of death in our society tend to be violent and sudden, hence distanced from us. "The crone shows us death as it more frequently is experienced, death from wasting disease and the slow degeneration of the body and mind."[28]

In a program note for her eightieth-birthday retrospective concert, Anna wrote:

In our culture, it seems as if we relate to death by hiding from it, romanticizing it or mythologizing it. Rather than interpret a concept, I want to convey what I have seen in others and felt within myself: feelings of fear, anger, sadness, regret, panic and even guilt. . . . What we as performers are trying to do is bypass our acquired belief systems and go directly to our physical bodies which hold all our life experiences.[29]

Without being conscious of it, Anna is using the voice of the crone here. She has learned the crone's language because she is now close enough to feel in her own body death's inexorable approach. The formula Anna is using here is one she has employed repeatedly over her career to give the contours of emotional realism to her dances. However, now she is attempting to give public shape to the one experience of which we can have only future— never past—knowledge: death.

In December 2000 the pair of Japanese-American dancers Eiko and Koma approached Anna about creating a collaborative work. Supported by a grant from Charles and Stephanie Reinhart, co-artistic directors for the American Dance Festival and dance at the Kennedy Center, the resulting dance premiered in October 2001 at the Kennedy Center in Washington, DC, with additional performances in January at the Joyce Theater in New York and at the Yerba Buena Theater in San Francisco. "Stephanie and I were the midwives for this project," Charles Reinhart said. "We went to Eiko and Koma, and said we'd like to commission you to do something with another artist. When they came up with Anna we jumped for joy!"[30] As

Eiko and Koma explained, "We have gotten so much from [Anna]: this is just a way of giving back." Even though, as Eiko indicated, the extent of their formal training with Anna was a single workshop in 1977, her significance in American postmodern dance has been formative for them. When pressed about the specifics of Anna's influence, Koma said simply, "We live in New York and we are crazy. Here we know there is another person on the West Coast even more crazy."[31]

Anna had never collaborated in this fashion with other dancers, and the process was difficult and prolonged as she advocated the dance evolve through her method of scoring while Eiko and Koma pushed to design it with more of an immediate emphasis on its visual impact. Over the next eight months Eiko and Koma commuted four times from New York to rehearse in Anna's indoor studio and outside on the dance deck. In one of the early rehearsals composer and renowned cellist Joan Jeanrenaud sat in the middle of the studio, her eyes gazing downward as she played double stops, pulling rich, resonant tones from her cello, occasionally hinting at a klezmer-like melody in little lyric runs. She focused on the task at hand, adumbrating death and relationships, the themes of this cross-cultural and cross-generational dance. Anna, for her part, followed Koma's instructions as she walked a few inches on her bare feet across the hardwood floor of her dance studio. From the other end of the room Koma called out to her softly, "Walk as if each step were on a carpet of tiny, tiny, flowers and you are not wanting to crush them. Feel the nice smell of the flowers in the upper body. And below, under your feet, destruction!" Anna tried again. This time she let her chest and head arch slightly backward and her arms float gently open, elbows bent, as she moved her feet in small steps, brushing them lightly across the top of the floor and then plowing them down in the imaginary flowers. "My balance isn't so good now, so walking slow is hard," she told the Japanese-born Koma, fifty-three, and his wife, Eiko, forty-nine, who crouched near her feet.[32]

For Anna this quip about balance was a rare admission about any age-imposed limitation on her remarkably lithe and limber old body. The previous day, for their first session together, Koma had asked Anna to "be an egg," which she dutifully did as a solitary exercise for one hour. Later, on that gray and chilly afternoon, the three had spent several hours, nude except for wrap-around skirts, improvising movement studies on the dance deck. Comfortable with nudity, they had been in quest of sculptural still-life images to evoke the implicit subjects of their collaboration—the navigation of relationships and the end of one's life.

The match was both logical and iconoclastic. Like Anna, Eiko and Koma work intuitively using nature as a springboard, coaxing out their choreographic designs rather than imposing them, letting the subject of their dance emerge quietly. Until this collaboration Eiko and Koma had always worked exclusively with each other with an acute eye toward form and images, whereas Anna focused on what she calls her holistic body, a conception of the body as part of a total environment in space. The resulting dance, *Be With*, was a document of a process, an emotional movement puzzle that kept spilling its pieces on the floor and reassembling them in a new order. In rehearsals death and tangled human bonds inhabited the studio improvisations through a sense of the body as a tremendously weighted and unwieldy freight whose steering grows increasingly perilous.

The *Be With* rehearsals were as much about finding motivation as inventing movement out of the poetry of decay. As the work evolved over the months, Anna immersed herself in Eiko and Koma's style of slow, sustained action, and they in turn were tugged into her steady questioning of motivations and the psychological and emotional texture of the dance. "In my work I don't start with emotion. I start with something that might elicit emotion," Anna told them.

The costumes began as lacy cheesecloth robes, which Koma hand-painted a fiery red and orange and then cut and tied until they resembled shredding skin. They imparted an eerie texture of decomposition to the dancers' crumpling walks along the mottled deep rust rear wall of the studio. *Be With* came to offer a mordant yet transcendent image of the dancing body stilled.

In performance, *Be With* courts, and then thwarts, narrative understanding. As Tobi Tobias, the dance critic for *New York* magazine, noted, "And all of a sudden, this stuff starts telling stories! Halprin appears to be the aged female of the tribe who must be escorted, willingly or no, to her death; a generic nurturing mother who brings solace to Eiko; a mother-in-law to Koma, who confronts her almost brutally, and perhaps sexually. Forty minutes of what might be taken by the irreverent for an ethnographic soap opera concludes with a contrived epiphany in which the three protagonists are raised on high, looking like statuary representing household gods." Although she called *Be With* "a worthy experiment," Tobias reflected on the ambiguity of its content:

What's going on? When they operate alone, Eiko and Koma are not characters in a narrative or even in a situation. They're more like elements of nature, life at a stage of development distinctly primordial, only slightly more apprehending than stones, rivers, and trees. Halprin's presence changes the nature of what occurs not because she is Caucasian but because her contribution has forced upon Eiko and Koma's private universe concerns and attitudes of Western culture innately alien to it.[33]

Anna struggled with *Be With*, and despite a generally favorable critical reception she remained dissatisfied—for her, as for Tobias, its real content remained elusive. Still, after the performance, she remarked, "I needed time for it to sink into my bones. Working with Eiko and Koma was a welcome challenge. I learned a lot and I admire their aesthetic. We remain wonderful friends."[34]

Anna continued working with Eeo Stubblefield until 2002. It is interesting that *Still Dance*, the only work Anna performed that was deliberately not created for a live audience, exists as one of the most heavily documented artifacts of her career. Not only did Stubblefield shoot hundreds of photographs of Anna, but Andy Abrahams Wilson documented their collaboration in *Returning Home*, a forty-five-minute film released in spring 2003. Wilson had followed and documented Anna's work for several years, beginning when he was a graduate student in visual anthropology at the University of Southern California in the late 1980s. One of his early projects was a documentary script about Anna, which concludes with a statement from her prophetically anticipating the aesthetic of dancing her immediate reality that *Returning Home* would chronicle:

> I don't think it's possible that I'll ever stop my work . . . unless I lose my mind. . . . One of the things I've noticed is how some dancers will just keep dancing the same dances as if they were the same age they were when they did those dances—and I've just never done that. I've always been very aware of where I am in my own personal life, and whatever I do in dance always reflects that.[35]

Fifteen years later, in the film *Returning Home*, Anna speaks frankly about the demands of her aesthetic choice to have her art follow her life:

> I'm aging. My body is not the same as a twenty-year-old's, and it doesn't have the prescribed quality of being in social places. But I think an aged

body has its own configurations of beauty. So the nakedness is its own metaphor. Working in nature stirs up very ancient memories that are just stored in the body. It makes me feel I am being true to nature by being sensitive to the natural world around me. The dances touch such deep places in me like a soul. That I would never have thought up. So they are always like little treasures. I come back feeling reborn in some way. Whenever I feel I need inspiration I always return to nature. Maybe it has to do with releasing to be able to come to terms with my own passing when the time comes.[36]

At the same time that Anna has been making her dances of aging and defying the rarity of encountering an old woman's body as the subject of dance, the growing cosmetic surgery industry has ironically focused public attention on the aesthetics of aging. In this context, the aged woman's body has become present by virtue of striving for its transformation backward in time to youthfulness.[37] "Instead of aging normally through their full life cycle, women are constrained to create an illusion that their growth process stopped in the first decade or two of adulthood," Barbara Walker has noted.[38] The aging adult is forced to think differently about her (or his) aging self. The hierarchy shifts: instead of using one's mental resolve to aggressively shape, discipline, and push one's body into the desired physical form, it is the body that begins dictating to the mind, cataloguing its limitations. As the philosopher Michel Foucault has observed, "The body the adult has to care for, when he is concerned about himself, is no longer the young body that needed shaping by gymnastics: it is a fragile, threatened body, undermined by petty miseries."[39]

Indirectly, the rhetoric that the aesthetic surgery industry uses to describe its goals for the aging body reveals some key beliefs about the performative aspects of oneself that are lost through aging, and potentially recoverable through "treatment." The cosmetic surgery industry prizes the body that defies change and instead enacts broadly cultural beauty ideals. An arrested state of continually performing the same immutable physical self becomes the goal. This is freighted with complexity, because, as the feminist theorist Kathleen Woodward has noted, "For its owner, the aging body is always a reality, always a fiction."[40] Our bodies are constantly growing older, yet we work continually to become stronger and healthier, as if growing in the opposite direction from death.

Anna's struggle with her body is not to preserve this myth of the unchanging self. Instead, she steadily works through dance to embody images showcasing change by continually adjusting to the mutability of her body and the evolving nature of her emotional preparedness for death. In *Still Dance* Anna prefigures death as a sensory experience rather than representing it as the most extreme form of sensory deprivation. Freud said that the compulsion to repeat was a substitute for the ability to access memory. Anna uses repetition in her choreographies of aging as a way to represent the memory of an experience that has not yet happened.

If, as Christopher Lasch observed in *The Culture of Narcissism,* despair of the future leads people to fixate on youth, then is it Anna's optimism about the future that propels her to embrace age?[41] She examines rage, sorrow, loss, fear, and guilt as emotional reactions to the approach of death, giving each a physical presence in her body. Her dances of aging are an attempt to recover through art the individual's authentic and true self, the same self that cosmetic surgery purports to reclaim. Elective medical interventions against aging, however, reclaim the body through erasure. Stalled aging is the goal, whereas Anna's portraits of aging aim to showcase the functional and true tractability of the old body. Perhaps aging and death lose their sting when made to work for an artist.

Anna also implicitly challenges a myth of the dance world—that one works steadily to change the body closer toward perfection during the years when one is training. Then, imperceptibly, at one point, one shifts, paralleling the goal of aesthetic procedures, to working toward *not* changing as one struggles to deny the effects of aging on the body's inner musculature, skin, response time to stimuli, speed, and precision.[42] Anna's dances of aging are in direct conflict with the impulse of aesthetic surgery, where medical intervention fictionalizes the exterior self to match the interior one. Anna's life project has been how to draft a nonfiction movement portrait where the inner and outer narratives mesh.

In several *Still Dance* series Stubblefield asked Anna to both experience internment and "perform" it, representing burial visually in such a way that the camera—and behind it, the spectator—shares the experience. Here the work lies midway between the theatricality of dance and the personal immediacy of performance art. In her video performance *Mitchell's Death* (1978), the performance artist Linda Montano "dances" her experience of one degree of separation from death. In this solo Montano, after inserting dozens of acupuncture needles in her face, recites an incantation about the details of the death by gunshot of her ex-husband Mitchell. The performance is an act of healing, but an experience of pain, particularly because in chanting her text she constantly has to move the muscles of her face instead of remaining still, as is customary in acupuncture treatments. Anna, in contrast, invites the body to perform and enact its emotions rather than allowing us to witness passive discomfort we can only hypothesize.

It is because Anna has defined so well the path into and out of the backrooms of our affective centers that her performance process has been as influential to the field of contemporary dance and theater as her actual choreography. Witnessing Anna today, in the costume of herself—that of an elderly woman on the edge of eternity—is ultimately comforting because it reminds us so vividly of the profound uses of live performance. Time and loss are essential elements in all choreographic works, and all the more in Anna's final body of works.

Even the notion of the beautiful is reassessed as an aesthetic value through the use of Anna's body as a site to recuperate disease, waste, and aging. This suggests that performance can be a mechanism for surviving and healing the displacement of physical decline. At the same time Anna gives us a different understanding of disappearance and death. In her late-in-life dances Anna presents her life as her work and her ideas offered for the next generation to develop. For much of her life Anna was preoccupied with using performance to describe the world she found. In these dances of aging she finally embraces performance to address the world she wants.

Since 2000, Anna has continued to perform *Intensive Care* both in the United States and in France, often pairing it with the part of *Parades and Changes* that features a group of young performers undressing and dressing.[43] In September 2004, thirty-nine years after she first performed in Europe, surprising audiences with her dance ritualizing everyday behavior, Anna took *Intensive Care* to Paris, the first time she had ever performed in France. She and a group of eight dancers performed at the Centre Pompidou as the opening dance event of the Festival d'Automne in what the French press called a "spectacle vivant," a designation that captured the spare yet lushly ceremonial quality of her program of *Parades and Changes* and *Intensive Care.*

In extensive advance coverage, Anna was heralded as a force parallel to Merce Cunningham in initiating postmodern dance. Every performance was sold out and hopeful ticket buyers clustered at the entrance to the theater. Unknown to the Pompidou authorities, Anna and her dancers offered a free, hour-long outdoor improvisation, *En Route,* nightly in the nearby Place Igor Stravinsky. Dressed in their *Parades and Changes* unisex suits, embellished with black bowler hats, umbrellas, and a boom box for portable sound, the dancers turned their nightly trip from the hotel to the theater into a processional echoing the irreverent whimsy of the animated sculptures of Niki de Saint Phalle and Jean Tinguely in the square's fountain. Inside the theater, the dancers again bridged the proscenium frame, greeting audience members on the aisles as they walked to their seats.[44]

In March 2006, shortly before her eighty-sixth birthday, Anna was featured in a half-hour *Spark* program on KQED-TV, the San Francisco–based PBS station. Before a camera crew filming her teaching in her studio, she elaborated her belief about what makes a dance meaningful: "There are essentially two ways of working with the body," she said. "One is when *mind* informs the body. When mind is telling you what to do. The other is when body itself informs the mind. It becomes your body and you are able to have experiences that go beyond conscious thinking."[45]

Experiences are the most complex and least predictable outcomes of a performance, and they can vary dramatically for the performer and the viewer. Anna's description of how to work with the body in a way that opens new experiences suggests her belief that even the most limited range of movement is potentially interesting if it is anchored in authenticity. This belief was the basis of a project Anna initiated in 2005, working with the oldest population of her career. Called *Seniors Rocking,* this project was a participatory workshop, and ultimately a performance event, for seniors, drawn primarily from assisted living communities and senior centers near the Halprin home in Marin County. "I wanted to work with people my own age and deal with issues that seniors deal with," she said of the genesis of *Seniors Rocking.* She remarked that she had spent her career working with young people and now wanted to return to working with peers because their issues were closer to her own. "I fuss around about death and dying in my mind," she admitted.[46]

Seniors Rocking was also prompted by her reaction to a film of the German choreographer Pina Bausch's 1998 restaging of her 1978 work *Kontakthof* for a cast of untrained people over sixty. Anna was distressed by Bausch's method of having these older dancers drilled to learn set choreography originally made for younger bodies. They are goaded to keep count, stay in formation, learn not to fidget, and memorize the steps by Jo Anne Endicott, who staged the work for Bausch in the film. Endicott comments, "Pina has always had a fantastic sense of what is 'in.' At the moment, old is 'in.'"[47]

For Anna, old is in *her* current repertoire because she herself is old and continually curious about what kind of new information she can still coax from her dancer's canvas. The *Kontakthof* process of watching an ordinary old body struggle to fit into a dance made for a young professional dancer seemed to her arrogant and insulting. "Not once did they leave a place for what was going on in these old people's own lives," Anna said about the film of Bausch's dance. In contrast, *Seniors Rocking* takes as its beginning, and end point, a modest range of movement actions tailor-made by each senior who turned out for the series of free workshops Anna offered. The simple act of rocking in a rocking chair, done as minimally or as maximally as the performer wants, is the choreographic center of Anna's dance for the seniors. "What can you do with the action of rocking?" she asked the group of men and women, aged sixty-five to their mid-nineties, seated in the carpeted social room during their first meeting in the Redwood Retirement Community Center in Mill Valley. She then led them to focus their attention on the prosaic act of rolling through the foot—pushing off with the ball, recovering by dropping the heel, then sequentially rolling back up to the toes to push off again. "It doesn't matter that the movement was limited in range—what came through was the spirit," she said.[48]

By the first of the two afternoon performances staged in early October 2005, the seniors *are* rocking, having found a remarkable range of movement interest and personal drama in their relationship to their rocking chairs. Prompted by an article about the dance in the local newspaper, the community has come forward to donate sixty-nine rocking chairs to support all the rocking seniors. The chairs have been set up on an island in the middle of a small lagoon at the Marin Civic Center. The presence of a Swiss film crew headed by Ruedi Gerber, who is making a documentary on Anna, adds to the ceremony of the event and signifies the international stature of the trim, curly-haired woman who many think is simply an unusually active elder. The finished performance is evocative and poignant without being nostalgic or overtly maudlin. There is a simple dignity to the mass of seniors as they sit in their rocking chairs, stretching their arms upward in a dance of softly waving arms that is both minimalist and childlike.

Using a cluster of performers to add interest to the same fundamental action of rocking, *Seniors Rocking* reveals both theatrical savvy and sensitivity to the performers' needs and limitations. A not-so-distant cousin to *Parades and Changes*, it offers a late-in-life equivalent to undressing—dancing in public. As is often the case with Anna's work, the results divide between private epiphanies and larger resonant questions staged with keen theatrical insight: Who should dance? Why? How?

"We are considered seniors—people who are 'done,'" a seventy-nine-year-old woman tells the recording crew after the performance. "But we are the next generation. Anna has given us an opportunity to just let it go. We aren't accepting cultural expectations for what we should do." Another woman fastens on the metaphoric power of the rocking chair: "There was a special moment as I was saying good-bye to the rocking chair that I realized it was a symbol of my life," she says, referring to the final moment in the dance when each elder rose from her or his chair, placed a flower on the seat, and slowly walked away. "There was sadness, depression but also joy," she continues. "I know now I would like to be able to celebrate dying the way I celebrate life. That's a gift that Anna has."[49]

By the summer of 2006 Anna is already onto her next project, having turned over the running of the ongoing Redwood seniors group to a former student who assisted her on *Seniors Rocking*. She speaks excitedly about her new topic—love—inspired by Auguste Rodin's famous sculptural studies of amorous passions. Several years earlier, she tellingly reflected on the source of her continual new projects and the tension between simplifying means and expanding possibilities that has propelled her:

> There is a secret to longevity in dance: I found a process, which enabled me to access my creativity through dance. . . . I stripped away many of the assumptions I had learned about dance, and re-invented it for myself. . . . I experimented with where dance could take place, and who could be a dancer. I danced on the streets and the beaches, and I danced with people who had never taken a dance class in their lives. . . . I started questioning what dance could be about and I started making dances that had to do with my life and the lives of the people who dance them. I have been playing for these many years in the open field of dance, where life experience is the fuel for my dancing, and dance is the fuel for my life experience.[50]

Anna resists the standard use of dance and, with it, a static notion of the artist and artistic style. In her career she has made a full circle back to the nature and role of dance in its most elemental use. Her one constant has been a vision of art as a continual transformation of experience, an opening of possibility, a hedge against the predictable. "I want you to imagine that you have one dance left to do," she once told an audience. "I want you to imagine what this dance would be. Money is no object. Production values are irrelevant. What is the dance you want to do—this last dance of your life?"[51]

ACKNOWLEDGMENTS

MY FIRST THANKS must go to Anna Halprin, who did not always agree with my perspective but who nonetheless gave me unlimited access to her extensive archives, files, letters, photographs, scores, and notes. She participated with unflagging generosity in countless interviews and telephone conversations during the fifteen years I worked on this project. I was allowed to observe Anna teaching workshops and classes for dancers, individuals challenging AIDS and cancer, health care providers, and seniors as well as in training sessions at Sea Ranch, retreats at Esalen, and performances and public addresses in the Bay Area and abroad. Lawrence Halprin was also very generous with his time, photographs, notebooks, scrapbooks, and memories. Both of them read the manuscript before it was edited and corrected some factual details. Beyond that, they had no direct involvement in the making of the book.

I owe an enormous debt of gratitude to the dancers, collaborators, and associates of Anna who generously shared their memories and often private letters, photographs, and clippings with me. They contributed immeasurably in giving me as vivid a sense as possible of the early workshops on the dance deck and many of the works of the 1950s, 1960s, and 1970s that have vanished. These individuals include Charles Amirkhanian, Jack Anderson, Paul Baum, Jeanne Hayes Beaman, Ruth Beckford, Miriam Raymer Bennett, Sunni Bloland, Rabbi Samuel Broude, Trisha Brown, Jim

Burns, Remy Charlip, Wanda Coleman, Bruce Conner, Maggie Creighton, Merce Cunningham, Doris Dennison, George Dorris, Eiko and Koma, Simone Forti, Kathelin Gray, Kim Hahn, Daria Halprin, Rana Halprin, Melinda West Harrison, Alma Hawkins, William Heick, Mary Hinkson, Luca Hoving, Jenny Hunter Groat, Warner Jepson, Rhodessa Jones, Kush, Jo Landor, Pearl Lang, Skip La Plante, Nina Lathrop, Norma Leistiko, Murray Louis, Sydney Luria, Jasmine Nash Lutes, Vera Maletic, Jamie McHugh, Nancy Cronenwelt Meehan, Meredith Monk, Robert Morris, Louise H'Doubler Nagel, Irving Penn, Yvonne Rainer, Robert Raymer, Larry Reed, Charles Reinhart, Terry Riley, John Rockwell, Juanita Sagan, Benito Santiago, Richard Schechner, Albert Schuman, Ida Schuman, Stanton Schuman, Ramon Sender, Kermit Sheets, Allan Stinson, Eeo Stubblefield, Morton Subotnick, Lynne Palmer Van Dam, Sir Lawrence Washington, James Woods, and La Monte Young. In particular, A.A. Leath responded from his home in the rainforest in Costa Rica with great generosity to my letters asking about the early works of the San Francisco Dancers' Workshop, sharing photos, films, and clippings from his own files, as did John Graham. Gail Randall Chrisman shared childhood letters, and Liam O'Gallagher provided a copy of the *Blue Planet Notebook*. Dee Mullen and Jeri Sulley helped with photographs and clippings in Larry's office archives.

I am also very grateful to Richard Schechner for his generosity in writing the elegant foreword. I extend special thanks to the photographers who allowed me to use their work, particularly Duane Beeson for Coni Beeson, Rick Chapman, the Imogene Cunningham Trust, Paul Fusco, Lawrence Halprin, William Heick, Warner Jepson, John Kokoska, Hattula Moholy-Nagy, Ron Partridge, Irving Penn, Casey Sonnabend, and Eeo Stubblefield, as well as Brigitte Carnochan for the author photograph. The Maison Européenne de la Photographie in Paris generously sent me a copy of the catalogue for Irving Penn's photographs of *The Bath*. The San Francisco Performing Arts Library and Museum kindly supplied digital files for the images of Ann Schuman in the 1920s, Ann Schuman in the Hillel Dance Group, Ann Halprin and Welland Lathrop in their studio, the 1960 summer workshop, *Ten Myths, Lunch*, Ann Halprin doing an outdoor improvisation in the 1970s, and the "Monster Dance" from *Circle the Earth*.

I owe a very special thanks to my friend the late Stephen Cobbett Steinberg, who, inspired by my early research on the Halprins, made the 1989 KQED-TV special dual portrait of the Halprins, *Inner Landscapes*. After Steve's death Joan Saffa, his associate at KQED-TV, allowed me to retrieve the dozens of background tapes that Steve had made, including video transfers of much of the archival footage of Anna's dances and Larry's projects, as well as extensive interviews with the Halprins and their associates, just before they were to be erased. I am very thankful to the staff of the San Francisco Performing Arts Library and Museum, and particularly Kirsten Tanaka and Tricia Roush, for their generosity in giving me access to the files and boxes of Anna Halprin's materials that were in the process of being transferred from her home to their San Francisco offices during the final period of this project. Monica Mosley at the Dance Collection of the New York Public Library was helpful in research I conducted there, as was the curator at the Steenbock Archives at the University of Wisconsin at Madison.

My colleague Peggy Phelan read an early draft of several chapters, and I have profited greatly from her insightful criticisms and conversations over several years. Mark Franko also made many helpful and important comments about the manuscript. Michele Pridmore Brown at the Michelle Clayman Institute for Gender Research at Stanford made perceptive comments on the chapter on aging. And Danny Walkowitz offered suggestions on an early chapter as well. Marcia Siegel was a supportive reader of the initial proposal of this book and offered valuable criticisms.

I am especially thankful to Joan Acocella, Mindy Aloff, Sally Banes, and Deborah Jowitt, each of whom offered their own form of encouragement at different important moments in the life of this project. Former and current students at Stanford also provided much appreciated assistance; these include Jill Antonides with her sharp editorial eye, Miguel de Bacca, and Emily Hite. And thanks to the Department of Drama, Zack, Daniel Sack, Arden Thomas, and Kathryn Syssoyeva, who also assisted me, as did Alice Kleeman, who transcribed hours of interviews over the years.

I would like to give profound thanks to the John Simon Guggenheim Memorial Foundation for its 2001 fellowship without which this book would probably never have been completed. A fellowship at the Stanford Humanities Center for 2001–2 was also critical to my completion of this project, allowing me time to write and research and to test out ideas among a remarkable community of scholars. The Djerassi Resident Artists Program offered me a month of splendid solitude to write in October 2002. The Institute for Research on Women and Gender at Stanford (now the Michelle Clayman Institute for Gender Research) also offered me a very collegial work community during the 2002–3 academic year. The Peninsula Community Foundation made possible the use of many of the photographs in the book with a greatly appreciated publication grant. The

Peninsula Community Foundation also helped support my time at Djerassi with an Outstanding Artist Foundation Fellowship. Finally, for a week each in the summers of 1992 and 1993, when my two children were quite young, the Cottages at Hedgebrook Women Writers Colony on Whidby Island, Washington, gave me my first fellowships that made possible the drafting of the prospectus for this book.

Some material from this book appeared earlier in different forms: material from chapter 4 appeared in "Anna Halprin and Improvisation as Child's Play," in Ann Cooper Albright and David Gere, eds., *Taken by Surprise: A Dance Improvisation Reader* (Wesleyan University Press/University Press of New England, 2003); material from chapter 6 appeared in "Anna Halprin and the 1960s: Acting in the Gap between the Personal, the Public and the Political," in Sally Banes and Andrea Harris, eds., *Reinventing Dance in the 1960s: Everything Was Possible* (University of Wisconsin Press, 2003); and material from chapters 6 and 10 appeared in "Anna Halprin's Urban Rituals," in *The Drama Review* (Summer 2004).

I cannot conclude without expressing my gratitude to my remarkable editors at UC Press. Doris Kretchmer was the first to have faith in the merit of the project, Sheila Levine graciously supported it, and Sue Heinemann spared no effort in improving each chapter with her unstinting editorial expertise and wealth of knowledge as a student of Anna Halprin's for many years. Her fastidious reading of the text has saved it from a great number of errors. My gratitude and love to my husband, Keith, son, Josh, and daughter, Maya, whose patience and understanding over the years get my final and most heartfelt thanks.

NOTES

Anna Halprin's archives are now located at the San Francisco Performing Arts Library and Museum. Stephen C. Steinberg's interviews with the Halprins, which he gave to the author, will also be available at SFPALM.

PREFACE

1. In 1972, after she survived a recurrence of her colorectal cancer, she adopted a modified version of her birth name, Hannah, anglicizing it to "Anna."

2. Ann Halprin, lecture-demonstration at Stanford University, Stanford, California, June 1961.

3. Susan L. Foster, *Choreography and Narrative Ballet's Staging of Story and Desire* (Bloomington: Indiana University Press, 1996), 261.

4. The dance historian Linda Tomko has noted how increasing circulation of Freud's theories in America refigured notions of what it was that bodies contained or deployed or needed to express. See her *Dancing Class: Gender, Ethnicity and Social Divides in American Dance 1890–1920* (Bloomington: Indiana University Press, 1999), 218.

5. Anna Halprin, in *Artists in Exile: A History of Modern Dance in San Francisco,* video documentary produced by Austin Forbord and Shelley Trott, San Francisco, 2000.

1. Stephen C. Steinberg's interview with Anna Halprin, San Francisco, 1988, no. 2, 18.

2. Irving Cutler, *The Jews of Chicago: From Shtetl to Suburb* (Urbana: University of Illinois Press, 1996), 50.

3. Ibid., 40.

4. Ibid., 65.

5. Ibid., 94.

6. Author's interview with Robert Raymer, Atherton, California, July 10, 1992.

7. Author's interview with Albert Schuman, Woodside, California, July 18, 1992. All subsequent quotations from Albert Schuman are from this interview.

8. Steinberg's interview with Anna Halprin, no. 2, 22.

9. Author's interview with Anna Halprin, Kentfield, California, June 30, 1992.

10. Howard Eilberg-Schwartz, *The Savage in Judaism: An Anthology of Israelite Religion and Ancient Judaism* (Bloomington: Indiana University Press, 1990).

11. Author's interview with Albert Schuman.

12. Steinberg's interview with Anna Halprin, no. 2, 16.

13. Ibid., 23.

14. Author's interview with Ida Schuman, Woodside, California, March 17, 1990.

15. Author's interview with Anna Halprin, June 30, 1992.

16. Ibid.

17. Ibid.

18. Ibid.

19. Ibid.

20. Noted by Robert Raymer in author's interview with Raymer, 1992.

21. Author's interview with Anna Halprin, June 30, 1992.

22. Author's interview with Albert Schuman.

23. Author's interview with Anna Halprin, June 30, 1992.

24. A. Zilversmit, *Changing School: Progressive Education Theory and Practice, 1930–1960* (Chicago: University of Chicago Press, 1993).

25. Carlton Washburne, *What Is Progressive Education? A Book for Parents and Others* (New York: John Day, 1952), 87, 144.

26. Author's interview with Anna Halprin, June 30, 1992.

27. Author's tour of the Winnetka schools and Halprin's home in August 1994. In an interview with the author (July 8, 1992), Miriam Raymer Bennett reported that there were two prominent Jewish families in Winnetka, the Loebs and the Strausses, who wanted, or succeeded in, it is unclear, passing local legislation that said neighbors had to approve a new family moving into a neighborhood. (She

believes this was an additional effort by the German Jews to keep the Eastern European ones out.)

28. Author's interview with Anna Halprin, June 30, 1992.

29. Washburne, *What Is Progressive Education?* 125.

30. Michel Foucault, *Discipline and Punish: The Birth of the Prison* (New York: Random House, 1977), 147.

31. Washburne, *What Is Progressive Education?* 124.

32. Author's interview with Anna Halprin, June 30, 1992.

33. Steinberg's interview with Anna Halprin, no. 2, 28.

34. Ibid.

35. Author's interview with Robert Raymer. All subsequent quotations from Raymer are from this interview.

36. Steinberg's interview with Anna Halprin, no. 2, 20.

37. Ibid., 28.

38. Author's interview with Anna Halprin, June 30, 1992.

39. Suzanne Shelton, *Divine Dancer: A Biography of Ruth St. Denis* (New York: Doubleday, 1981), 152–53.

40. Traditionally one is deemed Jewish by virtue of having been born to a Jewish mother.

41. Author's interview with Anna Halprin, June 30, 1992.

42. Steinberg's interview with Anna Halprin, no. 2, 31.

43. Author's interview with Anna Halprin, June 30, 1992.

44. Author's phone interview with Pearl Lang, September 20, 1992.

45. Author's interview with Anna Halprin, Kentfield, California, February 13, 2002.

46. Author's interview with Ida Schuman. Ida made this comment after a prompt from Anna, who was present at the interview.

47. In Doris Humphrey, *Doris Humphrey: An Artist First,* ed. Selma Jeanne Cohen (Middletown, CT: Wesleyan University Press, 1972), 133.

48. Marcia B. Siegel, *Days on Earth: The Dance of Doris Humphrey* (New Haven: Yale University Press, 1987), 151.

49. Humphrey, *Doris Humphrey,* 143.

50. Ann Halprin, unpublished notes, 1941, in Anna Halprin's archives.

51. Ibid.

52. Steinberg's interview with Anna Halprin, no. 2, 3.

53. Author's interview with Anna Halprin, February 13, 2002.

CHAPTER 2: THE SECRET GARDEN OF AMERICAN DANCE

The epigraph is from Richard Schechner, *Performance Studies: An Introduction* (New York: Routledge, 2002), 23.

1. Zvi Gitelman, *A Century of Ambivalence: The Jews of Russian and the Soviet Union, 1881 to the Present* (New York: Schocken Books, 1988).

2. "Harvard's Jewish Problem," www.jewishvirtuallibrary.org/jsource/antisemitism/harvard.html (September 24, 2002). The subsequent quote from Lowell is also from this source.

3. David O. Levin, *The American College and the Culture of Aspiration* (Ithaca, NY: Cornell University Press, 1986).

4. William James Lawson, ed., *Dance Magazine College Guide* (New York: Dance Magazine, 1988–89), 11.

5. Sali Ann Kriegsman, *Modern Dance in America: The Bennington Years* (Boston: G. K. Hall, 1981), 6. Ironically, it was reportedly the need for physical exercise and the lack of a gym, not Progressive ideals, that led the wife of Bennington's president Robert Devore Leigh to suggest that exercise classes might be offered as an art form—dance (ibid.).

6. Ibid., 79, 74.

7. Quoted in ibid., 75.

8. Janet Mansfield Soares, *Louis Horst: Musician in a Dancer's World* (Durham, NC: Duke University Press, 1992), 140.

9. Ibid., 142.

10. The ages of the students ranged from 16 to 41, and of the 180 participants, 100 were in the general program, with most of the others in the professional program. Kriegsman, *Modern Dance in America,* 78.

11. Author's interview with Anna Halprin, Kentfield, California, February 13, 2002. All quotations in this paragraph are from this interview.

12. Author's phone interview with Jeanne Hayes Beaman, September 26, 2002. All quotations from Beaman in this chapter are from this interview.

13. This was something Ann's college mentor Margaret H'Doubler once told a student. See Janice Ross, *Moving Lessons: Margaret H'Doubler and the Beginning of Dance in American Education* (Madison: University of Wisconsin Press, 2000).

14. Martha Hill, "Martha Hill Reminisces about Bennington," videotape of lecture delivered at Bennington College on July 25, 1985, in New York Public Library's Dance Collection, MGZHA 4–375: 1985.

15. Blanche Trilling, "History of Physical Education for Women at the University of Wisconsin, 1898–1946," 1951, University of Wisconsin–Madison Archives.

16. Author's phone interview with Mary Hinkson, March 3, 1997.

17. John Dewey, *Art as Experience* (New York: Capricorn Books, 1958 [1934]). Although *Art as Experience* was not published until 1934, Dewey had been ruminating on these ideas for decades.

18. Author's interview with Anna Halprin, Kentfield, California, April 14, 1999.

19. Quoted in Ross, *Moving Lessons,* 151.

20. Author's interview with Anna Halprin, April 14, 1999.

21. Ibid.

22. Author's interview with Anna Halprin, February 13, 2002.

23. Max Kadushin, *Organic Thinking: A Study in Rabbinic Thought* (New York: Bloch, 1938). Kadushin had trained in New York in the 1920s, when it was fashionable to find ways to organize knowledge in a discipline. He was part of a number of scientists and intellectuals who were finding ways to unify fields and organize apparently random information into a theory of "organic thinking."

24. Max Kadushin, *The Rabbinic Mind* (New York: Blaisdell, 1965), 111–12.

25. Stephen C. Steinberg's interview with Anna Halprin, San Francisco, 1988, no. 2, 13.

26. Ann Halprin, personal notes (1941), in Anna Halprin's archives. The dance was based on Walt Whitman's "The Hymn for Dead Soldiers."

27. Ben Stephansky, "Wisconsin Hillel Dance Idea," *The Hillel Review* (University of Wisconsin), November 27, 1941.

28. Kriegsman, *Modern Dance in America*. All quotations in this paragraph are from pages 82–83 in this source.

29. Author's interview with Anna Halprin, February 13, 2002.

30. Author's phone conversation with Anna Halprin, September 25, 2002.

31. Ted Sinitzky, "A Tribute to Excellence," *The Hillel Review* (University of Wisconsin), 1939. Around this time *The Daily Cardinal,* the University of Wisconsin student body newspaper, began devoting a weekly column to dance and dance activities on campus

32. Nik Krevitsky, "Orchesis Triumphs at U. of Wisconsin," *Chicago Dancer,* June 1941.

33. Ann Schuman, introductory speech given at University of Wisconsin, Madison, 1940; in Anna Halprin's archives.

34. J.A. Gray, "To Want to Dance: A Biography of Margaret H'Doubler," Ph.D. diss., University of Arizona, Tucson, 1978, 167.

35. Author's interview with Anna Halprin on teaching dance to children, Kentfield, California, March 12, 1994.

36. Ibid.

37. Gray, "To Want to Dance," 216.

38. Author's interview with Anna Halprin, April 14, 1999.

39. Stephen C. Steinberg's interview with Lawrence and Anna Halprin, Kentfield, California, 1988, reel 15.

40. Ibid.

41. Ibid.

42. Ibid.

43. Author's interview with Lawrence Halprin, San Francisco, July 10, 1992.

44. Ibid.

45. Author's interview with Sydney Luria, New York, November 10, 2000. All subsequent quotes from Sydney Luria are from this interview.

46. Stephen C. Steinberg's interview with Lawrence Halprin, San Francisco, 1988, 21–24.

47. Author's interview with Lawrence Halprin, July 10, 1992. Quotations in this paragraph and next are from this interview.

48. Ibid.

49. Note from Lawrence Halprin to author, June 28, 2004; author's interview with Lawrence Halprin, July 10, 1992.

50. Steinberg's interview with Lawrence and Anna Halprin, reel 15.

51. Author's interview with Lawrence Halprin, San Francisco, August 1, 1995.

52. Author's interview with Miriam Raymer Bennett, Atherton, California, July 8, 1992.

53. Author's interview with Anna Halprin, Kentfield, California, July 10, 1992.

54. Author's interview with Lawrence Halprin, August 1, 1995.

55. Ibid.

56. George M. Goodwin, "Wright's Beth Sholom Synagogue," *American Jewish History* 86 (Spring 1998): 1.

57. Steinberg's interview with Lawrence Halprin, 47.

58. Ibid., 48.

59. Steinberg's interview with Anna Halprin, no. 2, 13.

60. Ibid., 16–17.

61. Steinberg's interview with Lawrence and Anna Halprin, reel 15.

62. Ann Schuman Halprin, "Hebrews: A Dancing People: The Historical Development of Jewish Dance," senior thesis, University of Wisconsin, Madison, 1942, 97–98.

63. Ruth Hatfield, interviewed by Carol Murota, 1992, in Legacy Oral History Project, San Francisco Performing Arts Library and Museum.

64. Margaret H'Doubler, "A Question of Values and Terms," *Dance Observer* 12, no. 7 (August–September 1945).

CHAPTER 3: THE BAUHAUS AND THE SETTLEMENT HOUSE

The epigraph is quoted in Reginald Isaacs, *Walter Gropius: An Illustrated Biography of the Creator of the Bauhaus* (Boston: Little, Brown, 1983), 68.

1. Stephen C. Steinberg's interview with Lawrence Halprin, San Francisco, 1988, 53.

2. Christopher Tunnard, *Gardens in the Modern Landscape* (London: Architectural Press, 1938).

3. Author's interview with Lawrence Halprin, San Francisco, August 1, 1995. Subsequent quotations in this paragraph are also from this interview.

4. Isaacs, *Walter Gropius,* 238.

5. Ibid.

6. Ibid., 68.

7. Quoted in ibid., 228.

8. Author's interview with Lawrence Halprin, August 1, 1995.

9. Isaacs, *Walter Gropius,* 236.

10. Author's phone conversation with Anna Halprin, October 8, 2002.

11. Stephen C. Steinberg's interview with Anna Halprin, San Francisco, 1988, no. 2, 22.

12. Author's interview with Anna Halprin on teaching dance to children, Kentfield, California, March 12, 1994. All the subsequent quotations about her experience at Winsor (except for her program note) are from this interview.

13. Ibid. All the quotations about her experience at the settlement house are from this interview.

14. Thomas H. Johnson, *Oxford Companion to American History* (New York: Oxford University Press, 1966).

15. Steinberg's interview with Lawrence Halprin, 55–56.

16. Ann Halprin, personal notebook, 1943, in Anna Halprin's archives.

17. Author's interview with Anna Halprin, March 12, 1994.

18. Ann Halprin on Barbara Mettler's summer session, in her private journal, 1943; in Anna Halprin's archives.

19. Author's interview with Anna Halprin, March 12, 1994.

20. Author's phone conversation with Anna Halprin, October 8, 2002.

21. Robert Kraus, "William Steig at 80," *Publishers Weekly* (1987), available at www.williamsteig.com/article-pw87.htm.

22. Author's interview with Anna Halprin, Kentfield, California, February 13, 2002.

23. William Steig, *The Lonely Ones* (New York: Duell Sloan and Pearce, 1942).

24. In ibid., ii.

25. Program for *The Lonely Ones,* 1955, in Anna Halprin's archives. When Ann performed *The Lonely Ones* at the New York festival of the American National Theatre and Academy (ANTA) in 1955, Cazden played his piano score live at every performance.

26. Roger Angell, "The Minstrel Steig," *New Yorker* (February 20 and 27, 1995): 2.

27. Larry later described the lessons he had learned in this way: "Social problems and architecture were valid and important. Space and form are linked; the object you make has to be integrated into the landscape; the arts are not segmented—they are all one hunk; the arts are a way of creatively modifying and improving the world through creativity; and crafts and arts should not be separated" (from Steinberg's interview with Lawrence Halprin, 59).

28. See M. E. Harris, *The Arts at Black Mountain College* (Cambridge, MA: MIT Press, 1987), 17.

29 David Vaughan, *Merce Cunningham Fifty Years* (New York: Aperture, 1997), 27.

30. Steinberg's interview with Anna Halprin, no. 2, 2.

31. Author's phone conversation with Anna Halprin, October 8, 2002.

32. Steinberg's interview with Lawrence Halprin, 60.

33. Ann Halprin, letter to "Julie," April 1945, in Anna Halprin's archives.

34. Tilla Hevesi, "San Francisco Letter," *Dance Observer* (May 1945): 57.

CHAPTER 4: WESTERN SPACES

The epigraph is from Kenneth Rexroth, "San Francisco Letter" (1957) in *San Francisco Stories,* ed. John Miller (San Francisco: Chronicle Books, 1990), 179.

1. Anna Halprin, phone conversation with author, June 30, 2002.

2. "Celebration—Five Dead, 624 Injured," *San Francisco Chronicle,* August 16, 1945.

3. See, for example, Stanton Delapane, "S.F. Rioting Mob Is Out of Control; Sailors, Civilians, Girls in a Wild Bacchanalia," *San Francisco Chronicle,* August 16, 1945.

4. Peter Hartlaub, "Huge Crowds Avoided Deaths of Past Years," *San Francisco Examiner,* January 1, 2002; see www.sfgate.com/cgi-bin/article.cgi?file = / examiner/archive/2002/01/01.

5. Author's interview with Daria Halprin, Kentfield, California, September 20, 1991.

6. Anna Halprin, "A Report on *Citydance,*" in *Moving toward Life: Five Decades of Transformational Dance,* ed. Rachel Kaplan (Hanover, NH: Wesleyan University Press/University Press of New England, 1995), 170.

7. Richard Cándida Smith, *Utopia and Dissent: Art, Poetry, and Politics in California* (Berkeley: University of California Press, 1995), xviii.

8. Stephen C. Steinberg's interview with Lawrence Halprin, San Francisco, 1988, 5.

9. George Santayana, "The Genteel Tradition in American Philosophy" (1911), quoted in Kevin Starr, *Americans and the California Dream, 1850–1915* (New York: Oxford University Press, 1973), 422.

10. Edan Milton Hughes, *Artists in California 1786–1940,* 2nd ed. (San Francisco: Hughes Publishing, 1989), 4.

11. Starr, *Americans and the California Dream,* 312.

12. Quoted in ibid., 313.

13. Stephen C. Steinberg's interview with Anna Halprin, San Francisco, 1988, no. 2, 5.

14. This very useful phrase comes up in Foster's general discussion of ballet choreography and narrative, in her book *Choreography and Narrative Ballet's Staging of Story and Desire* (Bloomington: Indiana University Press, 1996). Foster has said that people "understand choreographic theorizations best when the bodies that enact them are engaged in distinct corporeal pursuits and are positioned in frictive encounter with dancing bodies" (xvi).

15. Dore Ashton, "An Eastern View of the San Francisco School," in *San Francisco Stories*, ed. John Miller (San Francisco: Chronicle Books, 1990), 211.

16. Ibid., 209.

17. Harold Rosenberg, *The Anxious Object: Art Today and Its Audience* (New York: Mentor Books, 1964), 212–13.

18. Dorothee Imbert, "Of Gardens and Houses as Places to Live: Thomas Church and William Wurster," in Marc Treib, ed., *An Everyday Modernism: The Houses of William Wurster* (Berkeley: University of California Press, 1995), 114.

19. Ibid.

20. Steinberg's interview with Lawrence Halprin, 7–9.

21. Ibid., 2.

22. Author's interview with Lawrence Halprin, San Francisco, August 1, 1995.

23. Ibid.

24. In Lawrence Halprin, *Lawrence Halprin: Changing Places*, exh. cat. (San Francisco: San Francisco Museum of Modern Art, 1986), 116.

25. Lawrence Halprin, "Landscaping a Small Plot," *Sunset*, November–December 1949, 105, 122.

26. *Los Angeles Times*, February 1949, from scrapbook of Lawrence Halprin.

27. Thomas Church and Lawrence Halprin, "You Have a Gold Mine in Your Backyard," *House Beautiful*, January 1949, 37–44.

28. In Treib, ed., *Everyday Modernism*, 127.

29. Steinberg's interview with Lawrence Halprin, 3.

30. Ibid., 7–8.

31. Halprin, *Lawrence Halprin: Changing Places*, 116.

32. "They Love to Dance," *Terpsichore* (April 1949).

33. Author's interview with John Graham, Stanford, California, September 21, 1992.

34. Author's interview with Nina Lathrop, San Francisco, August 20, 1992. Despite the fact that she was interviewed nearly forty years after Ann and Lathrop had dissolved their studio partnership, below the surface of Nina's clipped answers one could clearly sense her lingering defensiveness of her husband and resentment of Ann.

35. Alfred Frankenstein, "Ann Halprin Impressive in Dance Recital," *San Francisco Chronicle*, October 27, 1947, 13.

36. Alfred Frankenstein, "A Variety of Dance Programs," *San Francisco Chronicle*, 1947; in Anna Halprin's archives.

37. Spencer Barefoot, "Worthwhile Dance Program," *San Francisco Call Bulletin,* 1947.

38. Ibid.

39. Larry Cuban, *How Teachers Taught: Constancy and Change in American Classrooms 1880–1990* (New York: Teacher's College Press, 1993), 143.

40. Gale Randall Chrisman, e-mail to author, October 20, 2001.

41. Ibid., Chrisman kindly showed four photographs from Ann's classes.

42. Including a black student in a private dance class with whites was fairly radical at the time, some five years before the 1954 Supreme Court ruling that racial segregation was unconstitutional in public schools.

43. Chrisman, e-mail to author, October 20, 2001. Chrisman's parents were active Communists and in 1953, at the height of the blacklisting terror, they moved to Canada for several years. Ann continued to correspond with Chrisman during this time, giving her advice about the next steps to take in developing herself as a dancer. At one point, when Chrisman wanted to take ballet, Ann cautioned her against it, writing, "Why is it impossible for a teacher to do an honest job of directing students in both ballet and modern? In answering this question can you describe the difference between ballet and contemporary dance in terms of 1) technique, 2) choreography, 3) its values to the individual as an experience, 4) its values to society as we know it today" (letter from Ann Halprin to Gale Randall [Chrisman], December 14, 1954).

44. Lenore Peters Job, *Looking Back While Surging Forward* (San Francisco: Peters Wright Creative Dance, 1984), 80–81.

45. Chrisman, e-mail to author, October 20, 2001.

46. "Dancer Ann Halprin's Art Is a Philosophy of Life, Too," *San Francisco Chronicle,* 1950, 11; in Anna Halprin's archives.

47. Author's phone interview with Ruth Beckford, Oakland, California, September 8, 1994. Subsequent quotations from Beckford are also from this interview.

48. Murray Louis, "Editor's Note," *Impulse* (1948): 2.

49. Author's interview with Jenny Hunter Groat, Lagunitas, California, August 13, 1992. Subsequent quotations from Hunter Groat are also from this interview.

50. Yvonne Rainer, "Yvonne Rainer Interviews Anna Halprin," *Tulane Drama Review* 10, no. 5 (1965); reprinted in *Moving toward Life: Five Decades of Transformational Dance,* ed. Ruth Kaplan (Hanover, NH: Wesleyan University Press/University Press of New England, 1995), 77.

51. Author's interview with Graham.

52. Ann Halprin, "Intuition and Improvisation in Dance," *Impulse* (1955): 10–15.

53. Ibid.

54. Ann Halprin, "Children's Class," *Impulse* (1948): 27–29.

55. Ann Halprin, "Teaching Dance," *Impulse* (1949): 20.

56. Ibid.

57. Halprin, "Intuition and Improvisation in Dance," *Impulse* (1955): 11.

58. Ann Halprin, "Training for Expression," *Impulse* (1957): 39.

59. Author's interview with Doris Dennison, San Francisco, July 19, 1993.

60. Ibid.

61. Doris Dennison, "Improvisation and Dance Accompaniment," *Impulse* (1948): 13–15.

62. Murray Louis, *Inside Dance: Essays by Murray Louis* (New York: St. Martin's Press, 1980), 3.

63. Author's interview with Murray Louis, Arlee, Virginia, March 26, 2000.

64. Ibid.

65. Author's phone conversation with Anna Halprin, September 25, 2002.

66. Jennifer Dunning, "How Dance Can Shape a Child's View of Life," *New York Times,* December 1, 1997.

67. Mindy Aloff, "Arias," *The New Republic,* October 9, 2000, 6.

68. Author's phone conversation with Anna Halprin, September 25, 2002.

69. Jim Waring, "What Is the Ideal Technical Equipment for Today's Theater Dancer?" *Impulse* (1948): 18–20.

70. Author's interview with Anna Halprin, Kentfield, California, May 24, 2002.

71. Richard Ford, "Notes on Classes for Boys," *Impulse* 8 (1953).

72. Author's interview with Nancy Cronenwelt Meehan, New York, September 13, 2001. All the subsequent quotations from Meehan are also from this interview.

73. Author's interview with A.A. Leath, Madison, Wisconsin, September 8, 1992.

74. Lawrence Halprin, "The Choreography of Gardens," *Impulse* (1949): 31–32.

75. In *Sunset,* March 1955, from scrapbook of Lawrence Halprin.

76. Author's interview with Ann Halprin, May 24, 2002.

77. In Anna Halprin's archives.

78. Author's interview with Leath.

79. It seems appropriate that Ann met Jo Landor, a painter who worked for decades as her artistic consultant (becoming the artistic director for the San Francisco Dancers' Workshop), when Landor brought her two daughters to take dance classes with Ann (in this case, at the Union Street studio). One day Ann asked the mothers to make Indian costumes for the children, and when she saw Landor's rustic invention made out of old burlap potato sacks she quickly recruited her to make costumes for Ann and her adult dancers in an upcoming dance concert at San Francisco's Stern Grove. "It was the first time we collaborated," Lan-

dor said. "The dance was called *Madrona* and I began by gathering colors and fabrics the dancers could carry with them. I always felt that I worked as an artist and my materials were the space" (author's interview with Jo Landor, San Francisco, August 14, 1991).

80. Author's interview with Anna Halprin, Kentfield, California, January 25, 1996.

81. Clipping from *Dance Magazine,* 1957, in Anna Halprin's archives.

82. Author's interview with Anna Halprin, Kentfield, California, December 21, 1995.

83. From an undated document on the Marin Children's Dance Cooperative, in Anna Halprin's archives.

84. Author's interview with Anna Halprin, January 25, 1996.

85. From undated document on Marin Children's Dance Cooperative.

86. Author's interview with Anna Halprin, December 21, 1995.

87. Author's interview with Daria Halprin, Kentfield, California, January 2, 2002.

88. "Dancing in the Dark? Jobs and Futures for the College Dance Major," *Mademoiselle,* September 1950, 140–41.

89. Lawrence Halprin, "Structure and Garden Spaces Related in Sequence," *Progressive Architecture,* May 1958, 96–104.

90. Lawrence Halprin, "The Art of Garden Design," *Journal of Popular Culture,* July 1954, 226.

91. Ann Halprin, letter to Gale Randall [Chrisman], December 14, 1954.

92. Lawrence Halprin and Ann Halprin, "Dance Deck in the Woods," *Impulse* (1956): 24.

93. Steinberg's interview with Lawrence Halprin, 51.

94. Quoted in William L. Crosten, "Music Center Theater at Stanford University," *Impulse* (1959): 59.

95. Ben Belitt, "Poet in the Theater," *Impulse* (1959): 12.

96. Halprin and Halprin, "Dance Deck in the Woods," 23.

97. Ibid., 24.

98. Ibid.

99. In Stanley Eichelbaum, "The Kentfield Home of the Halprins—A Dwelling Built for a Dancer," *San Francisco Examiner* (1959): 11–13; in Anna Halprin's archives.

100. Author's interview with Anna Halprin, December 21, 1995.

101. Merce Cunningham, draft of lecture demonstration on Ann Halprin's dance deck, 1957; in Anna Halprin's archives.

102. Doris Humphrey, letter to Ann Halprin, October 11, 1953. When Ann wrote back, expressing interest, Humphrey supplied more details about the festival in a letter of October 20. Both letters in Anna Halprin's archives.

103. Ashton, "An Eastern View of the San Francisco School," 209.

104. Cándida Smith, *Utopia and Dissent*, 97. He is quoting Harold Rosenberg at the end.

105. Author's interview with Anna Halprin, Kentfield, California, July 19, 1999.

106. Humphrey, letter to Ann Halprin, October 20, 1953.

107. Author's interview with Anna Halprin, Kentfield, California, December 11, 1989.

108. John Martin, letter to Ann Halprin 1947; in Anna Halprin's archives.

109. John Martin, "Broadway Applauds Marin Dancer," quoted in *Marin Independent-Journal*, June 4, 1955, M6.

110. Author's interview with Anna Halprin, December 11, 1989.

111. Author's interview with Hunter Groat.

112. Author's interview with Leath.

113. P. Adams Sitney, "The Potted Psalm," in *Visionary Film: The American Avant-Garde* (New York: Oxford University Press, 1979), 82.

114. Ibid., 83.

115. Starr, *Americans and the California Dream*.

CHAPTER 5: INSTANTANEOUS EXPERIENCE, LUCY, AND BEAT CULTURE

The epigraph is quoted in Deborah Klotchko and Barbara Hitchcock, *Innovation/Imagination: Fifty Years of Polaroid Photography* (New York: Harry Abrams, 1999), 13.

1. Ibid., 16.

2. Ibid., 10.

3. Author's phone conversation with Anna Halprin, September 24, 2003.

4. Author's interview with Jenny Hunter Groat, Lagunitas, California, August 13, 1992.

5. Author's interview with Anna Halprin, Kentfield, California, January 22, 2005.

6. Stephen C. Steinberg's interview with James Broughton, 1988; in author's archives.

7. Ibid.

8. Quoted in P. Adams Sitney, "The Potted Psalm," in *Visionary Film: The American Avant-Garde* (New York: Oxford University Press, 1979), 83.

9. Steinberg's interview with Broughton. The subsequent quotation is also from this interview.

10. See Lori Landay, *Madcaps, Screwballs, and Con Women* (Philadelphia: University of Pennsylvania Press, 1998), 29, 161.

11. Author's interview with Jo Landor, San Francisco, August 14, 1991.

12. Author's interview with Anna Halprin, January 22, 2005.

13. Landay, *Madcaps, Screwballs, and Con Women*, 28. As Landay notes, *I Love Lucy* ran as a half-hour situation comedy from October 1951 to May 1957, and as thirteen hour-long shows from November 1957 until April 1960 (155).

14. Ibid., 29.

15. Ibid., 187.

16. Author's interview with Daria Halprin, Kentfield, California, January 2, 2002.

17. Author's interview with Simone Forti, Los Angeles, August 11, 2001.

18. Author's interview with Landor.

19. Author's interview with Daria Halprin.

20. Author's interview with Meredith Monk, Stanford, California, March 5, 2000.

21. Daniel Horowitz, *Betty Friedan and the Making of the Feminine Mystique* (Amherst: University of Massachusetts Press, 1998), 3. It should be noted that Ann's actions both repudiated and embraced contemporary feminist issues about "domestic discontents," and her social class enabled her always to have childcare and a housecleaner, giving her independence from full-time household duties. See M. Carson, "Domestic Discontents: Feminist Reevaluations of Psychiatry, Women and the Family," *Canadian Review of American Studies* (1992 Special Issue Part II): 171–91.

22. Susan M. Hartmann, *The Home Front and Beyond: American Women in the 1940s* (Boston: Twayne, 1982).

23. See Lisa Phillips, *Beat Culture and the New America 1950–1965*, exh. cat. (New York: Whitney Museum of American Art, 1996), 125.

24. Although (as noted in the previous chapter), in the late 1940s, just prior to the period this list covers, Waring did spend a couple of formative years in his development as a dancer studying at the Halprin-Lathrop School in San Francisco.

25. Quoted in Ann Charters, *Beat down to Your Soul* (New York: Penguin Books, 2001), 169.

26. See A. B. Levine, "The Body's Politics: Race and Gender in the Authentic Sixties," Ph.D. diss., University of Virginia, Charottesville, 1997, 221. Norman Mailer's "The White Negro," published in 1957, added to the masculinist mythology by conflating the avant-garde artist with the hipster so that what became glorified in the public consciousness was the artist as psychopath.

27. Author's interview with Anna Halprin, January 22, 2005.

28. Author's interview with Forti, 2001.

29. Richard Cándida Smith, *Utopia and Dissent: Art, Poetry, and Politics in California* (Berkeley: University of California Press, 1995), 220.

30. Michael McClure, *Scratching the Beat Surface* (San Francisco: North Point Press, 1982).

31. Halprin's style of "hanging" loosely with a group while being basically

independent can be also construed as a Beat posture. Halprin never had a "company"; instead, starting in 1955, she formed the San Francisco Dancers' *Workshop*, a loose collective of dancers and an actor with whom she improvised, discovering movement and exploring narratives of their lives together. In 1952 Herbert Blau had cofounded the San Francisco Actors' Workshop at San Francisco State with Jules Irving.

32. Quoted in Daniel Belgrade, *The Culture of Spontaneity: Improvisation and the Arts in Postwar America* (Chicago: University of Chicago Press, 1998), 89.

33. Cándida Smith, *Utopia and Dissent,* 151.

34. Quoted in ibid., 151.

35. Cándida Smith, *Utopia and Dissent,* 63.

36. Author's interview with Anna Halprin, Kentfield, California, September 1, 2003.

37. Author's interview with Hunter Groat.

38. Author's interview with Anna Halprin, January 22, 2005.

39. Author's interview with Forti, 2001. The following quote is also from this interview.

40. Author's phone conversation with Anna Halprin, September 24, 2003.

41. *Daughter of the Voice, The Prophetess,* and another dance of this period, *Emek,* which focus on Jewish heroines who became inspirational leaders for their people, fit into the post-Holocaust dances that Naomi Jackson describes as creating "uplifting, timeless images of a positive Jewish identity" (see her *Converging Movements: Modern Dance and Jewish Culture at the 92nd Street Y* [Hanover, NH: Wesleyan University Press, 2000]).

42. Author's interview with Anna Halprin, January 22, 2005.

43. Anna Halprin in "Yvonne Rainer Interviews Anna Halprin," *Tulane Drama Review* 10, no. 5 (1965): 77.

44. Author's interview with Forti, 2001.

45. Author's interview with A.A. Leath, Madison, September 8, 1992.

46. Author's interview with Forti, 2001.

47. Author's interview with Hunter Groat.

48. Author's interview with Forti, 2001.

49. Author's interview with Daria Halprin, September 5, 1991.

50. Author's phone interview with William (Bill) Heick, January 24, 2004.

51. Author's interview with Forti, 2001.

52. The evening also included a film Heick made of a Pomo Indian curing ceremony at Stewart's Point, on the Northern California coast, next to the future site of Sea Ranch (author's phone interview with Heick).

53. Note from William R. Heick to the author, July 7, 2004. These images and the dancers' air of hip nonchalance obliquely invoke and update 1930s photographs of Ted Shawn and his male dancers posing heroically with their muscled forms blending into the geometry of huge factory machinery.

54. Author's conversation with Paul Berliner, Stanford, California, May 12, 2002.

55. Author's interview with Forti, 2001.

56. Ibid.

57. Author's interview with John Graham, Stanford, California, September 21, 1992.

58. Quoted in H. George-Warren, ed., *The Rolling Stone Book of the Beats: The Beat Generation and American Culture* (New York: Hyperion, 1999), 354.

59. Ann Halprin, "Message to Our Audience from the Performers," mimeographed sheet, 1957; in Anna Halprin's archives.

60. David Sterritt, *Mad to Be Saved: The Beats, the Fifties, and Film* (Carbondale: Southern Illinois University Press, 1998).

61. Author's interview with Graham.

62. Author's phone conversation with Anna Halprin, September 24, 2003.

63. Author's interview with Simone Forti, Vermont, September 22, 1993.

64. Author's interview with Forti, 2001.

65. Author's interview with Forti, July 22, 1993. Trisha Brown recalls that the term *structured improvisation* developed in the early 1960s in New York out of things she and Forti were doing together (phone message to author, June 18, 2004).

66. This contrasted significantly with Grand Union's more egalitarian structure.

67. Author's interview with Leath.

68. Ibid.

69. Author's interview with Forti, July 22, 1993.

70. Edward Halsey Foster, *Richard Brautigan* (Indianapolis: Twayne, 1983), 21.

71. Michael Mason, "The Pancakes and the President: A Review of *The Tokyo Mountain Express,*" *Times Literary Supplement* (May 1, 1981): 483.

72. Robert Kern, "Williams, Brautigan, and the Poetics of Primitivism," *Chicago Review* 27, no. 1 (1975): 47–57.

73. Author's interview with Anna Halprin, January 22, 2005.

74. Program for *Flowerburger* at Contemporary Dancers Foundation, San Francisco, November 29–30 and December 1, 1959; in Anna Halprin's archives.

75. Peter Yates, "Visions of Dance—Part Two," *Arts and Architecture,* 1962, in Anna Halprin's archives.

76. J.B., "A Halprin Happening," *Open City Press,* November 18, 1964, 3.

77. Ann Halprin, "Program Notes of June 18, 1960," in Anna Halprin's archives.

78. Steinberg's interview with Broughton.

79. Ibid.

80. "Rainer Interviews Halprin," 3.

81. K. Robert Schwarz writes, "During the summer of 1958 [Young] composed his first mature composition, the *Trio for Strings*—a landmark in the history of twentieth-century music and the virtual fountainhead of American musical minimalism" (*Minimalists* [London: Phaidon Press, 1996], 3).

82. "Rainer Interviews Halprin," 6. Rainer interviewed Halprin in 1962, but the interview was not published in *TDR* until 1965.

83. This piece evokes Oskar Schlemmer's Bauhaus study, *Pole Dance* (1927), a choreographed solo in which a performer, in simple leotard and tights (the costume Ann used for *Birds*), with long poles affixed to each limb, navigates a black stage. The sticks swing like huge insect legs, shooting out from each body part.

84. Quoted in Richard Kostelanetz, "La Monte Young," in *The Theatre of Mixed Means: An Introduction to Happenings, Kinetic Environments, and Other Mixed-Means Performances* (New York: Dial Press, 1968), 191.

85. Author's interview with Terry Riley, Grass Valley, California, October 21, 2003.

86. Both letters mentioned in e-mail from Marian Zazeela to the author, June 21, 2004. These letters were researched by Jeremy Grimshaw, a Ph.D. student at the Eastman School in New York.

87. This statement comes from a letter Young wrote on April 7, 1960, to Leonard Stein, a noted pianist and one of Schoenberg's foremost disciples. (Stein had been Young's composition teacher at City College.) In the letter, Young noted that Ann "would have used us to do the program down there but she had already begun work with the other musicians before she met me." A few days later, though, he followed with another letter announcing that he and Terry Riley would be doing the music for Ann's UCLA March concert after all. In this second letter he laments that the dance in the concert will not be as fully improvisational as the workshops, noting that he and Riley will present a score that is "altogether improvised on the spot." (All these remarks are cited in the e-mail from Zazeela to author.)

88. Author's interview with Warner Jepson, San Francisco, December 17, 2001.

89. Quoted in Kostelanetz, "La Monte Young," 193.

90. Author's interview with Riley. Subsequent quotations are also from this interview.

91. Zazeela, e-mail to author.

92. A few weeks later, in a letter to Cage, Ann described more fully her continued support but growing concern about how the radicalness of their actions affected audiences. She noticed that "the sounds were of such a natue that in becoming involved as the audience was with them, they could not [see] the dance" (Ann Halprin, letter to John Cage, June 23, 1960; in Anna Halprin's archives).

93. Sally Banes, *Democracy's Body: Judson Dance Theatre, 1962–1964* (Durham, NC: Duke University Press, 1993), 12.

94. Yvonne Rainer, *Yvonne Rainer: Work 1961–73* (Halifax: Press of the Nova Scotia College of Art and Design, 1974), 312–13.

95. Yvonne Rainer, e-mail to author, August 21, 2001.

96. Kostelanetz, "La Monte Young," 77.

97. Ibid., 192.

98. Zazeela, e-mail to author.

99. Author's phone conversation with Anna Halprin, October 4, 2003.

100. Young's dance deck lecture may have been a model for the fragmented narratives in Ann's major work the following year, *The Four-Legged Stool*, for which Riley created what became known as his "Mescaline Mix" score.

101. Kostelanetz, "La Monte Young," 191.

102. Zazeela, e-mail to author.

103. Author's interview with Riley.

104. Ibid.

105. Eventually Young recorded two of the sounds from this period of work for Ann and released them as a tape composition, which Merce Cunningham used in his 1964 dance *Winterbranch*.

106. Yvonne Rainer, e-mail to author, August 16, 2001.

107. Robert Morris, e-mail to author, August 22, 2001.

108. Author's interview with Trisha Brown, 1993. The subsequent quotations from Brown are also from this interview.

109. Ann Halprin, "Program Notes of June 18, 1960," in Anna Halprin's archives.

110. Ann Halprin, "Statement for Jack Anderson," January 1961, in Anna Halprin's archives.

111. Ann Halprin, "Lecture-Demonstration for the University of British Columbia, Vancouver, Canada," February 1961, in Anna Halprin's archives.

112. Rainer, e-mails to author, August 21 and August 16, 2001.

113. Stephen Steinberg's interview with Yvonne Rainer, 2001, aired on KQED San Francisco; in author's archives.

114. Rainer, e-mail to author, August 21, 2001.

115. Ibid.

116. Simone Forti, *Handbook in Motion: An Account of an Ongoing Personal Discourse and Its Manifestations in Dance* (Halifax: Press of the Nova Scotia College of Art and Design, 1974), 32.

117. Author's interview with Forti, 2001.

118. Forti, *Handbook in Motion*, 32.

119. Author's interview with Forti, 2001.

120. Author's interview with Simone Forti, Larkspur, California, July 5, 1993.

121. Author's interview with Anna Halprin, September 24, 2003.

122. The other members of the workshop were Paulus Berenson, Marni Mahaffay, and Steve Paxton (Banes, *Democracy's Body*, 7).

123. Much of the information on Dunn in this paragraph comes from Banes, *Democracy's Body*, 3–4.

124. Author's interview with Forti, 2001; Morris, e-mail to author.

125. Rainer, e-mail to author, August 21, 2001.

126. Quoted in Banes, *Democracy's Body*, 8.

127. Banes, *Democracy's Body*, xviii.

128. Susan Leigh Foster, "Dancing Bodies," in *Meaning in Motion*, ed. Jane C. Desmond (Durham, NC: Duke University Press, 1997), 251. Foster's observations are about contact improvisation but apply to Ann Halprin in this instance.

CHAPTER 6: URBAN RITUALS

The epigraphs are from Diane Arbus, 1962 application to the John Simon Guggenheim Foundation, and Lenny Bruce, quoted in Maria Damon, "The Jewish Entertainer as Cultural Lightning Rod: The Case of Lenny Bruce," *Postmodern Culture* 7, no. 2 (January 1997): 5.

1. Martin Shepard, *Fritz* (Sagaponack, NY: Second Chance Press, 1975), 113.

2. Author's phone interview with Lynne Palmer Van Dam, 2002.

3. Stanley Eichelbaum, "Playhouse Dance Bedlam," *San Francisco Examiner*, May 7, 1962, 37.

4. Alfred Frankenstein, "Puzzle and Pathos of 'Five-Legged Stool,'" *San Francisco Chronicle*, 1962; in Anna Halprin's archives.

5. Author's interview with Anna Halprin, Kentfield, California, January 10, 2003.

6. Anna Halprin, Introduction to *Movement Ritual I*; reprinted in Rachel Kaplan, ed., *Moving toward Life: Five Decades of Transformational Dance* (Hanover, NH: Wesleyan University Press/University Press of New England, 1995), 37.

7. Roy A. Rappaport, "Ritual," in *Folklore, Cultural Performances and Popular Entertainments*, ed. R. Bauman (New York: Oxford University Press, 1992), 249–52, 255.

8. Nancy Stark Smith, "After Improv" (interview of Anna Halprin), in *Moving toward Life*, 203.

9. Victor Turner, *From Ritual to Theatre: The Human Seriousness of Play* (New York: Performing Arts Journal, 1982), 15.

10. James Miller, *Democracy Is in the Streets* (Cambridge, MA: Harvard University Press, 1994), 46.

11. Ibid.

12. Ann Halprin, "The Four-Legged Stool," unpublished production notes, 1961; in Anna Halprin's archives.

13. Merce Cunningham, draft of lecture demonstration on Ann Halprin's dance deck, 1957; in Anna Halprin's archives.

14. Author's interview with Palmer Van Dam.

15. Lawrence Halprin, "A Discussion of 'The Five-Legged Stool,'" *San Francisco Chronicle,* April 29, 1962, 3.

16. Ann Halprin, "The Four-Legged Stool."

17. Author's interview with Anna Halprin, Kentfield, California, April 14, 1999.

18. Lawrence Halprin, "A Discussion of the Five-Legged Stool," 3.

19. Chronology in Lawrence Halprin, *Lawrence Halprin: Changing Places,* exh. cat. (San Francisco: San Francisco Museum of Modern Art, 1986), 126.

20. Lawrence Halprin, "A Discussion of the Five-Legged Stool," 3.

21. Susan Sontag, "Looking at War: Photography's View of Devastation and Death," *New Yorker,* December 9, 2002, 97.

22. See Richard Schechner, *Between Anthropology and Theater* (Philadelphia: University of Pennsylvania Press, 1985), 6. Ann's performative exploration of the territory between theater and anthropology anticipated Schechner's and other scholars' theoretical exploration.

23. Anna Halprin, Introduction to *Movement Ritual I,* in *Moving toward Life,* 47.

24. Anna Halprin, *Dance as a Healing Art: A Teacher's Guide and Support Manual for People with Cancer* (Kentfield, CA: Tamalpa Institute, 1997), 37.

25. Jack Anderson, "Manifold Implications," *Dance Magazine* 36, no. 4 (April 1963): 45.

26. Berio interviewed in Alfred Frankenstein, "The Dance in the Galleries," *San Francisco Chronicle,* July 22, 1962.

27. Ibid.

28. Luciano Berio, letter to Ann Halprin, January 8, 1963.

29. Luciano Berio, letter to Alfred Frankenstein, June 25, 1962; in Anna Halprin's archives.

30. Diane Di Prima, "A Concert of Dance—Judson Memorial Church" (1962); reprinted in *The Floating Bear: A Newsletter, Numbers 1–37,* ed. Diane Di Prima and LeRoi Jones (La Jolla, CA: Laurence McGilvery, 1973), 239.

31. Rainer quoted in Sally Banes, *Democracy's Body: Judson Dance Theater, 1962–1964* (Durham, NC: Duke University Press, 1993), 67.

32. Banes, *Democracy's Body,* 66.

33. Diane Wakoski, "Letter to the Editor" (1962), reprinted in *The Floating Bear: A Newsletter,* 252.

34. Author's interview with Jack Anderson, San Francisco, October 29, 2001.

35. James Waring, "Letter to the Editor" (1962), reprinted in *The Floating Bear: A Newsletter,* 263.

36. Author's interview with Remy Charlip, San Francisco, December 21, 2001, and follow-up letter, June 25, 2004.

37. The original La Fenice, which translates as "The Phoenix," was built in 1792, but it burned to the ground in 1836 and was rebuilt the following year.

38. Author's interview with Melinda West Harrison, Sea Ranch, California, September 21, 2001.

39. Ann Halprin, "Esposizione," unpublished notes, 1962; in Anna Halprin's archives.

40. Luciano Berio, letter to Ann Halprin, December 1962; in Anna Halprin's archives.

41. Ann Halprin, letter to Luciano Berio, 1963; in Anna Halprin's archives. Ann later said she hated the solo, and she only performed it a few more times, in Rome and once in Zagreb (author's conversation with Anna Halprin, December 8, 2003).

42. Ann Halprin, letter to Berio.

43. Ann Halprin, "Esposizione."

44. Ann Halprin, letter to Berio.

45. First quotation from Ann Halprin, "Esposizione"; second from Ann Halprin's personal notes, 1963, in Anna Halprin's archives.

46. Ann Halprin, "Esposizione."

47. Ann Halprin, letter to Berio.

48. Jan Bark, "Happening i Venedig" (Stockholm, 1963); in Anna Halprin's archives.

49. Author's interview with Anna Halprin, Kentfield, California, April 13, 1999.

50. Alfred Frankenstein, "The Workshop's Tour," *San Francisco Chronicle*, 1963; in Anna Halprin's archives.

51. Ibid.

52. Author's interview with Vera Maletic, Warrenton, Virginia, March 25, 2000. Maletic's mother, Ana, who headed a Laban-based dance school in Zagreb, was also enlisted to help—she was called upon to collect the hundred wine bottles needed for the dance.

53. Ann Halprin, letter to her dancers, December 4, 1963; in Anna Halprin's archives.

54. Author's phone conversation with Ramon Sender, July 15, 2004.

55. Patric Hickey and Jo Landor worked on the costumes, decor, and props for this piece.

56. Alexander Fried, "A Tape Center Novelty—Is It a Parlor Trick?" *San Francisco Examiner*, 1964; in Anna Halprin's archives.

57. Author's interview with Anna Halprin, Kentfield, California, July 19, 1999.

58. Yvonne Rainer, "Yvonne Rainer Interviews Ann Halprin," *Tulane Drama Review* 10, no. 5 (1965).

59. Shepard, *Fritz*, 66. This biography is the source for much of the biographical information on Perls.

60. Fritz S. Perls, *Gestalt Therapy Verbatim* (Moab, Utah: Real People Press, 1969), 16.

61. Quoted in Shepard, *Fritz*, 129–30. Additional quotations are also from this source except as noted, for Anna Halprin later retold this story to the author with some slight modifications.

62. Author's interview with Anna Halprin, July 19, 1999.

63. Shepard, *Fritz*, 3.

64. Author's interview with Anna Halprin, July 19, 1999.

65. Shepard, *Fritz*, 22.

66. Quoted in ibid., 60.

67. Perls, *Gestalt Therapy Verbatim*, 53.

68. Author's interview with Anna Halprin, July 19, 1999. Subsequent quotations about this dream are also from this interview.

69. The Esalen Institute was founded in 1962 as an alternative educational center devoted to the exploration of what Aldous Huxley called the "human potential," the world of unrealized human capacities that lies beyond the imagination. Once home to a Native American tribe known as the Esselen, Esalen is located on twenty-seven acres of spectacular coastline with the Santa Lucia Mountains rising sharply behind, and it is blessed with natural hot springs. The institute soon became known for its blend of Eastern and Western philosophies in experiential and didactic workshops, taught by a steady influx of philosophers, psychologists, artists, and religious thinkers.

70. Fritz S. Perls, "A Session in Gestalt Therapy," 1968 videotape, Esalen Institute, Esalen, California, produced by Mediasync Corporation.

71. Anna Halprin, note to author, June 23, 2004; the following quotation is also from this note. Henderson, who also lived in Marin, continues to be friends with Larry and Anna forty or so years later.

72. Author's phone interview with Paul Baum, August 26, 1993.

73. Author's phone interview with Trisha Brown, June 11, 1993.

74. A.A. Leath, letter to author, January 13, 2004.

75. Author's interview with Brown, 1993.

76. Author's interview with Anna Halprin, Kentfield, California, July 30, 2001.

77. Author's phone interview with Carla Blank, June 28, 2004.

78. Author's interview with Meredith Monk, Palo Alto, California, March 1, 2000.

79. Meredith Monk, videotaped interview by Stephen Steinberg, 1991; in San Francisco Performing Arts Library and Museum.

80. Author's interview with Monk, 2000. The three-week August workshop in which Monk participated occurred just before Ann left for Sweden for the premiere of *Parades and Changes,* and most of the material she gave the workshop students to explore came directly from the sections of *Parades and Changes* she was fine-tuning. Ann actually left early, and A.A. Leath taught the final week of the workshop.

81. Ann Halprin, "Parades and Change (A Dancers' Workshop Production)," videotape, 1964–65; in Anna Halprin's archives.

82. Author's interview with Anna Halprin, July 19, 1999.

83. Ibid.

84. Rana Halprin remembers the Goldsmiths as being among the few Jewish families in Marin at that time: "Although I had many friends in the area, there were parents there who thought the scene [on the dance deck] was pretty weird and didn't want their kids playing with these Jews and artists" (phone interview with author, June 11, 2004).

85. Author's phone interview with Morton Subotnick, January 29, 1992.

86. Author's interview with John Graham, Stanford, California, September 21, 1992.

87. Author's interview with Jo Landor, San Francisco, August 14, 1991.

88. Author's phone interview with Kim Hahn, January 20, 1992.

89. Author's interview with Anna Halprin, Kentfield, California, June 30, 1992.

90. Author's phone interview with Carla Blank, June 22, 2004.

91. Ann Halprin, "Parades and Changes," 2.

92. Lawrence Halprin, *Halprin: Changing Places,* 129.

93. Folke Rabe, letter to Ann Halprin, June 22, 1965; in Anna Halprin's archives.

94. Stephen Steinberg's interview with Yvonne Rainer, 1990, for KQED, 1990; in author's archives.

95. Folke Rabe, in "Program Notes for *Parades and Changes,*" Stadsteater Publicity Department, Stockholm, 1965, 2; in Anna Halprin's archives.

96. Bengt Hager, in "Program Notes for Parades and Changes,"1.

97. Ryman, review of *Parades and Changes* (1965); translation from Swedish in Anna Halprin's archives.

98. Sven Kyberg, letter to Ann Halprin (via Swedish TV station), December 16, 1965; in Anna Halprin's archives. Julian Beck and Judith Malina of the Living Theater, who were living in Europe in exile from the United States from 1964 to 1969, also saw the Swedish television broadcast and wrote to Ann, praising her daring vision (noted in Marsha McMann Paludan, "Expanding the Circle: Anna Halprin and Contemporary Theater Practice," unpublished paper, 1994, in Anna Halprin's archives).

99. Hager, in "Program Notes for Parades and Changes,"1.

100. Madeline Kats, "Review of *Parades and Changes,*" *Expressen* (Stockholm), 1965; in Anna Halprin's archives.

101. Bengt Jahnsson, in *Dagen Nyheter,* September 1965; translation from Swedish in Anna Halprin's archives.

102. Robert J. Pierce, "The Ann Halprin Story," 1974; in Anna Halprin's archives.

103. Ann Halprin, "The Play Will Be Real—That Is, There Will Be No Play," *San Francisco Chronicle,* March 14, 1965.

104. Ibid.

105. Quoted in Rainer, "Yvonne Rainer Interviews Ann Halprin."

106. Quoted in N. E. Uber, "Ann Halprin: Towards a Biography," thesis, Sonoma State University, Sonoma, California, 1985, 133.

107. Richard Schechner, *Performance Studies: An Introduction* (New York: Routledge, 2002), 28.

108. Ann Halprin, "Program Notes for *Apartment 6*" (1965), in Anna Halprin's archives.

109. A.A. Leath, letter to author, January 13, 2004.

110. Uber, "Ann Halprin," 78.

111. Alfred Frankenstein, "Apartment 6—New Realism in Theater," *San Francisco Chronicle*, March 21, 1965, 7.

112. In Smith, "After Improv," 191.

113. Uber, "Ann Halprin," 79.

114. Ann Halprin, "Program Notes for *Apartment 6.*"

115. Author's interview with Anna Halprin, June 30, 1992.

116. Paludan, "Expanding the Circle," 145.

117. Author's interview with Anna Halprin, June 30, 1992.

118. George Dorris, e-mail to author, November 1, 2001.

119. Author's interview with Anderson.

120. Dorris, e-mail to author.

121. Meredith Monk was recruited to sign the invitations so that they had the imprimatur of the city's new arts community.

122. Clive Barnes, "Dance: The Ultimate in Bare Stages," *New York Times,* April 24, 1967, 38.

123. Author's interview with Anna Halprin, June 30, 1992.

124. Author's interview with Charlip.

125. Marcia B. Siegel, *At the Vanishing Point: A Critic Looks at Dance* (New York: Saturday Review Press, 1968), 301.

126. Author's interview with Daria Halprin, Kentfield, California, January 2, 2002.

127. Ann Halprin, "A New Development from the Rock Scene," press release, San Francisco Dancers' Workshop, October 1967; in Anna Halprin's archives.

128. Author's interview with Anna Halprin, June 30, 1992.

129. Dennis E. Showalter, "Archie Bunker, Lenny Bruce and Ben Cartwright: Taboo-Breaking and Character Identification in 'All in the Family,'" *Journal of Popular Culture* 9, no. 3 (Winter 1975): 618–21.

130. John Kifner, "No Joke! 37 Years after Death Lenny Bruce Receives Pardon," *New York Times,* December 24, 2003, A1, A20.

131. Damon, "The Jewish Entertainer," 6.

132. Author's interview with Anderson.

The epigraph is from author's interview with Anna Halprin, Kentfield, California, February 19, 2001.

1. Charles Perry, *The Haight-Ashbury: A History* (New York: Random House/Rolling Stone Press, 1984), 171.

2. Ibid., 175, 178.

3. Susan Bennett, *Theatre Audiences: A Theory of Production and Reception* (London: Routledge, 1990), 36–37.

4. Posted by Amanda Lyons in 2002 at www.uncwil.edu/com/rohler/all2.htm.2.

5. Perry, *Haight-Ashbury*, 171. In 1966 then-governor Ronald Reagan described a hippie as someone who "dresses like Tarzan, has hair like Jane, and smells like Cheetah" (Todd Gitlin, *The Sixties: Years of Hope, Days of Rage* [New York: Bantam Books, 1987], 217).

6. Wanda M. Corn, *The Great American Thing: Modern Art and National Identity, 1915–1935* (Berkeley: University of California Press, 1999), 73.

7. Peggy Phelan, *Unmarked: The Politics of Performance* (London: Routledge, 1993), 152.

8. Author's interview with Anna Halprin, Kentfield, California, September 5, 1991.

9. Ann Halprin, "Bath," undated choreographic notes, 1; in Anna Halprin's archives.

10. Author's interview with Anna Halprin, Kentfield, California, April 8, 1999.

11. Ann Halprin, "Bath," 1.

12. Anna Halprin, "What and How I Believe: Stories and Scores from the '60s," in *Moving toward Life: Five Decades of Transformational Dance*, ed. Rachel Kaplan (Hanover, NH: Wesleyan University Press/University Press of New England, 1995), 104, 106.

13. Author's phone conversation with Anna Halprin, February 13, 2002.

14. Ibid.

15. Ann Halprin, "Bath," 1–2.

16. Lawrence Halprin, *Lawrence Halprin: Changing Places*, exh. cat. (San Francisco: San Francisco Museum of Modern Art, 1986), 132. The month-long workshop in 1966 was the first of four collaborative sessions on group creativity Ann and Larry led on the dance deck in Kentfield, in the San Francisco studio, and on the beach at Sea Ranch over the next five years.

17. Lawrence Halprin, *Notebooks 1959–1971* (Cambridge: MIT Press, 1972), 158.

18. Ibid., 166, 179.

19. Author's phone conversation with Anna Halprin, March 22, 2002.

20. Author's interview with Anna Halprin, February 19, 2001.

21. Author's interview with Anna Halprin, April 8, 1999.

22. Ann Halprin, letter to Lars, n.d.; in Anna Halprin's archives.

23. Author's phone interview with Irving Penn, November 30, 1995.

24. William K. Zinsser, "Culture: The New Joy," *Look,* January 9, 1968, 8.

25. John Berger in his *Ways of Seeing* (London: Penguin Books, 1972) describes being *naked* as being oneself and being *nude* as a form of performing in a state of undress. Classical art depicts nudes, and naked images, such as Manet's *Déjeuner sur l'Herbe* have generally always made viewers uncomfortable.

26. Author's interview with Penn.

27. Edmonde Charles-Roux, introductory essay in Irving Penn, *Le Bain: Dancers' Workshop of San Francisco,* exh. cat. (Paris: Maison Européenne de la Photographie, 1997).

28. Postcard announcement for *Ten Myths,* September 1967, collection of John Rockwell. Rockwell had participated in several of Ann's workshops and studio events.

29. Ibid., 4.

30. Author's interview with Anna Halprin, February 19, 2001.

31. Gay McNulty notes that keeping performances in a theater building ensures that what happens in it comes under the control of civic authorities and prevents the contamination of the not real with the real (McNulty, *Space in Performance: Making Meaning in the Theatre* [Ann Arbor: University of Michigan Press, 1999], 279).

32. Ann Halprin, "Mutual Creation," *Tulane Drama Review* 13, no. 1 (Fall 1968): 166; reprinted in *Moving toward Life,* 133.

33. Ibid.

34. Author's interview with Anna Halprin, February 19, 2001.

35. The full series of *Ten Myths* included (1) Creation, (2) Atonement, (3) Trails, (4) Totem, (5) Maze, (6) Dreams, (7) Carry, (8) Masks, (9) Story Telling, and (10) Ome.

36. For more on H'Doubler's influential teaching, see Janice Ross, *Moving Lessons: Margaret H'Doubler and the Beginning of Dance in American Education* (Madison: University of Wisconsin Press, 2000), 161.

37. [John Rockwell], "Myths: An Explanation by Ann Halprin," press release, February 1, 1968, from Ralph Harper Silver Public Relations, San Francisco, 1; in Anna Halprin's archives. Although this press release is signed by Ann it was partially ghost-written by John Rockwell. It seems more of a combination feature and review than a bulleted news release. It reflects the perspective of an outsider, representing, perhaps even reveling in, the strangeness and potential controversy of the event.

38. Author's interview with Anna Halprin, Kentfield, California, December 19, 2001.

39. Ibid.

40. [John Rockwell], "Myths: An Explanation by Ann Halprin," 4.

41. Ann Halprin, in "An Interview with Ann Halprin by Douglas Ross," in "Mutual Creation," *Tulane Drama Review* 13, no. 1 (Fall 1968): 174; reprinted in *Moving toward Life*, 150.

42. Ibid.

43. Victor Turner, *From Ritual to Theatre: The Human Seriousness of Play* (New York: Performing Arts Journal, 1982), 47.

44. Ann Halprin, "Interview by Douglas Ross," 174.

45. Richard Schechner, "Performers and Spectators Transported and Transformed," *Kenyon Review* 3, no. 1 (1981): 106.

46. Author's interview with Anna Halprin, February 19, 2001.

47. Margaret H'Doubler initiated the use of blindfolds in the dance classroom in the second decade of the twentieth century as a way to get her students to attend to tactile and emotional stimuli rather than just visual cues (see Ross, *Moving Lessons*, 157). In a discussion between Ann and Margaret H'Doubler filmed on the Kentfield dance deck by filmmaker Connie Beeson in 1970, Ann describes a technique she uses in the studio of having her students cover their eyes with their hands "in order to turn off the mind and go into the body." H'Doubler responds excitedly, "That's why we worked with blindfolds in the classes you took with me." Ann agrees, "Yes."

48. The description of "Trails" is based on Ann Halprin, "Mutual Creation," 166.

49. Schechner, "Performers and Spectators," 90.

50. Ann Halprin, "Mutual Creation," 175.

51. Erving Goffman, *The Presentation of Self in Everyday Life* (New York: Doubleday/Anchor Books, 1956), 162.

52. Author's interview with Anna Halprin, February 19, 2001.

53. Ann Halprin, "Mutual Creation," 169, 170.

54. Author's interview with John Rockwell, New York, New York, November 10, 2000. Ann, who says she has no memory of this "Carry" episode, laughed good-naturedly at Rockwell's report of it, while not discounting it (author's interview with Anna Halprin, Kentfield, California, February 2, 2002). Yet Kathelin Gray (formerly Honey Hoffman), who participated in "Carry" in the 1960s, also remembered this incident (author's interview with Kathelin Gray, San Carlos, California, January 3, 2002).

55. Sally Banes, *Greenwich Village 1963* (Durham, NC: Duke University Press, 1993), 23.

56. Author's interview with Gray.

57. Author's interview with Rockwell.

58. Goffman, *Presentation of Self*, 51.

59. Author's interview with Anna Halprin, February 19, 2001.

60. Ann Halprin, interviewed in Vera Maletic, "The Process Is the Purpose," *Dance Scope* (Fall–Winter 1967–68): 13.

61. Stephen C. Steinberg, interview with Anna Halprin, San Francisco, 1988, no. 2, 24.

62. Author's interview with Anna Halprin, February 19, 2001.

63. Ibid.

64. Author's interview with Anna Halprin, Kentfield, California, August 24, 1993.

65. Paul Patai, *Myth and Modern Man* (Englewood, NJ: Prentice-Hall, 1972).

66. Author's phone interview with Anna Halprin, December 3, 2001.

67. Marc Manganaro, *Myth, Rhetoric, and the Voice of Authority: A Critique of Frazer, Eliot, Frye and Campbell* (New Haven, CT: Yale University Press, 1992), 161.

68. In [Rockwell], "Myths: An Explanation by Ann Halprin."

69. Turner, *From Ritual to Theatre*, 94.

70. Joseph Campbell, *The Hero with a Thousand Faces* (Princeton, NJ: Princeton University Press, 1949), 4.

71. Richard Schechner, *Essays in Performance Theory* (New York: Drama Books Specialists, 1977), 75ff; see also R. L. Grimes, *Ritual Criticism: Case Studies in Its Practice, Essays on Its Theory* (Columbia: University of South Carolina Press, 1990), 204–5.

72. Heuwell Tircuit, "Up and Down the Walls," *San Francisco Chronicle*, May 21, 1968.

73. Arthur Bloomfield, "When Nudity Is Defensible in Dancing," *San Francisco Sunday Examiner and Chronicle*, October 15, 1967, B4.

74. William Gilkerson, "Thursday Night Myths with Dancer Ann Halprin," *San Francisco Examiner*, March 31, 1968. The subsequent quotations are also from this article.

75. Antonin Artaud, quoted in McNulty, *Space in Performance*, 5.

76. McNulty, *Space in Performance*.

77. Ibid., 122.

78. Antonin Artaud, *The Theatre and Its Double* (New York: Grove Press, 1958 [1938]), 60.

79. "Rites: The Mythmaker," *Time*, January 24, 1969.

80. Banes, *Greenwich Village 1963*, 41. New York natives Beck, a painter, and Malina, an actress, had married in 1948 and began presenting the Living Theater in their apartment in the summer of 1951.

81. Ibid.

82. Author's phone conversation with Anna Halprin, December 12, 2001.

83. Ibid. This was confirmed by Kathelin Gray, who worked with the Living Theater in New York after studying with Ann (author's interview with Gray).

84. A.F. [probably Alfred Frankenstein], "Fillmore Abstraction—Light, Music, Dance," *San Francisco Sunday Examiner and Chronicle*, October 8, 1967, 29.

85. Gitlin, *The Sixties,* 206.

86. "Chronology of San Francisco Rock 1965–1969," www.sfmuseum.org/hist1/rock.html.

87. Philip Zimbardo, *The Psychology of Attitude Change and Social Influence* (New York: McGraw-Hill, 1991), 36.

88. Goffman, *Presentation of Self* (the subsequent quotation is also from this source). As Wanda Corn has argued, Duchamp's action offered important perceptual and conceptual lessons to Americans about their own national culture, its objects of originality, and its practices of consumption, and how the two are linked (see Corn, *The Great American Thing,* 48–49).

89. Artaud, *The Theatre and Its Double.* See also Richard Kostelanetz, *The Theatre of Mixed Means: An Introduction to Happenings, Kinetic Environments, and Other Mixed-Means Performances* (New York: Dial Press, 1968).

90. Author's phone conversation with Anna Halprin, November 15, 2001.

91. Artaud, *The Theatre and Its Double,* 32.

92. Jerzy Grotowski, *Towards a Poor Theatre* (New York: Simon and Schuster, 1968), 23.

93. Ibid.

94. Jennifer Kumiega, *The Theatre of Grotowski* (London: Methuen, 1985), 36.

95. Stephen Steinberg, interview with Richard Schechner, New York, 1988, 3; in San Francisco Performing Arts Library and Museum. Ann, however, has attributed her concept of witnessing to Native American dances.

96. Quoted in Kumiega, *The Theatre of Grotowski,* 54.

97. Allan Kaprow, *Assemblages, Environments and Happenings* (New York: Harry Abrams, 1966), 188.

98. Ibid.

99. Michael Kirby, "Happenings: An Introduction," in *Happenings and Other Acts,* ed. M. R. Sandford (London: Routledge, 1995), 3.

100. Kaprow, *Assemblages, Environments and Happenings,* 195–96.

101. Ibid., 196–97.

102. Author's interview with Ann Halprin, November 15, 2001.

103. Rush Rehm, *Greek Tragic Theatre* (London: Routledge, 1992), vii.

104. Herbert Blau, *The Audience* (Baltimore: Johns Hopkins University Press, 1990), 2.

105. Author's interview with Anna Halprin, April 8, 1999.

106. Marjorie Perloff, "cage:chance:change," in *Radical Artifice* (Philadelphia: University of Pennsylvania Press, 1996).

107. See Laura Mulvey, "Visual Pleasure and Narrative Cinema," *Screen* 16, no. 3 (1975): 6–18.

108. Hans Ulrich Gumbrecht, *Making Sense in Life and Literature* (Minneapolis: University of Minnesota Press, 1992).

109. Ibid.

110. Barbara Freedman, *Staging the Gaze: Postmodernism, Psychoanalysis, and Shakespearean Comedy* (Ithaca, NY: Cornell University Press, 1991), 3.

111. Marjorie Garber, *Symptoms of Culture* (New York: Routledge, 1998), 64.

112. Sally Banes has made an important analysis of the gaze in dance that complicates Mulvey's initial reading; see Banes's *Dancing Women: Female Bodies on Stage* (London: Routledge, 1998).

113. Quoted in Susan Manning, "The Female Dancer and the Male Gaze: Feminist Critiques of Early Modern Dance," in *Meaning in Motion*, ed. Jane C. Desmond (Durham, NC: Duke University Press, 1997), 156.

114. Susan L. Foster, "Dancing Bodies," in *Meaning in Motion*, 236–57.

115. Gumbrecht, *Making Sense in Life and Literature*, 287.

116. Goffman, *Presentation of Self.*

117. Ann Halprin, "Mutual Creation," in *Moving toward Life*, 149.

CHAPTER 8: CEREMONY OF MEMORY

The epigraphs are from Paul Connerton, *How Societies Remember* (Cambridge: Cambridge University Press, 1989), 72; Joseph Roach, *Cities of the Dead: Circum-Atlantic Performance* (New York: Columbia University Press, 1989), 286.

1. Fletcher Knebel, "Antonioni Found a Dancer for His Girl and a Carpenter for His Boy," *Look*, November 18, 1969, 37–40.

2. Ibid.

3. F. A. Villella, "Here Comes the Sun: New Ways of Seeing in Antonioni's Zabriskie Point," www.sensesofcinema.com/contents/00/4/zabriskie.html. 4 [accessed in 2002].

4. Virginia Westover, "'Nowest' Girl in Films," *San Francisco Chronicle*, January 22, 1969.

5. Daria Halprin, unpublished biographical statement, n.d.; in Anna Halprin's archives.

6. Calvin C. Hernton, *Coming Together: Black Power, White Hatred and Sexual Hang-ups* (New York: Random House, 1971), 36.

7. bell hooks, "Reflections on Race and Sex," in *Yearning, Race, Gender and Cultural Politics* (Boston: South End Press, 1990).

8. "Remembering Racial Change: The Civil Rights Movement in Fiction," presented at Black Liberation Conference, Stanford University, Stanford, California, November 3, 2001.

9. Alice Walker, *Meridian* (New York: Harcourt Brace Jovanovich, 1976), 165.

10. Lawrence Halprin, *Lawrence Halprin: Changing Places*, exh. cat. (San Francisco: San Francisco Museum of Modern Art, 1986), 135. The next quotation is also from this source.

11. Stephen C. Steinberg's interview with Lawrence Halprin, San Francisco, 1988, 30.

12. Lawrence Halprin, *Lawrence Halprin,* 134.

13. Douglas Davis, "The Golden Voyage," in ibid., 68.

14. Shannon Jackson, *Lines of Activity: Performance, Historiography, Hull-House Domesticity* (Ann Arbor: University of Michigan Press, 2000), 6.

15. Chip Lord interviewed by Paul Baum, in Lawrence Halprin and Jim Burns, *Taking Part: A Workshop Approach to Collective Creativity* (Cambridge, MA: MIT Press, 1974), 214.

16. Lawrence Halprin, introduction to *Taking Part.*

17. Author's phone interview with Jim Burns, August 26, 1993.

18. Halprin and Burns, *Taking Part,* 199.

19. Ibid.

20. Ibid., 206–7.

21. Ibid., 208–9.

22. Lawrence Halprin, e-mail to author, June 2, 2004.

23. See Lawrence Halprin, *The RSVP Cycles: Creative Processes in the Human Environment* (Cambridge, MA: MIT Press, 1969).

24. Author's interview with Lawrence Halprin, July 10, 1992.

25. Theodore Shank, "Framing Actuality: Thirty Years of Experimental Theater 1959–1989," in Enoch Brater and Ruby Cohn, eds., *Around the Absurd* (Ann Arbor: University of Michigan Press, 1990), 242–43.

26. Lawrence Halprin, *Notebooks 1959–1971* (Cambridge, MA: MIT Press, 1972), 263 (entry for December 20, 1967).

27. Author's interview with Anna Halprin, Kentfield, California, August 24, 1993.

28. Connerton, *How Societies Remember.*

29. Toni Morrison, *Playing in the Dark: Whiteness and the Literary Imagination* (Cambridge, MA: Harvard University Press, 1992), 9–10.

30. Morrison, *Playing in the Dark,* 17.

31. See Roach, *Cities of the Dead.*

32. Thomas C. Dent, Richard Schechner, and Gilbert Moses, eds., *The Free Southern Theater, by the Free Southern Theater: A Documentary of the South's Radical Black Theater* (Indianapolis: Bobbs-Merrill, 1969), 3.

33. Ngũgĩ wa Thiong'o, *Decolonising the Mind: The Politics of Language in African Literature* (London: James Currey, 1986).

34. The description that follows is based on David Sears and John McConahay, *The Politics of Violence: The Urban Blacks and the Watts Riot* (Boston: Houghton-Mifflin, 1973), 4–5.

35. Author's phone interview with Larry Reed, January 13, 2002.

36. Sears and McConahay, *Politics of Violence,* 196.

37. Shank, "Framing Actuality," 248.

38. Ann Halprin, "Lunch," performance notes, 1968, 1; in Anna Halprin's archives.

39. Author's interview with Norma Leistiko, Kentfield, California, June 21, 1992.

40. Author's interview with James Woods, Los Angeles, August 26, 1993.

41. William Glatkin, "The Art of Eating," *Sacramento Bee*, June 16, 1968.

42. Charles Amirkhanian, e-mail to author, December 3, 2001.

43. Ann Halprin, "Lunch," 1.

44. Todd Gitlin, *The Sixties: Years of Hope, Days of Rage* (New York: Bantam Books, 1987), 234.

45. Connerton, *How Societies Remember*, 83.

46. Author's phone interview with Charles Amirkhanian, August 26, 1993.

47. Bobby Seale, interviewed on *San Francisco in the 1960's*, KRON-TV (San Francisco), 1992.

48. Wavy Gravy, interviewed on *San Francisco in the 1960's*, KRON-TV (San Francisco), 1992.

49. This romance reached a peak in 1969, when Leonard Bernstein, music director of the New York Philharmonic, hosted a fund-raising party for a group of members of the militant Black Panther organization. Journalist Tom Wolfe wrote a celebrated article about the party for *New York* magazine, where he introduced the term "radical chic" in his title and discussion of the evening. Wolfe's point was that a surface appeal to social justice really masked a desire to be chic and trendy. The Panthers, whom Bernstein helped raise defense money for, were not nonviolent like Martin Luther King Jr., and Bernstein was criticized and picketed for endorsing this brand of race activism. See Joan Peyser, *Leonard Bernstein: A Biography* (New York: William Morrow, 1987), 408–9.

50. Author's interview with Woods. All subsequent quotations from Woods are from this interview.

51. Author's interviews with Anna Halprin, Kentfield, California, September 5, 1991, and August 24, 1993.

52. Author's phone interview with Wanda Coleman, August 27, 1993. All subsequent quotations from Coleman are from this interview unless otherwise noted. Unfortunately, despite repeated efforts over many months, it wasn't possible to locate any other Watts residents who participated in the workshops and performance.

53. Author's interview with Anna Halprin, August 24, 1993.

54. A poster for the Dancers' Workshop winter semester announced these tryouts, giving the first public mention of the Watts event: "Ann Halprin is conducting weekly workshops at STUDIO WATTS in Los Angeles in preparation for a new Dancers' Workshop production to be given in February at the Mark [Taper] Music Hall in Los Angeles. The group of performers will be a combined group of blacks from STUDIO WATTS with a new group from the San Francisco area."

55. Author's interview with Larry Reed. All subsequent quotations from Reed are from this interview.

56. Anna Halprin, note to author, June 23, 2004.

57. Author's interview with Anna Halprin, August 24, 1993. The subsequent quotation is also from this interview.

58. Author's phone interview with Melinda West Harrison, August 27, 1993. All subsequent quotations from West are from this interview.

59. Seth Hill, *Right On!* Dilexi Foundation Film, San Francisco, 1969. This sixty-minute film was broadcast in May 1969 on the local public broadcasting station, KQED-TV.

60. Author's phone interview with Liam O'Gallagher, August 26, 1993. Subsequent quotations are from this interview unless otherwise noted.

61. See Liam O'Gallagher, *The Blue Planet Notebooks* (San Francisco: X-Communications, 1972). O'Gallagher also wrote the words for a taped reading about the dancers' experiences.

62. Ann Halprin, "Ceremony of Us: Interview with Erika Munk," in *Moving toward Life: Five Decades of Transformational Dance,* ed. Rachel Kaplan (Hanover, NH: Wesleyan University Press/University Press of New England, 1995), 154.

63. Anna Halprin, note to author, June 23, 2004.

64. See Joel Makower, *Boom! Talkin' about Our Generation* (Chicago: Tilden Press, 1985), 205.

65. Author's interview with Anna Halprin, August 24, 1993.

66. See Paul Baum's comment on p. 180.

67. Author's interview with Rana Halprin, San Francisco, June 11, 2004. During this time Rana still went by the name Rana Schuman to mask her biological relationship to Ann. Indeed, Ann was so systematic in not disclosing that Daria and Rana were her daughters that forty years later, Kathelin Gray, one of the participants in Ann's mid-1960s events, still believed that Daria and Rana were adopted.

68. In Keneth Kinnamon and Michel Fabre, eds., *Conversations with Richard Wright* (Jackson: University Press of Mississippi, 1993), 224.

69. Author's interview with Anna Halprin, August 24, 1993.

70. Ibid.

71. Wanda Coleman, *A War of Eyes: And Other Stories* (Santa Rosa, CA: Black Sparrow Press, 1988), 170.

72. From Hill, *Right On!*

73. Ann Halprin, letter to Ida Schumann, May 19, 1969; in Anna Halprin's archives. She signed this letter with her mother's affectionate nickname for her, "Sister Dearie."

74. Anna Halprin, note to author, June 23, 2004.

75. Coleman, *War of Eyes,* 171.

76. Daria Halprin, phone conversation with author, June 7, 2004. Although Daria had at first been away filming *Zabriskie Point,* she returned to the Dancers' Workshop at her mother's request to participate in the final joint workshop and the performance at the Mark Taper Forum.

77. Ibid.

78. Paul Baum, letter to James Woods, January 1969; in Anna Halprin's archives.

79. Paul Baum, "The Day After," Los Angeles, report to Ann Halprin, 1969, 1; in Anna Halprin's archives.

80. Eldridge Cleaver, *Soul on Ice* (New York: Dell, 1968).

81. Ann would reprise this stomping movement twenty years later for the monster dance in *Circle the Earth: Dancing with Life on the Line.*

82. Anna Halprin, note to author, June 23, 2004.

83. For a more complete description of the score, see "Instructions to Performers: Ceremony of Us," in *Moving toward Life,* 161–65.

84. James T. Burns, "Microcosm in Movement," *The Drama Review* 13, no. 4 (Summer 1969).

85. Notes about post-performance meeting on *Ceremony of Us,* February 27, 1969, in Anna Halprin's archives.

86. Baum, "The Day After," 2–3.

87. Author's interview with Amirkhanian. Amirkhanian's score was created by recording rehearsals and encounters among the group of performers and then taking these dialogues and chopping them up and reordering them.

88. Ann Halprin, from transcript of *Ceremony of Us* discussion, 1969, Studio Watts School for the Arts, Los Angeles, 31.

89. Baum, "The Day After," 7.

90. Martin Bernheimer, "Ann Halprin Presents Dance Happening at Taper Forum," *Los Angeles Times,* March 1, 1969, 8.

91. John Rockwell, "Disappointing Experimental Dance," *Oakland Tribune,* March 1, 1969, 4.

92. John Rockwell, letter to Ann Halprin, March 1969; in Anna Halprin's archives.

93. See Joseph R. Roach, "Power's Body: The Inscription of Morality as Style," in *Interpreting the Theatrical Past: Essays in the Historiography of Performance,* ed. Thomas Postlewait and Bruce A. McConachie (Iowa City: University of Iowa Press, 1989), 100.

94. Here Ann might be seen as enacting the truism Roach describes of how the signifying body is constructed in theatrical representation beginning on the level of the techniques of preparing the body (see ibid., 101).

95. John Rockwell, "Ann Halprin Builds New Bridges in Dance," *Oakland Tribune,* March 1969.

96. Helen Flynn, "Sensuous Dancers in 'Turn-On' at UOP," *The Record* (Stockton, CA), March 1969.

97. Author's phone interview with Annie Hallett, June 22, 2004.

98. Author's interview with Anna Halprin, August 24, 1993.

99. The head of the Expansion Arts program, Van Witfield from Watts, had seen the *Ceremony of Us* performance at Mark Taper Forum and followed Ann's work closely after that.

100. Ann Halprin, letter to donors for 1969 summer session scholarships, August 1969; in Anna Halprin's archives.

101. Author's phone interview with Jasmine Nash Lutes, December 27, 2001.

102. Heuwell Tircuit, "An Award for Multi-racial Dance Research," *San Francisco Chronicle,* 1969; in Anna Halprin's archives.

103. Ann has since revealed that the anonymous donor was Roger Stevens, then the chair of the National Endowment for the Arts and a follower and fan of Ann's multiracial work, who by necessity had to keep a low profile about his enthusiasm (author's phone conversation with Anna Halprin, March 22, 2002).

104. Tircuit, "Award for Multi-racial Dance Research." The following description of the setup and lunch is also from this source..

105. "Tac Squad's Happening," *San Francisco Chronicle,* December 18, 1969, 4.

106. "Dancers' Workshop Bail Benefit Party," *San Francisco Chronicle,* December 31, 1969.

107. Author's interview with Anna Halprin, Kentfield, California, April 14, 1999.

108. In the spring of 1975 the French artist Daniel Buren staged a somewhat similar event, asking various people from the New York art world to walk through the Wall Street area carrying placards with nothing but vertical stripes.

109. Author's interview with Anna Halprin, August 24, 1993.

110. See John Sabini and Stanley Milgram, "*Candid Camera,*" *Society* 16, no. 6 (1969): 55–58.

111. Ann Halprin, "New Time Shuffle," diary entry, 1970; in Anna Halprin's archives.

112. Stanley Goree, letter to Ann Halprin, May 30, 1970; in Anna Halprin's archives.

113. Ann Halprin, "New Time Shuffle."

114. Ibid.

115. Ann Halprin in film footage of Ann Halprin and Margaret H'Doubler by Connie Beeson, 1970; in Anna Halprin's archives. All the quotations in this paragraph are from this source.

116. Ann Halprin, "New Time Shuffle."

117. Author's phone interview with Rabbi Samuel Broude, December 18, 2001. All subsequent quotations from Rabbi Broude are from this interview.

118. Author's interview with Nash.

119. Anna Halprin, "Three Decades of Transformative Dance," interview by Nancy Stark Smith, in *Moving toward Life*, 19.

120. Susi Oppenheimer, letter to the editor, *Temple Sinai Newsletter* (Oakland, CA), 1971.

121. Anna Halprin, note to author, June 23, 2004.

122. Author's phone interview with George Leonard, June 28, 2004.

123. Author's interview with Sir Lawrence Washington, San Francisco, August 17, 2001.

124. Ann Halprin, "Community Art as Life Process: The Story of the San Francisco Dancers' Workshop," in *Moving toward Life*, 126.

125. Richard Schechner, "Ann Halprin: A Life in Ritual," *The Drama Review* 33, no. 2 (1989).

126. Anna Halprin, note to author, June 23, 2004.

127. Ann Halprin, "Community Art as Life Process," 117.

128. Marcia B. Siegel, review reprinted in *At the Vanishing Point: A Critic Looks at Dance* (New York: Saturday Review Press, 1973), 301–2.

129. Robert J. Pierce, "The Ann Halprin Story," 1974; in Anna Halprin's archives.

130. Author's interview with Sydney Luria, New York, November 10, 2000.

131. Author's interview with Jack Anderson, San Francisco, October 29, 2001.

CHAPTER 9: ILLNESS AS PERFORMANCE

The epigraph is from Susan Sontag, *Illness as Metaphor and Aids and Its Metaphors* (New York: Anchor Books, 1990), 3. The essay "Illness as Metaphor" originally appeared in 1978.

1. Author's phone conversation with Anna Halprin, June 28, 2002; J. Williams, "Daria Halprin," *Pacific Sun* (San Rafael, California), April 29, 1977.

2. P. J. Growald, "Captain America Weds," *Washington Post*, May 16, 1972.

3. Author's interview with Sydney Luria, New York, November 10, 2000.

4. *Parade Magazine*, n.d.; in Anna Halprin's archives.

5. Author's interview with Daria Halprin, Kentfield, California, January 2, 2002.

6. Marianna Torgovnick, *Gone Primitive: Savage Intellects, Modern Lives* (Chicago: University of Chicago Press, 1990), 192.

7. Roger Copeland, *Merce Cunningham: The Modernizing of Modern Dance* (New York: Routledge, 2004), 122.

8. Torgovnick, *Gone Primitive*, 193.

9. See Ann Halprin, "Community Art as Life Process: The Story of the San Francisco Dancers' Workshop" (1973), in *Moving toward Life: Five Decades*

of Transformational Dance, ed. Rachel Kaplan (Hanover, NH: Wesleyean University Press/University Press of New England, 1995), 126.

10. Robert J. Landy, *Drama Therapy: Concepts and Practices* (Springfield, IL: Charles C. Thomas, 1985), 27. Just as the Living Theater chanted lines from the writings of the existential therapist R. D. Laing in their 1967 play *Paradise Now,* singing about madness as a visionary experience as they danced, Ann too borrowed from psychology, systematizing elements from Gestalt therapy in her workshops and performances. Connections between performance and the human potential movement begun in the 1960s were becoming more clearly established in this period of the early 1970s. Husband-and-wife psychologists Eugene and Juanita Sagan were not alone in sampling dance classes as a means toward different psychological insights.

11. Marsha McMann Paludan, "Expanding the Circle: Anna Halprin and Contemporary Theater Practice," unpublished manuscript, 1994, 268; in Anna Halprin's archives.

12. Ann Halprin, "My Experience of Cancer" (1993), in *Moving toward Life,* 65.

13. Anna Halprin, "Dance as a Self-Healing Art: Working with People Challenging HIV and Cancer," presented to the American Dance Association, April 1991, 1–3; in Anna Halprin's archives.

14. Author's interview with Anna Halprin, Kentfield, California, February 19, 2001.

15. Sontag, *Illness as Metaphor,* 17.

16. See Allen H. Postel, W. Robson, N. Grier, and S. Arthur Localio, "Training the Patient in the Bulb Syringe Method of Colostomy Irrigation: A Manual for Nurses," *Rehabilitation Monograph* 26 (1965): 1–25 (New York: Institute of Physical Medicine and Rehabilitation, New York University Medical Center).

17. Anna Halprin, "Circle the Earth: Myth and Ritual through Dance and the Environment," draft of manual, 1991, 84; in Anna Halprin's archives.

18. Ibid., 81.

19. Anna Halprin, "My Experience of Cancer," 66.

20. Ibid.

21. Sontag, *Illness as Metaphor,* 21.

22. Author's interview with Anna Halprin, Kentfield, California, January 23, 2004.

23. Author's phone conversation with Anna Halprin, July 2, 2006.

24. Anna Halprin, "My Experience of Cancer," 67.

25. Author's interview with Anna Halprin, January 23, 2004.

26. Margaret Shildrick, *Embodying the Monster: Encounters with the Vulnerable Self* (London: SAGE Publications, 2002), 5.

27. Ibid., 49, 52.

28. Lawrence Halprin, *Lawrence Halprin: Changing Places,* exh. cat. (San Francisco: San Francisco Museum of Modern Art, 1986), 141.

29. In ibid., 98.

30. Lawrence Halprin, *The RSVP Cycles: Creative Process in the Human Environment* (New York: George Braziller, 1969).

31. In 1976 Anna had returned to an active schedule of teaching, lecturing, leading workshops, and reviving her rituals. She guest-taught in Israel and Japan and led a summer solstice ritual at the pyramids in Egypt and a collective creativity workshop in Delphi. She resumed the practice she had been doing for several years of making a participatory dance for the American Humanistic Psychology Association's annual meeting based on the conference theme.

32. Another precedent was an exercise Anna used in one of her 1975 summer workshops, where participants divided into small groups and then moved around the city, paying special attention to the "dances" of everyone around them. At the end of the day they all came together again for a large group dance in Justin Herman Plaza, a downtown area designed by Larry (note to author from Sue Heinemann, a participant in the 1975 workshop, April 6, 2006).

33. Author's phone conversation with Ramon Sender, July 15, 2004. The score was reprinted in *TDR*.

34. Anna Halprin, James Burns, and James Nixon, "Citydance: Anna Halprin and San Francisco Dancers' Workshop 1977" (San Francisco: San Francisco Dancers' Workshop booklet, 1977), 7.

35. Anna Halprin, "A Report on *Citydance* 1977," in *Moving toward Life*, 170.

36. Anna Halprin, "A Workshop for San Francisco," unpublished talk, San Francisco, 1976; in Anna Halprin's archives.

37. Anna Halprin, Burns, and Nixon, "Citydance," 30.

38. Anna Halprin, "A Workshop for San Francisco."

39. Author's phone interview with Anna Halprin, July 2, 2006.

40. At Jewish funerals mourners used to distribute coins to the poor who came to the cemetery, and as they gave money away they chanted, "*Tzedakh* will save from death." The reminder to give is present at every major event in Jewish life. See Mark Zborowski and Elizabeth Herzog, *Life Is with People* (New York: Schocken Books, 1952).

41. Rachel Kaplan, "Introduction to 'Leaning into Ritual,'" in *Moving toward Life*, 184.

42. Author's interview with Daria Halprin, January 2, 2002.

43. Quoted in Sandy Park, "San Francisco Dancers' Workshop Training Program 1978 Documentation," unpublished manual, 108; in Anna Halprin's archives.

44. Anna Halprin, note to author, June 23, 2004.

45. All the quotations in this paragraph and the next are from Park, "Training Program," 108–9.

46. Author's interview with Anna Halprin, Kentfield, California, March 10, 2004.

47. Anna Halprin, "Circle the Earth," 16–17.

48. The drawing of the self-portrait, which was an important resource for Anna's "exorcism" dance, became a central part of the Tamalpa training, where one part of the program culminates in the performance of a self-portrait in front of an audience of workshop members.

49. Anna Halprin, *Dance as a Healing Art: A Teacher's Guide and Support Manual for People Living with Cancer* (Kentfield, Calif.: Tamalpa Institute, 1997), 18.

50. "Anna Halprin: A Life in Ritual: Interview by Richard Schechner" (1989), in *Moving toward Life*, 249.

51. Anna Halprin, "Planetary Dance," in *Moving toward Life*, 230.

52. Anna Halprin, "Circle the Earth," 9.

53. Quoted in Paludan, "Expanding the Circle," 298.

54. Author's conversation with Anna Halprin, Kentfield, California, May 2, 2000.

55. Author's interview with Anna Halprin, March 10, 2004.

56. Quoted in Jamie McHugh, "Circle the Earth: Dancing with Purpose," *In Dance* (February 1988): 3.

57. Ibid.

58. Richard Schechner, *Performance Studies—An Introduction* (New York: Routledge, 2002), 62.

59. Ibid., 71.

60. "Anna Halprin: A Life in Ritual: Interview by Richard Schechner," 251, 253.

61. Anna Halprin, *Dance as a Healing Art*, 137.

62. McHugh, "Circle the Earth: Dancing with Purpose," 4.

63. Anna Halprin, "Planetary Dance," 226.

64. Author's phone interview with Maggie Creighton, July 5, 2004.

65. Maggie Creighton, note to author, July 9, 2004.

66. Paludan, "Expanding the Circle," 318.

67. Anna Halprin, *Dance as a Healing Art*, 79; for subsequent material, see 89.

68. Author's interview with Allan Stinson, San Francisco, 1992.

69. Janice Ross, "Anna Halprin: A Performance Response to AIDS," *Dance USA/Journal* 9, no. 1 (1991): 12.

70. Author's phone interview with Jamie McHugh, July 1, 2004.

71. Quoted in Jamie McHugh, "Circle the Earth: Dancing with Life on the Line," *San Francisco Sentinel*, Spring 1991.

72. Author's interview with Anna Halprin, Kentfield, California, December 11, 1989.

73. David Gere, *How to Make Dances in an Epidemic: Tracking Choreography in the Age of AIDS* (Madison: University of Wisconsin Press, 2005).

74. Author's interview with Stinson.

75. Author's interview with Anna Halprin, June 30, 1992.

76. Quoted in Andy Abrahams Wilson, *Positive Motion*, videotape, Abrahams Wilson Productions, Sausalito, California, 1991.

77. Ibid.

78. Anna Halprin, "Circle the Earth," 10.

79. See, for example, Anna Halprin, *Dance as a Healing Art.*

80. "Anna Halprin: A Life in Ritual," 251.

81. Author's interview with Richard Schechner, New York, April 12, 2002.

82. Anna Halprin, "Circle the Earth," 114.

CHAPTER 10: CHOREOGRAPHING DISAPPEARANCE

The epigraphs are from Peggy Phelan, *Unmarked: The Politics of Performance* (London: Routledge, 1993), 147; Sylvia Plath, "Lady Lazarus," in *Collected Poems of Sylvia Plath* (London: Faber and Faber, 1981), 244. Special thanks to Michele Pridmore Brown of the Institute for Research on Women and Gender at Stanford for her insightful comments about women and aging in an earlier draft of this chapter.

1. Heidi Gilpin, "Lifelessness in Movement, or How Do the Dead Move? Tracing Displacement and Disappearance for Movement Performance," in *Corporealities: Dancing Knowledge, Culture and Power,* ed. Susan L. Foster (New York: Routledge, 1996), 110, 114.

2. Eugenio Barba, "From Learning to Learning to Learn," *Dictionary of Theater Anthropology,* ed. Eugenio Barba and Nicola Savarese (London: Routledge, 1991), 244.

3. Naomi Wolf, *The Beauty Myth: How Images of Beauty Are Used Against Women* (New York: Doubleday, 1991), 93.

4. Bonnie Sue Stein, "Twenty Years Ago We Were Crazy, Dirty and Mad," *The Drama Review* 30, no. 2 (1986): 107–26.

5. Richard Schechner, "Kazuo Ohno Doesn't Commute," *The Drama Review* 30, no. 2 (1986): 169.

6. Patricia Vertinsky, "Sporting Women in the Public Gaze: Shattering the Master Narrative of Aging Female Bodies," *Canadian Woman Studies* 21, no. 3 (2002): 59.

7. Simone de Beauvoir, *The Coming of Age,* trans. Patrick O'Brian (New York: Putnam's Sons, 1972), 297.

8. Wolf, *Beauty Myth,* 93–94.

9. De Beauvoir, *Coming of Age,* 300.

10. Abigail Solomon-Godeau, "The Legs of the Countess," *October* 39 (Winter 1986): 65–108.

11. Vertinsky, "Sporting Women in the Public Gaze," 59.

12. This phrase comes from Jacqueline Hayden in describing the public view

of the body; quoted in Kathleen Woodard, *Figuring Age: Women, Bodies, Generations* (Bloomington: Indiana University Press, 1999), 276.

13. Gilpin, "Lifelessness in Movement," 106.

14. Author's conversation with Anna Halprin, October 13, 1998.

15. Anna Halprin, post-performance discussion for "*Still* Moving," Theater Artaud, San Francisco, November 5, 1998; from author's notes.

16. Anna used a $30,000 grant she had received from the Irvine Foundation to support this collaboration.

17. Author's phone interview with Anna Halprin, January 12, 2002.

18. Author's phone conversation with Anna Halprin, April 10, 2003.

19. For information on Jewish burial traditions, see Mark Zborowski and Elizabeth Herzog, *Life Is with People: The Culture of the Shtetl* (New York: Schocken Books, 1952), 376, and Anita Diamant with Howard Cooper, *Living a Jewish Life: Jewish Traditions, Customs and Values for Today's Families* (New York: Harper-Collins, 1976), 291–92.

20. Some critics have also seen references to death in the underlying violence of some of Mendieta's imagery, especially in her silhouettes that are burnt into the ground.

21. Anna Halprin, quoted in brochure for the *Still Dance* photographs, 2001; in Anna Halprin's archives.

22. Author's phone interview with Eeo Stubblefield, January 23, 2003.

23. Eeo Stubblefield, quoted in brochure for the *Still Dance* photographs, 2001.

24. Barbara G. Walker, *The Crone: Woman of Age, Wisdom and Power* (New York: Harper and Row, 1985).

25. Allan Ulrich, "Halprin a Delight at Retrospective," *San Francisco Examiner,* June 6, 2000.

26. Author's phone conversation with Anna Halprin, January 12, 2000.

27. John Rockwell, "Bridging Past and Present," *New York Times,* June 11, 2000, 33.

28. Walker, *The Crone,* 29, 32, 33.

29. Anna Halprin, in program notes for Anna Halprin's Eightieth-Year Retrospective, Cowell Theater, Fort Mason, San Francisco, June 2000.

30. Author's phone interview with Charles Reinhart, January 5, 2001.

31. Janice Ross, "Landscaping Death," *New York Times,* January 27, 2002, "Arts and Leisure," 1.

32. Ibid.

33. Tobi Tobias, "Snow Motion," *New York,* February 18, 2002.

34. Anna Halprin, note to author, June 23, 2004.

35. Andy Abrahams Wilson, "Dance Is for Life: The Work of Anna Halprin," documentary script, University of Southern California, December 19, 1989, 79; in Anna Halprin's archives.

36. Anna Halprin in *Returning Home: Dances with the Earth Body,* film directed and produced by Andy Abrahams Wilson, 2003.

37. Deborah Caslav Covino, "Outside-In: Body, Mind and Self in the Advertisement of Aesthetic Surgery," *Journal of Popular Culture* 35, no. 3 (2001): 95.

38. Walker, *The Crone,* 23.

39. Quoted in Covino, "Outside-In," 95.

40. Kathleen Woodard, *Figuring Age,* 273.

41. Wolf cites this observation by Lasch in *The Beauty Myth* (130).

42. See Covino, "Outside-In," 93.

43. Although Anna does not maintain a company of dancers, she often works with a group called the Sea Ranch Collective, consisting of former students, a number of whom participated in this revival of *Parades and Changes.* The Sea Ranch Collective has also developed a number of environmental pieces, such as *Seasons* (begun in 2003).

44. See Janice Ross, "Halprin Takes Paris," *Dancemagazine,* February 2005, 20.

45. Anna Halprin on *Spark,* KQED-TV San Francisco, March 2006.

46. Author's phone interview with Anna Halprin, March 5, 2006.

47. Quoted in Judith Mackrell, "Growing Old Disgracefully: How a Bunch of Untrained 60-Somethings Are Breathing New Life into a Pina Bausch Classic," *Guardian,* November 27, 2002.

48. Author's phone conversation with Anna Halprin, November 20, 2005.

49. Interviews at Redwood Retirement Community Center, Mill Valley, California, October 12, 2005, recorded on tape "One Step"; in Anna Halprin's archives.

50. Anna Halprin, speech given at the University of California, Davis, in 2000, excerpted in "Arts and Healing Network News," March–April 2006, at www.artheals.org/news_2006/marApro6.html.

51. Ibid.

CHRONOLOGY OF PERFORMANCES, VIDEOS, AND FILMS

STUDENT DANCES

Pastoral, 1936 and 1938
   choreographed and performed by Ann Schuman; music: Francis Poulenc;
   location: Goodman Theatre, Chicago
Saga of Youth, 1938
   choreographed and performed by Ann Schuman; music: unnamed
   student; location: New Trier High School, Winnetka, Illinois
Air Primitive, 1938
   choreographed and performed by Ann Schuman; music: unnamed
   student; location: Bennington, Vermont
Elegy, or Hymn to Dead Soldiers, 1939
   choreography by Ann Schuman; performers: Ann Schuman, Orchesis;
   music: percussion; location: University of Wisconsin, Madison
Song of Youth or Refugees, 1939
   choreography by Ann Schuman; performers: Ann Schuman, Orchesis;
   music: voice; location: University of Wisconsin, Madison
Allegro Barbaro, 1939
   choreography by Ann Schuman; performers: Ann Schuman, Orchesis;
   music: Béla Bartók; location: University of Wisconsin, Madison
Dedication, 1939 *or* 1940
   choreography by Ann Schuman; performers: Ann Schuman, Orchesis;
   music: unnamed student; location: University of Wisconsin, Madison

Chaconne, 1939 or 1940
   choreography by Ann Schuman; performers: Ann Schuman, Orchesis;
   music: Johann Sebastian Bach, Ferruccio Bussoni; location: University of
   Wisconsin, Madison
War Hysteria, 1940
   choreography by Ann Schuman; performers: Ann Schuman, Orchesis;
   music: percussion; location: University of Wisconsin, Madison
Mat Dance, 1940
   choreography by Ann Schuman Halprin; performers: Ann Schuman
   Halprin and group; music: Karol Borsuk; location: Orchesis at the
   University of Illinois, Chicago
Three Pages from a Diary, ca. 1940
   choreographed and performed by Ann Schuman Halprin; music: Aaron
   Copland, Karol Borsuk; location: Orchesis at the University of Illinois,
   Chicago
Protest, 1941
   choreographed and performed by Ann Schuman Halprin; music: percus-
   sion; location: University of Wisconsin, Milwaukee
Shalom, 1942
   choreography by Ann Schuman Halprin; performers: Ann Schuman
   Halprin, Hillel Dance Group; location: University of Wisconsin, Madison
Folk Suite, 1942
   choreography by Ann Schuman Halprin; performers: Ann Schuman
   Halprin, Hillel Dance Group; location: University of Wisconsin, Madison
Ceremonial, 1942
   choreography by Ann Schuman Halprin; performers: Ann Schuman
   Halprin, Hillel Dance Group; location: University of Wisconsin, Madison
Prayer, 1942
   choreography by Ann Schuman Halprin; performers: Ann Schuman
   Halprin, Hillel Dance Group; location: University of Wisconsin, Madison
Wedding Dance, 1942
   choreography by Ann Schuman Halprin; performers: Ann Schuman
   Halprin, Hillel Dance Group; location: University of Wisconsin, Madison
Stella, 1942
   choreography by Ann Schuman Halprin; performers: Ann Schuman
   Halprin, Hillel Dance Group; location: University of Wisconsin, Madison

EARLY WORK IN NEW ENGLAND

Sketches, 1942
   choreography by Ann Halprin; performers: students; location: Mettler
   Estate, Franklin, New Hampshire

Jazz Fantasy, 1942
   choreography by Ann Halprin; performers: students; location: Mettler
   Estate, Franklin, New Hampshire
Death, 1942
   choreography by Ann Halprin; performers: students; location: Mettler
   Estate, Franklin, New Hampshire
New Hampshire Landscape, 1942
   choreography by Ann Halprin; performers: students; location: Mettler
   Estate, Franklin, New Hampshire
Feminine Intrigue, 1942
   choreography by Ann Halprin; performers: students; location: Mettler
   Estate, Franklin, New Hampshire
Epilogue, 1943
   choreographed and performed by Ann Halprin; location: Harvard School
   of Design, Cambridge, and South End Settlement House, Boston
Prologue, 1943
   choreographed and performed by Ann Halprin; location: Harvard School
   of Design, Cambridge, and South End Settlement House, Boston
Something Horizons, 1943
   choreography by Ann Halprin; location: Harvard School of Design,
   Cambridge, and South End Settlement House, Boston
The Lonely Ones, 1943
   choreographed and performed by Ann Halprin, based on cartoons of
   William Steig; music: Norman Cazden; costume: Lawrence Halprin;
   location: Harvard School of Design, Cambridge, and South End Settlement House, Boston

EARLY WORK IN CALIFORNIA (AND NEW YORK)

Bitter Herbs, 1945
   choreographed and performed by Ann Halprin; music: Norman Cazden;
   location: Kaufman Auditorium, New York
Interplay, 1946
   choreography by Ann Halprin; performers: Ann Halprin, Dick Ford, and
   Welland Lathrop; location: 1831 Union Street, San Francisco
Duet, 1946
   choreography by Ann Halprin; performers: Ann Halprin, Dick Ford, and
   Welland Lathrop; location: 1831 Union Street, San Francisco
Harmony at Evening, 1946
   choreographed and performed by Ann Halprin and Welland Lathrop;
   poem: James Broughton; location: 1831 Union Street, San Francisco

First Half Century or Life and Times of the Gadget, ca. 1947
  choreography based on an idea by Ann Halprin and realized by 1831 Union
  Street students; costumes: Lawrence Halprin, Welland Lathrop; music:
  Arthur Eisler; location: Marines Memorial Theatre, San Francisco
People Unaware, 1947
  choreography by Ann Halprin; performers: Ann Halprin, Paul Baum,
  Gladys Brower, Welland Lathrop, Georgiana Wiebenson, Richard Mait-
  land; music: Francean Campbell; location: Marines Memorial Theatre and
  1831 Union Street, San Francisco
Solitude—Quest, 1947
  choreography by Ann Halprin; performers: Maguerite Perego, Richard
  Maitland; music: Domenico Scarlatti; costumes: Mary Grant; location:
  1831 Union Street, San Francisco
Short Story, 1947
  choreography by Ann Halprin; location: 1831 Union Street, San Francisco
Entombment, 1947
  choreography by Ann Halprin; music: Cameron McGraw; costume:
  Welland Lathrop; set piece: Lawrence Halprin; location: Marines Memorial Theatre, San Francisco
The Prophetess, 1947
  choreographed and performed by Ann Halprin; music: Alan Hovhaness;
  costume: Lawrence Halprin; location: Marines Memorial Theatre, San
  Francisco; revival: ANTA Theater, New York, 1955
The Intruder, 1948
  choreographed and performed by Ann Halprin; location: Marines Memorial Theatre, San Francisco
Theme and Variations, 1949
  choreography by Ann Halprin; performers: Ann Halprin, Richard Ford,
  Welland Lathrop; music: Henry Purcell; costumes: Lawrence Halprin;
  location: Marines Memorial Theatre, San Francisco

PERFORMANCES FROM 1950S AND 1960S
Emek, 1951
  choreography by Ann Halprin; performers: Ann Halprin, Ruth Beckford,
  Stanley Brooks, Gladys Brower, Richard Ford, Welland Lathrop, Richard
  Maitland, Alec Rubin, Dulcy Stovner, James Sartin, Marta Skor, Georgiana Wiebenson; music: Leonard Ratner; costumes: Lawrence Halprin;
  premiere: March 25, 1951, Curran Theater, San Francisco
Coffee Pot, 1953
  choreographed and performed by Ann Halprin; music: vocal score;
  location: 1831 Union Street, San Francisco

Daughter of the Voice, 1953
  choreography by Ann Halprin; performers: Ann Halprin, Welland
  Lathrop, Avril Weber; music: Alan Hovhaness; costumes: Lawrence
  Halprin; decor: Keith Monroe; narrator: Alan Loew; premiere: April 24,
  1953, Veterans' Memorial Auditorium, San Francisco
People on a Slant, 1953
  choreography by Ann Halprin; performers: "Newspaper Stand": Ruth
  Beckford, Jenny Hunter (Groat), Robert La Crosse, A.A. Leath; "Pedes-
  trians on a Windy Day": Welland Lathrop, A.A. Leath, Jenny Hunter
  (Groat); "Figures in Collage": Ruth Beckford, Sherrill Cowgill, Jenny
  Hunter (Groat), Robert La Crosse, A.A. Leath; music: Doris Dennison;
  costumes: Lawrence Halprin; premiere: May 1, 1953, San Francisco
4 Variations, 1954
  choreographed and performed by Ann Halprin and San Francisco Dancers'
  Workshop (SFDW) including Dick Ford, Welland Lathrop; music: Henry
  Purcell; locations: toured the West Coast
Madrona, 1954
  choreographed and performed by Ann Halprin; music: Alan Hovhaness;
  costume: Jo Landor; location: Stern Grove, San Francisco
Steig People [The Lonely Ones], 1955
  choreographed and performed by Ann Halprin; music: Norman Cazden;
  costume: Ann Halprin; location: ANTA Theater, New York
Blind Song, 1956
  choreography by Ann Halprin; performers: Ann Halprin, A.A. Leath;
  location: the Pacific Coast Art Festival, Reed College, Portland, Oregon
Branch Dance, 1957
  choreography by Ann Halprin; performers: Ann Halprin, Simone Morris
  (Forti), A.A. Leath; location: Halprin dance deck, Kentfield, California
Hangar, 1957
  choreographed and performed by Ann Halprin, Simone Morris (Forti),
  Norma Leistiko, Jenny Hunter (Groat), A.A. Leath, John Graham;
  location: San Francisco Airport construction site, Millbrae, California
Flight, 1957
  choreography by Ann Halprin; performers: Ann Halprin, Jenny Hunter
  (Groat), A.A. Leath; music: Peter van Deuson; costumes: Jo Landor;
  location: Halprin dance deck, Kentfield, California
Lalezar, 1957
  choreographed and performed by Ann Halprin; music: Alan Hovhaness;
  premiere: December 3, 1957, University of Illinois, Chicago
Duet, 1958
  choreographed and performed by Ann Halprin, A.A. Leath; music: Pieter
  Van Deusen; location: Halprin dance deck, Kentfield, California

Trunk Dance, 1959
choreography by Ann Halprin; performers: Ann Halprin, John Graham, A.A. Leath, Simone Morris (Forti); premiere: San Francisco Playhouse, San Francisco

Four Square, 1959
choreographed and performed by Ann Halprin, John Graham, A.A. Leath, Simone Morris (Forti); location: San Francisco Playhouse, San Francisco

Flowerburger, 1959
choreographed and performed by Ann Halprin, John Graham, A.A. Leath; artistic director: Jo Landor; poetry: Richard Brautigan; lighting: Patric Hickey, Jo Landor; location: Jay Marks Contemporary Dance Theater, San Francisco; International Avant-Garde Festival, Vancouver

Rites of Women, 1959
choreographed and performed by Ann Halprin, Simone Forti, John Graham, A.A. Leath; music: Warner Jepson; songs: Ida Hodes; artistic director: Jo Landor; poetry: James Broughton; lighting: Patric Hickey; costumes: Eliza Pietsch, Sarah Pietsch; location: premiere: May 15, 1959, San Francisco Playhouse, San Francisco

Mr. and Mrs. Mouse, 1959
choreographed and performed by Ann Halprin, John Graham, Daria Halprin, A.A. Leath; music: Terry Riley, Warner Jepson; artistic director: Jo Landor; poetry: James Broughton; lighting: Patric Hickey; location: San Francisco Playhouse, San Francisco

Still Point, 1960
choreographed and performed by Ann Halprin, A.A. Leath, Hetty Mitchell; music: Terry Riley, La Monte Young; lighting: Patric Hickey; premiere: April 22, 1960, Schoenberg Hall, Los Angeles

Visions, 1960
choreographed and performed by Ann Halprin, John Graham, A.A. Leath, Hetty Mitchell, Sandy Piezer; music: Terry Riley, La Monte Young; lighting: Patric Hickey; premiere: April 22, 1960, Schoenberg Hall, Los Angeles

Birds of America, or Gardens Without Walls, 1960
choreographed and performed by Ann Halprin and SFDW including John Graham, Daria Halprin, Rana Halprin, A.A. Leath; music: La Monte Young *(Trio for Strings)*; artistic director: Jo Landor; lighting: Patric Hickey; location: International Avant-Garde Arts Festival, Vancouver; Teatro La Fenice, Venice; San Francisco Contemporary Dance Theatre, San Francisco

The Four-Legged Stool, 1961
choreographed and performed by Ann Halprin and Dancers' Workshop Company including John Graham, A.A. Leath, Lynne Palmer; music: Terry Riley; artistic director: Jo Landor; lighting: Patric Hickey; premiere: September, 24, 1961, San Francisco Playhouse, San Francisco

The Five-Legged Stool, 1962
  choreographed and performed by Ann Halprin and Dancers' Workshop Company including John Graham, Daria Halprin, Rana Halprin,
  A.A. Leath, Lynne Palmer; music: Morton Subotnick, David Tudor;
  artistic director: Jo Landor; lighting: Patric Hickey; premiere: April 29,
  1962, San Francisco Playhouse, San Francisco; toured to Rome, Zagreb,
  and Helsinki
Esposizione, 1963
  choreographed and performed by Ann Halprin, John Graham, Daria
  Halprin, Rana Halprin, A.A. Leath, Lynne Palmer; music: Luciano Berio;
  singer: Cathy Berberian; artistic director: Jo Landor; lighting: Patric
  Hickey; Sculptor: Jerry Walters; premiere: April, 18, 1963, 26th Festival
  Internazionale di Musica Contemporanea, Teatro La Fenice, Venice
Visage, 1963
  choreographed and performed by Ann Halprin; music: Luciano Berio;
  designer: Jo Landor; lighting: Patric Hickey; location: Teatro La Fenice,
  Venice; Teatro Eliseo, Rome; Muzicki Biennale, Zagreb, Yugoslavia
Yellow Cab, 1964
  choreographed and performed by Ann Halprin; music: Luciano Berio;
  artistic director: Jo Landor; lighting: Patric Hickey; premiere: May 4, 1964,
  San Francisco Tape Music Center, San Francisco
Procession, 1965
  choreographed and performed by Anna Halprin and Dancers' Workshop
  Company including John Graham, Daria Halprin, Rana Halprin, A.A.
  Leath, Lucy Lewis; music: Morton Subotnik; artistic director: Jo Landor;
  lighting: Patric Hickey; sculptor: Charles Ross; location: University of
  California, Los Angeles
Parades and Changes, 1965–67 (12 versions); revivals: 1995–2006
  choreographed and performed by Ann Halprin and SFDW including
  originally Larri Goldsmith, Paul Goldsmith, John Graham, Kim Hahn,
  Daria Halprin, Rana Halprin, A.A. Leath, Jani Novak; music: Folke Rabe,
  Morton Subotnik; costumes: Jo Landor; lighting: Patric Hickey; sculptor:
  Charles Ross; premiere: September, 5, 1965, Stockholm; other locations
  1965–67: Poland; University of California, Berkeley; University of Califor-
  nia, Los Angeles; San Francisco State University, San Francisco; "On the
  Mall," Fresno, California; Hunter College, New York; revivals: Footwork,
  San Francisco (1995); American Dance Festival, Durham, North Carolina
  (1997); Cowell Theater, San Francisco (2000); Centre Pompidou, Paris
  (2004); Jewish Community Center, San Francisco, and Contemporary
  Museum of Modern Art, Lyon, France (2006)
Trance Dance, 1965–78
  choreography by Ann Halprin; performers: open; locations: Dancers'

Workshop Studio, San Francisco; Ohio State University, Columbus; Dance Therapy Association, New York; Los Angeles

Apartment 6, 1965
choreographed and performed by Ann Halprin and SFDW including John Graham, A.A. Leath; sound: performers' vocal dialogue; designer: Jo Landor; lighting: Patric Hickey; sculptor: Charles Ross; premiere: March 19, 1965, San Francisco Playhouse, San Francisco; toured in Europe

The Bath, 1966–67
choreographed and performed by Ann Halprin and SFDW including Karen Ahlberg, Daria Halprin, Michael Katz, Morris Kelley, Kathy Peterson, Nancy Peterson, Peter Weiss; music: Pauline Oliveros; artistic director: Jo Landor; lighting: Patric Hickey; vocals: performers; premiere: November 4, 1966, SFDW Studio, San Francisco; February 1967, Wadsworth Atheneum, Hartford, Connecticut

Ten Myths, 1967–68
myths: Creation, Atonement, Trails, Totem, Maze, Dreams, Carry, Masks, Story Telling, Ome; choreographed and performed by Ann Halprin and SFDW with audience; music: Casey Sonnabend; lighting and environment designer: Patric Hickey; sculptor: Seymour Locks; location: SFDW Studio, San Francisco

Ome, 1968
choreographed and performed by Anna Halprin and SFDW; music: Casey Sonnabend; lighting: Patric Hickey; location: University of Oregon, Eugene

Lunch, 1968
choreographed and performed by Ann Halprin, Gary Hartford, Norma Leistiko, Larry Reed assisted by Kim Hahn, Annie Hallet, Daria Halprin, Rana Halprin; music: Charles Amirkhanian; designer: Jo Landor; lighting and environment designer: Patric Hickey; location: Associated Council of the Arts conference, Hilton Hotel, San Francisco

Look, 1968
choreographed and performed by Ann Halprin and SFDW with audience; music: performers; lighting: Patric Hickey; location: San Francisco Museum of Modern Art

Ceremony of Us, 1969
choreographed and performed by Ann Halprin, SFDW, and Studio Watts School for the Arts; music: Billy C. Jackson, Casey Sonnabend; designer: Jo Landor; lighting: Patric Hickey; premiere: February 27, 1969, Mark Taper Forum, Los Angeles; also performed at Laney College, Oakland, California

Event in a Chapel, 1969
   choreographed and performed by Ann Halprin and SFDW; music: Casey
   Sonnabend; lighting: Patric Hickey; location: University of the Pacific,
   Stockton, California
Event in a Mall, 1969
   choreographed and performed by Ann Halprin and SFDW; music: Ann
   Halprin; designer: Patric Hickey; location: San Jose State College, San
   Jose, California
The Bust, December 17, 1969
   choreographed and performed by Ann Halprin and SFDW; location:
   streets of San Francisco

PERFORMANCES FROM 1970S AND 1980S

Blank Placard Dance, 1970
   choreographed and performed by Ann Halprin and SFDW; location:
   streets of San Francisco
New Time Shuffle, 1970
   choreographed and performed by Ann Halprin and Reach Out; music: Bo·
   Conley, Richard Friedman; lighting: Patric Hickey; premiere: October 3,
   1970, Soledad Prison, Soledad, California; also at Harding Theatre, San
   Francisco, and in Oakland, Richmond, and Sausalito, California
Kadosh, 1971
   choreographed and performed by Ann Halprin and SFDW; collaborator:
   Rabbi Samuel Broude; designer: Patric Hickey; premiere: February 12,
   1971, Temple Sinai, Oakland, California
Orgonia, 1971
   choreographed and performed by Ann Halprin and SFDW; premiere:
   August 6, 1971, American Dance Festival, Connecticut College, New
   London
West/East Stereo, also called *Animal Ritual,* 1971
   choreographed and performed by Ann Halprin and SFDW; music:
   Richard Friedman, James Fletcher Hall; lighting: Patric Hickey;
   premiere: August 6–7, 1971, American Dance Festival, Connecticut
   College, New London; other locations: University Art Museum,
   Berkeley; George Washington University, Washington, DC; Williams
   College, Willamstown, Massacusetts; Virginia Museum of Fine Arts,
   Richmond, Virginia
Initiations and Transformations, 1971
   choreographed and performed by Ann Halprin and men of SFDW;
   location: New York City Center, New York

Ceremony of Signals, 1971
    choreographed and performed by Ann Halprin and Reach Out Company;
    location: Richmond, California
"Exorcism," or *"Dark Side" Dance,* 1975
    choreographed and performed by Ann Halprin; location: 321 Divisidero
    Street, San Francisco
Citydance, 1976–77
    choreographed and performed by Anna Halprin, SFDW, and people of
    the Bay Area; collaborators: Jim MacRitchie, Jim Burns; location: San
    Francisco
Ritual and Celebration, 1977
    choreographed and performed by Anna Halprin and SFDW with audi-
    ence; assistant: James Nixon; location: Berkeley, California
Male and Female Rituals, 1978
    choreographed and performed by Anna Halprin and SFDW with audi-
    ence; music: Natural Sound, Kirk Nurock; locations: City Center, New
    York; San Francisco Museum of Modern Art
Arcosanti Alive, 1978
    choreographed and performed by Anna Halprin, SFDW with architects
    and residents of Arcosanti, Arizona; collaborator: Paolo Soleri; location:
    Arcosanti, Arizona
Evolution of Consciousness through the Ages, 1979
    choreographed and performed by Anna Halprin and SFDW; music: Rody
    Marymore: location: boat cruise, Greece; Acropolis, Athens
Celebration of Life—Cycle of Ages, 1979
    choreographed and performed by Anna Halprin, Keijura Kimura, Norma
    Leistiko, and SFDW with members of the Western Gerontological Society
    of San Francisco; music: Rod Marymor, Sandy Hershman; designer: Patric
    Hickey; location: Hilton Hotel, San Francisco
Search for Living Myths and Rituals through Dance and Environment, 1980–81
    choreographed and performed by Anna Halprin and SFDW with people
    of the Bay Area; collaborator: Lawrence Halprin; designer: Patric Hickey;
    sponsor: Tamalpa Institute; location: College of Marin Fine Arts Theater,
    Kentfield, California, and other sites in Marin County; San Francisco
    Museum of Modern Art
In and On the Mountain, April 10–11, 1981
    created and led by Anna Halprin; performers: Tamalpa Institute dancers
    and workshop participants; music: Kirk Norwick; artistic director: Jo Lan-
    dor; lighting: Patric Hickey; set design: Joan Sommers; poet and narrator:
    Kush; sponsor: Tamalpa Institute; premiere: April 10, 1981, Mount Tamal-
    pais, Mill Valley, California; other location: College of Marin Fine Arts
    Theater, Kentfield, California

Thanksgiving Offerings (part of *Circle the Earth* series), 1982
poet and narrator: Kush; leaders: Anna Halprin, James Nixon; premiere:
April 15, 1982, Mount Tamalpais, Mill Valley, California
Return to the Mountain, April 30–May 1, 1983
created and led by Anna Halprin; performers: Tamalpa Institute dancers;
music: Bo Connley, Weldon McCarty, Shakti; set design: Joseph Stubble-
field; guest: Don Jose Mitsuwa; masks: Annie Hallet; narration: James
Cave and James Nixon; sponsor: Tamalpa Institute; location: Mount Tam-
alpais, Mill Valley, California; Redwood High School Gym, Larkspur,
California
Run to the Mountain, April 28–29, 1984
created and led by Anna Halprin; performers: Tamalpa dancers and Norma
Leistiko; set design: Joseph Stubblefield; poet and narrator: Kush; sponsor:
Tamalpa Institute; location: Mount Tamalpais, Mill Valley, California;
Redwood High School Gym, Larkspur, California
Circle the Mountain, April 6–14, 1985
created and led by Anna Halprin; performers: people from the Bay Area;
music: Brian Hand, Suru; set design: Joseph Stubblefield; workshop co-
leader: Jamie McHugh; poet and narrator: Kush; sponsor: Tamalpa Insti-
tute; location: Mount Tamalpais, Mill Valley, California; Redwood High
School Gym, Larkspur, California; Fort Mason Center, San Francisco
Earth Run (part of *Circle the Earth* series), June 21, 1985
created and led by Anna Halprin; performers: people from communities
worldwide; sponsor: New Wilderness Foundation; director: Marilyn
Woods; locations: Central Park and United Nations Plaza, New York; Los
Angeles, Big Sur, and Sausalito, California; Woodland Park, Lexington,
Kentucky; Baca Grande, Colorado; Berlin, Germany; also in Israel, Egypt,
Japan
Circle the Earth: A Dance in the Spirit of Peace, 1986
created and led by Anna Halprin; performers: people from the Bay Area
and around the world; musicians: John Gruntfest, Grant Rudolph, Weldon McCarty; guest composer: Terry Riley; poet and narrator: Kush; set
design: Joseph Stubblefield; altar: Eeo Stubblefield; location: Redwood
High School, Larkspur, California
Peace Meditation and Earth Run, June 18–22, 1986
created and led by Anna Halprin; sponsor: American Dance Festival;
location: Durham, North Carolina
Circle the Earth: A Peace Dance with the Planet, 1987
created and led by Anna Halprin; performers: people from the Bay Area
and around the world; guest singer: Susan Osborn; musician: Brian Hand;
set design: Joseph Stubblefield; altar: Eeo Stubblefield; location: Redwood
High School, Larkspur, California

Planetary Dance, 1987–
created and led by Anna Halprin; performers: people from the Bay Area and in communities all over the world; consultants: James Nixon and Russell Bass; locations: Mount Tamalpais, Mill Valley, California, and other locations around the world (see also 1990s on)
Circle the Earth: Dancing Our Peaceful Nature, 1988
presented by Anna Halprin and guest artists including James Nixon and Native spiritual leaders; participants: people from the Bay Area; location: Marin Headlands, California
Circle the Earth: Dancing with Life on the Line, 1989, 1991
led by Anna Halprin with Jamie McHugh and Tamalpa facilitators; musicians: Brian Hand, Mark Katz, Jason Serinus; vocals: Marcia Paludan and Carol Swann; performers: Steps Theater Company, Women with Wings; narration: Allan Stinson; set design: Joseph Stubblefield; location: Mount Tamalpais and Redwood High School, Larkspur, California

PERFORMANCES FROM 1990S ON

Planetary Dance and Earth Run (ongoing; see 1987)
yearly at Mount Tamalpais and other places; special locations: Mont Blanc (Milano), Italy, July 10, 1991; Min Tanaka Festival, Hakushu, Japan, July 25, 1991; Humanistic Medicine Conference, Garmisch, Germany, November 2, 1991; Tanz Atttuel, Berlin, November 3, 1991; Caldecott Field, Oakland, California, January 19, 1992 (directed by Anna Halprin for community members after the Oakland fire; titled *Earth Run after the Fire: Planting Seeds of Renewal*); Society of Dance History Scholars Conference, University of California, Riverside, February 16, 1992
Circle the Earth (ongoing from 1986)
led by Anna Halprin; location: Subud, Bali (1990); Essen, Germany (1991); Frieburg, Germany (1991; sponsored by Galli Institute)
Carry Me Home, 1990
created and led by Anna Halprin with Allan Stinson; dancers: Positive Motion participants; musicians: Jules Beckman and Norman Rutherford; premiere: June 16, 1990, Theater Artaud, San Francisco
The Grandfather Dance, 1994
choreographed and performed by Anna Halprin; music: Flying Klezmer Band; sponsor: Traveling Jewish Theater; premiere: February 2, 1994, Fort Mason Theater, San Francisco
Circle the Earth (Excerpts), Seventy-fifth Birthday Retrospective, 1996
choreographed by Anna Halprin; performers: Anna Halprin, Rachel Kaplan, Cydney Wilkes, Keith Hennessy, Jess Curtis, Jeff Rehg, Women

with Wings, Steps Theatre Company; musicians: Jules Beckman, Norman
Rutherford, and Billy Cauley; narrator: Jim Cave; location: Dancers'
Group Footwork, San Francisco
Still Dance with Anna Halprin, 1998–2002
conceived and directed by Eeo Stubblefield; performed by Anna Halprin;
various locations
From 5 to 110, 1999
created and performed by Anna Halprin; music: Ray Lynch; premiere:
"*Still* Moving," Theater Artaud, San Francisco, November 7, 1999;
other locations: Cowell Theatre, San Francisco (Part of "Memories from
My Closet"), 2000; Omega Institute, Rhinebeck, New York; "Art of
Aging" conference, San Francisco Hilton, San Francisco, 2004
Memories from My Closet: Four Dance Stories, Eightieth Birthday Retrospective,
2000
created and performed by Anna Halprin; assisted by David Greenaway;
dances: *From 5 to 110* (1998)/music: Ray Lynch, *The Courtesan and the
Crone* (2000)/music: Arcangelo Corelli, *The Grandfather Dance* (1995)/
music: Flying Klezmer Band, *Gratitude* (2000); location: Cowell Theatre,
San Francisco
Intensive Care: Reflections on Death and Dying, 2000–
choreographed and performed originally by Anna Halprin, Lakshmi Aysola,
David Greenaway, Jeff Rehg; music: Miguel Frasconi; voice: Carol Swann;
premiere: June 2, 2000, Cowell Theatre, San Francisco; later core perform-
ers: G. Hoffman Soto, Taira Restar, Brian Collentina; additional music:
"Gotham Lullaby" by Meredith Monk; other locations: Mountain Home
Studio (2004); Centre Pompidou, Paris (2004); Jewish Community
Center, San Francisco (2006)
Walking with the Dead, 2000–
ritual designed by Jeff Rehg with Anna Halprin; directed by Anna Halprin;
locations: Sea Ranch, California; Mountain Home Studio, Kentfield, California; Stinson Beach, California, memorial performance (October 2003)
Be With, 2001
choreographed and performed by Eiko and Koma with Anna Halprin;
music: Joan Jeanrenaud; costumes: Eiko, Koma; sets: Eiko, Koma; pre-
miere: Terrace Theatre, JFK Center for the Performing Arts, Washington,
DC; other locations: Yerba Buena Theater, San Francisco (2002); Joyce
Theater, New York, New York (2002)
Forest, 2002
created by Anna Halprin with members of the Sea Ranch Collective;
performed by members of the Sea Ranch Collective; costumes by Eeo
Stubblefield; premiere: March 2002, Falkirk Community Center, San
Anselmo, California

Seasons, Part 1: Summer, 2003
   created and performed by the Sea Ranch Collective; artistic director: Anna
   Halprin; music/soundscape: Billy Cauley; performance coordinator: Lynn
   Moody; rigging consultant: Karl Gillick; premiere: Mountain Home Studio
   (outdoor sites), Kentfield, California
El Dia de los Muertos, 2003
   created by Anna Halprin; performed by Terre Parker, Cindy Davis, Lesley
   Ehrenfeld, William McCandless, Grady Cousins, Amanda Royce; masks:
   Annie Hallatt; location: El Dia de los Muertos Parade, Canal Street, San
   Rafael, California
En Route, 2004–
   created by Anna Halprin with G. Hoffman Soto; originally performed by
   G. Hoffman Soto, Lakshmi Aysola, Boaz Barkan, Alain Buffard, Sherwood
   Chen, Anne Collod, Ivola Demange, Lesley Ehrenfeld, Frank Hediger,
   David Greenaway; assisted by Terre Unité Parker; costumes inspired by
   René Magritte; music: Ionel Petroï; premiere: Festival d'Automne, Paris,
   from Residence Hôtelière Citadine Les Halle to Centre Pompidou, Sep-
   tember 23–25, 2004
Seniors Rocking, 2005
   created by Anna Halprin; performers: seniors in Marin County; music:
   Billy Cauley; location: Marin Civic Center, San Rafael, California

FILMS AND VIDEOS
(Additional footage and archival films are contained in Anna Halprin's
archives at the San Francisco Performing Arts Library and Museum.)
"Princess Printemps," in Four in the Afternoon, 1951
   directed by James Broughton; performed by Ann Halprin (full film also
   includes dance by Welland Lathrop); music: William O. Smith; full film
   30 minutes, black-and-white
Children's Film, 1954
   documentary produced by KQED-TV, San Francisco; 20 minutes, black-
   and-white
Hangar, 1957
   documentary by William Heick of performance by Ann Halprin,
   Simone Forti, Norma Leistiko, A.A. Leath, John Graham, Jennifer
   Hunter (Groat); San Francisco Airport; 15 minutes, black-and-white
Procession, 1964
   documentary of performance; music: La Monte Young and Terry Riley;
   produced by University of California, Los Angeles; 30 minutes, black-
   and-white

Parades and Changes, 1965
   documentary of performance; directed by Arne Armbom; produced by National Swedish Television; 40 minutes, black-and-white
The Bed, 1968
   directed by James Broughton; performed by Ann Halprin and others; music: Warner Jepson; 20 minutes, color
Right On! (Ceremony of Us), 1969
   documentary directed by Seth Hill; produced by KQED-TV, San Francisco; 30 minutes, black-and-white
The Golden Positions, 1970
   directed by James Broughton; performed by Ann Halprin; 32 minutes, black-and-white and color
Ann: A Portrait, 1971
   filmed and directed by Coni Beeson; produced by American Film Institute; sound by Richard Friendman; 21 minutes, black-and-white
The Bust, 1971
   documentary of 1969 performance; directed by Paul Ryan; produced by KQED-TV, San Francisco; 15 minutes, black-and-white
How Sweet It Is, 1975
   directed by Lawrence Halprin with Paul Ryan; 12 minutes, black-and-white
"Exorcism" or *"Dark Side" Dance,* 1975
   documentary by Coni Beeson of performance by Ann Halprin; 15 minutes, black-and-white
Dance for Your Life and *A Ritual of Life/Death,* 1988
   documentaries with Steps Theater Company; 15 minutes each, color
Power of Ritual, 1988
   documentary produced by Thinking Allowed Productions; 30 minutes, color
Circle the Earth: Dancing with Life on the Line, 1989
   documentary produced by Media Arts West; 40 minutes, color
Lawrence and Anna Halprin: Inner Landscapes, 1991
   documentary directed by Joan Saffa; produced by KQED-TV, San Francisco; 60 minutes, color
Positive Motion: Challenging AIDS through Dance and Ritual, 1991
   documentary directed and produced by Andy Abrahams Wilson; 37 minutes, black-and-white
Embracing Earth: Dances with Nature, 1995
   directed and produced by Andy Abrahams Wilson; creator and executive producer: Anna Halprin; art director: Eeo Stubblefield; music: Norman Rutherford; 23 minutes, color

My Grandfather Dances, 1999
   directed by Douglas Rosenberg; 12 minutes, color
Returning Home: Dances with the Earth Body, 2003
   directed and produced by Andy Abrahams Wilson; artistic director and
   body art: Eeo Stubblefield; dancer: Anna Halprin; music: Fred Firth; 45
   minutes, color
Intensive Care: Reflections on Death and Dying, 2003
   created and performed by Anna Halprin in collaboration with Lakshmi
   Aysola, David Greenaway, and Jeff Rehg; directed and edited by Austin
   Forebord; artistic director: Josephine Landor; music, Miguel Frasconi;
   color
My Lunch with Anna, 2005
   directed by Alain Buffard; performed by Anna Halprin, Alain Buffard,
   Sherwood Chen, Lesley Ehrenfeld, and Karl Gillick; color
"Who Says You Have to Dance in the Theatre?" 2006
   documentary directed and produced by Jacqueline Caux; color
Spark: Anna Halprin, 2006
   documentary directed by Patrick Flaherty; produced by KQED-TV
   San Francisco; color (online at www.kqed.org/arts/people/spark/profile
   .jsp?id=5402)
Seniors Rocking, in process
   documentary directed and produced by Ruedi Gerber; color

SELECTED BIBLIOGRAPHY

Anna Halprin's personal collection of documents pertaining to her work is now housed in her archives at the San Francisco Performing Arts Library and Museum.

Albright, Ann Cooper. *Choreographing Difference: The Body and Identity in Contemporary Dance*. Hanover, NH: Wesleyan University Press, 1997.

Anderson, Jack. "Manifold Implications." *Dancemagazine* 36, no. 4 (April 1963): 44.

Banes, Sally. *Democracy's Body: Judson Dance Theatre, 1962–1964*. Durham, NC: Duke University Press, 1993.

———. *Greenwich Village 1963*. Durham, NC: Duke University Press, 1993.

Bassett, Gladys B. "Co-eds Find New Atmosphere in Lathrop Hall." *Wisconsin Alumni Magazine* (Wisconsin Women Edition, 1933). Steenbock Historical Archives, University of Wisconsin at Madison.

Bayer, Herbert, Ise Gropius, and Walter Gropius. *The Bauhaus: 1919–1928*. New York: Museum of Modern Art, 1938.

Belitt, Ben. "Poet in the Theatre." *Impulse* (1959): 12.

Bernheimer, Martin. "Ann Halprin Presents Dance Happening at Taper Forum." *Los Angeles Times*, March 1, 1969, sec. II, 8.

Bloomfield, Arthur. "When Nudity Is Defensible in Dancing." *San Francisco Sunday Examiner and Chronicle*, October 15, 1967, B4.

Burns, Stewart. *Social Movements of the 1960s: Searching for Democracy*. Boston: Twayne, 1990.

Burt, Ramsay. *Alien Bodies: Representations of Modernity, "Race," and Nation in Early Modern Dance.* London: Routledge, 1998.

———. *The Male Dancer: Bodies, Spectacle, Sexualities.* London: Routledge, 1995.

Butler, Judith. *Gender Trouble: Feminism and the Subversion of Identity.* London: Routledge, 1990.

Coleman, Wanda. *A War of Eyes.* Santa Rosa, CA: Black Sparrow Press, 1988.

Cutler, Irving. *The Jews of Chicago: From Shtetl to Suburb.* Urbana: University of Illinois Press, 1996.

Daly, Ann. *Done into Dance: Isadora Duncan in America.* Bloomington: Indiana University Press, 1995.

Damon, Maria. "The Jewish Entertainer as Cultural Lightning Rod: The Case of Lenny Bruce." *Postmodern Culture* 7, no. 2 (January 1997).

Dennison, Doris. "Improvisation and Dance Accompaniment." *Impulse* (1948): 13–15.

Desmond, Jane. "Dancing Out the Difference: Cultural Imperialism and Ruth St. Denis's Radha of 1906." In *Moving History/Dancing Cultures,* ed. Ann Cooper Albright and Ann Dils. Middletown, CT: Wesleyan University Press, 2001.

———. "Embodying Difference: Issues in Dance and Cultural Studies." In *The Routledge Dance Studies Reader,* ed. Alexandra Carter. London: Routledge, 1998.

Dewey, John. *Art as Experience.* New York: Capricorn Books, 1934.

Di Prima, Diane, and LeRoi Jones, eds. *The Floating Bear: A Newsletter, Numbers 1–37.* La Jolla, CA: Laurence McGilvery, 1973.

Diamant, Anita, and Howard Cooper. *Living a Jewish Life: Jewish Traditions, Customs and Values for Today's Families.* New York: Harper Collins, 1976.

Dils, Ann, and Ann Cooper Albright, eds. *Moving History/Dancing Cultures: A Dance History Reader.* Middletown, CT: Wesleyan University Press, 2001.

Douglas, Mary. *Implicit Meanings: Selected Essays in Anthropology.* London: Routledge, 2001.

———. "Jokes." In *Rethinking Popular Culture,* ed. Chandra Mukerji and Michael Schudson. Berkeley: University of California Press, 1991.

———. *Purity and Danger: An Analysis of Concepts of Pollution and Taboo.* London: Penguin Books, 1966.

Downing, Jack. *Gestalt Awareness.* New York: Harper and Row, 1976.

Duncan, Michael. "Tracing Mendieta." *Art in America* 87, no. 4 (April 1999): 110–13, 154.

Eichelbaum, Stanley. "Playhouse Dance Bedlam." *San Francisco Examiner,* May 7, 1962, 37.

Flacks, Richard. *Making History: The Radical Tradition in American Life.* New York: Columbia University Press, 1988.

———. *Youth and Social Change.* Chicago: Markham Publishing, 1971.

Ford, Richard. "Notes on Classes for Boys." *Impulse* (1953): 8.

Forti, Simone. *Handbook in Motion: An Account of an Ongoing Personal Discourse and Its Manifestations in Dance*. Halifax: Press of the Nova Scotia College of Art and Design, 1974.

Foster, Edward Halsey. *Richard Brautigan*. Boston: Twayne, 1983.

Foster, Susan Leigh. "Choreographies of Gender." In *Readers in Cultural Criticism: Performance Studies*, ed. Erin Striff. Hampshire, England: Palgrave Macmillan, 2003.

―――. "Dancing Bodies." In *Meaning in Motion*, ed. Jane Desmond. Durham, NC: Duke University Press, 1997.

Foucault, Michel. *The History of Sexuality: An Introduction*. New York: Random House, 1978.

Fowle, Farnsworth. "Rose Halprin Dies; Leading U.S. Zionist." *New York Times*, January 9, 1978.

Frankenstein, Alfred. "Ann Halprin Impressive in Dance Recital." *San Francisco Chronicle*, October 27, 1947, "Metropolis": 13.

―――. "Apartment 6—New Realism in Theatre." *San Francisco Chronicle*, March 21, 1965, 7.

―――. "Fillmore Abstraction—Light, Music, Dance." *San Francisco Sunday Examiner and Chronicle*, October 8, 1967, "This World": 29.

Gannon, Linda R. *Women and Aging: Transcending the Myth*. London: Routledge, 1999.

George-Warren, Holly, ed. *The Rolling Stone Book of the Beats: The Beat Generation and American Culture*. New York: Hyperion, 1999.

Gilpin, Heidi. "Lifelessness in Movement, or How Do the Dead Move? Tracing Displacement and Disappearance for Movement Performance." In *Corporealities: Dancing Knowledge, Culture and Power*, ed. Susan Leigh Foster. New York: Routledge, 1996, 106–28.

Gitlin, Todd. *The Sixties: Years of Hope, Days of Rage*. Toronto: Bantam, 1987.

Goffman, Erving. *The Presentation of Self in Everyday Life*. New York: Doubleday/Anchor Books, 1956.

Goode, Elizabeth. "The Dance at Mills College." *Dance Observer* 6, no. 5 (August–September 1939): 252.

Graff, Ellen. *Stepping Left: Dance and Politics in New York City 1928–1942*. Durham, NC: Duke University Press, 1997.

Gropius, Walter, and Arthur Wensinger. *The Theater of the Bauhaus*. Middletown, CT: Wesleyan University Press, 1961.

Grosz, Elizabeth. *Volatile Bodies: Toward a Corporeal Feminism*. Bloomington: Indiana University Press, 1994.

H'Doubler, Margaret Newell. *Dance: A Creative Art Experience*. Madison: University of Wisconsin Press, 1940.

―――. *The Dance and Its Place in Education*. New York: Harcourt, Brace, 1925.

―――. "Movement and Its Rhythmic Structure: An Educational Theory of Motor Learning." Mimeographed manuscript by Kramer Business Service, Madison, Wisconsin, 1946.

Halprin, Ann/Anna. "Children's Class." *Impulse* (Summer 1948): 27–29.

——. *Citydance 1977.* San Francisco: San Francisco Dancers' Workshop, 1977.

——. "Community Art as Life Process." *The Drama Review* 17, T-59 (1973): 64–80.

——. *Dance as a Healing Art: A Teacher's Guide and Support Manual for People with Cancer.* Kentfield, CA: Tamalpa Institute, 1997.

——. "Intuition and Improvisation in Dance." *Impulse* (1955): 10–15.

——. *Movement Ritual I.* Illustrations by Charlene Koonce. Kentfield, CA: San Francisco Dancers' Workshop/Tamalpa Institute, 1979.

——. *Moving toward Life: Five Decades of Transformational Dance,* ed. Rachel Kaplan. Hanover, NH: Wesleyan University Press/University Press of New England, 1995.

——. "Mutual Creation." *Tulane Drama Review* 13, no.·1 (Fall 1968): 163–75.

Halprin, Ann, and John Rockwell. "Myths, an Explanation by Ann Halprin." San Francisco: Ralph Harper Silver Public Relations, 1968.

Halprin, Lawrence. "The Art of Garden Design." *Journal of Popular Culture* (July 1954).

——. "The Choreography of Gardens." *Impulse* (1949): 30–34.

——. *Cities.* Cambridge, MA: MIT Press, 1963.

——. "A Discussion of the Five-Legged Stool." *San Francisco Chronicle* (1962); in Anna Halprin's archives.

——. "Landscaping a Small Plot." *Sunset,* November–December 1949, 105, 122.

——. *Lawrence Halprin: Changing Places,* exh. cat. San Francisco: San Francisco Museum of Modern Art, 1986.

——. "New York, New York: A Study of the Quality, Character and Meaning of Open Space in Urban Design." San Francisco: Lawrence Halprin Associates, 1968.

——. *Notebooks 1959–1971.* Cambridge, MA: MIT Press, 1972.

——. *The RSVP Cycles: Creative Process in the Human Environment.* New York: George Braziller, 1969.

——. *Sketchbooks of Lawrence Halprin.* Tokyo: Process Architecture, 1981.

——. "Structure and Garden Spaces Related in Sequence." *Progressive Architecture,* March 1958, 96–104.

Halprin, Lawrence, and Jim Burns. *Taking Part: A Workshop Approach to Collective Creativity.* Cambridge, MA: MIT Press, 1974.

Halprin, Lawrence, and Thomas Church. "You Have a Gold Mine in Your Backyard." *House Beautiful,* January 1949, 37–44.

Halprin, Lawrence, and Ann Halprin. "Dance Deck in the Woods." *Impulse* (1956): 21–25.

Harris, Mary Emma. *The Arts at Black Mountain College.* Cambridge, MA: MIT Press, 1987.

Hernton, Calvin C. *Coming Together: Black Power, White Hatred and Sexual Hang-ups.* New York: Random House, 1971.

Hevesi, T. "San Francisco Letter." *Dance Observer* 57 (May 1945).

Hill, Martha. *Martha Hill Reminisces about Bennington.* New York: NTSC Video Documentation of Dance Symposium, 1985.

Humphrey, Doris. *Doris Humphrey: An Artist First.* Middletown, CT: Wesleyan University Press, 1972.

"Invitation to Dance" (editorial). *San Francisco Chronicle,* August 21, 1962, 36.

Isaacs, Reginald. *Walter Gropius: An Illustrated Biography of the Creator of the Bauhaus.* Boston: Little, Brown, 1983.

Jacobs, Jane. *The Death and Life of Great American Cities.* New York: Random House, 1961.

Kadushin, Max. *Organic Thinking: A Study in Rabbinic Thought.* New York: Bloch, 1938.

———. *The Rabbinic Mind.* New York: Blaisdell, 1965.

Kaprow, Allan. *Assemblage, Environments and Happenings.* New York: Harry Abrams, 1966.

Kirby, Michael. "Happenings: An Introduction." In *Happenings and Other Acts,* ed. Mariellen R. Sandford. London: Routledge, 1995.

Kirby, Michael Stanley, ed. *The New Theatre: Performance Documentation.* New York: New York University Press, 1974.

Knebel, Fletcher. "Antonioni Found a Dancer for His Girl and a Carpenter for His Boy." *Look,* November 18, 1969, 37–40.

Kostelanetz, Richard. *The Theatre of Mixed Means: An Introduction to Happenings, Kinetic Environments, and Other Mixed-Means Performances.* New York: Dial Press, 1968.

Krevitsky, Nik. "Orchesis Triumphs at U. of Wisconsin." *Chicago Dancer,* June 1941.

Kriegsman, Sali Ann. *Modern Dance in America: The Bennington Years.* Boston: G. K. Hall, 1981.

Landay, Lori. *Madcaps, Screwballs, and Con Women.* Philadelphia: University of Pennsylvania Press, 1998.

Langer, Susanne K. *Feeling and Form.* New York: Charles Scribner's Sons, 1953.

———. *Problems of Art.* New York: Charles Scribner's Sons, 1957.

Leonard, George. "California, a New Game with New Rules." *Look,* June 28, 1966.

Lester, Elenore. "The Final Decline and Total Collapse of the American Avant-Garde." *Esquire* 71, no. 5 (1969): 142–51.

Makower, Joel. *Boom! Talkin' about Our Generation.* Chicago: Tilden Press, 1985.

Maletic, Vera. "The Process Is the Purpose." *Dance Scope,* Fall–Winter 1967–68, 11–17.

Manning, Susan. "The Female Dancer and the Male Gaze: Feminist Critiques of Early Modern Dance." In *Meaning in Motion*, ed. Jane C. Desmond. Durham, NC: Duke University Press, 1997.

Martin, John. "Broadway Applauds Marin Dancer." *Marin Independent-Journal*, June 4, 1955.

Miller, James. *Democracy Is in the Streets*. Cambridge, MA: Harvard University Press, 1994.

Modleski, Tania, ed. *Studies in Entertainment: Critical Approaches to Mass Culture*. Bloomington: Indiana University Press, 1986.

Moffett, James. "The Second Person." *Impulse* (1962).

Moore, Charles. "Still Pools and Crashing Waves." In *Lawrence Halprin: Changing Places*, exh. cat. San Francisco: San Francisco Museum of Modern Art, 1986.

Morrison, Toni. *Playing in the Dark: Whiteness and the Literary Imagination*. Cambridge, MA: Harvard University Press, 1992.

Neff, Renfreu. *The Living Theatre: USA*. Indianapolis: Bobbs-Merrill, 1970.

Nichols, Lewis. "Sing Out, Sweet Land!" *New York Times*, December 28, 1944.

O'Gallagher, Liam. *The Blue Planet Notebooks*. San Francisco: X-Communications, 1972.

Paludan, Marsha McMann. "Expanding the Circle: Anna Halprin and Contemporary Theatre Practice." Unpublished manuscript, 1994; in Anna Halprin's archives.

Park, Sandy. "SFDW Training Program 1978 Documentation." San Francisco: San Francisco Dancers' Workshop, 1979; in Anna Halprin's archives.

Perls, Frederick S. *Ego, Hunger and Aggression: A Revision of Freud's Theory and Method*. San Francisco: Orbit Graphic Arts, 1966.

———. *Gestalt Therapy Verbatim*. Moab, Utah: Real People Press, 1969.

———. *A Session in Gestalt Therapy* (audiovisual). Esalen, CA: Esalen Institute and Mediasync Corporation, 1968.

Perron, Wendy. "Moving, Joyfully and Carefully, into Old Age." *New York Times*, April 2, 2000, 8.

Perry, Charles. *The Haight-Ashbury: A History*. New York: Random House/Rolling Stone Press, 1984.

Phelan, Peggy. "Dance and the History of Hysteria." In *Corporealities: Dancing Knowledge, Culture and Power*, ed. Susan Leigh Foster. London: Routledge, 1996, 90–105.

———. *Unmarked: The Politics of Performance*. London: Routledge, 1993.

Phillips, Lisa. *Beat Culture and the New America 1950–1965*, exh. cat. New York: Whitney Museum of American Art, 1996.

Pierce, Robert J. "The Anna Halprin Story." Unpublished manuscript, 1974; in Anna Halprin's archives.

Rabe, Folke. "Program Notes for *Parades and Changes*." Stadsteater Publicity Department, Stockholm, 1965; in Anna Halprin's archives.

Rainer, Yvonne. "Yvonne Rainer Interviews Anna Halprin." *Tulane Drama Review* 10, no. 5 (Winter 1965).

———. *Yvonne Rainer Work 1961–73.* Halifax: Press of the Nova Scotia College of Art and Design, 1974.

Ramsay, Margaret Hupp. *The Grand Union (1970–76): An Improvisational Performance Group.* New York: Peter Lang, 1991.

Rexroth, Kenneth. "San Francisco Dancers' Workshop." Unpublished manuscript, 1970; in Anna Halprin's archives.

———. "San Francisco Letter" (1957). In *San Francisco Stories,* ed. John Miller. San Francisco: Chronicle Books, 1990.

Roach, Joseph R. "The Inscription of Morality as Style." In *Interpreting the Theatrical Past: Essays in the Historiography of Performance,* ed. Thomas Postelwart and Bruce A. McConachie. Iowa City: University of Iowa Press, 1989.

Rockwell, John. "Ann Halprin Builds New Bridges in Dance." *Oakland Tribune,* February 1969.

———. "Bridging Past and Present." *New York Times,* June 11, 2000, 33.

———. "Disappointing Experimental Dance." *Oakland Tribune,* March 1, 1969, B4.

Rorabaugh, William J. *Berkeley at War.* New York: Oxford University Press, 1989.

Ross, Janice. "Anna Halprin: A Performance Response to AIDS." *Dance USA Journal* 9, no. 1 (Summer 1991).

———. *Moving Lessons: Margaret H'Doubler and the Beginning of Dance in American Education.* Madison: University of Wisconsin Press, 2000.

Roszak, Theodore. *The Voice of the Earth.* New York: Simon and Schuster, 1992.

Roth, Leland M. *A Concise History of American Architecture.* New York: Harper and Row, 1979.

Sabini, John, and Stanley Milgram. "Candid Camera." *Society* 16, no. 6 (1969): 55–58.

Sagan, Juanita. "Institute for Creative and Artistic Development—How It All Began." El Cerrito, CA, Institute for Creative and Artistic Development, 1995.

Schechner, Richard. "Anna Halprin: A Life in Ritual." *The Drama Review* 33, no. 2 (Summer 1989).

———. *Essays in Performance Theory.* New York: Drama Books Specialists, 1977.

———. "Kazuo Ohno Doesn't Commute." *The Drama Review* 30 (Summer 1986): 163–69.

———. *Performance Studies: An Introduction.* New York: Routledge, 2002.

———. "Performers and Spectators Transported and Transformed." *Kenyon Review* 3, no. 1 (Winter 1981): 83–113.

———. "Training Interculturally." In *Dictionary of Theatre Anthropology,* ed. Eugenio Barba and Nicola Savarese. London: Routledge, 1991, 247–48.

Shepard, Martin. *Fritz.* Sagaponack, NY: Second Chance Press, 1975.

Shildrick, Margrit. *Embodying the Monster: Encounters with the Vulnerable Self.* London: Sage Publications, 2002.

Showalter, Dennis E. "Archie Bunker, Lenny Bruce and Ben Cartwright: Taboo-Breaking and Character Identification in 'All in the Family.'" *Journal of Popular Culture* 9, no. 3 (Winter 1975): 618–21.

Showalter, Elaine. *The Female Malady: Women, Madness, and English Culture, 1830–1980.* New York: Penguin Books, 1985.

Siegel, Marcia B. *At the Vanishing Point: A Critic Looks at Dance.* New York: Saturday Review Press, 1968.

———. *Days on Earth: The Dance of Doris Humphrey.* New Haven: Yale University Press, 1987.

Sitney, P. Adams. "The Potted Psalm." In *Visionary Film: The American Avant-Garde.* New York: Oxford University Press, 1979, 47–92.

Smith, Hilda L. "Cultural Constructions of Age and Aging: Age, a Problematic Concept for Women." *Journal of Women's History* 12, no. 4 (2001): 77–86.

Soares, Janet Mansfield. *Louis Horst: Musician in a Dancer's World.* Durham, NC: Duke University Press, 1992.

Sontag, Susan. *Illness as Metaphor and AIDS and Its Metaphors.* New York: Anchor Books, 1990.

———. "Looking at War: Photography's View of Devastation and Death." *New Yorker,* December 9, 2002, 92–98.

Starr, Kevin. *Americans and the California Dream, 1850–1915.* New York: Oxford University Press, 1973.

Steig, William. *The Lonely Ones.* New York: Duell, Sloan and Pearce, 1942.

"Tac Squad's Happening." *San Francisco Chronicle,* December 18, 1969, 4.

Torgovnick, Marianna. *Gone Primitive: Savage Intellects, Modern Lives.* Chicago: University of Chicago Press, 1990.

Tunnard, Christopher. *Gardens in the Modern Landscape.* London: Architectural Press, 1938.

Uber, Nancy E. "Anna Halprin: Towards a Biography." Sonoma, CA, Sonoma State University, MA thesis, December 16, 1985.

Vaughan, David. *Merce Cunningham: Fifty Years.* New York: Aperture, 1997.

Vertinsky, Patricia. "Sporting Women in the Public Gaze: Shattering the Master Narrative of Aging Female Bodies." *Canadian Woman Studies* 21, no. 3 (Winter–Spring 2002): 58–63.

Waring, Jim. "What Is the Ideal Technical Equipment for Today's Theatre Dancer?" *Impulse* (1948): 18–20.

Washburne, Carlton. *Winnetka: The History and Significance of an Educational Experiment.* Englewood Cliffs, NJ: Prentice-Hall, 1963.

Woodard, Kathleen. *Aging and Its Discontents: Freud and Other Fictions.* Bloomington: Indiana University Press, 1991.

———. *Figuring Age: Women, Bodies, Generations.* Bloomington: Indiana University Press, 1999.

Zborowski, Mark, and Elizabeth Herzog. *Life Is with People: The Culture of the Shtetl.* New York: Shocken Books, 1952.

Zimbardo, Philip. *The Psychology of Attitude Change and Social Influence.* New York: McGraw-Hill, 1991.

Zinsser, William K. "Culture: The New Joy." *Look,* January 9, 1968, 8.

Additional material was drawn from extensive interviews conducted by the author over a period of a decade and a half, from 1989 to 2006, with Anna Halprin and her colleagues, including Charles Amirkhanian, Jack Anderson, Paul Baum, Jeanne Hayes Beaman, Ruth Beckford, Miriam Raymer Bennett, Sunni Bloland, Rabbi Samuel Broude, Trisha Brown, Jim Burns, Remy Charlip, Gale Randall Chrisman, Wanda Coleman, Bruce Conner, Maggie Creighton, Merce Cunningham, Doris Dennison, George Dorris, Eiko and Koma, Simone Forti, Kathelin Gray, John Graham, Kim Hahn, Daria Halprin, Lawrence Halprin, Rana Halprin, Melinda West Harrison, Alma Hawkins, William Heick, Mary Hinkson, Luca Hoving, Jenny Hunter Groat, Warner Jepson, Rhodessa Jones, Kush, Jo Landor, Pearl Lang, Skip La Plante, Nina Lathrop, A.A. Leath, Norma Leistiko, Murray Louis, Sydney Luria, Jasmine Nash Lutes, Vera Maletic, Jamie McHugh, Nancy Cronenwelt Meehan, Meredith Monk, Robert Morris, Lousie H'Doubler Nagel, Liam O'Gallagher, Irving Penn, Yvonne Rainer, Robert Raymer, Larry Reed, Charles Reinhart, Terry Riley, John Rockwell, Juanita Sagan, Benito Santiago, Richard Schechner, Albert Schuman, Ida Schuman, Stanton Schuman, Ramon Sender, Kermit Sheets, Allan Stinson, Eeo Stubblefield, Morton Subotnick, Lynn Palmer Van Dam, Sir Lawrence Washington, James Woods, and La Monte Young.

INDEX

Photographs appear in two unnumbered insert sections.

Ashton, Dore, 74, 109
Asian Americans, 285, 291, 292
Associated Council of the Arts, 260
Auberg, Karen, 192, 228
Auden, W. H., 62
audience role, 160, 162, 185, 202, 257; in *Animal Ritual,* 296–98; in *The Bath,* 204, 205–6; in *Ceremony of Us,* 278–79, 282–83; in Happenings, 236–38; in *Lunch,* 260, 262; in *Ten Myths,* 208–21, 224, 232, 239, 240; as witnesses, 221–23, 313, 318, 328. *See also* community; participatory theater; spectatorship
Avalanche No. I, 141
Aysola, Lakshmi, 345

Bakar, Gerson, 310
Balanchine, George, 197
Ball, Lucille, 119–21
Ballet Russe de Monte Carlo, 19
Banes, Sally, 153, 166, 219, 227–28, 392n112
Barefoot, Spencer, 82, 83
Bark, Jan, 171, 187
Barnard College, 95
Barnes, Clive, 193
Barnes, Edward Larrabee, 49
Barthes, Roland, 1
Bath, The, 202–8, 247, 255, 319, 412, *photos*
Bauhaus, x, 49–52, 57–59, 61, 63, 65, 66, 173, 379n83
Baum, Paul, 174, 180, 249, 250, 257, 273, 277, 280–82
Bausch, Pina, *Kontakthof,* 354–55
Bayer, Herbert, 50
Beaman, Jeanne Hayes, 26
Beats, xiv, 74, 114, 122–25, 130–33, 145, 147, 159, 201, 377n31
Beauvoir, Simone de, *The Coming of Age,* 335
Bechtel Corporation, 129
Beck, Julian, 177, 227, 385n98
Beckett, Samuel, 188, 233; *Happy Days,* 169; *Waiting for Godot,* 157
Beckford, Ruth, 85–86, 286
Beckman, Jules, 327
Bed, The (film), 118, 419
Beeson, Coni, 307, 389n47
Belgrade Film Festival, 301
Bennett, Miriam Raymer, 8, 12, 15, 44, 66, 364n27

Bennington College, 23, 24, 366n5; School of the Dance, 24–28, 34, 43, 47, 65–66, 295
Bentley, Alys, 28
Berberian, Cathy, 169, 174
Berger, John, 207, 388n25
Berio, Luciano, 164–65, 169–74
Berliner, Paul, 131
Bernheimer, Martin, 282
Bernstein, Leonard, 394n49
Be With (Eiko and Koma with Anna Halprin), 349–50, 417
Big Brother and the Holding Company, 206
Bird, Bonnie, 65, 90
Birds of America, or Gardens Without Walls, 139–41, 143, 146, 169, 171, 379n83, 410
Bitter Herbs, 80, 407
Black Mountain College, 65
Black Panther Party, 264–65, 277, 394n49
Blank, Carla, 181, 185
Blank Placard Dance, 287, 289, 290, 413, *photo*
Blau, Herbert, 157, 169, 221, 238
Blind Song, 409
Blok, Helaine, 80
Bloland, Sunni, 144, *photo*
Bloomfield, Arthur, 225–26
Blow Up (film), 244
Blumkin, Rose, 34
B'nai B'rith, 35
Boal, Augusto, 258
Boas, Franz, 95
Boas, Franziska, 95, 190
Bolm, Adolph, 18
Booker T. Washington Community Center (San Francisco), 255
Boston Herald Traveler, 297
Branch Dance, 128, 409, *photo*
Brautigan, Richard, 123, 125, 137, 139
Breuer, Marcel, 50, 51
Broude, Samuel, 292, 293
Broughton, James, 74, 113–14, 117–18, 123, 125, 139, 212; *Musical Chairs,* 113
Brown, Trisha, 136, 144, 146–48, 151–53, 168, 180, 181, *photo*
Bruce, Lenny, 123, 154, 197–98
Buren, Daniel, 397n108
Burns, Jim, 249, 250–52, 254, 279
Bust, The, 287–89, 413, 419
Butler, Ethel, 34–35
Butoh, 334–35, 345

Café au Go Go (New York), 197
Cage, John, 65, 90, 91, 135, 141, 142, 144–46, 152, 160, 167, 237; *Fontana Mix*, 153
California, as creative space, 71–74
California Dance Educators Association, 338
Campbell, Joseph, 223–24
cancer: Anna Halprin's, 305–10, 315, 317, 321; Sontag on, 305; workshops for, 322–24
Cancer Support and Education Center, 323–24; "Moving toward Life" program, 324–25
Cándida Smith, Richard, 72, 109, 123–25
Candid Camera (television program), 230–32, 262, 289–90
Carry Me Home, 327–28, 416
Cassidy, Rosalind, 34–35
Castiglione, Countess de, 336
Catholics, 124
"Cathy Dance," 56–57, 63
Cazden, Norman, 63, 64, 369n26
Celebration of Life—Cycle of Ages, 414
Centre Pompidou (Paris), 353–54
Ceremonial, 406
Ceremony of Signals, 414
Ceremony of Us, 248, 266–84, 287, 289, 290, 293, 295, 296, 412, 419
Chaconne, 406
Chaikin, Joseph, 194, 254
Charlatans, 196
Charles-Roux, Edmonde, 208
Charlip, Remy, 167, 194, 195
Chicago Dance Council, 20, 21
Chicago Dancer, 35
Chicago Institute of Design, 65
Chicago Review, 123
Chicago World's Fair (1934), 20
children: classes for, 36, 53–59, 62, 65, 83–91, 97–101, *photo;* games of, 271–72, 279
Chrisman, Gale Randall, 83–85, 104, 372n43
Church, Thomas, 75–76, 78, 79
Circle the Earth, 164, 209, 315, 318–20, 322, 325–26, 328–30, 396n81, 415, 416, 419, *photo*
Circle the Mountain, 320, 415
Citizens for Interplanetary Activity (CIA), 230
City Center (New York), 298
City College of New York, 40
Citydance, xv, 71–72, 164, 309, 311–15, 414
City Lights bookstore (San Francisco), 123, 125, 312
City Scale environmental happening, 312

City University of New York, 192
Civil Rights Act (1964), 259
Claxton, Wayne, 44
Cleaver, Eldridge, 265; *Soul on Ice*, 277
Coffee Pot, 408
Cohen, Selma Jeanne, 19
Coleman, Wanda, 267–69, 274–75, 278, 280–82; "A War of Eyes," 276
collective creativity, 250, 253–54, 310, 333
Collins, Janet, 112
Columbia University, 249, 257; Teacher's College, 24, 28, 29
Communists, xi, 32, 372n43
community, 163, 27, 250–52, 254, 255, 258, 290; of artists, 53, 64, 74, 125; audience as, 242; black and white, 255–56 (*see also* racial issues); in *Bust*, 289; in *Circle the Earth*, 318–22, 325, 328–30; in *Citydance*, 311, 313–14; in *Lunch*, 260, 262. *See also* collective creativity
Congress of Wonders, 196
Connecticut College, 295
Conner, Bruce, 74, 123, 125
Connerton, Paul, 244, 256, 263–64
Copeland, Roger, 302
Corn, Wanda, 201, 391n88
Cornell University School of Agriculture, 38, 42
Cornish School (Seattle), 35, 66, 80, 90
Country Joe McDonald and the Fish, 265
Courtesan and the Crone, The, 346–47, 417
Cowell Theater (San Francisco), 345
Creighton, Magdalen (Maggie), 323
Cunningham, Merce, 87, 122, 142, 143, 145, 152, 167, 302, 353, *photo;* in Bennington summer program, 35, 65–6; Cage and, 65, 134–35, 160, 237; dance deck lecture demonstration by, 106–7; WORKS: *How to Pass, Kick, Fall, and Run*, 145; *Story*, 190; *Winterbranch*, 380n105
Cutler, Irving, 3

dadaism, 135, 238
Dagens Nyheter, 188
Dalcroze School of Eurythmics (London), 90
Dalí, Salvador, 310
Daly, Ann, 241
Dance as a Healing Art, 322, 324
dance deck, Halprins', 79, 103–7, 128, 160, 222, *photo*

Moholy-Nagy, László, 50, 51, 65
Mondrian, Piet, 49, 64
Monet, Claude, 335
Monk, Meredith, 121–22, 181, 384n80; *Break*, 181; "Gotham Lullaby," 345
Monroe, Marilyn, 207
monster, concept of, 309
"Monster Dance," 325, *photo*
Montano, Linda, *Mitchell's Death*, 352–53
Monterey Pop Festival, 230
Moore, Charles, 205
Morris, Robert, 143, 147, 152, 153, 185; *Tape Music*, 186
Morris, Simone. *See* Forti, Simone
Morrison, Toni, *Playing in the Dark*, 256
Moscone, George, 164, 314
Moses, Gilbert, 257
Moving toward Life, 217
Mulvey, Laura, 241, 392n112
Municipal Art Society of New York Certificate of Merit, 249
Muto, John, 296
Muzicki Biennale Zagreb, 172
Myers, David, 130
My Grandfather Dances (film), 420
My Lunch with Anna (film), 420
myth, 223–25, 234. *See also* Ten Myths

Nagrin, Daniel, 112
Nash, Jasmine, 259, 286, 292, 315–16
Nash, Xavier, 259, 269, 284, 286
National Endowment for the Arts, 310, 397n103; Expansion Arts Program of, 284–85
National Organization for Women, 264
Native Americans, 14, 35, 222, 223, 321, 384n69; Northwest Coast, 95. *See also* specific Native tribes
Nazism, x, 23, 33, 45, 50, 170
Neighborhood Playhouse School (New York), 80
Nelson, Lisa, 153
New Age movement, 298
New Bauhaus, 65
New Deal, 58
New Hampshire Landscape, 407
New School for Social Research, 152
Newsweek, 250
New Time Shuffle, 287, 291–92, 413
Newton, Huey P., 264, 265

New York City Board of Higher Education, 193–94
New York City Police Department, 193
New Yorker, 62
New York Herald-Tribune, 193
New York magazine, 349, 394n49
New York Stock Exchange, 41
New York Times, The, 92, 112, 193
Ngũgĩ wa Thiong'o, 258
Nielsen, Lavinia, 47, 111
Nijinsky, Vaslav, *Rite of Spring*, 304
Nikolais, Alwin, 92
Ninety-second Street Y (New York), 80
Noguchi, Isamu, 114
Nordness, Lee, 194
Northwestern University, 18
Novak, Jani, 118, 181, 183, 191
nudity, 220, 225–26; and *The Bath*, 203–4, 206–8; in *Parades and Changes*, 185, 186, 192–96, 251; in workshops/training program, 185, 251–53, 316–17

Oakland Tribune, xv, 192, 282
Oberlin College, 186
O'Connell, Jack, 244
O'Gallagher, Liam, 271
Oh! Calcutta! (musical), 194
Ohio State University, 172
Ohno, Kazuo, 334–35
Oklahoma! (musical), 68
Ome, 242–43, 412
O'Neal, John, 257
On the Town (musical), 67
Open Center (New York), 298
Open City Press, 138
Oppenheimer, Susi, 294
Orchesis dance group, 33, 35
Orgonia, 413
Overhoff, Jacques, 129

Palace of Fine Arts (San Francisco), 114
Palace of the Legion of Honor (San Francisco), 82
Palmer, Lynne, 155–56, 160–61, 173, 312
Pandor, Miriam, 80
Parade Magazine, 301
Parades and Changes, xiv, 113, 151, 181–88, 191–98, 201, 203, 234, 239, 251, 252, 319, 328, 346, 353–55, 384n80, 404n43, 411, 419, *photos*

Text: 11.25/13.5 Adobe Garamond
Display: Gill Sans Book
Compositor: Integrated Composition Systems
Printer and binder: Maple Vail Book Manufacturing Group